Annotated Instructor's Edition

Human Communication

Judy C. Pearson
North Dakota State University

Paul E. Nelson
North Dakota State University

Scott Titsworth
Ohio University

Lynn Harter
Ohio University

Boston   Burr Ridge, IL   Dubuque, IA   Madison, WI   New York   San Francisco   St. Louis
Bangkok   Bogotá   Caracas   Kuala Lumpur   Lisbon   London   Madrid   Mexico City
Milan   Montreal   New Delhi   Santiago   Seoul   Singapore   Sydney   Taipei   Toronto

McGraw-Hill Higher Education

A Division of The McGraw-Hill Companies

HUMAN COMMUNICATION

Published by McGraw-Hill, a business unit of The McGraw-Hill Companies, Inc., 1221 Avenue of the Americas, New York, NY 10020. Copyright © 2003, by The McGraw-Hill Companies, Inc. All rights reserved. No part of this publication may be reproduced or distributed in any form or by any means, or stored in a database or retrieval system, without the prior written consent of The McGraw-Hill Companies, Inc., including, but not limited to, in any network or other electronic storage or transmission, or broadcast for distance learning.

Some ancillaries, including electronic and print components, may not be available to customers outside the United States.

This book is printed on acid-free paper.

1 2 3 4 5 6 7 8 9 0 DOC/DOC 0 9 8 7 6 5 4 3 2

ISBN 0-07-256005-3 (student edition)
ISBN 0-07-256476-8 (annotated instructor's edition)

Publisher: *Phillip A. Butcher*
Senior sponsoring editor: *Nanette Kauffman*
Developmental editor II: *Jennie Katsaros*
Senior marketing manager: *Sally Constable, Daniel M. Loch*
Producer, media technology: *Jessica Bodie*
Project manager: *Rebecca Nordbrock*
Production supervisor: *Susanne Riedell*
Freelance design coordinator: *Gino Cieslik*
Lead supplement producer: *Marc Mattson*
Photo research coordinator: *Jeremy Cheshareck*
Photo researcher: *Julie Tesser*
Cover and interior design: *Ellen Pettengell*
Typeface: *10.5/12 New Aster*
Compositor: *Shepherd Incorporated*
Printer: *Von Hoffmann Press, Inc.*

Library of Congress Cataloging-in-Publication Data

Human communication / Judy C. Pearson . . . [et al.].
    p. cm.
    Includes index.
    ISBN 0-07-256005-3 (softcover : alk. paper)—ISBN 0-07-256476-8 (softcover : annotated instructor's edition)
    1. Communication. I. Pearson, Judy C.
P90 .H745 2003
302.2—dc21

2002069588

www.mhhe.com

dedication

We dedicate this book
Emma, Rebekah, Be
Christophe

brief contents

contents

PART **TWO** Communication Contexts 165

PART THREE Fundamentals of Public Speaking: Preparation and Delivery 363

CHAPTER **EIGHTEEN**

Persuasive Presentations 538

preface

As communication professors, the authors have spent many of their days in the classroom. Their commitment to the discipline, belief in the essential nature of communication to meet 21st Century challenges, and interest in extending their knowledge to others encouraged them to collaborate and coauthor this text. Although they cannot be physically present in multiple classrooms, they hope that this book will enhance learning and add to the excitement and fulfillment that people experience in the communication classroom.

Written for the basic course, *Human Communication* is a hybrid text that teaches principles and skills in interpersonal communication, small group discussion, organizational communication, public speaking, and mediated communication (including both mass media and computer-mediated communication). With its distinctive student-friendly voice, the text continues the tradition of Pearson and Nelson's *Understanding and Sharing* by coaching students through the foundations of human communication. With the new edition, the authors, Judy Pearson, Paul Nelson, Scott Titsworth, and Lynn Harter continue to place relevant skills, engaging theory, and energizing pedagogy at the forefront of the book.

Key Elements

Human Communication introduces students to the main contexts of human communication following these key themes:

- *A Student-Centered Approach*—We try to simplify complex ideas without significant distortion, to illustrate as much as possible, and to provide examples that will help students understand.

- *Cooperative and Collaborative Learning*—This text encourages active learning throughout the book by asking students to think about a concept, share their ideas with a classmate, and reveal their thinking to the class when invited to do so.

- *Learning Incrementally*—The text moves from simple to complex so students will not be overwhelmed with information overload.

- *Challenging Thought*—The text challenges students to think intelligently about communication concepts. Every chapter concludes with an issue that invites students to think more deeply about communication concepts, issues, and practices.

- *Practical Application*—This text presents practical knowledge, useful application, and skills that are highly valued in American culture.
- *Finding and Evaluating Information*—College-educated individuals know how to critically assess information. They know how to size up assertions, to weigh arguments and evidence, and to judge the value of information and ideas. This text teaches the trials and satisfaction of finding and evaluating information.
- *Behaving Ethically*—The text encourages positive, moral and ethical communication practices.
- *Using Technology*—Technology has changed the world of communication. Students are introduced to a variety of mediated forms of communication and are encouraged to critically assess the resources found on the Web.
- *Understanding Diversity*—Students will meet people of different cultural backgrounds in their professional and personal lives. This text encourages cultural competence by addressing diversity issues throughout the book and in a separate chapter on culture and co-cultural understanding.
- *Working in Teams*—Organizations thrive on collaborative and co-operative teams. In this book, college students will learn the skills necessary for successful work teams.
- *Using Visualization*—Some students learn best through visual images. This text is replete with images in the form of photos, illustrations, graphics, models, tables, figures, and stills of the animations found on the CD-ROM.

Edition Highlights

Human Communication includes a great deal of new and revised information. Research, examples, explanations, and exercises all have been updated. Some of the highlights are detailed here.

CD-ROM

The accompanying CD-ROM provides students and instructors with multiple tools for learning and teaching. These include:

- **Video *The Elliotts: Communicating Everyday.*** The six episodes of The Elliotts each run approximately 7 minutes. With consistent characters and plot lines that illustrate concepts discussed in the chapters, The Elliotts follows a television drama/sitcom format. Icons throughout the text indicate connections to this video series. And the "Video Link" features in the chapter review sections establish strategies for viewing specific episodes.

- **Animations.** The CD-ROM includes 18 dynamic animations that illustrate key concepts in the text. Written by the authors and created by renowned West Coast animator, Alexander Elko, these exclusive animations bring communication to life. The animations are represented in the text as illustrations, also created by Elko.

- **PowerPoint Tutorial.** Students will learn the rules of design and helpful tips on implementation when working with presentation software such as PowerPoint.

- **Self-Quizzes.** There are 15 multiple-choice and 5 true/false questions for each chapter. All questions include feedback for the student.

- **Flashcards with Sound, Business Document Templates, and Outline Tutor.** These tools enable students to prepare efficiently and professionally for exams, group projects, oral presentations, and actual assignments at work.

Chapter Features

Exciting, innovative chapter features include: *Team Challenges*, which are related to cooperative learning; *E-notes*, which highlight technology; *Think-Pair-Share*, which aids in critical thinking; *Cultural Notes*, which encourage sensitivity to diversity; and *Issues in Communication* vignettes, with real-life applications for critical thinking and further discussion.

Chapter Revisions

Human Communication is a first edition text. Nonetheless, the authors drew a great deal of material from previous editions of *An Introduction to Human Communication: Understanding and Sharing*. In this section of the preface, we provide the distinctive features of this book and the dramatic changes that have occurred.

Chapter 1: Introduction to Human Communication

- A new section on why the study of communication is essential is included.
- A definition and description of communication competence are added.
- A new section discusses ethics and includes the tenets of the National Communication Association Credo on Ethics.

Chapter 2: Perception, Self, and Communication

- This chapter has a new title: Perception, Self, and Communication. The title reflects a change in organization and approach, which relates perception, self, and communication in a coherent manner.
- A new section discusses errors that people make in their perceptions of others.
- Self-efficacy is defined and described in a new section.
- Impression management is defined and described.
- The component parts of impression management—actors, performance, and face—are explained in detail.

Chapter 3: Verbal Communication

- Language has been redefined and related concepts have been updated.
- A more complete description of the sets of rules that govern language use has been added.
- The richness of the relationship between language and culture is now explored.
- Communication on the Internet is an entirely new section and includes a discussion of the rules that guide communication on the Net—netiquette.
- In the past, the various forms of unique language that exist were described as providing barriers to communication; a new and more complete description reveals how they can also add beauty to language.
- A discussion of heterosexist language has been added.
- The discussion of differences between observations and inferences now leads into a natural discussion of differences between members of different cultures.
- Cultural competence is defined and a new section on cultural competence concludes the chapter.

Chapter 4: Nonverbal Communication

- This chapter is significantly updated with a new definition and description of nonverbal communication taken from contemporary scholarship.
- A discussion of emoticons—the symbols used in electronic communication to express emotions—is now incorporated into the discussion.

- The relationship between verbal and nonverbal communication is clearly delineated with sections on how they work together and how they are distinctive.
- New research on the accuracy of decoding nonverbal cues is added.
- Cultural differences in nonverbal communication have been added.
- New research on proxemics has been added.
- A discussion of expectancy violation theory has been added and current research, which tests this theory, has been included.
- A new section on chronemics, or the way that people organize and use time and the messages that are created because of our organization and use of it, is now included in this chapter.
- Silence—and all of its complexities—is the point of a new discussion in this chapter.

Chapter 5: Listening and Critical Thinking

- The definition of listening has been updated to reflect literature produced by the International Listening Association.
- A new section on "the importance of listening" addresses listening in students' personal and professional lives.
- A new section describes the relationship between listening and the thinking process (information processing theory), including how listening plays a role in attention, working memory, short-term memory, and long-term memory.
- The types of listening discussed in the chapter have been expanded to include reference to listening for enjoyment. The new section on "enjoyment listening" discusses interesting research on how enjoyment listening can help reduce pain!
- Examples in the "Barriers to Listening" section have been updated to be more relevant to traditional undergraduates.
- A new section has been added that covers listening strategies in specific situations including personal relationships, professional situations, classroom settings, and in mediated communication situations.

Chapter 6: Interpersonal Communication

- This chapter has been significantly changed, with dozens of new studies incorporated into the material.
- Interpersonal communication is defined differently than in the past.

- Distinctions between interpersonal and noninterpersonal communication are offered.
- The significance of interpersonal relationships is highlighted.
- The dark sides of interpersonal relationships are discussed.
- Why do people initiate new relationships? This chapter suggests some of the reasons as gleaned from the current literature.
- Uncertainty reduction theory is described and shown to apply to a variety of relationships; it is also shown to have limitations and potential weaknesses.
- The chapter reveals ways that people can maintain positive relationships over time.
- Dialectic theory is introduced and delineated.
- Co-cultural differences and conversational difficulties both mitigate against maintaining relationships, and these factors are depicted in detail.
- Why do people terminate relationships? This chapter identifies some of the individual's characteristics and some of the message characteristics that may lead to relational termination.
- The chapter concludes with a discussion of four essential interpersonal communication behaviors.
- The material on self-disclosure is totally rewritten to reflect more current thought and research.
- The importance of self-disclosure is given an updated perspective.
- The factors that affect appropriate self-disclosure are identified and described.
- A new section on affectionate and supportive communication has been added.
- A new section on influencing others in interpersonal settings has been included.
- The development of a unique relationship is described in detail.

Chapter 7: Intercultural Communication

- New material on Low Context and High Context Cultures is included.
- New material on P-Time Cultures and M-Time Cultures has been added.

Chapter 8: Interviewing

- This chapter was expanded from the appendix in the 8th edition of *Introduction to Human Communication: Understanding and Sharing*.
- An expanded section explains how interviewing is both similar and different from other contexts of communication.

- A new section has been added on using hypothetical and behaviorally-based questions.
- A section on employment interviews introduces the concept of anticipatory socialization.
- An integrated discussion of job descriptions and EEO laws can be found in the section on employment interviewing.
- The expanded discussion of résumés contains an integrated example.
- An example of a cover letter is included.
- The employment interviewing section includes a section on being prepared for "illegal" questions.
- An updated section on probing interviews is provided.

Chapter 9: The Dynamics of Small-Group Communication

- This chapter combines key elements of two small-group chapters found in Pearson and Nelson's *Understanding and Sharing*, 8th edition.
- Updated examples (including one of a group formed in response to the 9/11 tragedy) of how groups facilitate social change are presented.
- In addition to delineating between task-oriented (secondary) and relationship-oriented (primary) groups, the chapter distinguishes between assigned and emergent groups.
- A new section called "Embedding Groups in Our Lives" was added to illustrate how real-life groups blur boundaries between primary vs. secondary and assigned vs. emergent groups.
- Theoretical approaches to group leadership section have been condensed to focus on three broad themes: style approaches, contingency approaches, and distributed approaches.
- The section on culture in small groups makes a new distinction between observable and implicit within-group diversity.
- A new section on implicit characteristics of diversity discusses differences in cognitive paradigms and how they potentially influence group interaction.
- A section on groupthink has been added.
- A new section discusses group work that does not necessarily involve traditional problem-solving models. The section discusses the following concepts: decision-making, effecting social change, negotiating conflict, fostering creativity, and maintaining ties among stakeholders.
- How technology influences the group communication process is the topic of a new section, which includes a discussion of computer networking and group decision support systems.

Chapter 10: Communicating at Work

- This chapter is new.
- The section on "What is the Study of Organizational Communication" discusses structuration, types of organizations, bureaucratic structures, and information management.
- The section on "Internal Organizational Communication" discusses communication networks and organizational assimilation.
- The section on "External Organizational Communication" discusses organizational image, customer service, aggressive communication in the workplace, and sexual harassment.

Chapter 11: Mediated Communication and Media Literacy

- The chapter was retitled to emphasize a combined focus on both mass communication and computer-mediated communication.
- The role of mediated communication in the wake of 9/11 is discussed.
- The chapter discusses theoretical differences between mass communication (primarily linear) and computer-mediated communication (more interactive).
- The issue of television stations broadcasting faulty information in order to be first with the story uses 9/11 as a key example.
- The discussion of professional journals is enhanced by noting the importance of blind peer reviews.
- Research cited in the media effects section has been updated to reflect the findings of the comprehensive UCLA National TV Violence Study as well as current research in communication journals.
- The discussion of agenda setting has been augmented with the example of youth violence (e.g., Columbine and other school violence) as well as recent research on news reports of crime in general.
- Research discussing the issue of race and stereotypes in mass media has been updated.
- A new section on the cultivation effect (Gerbner's media cultivation theory) is included.
- A new primary section on computer-mediated communication (CMC) covers these general topics: (1) types of CMC including e-mail, bulletin board systems, instant messaging/chat, audio-video conferencing, and multi-user environments; (2) CMC and the communication process, which discusses the nature of CMC interactions, the role of CMC in community formation, and the relationship between CMC, gender, and culture.
- A new section on "Becoming a literate consumer of mediated communication" addresses both media literacy and CMC literacy.

Chapter 12: Communication Apprehension and Source Credibility

- This reconfigured chapter links two concepts that were in different chapters in the previous edition.
- Considerably more information on communication apprehension has been provided, with special attention to therapies for improvement and the cautions of communibiologists.
- The category of "identification" has been added to source credibility. It includes the influence of celebrity as an aspect of credibility.

Chapter 13: Topic Selection and Audience Analysis

- Some of the long lists of suggested topics have been shortened in favor of a focused selection of topics that are more attractive both to student audiences and to teachers.

Chapter 14: Finding Information

- A new section discusses how research plays a role in each step of the speech preparation process.
- The discussion of how to use the Internet effectively was greatly expanded.
- A new section on evaluating Web sources includes a table on how to decipher a domain name and Web address.
- Our discussion of verbal source citations has been expanded and includes a table illustrating common examples.
- A new section on evaluating the source of supporting material discusses issues of clarity, verification, competence, objectivity, and relevance.

Chapter 15: Organizing Your Presentation

- New examples of speech organization are provided.

Chapter 16: Delivery and Visual Resources

- This chapter has been reconfigured. In the prior edition, this chapter also included these two topics plus communication apprehension.
- Extensive coverage is provided of modes of delivery and methods of reinforcing the message through many types of visual resources—from blackboards to electronic transmissions.

Chapter 17: Informative Presentations

- The perspective has been changed from the informative speech to presenting information because students do not believe that they will give an informative speech outside the classroom, but they do anticipate having to present information.

- Principles of learning, information processing, and memory are included.

Chapter 18: Persuasive Presentations

- Called persuasive speaking in *An Introduction to Human Communication,* this chapter is now about how oral discourse functions in social influence—a bit broader, more current, and more interesting than persuasive speaking.

Katherine Dindia,
University of Wisconsin,
Milwaukee

Terre H. Allen,
California State University,
Long Beach

Richard West,
University of Southern Maine

Michael McDevitt,
University of New Mexico

Denise Solomon,
University of Wisconsin

Ronald L. Biddle,
Clovis Community College

Peggie Partello,
Keene State College

Joan M. Donnelly,
Keene State College

Linda Long,
North Lake College, Texas

Lonn Presnell,
Richland Community College,
Illinois

Marina Krcmar,
University of Connecticut

Nick Trujillo,
California State University,
Sacramento

Gail Medford,
Bowie State University, Maryland

Robert Brady,
University of Arkansas

Dori Barron,
Western Piedmont
Community College

Kim Smith,
Iowa State University

Kathryn Jones,
Northern Virginia
Community College

Danielle Powell,
James Madison University

Ernest Hakanen,
Drexel University

From the Authors

(left to right) Judy Pearson, Paul Nelson, Lynn Harter, and Scott Titsworth

Using Communication Studies to Make Sense of the World, Our Everyday Lives, and Our Relationships

Dear Colleagues:

Your students explore different perspectives on the world, their everyday lives, and their relationships with colleagues, friends, and family in many of their courses. But only in your communication class do they learn about how and why we relate to each other, why we are attracted to some people and not to others, why some relationships stand the test of time and others do not, and how to communicate effectively with each other. Unique among disciplines, communication helps students make sense of their everyday lives and make sense of the world.

We wrote *Human Communication* and produced its accompanying original video and animation series with two main goals: to capture the heart of classical and contemporary communication studies and to make this powerful body of work immediate and relevant to all your students.

USING COMMUNICATION STUDIES TO MAKE SENSE OF THE WORLD

The world changed on September 11, 2001. People became instantly more aware of the importance of communication principles. The events created information hunger, a concept familiar to communication scholars and professionals, and our students became more serious, more driven to comprehend the world. As teachers and as authors, we felt a responsibility to contribute to the level of understanding of this new world and immediately sought out books, articles, and information on the Internet from experts on terrorism, international organization, globalization, and intercultural understanding.

We believe that communication principles and practices play a key role in resolving disputes among nations as well as among friends and families. With this new text we want to make those concepts compelling for students through clear, relevant examples and interesting opportunities for debate and inquiry—all founded on the principles of our discipline.

Communication is consequential. And understanding the theories, research studies, and applications of communication in this way will, we believe, make significant differences in the lives of your students.

USING COMMUNICATION STUDIES TO MAKE SENSE OF OUR EVERYDAY LIVES

How can we take something as complex as the Enron debacle and make sense of it from the perspective of communication? Or, considering the recent debates on stem-cell research, how can we make sense of the scientific arguments, the political agendas, and the multiple ethical expectations of our culture?

We know you want to connect your course to the kinds of issues that make the headlines and affect everyday lives—at work, at school, and at home. And we know you want to show your students how communication studies can give them the background to research issues, analyze arguments, and assess credibility.

USING COMMUNICATION STUDIES TO MAKE SENSE OF OUR RELATIONSHIPS

For a good number of students the basic communication course seems to raise questions about relationships in general and their own in particular. If healthy people seek positive relationships with others, then why do relationships end or sometimes continue in dysfunctional ways? What does communication have to do with America's high rate of divorce? How might studies that look at communication behaviors like jealousy, deception, and aggression help your students make sense of their relationships?

We wrote *Human Communication* and created its original video and animation series to reflect the healthy curiosity of basic course students and to help cultivate positive communication methods that contribute to enriching relationships.

Throughout, our focus has been to "Make it Smart, Keep it Real." We hope you will agree that we have succeeded.

Judy Pearson, Paul Nelson, Scott Titsworth, Lynn Harter

Although the four authors of this book have different last names, they are married couples. Their common love of communication studies, undergraduate instruction, and translating complex research into useful applications drove this enterprise. Paul and Judy began work on this project nearly 30 years ago as a young married couple with tiny son Ben to distract them. Today, the project continues with Scott, Lynn, and their daughter Emma. As the field of communication continues to grow and develop, these two professional couples manage to honor the past and celebrate the future.

A COMPLETE LEARNING PACKAGE INTEGRATES THE TEXTBOOK WITH ORIGINAL MULTIMEDIA

INNOVATIVE BUILT-IN ACTIVITIES MAKE THE TEXT BOTH INTERACTIVE AND INNOVATIVE . . .

TRY ▶ THIS

Make a list of the jargon used in your area of study or in a job you have or have had in the past. Ask a friend to do the same. Do you know what the words on your friend's list mean? Can he or she determine what the words on your list mean?

. . . with features that encourage critical thinking through cooperative learning experiences and discussion of real issues.

Team Challenge

THE PERCEPTUAL PROCESS

With a group of people from your class, identify a place on campus or in your community and a time to engage in group observation. Spend at least 10 minutes with your group at this location in complete silence. Try to select a location that has multiple people and events to observe. During the 10 minutes of silence, record everything that you perceive. Do not share your perceptions with others until the time has lapsed.

After 10 minutes, take turns sharing your observations with group members. Look for common perceptions and unique perceptions. Describe how the processes of selection, organization, and interpretation influenced your perceptions. Did individuals use figure and ground, closure, proximity, and similarity in their perceptions? Describe your experience to the rest of the class in your next class meeting.

Think, Pair, Share

MANAGING RELATIONAL DIALECTICS

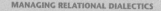

How do people manage the dialectics they find in their interpersonal relationships? Baxter (1990) studied people like you to learn that relational couples generally rely on four strategies:

selection
Managing dialectics by choosing one need over the other.

1. **Selection**—*couples choose one of their needs over the other.* They decide that their time together is far more important than time they spend alone and try to spend every waking moment together, for example. Or they decide that predictability is more important than novelty and enjoy dinner at the same restaurant every Friday evening.

separation
Managing dialectics by fulfilling one need in some situations and the other in different situations.

2. **Separation**—*contradictory needs are met by fulfilling one in some situations and the other in different situations.* For instance, the couple decides that during the workday, they will interact with others and maintain their independence. However, every evening must be spent together. Or they decide that the quick meals they catch together will be at a multitude of different fast-food restaurants, but that celebratory meals are always at one favorite restaurant.

neutralization
Managing dialectics by compromise.

3. **Neutralization**—*contradictory needs are not met completely, but a compromise is struck.* The couple provides private information about some matters, but not about others. Or they spend about half of their free time with each other and about half of it with others.

reframing
Managing dialectics by transformation of needs so they are no longer regarded as opposites.

4. **Reframing**—*contradictory needs are transformed so they no longer are regarded as opposites.* Commuting couples sometimes explain that being apart so much leads to greater intimacy and closeness. The couple who is always living on the edge and exploring new personal ground describe their behavior as predictable or routine.

Consider one of your personal relationships—with a family member, close friend, or intimate partner. Which of these strategies do you use? Think of examples that illustrate what you do. After you have spent a few minutes identifying some of the strategies to manage contradictions in your relationship, share them with a partner in class. How do you differ? How are you similar in relational management? What have you learned from sharing your ideas with a classmate?

ANIMATION AND VIDEO BRING COMMUNICATION TO LIFE

ANIMATIONS

A series of 18 developed by the text authors and renowned West Coast animator Alexander Elko.

1 Perspectives on Communication
2 The Perception Process
3 Denotative and Connotative Meaning
4 Zones of Space
5 The Listening Process
6 Relationship Development
7 Cultural Differences
8 The Employment Interview Process
9 Small-Group Problem Solving
10 Formal Communication Flow
11 Models of Mediated Communication
12 The Sleeper Effect
13 Selecting and Narrowing a Topic
14 The Research Process
15 Planning a Speech Introduction
16 Effective Delivery Behaviors
17 Behavior Purposes and Informative Speaking
18 Monroe's Motivated Sequence

Each animation connects directly to an illustration in the textbook. →

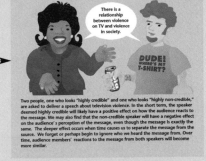

Two people, one who looks "highly credible" and one who looks "highly non-credible," are asked to deliver a speech about television violence. In the short term, the speaker deemed highly credible will likely have a positive effect on how the audience reacts to the message. We may also find that the non-credible speaker will have a negative effect on the audience's perception of the message, even though the message is exactly the same. The sleeper effect occurs when time causes us to separate the message from the source. We forget or perhaps begin to ignore who we heard the message from. Over time, audience members' reactions to the message from both speakers will become more similar.

Figure 12.1   The sleeper effect.

VIDEO

The Elliotts: Communicating Everyday
Available on the student CD-ROM and in VHS format.

The six episodes of The Elliotts: Communicating Everyday video present key communication concepts in the style of a contemporary television drama.

AUDIO FLASHCARDS

Flashcards present key terms for each chapter using text and sound.

PREVIOUS ● NEXT	**communication**

CLICK TO SEE DEFINITION

The process by which meaning is exchanged between individuals through a common system of symbols, signs, or behavior.

4 of 33

MARK   VIEW: ALL   ● VIEW BY: TERM

INTEGRATED THROUGHOUT THE TEXT: COMPUTER-MEDIATED COMMUNICATION

Features chapter 11, Mediated Communication and Media Literacy, including a discussion of the role of media in the wake of 9/11.

Mediated Communication and Media Literacy

What will you learn?

When you have read and thought about this chapter, you will be able to:

1. Explain the importance of studying mediated communication.
2. Define mediated communication and explain the differences between mass communication and computer-mediated communication.
3. Identify types of mass communication.
4. Discuss ways in which the mass media affect our culture and us.
5. Identify types of computer-mediated communication.
6. Explain the difference between synchronous and asynchronous communication.
7. Discuss how CMC affects the communication process.
8. Understand strategies for becoming a critical consumer of mediated messages.

We all participate in **mediated communication,** which is *any communication interaction using technology as the primary channel.* The two predominant types of mediated communication—mass communication and computer-mediated communication—inform, entertain, persuade, and provide a means for connecting people. In this chapter you will learn the importance of mediated communication, how mediated communication affects us through the communication process, and how to be a more critical consumer of mediated messages.

Discusses the influence of technology on the group communication process.

Chapter Nine   The Dynamics of Small-Group Communication   293

As you can see, groups exist for many reasons. Although the heart of group activity may indeed be problem solving, not all groups exist solely for that purpose.

Technology and Group Communication Processes

Throughout this book we have explored how various forms of technology impact human communication. In small-group communication, technology can be used for facilitating communication as well as for sharing strategic information necessary for decision making. One form of group technology is decision support systems.

A **group decision support system (GDSS)** is *an interactive network of computers with specialized software allowing users to generate solutions for unstructured problems* (Sosik, Avolio, & Kahai, 1997). Although the exact nature of the GDSS environment can be tailored to specific situations, most GDSS-based group interactions are used to facilitate brainstorming and evaluation of alternatives. In a typical GDSS session members anonymously post ideas using a personal computer. Although postings are anonymous, each member of the group can see ideas posted by other members. By doing this, ideas generated by one person may generate additional ideas by someone else. After a predetermined length of time for brainstorming, members can anonymously rank and/or rate each idea. The software summarizes the results of members' ranking and/or ratings. Most GDSSs also allow members to anonymously vote to indicate their choice for the best alternative. Some GDSSs also allow for anonymous text-based discussions using the computer.

The key characteristics of GDSSs are anonymity and efficiency. Because individuals' ideas are anonymous, discussions using GDSSs tend to result in better information sharing and critical analysis of ideas than face-to-face interactions (Lam & Schaubroek, 2000). Although GDSSs tend to encourage minority viewpoints to be expressed more frequently, those viewpoints may have less impact on others' opinions in GDSS environments than in face-to-face environments (McLeod, Baron, Weighner, & Yoon, 1997). In addition to being anonymous, GDSSs are also efficient. In reviewing more than 28 experimental studies comparing GDSS discussion groups to face-to-face groups, Hwang (1998) concluded that GDSSs resulted in significantly more ideas generated than traditional face-to-face groups. Thus in the same amount of time the efficiency of brainstorming is significantly improved by GDSS-based discussions. Aiken and Martin (1994) also suggested that GDSSs have the potential to reduce the likelihood of groupthink because alternative opinions can be presented anonymously.

Computers can be used to facilitate group communication.

group decision support systems (GDSS) Interactive network of computers with specialized software allowing users to generate solutions for unstructured problems.

Reveals how technology is changing the ways we communicate with each other.

E-Note

TESTING YOUR INTERPERSONAL SKILLS

www.queendom.com is a site for multiple tests on relationships, personality, health, career, and intelligence. Although the validity and reliability information on the tests is not provided, the tests do provide an interesting starting point to think about how your personality and relationship scores might affect your interpersonal relationships and communication with others. Relevant to this chapter are tests on arguing, assertiveness, commitment readiness, communication skills, conflict management, coping skills, jealousy, relationship attachment, relationship satisfaction, romantic personality, romantic space, and self-disclosure. You might wish to take one or more of these tests with someone with whom you have an interpersonal relationship. Share your responses with each other and determine the perceived accuracy of the test results with your partner. Does your partner see you differently or similarly to how you perceive yourself? How could differences in perception affect your relationship?

Challenges students to think critically in evaluating Web sources and includes a table on how to decipher a domain name and Web address.

TABLE 14.3   BREAKING DOWN WEB ADDRESSES

ELEMENTS OF A WEB ADDRESS

http://iwin.nws.noaa.gov/iwin/iwdspg1.html

Server | Server extension | Exact location on server

COMMON SERVER EXTENSIONS

EXTENSION	DESCRIPTION	EXAMPLE
.edu	Primarily college and university websites	www.ohio.edu Website for Ohio University
.com	Primarily commercial or for-profit websites	www.mhhe.com Website for McGraw-Hill Publishing Company
.gov	Government websites	www.ed.gov Website for the U.S. Department of Education
.net	Primarily Internet service provider public sites, sometimes used as an alternative when a ".com" name has already been taken	www.maui.net Website for Island of Maui Tourism
.org	Primarily not-for-profit organizations	www.helping.org A resource site for volunteerism and nonprofit organizations

INTEGRATED THROUGHOUT THE TEXT: CULTURE AND ETHICS

Encourages cultural competence and understanding by exploring issues of diversity throughout the book

CHAPTER SEVEN

Human beings draw close to one another by their common nature, but habits and customs keep them apart.
CONFUCIAN SAYING

Human culture without language is unthinkable.
CLYDE KLUCKHOHN

The thing I like most about Brooklyn is all the different people who live there. The thing I like least about Brooklyn is that these people do not get along with each other.
ELDERLY AFRICAN-AMERICAN BROOKLYN RESIDENT

Active listening differs from culture to culture.

Cultural Note

DIFFERENCES IN ACTIVE LISTENING

The way a person actively listens can vary from culture to culture. College students in Finland, for example, listen carefully and take notes but do not respond overtly while being addressed by the professor. In fact, they remain quite expressionless. In some Native American tribes and in some Hispanic groups, people avert their eyes when listening; but in groups such as northern whites and blacks, people tend to maintain eye contact while actively listening. How would you describe the norms of listening in your culture, community, or school?

Covers cultural stereotypes in mass media

- The media generally do not represent older adults. In a content analysis of more than 750 advertisements appearing in national news magazines over a one-year period, McConatha, Schnell, and McKenna (1999) found that when older adults were depicted, they were often in passive or dependent roles.
- Native Americans are also relatively invisible in the media. When depicted at all, male Native Americans are depicted as aggressive, and female Native Americans are sexualized (Bird S., 1999).
- Latino Americans are often depicted in films and television as servants, "illegal" aliens, and drug dealers (Pachon, 2001).

Invites students to consider ways of incorporating ethical considerations in their relationships and in the everyday contexts of school and work

Ethical Communication

A second goal of studying communication lies in its ethical dimension. **Ethics** may be defined as *a set of moral principles or values.* Ethical standards may vary from one discipline to another just as they differ from one culture to another. Within the communication discipline, a set of ethics has been adopted. The National Communication Association created the following set of ethics.

Chapter 1 introduces students to the National Communication Association Credo on Ethics.

NCA Credo for Communication Ethics

Questions of right and wrong arise whenever people communicate. Ethical communication is fundamental to responsible thinking, decision making, and the development of relationships and communities within and across contexts, cultures, channels, and media. Moreover, ethical communication enhances human worth and dignity by fostering truthfulness, fairness, responsibility, personal integrity, and respect for self and others. We believe that unethical communication threatens the quality of all communication and consequently the well-being of individuals and the society in which we live. Therefore we, the members of the National Communication Association, endorse and are committed to practicing the following principles of ethical communication:

We advocate truthfulness, accuracy, honesty, and reason as essential to the integrity of communication.

COMMUNICATING IN THE WORKPLACE

Two chapters, Interviewing and Communicating at Work, are designed to relate to the current work lives of students and to cultivate skills for their careers.

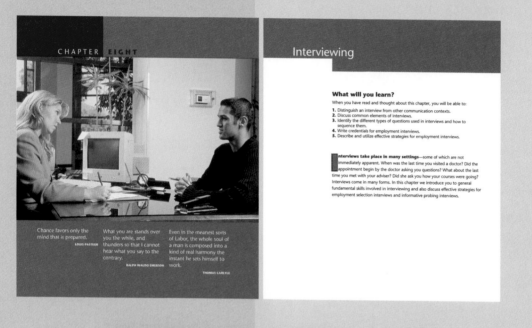

CHAPTER EIGHT

Chance favors only the mind that is prepared.
LOUIS PASTEUR

What you are stands over you the while, and thunders so that I cannot hear what you say to the contrary.
RALPH WALDO EMERSON

Even in the meanest sorts of Labor, the whole soul of a man is composed into a kind of real harmony the instant he sets himself to work.
THOMAS CARLYLE

Interviewing

What will you learn?

When you have read and thought about this chapter, you will be able to:

1. Distinguish an interview from other communication contexts.
2. Discuss common elements of interviews.
3. Identify the different types of questions used in interviews and how to sequence them.
4. Write credentials for employment interviews.
5. Describe and utilize effective strategies for employment interviews.

Interviews take place in many settings—some of which are not immediately apparent. When was the last time you visited a doctor? Did the appointment begin by the doctor asking you questions? What about the last time you met with your adviser? Did she ask you how your courses were going? Interviews come in many forms. In this chapter we introduce you to general fundamental skills involved in interviewing and also discuss effective strategies for employment selection interviews and informative probing interviews.

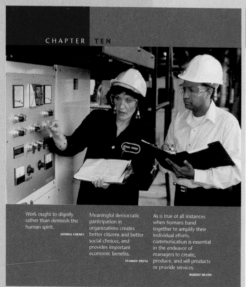

CHAPTER TEN

Work ought to dignify rather than diminish the human spirit.
GEORGE CHENEY

Meaningful democratic participation in organizations creates better citizens and better social choices, and provides important economic benefits.
STANLEY DEETZ

As is true of all instances when humans band together to amplify their individual efforts, communication is essential in the endeavor of managers to create, produce, and sell products or provide services.
ROBERT HEATH

Communicating at Work

What will you learn?

When you have read and thought about this chapter, you will be able to:

1. Define organizational communication.
2. Recognize different organization types.
3. Explain how structures develop in organizations.
4. Identify different types of organizational structure.
5. Identify types of communication in organizational networks.
6. Describe the process of organizational socialization.
7. Explain how organizational images are created through public relations and crisis management efforts.
8. Utilize communication skills necessary for effective customer service.
9. Recognize and avoid aggressive communication in the workplace, including sexual harassment.

The very fabric of our social, cultural, and economic worlds is organizationally based, thus the need for us to be competent communicators in organizational settings is undeniable. Organizational communication practices can enhance, or diminish, our role in inventing a better future and maintaining some degree of control over our work environment. In this chapter we introduce you to the study of organizational communication, including internal and external organizational communication, the dark side of communication in organizations, and ethical approaches to competent communication in organizational settings.

SUPPLEMENTS:
A COMPREHENSIVE PACKAGE

RESOURCES FOR THE STUDENT

The Student CD-ROM is a powerful extension of the text, offering

- Chapter self-quizzes (15 multiple-choice and 5 true/false) with feedback.
- Flashcards of chapter key terms with sound.
- The Elliotts: Communicating Everyday—6 video episodes presenting key communication concepts in the style of a contemporary television drama.
- 18 new, original animations that provide step-by-step explanations of communication models.
- Business Document Template with templates for cover letters, résumés, agendas, and memos.
- Outline Tutor provides a template for writing speech outlines and organizing presentations.
- PowerPoint Tutorial presents the basic steps to create and use PowerPoint effectively in presentations.

The Online Learning Center, a FREE text-specific website at www.mhhe.com/pearson, offers students additional resources and activities. No password is required.

- Chapter self-quizzes with feedback for each chapter.
- Key terms crossword puzzles for each chapter.
- Internet exercises for each chapter.
- PowerPoint slides for each chapter.

SUPPLEMENTS:
A COMPREHENSIVE PACKAGE

RESOURCES FOR THE INSTRUCTOR
Annotated Instructor's Edition
(0-07-256476-8)

Marginal annotations throughout the Instructor's Edition provide suggestions on how to integrate technology, media literacy, critical thinking, activities and the text's videos and animations into the classroom. The notations also provide links to the instructor's resource integrator.

Instructor's Resource Integrator
(0-07-256475-X)

Pulling together student and instructor resources with an eye toward curriculum planning and course management, the authors suggest resources from the text package according to key concepts and instructional strategies for each chapter. While the Resource Integrator functions basically like an Instructor's Manual, it is an enhanced model that also serves to coordinate the package so that the instructor can make practical and outcome-oriented choices about which activities and multimedia components to use. It also includes the Test Bank and full, annotated scripts of the video: The Elliotts: Communicating Everyday.

Instructor's Resource CD-ROM with Computerized Test Bank and PowerPoint Slides (0-07-256478-4)

Video: The Elliotts: Communicating Everyday

In VHS (0-07-256479-2) and CD-ROM (0-07-256474-1)

Video: Communication Concepts (0-07-236543-9)

Online Learning Center

A FREE text-specific website at www.mhhe.com/pearson offering a variety of resources and activities for instructors and students. No passcard is required.

PageOut

Instructors can create a custom course website using the PageOut template. PageOut is fully compatible with most course management websites, including Blackboard and WebCT. For more information visit mhhe.com/solutions.

PowerWeb (0-07-256477-6)

Offered free with the text, *PowerWeb* is a password-protected website developed by McGraw-Hill that provides instructors and students with primary source readings, course-specific study materials and current, relevant, and validated Web content. Accessible from a link on the Pearson Online Learning Center, *PowerWeb* helps students with online research by directing them to more than 6,000 high-quality academic sources.

Telecourse Faculty Guide and Student Study Guide

This text supports the GPN Human Communication Telecourse. The Telecourse Faculty Guide (0-07-283223-1) and Student Study Guide (0-07-283222-3) have been revised with this edition of *Human Communication*. Bookstores and instructors should order these guides from McGraw-Hill. However McGraw-Hill does not license the telecourse itself or sell the telecourse videos. Instead, please contact GPN in Lincoln, Nebraska at 1-800-228-4630, gpn@unl.edu or www.gpn.unl.edu.

Have you ever wondered how communication works, why it often fails, and why it is important to study it? Chapter 1, Introduction to Human Communication, provides some answers to those questions by introducing you to the terms, the models, and the contexts of communication.

Chapter 2, Perception, Self, and Communication, reveals how perception functions in communication, how the way you see others and yourself affects your communication, and how the messages you provide and receive affect the way you see yourself.

PART ONE

Fundamentals of Communication Studies

Chapter 3, Verbal Communication, addresses the role language plays in communication, how language relates to meaning, how language can be both an enhancement and an obstacle to communication, and how people reach shared meaning through language.

In Chapter 4, Nonverbal Communication, you will learn how nonverbal and verbal codes are related. You will also learn about the major nonverbal codes that people use to communicate, such as body movement and facial expression, bodily appearance, space, time, touching, and vocal cues. You will also learn how to improve your nonverbal communication with others.

Chapter 5, Listening and Critical Thinking, discusses the listening process by explaining the importance of listening, common barriers to listening, and strategies for becoming a better listener in various situations including interpersonal conversations, business meetings, and even online conversations.

CHAPTER ONE

Americans report that their greatest fear is the fear of speaking in front of a group.

BRUSKIN REPORT

A world community can exist only with world communication, which means . . . common understanding, a common tradition, common ideas, and common ideals.

ROBERT M. HUTCHINS

Speech is civilization itself. The word, even the most contradictory word, preserves contact—it is silence which isolates.

THOMAS MANN

Introduction to Human Communication

What will you learn?

When you have read and thought about this chapter, you will be able to:

1. State reasons why the study of communication is essential.
2. Define communication.
3. Explain some principles of communication.
4. Name the components of communication.
5. Differentiate among the action, interaction, transaction, and constructivist models.
6. Explain the ways in which intrapersonal, interpersonal, public, and mass communication differ from each other.
7. Define communication competence.
8. Name some of the tenets of the National Communication Association Credo on Ethics.

n this chapter you will be introduced to communication, including some of the fundamental concepts and terms you will need to know for the remainder of this text. You will learn why it is important to study communication and how communication is defined. This chapter will show you how communication begins with you and extends to other people, and it will identify the components of communication. Finally, you will learn about four communication models and the characteristics of the various communication contexts.

Jan Johnson was delighted when her executive manager chose her to be the team leader for the Phoenix Project. After all, Phoenix, Inc., was one of the firm's most important customers, and heading this project would give Jan an opportunity to prove her leadership abilities so that she could advance in the company. Although Jan looked forward to the challenge of her new assignment, she was also a little nervous. It was a big project, and she had never been a team leader before. She wondered if the others in the group would take her seriously. She also worried about the presentation she would have to give to her executive manager and to Phoenix's upper management.

Rudolpho Alvarez, a senior at Miami Dade Community College, was nervous about an employment interview for his first professional job. As a high school and college student he had interviewed successfully for jobs, but this was his first interview for a position in his major field. He had high hopes that this interview would lead to his first job in what would be a long career in business. Rudolpho was worried about the questions the interviewer might ask. "What if he asks about my so-so grades or my marginal computer skills?" Rudolpho wondered. He was afraid he'd be so nervous on the day of the interview that the interviewer would be able to see the sweat beads on his face. Rudolpho didn't get much sleep the night before the interview. He lay awake fretting about the various questions that might be asked and how he'd respond to them.

Jan and Rudolpho are dealing with different communication contexts. This chapter will introduce you to valuable terminology, including communication contexts, which you will need to know as you study communication.

Communication Is Essential

Studying communication is essential for you. Communication is central to your life. Effective communication can help you solve problems in your professional life and improve your relationships in your personal life. Communication experts believe that poor communication is at the root of many problems and that effective communication is one solution to these problems.

Communication is consequential. Understanding the theory, research, and application of communication will make significant differences in your life and the lives of people around the world. The world changed on September 11, 2001, and people became far more aware of the importance of communication principles—particularly intercultural communication principles. Communication principles and practices can resolve disputes among nations as well as among friends and family. Effective communication may not solve all the world's problems, but better communication practices probably can begin to solve or avoid many problems.

Teaching Tip

Before discussing important concepts or questions in class, have students prepare a 3- to 5-minute free write on the topic or question. Giving students time to make note of their ideas will increase the depth of discussions.

Communication is ubiquitous. You cannot avoid communication and you will engage in communication nearly every minute of every day of your life. In addition, communication plays a major role in nearly every aspect of your life.

Regardless of your interests and goals, the ability to communicate effectively will enhance and enrich your life. But learning *how* to communicate is just as important as learning *about* communication. Studying communication comprehensively offers a number of advantages:

1. *Studying communication can improve the way you see yourself.* Communication is "vital to the development of the whole person" (Morreale, Osborn, & Pearson, 2000, p. 4). As we will see in chapter 2, most of our self-knowledge comes from the communicative experience. As we engage in thought (intrapersonal communication) and interactions with significant other people (interpersonal communication), we learn about ourselves. People who are naive about the communication process and the development of self-awareness, self-concept, and self-efficacy may not see themselves accurately or may be unaware of their own self-development. Knowing how communication affects self-perception can lead to greater awareness and appreciation of the self.

Learning communication skills can improve the way you see yourself in a second way. As you learn how to communicate effectively in a variety of situations—from interpersonal relationships to public speeches—your self-confidence will increase. In a study based on the responses from 344 students at a large public university, students who completed a communication course perceived their communication competence to be greater in the classroom, at work, and in social settings. Most dramatic were their perceived improvements in feeling confident about themselves, their feeling comfortable with others' perceptions of themselves, reasoning with people, and using language appropriately (Ford & Wolvin, 1993). Based on such research, you can conclude that your success in interacting with other people in social situations and your achievements in professional settings will lead to more positive feelings about yourself.

2. *Studying communication can improve the way others see you.* In chapter 2 we will discuss self-presentation, image management, and locus of control. You will learn that you can to a considerable extent control your own behavior, which will lead to positive outcomes with others. You will find that your interactions can be smoother and that you can achieve your goals more easily as you manage the impression you make on others.

You can improve the way others see you a second way. Generally, people like communicating with others who can communicate well. Compare your interactions with someone who stumbles over words, is awkward, falls silent, interrupts, and uses inappropriate language to express a

Side Note: A free write allows students to note their thoughts before trying to verbally answer or discuss something. They are called free writes because points are not assigned (thus, "free").

Discussion Question

Have students do a 2- to 3-minute free write on why they think studying communication is important. As a class, discuss the most common reasons. How do students' personal reasons relate to the list of general reasons identified in the book?

thought to your interactions with someone who has a good vocabulary, listens when you speak, reveals appropriate personal information, and smoothly exchanges talk turns with you. Which person do you prefer? Most of us prefer competent communicators. As you become increasingly competent, you will find that others seek you out for conversations, for assistance, and for advice.

3. *Studying communication can increase what you know about human relationships.* The field of communication includes learning about how people relate to each other and about what type of communication is appropriate for a given situation. Most people value human relationships and find great comfort in friendships, family relationships, and community relationships. Within these relationships we learn about trust, intimacy, and reciprocity.

Human relationships are vital to each of us. Human babies thrive when they are touched and when they hear sounds; similarly, adults who engage in human relationships appear to be more successful and satisfied than do those who are isolated. Human relationships serve a variety of functions. They provide us with affection (receiving and providing warmth and friendliness), inclusion (feelings that we belong and providing others with messages that they belong), pleasure (to share happiness and fun), escape (for diversion), and control (to manage our lives and to have influence) (Rubin, Perse, & Barbato, 1988).

We learn about the complexity of human relationships as we study communication. We learn, first, that other people in relationships are vastly different from each other. We learn that the other person in a relationship may be receptive or dismissive toward us. We learn that others behave as if they were superior or inferior to us. They might be approachable or highly formal. People are clearly not interchangeable with each other.

We learn that the interactions we have with others may be helpful or harmful. Communicators can share personal information that builds trust and rapport. The same personal information can be used outside the relationship to humiliate or shame the other person. While some relationships enhance social support, others are riddled with deception and conflict. Interactions are not neutral.

We learn that people co-construct the reality of the relationship. Families, for example, love to tell stories of experiences they have had on vacation, when moving across the country, or when some particularly positive or negative event occurred. Indeed, they often take turns "telling the story." Couples, too, create and tell stories of their lives. Couples' stories may be positive as the couple emphasizes their feelings of belongingness and their identity as a couple. On the other end of the spectrum, stories may be highly negative as people deceive others with information that allows them to cover up criminal acts including drug use, child abuse, or murder.

Human relationships are complex. As you study communication you clarify the variables involved in relationships—other people, the verbal and nonverbal cues provided, the effect of time, the nature of the relationship, and the goals of the participants. You will be far better equipped to engage in relationships with an understanding of the communication process.

4. *Studying communication can teach you important life skills.* Studying communication involves learning important skills that everyone will use at some point in his or her life, such as critical thinking, problem solving, decision making, conflict resolution, team building, media literacy, and public speaking. Allen, Berkowitz, Hunt, and Louden (1999) analyzed dozens of studies and concluded that "communication instruction improves the critical thinking ability of the participants." Our visual literacy is improved as we understand the technical and artistic aspects of the visual communication medium (Metallinos, 1992).

Studying communication early in your college career can enhance your success throughout college. Consider the centrality of oral communication to all of your college classes. You regularly are called on to answer questions in class, to provide reports, to offer explanations, and to make presentations. In addition, your oral and written work both depend on your ability to think critically and creatively, to solve problems, and to make decisions. Most likely, you will be engaged in group projects where skills such as team building and conflict resolution will be central. These same skills will be essential throughout your life.

5. *Studying communication can help you exercise your constitutionally guaranteed freedom of speech.* Few nations have a bill of rights that invites people to convey their opinions and ideas, yet freedom of speech is essential to a democratic form of government. Being a practicing citizen in a democratic society involves knowing about current issues and being able to speak about them in conversations, in speeches, and through the mass media; it also involves being able to critically examine messages from others.

Our understanding of communication shapes our political lives. Mass communication and communication technology have sharply altered the political process. Today many more people have the opportunity to receive information than ever before. Through the mass media, people in remote locations are as well-informed as those in large urban centers. The public agenda is largely set through the media. Pressing problems are given immediate attention. Blumer (1983) notes, "At a time when so many forces—volatility, apathy, skepticism, a sense of powerlessness, and intensified group hostility—appear to be undermining political stability, media organizations have become pivotal to the conduct of human affairs."

Teaching Tip

If you plan to use activity boxes as in-class activities, warn students the day before so they can think about the activity prior to class.

Think, Pair, Share

Does public discourse today operate in an open forum in which a variety of perspectives can be offered on public issues? After you have considered this question and offered arguments for both sides of the issue, share your responses with a member of the class. How do you agree? How do you disagree? For advanced reading on methods of mapping the universe of discourse, see Anderson and Prelli (2001).

Discussion Question

Did the terrorism acts of September 11 teach us anything about communication? Potential topics: lack of communication between government agencies prior to the attack, role of the mass media in informing citizens, how communication and relationships help us manage crises.

While people may feel more enfranchised by the common denominator of the media, others feel more alienated as they become increasingly passive in the process. Whereas face-to-face town meetings were the focus of democratic decision making in times past, today people receive answers to questions, solutions to problems, and decisions about important matters from the media. Many feel powerless and anonymous.

In the wake of the terrorism of September 11, 2001, Americans began to rediscover and recognize the value of a democratic form of government. At the same time, they recognized how vulnerable they were to people who did not endorse basic democratic principles. Americans also learned that terrorist dictators could use the media as easily as could those who came from more reasonable and more democratic ideologies.

The study and understanding of communication processes is profoundly political. Hart (1993) opines that "Those who teach public address and media studies teach that social power can be shifted and public visions exalted if people learn to think well and speak well" (p. 102). Paraphrasing the ancient Isocrates, Hart notes, "To become eloquent is to activate one's humanity, to apply the imagination, and to solve the practical problems of human living" (p. 101). Freedom goes to the articulate.

You have the opportunity of being a fully functioning member of a democratic society. You also have the additional burden of understanding the media and other information technologies. Studying communication will help you learn how to speak effectively, analyze arguments, synthesize large quantities of information, and critically consume information from a variety of sources. The future of our government demands such responsibility.

6. *Studying communication can help you succeed professionally.* A look at the job postings in any newspaper will give you an immediate understanding of the importance of improving your knowl-

edge and practice of communication. The employment section of *The Washington Post* provides some examples (Today's Employment, 1998):

- "We need a results-oriented, seasoned professional who is a good communicator and innovator" reads one ad for a marketing manager.
- Another ad, this one for a marketing analyst, reads, "You should be creative, inquisitive, and a good communicator both in writing and orally."
- An ad for a training specialist calls for "excellent presentation, verbal, and written communication skills, with ability to interact with all levels within organization."

As a person educated in communication, you will be able to gain a more desirable job (Bardwell, 1997; Cockrum, 1994; Peterson, 1997; Ugbah & Evuleocha, 1992). Your interviewing skills will be enhanced. Further, personnel interviewers note that oral communication skills, in general, significantly affect hiring decisions (Peterson, 1997). One survey showed that personnel managers identified effective speaking and listening as the most important factors in hiring people (Curtis, Winsor, & Stephens, 1989). In another survey, employers identified the most important skills for college graduates as oral communication, interpersonal skills, teamwork, and analytical abilities (Collins & Oberman, 1994).

Employers view your written and oral communication competencies and your ability to listen and analyze messages as essential job skills (Carnevale, Gainer, & Meltzer, 1990; Curtis, Winsor, & Stephens, 1989; Maes, Weldy, & Icenogle, 1997; Parnell, 1996; Winsor, Curtis, & Stephens, 1997). Similarly, college graduates perceive communication coursework as essential (Pearson, Sorenson, & Nelson, 1981). Communication competence is important in general and has also been identified as essential in specific careers. Professionals in fields including accounting, auditing, banking, counseling, engineering, industrial hygiene, information science, public relations, and sales have all written about the importance of oral communication skills (Hanzevack & McKean, 1991; Horton & Brown, 1990; LaBar, 1994; Leathers, 1988; Messmer, 1997; Nisberg, 1996; Ridley, 1996; Simkin, 1996).

Communication skills are not only important at the beginning of your career. They continue to be important throughout the work life span. Dauphinais (1997) observes that communication skills can increase upward mobility in one's career. Business executives note the importance of communication competence (Argenti & Forman, 1998; Reinsch & Shelby, 1996). Finally, communication skills are among the top priorities for entrepreneurs.

Communication: The Process of Exchanging Meaning

Now that you have considered why learning about communication is important, you need to know exactly what the term means. Over the years, scholars have created hundreds of definitions of communication. How they define the term can limit or expand the study of the subject. In this text, the definition is simple and broad—simple enough to allow understanding and broad enough to include many contexts of communication.

Communication comes from the Latin word *communicare*, which means "to make common" or "to share." The root definition is consistent with our definition of communication. In this book, **communication** is defined as *the process by which meaning is exchanged between individuals through a common system of symbols, signs, or behavior.* Communication is considered a **process** because it is *an activity, an exchange, or a set of behaviors*—not an unchanging product. Communication is not an object you can hold in your hands—it is an activity in which you participate. David Berlo (1960), a pioneer in the field of communication, probably provided the clearest statement about communication as a process:

> If we accept the concept of process, we view events and relationships as dynamic, ongoing, ever changing, continuous. When we label something as a process, we also mean that it does not have a beginning, an end, a fixed sequence of events. It is not static, at rest. It is moving. The ingredients within a process interact; each affects all the others.

What is an example of how process works in everyday communication? Picture three students meeting on the sidewalk between classes and exchanging a few sentences. This "snapshot" does not begin and end with the students' first word and last sentence. Since they all stopped to chat with each other, you might assume that their relationship began before this encounter. Since they all seem to have a common understanding of what is being said, you might assume that they share experiences that similarly shape their perceptions. You also might assume that this brief encounter does not end when the students leave each other but, rather, that they think about their conversation later in the day or that it leads to another meeting later in the week. In other words, a snapshot cannot capture all that occurs during communication, a process that starts before the words begin and ends long after the last words end.

Communication involves **meaning**, which is *the shared understanding of the message.* Suppose a professor asks a student, "What is the ontogeny of your misogyny?" Although the student hears the words, he or she may not understand what the professor is asking if the meaning of *ontogeny* or *misogyny* is not known. (The professor is asking, "What is the origin of your hatred of women?")

communication

The process by which meaning is exchanged between individuals through a common system of symbols, signs, or behavior.

process

An activity, exchange, or set of behaviors that occurs over time.

Teaching Tip

If you plan to use activity boxes as in-class activities, warn students the day before so they can think about the activity prior to class.

meaning

The shared understanding of the message constructed in the minds of the communicators.

THE NATIONAL COMMUNICATION ASSOCIATION

The discipline, or academic study, of communication traces its roots to the ancient Greek and Roman eras. As an association, communication first emerged in 1914 when a small group of teachers of speech broke away from a larger group of teachers of English. The National Communication Association (NCA), as it is known today, now has approximately 8,000 members and provides a variety of services to educators and practitioners in the communication discipline. Find the NCA on the Web at **www.natcom.org**. Learn about one or two features of the organization that you can share with the class. Would you benefit by being a member of this organization? What can you learn about the study of communication from the website?

Understanding emerges from shared meanings.

Class Activity

Have students form groups and develop guidelines defining "short research papers." Many teachers use such assignments, but their expectations vary. As a class, use groups' descriptions of short research papers to emphasize why shared meaning is important. Alternatively, pick an assignment you plan to use later in the semester rather than the generic "short research paper."

Understanding the meaning of another person's message does not occur unless the two communicators can elicit common meanings for words, phrases, and nonverbal codes.When you use language, meaning facilitates an appropriate response that indicates that the message was understood. For example, you ask a friend for a sheet of paper. She says nothing and gives you one sheet of paper. You and your friend share the same meaning of the message exchanged. But a message can be interpreted in more than one way, especially if the people involved have little shared experience. In such a case, a more accurate understanding of the intended meaning can be discerned by *negotiating*, that is, by asking questions.

Communication Principles

A definition of communication may be insufficient to clarify the nature of communication. To explain communication in more detail, we consider here some principles that guide our understanding of communication.

Communication Begins with the Self

Discussion Question

What is one personal characteristic that influences how you communicate? Use the free-write technique to give students an opportunity to think about their answers.

Video Activity

Ask students to watch the video segment titled "The Hospital." Discuss how Susan's mother's sense of self influenced the way she communicated with Susan about the grandmother's hospital visit.

How you see yourself can make a great difference in how you communicate. Carl Rogers (1951) wrote, "Every individual exists in a continually changing world of experience of which he [or she] is the center" (p. 483). For instance, when people are treated as though they are inferior, intelligent, gifted, or attractive, they will often begin acting accordingly. Many communication scholars and social scientists believe that people are products of how others treat them and of the messages others send them.

The theory behind this point of view was developed about 30 years ago by Dean Barnlund, a communication theorist. He introduced the idea that individuals "construct" themselves through the relationships they have, wish to have, or perceive themselves as having. Barnlund (1970) also developed the idea that "six persons" are involved in every two-person communication situation. Figure 1.1 shows that these six persons emerge from

1. How you view yourself.
2. How you view the other person.
3. How you believe the other person views you.
4. How the other person views himself or herself.
5. How the other person views you.
6. How the other person believes you view him or her.

An example may clarify Barnlund's six-person concept. Suppose you see yourself as an enthusiastic, highly motivated student (person 1). You perceive your best friend as very intelligent, yet judgmental (2). She sees you as fun-loving and achievement-oriented, yet somewhat rigid (5); she views herself as moderately intelligent and a good conversationalist (4). Your tendency may be to downplay your goals and accomplishments and to emphasize your sense of humor (3) when you are with your friend. You frequently turn to your friend for advice on academic matters, yet discount any negative messages in other areas. She, in turn, frequently offers advice but fails to share her opinions (6). Barnlund encourages us to con-

Figure 1.1   Barnlund's "six people" involved in every two-person communication.

sider the various perspectives involved in communication and to recognize the centrality of the self in communication.

As persons, our understanding of the world is limited by our experiences with it. Shotter (2000) suggests that we cannot understand communication through external, abstract, and systematic processes. Instead, he describes communication as a "ceaseless flow of speech-entwined, dialogically structured, social activity" (p. 119). In other words, our understanding of communication is participatory. We are actively involved and relationally responsive in our knowledge of communication. Shotter would contrast his perspective of a participatory-wholistic view of communication with one that is abstract and systematic.

To apply this perspective, let us consider an example. You have a roommate who is from another country. The roommate's religion, belief system, and daily habits challenge your perspective, derived from interacting primarily with people in the United States who hold Western and Christian values. To the extent that you each try to impose your own preunderstandings on the communication you share, you may be dissatisfied and experience great conflict. By preimposing "rules" of communication derived from your earlier experiences in two distinctive cultures, you are bound to fail in this new relationship. If you are able to move beyond such a view and allow your perception of your communication to become a product of your interactions, you may be able to communicate in interesting and effective ways.

Every day we experience the centrality of ourselves in communication. As a participant in communication, you are limited by your own view of the situation. A student, for instance, may describe a conflict with an instructor as unfair treatment: "I know my instructor doesn't like the fact that I don't agree with his opinions, and that's why he gave me such a poor grade in that class." Conversely, the instructor might think, "That student doesn't understand all the factors that go into a final grade." Each person may believe that he is correct and that the other person's view is wrong. As you study communication, you will learn ways to better manage such conflict.

Communication Involves Others

George Herbert Mead (1967) said that the self originates in communication. Through verbal and nonverbal symbols, a child learns to accept roles in response to the expectations of others. For example, Dominique Moceanu, a successful Olympic gymnast, was influenced quite early in life by what others wanted her to be. Both her parents had been gymnasts, and apparently her father told her for years that her destiny was to be a world-class gymnast (Hamilton, 1998). Most likely she had an inherent ability to be a good one, but she may not have become an accomplished, medal-winning gymnast without the early messages she received from her parents and trainers. Like Moceanu, you establish self-image, the sort of person you believe you are, by the ways others categorize you. Positive, negative, and neutral messages that you receive from others all play a role in determining who you are.

dialogue

The act of taking part in a conversation, discussion, or negotiation.

Communication itself is probably best understood as a dialogic process. A **dialogue** is simply *the act of taking part in a conversation, discussion, or negotiation.* When we describe and explain our communicative exchanges with others, we are doing so from a perspective of self and from a perspective derived from interacting with others. Our understanding of communication does not occur in a vacuum but in light of our interactions with other people. (For further reading, see Czubaroff, 2000.)

In a more obvious way, communication involves others in the sense that a competent communicator considers the other person's needs and expectations when selecting messages to share. The competent communicator understands that a large number of messages can be shared at any time, but sensitivity and responsiveness to the other communicators are essential. Thus we observe that communication begins with the self, as defined largely by others, and involves others, as defined largely by the self.

Communication Is Complicated

Communication, some believe, is a simple matter of passing information from one source to another. In a sense, communication defined in this way would occur whenever you accessed information on the Web. However, you know that even in this most simple example, communication does not necessarily occur. For example, if you access a homepage written in a language that you do not understand, no communication occurs. If the material is highly complex, you might not understand its message. Similarly, you might be able to repeat what someone else has spoken to you, but with absolutely no understanding of the intent, or the content, of the message.

Communication is far more than simple information transmission. Communication involves choices about the multiple aspects of the message—the verbal, nonverbal, and behavioral aspects, the choices surrounding the transmission channels used, the characteristics of the speaker, the relationship between the speaker and the audience, the characteristics of the audience, and the situation in which the communication occurs. A change in any one of these variables affects the entire communication process. We will discuss each of these components of communication in a later section in this chapter.

An Increased Quantity of Communication Does Not Increase the Quality of Communication

You might believe that a textbook on communication would stake claims on the importance of increased communication. You may have heard counselors or therapists encouraging people to communicate more: "What we need is more communication." However, greater amounts of communication do not lead to more harmony or more accurate and shared meanings. Sometimes people disagree, and the more they talk, the more they learn that they are in conflict. At other times, people have very poor listening or empathy skills and they misunderstand vast quantities of information. Communication, defined simply as verbiage, does not necessarily lead to positive outcomes.

TRY ►THIS

Try to recall an experience in which you and another person tried to resolve a conflict by talking about it, only to find that your conflict escalated instead of being resolved.

"Communication Is Inevitable, Irreversible, and Unrepeatable" (DeVito, 1999, p. 30)

Although communication is complicated and more communication is not necessarily better communication, communication occurs almost every minute of your life. If you are not communicating with yourself (thinking, planning, reacting to the world around you), you are observing others and drawing inferences from their behavior. Even if the other person did not intend a message for you, you gather observations and draw specific conclusions. A person yawns and you believe that person is bored with your message. A second person looks away from you and you conclude that person is not listening to you. A third person smiles (perhaps because of a memory of a joke he heard recently) and you believe that he is attracted to you. We are continually gleaning meanings from others' behaviors and we are constantly providing behaviors that have communicative value for them.

Communication Cannot Be Reversed

Have you ever insulted someone accidentally? You may have tried to explain that you did not intend to insult anybody. You may have told the other person that you were sorry for your statement. You may have made a joke out of your misstatement. Nonetheless, your comment lingers both in the mind of the other person and in your own mind. As you understand the irreversibility of communication, you may become more careful in your conversations with others and you may take more time preparing public speeches. We cannot go back in time and erase our messages to others.

Communication Cannot Be Repeated

Have you ever had an incredible evening with someone and remarked, "Let's do this again." When you tried to recreate the ambience, the conversation, and the setting, nothing seemed right. Your second experience with a similar setting and person yielded far different results. Just as you cannot repeat an experience, you cannot repeat communication.

To summarize the principles we identified in this section, communication begins with the self, involves others, and is complicated. An increased quantity of communication does not increase the quality of communication. Communication is inevitable, irreversible, and unrepeatable.

Components of Communication

In this section you will learn how communication in action really works. The components of communication are people, messages, codes, channels, feedback, encoding and decoding, and noise.

People

source

A message initiator.

receiver

A message target.

People are involved in the human communication process in two roles. They serve as both the sources and the receivers of messages. A **source** *initiates a message,* and a **receiver** is *the intended target of the message.* In-

WHAT'S IN A NAME?

Americans name their children after relatives, entertainers, famous people, and biblical figures. Many Spanish-speaking males are named after Jesus, and thousands of Muslim males are named after Mohammed. In China, too, names have meaning that can influence how a person feels about himself or herself. Wen Shu Lee (1998), a professor originally from Taiwan, published an article about the names of women in China. She claims that naming practices often reflect gender- and class-based oppression. The name *Zhao Di,* for example, "commands a daughter to bring to the family a younger brother, while 'expelling' more younger sisters." The name reflects a higher value on male children. Does your name influence what you think of yourself? Does your name affect how, when, and with whom you communicate? What's in a name?

dividuals do not perform these two roles independently. Instead, they are the sources and the receivers of messages simultaneously and continually.

People do not respond uniformly to all messages, nor do they always provide the same messages in exactly the same way. Individual characteristics of people, including race, sex, age, culture, values, and attitudes, affect the way they send and receive messages. (Throughout this text, you will find discussions about the ways in which culture and sex affect communication.)

The Message

The **message** is *the verbal and nonverbal form of the idea, thought, or feeling that one person (the source) wishes to communicate to another person or group of people (the receivers).* The message is the content of the interaction. The message includes the symbols (words and phrases) you use to communicate your ideas, as well as your facial expressions, bodily movements, gestures, touch, tone of voice, and other nonverbal codes. The message may be relatively brief and easy to understand or long and complex. Some experts believe that real communication stems only from messages that are intentional, or have a purpose. However, since intent is sometimes difficult to prove in a communication situation, the authors of this text believe that real communication can occur through either intentional or unintentional messages.

message

The verbal or nonverbal form of the idea, thought, or feeling that one person (the source) wishes to communicate to another person or group of people (the receivers).

channel

The means by which a message moves from the source to the receiver of the message.

feedback

The receiver's verbal and nonverbal response to the source's message.

Class Activity

Have students form groups and identify a list of different channels that could be used in communication. For each item, students should identify one advantage and one disadvantage of the channel. This activity illustrates how communicators must think strategically about which channel to use and also foreshadows topics discussed in subsequent chapters.

code

A systematic arrangement of symbols used to create meanings in the mind of another person or persons.

syntax

The rules of arrangement in language.

grammar

The rules of function in language.

The Channel

The **channel** is *the means by which a message moves from the source to the receiver of the message.* A message moves from one place to another, from one person to another, by traveling through a medium, or channel. Airwaves, sound waves, twisted copper wires, glass fibers, and cable are all communication channels. Airwaves and cable are two of the various channels through which you receive television messages. Radio messages move through sound waves. Computer images (and sound, if there is any) travel through light waves, and sometimes both light and sound waves. In person-to-person communication, you send your messages through a channel of sound waves and light waves that enable receivers to see and hear you.

Feedback

Feedback is *the receiver's verbal and nonverbal response to the source's message.* Ideally, you respond to another person's messages by providing feedback so that the source knows the message was received as intended. Feedback is part of any communication situation. Even no response, or silence, is feedback, as are restless behavior and quizzical looks from students in a lecture hall. Say you're in a building you've never been in before, looking for a restroom. You ask a person quickly passing by, "Excuse me, can you tell me . . . ," but the person keeps on going without acknowledging you. In this case, the intended receiver did not respond, yet even the lack of a response provides you with some feedback. You may surmise that perhaps the receiver didn't hear you or was in too much of a hurry to stop.

Code

A computer carries messages via binary code on cable, wire, or fiber; similarly, you converse with others by using a code called language. A **code** is *a systematic arrangement of symbols used to create meanings in the mind of another person or persons.* **Syntax**—*rules of arrangement*—and **grammar**—*rules of function*—in language result in the "systematic arrangement" that becomes a code. Words, phrases, and sentences become "symbols" that are used to evoke images, thoughts, and ideas in the mind of others. If someone yells "Stop" as you approach the street, the word *stop* has become a symbol that you are likely to interpret as a warning of danger.

Verbal and nonverbal codes are the two types of code used in communication. **Verbal codes** consist of *symbols and their grammatical arrangement.* All languages are codes. **Nonverbal codes** consist of *all symbols that are not words, including bodily movements, your use of space and* *time, your clothing and other adornments, and sounds other than words.* Nonverbal codes should not be confused with nonoral codes. All nonoral codes, such as bodily movement, are nonverbal codes. However, nonverbal codes also include *oral* codes, such as pitch, duration, rate of speech, and sounds like *eh* and *ah.*

Encoding and Decoding

If communication involves the use of codes, the process of communicating can be viewed as one of encoding and decoding. **Encoding** is defined as *the act of putting an idea or a thought into a code.* **Decoding** is *assigning meaning to that idea or thought.* For instance, suppose you are interested in purchasing a new car. You are trying to describe a compact model to your father, who wants to help you with your purchase. You might be visualizing the car with the black interior, sporty design, and red exterior that belongs to your best friend. Putting this vision into words, you tell your father you are interested in a car that is "small and well designed." You encode your perceptions of a particular car into words that describe the model. Your father, on hearing this, decodes your words and develops his own picture. His love of larger cars affects this process. As a result of your definition, he envisions a sedan. As you can see, misunderstanding often occurs because of the limitations of language and the inadequacy of descriptions. Nonetheless, encoding and decoding are essential in sharing your thoughts, ideas, and feelings with others.

Noise

In the communication process, **noise** is *any interference in the encoding and decoding processes that reduces the clarity of a message.* Noise can be physical noise, such as loud sounds; distracting sights, such as a piece of food between someone's front teeth; or an unusual behavior, such as someone standing too close for comfort. Noise can be mental, psychological, or semantic, such as daydreams about a loved one, worry about the bills, pain from a tooth, or uncertainty about what the other person's words are supposed to mean. Noise can be anything that interferes with receiving, interpreting, or providing feedback about a message.

Discussion Question

What are examples of feedback strategies we use during communication? Potential topics include various forms of verbal and nonverbal feedback.

verbal codes

Symbols and their grammatical arrangement, such as languages.

nonverbal codes

All symbols that are not words, including bodily movements, use of space and time, clothing and adornments, and sounds other than words.

encoding

The process of translating an idea or thought into a code.

decoding

The process of assigning meaning to the idea or thought in a code.

noise

Any interference in the encoding and decoding processes that reduces message clarity.

TRY ◄►THIS

Think of as many examples as you can of noise that interferes with communication.

Team Challenge

Academic disciplines such as English, history, physics, and biology all have agreed-on rules about what constitutes knowledge. Concepts like validity, reliability, narrative fidelity, precision, parsimony, and simplicity guide these decision rules. Communication is an academic discipline and has standards for the generation, and acceptability, of knowledge. Because communicative behavior is so familiar, many people believe they are experts when they know very little. In some colleges and universities, for example, oral communication is taught "across the curriculum," and professors of engineering, science, and math teach and evaluate oral communicative performance. These same professors would be mortified if they learned that quantum mechanics, physics, or chemistry was being taught and evaluated across the curriculum by professors of humanities and fine arts.

How do we know whether information we read and hear about communication is accurate? What constitutes valid and reliable information? These questions loom even larger today as the Internet spews larger and larger quantities of information to users each day.

After you have had some time to look at books and Internet sources on communication research and theory, identify some rules that you believe that a student of communication should follow in gaining accurate and useful information on communication. Then, in a group of students in class, put together some agreed-on conventions for assessing the validity (accuracy) and reliability (consistency) of claims that are offered about communication.

As you progress through this course, remember to apply these principles to information that you read, see, and hear about communication.

How Does Communication Occur?

Barnlund's six-person theory of communication presented earlier is a model, a pictorial depiction of how communication would look drawn. This simplified model serves as a predictor of how communication might occur. Earlier models—the action model, the interaction model, and the transaction model—reveal how communication models have evolved over time. We should note that all of the models presented here are culturally bound; that is, they are limited by Western thought. A person from an Eastern culture might view communication very differently.

The Action Model

In the past, people believed communication could be viewed as action; thus, in the **action model,** *one person sends a message and another person (or persons) receives it.* Experts in communication derided this simple model (Figure 1.2) by calling it the "inoculation model" because it seemed to depict a speaker injecting an audience with a message. The model is linear, with movement in only one direction, and it was faulted for not revealing anything about how audiences influence speakers. The action model seems to depict a public-speaking situation, but even in that context audiences affect speakers through nonverbal and verbal feedback, which is not reflected in the action model.

The Interaction Model

The interaction model of communication adds another dimension to the action model. In the **interaction model,** *one person sends a message to a second person, who receives it and responds with another message.* This model (Figure 1.2) seems to depict a conversation between two people in which the communicators take turns sending and receiving messages. Communication of this type can be compared to a basketball game. Just as a basketball cannot be thrown back until it is caught, in the interaction model, the receiver cannot return a message until the speaker's message is received.

The Transaction Model

Rather than act exclusively as senders or receivers, in the **transaction model** of communication, *communicators simultaneously send and receive messages* (Figure 1.2). Thus sending and receiving are no longer separate activities, and they do not occur one at a time. According to the transactional view, people are continually sending and receiving messages; they cannot avoid communication. With this model, communication becomes a confusing ball game in which a person catches and throws an unlimited number of balls at any time, in any direction, and to any person. Whether or not an individual throws a ball is not dependent on his or her ability to catch one first. Individuals do not have to take turns in this game. The game has some rules and predictability, but from time to time balls fly through the air without preparation. Similarly, in the transaction model messages are everywhere. So the person talking to you on the sidewalk can also be nodding to a passerby. How you look, what you say, how receptive you are, and what is happening around you all are part of the transactional model.

CD-ROM Activity

Have students view the animation "Perspectives on Communication" contained on the student CD-ROM. The animation describes similarities and differences between the various models of communication.

action model

A depiction of communication as one person sending a message and another person or group of persons receiving it.

interaction model

A depiction of communication as one person sending a message and a second person receiving the message and then responding with a return message.

transaction model

A depiction of communication as communicators simultaneously sending and receiving messages.

Figure 1.2 Perspectives on communication.

The Constructivist Model

The first three models—action, interaction, and transaction—are mechanistic models that are limited in that they simply show the direction of communication movement: source to receiver, source to receiver to source, or source and receiver simultaneously. In the constructivist model, the focus shifts from sources, messages, receivers, and feedback to what occurs in the minds of the communicators: interpreting meaning.

The **constructivist model** posits that *receivers create their own reality in their minds* (Figure 1.2). The sender's words are symbols to be interpreted, and the receiver constructs his or her own meaning. However, the receiver's interpretation of the sender's message may or may not be the same as what the sender intended it to be. The only way to reach agreement about the message is by discussing what the sender intended and what the receiver interpreted. This is called *negotiating meaning.*

The constructivist model significantly reframes the communication process. The message is no longer something that is simply sent one way to a passive audience that receives it like an injection; it is no longer passed back and forth like a basketball; and it is no longer tossed about in a confusing game whose participants might be bombarded with multiple balls. In this model, the ball (or the message) may be something else by the time it is received and interpreted. Communication becomes more confusing under this model. But in reality, communication isn't as easy as the earlier models described it as being. Under the best of communication circumstances the two people involved learn to manage meaning by negotiating what each believes the message to be.

constructivist model

A theory of communication which posits that receivers create their own reality in their minds.

Class Activity

To help students review the various communication models, have groups create a narrative or fictional case study of a communication situation illustrating one of the models (each group should be assigned a different model). Discuss the narratives in class.

What Are Communication Contexts?

Communication occurs in a **context,** *a set of circumstances or a situation.* Communication occurs between two friends, among five business acquaintances in a small-group setting, and between a lecturer and an audience that fills an auditorium. At many colleges and universities, the communication courses are arranged by context: interpersonal communication, interviewing, small-group communication, public speaking, and mass communication. The number of people involved in communication affects the kind of communication that occurs. You may communicate with yourself, with another person, or with many others. The differences among these situations affect your choices of the most appropriate verbal and nonverbal codes.

context

A set of circumstances or a situation.

Intrapersonal Communication

intrapersonal communication

The process of understanding and sharing meaning within the self.

Intrapersonal communication is *the process of understanding and sharing meaning within the self.* Intrapersonal communication is the communication that occurs within your own mind. For example, suppose you and the person you've been dating for two years share the same attitude toward education and a future career. After the two of you finish your undergraduate degrees, you both plan to attend graduate school together and later to operate your own business. One day, your partner informs you that he or she has decided to work in the family's business immediately after graduating. In your opinion, this action changes everything, including you and your partner's future together. When you begin to share your feelings with your partner, he or she becomes angry and says your attitude is just another example of your inflexibility. You tell your partner that you can't discuss the issue with him or her now and that you need to think things over for a while. You leave, thinking about what has just happened and what the future holds for you and your partner. You are engaged in intrapersonal communication.

Intrapersonal communication occurs, as this example suggests, when you evaluate or examine the interaction that occurs between yourself and others, but it is not limited to such situations. This form of communication occurs before and during other forms of communication as well. For instance, you might argue with yourself during a conversation in which some-

Intrapersonal communication occurs in our reflections.

24

one asks you to do something you don't really want to do: Before you accept or decline, you mull over the alternatives in your mind.

Intrapersonal communication also includes such activities as solving problems internally, resolving internal conflict, planning for the future, and evaluating yourself and your relationships with others. Intrapersonal communication—the basis for all other communication—involves only the self.

Each one of us is continually engaged in intrapersonal communication. Although you might become more easily absorbed in talking to yourself when you are alone (while walking to class, driving to work, or taking a shower, for instance), you are also likely to be involved in this form of communication in crowded circumstances as well (such as during a lecture, at a party, or when visiting friends). Think about the last time you looked at yourself in a mirror. What were your thoughts? Although intrapersonal communication is almost continuous, people seldom focus on this form of communication.

Indeed, not all communication experts believe intrapersonal communication should be examined within communication studies. The naysayers believe that communication requires two or more receivers of a message, and since there are no receivers in intrapersonal communication, no communication actually occurs. They reason that intrapersonal communication should be studied in a discipline such as psychology or neurology—some field in which experts study the mind or the brain. Nonetheless, intrapersonal communication is recognized by most scholars within the discipline as one context of communication.

Interpersonal Communication

When you move from intrapersonal communication to interpersonal communication, you move from communication that occurs within your own mind to communication that involves one or more other persons. **Interpersonal communication** is *the personal process of coordinating meaning between at least two people in a situation that allows mutual opportunities for both speaking and listening.* Like intrapersonal communication, interpersonal communication occurs for a variety of reasons: to solve problems, to resolve conflicts, to share information, to improve your perception of yourself, or to fulfill social needs, such as the need to belong or to be loved. Through our interpersonal communication, people are able to establish relationships with others that include friendships and romantic relationships.

Dyadic and small-group communication are two subsets of interpersonal communication. **Dyadic communication** or *two-person communication,* includes interviews with an employer or a teacher; talks with a parent, spouse, or child; and interactions among strangers, acquaintances,

interpersonal communication

The personal process of coordinating meaning between at least two people in a situation that allows mutual opportunities for both speaking and listening.

dyadic communication

Two-person communication.

small-group communication

The interaction of a small group of people to achieve an interdependent goal.

and friends. **Small-group communication** is *the interaction of a small group of people to achieve an interdependent goal* (Brilhart & Galanes, 1998). Small-group communication occurs in families, work groups, support groups, religious groups, and study groups. Communication experts agree that two people are a dyad and more than two people are a small group if they have a common purpose, goal, or mission. However, disagreement emerges about the maximum number of participants in a small group. Technology also poses questions for communication scholars to debate: Does a small group have to meet face-to-face? That teleconferences can be small-group communication is uncontroversial, but what about discussions in chat rooms on the Internet? Small-group communication is discussed in greater detail later in this text.

Public Communication

public communication

The process of generating meanings in a situation where a single source transmits a message to a number of receivers who give nonverbal and, sometimes, question-and-answer feedback.

Public communication is *the process of generating meanings in a situation where a single source transmits a message to a number of receivers who give nonverbal and, sometimes, question-and-answer feedback.* In public communication the source adapts the message to the audience in an attempt to achieve maximum understanding. Sometimes, virtually everyone in the audience understands the speaker's message; other times, many people fail to understand.

Public communication, or public speaking, is recognized by its formality, structure, and planning. You probably are frequently a receiver of public communication in lecture classes, at convocations, and at religious services. Occasionally, you also may be a source: when you speak in a group, when you try to convince other voters of the merits of a particular candidate for office, or when you introduce a guest speaker to a large audience. Public communication most often informs or persuades, but it can also entertain, introduce, announce, welcome, or pay tribute.

Mass Communication

mass communication

Communication mediated, via a transmission system, between a source and a large number of unseen receivers.

Mass communication, or *communication mediated between a source and a large number of unseen receivers,* always has some transmission system (mediator) between the sender and the receiver. When you watch your favorite TV show, the signals are going from a broadcast studio to a satellite or cable system and then from that system to your TV set: The mediator is the channel, the method of distribution. This type of communication is called "mass" because the message goes to newspaper and magazine readers, TV watchers, and radio listeners. Mass communication is often taught in a college's or university's department of mass communication, radio and television, or journalism.

The various communication contexts can be determined by several factors: the number of people involved, the degree of the setting's formality or intimacy, the opportunities for feedback, the need for restructuring

TABLE 1.1   DIFFERENCES AMONG COMMUNICATION CONTEXTS

CONTEXTS	INTRAPERSONAL COMMUNICATION	DYADIC COMMUNICATION	INTERPERSONAL COMMUNICATION		
			SMALL-GROUP COMMUNICATION	PUBLIC COMMUNICATION	MASS COMMUNICATION
NUMBER OF PEOPLE	1	2	Usually 3 to 10; maybe more	Usually more than 10	Usually thousands
DEGREE OF FORMALITY OR INTIMACY	Most intimate	Generally intimate; interview is formal	Intimate or formal	Generally formal	Generally formal
OPPORTUNITIES FOR FEEDBACK	Complete feedback	A great deal of feedback	Less than in intrapersonal communication but more than in public communication	Less than in small-group communication but more than in mass communication	Usually none
NEED FOR PRESTRUCTURING MESSAGES	None	Some	Some	A great deal	Almost totally scripted
DEGREE OF STABILITY OF THE ROLES OF SPEAKER AND LISTENER	Highly unstable; the individual as both speaker and listener	Unstable; speaker and listener alternate	Unstable; speakers and listeners alternate	Highly stable; one speaker with many listeners	Highly stable; on-air speakers, invisible listeners

messages, and the degree of stability of the roles of speaker and listener. Table 1.1 compares the contexts on the basis of these factors.

What Are the Goals of Communication Study?

You learned the importance of studying communication at the beginning of this chapter. You will derive many benefits: You can improve the way you see yourself and the ways others see you, you can increase what you know about human relationships, you can learn important life skills, you can better exercise your constitutionally guaranteed freedom of speech, you can increase your chances of succeeding professionally. How will you achieve these outcomes? To the extent that you become a more effective and ethical communicator, you will enhance the likelihood of these positive results.

Class Activity
Table 1.1 suggests relationships between the number of people involved in a communication situation and other elements of communication. For example, as the number of people involved in the communication event increases, the need for prestructuring messages also increases. Have groups develop a list of "propositions" pointing out these relationships.

communication competence

The ability to effectively exchange meaning through a common system of symbols, signs, or behavior.

ethics

A set of moral principles or values.

Class Activity
As a class develop your own credo of ethical behavior. How should students act as speakers in the class? How should listeners behave in the class? Post the credo you developed in the classroom.

Effective Communication

Effective communication is also known as communication competence. **Communication competence** is defined simply as *the ability to effectively exchange meaning through a common system of symbols, signs, or behavior.* As you will learn in this textbook, communication competence is not necessarily easy to achieve. Communication competence can be difficult because your goals and others' goals may be discrepant. Similarly, you and the others with whom you communicate may have a different understanding of your relationship. Cultural differences may cause you to view the world and other people differently. Indeed, people's different perspectives about communication may themselves create problems in your interactions with others. As you read this text, you will learn about the multiple variables involved in communication and you will become more competent in your communication.

You need to recognize now that while communication competence is the goal, the complexity of communication will encourage you to be a student of communication over your lifetime. In this course you begin to learn the terminology and the multiple variables that comprise communication. Although you will not emerge from the course as totally effective, you should begin to see significant changes in your communication abilities. The professional public speaker or comedian, the glib reporter on television, and the highly satisfied spouse in a long-term marriage make communication look easy. However, as you will learn, their skills are complex and interwoven with multiple layers of understanding.

Ethical Communication

A second goal of studying communication lies in its ethical dimension. **Ethics** may be defined as *a set of moral principles or values.* Ethical standards may vary from one discipline to another just as they differ from one culture to another. Within the communication discipline, a set of ethics has been adopted. The National Communication Association created the following set of ethics.

NCA Credo for Communication Ethics

Questions of right and wrong arise whenever people communicate. Ethical communication is fundamental to responsible thinking, decision making, and the development of relationships and communities within and across contexts, cultures, channels, and media. Moreover, ethical communication enhances human worth and dignity by fostering truthfulness, fairness, responsibility, personal integrity, and respect for self and others. We believe that unethical communication threatens the quality of all communication and consequently the well-being of individuals and the society in which we live. Therefore we, the members of the National Communication Association, endorse and are committed to practicing the following principles of ethical communication:

We advocate truthfulness, accuracy, honesty, and reason as essential to the integrity of communication.

We endorse freedom of expression, diversity of perspective, and tolerance of dissent to achieve the informed and responsible decision making fundamental to a civil society.

We strive to understand and respect other communicators before evaluating and responding to their messages.

We promote access to communication resources and opportunities as necessary to fulfill human potential and contribute to the well-being of families, communities, and society.

We promote communication climates of caring and mutual understanding that respect the unique needs and characteristics of individual communicators.

We condemn communication that degrades individuals and humanity through distortion, intimidation, coercion, and violence, and through the expression of intolerance and hatred.

We are committed to the courageous expression of personal convictions in pursuit of fairness and justice.

We advocate sharing information, opinions, and feelings when facing significant choices while also respecting privacy and confidentiality.

We accept responsibility for the short- and long-term consequences of our own communication and expect the same of others.

These "Nine Commandments" are actually quite straightforward. They suggest that we should be open, honest, and reasonable. They affirm our belief in the First Amendment to the Constitution of the United States of America. Respect for other people and their messages is essential. Access to information and to people is acknowledged. Finally, responsibility for our behavior is identified as important.

These ideals are derived from Western conceptions of communication and with a belief in democratic decision making. They also reflect ideologies of people within the communication discipline. We acknowledge that these standards might not be consistent with other cultures, belief systems, religions, or even academic disciplines. Murray (2000), for example, would suggest that we more properly should derive ethical standards in dialogue with others combining one's own answerability with the calls to responsibility from others.

While we hold the NCA Credo as the best set of ethical conventions guiding communication, we recognize that others might not view these ideals as appropriate for all of us or appropriate at all times. Throughout this text we will consider the importance of ethics and we will make reference to this credo.

TRY ◄►THIS

Our communication, and that of others, is not always effective or ethical. Identify an experience in which communication between you and another person was not effective. Identify another experience in which it was not ethical.

Chapter Review

SUMMARY

In this chapter you have learned the following:

- Communication is essential because
  - Understanding communication can improve the way people view themselves and the way others view them.
  - People learn more about human relationships as they study communication and they learn important life skills.
  - Studying communication can help people exercise their constitutionally guaranteed freedom of speech.
  - An understanding of communication can help people succeed professionally.
- Communication is the process by which meaning is exchanged between individuals through a common system of symbols, signs, or behavior.
  - Communication begins with the self and involves others.
  - Increased quantity of communication does not necessarily increase the quality of communication.

- Communication is inevitable, irreversible, and unrepeatable.

- The components of communication are people, messages, channels, feedback, codes, encoding and decoding, and noise.
- Four communication models exist: action, interaction, transaction, and the constructivist model.
- Communication occurs in intrapersonal, interpersonal, public, and mass contexts. The number of people involved, the degree of formality or intimacy, the opportunities for feedback, the need for prestructuring messages, and the degree of stability of the roles of speaker and listener all vary with the communication context.
- Communication behavior should be effective and ethical.

⊙ VIDEO LINK: EXCHANGING MEANING

Video Episodes 1 and 2: "Sam's Graduation Party" and "The Hospital"

Have you ever wished that homework assignments were as enjoyable as watching television? Think about it: If assignments were as entertaining as classic episodes of "Friends," we would be honor students, right? We cannot change all homework, but we can recommend some homework that may be entertaining. Accompanying your textbook is a CD-ROM containing a video telling the story of Susan Elliott, a student much like yourself. In the video you will see Susan attend a graduation party for her brother where tension mounts because people violate social norms. You will also learn why Susan's mother gets so upset over a visit to the hospital. Through the various segments you will meet interesting characters like Vivian Min and Enrique Roberts. As you meet these people, our hope is that you begin to recognize the relevance of communication in your own life. We encourage you to begin by watching all of the video segments. Besides entertaining you, the complete initial viewing will also provide a context for questions we pose about the video at the end of each chapter. Enjoy!

Communication is the process by which meaning is exchanged between individuals through a common system of symbols, signs, or behavior. This chapter identifies several principles to further explain communication. One principle is that communication begins with the self. Stated simply, how you see yourself can make a great difference in how you communicate, or exchange meaning with others. Watch, "The Hospital," and analyze how Susan's mom's perception of herself influenced her communication with Susan about the grandmother's hospitalization. Also, did knowledge of the mother's self-perception change the way Susan assigned meaning to her mother's statements? Watch "Sam's Graduation Party" and analyze how mom's self-perception influenced her behavior toward her husband and Dr. Stern.

ISSUES IN COMMUNICATION: A BUSINESS SUCCESS?

This Issues in Communication narrative is designed to provoke individual thought or discussion about key concepts raised in the chapter.

Kyle Gorton was one of the founders of a successful company, KyMo, which created virtual-reality software. Before the company was sold, Kyle often worked 18-hour days. He sold products, wrote business plans, handled the company's finances, oversaw production, and was familiar with all aspects of the operation. While Kyle did most of the behind-the-scenes work, his cofounder, Morton Giamani, made presentations to trade shows and venture capitalists. Morton recruited potential employees, but Kyle interviewed them, and if they were hired, he often took them under his wing and became their mentor. Because he thought all his employees had valuable skills and ideas to contribute to the company, he frequently employed work teams. As a result, the employees of KyMo thought highly of him. However, because Morton was the one who was out meeting all the movers and shakers in the industry, the industry leaders believed that Morton was primarily responsible for the company's success.

Now that the company has been sold, Kyle must decide what to do with his future. Although Kyle and Morton's company was successful, Kyle doesn't have the contacts in the industry that Morton has, so very few would associate his name with the company. Although Kyle knows he's intelligent and hardworking, he finds himself comparing himself to Morton and doubting his own abilities. Kyle thinks, "Why couldn't I have been more of a charismatic people-person like Morton? I should have spent more time writing articles, giving speeches, and rubbing shoulders with venture capitalists. But then again, I just don't think I'm as good as Morton at that sort of thing. I have my strengths, and he has his. We were a great team. I don't know why, but we really haven't talked about starting up another company together. I think I'm going to take the initiative and talk to him about it."

The next day Kyle and Morton begin discussing what kind of company they'd like to start next.

Apply what you have learned about communication as you ponder and discuss the following questions: Which communication context(s) do you think Kyle was most comfortable in as the head of KyMo? Which one(s) do you think Morton was the most comfortable in? How does intrapersonal communication help Kyle?

KEY TERMS

 Use the *Human Communication* CD-ROM and the *Online Learning Center* at www.mhhe.com/pearson to further your understanding of the following terminology.

Action model
Channel
Code
Communication
Communication
  competence
Constructivist model
Context
Decoding
Dialogue
Dyadic communication
Encoding

Ethics
Feedback
Grammar
Interaction model
Interpersonal
  communication
Intrapersonal
  communication
Mass communication
Meaning
Message
Noise

Nonverbal codes
Process
Public communication
Receiver
Small-group
  communication
Source
Syntax
Transaction model
Verbal codes

SELF-QUIZ

 Go to the self-quizzes on the *Human Communication* CD-ROM and the *Online Learning Center* at www.mhhe.com/pearson to test your knowledge.

REFERENCES

Allen, M., Berkowitz, S., Hunt, S., & Louden, A. (1999). A meta-analysis of the impact of forensics and communication education on critical thinking. *Communication Education, 48,* 18–30.

Anderson, F. D., & Prelli, L. J. (2001). Pentadic cartography: Mapping the universe of discourse. *Quarterly Journal of Speech, 87,* 73–95.

Argenti, P. A., & Forman, J. (1998). Should business schools teach Aristotle? *Strategy & Business.* Retrieved from *http://www.strategy-business.com/briefs/98312.*

Bardwell, C. B. (1997). Standing out in the crowd. *Black Collegian, 28,* 71–79.

Barnlund, D. (1970). A transactional model of communication. In K. K. Sereno & C. D. Mortensen (Eds.), *Foundations of communication theory* (pp. 98–101). New York: Harper & Row.

Berlo, D. (1960). *The process of communication.* New York: Holt, Rinehart and Winston.

Blumer, J. G. (1983). Communication and democracy: The crisis beyond and the ferment within. *Journal of Communication, 33,* 166–173.

Brilhart, J. K., & Galanes, G. J. (1998). *Effective group discussion* (9th ed.). New York: McGraw-Hill.

Carnevale, A. P., Grainer, L. J., & Meltzer, A. S. (1990). Workplace basics: The essential skills employers want. San Francisco: Jossey-Bass.

Cockrum, K. V. (1994). Role-playing the interview. *Vocational Education Journal, 69,* 15–16.

Collins, M., & Oberman, D. (1994). What's the job outlook for '94? *Journal of Career Planning and Employment, 54,* 57–58.

Curtis, D. B., Winsor, J. L., & Stephens, R. D. (1989). National preferences in business and communication education. *Communication Education, 38,* 6–14.

Czubaroff, J. (2000). Dialogical rhetoric: An application of Martin Buber's philosophy of dialogue. *Quarterly Journal of Speech, 86,* 168–189.

Dauphinais, W. (1997). Forging the path to power. *Security Management, 41,* 21–23.

DeVito, J. A. (1999). *Essentials of human communication.* New York: Longman.

Ford, W. S. Z., & Wolvin, A. D. (1993). The differential impact of a basic communication course on perceived communication competencies in class, work, and social contexts. *Communication Education, 42,* 215–233.

Hamilton, K. (1998, November 2). A very ugly gym suit. *Newsweek,* p. 52.

Hanzevack, E. L., & McKean, R. A. (1991). Teaching effective oral presentations as part of the senior design course. *Chemical Engineering Education, 25,* 28–32.

Hart, R. P. (1993). Why communication? Why education? Toward a politics of teaching. *Communication Education, 42,* 97–105.

Horton, G. E., & Brown, D. (1990). The importance of interpersonal skills in consultee-centered consultation: A review. *Journal of Counseling and Development, 68,* 423–426.

LaBar, G. (1994). Putting together the complete hygienist. *Occupational Hazards, 56,* 63–66.

Leathers, D. G. (1988). Impression management training: Conceptualizing and application to personal selling. *Journal of Applied Communication Research, 16,* 126–145.

Lee, W. S. (1998). In the names of Chinese women. *Quarterly Journal of Speech, 84,* 283–302.

Maes, J. D., Weldy, T. G., & Icenogle, M. L. (1997). A managerial perspective: Oral communication competency is most important for business students in the workplace. *Journal of Business Communication, 34,* 67–80.

Mead, G. H. (1967). *Mind, self, and society from the standpoint of a social behaviorist.* Charles W. Morris (ed.). Chicago: University of Chicago Press.

Messmer, M. (1997, August). Career strategies for accounting graduates. *Management Accounting,* pp. 4–10.

Metallinos, N. (1992, September–October). *Cognitive factors in the study of visual image recognition standards.* Paper presented to the Annual Conference of the International Visual Literacy Association, Pittsburgh, PA. (ERIC Document Reproduction Service No. ED 352 936).

Morreale, S. P., Osborn, M. M., & Pearson, J. C. (2000). Why communication is important: A rationale for the centrality of the study of communication. *Journal of the Association for Communication Administration, 29,* 1–25.

Murray, J. W. (2000). Bakhtinian answerability and Levinasian responsibility: Forging a fuller dialogical communicative ethics. *Southern Communication Journal, 65,* 133–150.

Nisberg, J. N. (1996). Communication: What we hear, what we say vs. what they hear, what they say. *The National Public Accountant, 41,* 34–38.

Parnell, C. L. (1996). Effective business communications: It is not just for the communications department. *Executive Speeches, 11,* 9–13.

Pearson, J. C., Sorenson, R. L., & Nelson, P. E. (1981). How students and alumni perceive the basic course. *Communication Education, 30,* 296–299.

Peterson, M. S. (1997). Personnel interviewers' perceptions of the importance and adequacy of applicants' communication skills. *Communication Education, 46,* 287–291.

Reinsch, L., & Shelby, A. N. (1996). Communication challenges and needs: Perceptions of MBA students. *Business Communication Quarterly, 59,* 36–52.

Ridley, A. J. (1996). A profession for the twenty-first century. *Internal Auditor, 53,* 20–25.

Rogers, C. (1951). *Client-centered therapy.* Boston: Houghton Mifflin.

Rolls, J. (1998, June). Facing the fears associated with public speaking. *Business Communication Quarterly, 61* (2), 103–104.

Rubin, R. B., Perse, E. M., & Barbato, C. A. (1988). Conceptualization and measurement of interpersonal communication motives. *Human Communication Research, 14,* 602–628.

Severin, W., & Tankard, J., Jr. (1997). *Communication theories: Origins, methods, and uses in the mass media* (4th ed.). New York: Longman.

Shotter, J. (2000). Inside dialogical realities: From an abstract-systematic to a participatory-wholistic understanding of communication. *Southern Communication Journal, 65,* 119–132.

Simkin, M. G. (1996). The importance of good communication skills on "IS" career paths. *Journal of Technical Writing & Communication, 26,* 69–78.

Today's Employment. (1998, October 18). *The Washington Post,* pp. K33, K49.

Ugbah, S. D., & Evuleocha, S. U. (1992). The importance of written, verbal, and nonverbal communication factors in employment interview decisions. *Journal of Employment Counseling, 29,* 128–137.

Winsor, J. L., Curtis, D. B., & Stephens, R. D. (1997). National preferences in business and communication education. *Journal of the Association for Communication Administration, 3,* 170–179.

Wood, J. (1997). *Communication theories in action.* Belmont, CA: Wadsworth.

CHAPTER TWO

Everyone has his own set
of goggles.

MARSHALL MCLUHAN

Know thyself.

THALES

To love oneself is the
beginning of a life-long
romance.

OSCAR WILDE

Perception, Self, and Communication

What will you learn?

When you have read and thought about this chapter, you will be able to:

1. Explain some of the reasons why differences in perception occur.
2. Describe how selection, organization, and interpretation occur during perception.
3. Differentiate figure and ground, proximity, closure, and similarity.
4. Identify errors that we might make when we perceive others.
5. Understand how self-awareness is related to communication.
6. Differentiate self-awareness, self-fulfilling prophecies, self-concept, self-image, self-esteem, and self-efficacy.
7. Provide examples of confirmation, rejection, and disconfirmation.
8. List steps you can take to improve your self-concept.
9. Define impression management and explain the component parts of actors, performance, and face.

This chapter introduces you to the role of perception and the role of the self in communication. The chapter opens by explaining what perception is; then it describes why differences in perception occur and what occurs during perception. Next, the chapter moves to our perceptions of others, including errors we occasionally make in those perceptions. A discussion of self-awareness, self-concept (which includes self-image and self-esteem), self-efficacy, and self-presentation completes the chapter. After you read this chapter you will have a better understanding of the communicative importance of how you see yourself and how you see others.

Myron, a reporter for the campus newspaper, is trying to get the scoop on an accident that occurred this morning on campus. He's having difficulty determining what actually happened because he's getting conflicting stories from his sources. The police report said, "A late-model blue sedan was involved in a collision with a red 10-speed bicycle. The bicyclist took the blame for the accident, saying he failed to stop for a red light. Police issued a warning and the driver, who was uninjured, pressed no charges. The bicyclist suffered superficial wounds, and refused medical assistance."

However, the only eyewitness said, "It was clearly the driver's fault. He accelerated when he saw the light ahead turning yellow, and he actually ended up going through it when it was red."

How will Myron determine whose story is correct? Neither individual experiences nor perceptions are identical—even regarding the same event.

Ana has decided to attend an assertiveness training workshop because she feels she is often unable to talk with her husband, Stefan, about things that are bothering her. One example of a "problem topic" is their personal finances. During their 10-year marriage, Stefan has always taken care of the finances, but after several financial mishaps, Ana understood that he simply wasn't good with money. Every time a problem occurred, Ana tried to talk with Stefan, but he always acted sullen and withdrawn. As a result, Ana kept her thoughts and ideas to herself, even though she thought she could do a better job. Ana needed to become better at confronting Stefan and at talking to him in a way that would get him to open up.

When Ana and her husband finally talked openly about the situation, she discovered that he didn't really like handling the money because he knew he wasn't good at it. Stefan said he kept doing it for all these years because he thought she thought it was the man's responsibility to handle the finances. He had been sullen and withdrawn before because he was embarrassed by his incompetence in this area. Once Ana started managing their finances, she discovered she was quite good at it.

Ana's and Stefan's self-concepts and their perceptions of each other played a crucial role in their ability to communicate with each other.

Teaching Tip
This chapter potentially raises tough questions for students. Topics like self-image and self-presentation can be particularly important for younger students new to college. This might be a good opportunity to introduce students to services offered by your campus counseling center. Beyond offering support services, your counseling center may have teaching resources like personality surveys and instructional videos.

What Is Perception?

In this chapter we focus on perception, the self, and communication. Differences in perception affect the way we understand events, others, and ourselves. Consequently, perception affects self-concept, self-efficacy, and our presentation of self. In turn, perception influences our experience and assessment of others and our communication with them. The way you sense the world—the way you see, hear, smell, touch, and taste—is subjective, uniquely your own. Nobody else sees the world the way you do, and nobody experiences events exactly as you do. The uniqueness of human experience is based largely on differences in **perception,** *the process of becoming aware of objects and events from the senses*" (DeVito, 1986). Since our perceptions are unique, communication between and among people becomes complicated.

At one time, experts tended to see perception as passive. **Passive perception** means that, like video recorders, *people are simply recorders of stimuli.* Today perception is considered to be more active. **Active perception** means that *your mind selects, organizes, and interprets that which you sense.* So each person is a different video camera, and each person aims the camera at different things; each person's lens is different; each person sees different colors; and each person's audio picks up different sounds. Perception is subjective in that you interpret what you sense; you make it your own, and you add to and subtract from what you see, hear, smell, and touch. **Subjective perception** is *your uniquely constructed meaning attributed to sensed stimuli.* As depicted in Figure 2.1, your perception of an apple is not the same as anyone else's perception of an apple.

Consider how much your inner state affects your perceptions. If you have a bad headache, the pain probably will affect the way you treat your children, the way you respond to your instructor's giving a pop quiz, and even the way you see yourself in the mirror. Consider also how complicated communication becomes when you know that everyone has his or her own view, uniquely developed and varying by what is happening both outside and inside the mind. Finally, consider what happens to Barnlund's six-person model from chapter 1 when you add to the equation all the variations that occur with perception. Perception is just one of the many factors that complicate communication.

How do you see the world around you? Perhaps to compare the way your mind works to the way a computer works would help. Think of your conscious experiences as the images that appear on your computer monitor. Think of what you sense with your eyes, nose, tongue, ears, and fingertips as that which is read off your computer disk. The picture you see on the screen is not the same as the bits on the disk; instead, an image is generated from the bits to create something you can see. "What we perceive in the world around us is not a direct and faithful representation of that world itself, but, rather, a 'computer-enhanced' version based upon very limited data from that world" according to Wright (1994).

perception

The process of becoming aware of objects and events from the senses.

passive perception

Perception in which people are simply recorders of stimuli.

active perception

Perception in which our minds select, organize, and interpret that which we sense.

subjective perception

Your uniquely constructed meaning attributed to sensed stimuli.

Class Activity

To illustrate active perception, show students a picture from a magazine or newspaper or a photograph (I sometimes use old family photos). Ask them to write a brief description of what they see. Discuss students' answers and use this as an opportunity to discuss the role of perception.

Figure 2.1   The perception process.

Perception is subjective, active, and creative. Differences in perception may be the result of physiological factors, people's past experiences and roles, their cultures and co-cultures, and their present feelings and circumstances.

Why Do Differences in Perception Occur?

TRY ◄ ►THIS

Think of an event that recently occurred in your life in which your perception of what happened might be quite different from the perceptions of others.

Physiological Factors

You are not physiologically identical to anyone else. People differ from each other in height, weight, body type, sex, and senses. You may be tall or short, have poor eyesight, or have impaired hearing; you may be particularly sensitive to smells; or your body temperature may be colder than the rest of your family's body temperatures.

Sex is another physiological factor that may lead to perceptual differences. Some authors have suggested that hemispheric differences in the cerebral cortex of the brain are sex-linked. One study showed that these differences account for females' language facility and fine hand control and males' spatial and mathematical abilities, as well as their increased likelihood of dyslexia, stuttering, delayed speech, autism, and hyperactivity (Restak, 1984). Regardless of these findings, experts have found no conclusive evidence establishing an anatomical difference between the brain structures of human females and males.

Differences in perception also may arise from temporary conditions. A headache, fatigue, or a pulled muscle can cause you to perceive a critical comment when a friendly one is being offered. You may not see a stop sign if your thoughts are elsewhere. Similarly, if you are tired, you may perceive stimuli differently than you do when you are well rested. Other physiological needs, such as hunger and thirst, may also affect your perceptive skills.

Past Experiences and Roles

Just as your size, sex, and physical needs can affect your perceptions, so can your past experiences and your various roles.

The concept that best explains the influence of your past experiences on your perceptions is **perceptual constancy:** the idea that *your past experiences lead you to see the world in a way that is difficult to change; your*

Discussion Question

Have students do a free write on how their own psychological factors, past experiences, and culture/co-culture affect their perceptions. This free write should be at least 5 minutes. Discuss answer as a class.

perceptual constancy

The idea that our past experiences lead us to see the world in a way that is difficult to change; that is, our initial perceptions persist.

role

The part an individual plays in a group; an individual's function or expected behavior.

initial perceptions persist. What happened to you in the past influences your perception of the present and the future. A bad experience in a given situation may cause you to avoid that situation in the future. Your experiences affect how you respond to professors, police, politicians, and lawyers.

Roles also influence perceptions. A **role** is *"the part an individual plays in a group; an individual's function or expected behavior"* (DeVito, 1986, p. 269). You may be a student, a single mother or father, a political leader, or a business major. Your roles affect your communication: whom you talk to, how you talk to people, the language you use, and the way you respond to feedback. A good example of how perceptual constancy and role are related is how parents treat their children. Even after some people become adults, their parents still treat them like they did when they were growing up. Roles also tend to change with context: in your parents' home you are a son or daughter; in your own home you may be a roommate or a mother or father; in the classroom you are a student; and at work you may be an editor or a manager.

culture

A system of shared beliefs, values, customs, behaviors, and artifacts that the members of a society use to cope with one another and with their world.

Culture and Co-culture

The ways people greet each other, position themselves when they talk, and even eat and sleep are all influenced by culture. **Culture** can be defined as *a system of shared beliefs, values, customs, behaviors, and artifacts that the members of a society use to cope with one another and with their world.* Marshall R. Singer (1982), an intercultural communication researcher, maintains that what people see, hear, taste, touch, and smell are conditioned by their culture. He says that people's perceptions are largely learned; the greater the experiential differences among people, the greater the disparity in their perceptions. Conversely, the more similar their backgrounds, the more similarly they perceive the world.

Differences in perception that are created by cultural differences can be overcome in our interaction with others.

co-culture

A group whose beliefs or behaviors distinguish it from the larger culture of which it is a part and with which it shares numerous similarities.

To complicate matters further, your co-culture also affects your perceptions of the world. A **co-culture** is *"a group whose beliefs or behaviors distinguish it from the larger culture of which it* *is a part and with which it shares numerous similarities"* (DeVito, 1986). Four of the more common co-cultures in the United States today are Latinos, African Americans, women, and gays and lesbians (Samovar, Porter, & Stefani, 1998). Women and men, for example, tend to see the world differently, communicate about it differently, and even practice and perceive communication itself differently. Women tend to see talk as relational, as a way to share and understand feelings, and men tend to see talk as instrumental, as a way to achieve a task (Pearson, 1995). Culture and co-culture are discussed in greater detail in chapter 7.

Class Discussion

How does your college or university act as a co-culture within your community and state? What unique qualities define your school?

TRY ◄ ► THIS

Think of ways your cultural or co-cultural affiliation affects the way you perceive the world.

Present Feelings and Circumstances

Your daily, monthly, or yearly cycle may affect how you perceive stimuli. If you are an "evening person," you might not be able to discriminate among multiple-choice answers on an exam at 8 A.M. as well as you could later in the day. If you are having a bad week, you might be offended by the humor of one of your friends; later in the month, you might find the same remark very funny. You might perceive stimuli more acutely in the cooler months of winter than you do in the warmer summer months.

If you have ever spent a night alone in a large house, a deserted dormitory, or an unfamiliar residence, you probably understand that perceptions are altered by circumstances. Most people experience a remarkable change in their hearing at night when they are alone. They hear creaking, whining, scraping, cracking sounds at night but not during the day. The lack of other stimuli—including light, other sounds, and other people with whom to talk—coupled with a slight feeling of anxiety provides circumstances that result in more acute hearing.

What Occurs in Perception?

You engage in three separate activities during perception: selection, organization, and interpretation. No one is aware of these separate processes because they occur quickly and almost simultaneously. Nonetheless, each activity is involved in perception.

E-Note

PERCEPTION ACTIVITIES ON THE WEB

Sensation and perception are interesting in themselves. For an entertaining look at sensation and perception, go to **http://psych.hanover.edu/Krantz/sen_tut.html.** You will find a variety of activities related to visual information in art, size constancy, Gestalt laws of organization, aftereffects, and motion and depth.

selection

The process of neglecting some stimuli in the environment to focus on other stimuli.

selective exposure

The tendency to expose ourselves to information that reinforces rather than contradicts our beliefs or opinions.

selective attention

The tendency, when we expose ourselves to information and ideas, to focus on certain cues and ignore others.

Selection

No one perceives all the stimuli in his or her environment. Through **selection**, *you neglect some stimuli in your environment to focus on other stimuli.* For example, when you drive or walk to your classes, you are probably bombarded with sights, sounds, smells, and other sensations. At the time, you elect to perceive some of the stimuli and to disregard others. You smell steak cooking as you walk by a restaurant, but you ignore the dimness of the evening. Afterward, it's likely you will recall the stimuli you perceived but will have forgotten the other stimuli.

You also select the messages to which you attend. You might not hear one of your parents admonishing you, but you do hear the much softer sound of your name being called from a distance. You may "tune out" one of your professors while you listen to the hard rainfall outside the classroom window. You might listen to the criticism a friend offers you, but not the corresponding praise.

Four types of selectivity are selective exposure, selective attention, selective perception, and selective retention. In **selective exposure**, *you expose yourself to information that reinforces, rather than contradicts, your beliefs or opinions* (Wilson & Wilson, 1998). In other words, conservative Republicans are more likely than liberal Democrats to listen to Rush Limbaugh and Oliver North on the radio and to read editorials by George Will. Liberal Democrats, on the other hand, are more likely to avoid these sources of information and listen to sources that support their beliefs.

In **selective attention**, even when you do expose yourself to information and ideas, *you focus on certain cues and ignore others.* In class, you might notice the new outfit your friend is wearing but not the earring worn by the man three seats in front of you. At a buffet table, you might be drawn to the smells and the foods that you recognize and select only those. In an elevator, you may notice the conversation between the two other people in the elevator with you but not the music that's being piped in overhead.

In communication, we do not treat all sounds, words, phrases, and sentences equally. We might attend to a sound that is similar to our names because of familiarity. We might hear a word that we view as ob-

Think, Pair, Share

SIMILAR OR DIFFERENT?

To whom do you listen and to what do you direct your attention? You might believe that your classmates make choices that are similar to yours. By yourself, list the type of music you prefer and three of the top musical groups you enjoy. Identify your favorite reading material. What television programs do you normally watch? What is your favorite website? What is the primary purpose for your use of the Internet? If you were going to spend time conversing with one other person, whom would you choose? If you were going to participate in a discussion, which three people would you prefer to communicate with? After you have compiled your individual answers, pair up with another person in your class and share your answers. Consider similarities and differences in your responses. Are you surprised by some of the differences? How do you account for the similarities?

scene or novel because of its nature. We might focus on an unfamiliar comparison or a humorous cliché. We might attend to a sentence that is striking or provocative. Selective attention is as central to communication as it is to other perceived entities.

After you expose yourself to a message and then select it for further attention, you see that message through your own special lens. **Selective perception** is *the tendency to see, hear, and believe only what you want to see, hear, and believe* (Wilson & Wilson, 1998). If someone accused your trustworthy, law-abiding friend of 20 years of stealing, would you believe that person? You may not listen to the accusations, or even look at the evidence, because you believe it simply is not possible that your friend would ever do such a thing.

A recent example of selective perception occurred in the aftermath of the "attack on America" on September 11, 2001. Immediately after the event, reporters and people on the street reviewed the horrific event as occurring out of context. They did not perceive the other acts of terrorism to the United States or Israel that led up to the destruction of the World Trade Center and a portion of the Pentagon. Even more strikingly, many Americans did not perceive that U.S. actions in the past might be perceived by others to be aggressive or harmful. As a nation, Americans engaged in selective perception.

Finally, you select the stimuli you will recall or remember. **Selective retention** is *the tendency to remember better the things that reinforce your beliefs than those that oppose them* (Wilson & Wilson, 1998). For example, make a list of some of the bad qualities of someone you dislike and a list

selective perception

The tendency to see, hear, and believe only what we want to see, hear, and believe.

CD-ROM Activity

Ask students to view the animation titled "The Perception Process" found on the student CD-ROM. The animation illustrates the process of active perception.

selective retention

The tendency to remember better the things that reinforce our beliefs than those that oppose them.

45

Video Activity

Ask students to view the video segment "Sam's Graduation Party." As a class or in groups have students discuss things they "picked up on" during the segment. This discussion will illustrate how certain stimuli are selected (i.e., what the students "picked up on").

of some of the bad qualities of someone you admire. Compare your lists. Usually, people can easily think of the negative qualities of someone they dislike, but they often find it difficult to think of an admirable person's negative qualities (Wilson & Wilson, 1998).

All of us recall conversations that we have had with other people. Over time, those recollections are probably affected by selective retention. We recall critical comments that someone had made about our abilities when we later proved them to be wrong. We remember (and perhaps even exaggerate) honorific remarks that were made. We enjoy retelling conversations that paint a picture that is consistent with our beliefs about ourselves and others.

Selection is the first process that occurs during perception; the next is organization.

Organization

organization

The grouping of stimuli into meaningful units or wholes.

Each person organizes the stimuli in his or her environment. **Organization** is *the grouping of stimuli into meaningful units or wholes.* You organize stimuli in a number of ways, through figure and ground, closure, proximity, and similarity.

Figure and Ground

figure

The focal point of a person's attention.

ground

The background against which a person's focused attention occurs.

One organization method is to distinguish between figure and ground. **Figure** is *the focal point of your attention,* and **ground** is *the background against which your focused attention occurs.* When looking at Figure 2.2, some people might perceive a vase or a candlestick, whereas others perceive twins facing each other. People who see a vase identify the center of the drawing as the figure and the area on the right and left as the ground, or background. Conversely, people who see twins facing each other see the center as the background and the area on the right and left as the figure.

Figure 2.3 is another illustration of the principle of figure and ground. As you first glance at the drawing, you probably perceive only ink blobs—nothing is clearly distinguishable as either figure or ground. However, if you continue to look at the drawing, you perceive the face of a bearded man at the center of the picture. When you see the face, it becomes the figure; the rest of the drawing becomes the ground.

How do figure and ground work in communication encounters? In your verbal and nonverbal exchanges you perform a similar feat of focusing on some parts (figure) and distancing yourself from others (ground). When you hear your name in a noisy room, your name becomes figure and the rest becomes ground; on a posted grade list, your student identification number becomes figure and the other numbers become ground. Here's another example: During a job evaluation, your employer may talk about your weaknesses and strengths, but the so-called weaknesses may make you so angry that you don't even remember the strengths. The messages about weaknesses were figure, and the ones about strengths were

Figure 2.2   An example of figure and ground: a vase or twins?

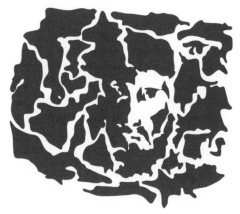

Figure 2.3   An example of figure and ground: ink blobs or a bearded man?

Figure 2.4   An example of closure: ink blobs or a cat?

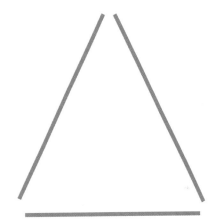

Figure 2.5   An example of closure: triangle or straight lines?

ground. Because of who and what you are, and because of your own unique perceptual processes, your attention focuses and fades, and you choose the figure or ground of what you see, hear, smell, touch, and taste.

Closure

Another way of organizing stimuli is **closure,** *the tendency to fill in missing information in order to provide the appearance of a complete unit.* If someone were to show you Figure 2.4 and ask you what you see, you might say it is a picture of a cat. But as you can see, the figure is incomplete. You see a cat only if you are willing to fill in the blank areas. Additional examples of closure appear in Figures 2.5 and 2.6. Most people

closure

The tendency to fill in missing information in order to complete an otherwise incomplete figure or statement.

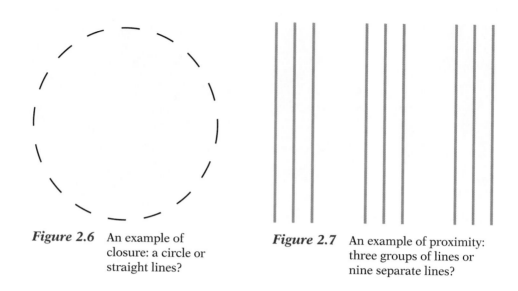

Figure 2.6   An example of
closure: a circle or
straight lines?

Figure 2.7   An example of proximity:
three groups of lines or
nine separate lines?

would identify Figure 2.5 as a triangle and Figure 2.6 as a circle, rather than seeing both as simply a number of short lines.

Closure also functions in your communication interactions. You see two people standing face-to-face and looking deeply into each other's eyes, and you "fill in" your inference that they are lovers. A public speaker says, "We need to preserve our neighborhoods," and you assume she is against the proposed low-income housing. Visual closure might be completing the circle or seeing the cat, but mental closure means filling in the meaning of what you hear and observe.

Proximity

proximity

The principle that objects that are physically close to each other will be perceived as a unit or group.

You also organize stimuli on the basis of their proximity. According to the principle of **proximity,** *objects physically close to each other will be perceived as a unit or group* (DeVito, 1986). This principle is at work in Figure 2.7. You are most likely to perceive three groups of three lines, rather than nine separate lines.

Proximity works verbally and nonverbally in communication. Some nonverbal examples include thinking that the person standing next to the cash register is the cashier or assuming that the two people entering the room at the same time are a couple. And here is a verbal example: Suppose your boss announces that due to an economic downturn he is forced to lay off 25 employees, and one hour later he calls you into his office—the proximity of the messages leads you to believe that you will be laid off.

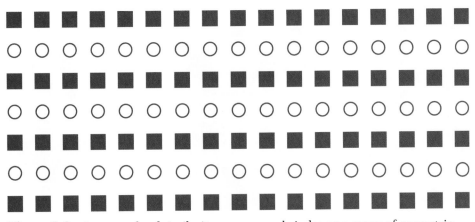

Figure 2.8   An example of similarity: squares and circles or a group of geometric shapes?

Similarity

Similarity is probably one of the simplest means of organizing stimuli. On the basis of **similarity**, *elements are grouped together because they resemble each other in size, color, shape, or other attributes.* The saying "Birds of a feather flock together" can hold true as well for human groups, who often organize by ethnicity, religion, political leaning, or interest. In Figure 2.8, you probably perceive circles and squares, rather than a group of geometric shapes, because of the principle of similarity.

To understand the relationship between the organization of stimuli and communication, think about a classroom setting. When you enter the room, your tendency is to organize the stimuli, or people there, into specific groups. Your primary focus is on acquaintances and friends—the *figure*—rather than on the strangers, who function as the *ground.* You talk to friends sitting near the doorway as you enter, due to their *proximity.* You then seat yourself near a group of students you perceive as having interests identical to yours, thus illustrating *similarity.* Last, you notice your instructor arrive with another professor of communication. They are laughing, smiling, and conversing enthusiastically. *Closure* is a result of your assumption that they have a social relationship outside the classroom.

Interpretation

The third activity you engage in during perception is **interpretation,** *the assignment of meaning to stimuli.* **Interpretive perception,** then, is *a blend of internal states and external stimuli.* The more ambiguous the stimuli, the more room for interpretation. The basis for the well-known

similarity

The principle that elements are grouped together because they share attributes such as size, color, or shape.

Class Activity

Have groups of students develop examples or narratives illustrating one of the four methods of organizing stimuli. Discuss the examples in class.

interpretation

The process of assigning meaning to stimuli.

interpretive perception

Perception that involves a blend of internal states and external stimuli.

Figure 2.9   An example of interpretation: the inkblot.

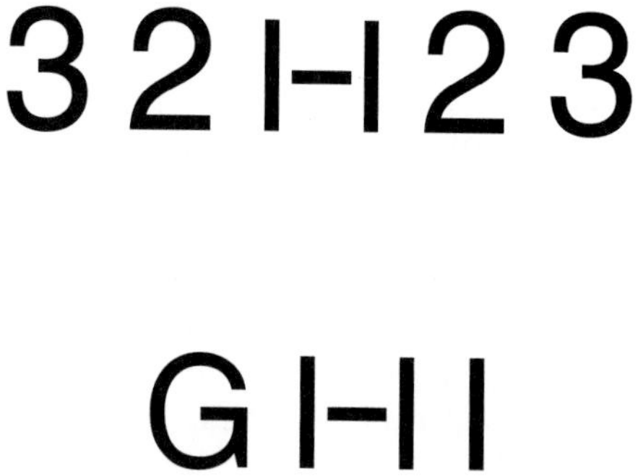

3 2 I-I 2 3

G I-I I

Figure 2.10   An example of the usefulness of context in the interpretation
of stimuli.

inkblot test lies in the principle of interpretation of stimuli. Figure 2.9
shows three inkblots that a psychologist might ask you to interpret. The
ambiguity of the figures is typical.

When interpreting stimuli, people frequently rely on the context in
which the stimuli are perceived or they compare the stimuli to other
stimuli (Figure 2.10). Sometimes context helps, but other times it can create confusion in interpretation. You have probably seen Figures 2.11 and
2.12 before. When looking at these figures, you probably perceive differences in the length of the lines in Figure 2.11 and in the height and width
of the candleholder in Figure 2.12. However, no differences exist.

You can become so accustomed to seeing people, places, and situations
in a certain way that your senses do not pick up on the obvious. Many people who read the following sentence will overlook the problem with it:

The cop saw the man standing on the the street corner.

We achieve closure on the sentence and interpret its meaning without
consciousness of the details, so the repeated *the* is overlooked. Context

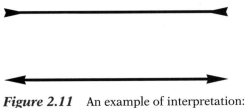

Figure 2.11   An example of interpretation: Which line is longer?

Figure 2.12   An example of interpretation: Is the width of the holder the same length as the candle?

provides cues for how an action, an object, or a situation is to be interpreted or perceived. Not seeing the double *the* in the sentence would be no problem for a reader trying to comprehend meaning, but a proofreader's job would be in jeopardy if such an error was missed often.

How Do We Perceive Others?

Once we understand the active nature of perception and that people hold unique perceptions as a consequence, we can understand that we might make errors when we perceive other people. Attribution, in general, is the ascribing of something to somebody or something. When we consider our perceptions of others, **attribution** refers to *the assignment of meaning to their behavior.* Attributions may vary based on our relationship with the other person (Manusov, Trees, Reddick, Rowe, & Easley, 1998). In this section of the chapter, we will consider some of the common attributions that we make in understanding other people that may lead us to perceptual errors. You will determine that these errors are a result of the processes of perception discussed earlier in this chapter.

Attribution Errors

Fundamental Attribution Error

The **fundamental attribution error** occurs *when we make judgments about other people's successes and failures: When other people fail, we assume it is*

attribution

The assignment of meaning to people's behavior.

fundamental attribution error

In judging other people, the tendency to attribute their successes to the situation and their failures to their personal characteristics.

Team Challenge

THE PERCEPTUAL PROCESS

With a group of people from your class, identify a place on campus or in your community and a time to engage in group observation. Spend at least 10 minutes with your group at this location in complete silence. Try to select a location that has multiple people and events to observe. During the 10 minutes of silence, record everything that you perceive. Do not share your perceptions with others until the time has lapsed.

After 10 minutes, take turns sharing your observations with group members. Look for common perceptions and unique perceptions. Describe how the processes of selection, organization, and interpretation influenced your perceptions. Did individuals use figure and ground, closure, proximity, and similarity in their perceptions? Describe your experience to the rest of the class in your next class meeting.

Writing Assignment

Have students develop a short essay analyzing perceptual errors in a sitcom or TV drama. Shows like *Friends* and *Frasier* are often rife with perception errors.

because of their personal failure; when they succeed, we assume it is because of the situation in which they find themselves. Imagine that a friend of yours loses a state beauty contest. Most likely you would conclude that it is a result of her physical features, weight, personality, or other characteristics. On the other hand, her success would not be evaluated on these same qualities. Instead, you might conclude that she was "lucky," "few contestants competed this year," or that some other circumstance accounts for her success.

Self-Serving Bias

self-serving bias

In assessing ourselves, the tendency to attribute our own successes to our personal qualities and our failures to the circumstances.

Although other people's successes are often viewed as situational and their failures are seen as personal failures, we attribute our own successes and failures in exactly the opposite way. The **self-serving bias** maintains that *our successes are due to our personal qualities*—intelligence, wit, political savvy—*and our failures occur because of our circumstances*—the teacher did not like me, no one received grades of A, the class was too difficult for undergraduate students, my adviser did not explain that I needed a prerequisite, and the departmental chair is a bigot.

Perceptual Errors

Many perceptual errors exist. We will consider nine of the most common errors: stereotyping, first impressions, projection, perceptual defense, halo effect, leniency, central tendency, recency, and contrast effects.

Stereotyping

Stereotyping occurs *when we offer an oversimplified or standardized image of a person because of her or his group membership.* How does stereotyping work? First, we categorize other people into groups based on a variety of criteria—age, race, gender, sexual affectional orientation, occupation, region of the country, or physical abilities. Next, we infer that everyone within that group has the same characteristics. For instance, we might conclude that all lesbians are masculine, that people on the East Coast are fast-talking and fast-paced, or that older people are conservative.

Our expectations and our interpretations of the behavior of others are then guided by these perceptions. When we observe people from other groups, we exaggerate, or overestimate, how frequently they engage in the stereotypic behaviors we believe they hold. We ignore, or underestimate, how frequently they engage in the behaviors that we do not believe that they hold.

Our explanations for the expected and unexpected behaviors are frequently in error as we assume situational reasons for unexpected outcomes and personal reasons for expected outcomes. For example, if we believe that teenagers are foolhardy and high risk takers, we explain the behavior of a careful and conservative teenager by concluding that this is her "public behavior" and that she actually behaves differently in private.

Finally, we differentiate ourselves from people whom we stereotype. The woman who has some African-American heritage, but does not identify with it, might view other black people as possessing qualities that are different from her own. The man who has only the slightest Hispanic background, but is proud of this heritage, may see Caucasians as boring and too prudent.

stereotyping

Oversimplifying or standardizing a person because of her or his group membership

Video Activity
Have students view the video segment "The Right Kind of Care." Ask students whether stereotyping played a role in Susan's and her grandmother's reactions to Mr. Chamberlin or Ms. Min.

First Impressions

Each of us seeks to form a **first impression** of others—*an initial opinion about people upon meeting them.* These impressions are powerful and lead to errors in our assessments of people. They may be affected by the situation or other specific circumstances that the other person is experiencing.

first impression

Our initial opinion about people upon meeting them.

Nonetheless, we tend to cling to these impressions in future interactions. When information is provided to us which does not conform to our initial impressions, we filter that new information out. Imagine that you met a friend's mother on the occasion of a holiday. Your friend's mother drank a great deal and was highly gregarious. You conclude that she enjoys parties and is very friendly. On your next encounters with the friend's mother, she seems quiet and businesslike. Nonetheless, you adhere to your original conclusion that she is a fun-loving and talkative individual.

Projection

projection

Our belief that others are fundamentally like us.

Do you believe that others are fundamentally like you or different from you? If you are like most people, you are prone to **projection:** *You assume others have characteristics and feelings that are similar to your own.* If you are a generous person, you perceive their tendency to be filled with generosity. If you are self-absorbed, you might view others around you as self-absorbed as well.

Perceptual Defense

perceptual defense

A defense mechanism in which you ignore or minimize damaging or harmful information.

Perceptual defense is *a kind of defense mechanism in which you ignore or minimize damaging or harmful information.* Suppose that someone tells you that a friend who lives close by has had trouble with the law in the past. This person suggests that she was arrested for shoplifting, that she wrote bad checks, and that she is currently suspected of bilking money from unsuspecting older women. What is your most likely response? You probably would categorize the information as "gossip" and dismiss it. Most of us do not want to believe negative information.

On September 11, 2001, many people watching television saw the second World Trade Center tower literally fall to the ground—but they did not believe it. They concluded that it was a media experiment, similar to the radio broadcast of H. G. Wells' *The War of the Worlds* that was first aired in 1938. Many hoped that it was a hoax and not real. The enormity and horror of the event was too dramatic and negative to accept.

Halo Effect

halo effect

A generalization of all attributes based on one attribute, which can be negative or positive.

The **halo effect** is similar to stereotyping in that the halo effect is *a generalization of all attributes based on one attribute.* The halo effect can be negative or positive. Generally the impression a person holds about another is used to bias ratings about all other aspects of him or her. Imagine that you sit next to someone in class who uses a cologne that is familiar to you and that you like. You conclude that the person is warm, kind, fun, interesting, and might be a good person to date. Are you likely to be wrong? Probably, since you are making all of these judgments based on a choice of cologne.

Leniency

Leniency occurs *when we consistently evaluate other people (or objects) in an overly positive manner.* A parent who forgives and forgets every wrongdoing of his or her child, no matter how terrible, engages in leniency. The professor who gives all of the students grades of A is similarly behaving with leniency.

leniency

The consistent evaluation of people (or objects) in an overly positive manner.

Central Tendency

Central tendency, somewhat different from leniency, occurs *when someone makes a perceptual error of viewing everyone as average or neutral.* The person makes no extreme judgments—positive or negative. The parent who makes this perceptual error would view all of his or her children similarly and would not single out acts of greatness or misconduct as anything but ordinary. The professor who made this perceptual error would give C grades to everyone.

central tendency

The perceptual error of viewing everyone as average or neutral.

Recency

Recency occurs *when a person recalls recent information and allows it to affect his assessment of a person at the current time.* Imagine that you come to class late and the professor is irritated by your tardiness. During the class period you give a short speech and the professor grades you harshly even though the speech is quite good. The professor might be making the perceptual error of recency—remembering your belated arrival and giving you a lower grade as a result.

recency

Assessment of a person at the current time on the basis of the recollection of recent information.

Contrast Effects

Contrast effects occur *when you compare people or their behavior with the characteristics or behavior of other people.* For example, your older brother had several fairly serious accidents just after receiving his driver's license. You have a small accident and your parents assure you that "this is nothing." The professor who hears three poor speeches may grade the good speech more highly than if the professor had not heard the poorer speeches for contrast.

contrast effects

Comparison of people or their behavior with the characteristics or behavior of other people.

What can we conclude about attribution and perceptual errors? First, we recognize that all of us have distorted views of others from time to time. Some of us are more likely to err in one or more of these ways while others exemplify different errors. You might make leniency errors because you are a positive and upbeat person. One of your parents may use projection frequently while a younger brother errs by judging people on the basis of first impressions.

At the same time, we need to acknowledge that all of our assessments of others are not necessarily distorted. A classmate who regularly misses class, does not read the text and other materials, and has no interest in the subject matter of the course may fail because of his or her own behavior, not because we are making an attribution error.

Understanding that our perceptions of others rest on a subjective, active, and creative perceptual process is important. Our perceptions of others are unique, and individuals are perceived in multiple ways by multiple interactants. We can more fairly appraise others and their behavior by understanding common attribution and perceptual errors and the extent to which we are engaged in them. We can also determine the reliability of our perceptions by asking other people how they feel about others and their behavior. Finally, we can develop cultural competence, which is discussed later in this book.

What Is Self-Awareness?

The discussion of perception naturally leads to a look at self-perception or self-awareness. How you perceive yourself plays a central role in communication, regardless of whether the communication is in a daydream, in a journal, in a small group, or at a podium. An early step in considering yourself a communicator is to contemplate your **self-awareness,** *an understanding of the self, including your attitudes, values, beliefs, strengths, and weaknesses* (DeVito, 1986, p. 274). Self-awareness is linked to your past, present, and future. Your past goes all the way back to how you were reared, or the way your family taught you to think, believe, and behave. You began as a spontaneous creature who cried when hungry or frustrated, lashed out at others when angry, and giggled and beamed when happy. Over time, adults took away some of your spontaneity until you behaved like an adult—until you ate at mealtimes, held your anger in check with your teachers, laughed when appropriate, and cried little if at all. Your emotions, as well as your physical responses, were altered to make you responsible for your own behavior.

Self-awareness develops in our *communication with ourselves,* which is known as *intrapersonal communication.* Shedletsky (1989) writes that intrapersonal communication includes "our perceptions, memories, experiences, feelings, interpretations, inferences, evaluations, attitudes, opinions, ideas, strategies, images, and states of consciousness." Intrapersonal communication may be viewed as "talking to ourselves"; it is also synonymous with thinking. Intrapersonal communication appears to be the most common context of communication, the foundation for the other contexts.

Self-awareness also develops in our communication with others. Once you mastered language, symbolic interactionism shaped you in ways that made you what you are today. The term **symbolic interactionism** refers to *the development of the self through the messages and feedback received from others* (Mead, 1934). You may have been punished for acting up in

self-awareness

An understanding of and insight into one's self, including one's attitudes, values, beliefs, strengths, and weaknesses.

symbolic interactionism

The process in which the self develops through the messages and feedback received from others.

class, rewarded for athletic skill, or ignored for saying too little. The result is the person you see in the mirror today.

An aspect of symbolic interactionism is the **self-fulfilling prophecy,** the idea that *you behave and see yourself in ways that are consistent with how others see you* (Wood, 1997, p. 383). Through a number of studies on academic performance, Rosenthal and Jacobson (1968) found that students who were expected to do well actually performed better than students who were not expected to perform well. In other words, "We learn to see ourselves in terms of the labels others apply to us. Those labels shape our self-concepts and behaviors" (Wood, 1997, p. 128).

self-fulfilling prophecy

The idea that we behave and see ourselves in ways that are consistent with how others see us.

Indeed, your concept of yourself originated in the responses you received when you were young, and, to some extent, self-fulfilling prophecies help maintain your self-concept. In many ways, individuals attempt to behave in ways consistent with other people's expectations, regardless of whether those expectations are positive or negative. But the self-fulfilling prophecy is not a simple, straightforward concept: Individuals do not simply and routinely behave in the ways other people expect. For you, it may be that other people's expectations play a more important role than your own or, conversely, that you see your own expectations as more relevant. In either case, however, others' observations about who and what you are can have a powerful influence on the self.

Perhaps you now understand why the ancients said, "Know thyself." They, like people today, believed that self-awareness is a discovery worth making. It tells you which choices are open to you and which ones are not. If you are bad at math, you will not have a future as an accountant. If you hate chemistry, you should not become a physician or pharmacist. If you like to write and are good at it, you may have a future as a writer. If you are skillful at athletics, perhaps you can exploit that talent with scholarships, varsity sports, and professional teams. What you have learned about yourself in the past, and what you learn about yourself today, will affect your future.

In the here-and-now you should be aware of what kind of person you are. Are you timid, shy, unassertive? Are you healthy, vigorous, energetic? Do you welcome change, adventure, and risk? Do you see yourself as capable, unstoppable, and hard-driving? The answers to these and many other questions are the key to

New experiences may lead to increased self-knowledge.

your self-awareness. Will Schutz (1982) wrote, "Given a complete knowledge of myself, I can determine my life; lacking that mastery, I am controlled in ways that are often undesirable, unproductive, worrisome, and confusing" (p. 1).

Joseph O'Connor was a high school junior when he spent two weeks in the Sierra Nevada mountain range of northeastern California—a challenge that changed his level of self-awareness. Rain poured, hail pelted, and the beauty of dawn at 13,000 feet entranced him. Writing about his self-awareness in an article entitled "A View from Mount Ritter: Two Weeks in the Sierras Changed My Attitude toward Life and What It Takes to Succeed," O'Connor (1998) stated:

> The Wonder of all I'd experienced made me think seriously about what comes next. "Life after high school," I said to myself. "Uh-oh." What had I been doing the last three years? I was so caught up in defying the advice of my parents and teachers to study and play by the rules that I hadn't considered the effects my actions would have on me. (p. 17)

O'Connor's experience changed his self-awareness, and he went from being a D student to one who made the honor roll.

You don't have to go to the mountains to come to a new awareness of yourself. You can act in a community play, finish your undergraduate degree after years away from school, accept your employer's invitation to lead a work team, or decide to quit your paying job to care for your children. The more you can learn about yourself, the easier it will be to learn how and why you communicate with others. Your self-awareness also concerns your potential, your future prospects. Abraham Maslow (1970) called this concept **self-actualization**—*the fulfillment of one's potential as a person*—and saw it as the highest level in the hierarchy of human needs. Carl Rogers labeled the self-actualized person as the "fully functioning person"; Sidney Jourard called it the "disclosed self"; and Charles Morris identified it as the "open self." All these writers recognized that self-awareness leads to self-actualization.

self-actualization

According to Maslow, the fulfillment of one's potential as a person.

What Is Self-Concept?

self-concept

An individual's evaluation of himself or herself, that is, an individual's self-appraisal.

Self-concept is *each person's evaluation of himself or herself, that is, self-appraisal* (DeVito, 1986, p. 275). Your self-concept develops from words and actions (symbolic interactionism); from what others say to you and do with you (self-fulfilling prophecies); and from the way you perceive yourself (self-concept). The self is socially constructed through communication; that is, your self is a result of how others speak to you and treat you and how you see yourself. Self-concept is composed of two parts: self-image and self-esteem.

CULTURAL DIFFERENCES IN MEMORY

New research by Qi Wang and her associates (in press; Wang & Leichtman, 2000; Wang, Leichtman, & Davies, 2000; Wang, Leichtman, & White, 1998; Han, Leichtman, & Wang, 1998) shows that American adults and preschool children recall their personal memories differently than do the indigenous Chinese. Since our self-concept is dependent on our self-awareness, these cultural differences are important.

"Americans often report lengthy, specific, emotionally elaborate memories that focus on the self as a central character," said Qi Wang. "Chinese tend to give brief accounts of general routine events that center on collective activities and are often emotionally neutral. These individual-focused vs. group-oriented styles characterize the mainstream values in American and Chinese cultures, respectively" (www.news.cornell.edu/Chronicles/6.28.01/memory-culture.html).

Wang and Leichtman (2000) also investigated the fictional events and personal experiences of American and Chinese six-year-olds. They found that Chinese children were more concerned with moral correctness and authority and American children had a greater sense of independence in their narratives. Cultural values and differences were obvious. "These findings indicate that cultural differences in autobiographical memory are apparently set by early preschool years and persist into adulthood. They are formed both in the larger cultural context that defines the meaning of the self and in the immediate family environment," Wang concludes. "The self and autobiographical memory are intertwined not only within an individual but also in the overarching cultural system" (www.news.cornell.edu/Chronicles/6.28.01/memory-culture.html).

Self-Image

Self-image is *the picture you have of yourself, the sort of person you believe you are.* Included in your self-image are the categories in which you place yourself, the roles you play, and other similar descriptors you use to identify yourself. If you tell an acquaintance you are a grandfather who recently lost his wife and who does volunteer work on weekends, several elements of your self-image are brought to light—the roles of grandparent, widower, and conscientious citizen.

self-image

The picture an individual has of himself or herself; the sort of person an individual believes he or she is.

Homework Activity

Have students create posterboard collages of pictures, objects, and other images that help them define their own self-image. Have students informally discuss their posters with the class.

confirmation

Feedback in which others treat us in a manner consistent with who we believe we are.

rejection

Feedback in which others treat us in a manner that is inconsistent with our self-definition.

disconfirmation

Feedback in which others fail to respond to our notion of self by responding neutrally.

But self-image is more than how you picture yourself; it also involves how others see you. Michael Argyle (1969) noted that self-image is originally based on characterizations by others and that others characterize us most often by family roles, followed by occupation, marital status, and religious affiliation.

Three types of feedback from others are indicative of how they see us: confirmation, rejection, and disconfirmation (Watzlawick, Beavin, & Jackson, 1967). **Confirmation** occurs when *others treat you in a manner consistent with who you believe you are.* You see yourself as intelligent, and your parents praise you for your excellent grades in school; you believe you have leadership abilities, and your boss puts you in charge of a new work team. Confirmation can occur through humor or even teasing (Heisterkamp & Alberts, 2000).

On the other hand, **rejection** occurs when *others treat you in a manner that is inconsistent with your self-definition.* Pierre Salinger was appointed senator from California but subsequently lost his first election. He thought he was a good public official, but the voters obviously thought otherwise—their vote was inconsistent with his self-concept.

The third type of feedback is **disconfirmation,** which occurs when *others fail to respond to your notion of self by responding neutrally.* A small child repeatedly tries to get a parent to look at something he has drawn, but the parent gives it only a cursory glance and buries her head back in her newspaper. A student writes what he thinks is an excellent composition, but the teacher writes no encouraging remarks. Rather than relying on how others classify you, consider how you identify yourself. The way in which you identify yourself is the best reflection of your self-image.

TRY ◄ ► THIS

When meeting people for the first time, observe how they identify themselves. What does their self-description tell you about their self-concept? How do you identify yourself when meeting people for the first time? What does your self-description tell you about your own self-concept?

---

self-esteem

The feeling an individual has about his or her self-concept, that is, how well the individual likes and values himself or herself.

Self-Esteem

The second part of self-concept is **self-esteem**—*how you feel about yourself, how well you like and value yourself.* Self-esteem is usually based on perceptions of your successes or failures. Think of self-esteem as the plus or minus you place on your self-perception. If you have an unfavorable perception of yourself, you are said to have low self-esteem; if you have a favorable perception of yourself, you have high self-esteem.

But perception and communication are affected regardless of whether self-esteem is high or low. For example, Baumgardner and Levy (1988) found that people with high self-esteem tend to view others who are motivated as bright people and those who are not motivated as less bright. In other words, they think people who put forth effort also have great ability. People with low self-esteem do not make this distinction. This lack of discrimination may prevent people with low self-esteem from understanding the behaviors necessary for succeeding.

Although self-esteem is important, some critics believe educators have spent too much time and effort trying to get young people to feel good about themselves and too little time and effort trying to get them to earn the right to those good feelings. For example, Shaw (1994) showed that although self-esteem had risen among young people to all-time highs, test scores had plummeted to new lows.

You communicate in a variety of ways whether or not you value yourself. At the same time, what other people say about you can affect your self-esteem.

Discussion Question

As a class or in groups discuss how self-esteem can affect communication in interpersonal, small-group, and public-speaking situations.

Improving Self-Concept

Numerous people have made dramatic changes in their lifestyle, their behavior, and, in turn, their self-concept. The news is filled with stories of former convicts who become responsible members of the community, alcoholics who are able to abstain from drinking, and highly paid television, movie, and rock stars who are able to overcome their fame and have fairly normal family lives. Dramatic changes occur in people. Although you might not choose to follow the paths of those in the news, their stories do provide evidence that people can change.

Usually people want to change their self-concept when it is inhibiting their development as an individual, as an upwardly mobile employee, or as a member of a family. Perhaps you have never been comfortable in conversations with strangers; as a result, you often feel inadequate at receptions, parties, and business social events. Maybe you have never worked well in groups and thus have a hard time picturing yourself as part of a work team. Your inability to work with others can be regarded as a detriment to professional advancement. Or perhaps you bicker often with your spouse or partner, and you worry about how your argumentative style affects your relationship not only with that person but with others as well. A sensed need to change is what inspires people to improve their self-concept.

If you wish to change your self-concept in order to improve your ability to communicate with others, at least two steps are essential. First, you need to become aware of yourself; second, you need to establish a positive attitude toward yourself and toward others. The first step is not an

Writing Assignment

Have students do a short reflection paper identifying one thing they will focus on during the semester to help improve their self-concept.

automatic, natural process. People are conditioned to be out of touch with themselves.

To acknowledge all of your feelings is essential. People are usually more familiar with certain aspects of themselves than with others. If you have low self-esteem, you probably focus on aspects of yourself that you see as problems or deficiencies. If you have high self-esteem, you probably ignore your liabilities and focus on your assets. Each person has negative and positive characteristics, and to recognize both aspects is important.

To become more aware of yourself, you need to focus on yourself, rather than on others. Instead of using your parents' perception of you, try to establish your own viewpoint. Rather than deciding who you are on the basis of cultural standards and norms, try to assess yourself on the basis of your own standards.

Establishing a positive attitude toward yourself and others—the second step in changing your self-concept—is more difficult than increasing self-awareness. If you are to alter your self-concept, you must strive to believe that you, and others, are worthy of being liked and accepted. You need to reject highly critical attitudes about yourself and others. You need to develop the belief that you, and others, have potentialities worthy of respect. You need to rid yourself of anxiety, insecurity, cynicism, defensiveness, and the tendency to be highly evaluative. Your goal should be to free yourself so that you can establish meaningful relationships with yourself and others.

Barriers to Improving Self-Concept

Altering your self-concept is not a simple matter. One of the factors that makes change difficult is that people who know you expect you to behave in a certain way. In fact, they helped create and maintain your self-concept. These people may continue to insist that you maintain a particular self-concept, even when you are attempting to change.

Sometimes, people work against themselves when they try to change their self-concept. For example, you might label yourself "passive"; that is, even when others voice opinions contrary to yours or attack values you hold, you say nothing in defense. This passivity may be consistent with other aspects of your self-concept such as "open-minded" and "nonargumentative." You can alter one aspect of your self-concept only to the extent that it does not contradict other aspects. If your passivity fits with your self-concept of being warm and supportive of others, you may find that becoming more assertive is difficult unless you are also willing to be less supportive on some occasions.

What Is Self-Efficacy?

In 1986, Albert Bandura coined the term "self-efficacy." **Self-efficacy** was defined as *"the belief in one's capabilities to organize and execute the sources of action required to manage prospective situations"* (Bandura, 1986; www.emory.edu/EDUCATION/mfp/effpage.html). Self-efficacy is not the same as self-concept. Self-concept is our evaluation of ourselves over multiple dimensions. It is a general self-appraisal. Self-efficacy is a context-specific evaluation of one's ability to perform a specific undertaking or a range of tasks within a specific area. If you are expressing self-concept, you might state that you are a superb speaker but a poor mathematician. If you are expressing self-efficacy, you might explain that you can give classroom speeches that are organized, but that you cannot solve the word problems that your physics professor provides.

Self-concept centers on your self-worth, whereas self-efficacy focuses on your confidence to perform a specific act. Self-concept is neither sensitive to the context nor specific to a particular task, whereas self-efficacy is context-specific and can be task-specific as well. Self-concept provides a sense of being or feeling, whereas self-efficacy provides a sense of whether or not one can do or perform a certain behavior. Self-concept develops through interactions with others; self-efficacy may develop similarly but can also occur through one's mastery of an experience. Clearly, self-efficacy affects our choices, how much effort we provide, our levels of persistence, and how we feel (Bandura, 1977, 1986, 1995, 1997, 1998, 2000).

self-efficacy

The belief in one's capabilities to organize and execute the sources of action required to manage prospective situations.

Group Activity

Assign groups of students to observe behaviors related to self-presentation by picking a public place, going there to observe people, and noting observed behaviors that are evidence of self-presentation. You can also use this activity to illustrate how perception influences our own interpretation of other people's behavior.

What Is Self-Presentation?

In this chapter we have shown the relationship between perception, self-perception, and communication. Communication and perception influence each other. Communication is largely responsible for our self-perceptions. Communication can also be used to change the perceptions that others have of us. We attempt to influence other's perceptions of ourselves through self-presentation.

In our daily interactions we present ourselves to people, both consciously and unconsciously. **Self-presentation** may be defined as *the way we portray ourselves to others.* Generally, our self-presentation is consistent with an ideal self-image, allows us to enact an appropriate role, may influence others' view of us, permits us to define the situation in our terms, and/or influences the progress of an interaction.

self-presentation

The way we portray ourselves to others.

impression management

The control (or lack of control) of the communication of information through a performance.

high self-monitors

Individuals who are highly aware of their impression management behavior.

low self-monitors

Individuals who communicate with others with little attention to the responses to their messages.

face

The socially approved and presented identity of an individual.

facework

Verbal and nonverbal strategies that are used to present one's own varying images to others and to help them maintain their own images.

positive face

The desire to be liked and respected.

negative face

The desire to be free from constraint and imposition.

Erving Goffman (1959, 1974, 1981) first described the process of self-presentation. Goffman adopted the symbolic interactionist perspective described earlier. He described everyday interactions through a dramaturgical, or theater arts, viewpoint. His theory includes individual identity, group relationships, the context or situation, and the interactive meaning of information. Individuals are viewed as "actors" and interaction is seen as a "performance" shaped by the context and situation and constructed to provide others with "impressions" consistent with the desired goals of the actor. **Impression management** is thus defined as *the control (or lack of control) of the communication of information through a performance.* In impression management, people try to present an "idealized" version of themselves in order to reach desired ends.

You may believe that you do not engage in impression management. However, a number of research studies illustrate that people act differently when they are being viewed than when they are not seen. For example, people speaking on a telephone who are expressing empathy or shared emotions do not engage in facial responsiveness, whereas people expressing the same sentiments in face-to-face encounters do (Chovil, 1991). Investigations in this area suggest that people generally do engage in impression management in their face-to-face interactions.

Why might you believe that you do not engage in impression management? You have engaged in this behavior over your entire life. You were rewarded for it when you engaged in it and you were punished when you deviated from it. At this point, impression management may be unconscious and second nature. **High self-monitors** are those *individuals who are highly aware of their impression management behavior* (Snyder, 1979).

On the other hand, we know that some people are unaware of the importance of impression management. They have little idea about how others perceive them and they know even less about how to interact with others. These **low self-monitors** *communicate with others with little attention to the responses to their messages.* Still others believe that impression management is somehow unethical or deceptive. To understand the importance of impression management, we return to the theory.

In addition to the concepts of "actors" and "performance," Goffman introduced the notion of "face." **Face** can be defined as *the socially approved and presented identity of an individual.* Each of us has several "faces" that we present, depending on the group in which we interact and the context or situation in which we find ourselves. You may see yourself as a part-time worker, a full-time student, a great dancer, an athlete, a studious and serious scholar, and a poet. You engage in **facework,** or *verbal and nonverbal strategies used to present these varying images to others and to help them maintain their own images.*

Penelope Brown and Stephen C. Levinson (1987) extended the ideas of Goffman in their contribution of "politeness theory." Politeness theory states that we have an interest in **positive face**—*the desire to be liked and respected*—and **negative face**—*the desire to be free from constraint and*

ELECTRONIC SELF-PRESENTATION

Although Goffman's work centered on face-to-face interaction, electronic communication allows us to consider applications of his theory beyond interpersonal communication. The World Wide Web has developed quickly and has revolutionized communication between people. Today, many people have their own home pages in which they present themselves to others with new resources. Stone (1998) has discussed the nature of our "electronic selves." What do home pages communicate? Find five Web pages and analyze the differences among them. What impressions do you have about the person who created the Web page?

imposition. Positive face is threatened when we let someone else know—directly or indirectly—that we do not approve of their behavior or of them. Negative face is threatened when we order other people to do things or when we ask people to give up freedoms that they would normally hold. Generally people try to support both the positive and negative face of others because they do not want the other person to feel embarrassed. When we witness one person causing a second person to lose face, we feel embarrassed for the second person and we might take action against the first. **Politeness,** then, is comprised of *our efforts to save face for others.*

William L. Benoit (1995) made an important contribution to this work when he offered a "theory of image restoration." Benoit observed that people encounter damage to their reputation because of their own wrongdoing or when they are suspected of wrongdoing. He suggests that people engage in "communicative behavior designed to reduce, redress, or avoid damage to their reputation (or face or image)" (p. vii). Upon reflection, Benoit renamed the theory "image repair" because restoration suggests that the image may have been restored to its prior state (Benoit, 2000; Burns & Bruner, 2000). Table 2.1 summarizes the five general strategies and the tactics that Benoit discovered.

Impression management is important, then, because it helps us save embarrassment for ourselves and others. In addition, impression management allows us to achieve our goals through our communicative behavior. When we use language appropriate for the occasion, when we demonstrate empathy through facial expression and bodily movement, when we use self-disclosure appropriately, and when we wear clothing that is within appropriate guidelines, we increase the likelihood we will be viewed as credible and achieve our goals.

In the next two chapters you will learn more about verbal and nonverbal communication. Your understanding of these symbolic means of

politeness

Our efforts to save face for others.

TABLE 2.1   IMAGE REPAIR STRATEGIES

Strategy/Tactic	Key Characteristic	Example
Denial		
Simple denial	Did not act (or act did not occur)	Coke does not charge McDonald's less
Shift blame	Another did act	Tylenol did not poison capsules
Evade Responsibility		
Provocation	Act was a response to another's offense	Firm moved the plant because of new taxes
Defeasibility	Lack of information or ability	Person not told meeting moved
Accident	Act was a mishap	Sears unneeded repairs inadvertent
Good intentions	Act was meant well	Sears claimed no willful overcharges
Reduce Offensiveness		
Bolster	Stress good traits	Exxon claimed swift/competent action
Minimize	Act not serious	Exxon: few animals were killed
Differentiate	Act less serious than similar ones	Borrowed car; did not steal it
Transcend	More important considerations	Helping humans justifies animal tests
Attack accuser	Reduce credibility of attacker	Pepsi: Coke charges McDonald's less
Compensate	Reimburse victims	Free travel to airline passengers when flight overbooked
Corrective Action	Plan to solve or to prevent recurrence	AT&T promised to improve service
Mortification	Apology	AT&T apologized

SOURCE: www.missouri.edu/~commwlb/html/image_repair_strategies.html.

communicating will be enhanced by your understanding of impression management. Wiggins, Wiggins, and Vander Zanden (1993) suggest that three essential types of communication are used to manage impressions. They include manner, appearance, and setting. Manner includes both verbal and nonverbal codes. Your manner might be seen as brusque, silly, businesslike, immature, friendly, warm, or gracious. Your appearance may suggest a role that you are playing (lab assistant), a value that you hold (concern for the environment), your personality (relaxed), or how important you view the communication setting (unimportant). Setting includes your immediate environment (the space in which you communicate) as well as other public displays of who you are (the kind of home in which you live, the type of automobile you drive).

Chapter Review

SUMMARY

In this chapter you have learned the following:

- Perception is important in communication because perception affects the way we understand events, others, and ourselves.

- Our perceptions are unique because of physiological factors, past experiences, culture and co-culture, and present feelings and circumstances.

- During perception, three separate activities are occurring: selection, organization, and interpretation.
  - Through selection, you neglect some stimuli in your environment and focus on others. Four types of selectivity are selective exposure, selective attention, selective perception, and selective retention.
  - The stimuli that you focus on are organized in a number of ways—through figure and ground, closure, proximity, and similarity.

- We often make errors in our perceptions of others.
  - We make attributional errors, including the fundamental attribution error and the self-serving bias.
  - We engage in perceptual errors such as stereotyping, first impressions, projection, perceptual defense, halo effect, leniency, central tendency, recency, and contrast effects.

- How you perceive yourself plays a central role in communication.
  - Self-awareness is an understanding of the self—your attitudes, values, beliefs, strengths, and weaknesses.
  - Self-awareness involves the important concepts of symbolic interaction-ism, self-fulfilling prophecy, and self-actualization.

- Self-concept, defined as each person's evaluation of himself or herself, consists of self-image and self-esteem.

- Self-image is the picture you have of yourself and involves how others see you.

- Three types of feedback from others indicate how they see you: confirmation, rejection, and disconfirmation.

- Self-esteem, the second part of self-concept, is how you feel about yourself.

- You can improve your self-concept.

- Self-efficacy is defined as the belief in one's capabilities to organize and execute the sources of action required to manage prospective situations.

- Impression management is the control (or lack of control) of the communication of information through a performance.
  - People who are high self-monitors are well aware of their impression management behavior, whereas people who are low self-monitors communicate with others with little attention to the responses to their messages.
  - One's face is the socially approved identity an individual presents.
  - Facework includes the verbal and nonverbal strategies that are used to present one's own varying images to others and to help them maintain their own images.
  - Our positive face is the desire to be liked and respected; our negative face is our desire to be free from constraint and imposition. Politeness is defined as our efforts to save face for others.

● VIDEO LINK: THE INFLUENCE OF CULTURE ON PERCEPTION

Video Episode 3: "The Right Kind of Care"

As people interact, the more similar their cultural backgrounds are, the more likely they are to share similar perceptions. Watch "The Right Kind of Care" to see the influence of culture on perception. In that segment, Susan Elliott and her grandmother interview two home care assistants for Susan's grandmother. The two interviewees, Donell Chamberlin and Vivian Min, are of different ethnic backgrounds. How do cultural differences affect Susan and her grandmother's perceptions of the two interviewees? Do Susan and her grandmother share similar perceptions with the two candidates? Do similarities or differences in perception affect the final hiring decision?

ISSUES IN COMMUNICATION: THE IMPORTANCE OF SELF-CONCEPT

This Issues in Communication narrative is designed to provoke individual thought or discussion about concepts raised in the chapter.

During the last part of the nineteenth century, a prestigious Ohio banker raised his daughter Florence as if she were the son he would never have. He trained her in the ways of business, instilling in her a sense of independence and a spirit of self-reliance. This upbringing proved effective when she gravitated toward male-dominated courses in school such as math, surveying, and science. A talented musician as well, she enrolled in the Cincinnati Conservatory at 17 to study piano.

Her ambitious plans for a career in the arts ended abruptly when her mother's illness forced her to return home. Embittered, disdainful of housework, and plagued by quarrels with her dominating father, Florence didn't remain home long. At 19, she was rebellious, pregnant, and unmarried. It was not until she was 30 that this single mom found her ideal husband. The good-

looking editor of the local paper, and five years her junior, he shared her many interests.

Florence, always an independent soul, refused to wear a wedding band (she would never "belong" to anyone) and at the wedding reception announced her goal to make her husband president of the United States. Appropriately he gave her the nicknames "Boss" and "Duchess." Florence's opinionated father could not help but broadcast his view that his new son-in-law, Warren, would not amount to much. Warren's well-known reputation as a salacious lady's man was reconfirmed throughout his marriage by his highly publicized philandering and rumors of several illegitimate children. The prophecy of his failure might have come true but for Florence's persistence.

Overlooking his indiscretions, she used her position as his wife to advance the cause of women, keep racists out of appointed offices, and to reform prisons. When Warren G. Harding died in office, Florence was at his side not just as his wife but as the First Lady who reopened the

White House to the public, became a master of presidential public relations, and was the architect of her husband's short-lived presidency.*

Apply what you have learned about self-awareness and self-concept as you ponder and discuss the following questions: How did the feedback Florence received from her father appear to affect her self-concept? What type of feedback did he give her? How do you think Florence would describe her self-concept? How has your family influenced your self-concept?

*Based on Sylvia Jukes Morris, "Standing by Her Man" [review of Carl S. Anthony's *Florence Harding: The First Lady, the Jazz Age, and the Death of America's Most Scandalous President*]. *The Washington Post Book World*, July 5, 1998, pp. 3, 11.

KEY TERMS

Use the *Human Communication* CD-ROM and the *Online Learning Center* at www.mhhe.com/pearson to further your understanding of the following terminology.

Active perception	Impression management	Selection
Attribution	Interpretation	Selective attention
Central tendency	Interpretive perception	Selective exposure
Closure	Leniency	Selective perception
Co-culture	Low self-monitors	Selective retention
Confirmation	Negative face	Self-actualization
Contrast effects	Organization	Self-awareness
Culture	Passive perception	Self-concept
Disconfirmation	Perception	Self-efficacy
Face	Perceptual constancy	Self-esteem
Facework	Perceptual defense	Self-fulfilling prophecy
Figure	Politeness	Self-image
First impression	Positive face	Self-presentation
Fundamental attribution error	Projection	Self-serving bias
	Proximity	Similarity
Ground	Recency	Stereotyping
Halo effect	Rejection	Subjective perception
High self-monitors	Role	Symbolic interactionism

SELF-QUIZ

Go to the self-quizzes on the *Human Communication* CD-ROM and the *Online Learning Center* at www.mhhe.com/pearson to test your knowledge.

REFERENCES

Argyle, M. (1969). *Social interaction*. New York: Atherton.

Bandura, A. (1977, March). Self-efficacy: Toward a unifying theory of behavioral change. *Psychological Review, 84,* 191–215.

Bandura, A. (1986). *Social foundations of thought and action: A social cognitive theory*. Englewood Cliffs, NJ: Prentice Hall.

Bandura, A. (1997). *Self-efficacy: The exercise of control*. New York: W. H. Freeman.

Bandura, A. (1998). Personal and collective efficacy in human adaptation and change. In J. G. Adair & D. Belanger (Eds.), *Advances in psychological science, Vol. 1: Social, personal, and cultural aspects* (pp. 51–71). Hove, England: Psychology Press.

Bandura, A. (2000). Self-efficacy: The foundation of agency. In W. J. Perrig (Ed.), *Control of human behavior, mental processes, and consciousness* (pp. 17–33). Mahwah, NJ: Lawrence Erlbaum Associates.

Bandura, A. (Ed.) (1995). *Self-efficacy in changing societies.* New York: Cambridge University Press.

Barnett, H. (1998). *Maintaining the self in communication: Concept and guidebook.* Novato, CA: Alpha and Omega.

Baumgardner, A. H., & Levy, P. E. (1988). Role of self-esteem in perceptions of ability and effort: Illogic or insight? *Personality and Social Psychology Bulletin, 14,* 429–438.

Bell, N. J., & Carver, W. (1980). A reevaluation of gender label effects: Expectant mothers' responses to infants. *Child Development, 51,* 925–927.

Benoit, W. L. (1995). Accounts, excuses, and apologies: A theory of image restoration discourse. Albany: State University of New York Press.

Benoit, W. L. (2000). Another visit to the theory of image restoration strategies. *Communication Quarterly, 48,* 40–44.

Brown, P., & Levinson, S. C. (1987). *Politeness: Some universals in language usage.* Cambridge, England: Cambridge University Press.

Burns, J. P., & Bruner, M. S. (2000). Revisiting the theory of image restoration strategies. *Communication Quarterly,* 48, 27–39

Chovil, N. (1991). Social determinants of facial displays. *Journal of Nonverbal Behavior, 15,* 141–154.

DeVito, J. A. (1986). *The communication handbook: A dictionary.* New York: Harper & Row.

Goffman, E. (1959). *The presentation of self in everyday life.* New York: Doubleday Anchor.

Goffman, E. (1974). *Frame analysis: An essay on the organization of experience.* New York: Harper & Row.

Goffman, E. (1981). *Forms of talk.* Oxford: Basil Blackwell.

Han, J. J., Leichtman, M. D., & Wang, Q. (1998). Autobiographical memory in Korean, Chinese, and American children. *Developmental Psychology, 34*(4), 701–713.

Heisterkamp, B. L., & Alberts, J. K. (2000). Control and desire: Identity formation through teasing among gay men and lesbians. *Communication Studies, 51,* 388–403.

Manusov, V., Trees, A. R., Reddick, L. A., Rowe, A. M. C., & Easley, J. M. (1998). Explanations and impressions: Investigating attributions and their effects on judgments for friends and strangers. *Communication Studies, 49,* 209–223.

Maslow, A. H. (1970). *Motivation and personality* (2nd ed., pp. 35–72). New York: Harper & Row.

Mead, G. H. (1934). *Mind, self, and society.* Chicago: University of Chicago Press.

O'Connor, J. T. (1998, May 25). A view from Mount Ritter: Two weeks in the Sierras changed my attitude toward life and what it takes to succeed. *Newsweek,* p. 17.

Pearson, J. C. (1995). *Gender and communication* (3rd ed.). Madison, WI: Brown & Benchmark.

Restak, R. (1984). *The brain.* New York: Bantam Books.

Rosenthal, R., & Jacobson, L. (1968). *Pygmalion in the classroom.* New York: Holt, Rinehart and Winston.

Samovar, L. A., Porter, R. E., & Stefani, L. (1998). *Communication between cultures.* Belmont, CA: Wadsworth.

Schutz, W. (1982). *Here comes everyone* (2nd ed.). New York: Irvington.

Seegmiller, B. R. (1980). Sex typed behavior in pre-schoolers: Sex, age, and social class effects. *Journal of Psychology, 104,* 31–33.

Shaw, P. (1994, Summer). Self-esteem rises to all-time high; Test scores hit new lows. *Antioch Review,* pp. 467–474.

Shedletsky, L. J. (1989). The mind at work. In L. J. Shedletsky (Ed.), Meaning and mind: An intrapersonal approach to human communication. ERIC and The Speech Communication Association.

Singer, M. R. (1982). Culture: A perceptual approach. In L. A. Samovar & R. E. Porter (Eds.), *Intercultural communication: A reader* (3rd ed.). Belmont, CA: Wadsworth, pp. 54–61.

Snyder, M. (1979). Self-monitoring processes. In L. Berkowitz (Ed.), *Advances in experimental social psychology.* New York: Academic Press.

Stone, A. R. (1998). *The war of desire and technology at the close of the mechanical age.* Cambridge, MA: The MIT Press.

Tibbits, S. (1975). Sex role stereotyping in the lower grades: Part of a solution. *Journal of Vocational Behavior, 6,* 255–261.

Wang, Q. (in press). Cultural effects on adults' earliest childhood recollection and self-description: Implications for the relation between memory and the self. *Journal of Personality and Social Psychology.*

Wang, Q., & Leichtman, M. D. (2000). Same beginnings, different stories: A comparison of American and Chinese children's narratives. *Child Development, 71*(5), 1329–1346.

Wang, Q., Leichtman, M. D., & Davies, K. I. (2000). Sharing memories and telling stories: American and Chinese mothers and their 3-year-olds. *Memory, 8*(3), 159–177.

Wang, Q., Leichtman, M. D., & White, S. H. (1998). Childhood memory and self-description in young Chinese adults: The impact of growing up an only child. *Cognition, 69*(1), 73–103.

Watzlawick, P., Beavin, J. H., & Jackson, D. D. (1967). *Pragmatics of human communication: A study of interactional patterns, pathologies, and paradoxes.* New York: Norton.

Wiggins, J. A., Wiggins, B. B., & Vander Zanden, J. (1993). *Social psychology* (4th ed.). New York: McGraw-Hill.

Wilson, J., & Wilson, S. (Eds.). (1998). *Mass media/mass culture.* New York: McGraw-Hill.

Wood, J. T. (1997). *Communication theories in action.* Belmont, CA: Wadsworth.

Wright, R. (1994, July–August). That never really happened. *The Humanist,* pp. 30–31.

CHAPTER THREE

Kind words can be short and easy to speak, but their echoes are truly endless.

MOTHER TERESA

Tell me how much a nation knows about its own language, and I will tell you how much that nation cares about its own identity.

JOHN CIARDI

When ideas fail, words come in very handy.

JOHANN WOLFGANG VON GOETHE

Verbal Communication

What will you learn?

When you have read and thought about this chapter, you will be able to:

1. Define language and state several of its characteristics.
2. Identify three sets of rules that govern language use.
3. Explain how language and culture are intertwined.
4. List some of the rules for communicating on the Net.
5. Describe the various forms of unique language and how they can provide both beauty and barriers to communication.
6. Use specific techniques, like paraphrasing and dating, to demonstrate your verbal communication skills.

This chapter is about the importance of language and how language functions in communication. In this chapter, you will learn about the world of language, including the definition of language and its many characteristics. You will learn that language can be both an enhancement and an obstacle to communication. Finally, specific suggestions are provided for improving your verbal skills.

Nathan had his first big job interview for a sales representative position with a national computer-software company. He wanted to be certain he looked professional, so he bought a new suit and a new briefcase for the interview. He arrived for the interview early and then waited patiently in the reception area for the interviewer to come for him. When Mr. Baughman arrived, Nathan rose, shook his hand with a firm grip, and looked him directly in the eye as he said, "Nice to meet you Mr. Baughman." They sat down in Mr. Baughman's office, and the interview began.

"So, Nathan. Tell me why you're interested in a job with our company," said Mr. Baughman.

"Well, I, ah, umm . . . Like, you know Mr. Baughman. I just think it would be awesome to work for a company like this. I mean, who wouldn't want a job with this company?"

"Awesome, huh?" Mr. Baughman, surprised by Nathan's response, paused for a few moments before he posed his next question: "It says here that you'll be graduating with a business degree in May. Explain how your experiences as an undergraduate make you qualified to work as a sales representative for our company."

"Well, geez man. I mean, I've had to work on computers nearly every day for four years. Every paper I've done has been on a computer, and I've even used your software. I also sell some of your software at the electronics store I work at now. We sell some other stuff too, of course."

Not surprisingly, Nathan did not get the job. When one of his friends asked him what he thought went wrong, he said, "I don't know man. I just don't think we spoke the same language." While Nathan recognized the importance of looking professional, he had failed to recognize the effect his verbal communication skills would have on the interview.

Class Activity

Have students write down the terms *always, almost always, sometimes, almost never, and never* and then assign a percentage to each term. For example, what percent of the time would you "almost always" do something? Do "never" and "always" really mean 100 percent? Compare percentages in groups or as a class and discuss how differences in meaning, as exemplified in the activity, could lead to miscommunication.

What Is Language?

Language is *a collection of symbols, letters, or words with arbitrary meanings that are governed by rules and used to communicate.* Language consists of words or symbols that represent things without being those things. The word *automobile* is a symbol for a vehicle that runs on gasoline, but the symbol is not the vehicle itself. When you listen to others' verbal communication, you **decode** *(assign meaning to)* their words in order to translate them into thoughts of your own. Because language is an imperfect means of transmission, the thoughts expressed by one person never exactly match the thoughts decoded by another.

Verbal communication is essential in virtually all of our endeavors from the very private to the most public. Both writing and speaking rely on the use of language. Verbal communication comprises one of the two major codes of communication; the other is nonverbal communication,

language

A code consisting of symbols, letters, or words with arbitrary meanings that are governed by rules and used to communicate.

which we will discuss in the next chapter. In chapter 4 we will consider the similarities and differences of these two codes.

The definition on page 74 tells you that language consists of words or symbols, has rules, and is arbitrary, but the definition does not reveal some of the other important characteristics of language. Language is also intertwined with culture, organizes and classifies reality, and is abstract. The following section is a closer look at each of these characteristics.

Language Has Rules

Language has multiple rules. Three sets of rules are relevant to our discussion: semantic rules, syntactic rules, and pragmatic rules. **Semantics** is *the study of the way humans use language to evoke meaning in others.* Semantics focuses on individual words and their meaning. Semanticists—people who study semantics—are interested in how language and its meaning change over time.

While semantics focuses on the definition of specific words, **syntax** is *the way in which words are arranged to form phrases and sentences.* For example, in the English language the subject is usually placed before the verb and the object after the verb. Other languages have different rules of syntax, including reading from right to left. You **encode** by *translating your thoughts into words.* Syntax changes the meaning of the same set of words. For example, the declarative statement "I am going tomorrow" uses syntax to signal that someone is leaving the next day. If you change the word arrangement to "Am I going tomorrow?" the statement becomes a question and acquires a different meaning.

Pragmatics is *the study of language as it is used in a social context, including its effect on the communicators.* Messages are variable, depending on the situation. Ambiguous messages such as "How are you?" "What's new?" and "You're looking good" have different meanings, depending on the context. For example, many people use such phrases as **phatic communication,** or *communication that is used to establish a mood of sociability rather than to communicate information or ideas.* Indeed, they would be surprised if someone offered a serious or thoughtful answer to such questions or statements. On the other hand, if you are visiting your grandmother who has been ill, your questions about how she is feeling are sincere and designed to elicit information. Similarly, you might genuinely be complimenting another person's new haircut, new tattoo, or new tongue bolt when you tell them they are looking good. Pragmatic rules help us interpret meaning in a specific context.

Language and Culture Are Intertwined

Although we will talk about the role of intercultural communication in a later chapter, to note the relationship between language and culture is

decode

The process of assigning meaning to others' words in order to translate them into thoughts of your own.

semantics

The branch of language study that is concerned with meaning.

syntax

A set of rules about language that determines how words are arranged to form phrases and sentences.

encode

The process of translating your thoughts into words.

pragmatics

The study of language as it is used in a social context, including its effect on the communicators.

phatic communication

Communication that is used to establish a mood of sociability rather than to communicate information or ideas.

Team Challenge

CULTURAL DIFFERENCES AT WORK

Working together with a group of classmates, identify a particular context in which communication occurs and in which you might work as a career field. You might select education, the law, medicine, retail sales, community agencies, mass communication, or another context. With your classmates, and the aid of the Internet, identify specific problems that could ensue within your selected context if people speak different first languages and/or come from distinctive cultures. You will find that in some situations, these problems may create life and death issues and, in other circumstances, they could be the source of humor.

culture

The socially transmitted behavior patterns, beliefs, attitudes, and values of a particular period, class, community, or population.

Sapir-Whorf hypothesis

A theory that our perception of reality is determined by our thought processes and our thought processes are limited by our language and, therefore, that language shapes our reality.

essential now. **Culture** may be defined as *all of the socially transmitted behavior patterns, beliefs, attitudes, and values of a particular period, class, community, or population.* We often think of the culture of a country (Greek culture), institution (the culture of higher education), organization (the IBM culture), or group of people (the Hispanic culture). Culture and language are thus related as the transmission of culture occurs through language.

Language and culture are related in a second way. Culture creates a lens through which we perceive the world and create shared meaning. Language thus develops in response to the needs of the culture or to the perceptions of the world. Edward Sapir and Benjamin Lee Whorf were among the first to discuss the relationship between language and perception. The **Sapir-Whorf hypothesis,** as their theory has become known, states that *our perception of reality is determined by our thought processes and our thought processes are limited by our language and, therefore, language shapes our reality* (Whorf, 1956). Similarly, European scholars like Derrida (1974), Foucault (1980), Habermas (1984), and Lucan (1981) assume that language creates reality. Language is the principal way that we learn about ourselves, others, and our culture (Bakhurst & Shanker, 2001; Cragan & Shields, 1995; Wood, 1997).

The Sapir-Whorf hypothesis has been demonstrated in multiple cultures (Samovar & Porter, 2000; Whorf, 1956). The Hopi language serves as an early example. The Hopi people do not distinguish between nouns and verbs. In many languages, nouns are given names that suggest that they remain static over time. For example, we assume that words like *professor, physician, lamp,* and *computer* refer to people or objects that are relatively unchanging. Verbs are action words that suggest change. When we use words like *heard, rehearsed, spoke,* and *ran,* we assume alterations and movement. The Hopi, by avoiding the distinction between nouns and verbs, thus refer to people and objects in the world as always changing.

CHAPTER FOUR

Listen to a woman when
she looks at you.

KAHLIL GIBRAN

You cannot shake hands
with a clenched fist.

INDIRA GANDHI

When one is pretending,
the entire body revolts.

ANAÏS NIN

Nonverbal
Communication

What will you learn?

When you have read and thought about this chapter, you will be able to:

1. Define nonverbal communication.
2. Describe how verbal and nonverbal codes work in conjunction.
3. Explain how nonverbal and verbal codes are distinctive.
4. Identify three problems people have in interpreting nonverbal codes.
5. Define and identify nonverbal codes.
6. Recognize the types of bodily movement in nonverbal communication.
7. Describe the role of bodily appearance in communication.
8. State the factors that determine the amount of personal space you use.
9. Explain how people view time differently.
10. State the factors that influence the meaning and use of touch.
11. Understand how objects are used in nonverbal communication.
12. Utilize strategies for improving your nonverbal communication.

This chapter focuses on the role of nonverbal codes in communication. The chapter first looks at the problems that can occur in interpreting nonverbal codes. Next, some of the major nonverbal codes are identified and defined, including bodily movement and facial expression, bodily appearance, space, time, touching, and vocal cues. The chapter concludes with a discussion of some solutions to the problems you might encounter in interpreting nonverbal codes.

On any given weekday, most high school students gather together to talk between classes. Marla and her friends are no exception. Their discussions are often animated, and they touch each other occasionally when one person is speaking to another. You can tell when they're talking about something serious or personal because their voices drop, they gather more closely together, and their eyes occasionally dart suspiciously at others outside their group. Marla and her friends dress alike (they often borrow each other's clothing), and even their hairstyles are similar.

As they stand together talking, someone occasionally approaches the group. Today, Sam, a boy Marla has been seeing, approaches the group. Marla immediately stops talking and moves away from the group and toward Sam. Marla and Sam begin conversing with each other. Sam keeps his baseball-cap-covered head down, they speak in quiet tones, and they do not touch each other. Marla looks at Sam's face intently as he speaks, apparently trying to establish some sort of eye contact. Twice, she moves closer to him, but she maintains enough distance that they never physically touch each other. After Sam leaves, Marla's friends gather around her, asking her what she and Sam will be doing this weekend. "I have no idea," she replies. "I don't know if he even wants to go out with me again. I just can't read him."

Marla's problem is not unique. Most of us have difficulty interpreting the nonverbal cues of others.

Group Discussion

Have students form groups and discuss whether they think nonverbal communication must be intentional. In other words, can unintended nonverbal signals be defined as communication?

What Is Nonverbal Communication?

nonverbal communication

The behaviors of people, other than their use of words, which have socially shared meaning, are intentionally sent or interpreted as intentional, are consciously sent or consciously received, and have the potential for feedback from the receiver.

This chapter will define nonverbal communication and will discuss the relationship between nonverbal and verbal communication. You will learn why nonverbal cues sometimes create misunderstanding. The chapter should help you make sense of the most frequently seen nonverbal codes, as well as provide you with some suggestions for improving your nonverbal communication. Let us begin with a definition and a brief discussion on the significance of nonverbal communication.

Nonverbal communication is defined as the "*attributes or actions of humans, other than the use of words themselves, which have socially shared meaning, are intentionally sent or interpreted as intentional, are consciously sent or consciously received, and have the potential for feedback from the receiver*" (Burgoon & Saine, 1978, pp. 9–10). Communication is complex. We cannot quantify the relative contribution of nonverbal communication to verbal communication (Lapakko, 1997), but nonverbal communication often provides much more meaning than people realize. Indeed, when we are not certain about another person's feelings or our feeling about him or her, we may rely far more on nonverbal cues and less on the words that are used (Mehrabian & Ferris, 1967; Mehrabian & Wiener, 1967).

Team Challenge

REFINING THE DEFINITION OF NONVERBAL COMMUNICATION

Nonverbal communication was defined in this text as "attributes or actions of humans, other than the use of words themselves, which have socially shared meaning, are intentionally sent or interpreted as intentional, are consciously sent or consciously received, and have the potential for feedback from the receiver" (Burgoon & Saine, 1978, pp. 9–10). In a group, consider communication that would not fit within this definition. For example, would unintentional messages be included? Do animals that are not human communicate nonverbally? Does thinking constitute nonverbal communication? If no one receives a nonverbal message that you send, does your behavior represent nonverbal communication? If you engage in eccentric or distinctive behavior, does it form an example of nonverbal communication? After you have agreed upon the definitions of the behaviors that do, and do not, count as nonverbal communication, place some behaviors in each category and explain why you placed them there.

You know the importance of nonverbal communication in your own life. Imagine how difficult communication would be if you could not see the people with whom you are communicating, hear their voices, or sense their presence. Actually, this is what occurs when you are sending e-mail or instant messages or chatting with others online. As electronic forms of communication have become more prevalent, people have found creative ways to communicate feeling and emotions. *Emoticons* are sequences of characters composed in two-dimensional written formats for the purpose of expressing emotions. The most common example of the emoticon is the "smiley" or "smiley face." Emoticons are a form of nonverbal communication and they illustrate the importance of this means of communication, no matter the context.

How Are Verbal and Nonverbal Communication Related?

In the last chapter we examined verbal communication and verbal codes. Both verbal and nonverbal communication are essential for effective interactions with others. How are the two related? We will consider the way nonverbal codes work in combination with verbal codes first. Then we will examine how the two are dissimilar.

E-Note

Emoticons are important tools when you are trying to convey your feelings to another person electronically. Without vocal inflections, facial expression, and bodily movement, your emotions are difficult to interpret. Emoticons can be helpful in avoiding misunderstanding. No absolute and standard definitions exist for individual emoticons, but many people have common understandings for a variety of these symbols. Generally, emoticons are made to resemble a face. Four examples are provided here. You can easily find additional examples online by using a search engine and the key word *emoticons*.

:-) Happiness or humor

:-I Indifference

:-Q Confusion

:-O Surprise

Nonverbal and Verbal Codes Work Together

Nonverbal communication works in conjunction with the words that we utter in six ways: to repeat, to emphasize, to complement, to contradict, to substitute, and to regulate. Let us consider each of these briefly.

repetition

The same message is sent both verbally and nonverbally.

Repetition occurs *when the same message is sent verbally and nonverbally.* For example, you frown at the PowerPoint presentation while you ask the speaker what he means. You direct a passing motorist by pointing at the next street corner and explaining where she should turn.

emphasis

Nonverbal cues strengthen verbal messages.

Emphasis is *the use of nonverbal cues to strengthen your message.* Hugging a friend and telling him that you really care about him is a stronger statement than using either words or bodily movement alone.

complementation

Nonverbal and verbal codes add meaning to each other and expand the meaning of either message alone.

Complementation is different from repetition in that it goes beyond duplication of the message in two channels. It is also not a substitution of one channel for the other. *The verbal and nonverbal codes add meaning to each other and expand on either message alone.* Your tone of voice, your gestures, and your bodily movement can all indicate your feeling, which goes beyond your verbal message.

contradiction

Verbal and nonverbal messages conflict.

Contradiction occurs *when your verbal and nonverbal messages conflict.* Often this occurs accidentally. If you have ever been angry at a teacher or parent, you may have stated verbally that you were fine—but your bodily movements, facial expression, and use of space may have "leaked" your actual feelings. Contradiction occurs intentionally in humor and sarcasm. Your words provide one message, but your nonverbal delivery tells how you really feel.

Substitution occurs *when you use no verbal language at all.* You roll your eyes, you stick out your tongue, you gesture thumbs down, or you shrug. In most cases, your intended message is fairly clear.

Regulation is used to *monitor and control interactions with others.* You look away when someone else is trying to talk and you are not finished with your thought. You walk away from someone who has hurt your feelings or made you angry. You shake your head and encourage another person to continue talking. While verbal and nonverbal codes often work in concert, they also exhibit differences that we will consider next.

Nonverbal and Verbal Codes Are Distinctive

Although nonverbal and verbal codes often work together, nonverbal communication may be viewed as different from verbal communication in four basic ways. First is the *number of channels available in each.* In verbal communication, one channel—the stream of utterances we offer—is all we have. In nonverbal communication, communication channels are multiple and simultaneous. We receive messages from others' eyes, face, body, movement, and other nonverbal cues.

Second is the *difference in coding systems.* You are familiar with the terms digital and analog because of the recent and rapid developments in information technology. **Digital** refers to *discrete or separate items.* For example, a digital clock is one that displays specific numbers rather than a more accurate, continual reading of time. **Analog** refers to *continual variable, measurable, physical quantities,* such as height, weight, or pressure. Verbal language is digital and consists of discrete and separate words. Nonverbal communication, alternatively, is analogic and continual. Often no beginning or end can be provided to someone's expression of an emotion through nonverbal cues. Similarly, most people do not use facial expression or use no facial expression; instead, they provide interesting blends of multiple facial movement.

A third difference between the two channels of communication is the *type of content for which they are best suited.* Nonverbal communication is ideal for expressing emotions. Verbal communication can provide a message with virtually no emotional content. Verbal communication can also be used to explain, argue, or tell a story. Verbal communication has the capacity to be *self-reflexive,* or to talk about itself. Nonverbal communication does not have this capability. Verbal communication can *distinguish tense* and contrast the past, present, and future, but nonverbal communication cannot. Finally, verbal communication can discuss the absence, or *reference the negative,* of something, whereas nonverbal communication has no capacity to do this.

A final difference between nonverbal and verbal communication centers on the *rule structure.* Generally, verbal communication, or language, has far more rules than does nonverbal communication.

substitution

Nonverbal codes are used instead of verbal codes.

regulation

Nonverbal cues are used to monitor and control interactions with others.

digital

Discrete or separate items; words are digital.

analog

Continual variable, measurable, physical quantities; nonverbal communication is analogic.

Group Activity

In groups have students identify or list various rules governing nonverbal behavior. Are rules more constant in verbal or nonverbal communication codes?

Language has a multifaceted and multilayered structure. The difference in the rule structure between the two channels suggests that nonverbal communication may be more difficult to understand and interpret than is verbal communication. Indeed, in the next section of the chapter we will determine exactly why nonverbal communication is the source of so much confusion.

Why Are Nonverbal Codes Difficult to Interpret?

Nonverbal communication is responsible for much of the misunderstanding that occurs during communication. Just as people have difficulty interpreting verbal symbols, so do they struggle to interpret nonverbal codes. The ambiguity of nonverbal communication occurs for three reasons: people use the same code to communicate a variety of meanings, they use a variety of codes to communicate the same meaning, and people have different interpretations of the purpose of nonverbal codes.

One Code Communicates a Variety of Meanings

Writing Assignment

Have students write a short paper explaining how difficulty in interpreting nonverbal communication has posed communication challenges in their own lives.

The ambiguity of nonverbal codes occurs in part because one code may communicate several different meanings. Two examples of situations in which one code communicates a variety of meanings will clarify this problem. The nonverbal code of raising your right hand may mean that you are taking an oath, you are demonstrating for a cause, you are indicating to an instructor that you would like to answer a question, a physician is examining your right side, or you want a taxi to stop for you. You may stand close to someone because of a feeling of affection, because the room is crowded, or because you have difficulty hearing.

Although people in laboratory experiments have demonstrated some success in decoding nonverbal behavior accurately (Druckmann, Rozelle, & Baxter, 1982), in actual situations, receivers of nonverbal cues can only guess about the meaning of the cue (Motley & Camden, 1988). Several lay authors have been successful in selling books which suggest that observers can learn to easily and accurately distinguish meaning from specific nonverbal cues. Unfortunately, these authors have not been able to demonstrate any significant improvement among their readers. Single cues can be interpreted in multiple ways.

A Variety of Codes Communicate the Same Meaning

Nonverbal communication is not a science: Any number of codes may be used to communicate the same meaning. One example is the many nonverbal ways by which adults communicate love or affection. You may sit or stand more closely to someone you love. You might speak more softly, use a certain vocal intonation, or alter how quickly you speak when you communicate with someone with whom you are affectionate. Or perhaps you may choose to dress differently when you are going to be in the company of someone you love.

Cultural differences are especially relevant when we consider that multiple cues may be used to express a similar message. How do you show respect to a speaker in a public-speaking situation? In some cultures, respect is shown by listeners when they avert their eyes; in other cultures, listeners show respect and attention by looking directly at the speaker. You may believe that showing your emotions is an important first step in resolving conflict, whereas a classmate may feel that emotional responses are an interference to conflict resolution.

Interpretations of Intentionality Vary

Intentionality, or *the purposefulness of nonverbal codes* (Malandro, Barker, & Barker, 1989), has four possible interpretations. First, *intentional nonverbal communication may be interpreted as intentional*, such as when you hug a friend. The hug is nonverbal, purposeful, and perceived as an intended message: I am so glad to see you. In this case, no misunderstanding occurs.

Second, *an intentional code may be misperceived as having another intention*, such as when a man is reading the message printed on a woman's T-shirt and she covers her chest and quickly turns away. The reading of the shirt, a nonverbal code, is perceived as intentional lust. Third, *an unintentional code may be perceived as intentional*, such as when someone forgets that the turn signal is on and another driver thinks that person intends to turn. Fourth, *a code may be sent and received unintentionally*, such as when a man accidentally leaves a price tag on a new tie or a person wears mismatched socks. The code is noticed, but it is perceived as unintentional and discounted as meaningless.

In the study of nonverbal communication, the focus is on nonverbal codes that are intentionally sent or received.

intentionality

The purposefulness of nonverbal codes.

Video Activity

Ask students to view the video segment "Sam's Graduation Party," which illustrates several types of nonverbal code.

What Are Nonverbal Codes?

Nonverbal codes are *codes of communication consisting of symbols that are not words, including nonword vocalizations.* Bodily movement, facial expression, bodily appearance, the use of space, the use of time, touching, vocal cues, and clothing and other artifacts are all nonverbal codes. Let us consider these systematic arrangements of symbols that have been given arbitrary meaning and are used in communication.

nonverbal codes

Codes consisting of symbols that are not words, including nonword vocalizations.

Bodily Movement and Facial Expression

kinesics

The study of bodily movements, including posture, gestures, and facial expressions.

The study of posture, movement, gestures, and facial expression is called **kinesics,** a word derived from the Greek word *kinesis,* meaning movement. Some popular books purport to teach you how to "read" nonverbal communication so that you will know, for example, who is sexually aroused, who is just kidding, and whom you should avoid. Nonverbal communication, however, is more complicated than that. Interpreting the meaning of nonverbal communication is partly a matter of assessing the other person's unique behavior and considering the context. You don't just "read" another person's body language; instead, you observe, analyze, and interpret before you decide the probable meaning.

Assessing another person's unique behavior means that you need to know how that person usually acts. A quiet person might be unflappable even in an emergency situation. A person who never smiles may not be unhappy, and someone who acts happy might not actually be happy. You need to know how the person expresses emotions before you can interpret what his or her nonverbal communication means.

Considering the context means that the situation alters how you interpret nonverbal communication. Many people become talkative, candid, and sometimes stupid when they drink alcoholic beverages. Finding someone excessively friendly at a long party might be more attributable to the proof of the drinks than to anything else. People tend to be formally polite at ceremonies, emotionally unguarded in their homes, and excessively prudent when applying for a job.

To look more deeply into interpreting nonverbal communication, let us consider the work of some experts on the subject: Albert Mehrabian, Paul Ekman, and Wallace Friesen.

Mehrabian (1971) studied nonverbal communication by examining the concepts of liking, status, and responsiveness among the participants in communication situations.

Homework Assignment

Have students find magazine and newspaper pictures illustrating Mehrabian's (1971) notions of liking, status, and responsiveness. Students should be prepared to show pictures in class.

1. *Liking* was often expressed by leaning forward, a direct body orientation (e.g., standing face to face), close proximity, increased touching, relaxed posture, open arms and body, positive facial expression, and eye contact (i.e., looking directly at the other person). For example, look at how a group of males act when drinking beer and watching a game on television, or watch newly matched couples in the spring.

2. *Status,* especially high status, is communicated nonverbally by bigger gestures, relaxed posture, and less eye contact. Male bosses sometimes put their feet up on their desks when talking to subordinates, but subordinates rarely act that way when talking to their boss.

GREETINGS

Chinese, Japanese, and Koreans bow, and Thais bow their heads while holding their hands in a prayerlike position. The bumi putra, or Muslim Malaysians, have a greeting of their own: They shake hands as westerners do, but they follow up by touching their heart with their right hand to indicate that they are greeting you "from the heart."

3. *Responsiveness* in nonverbal communication is exhibited by moving toward the other person, by spontaneous gestures, by shifting posture and position, and by facial expressiveness. In other words, the face and body provide positive feedback to the other person.

Ekman (1993, 1997, 1999a, 1999b) and Ekman and Friesen (1969) categorized movement on the basis of its functions, origins, and meanings. Their five categories include emblems, illustrators, affect displays, regulators, and adaptors.

1. **Emblems** are *movements that substitute for words and phrases.* Examples of emblems are a beckoning first finger to mean "come here," an open hand held up to mean "stop," and a forefinger and thumb together to mean "OK." Be wary of emblems; they may mean something else in another culture.

2. **Illustrators** are *movements that accompany or reinforce verbal messages.* Examples of illustrators are nodding your head when you say yes, shaking your head when you say no, stroking your stomach when you say you are hungry, and shaking your fist in the air when you say "Get out of here." These nonverbal cues tend to be more universal than many of the other four categories of movement.

3. **Affect displays** are *movements of the face and body used to show emotion.* Watch people's behavior when their favorite team wins a game, listen to the door slam shut when an angry person leaves the room, and watch men make threatening moves when they are very upset with each other but don't dare fight openly.

4. **Regulators** are *nonverbal moves that control the flow or pace of communication.* Examples of regulators are starting to move away when you want the conversation to stop, looking at the floor or

emblems

Nonverbal movements that substitute for words and phrases.

illustrators

Nonverbal movements that accompany or reinforce verbal messages.

affect displays

Nonverbal movements of the face and body used to show emotion.

regulators

Nonverbal movements that control the flow or pace of communication.

looking away when you are not interested, or yawning and looking at your watch when you are bored.

5. **Adaptors** are *movements that you might perform fully in private but only partially in public.* For example, you might rub your nose in public, but you would probably never pick it.

adaptors

Nonverbal movements that you might perform fully in private but only partially in public.

Finally, Ekman and Friesen (1967) determined that a person's facial expressions provide information to others about how he or she feels, whereas the person's body orientation suggests how intensely he or she feels. Put facial expression and body orientation together, and your interpretation of nonverbal messages will become more accurate.

To illustrate the importance of nonverbal communication, consider the finding that audiences who can see the speaker understand more of the message than audiences who cannot see the speaker (Kramer & Lewis, 1951). Apparently, bodily movement and facial expression increase the ability to interpret meaning.

Bodily Appearance

Closely related to kinesics are the physical qualities, or bodily appearance, that we possess. Both our body type (which includes our height, weight, and muscularity) and our physical attractiveness hold communication potential.

somatotype

Body type which is comprised of a combination of height, weight, and muscularity.

ectomorph

Body type that is characterized by a tall, thin, and sometimes frail person.

mesomorph

Body type that is proportioned, average in height, athletic, trim, and muscular.

endomorph

Body type that tends to be short, soft, and round.

Body Type

Body type, or **somatotype,** is comprised of *a combination of height, weight, and muscularity* (see, for reference, www.fitnesszone.com/features/archives/body-types.html). Body types have been categorized into three overall types: ectomorph, mesomorph, and endomorph. An **ectomorph** is a tall, thin, and sometimes frail person. Generally this person possesses low body fat, small bone size, a high metabolism, and a small amount of muscle mass and muscle size. A **mesomorph** is *proportioned, average in height, athletic, trim, and muscular.* Typically, this individual has low to medium body fat, medium to large bone size, a medium to high metabolism, and a large amount of muscle mass and muscle size. An **endomorph** is *short, soft, and round.* Endomorphs often possess high body fat, large bone size, a slow metabolism, and a small amount of muscle mass and muscle size.

Most of us do not possess "pure" body types and are some combination of these three. To make a rough estimate of your body type, you can rate yourself on the three body types. Give yourself a score between 1 and 7 for each of the possible body types. If you are a college athlete, you might be a 2/7/1. If you are tall and thin with small bones, you might rate as a 7/1/1. Most of us have scores that illustrate that we are combinations of the three.

Ectomorphic women and mesomorphic men may be the cultural ideal; however, many people in the United States tend to be endomorphic because of obesity. When people are endomorphic, they are often judged negatively. These negative assessments carry with them ideas about individuals' personalities and their interest in how they present themselves. They also set the stage for eating disorders (Cash, 1997; Cash & Roy, 1999; Cash & Strachan, 1999). Diet and exercise can lead to some modification of our somatotype and positive outcomes, but they can also be overdone. In addition, our body type is something we inherit, and we cannot change it completely.

We should observe that height, on its own, affects others' impressions of us, too. Tall people are generally more successful in a variety of contexts. For instance, when two men of different heights are candidates for the U.S. presidency, the taller man generally wins the election. Taller people are also more likely to be hired in employment interviews and they tend to make more income, as well (Hensley, 1992; Knapp & Hall, 1992). On the other hand, although women prefer tall men over short ones, they generally view men of medium height as the most attractive, dateable, and likable (Graziano, Brothen, & Berscheid, 1978).

Physical Attraction

Beauty, it has been noted, is in the eye of the beholder. However, some research has suggested that particular characteristics—bright eyes, symmetrical features, and thin or medium build—are generally viewed to be associated with physical attraction (Cash, 1980; Kowner, 1996). Moreover, such characteristics may not be limited to our culture, but may be universal (Brody, 1994).

Although we may want to believe that physical attractiveness is irrelevant to other aspects of our lives, we cannot deny the evidence. Our culture is obsessed with the concept of beauty. The influence of physical appearance begins when we are young. By the age of four, children are treated differently based on their physical appearance by their daycare teachers (Cash, 1980; Langlois & Downs, 1979). When children misbehave, their behavior is viewed as an isolated, momentary aberration if they are physically attractive, but as evidence of a chronic tendency to be bad if they are unattractive. These patterns continue throughout childhood and adolescence (Knapp & Hall, 1992).

Physical attractiveness generally leads to more social success in adulthood. Women who are attractive report a larger number of dates in college. Both women and men who are attractive are seen as more sociable and sensitive (Knapp & Hall, 1992). Attractive people receive higher initial credibility ratings than do those who are viewed as unattractive (Widgery, 1974).

Physically attractive people are generally more likely to succeed at work, too. They are more likely to be hired and they receive higher salaries when they are hired (Knapp & Hall, 1992; Schneider, 2001). Some studies suggest that these conclusions might not be equally true for women and men. Attractive females are sometimes judged as less competent than are unattractive females. In some instances, "beauty and brains do not mix" for women. For males, attractiveness either shows no difference on competence or attractive men are viewed as more competent (Kaplan, 1978).

Space

proxemics

The study of the human use of space and distance.

Anthropologist Edward T. Hall (1966) introduced the concept of **proxemics,** *the study of the human use of space*, in his book *The Hidden Dimension.* This researcher and others, such as Werner (1987), have demonstrated the role space plays in human communication. Two concepts considered essential to the study of the use of space are territoriality and personal space:

Discussion Question

Ask students to discuss the impact of increasing multiculturalism in the United States on the nonverbal use of space. Based on statistics discussed in chapter 7, will American's use of space begin to change?

CD-ROM Activity

Ask students to view the animation titled "Zones of Space" on the student CD-ROM. The animation illustrates Hall's notions of intimate, personal, social, and public distance.

TRY◀▶THIS

Next time you go to a party, notice how the size of the room and the seating arrangement affect the way people are grouped and how they communicate.

---

1. *Territoriality* refers to your need to establish and maintain certain spaces as your own. In a shared dormitory room, the items on the common desk area mark the territory. On a cafeteria table, the placement of the plate, glass, napkin, and eating utensils marks the territory. In a neighborhood, it might be fences, hedges, trees, or rocks that mark the territory. All are nonverbal indicators that signal ownership.
2. *Personal space* is the personal "bubble" of space that moves around with you. It is the distance you maintain between yourself and others, the amount of room you claim as your own. Large people usually claim more space because of their size, and men often take more space than women. For example, in a lecture hall, observe who claims the armrests as part of their personal bubbles.

TRY◀▶THIS

Purposefully overstep someone's personal space and watch his or her reaction. Does the person become uncomfortable, move back, or not even notice?

Figure 4.1 Zones of space.

Active Art

Hall (1966) was the first to define the four distances people regularly use while they communicate. His categories have been helpful in understanding the communicative behavior that might occur when two communicators are a particular distance from each other. Beginning with the closest contact and the least personal space, and moving to the greatest distance, Hall's four categories are intimate distance, personal distance, social distance, and public distance (see figure above).

1. *Intimate distance* extends from you outward to 18 inches, and it is used by people who are relationally close to you. Used more often in private than in public, this intimate distance is employed to show affection, to give comfort, and to protect. Graves and Robinson (1976) and Burgoon (1978) say that intimate distance usually shows positive response because individuals tend to stand and sit close to people to whom they are attracted.

2. *Personal distance* ranges from 18 inches to 4 feet, and it is the distance used by most Americans for conversation and other nonintimate exchanges.

Video Activity

Ask students to view the video segment "Sam's Graduation Party." Have students discuss how various characters used space and established territoriality.

3. *Social distance* ranges from 4 to 12 feet, and it is used most often to carry out business in the workplace, especially in formal, less personal situations. The higher the status of one person, the greater the distance.
4. *Public distance* exceeds 12 feet and is used most often in public speaking in such settings as lecture halls; churches, mosques, and synagogues; courtrooms; and convention halls. Professors often stand at this distance while lecturing.

Distance, then, is a nonverbal means of communicating everything from the size of your personal bubble to your relationship with the person to whom you are speaking or listening. A great deal of research has been done on proxemics (see, for example, Andersen, Guerrero, Buller, & Jorgensen, 1998; Grammer, Kruck, & Magnusson, 1998; Tucker & Anders, 1998). Sex, size, and similarity seem to be among the important determiners of your personal space.

Men tend to take more space because they are often larger than women (Argyle & Dean, 1965). Women take less space, and children take and are given the least space. Women exhibit less discomfort with small space and tend to interact at closer range (Addis, 1966; Leventhal & Matturro, 1980; Snyder & Endelman, 1979). Perhaps because women are so often given little space, they come to expect it. Also, women and children in our society seem to desire more relational closeness than do men.

Your relationship to other people is related to your use of space (Guardo, 1969). You stand closer to friends and farther from enemies. You stand farther from strangers, authority figures, high-status people, physically challenged people, and people from racial groups different from your own. You stand closer to people you perceive as similar or unthreatening because closeness communicates trust.

The physical setting also can alter the use of space. People tend to stand closer together in large rooms and farther apart in small rooms according to Sommer (1962). In addition, physical obstacles and furniture arrangements can affect the use of personal space.

The cultural background of the people communicating also must be considered in the evaluation of personal space. Hall (1963) was among the first to recognize the importance of cultural background when he was training American service personnel for service overseas. He wrote:

Americans overseas were confronted with a variety of difficulties because of cultural differences in the handling of space. People stood "too close" during conversations, and when the Americans backed away to a comfortable conversational distance, this was taken to mean that Americans were cold, aloof, withdrawn, and disinterested in the people of the country. USA housewives muttered about "waste-space" in houses in the Middle East. In England, Americans who were used to neighborliness were hurt when they discovered that their neighbors were no more accessible or friendly than other people, and in Latin America, exsuburbanites, accustomed to unfenced yards, found that the high walls there made them feel "shut out." Even in Germany, where so many of my countrymen felt at home, radically different patterns in the use of space led to unexpected tensions. (Hall, 1963, p. 422)

Cultural background can result in great differences in the use of space and in people's interpretation of such use. As our world continues to shrink, more people will be working in multinational corporations, regularly traveling to different countries, and interacting with others from a variety of backgrounds. Sensitivity to space use in different cultures and quick, appropriate responses to those variations are imperative.

Although considerable research has documented appropriate personal space and variations in personal space, sometimes people are not sensitive to the norms of personal space. Burgoon and her colleagues (Burgoon, 1978; 1993; 1995; Burgoon & LePoire, 1993; Floyd, Ramirez, & Burgoon, 1999) have explored this phenomenon by offering the expectancy violation theory and testing it in a variety of contexts. The **expectancy violation theory** centers on *the relationship between "personal space expectations and the communicative impact of violations of those expectations"* (Burgoon, 1978, p. 129).

Communication outcomes are affected by violations of personal space. For example, when someone acts in an unexpected way, but in a way that is favorably interpreted and with a positive evaluation, more favorable outcomes occur than if the same act was expected. To illustrate this finding, imagine two situations. In the first, an attractive stranger on a plane leans unexpectedly close to you as you converse. In the second, one of your parents has a converation with you at a similar close space. The expectancy violation theory would posit that you would respond more favorably in the first instance than in the second. Both situations have a favorable interpretation and both have a positive evaluation, but the unexpected nature of the first situation leads to more favorable outcomes.

Research on the expectancy violation theory also shows generally that people who are rewarding in their interactions with us continue to maintain positive outcomes, even when they move closer to us than normal. Too, they can interact much more closely and still have positive results than can those communicators who we find to be punishing. Violations of personal space are thus more serious in punishing situations.

Time

Temporal communication, or **chronemics,** refers to *the way that people organize and use time and the messages that are created because of our organization and use of it* (for more explanation, see www.agricola. umn.edu/Library/Chronemics.htm; www.walther.llc.rpi.edu/vita/pubs/ chronem.htm; www.cbpa.louisville.edu/bruce/mgmtwebs/commun_f98/ chronemics.htm). Time can be examined on a macro level. How do you perceive the past, future, and present? Some people value the past and collect

Writing Assignment

Ask students to select a culture or co-culture and write a short paper on how that culture's nonverbal codes may differ from American dominant culture.

expectancy violation theory

The communicative impact of violations of personal space expectations

chronemics

Also called temporal communication, is the way people organize and use time.

Think, Pair, Share

Consider how one (or more) of your family members, one (or more) of your roommates, and one (or more) of your teachers view time. Do they arrive early and leave events early? Are they regularly later than you are? With whom do you experience conflicts because of their use of time? How do you manage these conflicts? After you have had time to reflect on these differences in the use of time, share your perceptions with another classmate. Does the second person have ideas on how you can more successfully navigate issues surrounding time with those with whom you interact?

photographs and souvenirs to remind themselves of time in the past. They emphasize how things have been. Others live in the future and are always chasing dreams or planning future events. They may be more eager when planning a vacation or party than they are when the event arrives. Still others live in the present and savor the current time. They try to live each day to its fullest and neither lament the past nor show concern for the future.

Our use of time communicates several qualities. Our urgency or casualness with the starting time of an event could be an indication of our personality, our status, or our culture. Relaxed, relational people may arrive and leave late, whereas highly structured, task-oriented counterparts may arrive and leave on time or even early. People with high status are generally granted the opportunity of arriving late, whereas those with low status are expected to arrive on time. Punctuality is more important in North America than in South America. Dinner guests in eastern United States urban areas may view a suggested time of arrival more flexibly than do rural people in the Upper Midwest.

Touching

tactile communication

The use of touch in communication.

Tactile communication is *the use of touch in communication.* Because touch always involves invasion of another's personal space, it commands attention. It can be welcome, as when a crying child is held by a parent, or unwelcome, as in sexual harassment, and our need for, and appreciation of, tactile communication starts early in life. Schutz (1971) observed:

> The unconscious parental feelings communicated through touch or lack of touch can lead to feelings of confusion and conflict in a child. Sometimes a "modern" parent will say all the right things but not want to touch the child very much. The child's confusion comes from the inconsistency of levels: if they really approve of me so much like they say they do, why don't they touch me? (p. 16)

Touch is part of many rituals.

Insufficient touching can lead to health disorders, such as allergies and eczema, speech problems, and even death. Researchers have found that untouched babies and small children can grow increasingly ill and die (Montagu, 1971).

For adults, touch is a powerful means of communication (Aguinis, Simonson, & Pierce, 1998; Fromme et al., 1989). Usually, touch is perceived as positive, pleasureful, and reinforcing. The association of touch with the warmth and caring that began in infancy carries over into adulthood. People who are comfortable with touch are more likely to be satisfied with their past and current lives. They are self-confident, assertive, socially acceptable, and active in confronting problems.

TRY ◀▶ THIS

Think about how you use nonverbal communication. Are you comfortable touching and being touched? Do you frequently hug others or shake hands with others? Why or why not?

Touch is part of many important rituals. In baptism, the practice in many churches is as little as a touch on the head during the ceremony to as much as a total immersion in water. Prayers in some churches are said with the pastor's hand touching the person being prayed for. In fundamentalist Christian churches, the healer might accompany the touch with a mighty shove, right into the hands of two catchers. Physician Bernie Siegel (1990) wrote the following in his book on mind–body communication:

> I'd like to see some teaching time devoted to the healing power of touch—a subject that only 12 of 169 medical schools in the English-speaking world deal with at all . . . despite the fact that touch is one of the most basic forms of communication between people. . . . We need to teach medical students how to touch people. (p. 134)

Religion and medicine are just two professions in which touch is important for ceremonial and curative purposes.

Touch varies within each co-culture. The findings relating touch with gender indicate that

- Women value touch more than men do (Fisher, Rytting, & Heslin, 1976).
- Women are touched more than men, beginning when they are six-month-old girls (Clay, 1968; Goldberg & Lewis, 1969).
- Women touch female children more often than they touch male children (Clay, 1968; Goldberg & Lewis, 1969).
- Men and their sons touch each other the least (Jourard & Rubin, 1968).
- Female students are touched more often and in more places than are male students (Jourard, 1966).
- Males touch others more often than females touch others (Henley, 1973–1974).
- Males may use touch to indicate power or dominance (Henley, 1973–1974).

On the last point, to observe who can touch whom among people in the workplace is interesting. Although fear of being accused of sexual harassment has eliminated a great deal of touch except for handshaking, the general nonverbal principle is that the higher-status individual gets to initiate touch, but touch is not reciprocal: The president might pat you on the back for a job well done, but in our society you don't pat back.

Further, both co-culture and culture determine the frequency and kind of nonverbal communication. People from different countries handle nonverbal communication differently—even something as simple as touch. Sidney Jourard (1968) determined the rates of touch per hour among adults from various cultures. In a coffee shop, adults in San Juan, Puerto Rico, touched 180 times per hour, while those in Paris, France, touched about 110 times per hour, followed by those in Gainesville, Florida, who touched about 2 times per hour, and those in London, En-

Discussion Topic

Rules for touch are different from one situation to the next. Discuss how touching rules differ in the following contexts: a classroom, a bar or dance, the mall, and a TV lounge in a dorm.

gland, who touched only once per hour. North Americans are more frequent touchers than are the Japanese (Barnlund, 1975).

Touch sends such a powerful message that it has to be handled with responsibility. When the right to touch is abused, it can result in a breach of trust, anxiety, and hostility. When touch is used to communicate concern, caring, and affection, it is welcome, desired, and appreciated.

Vocal Cues

Nonverbal communication includes some sounds, as long as they are not words. We call them **paralinguistic features,** *the nonword sounds and nonword characteristics of language, such as pitch, volume, rate, and quality.* The prefix *para* means "alongside" or "parallel to," so *paralinguistic* means "alongside the words or language."

The paralinguistic feature examined here is **vocal cues,** *all of the oral aspects of sound except words themselves.* Vocal cues include

- **Pitch:** *the highness or lowness of your voice.*
- **Rate:** *how rapidly or slowly you speak.*
- **Inflection:** *the variety or changes in pitch.*
- **Volume:** *the loudness or softness of your voice.*
- **Quality:** *the unique resonance of your voice,* such as huskiness, nasality, raspiness, and whininess.
- **Nonword sounds:** *mmh, huh, ahh, and the like, as well as pauses or absence of sound* used for effect in speaking.
- **Pronunciation:** *whether or not you say a word correctly.*
- **Articulation:** *whether or not your mouth, tongue, and teeth coordinate to make a word understandable* to others (e.g., a lisp).
- **Enunciation:** *whether or not you combine pronunciation and articulation to produce a word with clarity* and distinction so it can be understood. A person who mumbles has an enunciation problem.
- **Silence:** *the lack of sound.*

These vocal cues are important because they are linked in our minds with a speaker's physical characteristics, emotional state, personality characteristics, gender characteristics, and even credibility.

According to Kramer (1963), vocal cues frequently convey information about the speaker's characteristics, such as age, height, appearance, and body type. For example, people often associate a high-pitched voice with someone who is female; someone who is younger; and someone who is smaller, rather than larger. You may visualize someone who uses a loud voice as being tall and large or someone who speaks quickly as being nervous. People who tend to speak slowly and deliberately may be perceived as being high-status individuals or as having high credibility.

paralinguistic features

The nonword sounds and nonword characteristics of language, such as pitch, volume, rate, and quality.

vocal cues

All of the oral aspects of sound except words themselves; part of paralinguistic features.

pitch

The highness or lowness of one's voice.

rate

The pace of one's speech.

inflection

The variety or changes in pitch.

volume

The loudness or softness of one's voice.

quality

The unique resonance of one's voice, such as huskiness, nasality, raspiness, and whininess.

nonword sounds

Sounds such as *mmh, huh,* and *ahh* and pauses or absence of sound used for effect in speaking.

pronunciation

The correct way to say a word.

articulation

Coordination of the mouth, tongue, and teeth to make a word understandable to others.

enunciation

Pronunciation and articulation to produce a word with clarity and distinction so it can be understood.

silence

The lack of sound.

Group Activity

Have students bring in audiotapes of a friend talking (2–3 minutes). Each group should have a tape player. Students will take turns playing their audiotape and other group members will identify paralinguistic behaviors and try to guess the age, gender, appearance, etc., of the person talking in each tape.

A number of studies have related emotional states to specific vocal cues. Joy and hate appear to be the most accurately communicated emotions, whereas shame and love are among the most difficult to communicate accurately (McCroskey, Larson, & Knapp, 1971). Joy and hate appear to be conveyed by fewer vocal cues, and this makes them less difficult to interpret than emotions such as shame and love, which are conveyed by complex sets of vocal cues. "Active" feelings such as joy and hate are associated with a loud voice, a high pitch, and a rapid rate. Conversely, "passive" feelings, which include affection and sadness, are communicated with a soft voice, a low pitch, and a relatively slow rate (Kramer, 1963).

Personality characteristics also have been related to vocal cues. Dominance, social adjustment, and sociability have been clearly correlated with specific vocal cues (Bateson, Jackson, Haley, & Weakland, 1956).

Although the personality characteristics attributed to individuals displaying particular vocal cues have not been shown to accurately portray the person, as determined by standardized personality tests, our impressions affect our interactions. In other words, although you may perceive loud-voiced, high-pitched, fast-speaking individuals as dominant, they might not be measured as dominant by a personality inventory. Nonetheless, in your interactions with such people, you may become increasingly submissive because of your perception that they are dominant. In addition, these people may begin to become more dominant because they are treated as though they have this personality characteristic.

Vocal cues can help a public speaker establish credibility with an audience and can clarify the message. Pitch and inflection can be used to make the speech sound aesthetically pleasing, to accomplish subtle changes in meaning, and to tell an audience whether you are asking a question or making a statement, being sincere or sarcastic, or being doubtful or assertive. A rapid speaking rate may indicate you are confident about speaking in public or that you are nervously attempting to conclude your speech. Variations in volume can be used to add emphasis or to create suspense. Enunciation is especially important in public speaking because of the increased size of the audience and the fewer opportunities for direct feedback. Pauses can be used in a public speech to create dramatic effect and to arouse audience interest. Vocalized pauses—*ah, uh-huh, um,* and so on—are not desirable in public speaking and may distract the audience.

Silence is a complex behavior steeped in contradictions. To be sure, silence is far better than vocalized pauses in public speaking. Too, silence may signal respect and empathy when another person is speaking or disclosing personal information. One observer noted: "Sometimes silence is best. Words are curious things, at best approximations. And every human being is a separate language. . . . [Sometimes] silence is best" (Hardman, 1971). On the other hand, silence may signal the dark side of communication. People in power, in dominant cultures, or in positions of authority may silence others. Those with whom they come in contact may be marginalized or embarrassed and feel that they must remain silent because of sexism, racism, taboo, incidents of violence or abuse, shame, or a hostile environment (Olson, 1997).

TRY ◄►THIS

When you picture people you talk to on the telephone before meeting them, does your expectation of how they will look usually turn out to be accurate? What vocal cues did they use that led to your picture of how they would look?

Clothing and Other Artifacts

Objectics, or **object language,** refers to *the study of the human use of clothing and other artifacts as nonverbal codes.* **Artifacts** are *ornaments or adornments we display that hold communicative potential,* including jewelry, hairstyles, cosmetics, automobiles, canes, watches, shoes, portfolios, hats, glasses, tattoos, body piercings, and even the fillings in teeth. Your clothing and other adornments communicate your age, gender, status, role, socioeconomic class, group memberships, personality, and relation to the opposite sex. Dresses are seldom worn by men, low-cut gowns are not the choice of shy women, bright colors are avoided by reticent people, and the most recent Paris fashion is seldom seen in the small towns of mid-America.

These cues also indicate the time in history, the time of day, and the climate. Clothing and artifacts provide physical and psychological protection, and they are used for sexual attraction and to indicate self-concept. Your clothing and artifacts clarify the sort of person you believe you are (Fisher, 1975). They permit personal expression (Proctor, 1978), and they satisfy your need for creative self-expression (Horn, 1975). A person who exhibits an interest in using clothing as a means of expression may be demonstrating a high level of self-actualization (Perry, Schutz, & Rucker, 1983). For example, an actress who always dresses in expensive designer dresses may be showing everyone that she is exactly what she always wanted to be.

TRY ◄►THIS

Observe others' clothing and determine what their choices tell you about their personality.

Discussion Question

How do people use ornaments like jewelry to communicate? What is the meaning of various types and styles of jewelry? Does body piercing follow the same rules for assigning meaning as other forms of jewelry? Why or why not?

objectics

Also called object language, is the study of the human use of clothing and other artifacts as nonverbal codes.

artifacts

Ornaments or adornments we display that hold communicative potential.

What do you conclude about this person based on his artifacts?

Many studies have established a relationship between an individual's clothing and artifacts and his or her characteristics. Conforming to current styles is correlated with an individual's desire to be accepted and liked (Taylor & Compton, 1968). In addition, individuals feel that clothing is important in forming first impressions (Henricks, Kelley, & Eicher, 1968).

Perhaps of more importance are the studies that consider the relationship between clothing and an observer's perception of that person. In an early study, clothing was shown to affect others' impressions of status and personality traits (Douty, 1963). People also seem to base their acceptance of others on their clothing and artifacts. In another early study, women who were asked to describe the most popular women they knew used clothing as the most important characteristic (Williams & Eicher, 1966).

What Are Some Ways to Improve Nonverbal Communication?

Teaching Tip

Emphasize that in any communication situation the context determines, in part, how meaning is assigned to messages. This is particularly true with nonverbal communication.

Sensitivity to nonverbal cues is highly variable among people (Rosenthal, Hall, Matteg, Rogers, & Archer, 1979). You can improve your understanding of nonverbal communication, though, by being sensitive to context, audience, and feedback.

The *context* includes the physical setting, the occasion, and the situation. In conversation, your vocal cues are rarely a problem unless you stutter, stammer, lisp, or suffer from some speech pathology. Paralinguistic features loom large in importance in small-group communication, where you have to adapt to the distance and to a variety of receivers. These features are, perhaps, most important in public speaking because you have to adjust volume and rate, you have to enunciate more clearly, and you have to introduce more vocal variety to keep the audience's attention. The strategic use of pauses and silence is also more apparent in public speaking than it is in an interpersonal context in conversations or small-group discussion.

The occasion and physical setting also affect the potential meaning of a nonverbal cue. For example, when would it be appropriate for you to wear a cap over unwashed, uncombed hair and when would it be interpreted as inappropriate? The distance at which you communicate may be different based on the setting and the occasion: You may stand farther away from people in formal situations when space allows, but closer to family members, or others, in an elevator.

The *audience* makes a difference in your nonverbal communication, so you have to adapt. When speaking to children, you must use a simple vocabulary and careful enunciation, articulation, and pronunciation. With an older audience or with younger audiences whose hearing has been impaired by too much loud music, you must adapt your volume. Generally, children and older people in both interpersonal and public-speaking situations appreciate slower speech. Also, adaptation to an audience may determine your choice of clothing, hairstyle, and jewelry. For instance, a shaved head, a ring in the nose or lip, and a shirt open to the navel do not go over well in a job interview unless you are trying for a job as an entertainer.

Your attention to giving *feedback* can be very important in helping others interpret your nonverbal cues that might otherwise distract your listeners. For example, some pregnant women avoid questions and distraction by wearing a shirt that says, "I'm not fat, I'm pregnant"; such feedback prevents listeners from wondering instead of listening. Similarly, your listener's own descriptive feedback—quizzical looks, staring, nodding off—can signal you to talk louder, introduce variety, restate your points, or clarify your message.

Chapter Review

SUMMARY

In this chapter you have learned the following:

- Verbal and nonverbal codes work in conjunction and are distinctive.
- People often have difficulty interpreting nonverbal codes because
  - They use the same code to communicate a variety of meanings.
  - They use a variety of codes to communicate the same meaning.
  - They have different interpretations of intentionality.
- Nonverbal codes consist of nonword symbols:
  - Bodily movements and facial expression
  - Bodily appearance
  - Personal space
  - Time
  - Touching
  - Vocal cues
  - Clothing and artifacts
- You can solve some of the difficulties in interpreting nonverbal codes if you
  - Consider all of the variables in each communication situation.
  - Consider all of the available verbal and nonverbal codes.
  - Use descriptive feedback to minimize misunderstandings.

⊙ VIDEO LINK: GOING TO A PARTY WITH NONVERBAL COMMUNICATION

Video Episode 1: "Sam's Graduation Party"

We constantly use nonverbal communication to intentionally or unintentionally communicate messages to others. An intentional choice of clothing, a warm hug, and the choice to wear perfume or cologne are all examples of nonverbal communication, and there are many others. Watch "Sam's Graduation Party" and observe the nonverbal behaviors exhibited by those in attendance. Based on nonverbal behaviors, what impressions can you draw about the various characters? Does the choice of clothing influence your perceptions about people in the clip? How do the characters use space and touch to express meaning? What other nonverbal behaviors catch your attention?

ISSUES IN COMMUNICATION: A CHINESE GOODBYE

This Issues in Communication narrative is designed to provoke individual thought or discussion about concepts raised in the chapter.

Peter Nelson, an American, was recently faced with a six-hour layover in Taiwan's international airport. A long layover in any airport is usually a dreadful prospect, but in this case it was particularly difficult. Passengers transferring from one flight to another were banned from the shopping area. Additionally, there was only a single vending machine and a television tuned to Airport CNN.

Peter occupied much of his time "people watching." He sat in a high balcony over an area where outgoing passengers left their loved ones to board international flights. He noticed that when Chinese couples approached the boarding gate, the partners usually looked at each other (sometimes bowing slightly) and said a few words, then parted as one entered a gate where nonpassengers were not allowed. During two hours of observation, only one couple—a young Chinese male and a youthful American female—actually embraced, hugged, and kissed. Otherwise, couple after couple repeated the same ritual, with the partners usually not touching each other or occasionally touching with just a quick hand on the shoulder.

A second part of the ritual became apparent to Peter only after he had watched for a while. After passengers went through the passengers-only gate, their loved ones lingered behind a glass partition where they could see the passengers standing in line to receive boarding passes. During this time, the people in line never looked back at their loved ones, even though they sometimes waited in line for 5 or 10 minutes. Only before disappearing down the corridor to the airplane would a passenger turn to wave quickly to his or her loved one waiting behind the glass. Then both would turn and leave.

Only once during the two-hour period that Peter was watching did the routine not play out this way, and that was with the Chinese male and American female who embraced and kissed before the man entered the passengers-only gate. Just like the other people, the American woman waited behind the glass partition as her Chinese companion waited in line for his boarding pass. When he finally got his boarding pass, he waved goodbye and then disappeared swiftly down the corridor. The woman, however, lingered and watched him disappear. When she turned to leave, Peter noticed tears rolling down her face.

Apply what you have learned about nonverbal communication as you ponder and discuss the following questions: In what ways are the nonverbal codes the Chinese use to say goodbye to their loved ones in an airport different from the ways Americans say goodbye in an airport? In general, how does culture influence nonverbal communication? (If you're aware of any specific examples not included in the chapter, be sure to state those too.) Compare the nonverbal communication you use when saying goodbye to a loved one with your nonverbal communication when waiting for your flight or when chatting with someone waiting for the same flight as you.

KEY TERMS

Use the *Human Communication* CD-ROM and the *Online Learning Center* at www.mhhe.com/pearson to further your understanding of the following terminology.

Adaptors	Artifacts	Digital
Affect displays	Chronemics	Ectomorph
Analog	Complementation	Emblems
Articulation	Contradiction	Emphasis

Endomorph
Enunciation
Expectancy violation theory
Illustrators
Inflection
Intentionality
Kinesics
Mesomorph
Nonverbal codes

Nonverbal communication
Nonword sounds
Objectics
Paralinguistic features
Pitch
Pronunciation
Proxemics
Quality
Rate

Regulation
Regulators
Repetition
Silence
Somatotype
Substitution
Tactile communication
Vocal cues
Volume

SELF-QUIZ

Go to the self-quizzes on the *Human Communication* CD-ROM and the *Online Learning Center* at www.mhhe.com/pearson to test your knowledge.

REFERENCES

Addis, B. R. (1966). *The relationship of physical interpersonal distance to sex, race, and age.* Unpublished master's thesis, University of Oklahoma.

Aguinis, H., Simonsen, M. M., & Pierce, C. A. (1998). Effects of nonverbal behavior on perceptions of power bases. *Journal of Social Psychology, 138*(4), 455–475.

Andersen, P. A., Guerrero, L. K., Buller, D. B., & Jorgensen, P. F. (1998). An empirical comparison of three theories of nonverbal immediacy exchange. *Human Communication Research, 24*(4), 501–536.

Argyle, M., & Dean, J. (1965). Eye-contact, distance, and affiliation. *Sociometry, 28,* 289–304.

Bailey, W., Nowcki, S., & Cole, S. P. (1998). The ability to decode nonverbal information in African American, African and Afro-Caribbean, and European American adults. *Journal of Black Psychology, 24*(4), 418–432.

Barnlund, D. C. (1975). Communicative styles of two cultures: Public and private self in Japan and the United States. In A. Kendon, R. M. Harris, & M. R. Key (Eds.), *Organization of behavior in face-to-face interaction.* The Hague: Mouton.

Bateson, G., Jackson, D. D., Haley, J., & Weakland, J. H. (1956). Toward a theory of schizophrenia. *Behavioral Science, 1,* 251–264.

Brody, J. E. (1994, March 21). Notions of beauty transcends culture, new study suggests. *The New York Times,* p. A14.

Burgoon, J. K. (1978). A communication model of personal space violations: Explication and an initial test. *Human Communication Research, 4,* 129–142.

Burgoon, J. K. (1993). Interpersonal expectations, expectancy violations, and emotional communication. *Journal of Language and Social Psychology, 12,* 30–48.

Burgoon, J. K. (1995). Cross-cultural and intercultural applications of expectancy violations theory. In R. L. Wiseman (Ed.), *Intercultural communication theory* (International and Intercultural Communication Annual, Vol. 19, pp. 194–214). Thousand Oaks, CA: Sage.

Burgoon, J. K., & Le Poire, B. A. (1993). Effects of communication expectancies, actual communication, and expectancy disconfirmation on evaluations of communicators and their communication behavior. *Human Communication Research, 20,* 75–107.

Burgoon, J. K., & Saine, T. (1978). *The unspoken dialogue: An introduction to nonverbal communication.* Boston: Houghton Mifflin.

Cash, T. F. (1980, July 7). If you think beautiful people hold all the cards, you're right says a researcher. *People Weekly, 14,* 74–79.

Cash, T. F. (1997). The emergence of negative body images. In E. Blechman & K. Brownell (Eds.), *Behavioral medicine for women: A comprehensive handbook* (pp. 386–391). New York: Guilford.

Cash, T. F., & Roy, R. E. (1999). Pounds of flesh: Weight, gender, and body images. In J. Sobal & D. Maurer (Eds.), *Interpreting weight: The social management of fatness and thinness* (pp. 209–228). Hawthorne, NY: Aldine de Gruyter.

Cash, T. F., & Strachan, M. D. (1999). Body images, eating disorders, and beyond. In R. Lemberg (Ed.), *Eating disorders: A reference sourcebook* (pp. 27–36). Phoenix, AZ: Oryx Press.

Clay, V. S. (1968). The effect of culture on mother–child tactile communication. *Family Coordinator, 17,* 204–210.

Douty, H. I. (1963). Influence of clothing on perception of persons. *Journal of Home Economics, 55,* 197–202.

Druckman, D., Rozelle, R. M., & Baxter, J. C. (1982). *Nonverbal communication: Survey, theory, and research.* Newbury Park, CA: Sage.

Ekman, P. (1993). Facial expression of emotion. *American Psychologist, 48,* 384–392.

Ekman, P. (1997). Should we call it expression or communication? *Innovations in Social Science Research, 10,* 333–344.

Ekman, P. (1999a). Basic emotions. In T. Dalgleish & T. Power (Eds.), *The handbook of cognition and emotion* (pp. 45–60). Sussex, UK: John Wiley & Sons.

Ekman, P. (1999b). Facial expressions. In T. Dalgleish & T. Power (Eds.), *The handbook of cognition and emotion* (pp. 301–320). Sussex, UK: John Wiley & Sons.

Ekman, P., & Friesen, W. V. (1967). Head and body cues in the judgment of emotion: A reformulation. *Perceptual and Motor Skills, 24,* 711–724.

Ekman, P., & Friesen, W. V. (1969). The repertoire of nonverbal behavior: Categories, origins, usage, and coding. *Semiotica, 1,* 49–98.

Fisher, J. D., Rytting, M., & Heslin, R. (1976). Hands touching hands: Affective and evaluative effects of interpersonal touch. *Sociometry, 3,* 416–421.

Fisher, S. (1975). Body decoration and camouflage. In L. M. Gurel & M. S. Beeson (Eds.), *Dimensions of dress and adornment: A book of readings.* Dubuque, IA: Kendall/Hunt.

Floyd, K., Ramirez, A., Jr., & Burgoon, J. K. (1999). Expectancy violations theory. In L. A. Guerrero, M. Hecht, & J. DeVito (Eds.), *The nonverbal communication reader* (2nd ed., pp. 437–444). Prospect Heights, IL: Waveland Press.

Fromme, D. K., Jaynes, W. E., Taylor, D. K., Hanold, E. G., Daniell, J., Rountree, J. R., & Fromme, M. L. (1989). Nonverbal behavior and attitudes toward touch. *Journal of Nonverbal Behavior, 13,* 3–14.

Goldberg, S., & Lewis, M. (1969). Play behavior in the year-old infant: Early sex differences. *Child Development, 40,* 21–31.

Grammer, K., Kruck, K. B., & Magnusson, M. S. (1998). The courtship dance: Patterns of nonverbal synchronization in opposite-sex encounters. *Journal of Nonverbal Behavior, 22*(1), 27.

Graves, J. R., & Robinson, J. D. (1976). Proxemic behavior as a function of inconsistent verbal and nonverbal messages. *Journal of Counseling Psychology 23,* 333–338.

Graziano, W., Brothen, T., & Berscheid, E. (1978). Height and attraction: Do men and women see eye to eye? *Journal of Personality, 46,* 128–145.

Guardo, C. J. (1969). Personal space in children. *Child Development, 40,* 143–151.

Hall, E. T. (1963). Proxemics: The study of man's spatial relations and boundaries. In I. Galdston (Ed.), *Man's image in medicine and anthropology* (pp. 422–445). New York: International Universities Press.

Hall, E. T. (1966). *The hidden dimension.* New York: Doubleday.

Hardman, P. (1971, September). Every human being is a separate language. *The Salt Lake Tribune.*

Henley, N. (1973–1974). Power, sex, and nonverbal communication. *Berkeley Journal of Sociology, 18,* 10–11.

Henricks, S. H., Kelley, E. A., & Eicher, J. B. (1968). Senior girls' appearance and social acceptance. *Journal of Home Economics, 60,* 167–172.

Hensley, W. (1992). Why does the best looking person in the room always seem to be surrounded by admirers? *Psychological Reports, 70,* 457–469.

Horn, M. J. (1975). Carrying it off in style. In L. M. Gurel & M. S. Beeson (Eds.), *Dimensions of dress and adornment: A book of readings.* Dubuque, IA: Kendall/Hunt.

Jourard, S. M. (1966). An exploratory study of body accessibility. *British Journal of Social and Clinical Psychology, 5,* 221–231.

Jourard, S. M. (1968). *Disclosing man to himself.* Princeton, NJ: Van Nostrand.

Jourard, S., & Rubin, J. E. (1968). Self-disclosure and touching: A study of two modes of interpersonal encounter and their inter-relation. *Journal of Humanistic Psychology, 8,* 39–48.

Kaplan, R. M. (1978). Is beauty talent? Sex interaction in the attractiveness Halo Effect. *Sex Roles, 4,* 195–204.

Knapp, M. L., & Hall, J. A. (1992). *Nonverbal communication in human interaction,* (3rd ed.). Fort Worth: Harcourt Brace Jovanovich.

Kowner, R. (1996, June). Facial asymmetry and attractiveness judgment in developmental perspective. *Journal of Experimental Psychology, 22,* 662–675.

Kramer, E. (1963). The judgment of personal characteristics and emotions from nonverbal properties of speech. *Psychological Bulletin, 60,* 408–420.

Kramer, E. J. J., & Lewis, T. R. (1951). Comparison of visual and nonvisual listening. *Journal of Communication, 1,* 16–20.

Langlois, J. H., & Downs, A. C. (1979). Peer relations as a function of physical attractiveness: The eye of the beholder or behavioral reality? *Child Development, 59,* 409–418.

Lapakko, D. (1997). Three cheers for language: A closer examination of a widely cited study of nonverbal communication. *Communication Education, 46,* 63–67.

Leventhal, G., & Matturro, M. (1980). Differential effects of spatial crowding and sex on behavior. *Perceptual and Motor Skills, 51,* 111–119.

Malandro, L. A., Barker, L., & Barker, D. A. (1989). *Nonverbal communication.* New York: Random House.

McCroskey, J. C., Larson, C. E., & Knapp, M. L. (1971). *An introduction to interpersonal communication.* Englewood Cliffs, NJ: Prentice Hall.

Mehrabian, A. (1971). *Silent messages.* Belmont, CA: Wadsworth.

Mehrabian, A., & Ferris, S. (1967). Inference of attitudes from nonverbal communication in two channels. *Journal of Consulting Psychology, 31,* 248–252.

Mehrabian, A., & Wiener, M. (1967). Decoding of inconsistent communications. *Journal of Personality and Social Psychology, 6,* 109–114.

Montagu, A. (1971). *Touching: The human significance of the skin.* New York: Harper & Row.

Motley, M. T., & Camden, C. T. (1988). Facial expression of emotion: A comparison of posed expressions versus spontaneous expressions in an interpersonal communication setting. *Western Journal of Speech Communication, 52,* 1–22.

Olson, L. C. (1997). On the margins of rhetoric: Audre Lorde transforming silence into language and action. *The Quarterly Journal of Speech, 83,* 49–70.

Perry, M. O., Schutz, H. G., & Rucker, M. H. (1983). Clothing interest, self-actualization and demographic variables. *Home Economics Research Journal, 11,* 280–288.

Proctor, L. (1978). *Fashion and anti-fashion.* London: Cox and Wyman.

Rosenthal, R., Hall, J. A., Matteg, M. R. D., Rogers, P. L., & Archer, D. (1979). *Sensitivity to nonverbal communication: The PONS Test.* Baltimore, MD: Johns Hopkins University Press.

Schneider, D. (2001). *Attractiveness.* Retrieved from http://www.ruf.rice.edu/~sch/social%20course/Attractiveness.htm.

Schutz, W. C. (1971). *Here comes everybody.* New York: Harper & Row.

Siegel, B. S. (1990). *Peace, love and healing: Bodymind communication and the path to self-healing: An exploration.* New York: Harper Perennial.

Snyder, C. R., & Endelman, J. R. (1979). Effects of degree of interpersonal similarity on physical distance and self-reinforcement theory predictions. *Journal of Personality, 47,* 492–505.

Sommer, R. (1962). The distance for comfortable conversation: A further study. *Sociometry, 25,* 111–116.

Taylor, L. C., & Compton, N. H. (1968). Personality correlates of dress conformity. *Journal of Home Economics, 60,* 653–656.

Tucker, J. S., & Anders, S. L. (1998). Adult attachment style and nonverbal closeness in dating couples. *Journal of Nonverbal Behavior, 22*(2), 109–125.

Werner, C. M. (1987). Home interiors: A time and place for interpersonal relationships. *Environment and Behavior, 19,* 169–179.

Widgery, R. N. (1974). Sex of receiver and physical attractiveness of source as determinants of initial credibility perception. *Western Speech, 38,* 13–17.

Williams, M. C., & Eicher, J. B. (1966). Teenagers' appearance and social acceptance. *Journal of Home Economics, 58,* 457–461.

CHAPTER FIVE

It is the province of knowledge to speak and it is the privilege of wisdom to listen.

OLIVER WENDELL HOLMES

I like to listen. I have learned a great deal from listening. Most people never listen.

ERNEST HEMINGWAY

I know you believe you understand what you think I said, but I am not sure you realize that what you heard is not what I meant.

ANONYMOUS

Listening and Critical Thinking

What will you learn?

When you have read and thought about this chapter, you will be able to:

1. Differentiate between hearing and listening.
2. Discuss three reasons why listening is important in our lives.
3. Define and discuss examples of active, empathic, critical, and enjoyment listening.
4. Analyze barriers to effective listening, including internal and external noise, perceptions of others, and yourself.
5. Use strategies for critical thinking to evaluate both the communication situation and the message of the speaker.
6. Discuss several strategies for using verbal and nonverbal communication to improve your listening effectiveness.
7. Adapt general strategies for effective listening to specific listening situations.

Listening is our most frequently used and least studied communication skill. In this chapter you will learn about the listening process, some factors that can inhibit effective listening, different types of listening, and strategies for becoming a more effective listener. Our hope is that you will learn that listening, like any other communication behavior, is a skill that must be developed through forethought and practice.

After taking seven years off from school, Ted was finally ready to finish the last class he needed to complete his degree in construction management. Besides finishing this class, Ted was employed full time with a local construction company. He and his wife, Casey, have two children, Tyler and Greg.

Working full time while taking a class and meeting the needs of his family was beginning to take its toll on Ted. Before class one evening Ted was sitting in the commons and decided to call home to check on Casey and Tyler, who had both come down with the flu. While he was on the phone, a person sitting at Ted's table spilled coffee perilously close to Ted's laptop computer. If that were not enough, the commons area is always very loud and it had been difficult for Ted to memorize the information he needed to know for tonight's quiz. In retrospect, calling home at this moment could not have been a worse choice.

"Ted," exclaimed Casey, "I'm soooo glad you called! I am feeling a little better, but Tyler is still feeling very sick. The doctor said we should give him a type of sports drink that has. . . ."

As Casey continued to explain the message from the doctor, Ted found his mind wondering. He saw the coffee inching closer to the computer he was still paying for and he wondered whether he should call Casey back and help clean up the mess. Suddenly, Ted caught himself and tried to refocus on the conversation. "So you are feeling better," said Ted. "Have you and the boys had anything to eat?"

"We really haven't. I only felt like being close to food in the last hour or so. Poor Greg has been munching on popcorn and chips the whole evening. We have things here, but none of us will feel like fixing it. I really think you should pick something up on the way home."

"How about getting some soup from the deli? A little chicken soup might be good for you and Tyler." Ted was very proud of his suggestion—he usually opted for tacos at times like these! As he thought that, he remembered that he only had a few more minutes before class—and the quiz.

"That sounds great. Hurry home Ted."

"Bye hon. Tell the boys hi."

Ted survived the rest of the night class and headed home. He stopped by the deli and picked up four bowls of steaming chicken noodle soup. As he walked in the door, Casey hugged him, looked at the bag, and said: "What about Tyler's sports drink—he's already dehydrated—geez Ted, weren't you listening?"

Listening, an important key to successful communication, is one of the primary ways in which we discover others, enrich our relationships, and broaden our knowledge. Being a good listener involves actively attending to and understanding the messages we hear. If Ted had actively listened to the message his partner gave him, he might have recalled the most important part of the message—the message from the doctor. This chapter will help you develop your listening skills so that you can become a more competent communicator.

INTERNATIONAL LISTENING ASSOCIATION

The International Listening Association (ILA) is the scholarly organization devoted to the study and teaching of listening behaviors. The ILA website has a wide variety of information about listening including quotations, bibliographies, and links to research articles. The Web address for the ILA is **www.listen.org.**

What Is Listening?

Have you ever had the embarrassing experience of having someone ask you a question during a conversation when you were only pretending to listen? You have no idea what the question was, so you have no idea what the answer should be. Have you had someone ask you to do something that was important to that person but unimportant to you—so you forgot to do it? The sounds can go into your ears, but that does not mean that your brain interprets those sounds; nor does it mean that your mind stores the message or that your body does what the message requested. Sometimes you hear, you listen, and you even understand the message, but you do not obey. The listening process is complicated. Much happens between the reception of sounds and an overt response by the receiver.

The first step in learning about listening is to understand the distinction between hearing and listening. **Hearing** is simply *the act of receiving sound.* You can close your eyes to avoid seeing, cover your nose to avoid smelling, and shrink away to avoid touch, but your ears have no flaps to cover them. Their structure suggests that for your own protection, your ears should never be closed, even when you sleep. Because you cannot close your ears, you receive and hear sounds constantly. However, hearing is not the same as listening. **Listening,** as defined by the International Listening Association (ILA),

> *is the active process of receiving, constructing meaning from, and responding to spoken and/or nonverbal messages. It involves the ability to retain information, as well as to react empathically and/or appreciatively to spoken and/or nonverbal messages.* (An ILA Definition of Listening, 1995, p. 1)

As you can see, listening involves more than simply hearing. Notably, listening is an active process involving the construction, retention, and reaction to meanings we assign to information. As you reflect on the ILA definition of listening, its commonsense point becomes clear: Although hearing happens naturally for most of us, listening requires our sustained attention and focus.

Discussion Question

What are situations where you might hear but not listen? Do you have to listen all the time to be an effective communicator?

hearing

The act of receiving sound.

listening

The active process of receiving, constructing meaning from, and responding to spoken and/or nonverbal messages. It involves the ability to retain information, as well as to react empathically and/or appreciatively to spoken and/or nonverbal messages.

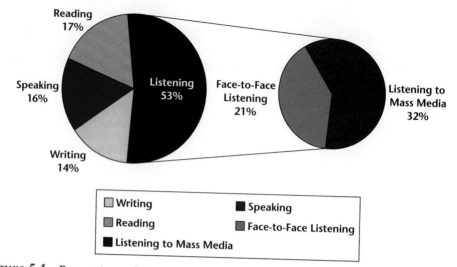

Figure 5.1   Proportions of time spent by college students in communication activities.

The Importance of Listening in Our Lives

Class Activity

Have students compile a schedule of their activities during a 24-hour day. Ask them to estimate how much time was spent writing, speaking, reading, listening face-to-face, and listening to mass media. Students should create a pie chart to represent their behaviors. Have students form groups and discuss how their percentages compare to those in Figure 5.1.

Given our basic understanding of listening, listening is clearly an essential skill for effective communicators. A classic study of listening showed that Americans spend more than 40 percent of their time listening (Rankin, 1926). Weinrach and Swanda (1975) found that business personnel, including those with and without managerial responsibilities, spend nearly 33 percent of their time listening, almost 26 percent of their time speaking, nearly 23 percent of their time writing, and almost 19 percent of their time reading. When Werner (1975) investigated the communication activities of high school and college students, homemakers, and employees in a variety of other occupations, she determined that they spend 55 percent of their time listening, 13 percent reading, and 8 percent writing. Figure 5.1 shows how much time college students spend in various communication activities each day. According to these studies, you spend over half your time (53 percent) listening either to the mass media or to other people.

TRY◀THIS

For three hours keep a communication journal tracking what types of communication activities you take part in (talking, reading, listening face-to-face, listening to media). What percentage of your time was devoted to each behavior? How do your results compare to those reported in Figure 5.1?

The importance of listening is even clearer when we consider how we use it in our personal and professional lives. Listening helps us build and maintain relationships and can even help us determine whether the person we are talking to is being deceitful (di Batista, 1997). Listening is also recognized as an essential skill for business success (Goby, 2000). Because of effective listening we are able to improve workplace relationships and be more productive (Salopek, 1999).

TRY ◀▶ THIS

The next time you interact with a salesperson, note listening behaviors that he or she displays which are effective or ineffective. Would you evaluate that person as generally effective or ineffective at listening? What led you to your evaluation?

The Listening Process

The final reason why listening is so important is that listening is directly connected to our ability to think about and remember information. The process of listening is summarized in Figure 5.2. As the illustration shows, we receive stimuli (such as music, words, or sounds) in the ear, where the smallest bones in the body translate the vibrations into sensations registered by your brain. The brain, using what is referred to as attention and working memory, focuses on the sensations and gives them meaning. Your brain might, for example, recognize the first few bars of a favorite song, the voice of a favorite artist, or the recognizable sound of a police siren. Upon hearing these sounds, you immediately know what they mean. Your interpreted message is then stored in short-term memory for immediate use or long-term memory for future recall (Hauser & Hughes, 1988; Schab & Crowder, 1989).

As we discuss later, people create many obstacles to effective listening. Not all obstacles, however, are the fault of lazy, unethical, or ineffective listeners. Because listening is a process, natural barriers present themselves at various stages. These natural barriers are explained for each major step in the listening process: attention, working memory, short-term memory, and long-term recall.

Feedback, which demonstrates active listening, may be verbal or nonverbal, positive or negative.

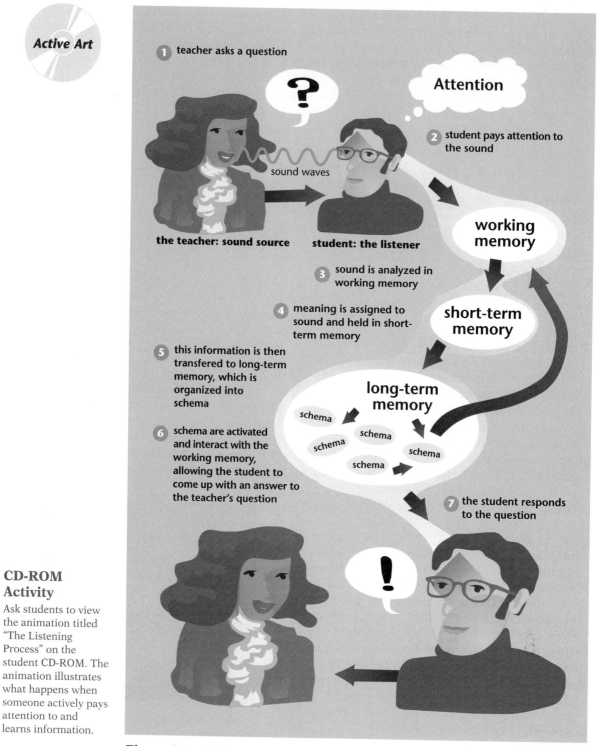

**CD-ROM
Activity**

Ask students to view
the animation titled
"The Listening
Process" on the
student CD-ROM. The
animation illustrates
what happens when
someone actively pays
attention to and
learns information.

Figure 5.2   The listening process.

Attention

After the ear receives sound waves, the brain sorts them by importance. Think of the last time you had a conversation in the mall or cafeteria. Your brain was being bombarded by aural stimuli, or sounds, but your mind was able to block out the other sounds and focus on your friend's voice. In most circumstances this process of "blocking out" irrelevant stimuli and "focusing" on important stimuli is volitional, or voluntary. That is, we want to selectively hear what our friend has to say rather than the fragmented chatter of the adolescents ahead of us. In other situations, our attention is automatic rather than selective. We automatically focus attention in the direction of a loud bang, a siren, or the cry of a baby.

Attention, then, can be selective or automatic. **Selective attention** is *the sustained focus we give to stimuli we deem important.* We selectively pay attention to our favorite television show, the voice of our friends during conversation, and (we hope) the professors in our classes. Selective attention can be impeded by our mind's instinct to pay automatic attention to certain stimuli. **Automatic attention** is *the instinctive focus we give to stimuli signaling a change in our surroundings (like a person walking into the room), stimuli that we deem important (our name being shouted from across the room), or stimuli that we perceive to signal danger (like a siren or loud bang).* The problem faced by all of us is that automatic attention competes with selective attention. When we are trying to selectively pay attention to one stimulus (like our professor's lecture), other stimuli naturally draw our automatic attention.

TRY ▶ THIS

In your next class make a list of all stimuli in the communication environment that could draw your automatic attention. What are strategies you could use to eliminate the potential for distraction?

Working Memory

Once we have paid selective attention to relevant sounds and stimuli, our brain must initially process and make sense of those stimuli. **Working memory** is *the part of our consciousness that interprets and assigns meaning to stimuli we pay attention to.* Most of us use our working memory without "thinking" about it. When you see or hear words, you automatically know what they mean in most circumstances. Notably, our working memory looks for shortcuts when processing information. Rather than trying to interpret each letter in a word, our working memory quickly recognizes the pattern of letters and assigns meaning. Likewise, when you hear the sounds of a word, your working memory recognizes the pattern

Group Activity

In groups students should make a list of things that can capture our automatic attention in a classroom situation. What strategies can we use to prevent these distractions from drawing our selective attention away from the teacher or learning task?

selective attention

The sustained focus we give to stimuli we deem important.

automatic attention

The instinctive focus we give to stimuli signaling a change in our surroundings, stimuli that we deem important, or stimuli that we perceive to signal danger.

Teaching Tip

See activities in the instructor's manual dealing with attention, working memory, and short-term memory.

working memory

The part of our consciousness that interprets and assigns meaning to stimuli we pay attention to.

of sounds rather than trying to process each sound separately. On a larger scale, our working memory can recognize patterns of words. If you watch the game show *Wheel of Fortune*, your working memory helps you look for patterns of words combined into phrases, even when all of the letters and words are not visible.

Because the recognition of patterns is an essential function of working memory, your working memory must work in conjunction with long-term memory. Although we discuss long-term memory in detail later, understand that working memory looks for connections between newly heard information and information stored in long-term memory. If your mind finds connections, patterns are more easily distinguished and listening is more efficient. Without such connections, patterns may not be found and your working memory must process information in smaller units. If you have ever missed a day or two in a difficult class, you have encountered this problem with working memory. Because most classes build on information learned during previous days, missing one or two class periods prevents understanding how new information connects to what you already know.

Short-Term Memory

short-term memory

A part of memory that acts as a temporary storage place for information

Information once interpreted in working memory is sent to either short-term or long term memory. **Short-term memory** is *a temporary storage place for information*. All of us use short-term memory to retain thoughts that we want to use immediately but do not necessarily want to keep for future reference. You might think of short-term memory as being similar to a Post-it note. You will use the information on the note for a quick reference but will soon discard or decide to write it down in a more secure location. During the listening process we use short-term memory for a variety of purposes. If you have ever had a question pop into your mind during a lecture or tried to remember a phone number while walking back to your dorm room, you have likely used sort-term memory.

bit of information

Any organized unit of information including sounds, letters, words, sentences, or something less concrete like ideas.

We constantly use short-term memory, but it is the least efficient of our memory resources. Classic studies in the field of psychology have documented that short-term memory is limited in the quantity of information stored as well as the length of time information is retained (Miller, 1994). For quantity, short-term memory is limited to 7 ± 2 bits of information. A **bit of information** is *any organized unit of information including sounds, letters, words, sentences, or something less concrete like ideas*, depending on the ability of your working memory to recognize patterns. If your short-term memory becomes overloaded (for average people more than 9 bits of information), you begin to forget. Short-term memory is also limited to about 20 seconds in duration unless some strategy like rehearsal is used. If you rehearse a phone number over and over until you reach your dorm room, you can likely remember it. However, if something breaks your concentration and you stop rehearsing, the number will likely be lost.

Unfortunately, many listeners over-rely on short-term memory during the listening process. Researchers in the field of communication have found that individuals recall only 50 percent of a message immediately after listening to it and only 25 percent after a short delay (Gilbert, 1988).

Long-Term Recall

Information processed in working memory can also be stored in long-term memory for later recall. Similarly, information temporarily stored in short-term memory can be deemed important and subsequently stored in long-term memory. If short-term memory is the Post-it note in the listening process, long-term memory is the supercomputer. **Long-term memory** is *our permanent storage place for information including but not limited to past experiences, language, values, knowledge, images of people, memories of sights, sounds, and smells, and even fantasies.* Unlike short-term memory, long-term memory has no known limitations on the quantity or duration of stored information.

Explanations of how long-term memory works are only speculative; however, researchers hypothesize that our thoughts are organized according to **schema,** which are *organizational "filing systems" for our thoughts.* We might think of schema as an interconnected web of information. Our ability to remember information in long-term memory is dependent on finding connections to the correct schema containing the particular memory, thought, idea, or image we are trying to recall.

In theory, people with normal functioning brains never lose information stored in long-term memory. How is it then that we often forget things we listen to? When we try to access information in long-term memory we access schema holding needed information through the use of **stimulus cues,** which could be *words, images, or even smells and tastes.* If the cue we receive does not give us enough information to access the corresponding schema, we may be unable to recall the information. Consider, for example, a situation where you see a person who looks familiar. In this situation you recognize the person (a visual cue); however, that stimulus does not provide you with enough information to recall whom the person is. If you hear the person's voice or if the person mentions a previous encounter with you, you may then have enough information to activate the correct schema and recall specific details about the person.

Long-term memory plays a key role in the listening process. As we receive sounds, our working memory looks for patterns based on schema contained in our long-term memory. Thus our ability to use language, our ability to recognize concepts, and our ability to interpret meaning is based on the schema we accumulate over a lifetime. If we encounter new information that does not relate to preexisting schema, our working memory instructs our long-term memory to create new schema to hold the information. The heavy broken arrows in Figure 5.2 depict this working relationship between schema and working memory.

long-term memory

Our permanent storage place for information including but not limited to past experiences, language, values, knowledge, images of people, memories of sights, sounds, and smells, and even fantasies.

schema

Organizational "filing systems" for thoughts held in long-term memory.

stimulus cues

Words, images, smells, and/or tastes that signal us to activate information held in schema.

Four Types of Listening

Listening is classified into four main types: active listening, empathic listening, critical listening, and listening for enjoyment.

Active listening is *"involved listening with a purpose"* (Barker, 1971). Active listening involves the steps of (1) listening carefully by using all available senses, (2) paraphrasing what is heard both mentally and verbally, (3) checking your understanding to ensure accuracy, and (4) providing feedback. **Feedback** consists of *the listener's verbal and nonverbal responses to the speaker and the speaker's message.* Feedback can be **positive,** where *the speaker's message is confirmed,* or **negative,** where *the speaker's message is disconfirmed.* Valued in conversation, small-group discussion, and even question-and-answer sessions in public speaking, active listening is a communication skill worth learning.

Empathic listening is a form of active listening where *you attempt to understand the other person.* You engage in empathic listening by using both **mindfulness,** which is *being "fully engaged in the moment"* (Wood, 1977), and **empathy,** which is *the ability to perceive another person's worldview as if it were your own.*

In **critical listening** you *challenge the speaker's message by evaluating its accuracy, meaningfulness, and utility.* Critical listening and critical thinking really go hand in hand: You cannot listen critically if you do not think critically. Skills in critical listening are especially important because we are constantly bombarded with commercials, telemarketing calls, and other persuasive messages. Later in the chapter we discuss several strategies one can use to listen and think critically.

Finally, we listen for enjoyment. Whether we are listening to our favorite musical artist, our favorite television show, or our group of friends talking about an upcoming concert, we continue listening because we enjoy it. Besides helping you relax, studies have shown that listening to enjoyable music can even reduce pain for hospital patients (A dose of music may ease the pain, 2000).

active listening

Involved listening with a purpose.

feedback

The listener's verbal and nonverbal responses to the speaker and the speaker's message.

positive feedback

Verbal and nonverbal responses intended to affirm the speaker and the speaker's message.

negative feedback

Verbal and nonverbal responses intended to disconfirm the speaker and the speaker's message.

empathic listening

Listening with a purpose and attempting to understand the other person.

mindfulness

Being fully engaged in the moment.

empathy

The ability to perceive another person's worldview as if it were your own.

Listening for enjoyment is an easy way to relax.

Barriers to Listening

Although you might agree that listening is important, you may not be properly prepared for effective listening. A survey conducted by a corporate training and development firm noted that 80 percent of corporate executives taking part in the survey rated listening as the most important skill in the work force. Unfortunately, nearly 30 percent of those same executives said that listening was the most lacking communication skill among their employees (Salopek, 1999). In the section explaining the connection between listening and thinking we discussed several natural impediments to listening. In this section we explain barriers we create for ourselves in the listening process. In Table 5.1, we identify noise, perceptions of others, and yourself as potential listening barriers.

critical listening

Listening that challenges the speaker's message by evaluating its accuracy, meaningfulness, and utility.

TRY ◄►THIS

What slights, slurs, or implications through words or gestures would cause you to stop listening and start distracting you from listening to another person? What are the "red flag" words that set you off and keep you from listening?

Listeners are sometimes distracted by noise and cannot listen to the speaker's message. Careful attention to the speaker allows listeners to avoid distractions.

Class Activity

Watch a show like *Friends* or *Frasier*. Ask students to identify examples of positive and negative feedback. How did such feedback influence communication in the show?

Video Activity

Ask students to view the video segment "Senior Seminar." What types of feedback did the various characters in this segment use? Did some characters use positive feedback? Were there examples of negative feedback?

Video Activity

Ask students to view the video segment "The Hospital." The dialogue between Susan and her mother illustrates empathic listening.

Video Activity

Ask students to view the video segment "On the Air with Campus-Community Connection." Have students listen critically to the arguments made by the two speakers in this segment.

Discussion Question

What are situations where you listen for enjoyment? What types of things do you listen to?

Writing Assignment

Each student should prepare a short essay discussing strategies he or she could personally use to overcome each barrier to effective listening. Examples should be provided in the essays as appropriate. Students should discuss their strategies in groups.

Video Activity

Ask students to view the video segment titled "Sam's Graduation Party." How did Dr. Stern's status as Sam's adviser effect the way people listened to her?

TABLE 5.1	BARRIERS TO LISTENING
TYPE OF BARRIER	**EXPLANATION AND EXAMPLE**
NOISE	
Physical Distractions	All the stimuli in the environment that keep you from focusing on the message. Example: Loud music playing at a party.
Mental Distractions	The wandering of the mind when it is suppose to be focusing on something. Example: Thinking about a lunch date while listening to teacher.
Factual Distractions	Focusing so intently on the details that you miss the main point. Example: Listening to all details of a conversation but forgetting the main idea.
Semantic Distractions	Overresponding to an emotion-laden word or concept. Example: Not listening to a teacher when she mentions the word "Marxist theory."
PERCEPTION OF OTHERS	
Status	Devoting attention based on the social standing, rank, or perceived value of another. Example: Not listening to a freshman in a group activity.
Stereotypes	Treating individuals as if they are the same as others in a given category. Example: Assuming all older people have similar opinions.
Sights and Sounds	Letting the appearance or voice qualities affect your listening. Example: Not listening to a person with a screechy voice.
YOURSELF	
Egocentrism	Excessive self-focus or seeing yourself as the central concern in every conversation. Example: Redirecting conversations to your problems.
Defensiveness	Acting threatened and feeling like you must defend what you have said or done. Example: Assuming others' comments are veiled criticisms of you.
Experiential Superiority	Looking down on others as if their experience with life is not as good as yours. Example: Not listening to those with less experience.
Personal Bias	Letting your own predispositions, or strongly held beliefs, interfere with your ability to interpret information correctly. Example: Assuming that people are generally truthful (or deceitful).

TRY ◀▶ THIS

The next time you interact with a stranger, make note of whether you generally think he or she is truthful or deceitful. What behaviors or impressions led you to that conclusion?

A Strategy for Becoming a Better Listener

So far in this chapter we have tried to emphasize the importance of listening while at the same time pointing out both natural and self-taught barriers to effective listening. Faced with this knowledge, you might wonder how any of us can hope to become effective listeners. After all, the potential barriers are many. Fortunately, each of us can take several steps to overcome these barriers to good listening. In this section we highlight general strategies you can use in any listening situation as well as specific strategies you can use in personal, professional, classroom, and online listening situations.

General Strategies

Effective listening, much like effective speaking and effective writing, is a skill that one develops throughout life. No magic list of behaviors can help an ineffective listener become a listening expert overnight. In this section we discuss three key categories of skills that each of us should monitor and improve upon to become more effective listeners.

Listen and Think Critically

Critical listening and critical thinking go hand in hand: You cannot listen critically without also thinking critically. We have already noted that critical listening is a form of active listening where you carefully analyze the accuracy, meaningfulness, and utility of a speaker's message. Similarly, **critical thinking** is where you *analyze the speaker, the situation, and the speaker's ideas to make critical judgments about the message being presented.* Although we discuss critical thinking in terms of its relationship to critical listening, you also use critical thinking when reading, watching television, or even when you try to analyze the ingredients of a tasty meal.

One way to think critically is to analyze the **communication situation,** or *the context in which communication is occurring.* One of our students recently attended a job interview for a position requiring "excellent public speaking skills." As a communication major, our student was excited about this prospect for a job in speaking. At the interview she found herself surrounded by nearly 50 other applicants. During a presentation she

critical thinking

Analyzing the speaker, the situation, and the speaker's ideas to make critical judgments about the message being presented.

communication situation

The context in which communication is occurring.

Homework Assignment

Have students collect controversial stories from local newspapers. Ask them to review several articles and write a brief assessment of procedures used by the reporter to ensure accuracy and truth. How can this same process be applied in critical listening situations?

message analysis

Evaluating the process by which information or knowledge was discovered as well as evaluating specific elements of the message content.

observations

Descriptions based on phenomena that can be sensed.

inferences

Generalizations from or about information received through the senses.

first-person observation

Observations based on something that you personally have sensed.

second-person observation

A report of what another person observed.

learned that the company sold "natural" products like filtered water, organic toothpaste, and even chemical-free moist wipes for babies. Through a little critical thinking and listening, our student quickly figured out that the company was actually a type of pyramid scheme and the "interview" was an attempt to get her to purchase bulk quantities of the products and then "market" those products to her friends and family. The people explaining the products were indeed experts, but her analysis of the situation told her that this job was not the one for her.

The second general strategy for engaging in critical listening and thinking is to carefully analyze the speaker's ideas. The first step in analyzing the speakers' ideas is **message analysis,** which requires *evaluating the process by which information or knowledge was discovered as well as evaluating specific elements of the message content.* When evaluating the message, you essentially want to ensure that factual information contained in the message is accurate and that the speaker has drawn reasonable conclusions from that information.

The first step in message analysis is evaluating the accuracy of factual information. If the speaker is using evidence from other sources, you should question the qualifications of those sources much like you should question the qualifications of the speaker. Does the speaker identify the sources, along with qualifications for those sources? Are the sources recognized as having expertise with the topic in question because of either professional qualifications or extensive experience? Do the sources have any potential bias that would diminish the credibility of their statements? We view these questions as critical for effective critical listening, especially given the rapid rise of the Internet as a source of information. For any number of topics, literally thousands of Web pages provide potentially relevant information. Our experience is that many Internet sources not only are of poor quality but also intentionally distort information.

One of our students gave a persuasive speech on vegetarianism. After listening to the speech it was obvious that the student had directly quoted several Web pages without giving credit in her speech—an obvious example of plagiarism. Looking at the Web pages she used revealed that several not only plagiarized each other, but also presented what was likely fabricated evidence about vegetarianism. Even if the student had not plagiarized, she would have based her speech on inaccurate and unethical information. We cannot stress enough the importance of questioning the credentials of information sources.

In addition to analyzing the credibility of sources, we also suggest the following techniques for analyzing factual information:

- *Distinguish between observations and inferences.* **Observations** are *descriptions based on phenomena that can be sensed*—seen, heard, tasted, smelled, or felt. On the other hand, **inferences** are *generalizations from or about information you have received through your senses.* You might observe that a number of people who are homeless live in your community. Based on that observation, you might infer that your community does not have enough affordable housing. Observations are more likely to be agreed upon by observers; inferences vary widely in terms of agreement between individuals (Brooks & Heath, 1989).

- *Distinguish between first-person and second-person observations. A* **first-person observation** *is based on something that was personally sensed; a* **second-person observation** *is a report of what another person observed.* First-person observations are typically more accurate because they are direct accounts rather than inferences drawn from others' accounts.

The second step in analyzing the message is to evaluate the arguments presented by the speaker. **Arguments** made during a presentation or conversation consist of **propositions,** which are *statements the speaker is trying to prove,* and **justification,** which is *the evidence used to support those statements.* One form of justification is **emotional proof** (also called *pathos*), which is *proof based on feelings and emotions.* An example of emotional proof is when a man tells his wife "I will be sad if we are not able to buy the car I want because we have not paid off our credit cards." This simple statement potentially contains several emotions relevant to that couple. The man is obviously trying for sympathy, and perhaps the goal of purchasing a new car is an important dream for the couple.

Unlike emotional proof, **logical proof** (also called *logos*) is *proof based on reasoning.* Reasoning (the thought process behind arguments) can come in two forms: inductive reasoning and deductive reasoning. **Inductive arguments** *use specific pieces of evidence to draw general conclusions.* For example, after noting that three of my friends jog and they are very healthy, I might generally infer that jogging makes one healthy. You must critically evaluate inductive arguments by deciding if the observations are accurate and are sufficient to justify the generalization. **Deductive arguments** *use general propositions to make conclusions about a specific instance.* Deductive arguments typically follow the form of a **syllogism,** *which has a major premise, a minor premise, and a conclusion.* An example of a syllogism is:

People who drive while they are intoxicated are more likely to have accidents than those who drive only when sober. [major premise]

Jack regularly drives while intoxicated. [minor premise]

Therefore, Jack is more likely to have an accident than other people who drive sober. [conclusion]

For deductive arguments to be **valid,** *the conclusion must logically flow from the logical combination of the major and minor premises.* For instance, in the previous syllogism, to conclude that Jack should stop drinking would be invalid. Though a very practical suggestion, it does not flow

arguments

Statements consisting of propositions and justification for propositions.

propositions

Statements the speaker is trying to prove.

justification

The evidence used to support propositions.

emotional proof

Also called pathos, is proof based on feelings and emotions.

logical proof

Also called logos, is proof based on reasoning.

inductive arguments

Arguments using specific pieces of evidence to draw general conclusions.

deductive arguments

Arguments using general propositions to make conclusions about a specific instance.

syllogism

Deductive arguments that have a major premise, a minor premise, and a conclusion.

valid

In deductive arguments, when the conclusion logically flows from the logical combination of the major and minor premises.

accurate

The extent to which premises in deductive arguments are truthful and verifiable.

enthymemes

Deductive arguments in which one or more parts are left out.

personal proof

Also called ethos, is based on personal expertise or authority.

source credibility

The extent to which the speaker is perceived as competent to make the claims he or she is making.

Writing Assignment

Ask students to select an editorial from a newspaper and write a brief essay analyzing arguments made in the editorial. What type of proof was most predominant?

directly from the combination of major and minor premises. In addition to being valid, major and minor premises must be **accurate,** which means that *they must be truthful and verifiable.* If, for example, we find out that Jack has never taken a drink of any kind, the entire argument becomes flawed. In many listening situations you should recognize that speakers may not present the full form of the syllogism. Rather, they may *leave out one or more parts of the deductive argument—leaving you, the listener, to fill in the missing information.* These types of deductive arguments are called **enthymemes** rather than syllogisms. An example of an enthymeme is "Jack is more likely to be involved in a car accident because he drinks." In this enthymeme, the major premise as well as parts of the minor premise are not included, yet the reasoning is still implicit in the argument.

The third form of proof to analyze in a listening situation is **personal proof** (also called *ethos*), which is *based on personal expertise, authority, or source credibility.* One way to analyze personal proof is to think about it in terms of source credibility. **Source credibility** is *the extent to which the speaker is perceived as competent to make the claims he or she is making.* If you wanted to know what procedures were required to study in Europe for a semester, who would give you the best information? Would you be more likely to trust your roommate, who heard about foreign exchange programs during freshman orientation; your adviser, who had an exchange student a few years back; or the director of international programs on your campus? If your car ran poorly, would you trust your neighbor's advice or the advice of an auto mechanic? The choice seems obvious in these situations. When assessing the credibility of a speaker you should determine whether the speaker has qualifications, whether the speaker has experience, and whether the speaker has any evident bias or ulterior motive for taking a certain position.

As you can see, critical listeners must evaluate several aspects of the communication situation, the speaker's message, and even the speaker's credibility. Critical thinking and listening is a skill that each of us can develop with practice. The next time you hear a classmate present information, a teacher lecture over a concept, or a friend discuss options for evening entertainment, you have a perfect opportunity to practice critical thinking and listening. As with any skill, diligent practice now will allow those skills to become automatic in the future.

TRY ►THIS

Watch television commercials and find examples of emotional, logical, and personal proof. In general, which type of proof do you find most persuasive in commercials? Do some types of proof tend to "bother" you because of the way they are used?

Use Verbal Communication Effectively

The notion of verbal components of listening may seem strange to you. You may reason that if you are engaged in listening, you cannot also be speaking. However, transactional communication assumes that you are simultaneously a sender and receiver. That is, you can make verbal responses while you are deeply involved in listening. To determine your current competence in this area, consider the skills you regularly practice:

1. *Invite additional comments.* Suggest that the speaker add more details or give additional information. Phrases such as "Go on," "What else?" "How did you feel about that?" and "Did anything else occur?" encourage the speaker to continue to share ideas and information.

2. *Ask questions.* One method of inviting the speaker to continue is to ask direct questions, requesting more in-depth details, definitions, or clarification.

3. *Identify areas of agreement or common experience.* Briefly relate similar past experiences, or briefly explain a similar point of view that you hold. Sharing ideas, attitudes, values, and beliefs is the basis of communication. In addition, such comments demonstrate your understanding.

4. *Vary verbal responses.* Use a variety of responses such as "Yes," "I see," "Go on," and "Right" instead of relying on one standard, unaltered response such as "Yes," "Yes," "Yes."

5. *Provide clear verbal responses.* Use specific and concrete words and phrases in your feedback to the speaker. Misunderstandings can occur if you do not provide easily understood responses. In the following example, Jayne's vague response to Erika's question confuses the issue:

Erika: Jayne, what time do you want to go to the commons for dinner?

Jayne: Well, I have to finish writing this essay and then John is supposed to call.

Erika: We have about an hour and a half before it closes.

Jayne: Have you seen Tricia? She was going to give me an article I needed for the essay.

Erika: I haven't seen her lately. She might be on third floor with Andy. What about dinner?

Jayne: It will have to wait until I get all my work done.

Erika: [laughing] You are worse than a guy when it comes to making decisions!

In this example, Jayne was vague when responding to Erika's question. At the end of the conversation, Erika was no closer to knowing when Jayne wanted to eat than at the beginning. Notice, however, the way Erika tried to use verbal statements to indicate to Jayne that her responses were unclear. In the following dialogue, two coworkers are discussing statements made by a supervisor, but the listener offers little clear feedback—the overused and ambiguous words are too general to supply the speaker with satisfaction:

Hyun-Su: I just had my performance appraisal interview with Jim.

Fred: Oh.

Hyun-Su: He said that I am not making my quota on sales this month.

Fred: That's something.

In both dialogues, the listeners fail to supply clear responses to the other communicator. If Jayne in the first dialogue had answered Erika's questions directly, and if Fred had offered specific comments, these conversations would have been greatly improved through active listening.

6. *Use descriptive, nonevaluative responses.* Better to say "Your statistics are from an organization that is biased against gun control" (descriptive) than to say "Your speech was a bunch of lies" (evaluative). Trivializing or joking about serious disclosures suggests a negative evaluation of the speaker. Similarly, derogatory remarks are seen as offensive. Attempting to be superior to the speaker by stating that you believe you have a more advanced understanding suggests an evaluative tone. The conversation between Hyun-Su and Fred degenerates. Not only does Fred respond with ambiguous comments, but he also appears to act superior to Hyun-Su:

Hyun-Su: Hasn't this ever happened to you?

Fred: No.

Hyun-Su: I thought you had been having fewer sales this month.

Fred: Yes, but my situation is different. You see, I have been spending part of my time training on the new automated dialing system!

Hyun-Su probably feels defensive because of Fred's act of superiority and demonstrates his frustration with the somewhat aggressive question about Fred's job performance.

7. *Provide affirmative and affirming statements.* Comments such as "Yes," "I see," "I understand," and "I know" provide affirmation. Offering praise and specific positive statements demonstrates concern.

8. *Avoid complete silence.* The lack of any response suggests that you are not listening to the speaker. The "silent treatment" induced by sleepiness or lack of concern may result in defensiveness or anger on the part of the speaker. Appropriate verbal feedback demonstrates your active listening.

9. *Allow the other person the opportunity of a complete hearing.* When you discuss common feelings or experiences, avoid dominating the conversation. Allow the other person to go into depth and detail; allow the other person the option of changing the topic under discussion; allow the other person to talk without being interrupted. One woman reported the following conversation that she had with her roommate's brother. She stated that she felt very frustrated because she was unable to complete any of her thoughts and Jerry had not listened to her.

Jerry: So you and Maggie are going to move out of the house?

Char: Yeah, we're thinking about . . .

Jerry: Well, I think it's wrong. Have you talked with your folks about it?

Char: Yes, I talked to . . .

Jerry: Is it what they want?

Char: Yes . . .

Jerry: How do you know?

Char: Well, my mom said . . .

Jerry: What?

Char: [hesitating because of the continuing frustration she is feeling] . . . That it was up to me to make my own decisions about where I live.

Jerry: Well, that's not what she wants at all. She's just saying that because she knows that you are so headstrong and won't do what she wants anyway.

Char: I can't talk to you anymore about this now. I'll see you later.

Because of her frustration in this conversation, Char lowered her opinion of Jerry. After a number of similar conversations, she began to avoid him completely.

10. *Restate the content of the speaker's message.* Use repetition of key words, phrases, and ideas to demonstrate your understanding of the conversation. Such restatements should be brief.

11. *Paraphrase the content of the speaker's message.* Restate the speaker's message in your own words to determine if you understand the content of the message. Your goals in paraphrasing should be to completely understand the other person, rather than to disagree or to state your own point of view.

12. *Paraphrase the intent of the speaker's message.* People generally have a reason for making statements or disclosing information. Demonstrate your understanding of the speaker's intention by attempting to state that intention concisely in your own words.

Use Nonverbal Communication Effectively

Although you demonstrate active listening through verbal skills, the majority of your active-listening ability is shown through nonverbal communication. The following nonverbal skills are essential in your ability to demonstrate active listening. As you listen to another person, have a friend observe you to determine if you are practicing these skills:

1. *Demonstrate bodily responsiveness.* Use movement and gestures to show your awareness of the speaker's message. Shaking your head in disbelief, checking the measurements of an object by indicating the size with your hands, and moving toward a person who is disclosing negative information demonstrate appropriate bodily responsiveness.

2. *Lean forward.* By leaning toward the speaker, a good listener demonstrates interest in the speaker. A forward lean suggests responsiveness as well as interest. In addition, leaning places the listener in a physical state of readiness to listen to the speaker.

3. *Use direct body orientation.* Do not angle yourself away from the speaker; instead, sit or stand so that you are directly facing him or her. A parallel body position allows the greatest possibility for observing and listening to the speaker's verbal and nonverbal messages. When you stand or sit at an angle to the speaker, you may be creating the impression that you are attempting to get away or that you are moving away from the speaker. An angled position also blocks your vision and allows you to be distracted by other stimuli in the environment.

4. *Use relaxed, but alert, posture.* Your posture should not be tense or "proper," but neither should it be so relaxed that you appear to be resting. Slouching suggests unresponsiveness; a tense body position suggests nervousness or discomfort; and a relaxed position accompanied by crossed arms and legs, a backward lean in a chair, and a confident facial expression suggests arrogance. Your posture should suggest to others that you are interested and that you are comfortable talking with them.

5. *Establish an open body position.* Sit or stand with your body open to the other person. Crossing your arms or legs may be more comfortable, but that posture frequently suggests that you are closed off psychologically, as well as physically. In order to maximize your nonverbal message to the other person that you are "open" to him or her, you should sit or stand without crossing your arms or legs.

6. *Use positive, responsive facial expressions and head movement.* Your face and head will be the speaker's primary focus. The speaker will be observing you, and your facial expression and head movement will be the key. You can demonstrate your concern by nodding your head to show interest or agreement. You can use positive and responsive facial expressions, such as smiling and raising your eyebrows.

7. *Establish direct eye contact.* The speaker will be watching your eyes for interest. One of the first signs of a lack of interest is the listener's tendency to be distracted by other stimuli in the environment. For example, an instructor who continually glances out the door of her office, a roommate who glances at the television program that is on, or a business executive who regularly looks at her watch is, while appearing to listen, indicating lack of interest. Try to focus on and direct your gaze at the speaker. When you begin to look around the room, you may find any number of other stimuli to distract your attention from the speaker and the message.

8. *Sit or stand close to the speaker.* Establishing close proximity to the speaker has two benefits. First, you put yourself in a position that allows you to hear the other person and that minimizes the distracting noises, sights, and other stimuli. Second, you demonstrate your concern or your positive feelings for the speaker. You probably do not stand or sit close to people you do not like, you do not respect, or with whom you do not have common experiences. Close physical proximity allows active listening to occur.

9. *Be vocally responsive.* Change your pitch, rate, inflection, and volume as you respond to the speaker. Making appropriate changes and choices shows that you are actually listening, in contrast to responding in a standard, patterned manner that suggests you are only appearing to listen. The stereotypical picture of a husband and wife at the breakfast table with the husband, hidden behind a newspaper, responding, "Yes, yes, yes" in a monotone while the wife tells him their son has shaved his hair, she is running off with the mail carrier, and the house is on fire provides a familiar example of the appearance of listening while one is actually far away from the speaker's message.

10. *Provide supportive utterances.* Sometimes you can demonstrate more concern through nonverbal sounds such as "Mmm," "Mmm-hmm," and "Uh-huh" than you can by stating "Yes, I understand." You can easily provide supportive utterances while others are talking or when they pause. You are suggesting to them that you are listening but you do not want to interrupt with a verbalization of your own at this particular time. Such sounds encourage the speaker to continue without interruption.

Strategies for Specific Situations

Active listening requires a great deal of energy and sensitivity to the other person, but this skill can be learned. The behaviors previously outlined should assist you in listening more actively to others. You should also recognize that active listening behaviors must be adapted to the situation at hand. In this section we provide specific suggestions for effective listening behaviors in four common communication contexts: personal relationships, professional situations, classroom settings, and online communication.

Effective Listening in Personal Relationships

How many times have you engaged in a personal conversation with someone and felt like you were communicating with a brick wall? As we mentioned at the beginning of this chapter, active listening is not only essential for building relationships, but it is also essential for maintaining healthy relationships. Consider the following conversation between Molly and Tim:

Tim: Molly, we are both going to graduate in a month. Have you thought about what we are going to do after graduation? After all, we have been dating for three years now . . .

Molly: I know that I want to get a job someplace away from here. I have lived in this town for six years now, and it is time for a change!

Tim: I know you want to leave. My family is here and it is really important to me that I am near them. But I love you and . . .

Molly: Tim, you are the best accounting student in the department. Your teachers love you and you already have great contacts in town from your internship. You won't have any trouble finding a job. Now let's stop talking and get going. I need to be on campus in 15 minutes or I'll be late for a group meeting.

Tim: OK, I guess you are right. I want to talk about this more though.

In this conversation you can see that Tim might feel like Molly was missing the point of the talk. Although Molly responded to what Tim was saying, she was not responding to his concerns about where the two of them want to live after graduation. In this conversation, we might say that Molly was *hearing,* but she was not *listening.*

Communication in personal relationships involves both content and relational messages. A **content message** refers to *the actual facts and ideas contained in the spoken statements of a communicator.* In the previous dialogue, the content of Tim's message appears to be concern for what will happen to him after graduation. In contrast, **relational messages** are *more implicit and address the feelings of one person in relation to another or the feelings of one person about the relationship he or she has with another.* In the dialogue between Tim and Molly, Tim's relational message expressed concern about the future of their relationship—he was afraid that they would be separated. Although Molly heard both messages (content and relational), she listened to the content part of the message only.

Active listening in interpersonal relationships requires you to hear, listen to, and respond to both content and relational messages. If Molly had listened to both messages, the dialogue might go like this:

Tim: Molly, we are both going to graduate in a month. Have you thought about what we are going to do after graduation? After all, we have been dating for three years now . . .

---

content message

The actual facts and ideas contained in the spoken statements of a communicator.

relational messages

Messages which address the feelings of one person in relation to another or the feelings of one person about the relationship he or she has with another.

Molly: I know that I want to get a job someplace away from here. I have lived in this town for six years now, and it is time for a change!

Tim: I know you want to leave. My family is here, and it is really important to me that I am near them. But I love you and . . .

Molly: Tim, you are the best accounting student in the department. Your teachers love you and you already have great contacts in town from your internship. You won't have any trouble finding a job. Are you concerned about that or are you worried about us being together?

Tim: Well, I guess it's more us than the job thing.

Molly: Tim, I know that you are worried about this. You mean so much to me, and I can't imagine being without you in my life. We have some different ideas about where we want to live, but we will find a way to work that out. I want to talk about this more, but right now I have to get to school. Let's talk about this more when I get home.

Tim: Thanks Molly.

In this example, Molly engaged in more effective listening skills. Notice that she responded to the content meaning of Tim's message ("you are the best accounting student") and also asked a question to clarify her perceptions of Tim's relational message ("are you worried about us being together?"). Later in the dialogue Molly responds to Tim's relational message by affirming his feelings ("I know you are worried") and providing a clear intent for additional action ("Let's talk more when I get home"). By recognizing and responding to both content and relational messages from Tim, Molly was a more effective listener.

Effective Listening in Professional Situations

As our economy has shifted from an industrial-based economy to an information-based economy, effective listening has become recognized as an essential skill for workers. The U.S. Bureau of Labor (Bureau of Labor Statistics, 2000) reported that just over 80 percent of the U.S. work force in 1999 was employed in service-oriented industries. This statistic means that the majority of jobs are the types of jobs requiring employee–customer interaction—jobs where listening skills on the part of employees translate into revenue.

To become a more effective listener in professional situations you need only apply several of the suggestions mentioned previously. Jennifer Salopek (1999), the president of a corporate training firm, suggests that you

- Be aware of when you are not listening.
- Monitor your nonverbal behaviors to determine whether you are giving appropriate feedback to the person speaking.

- Hear people out and minimize interruptions.
- Learn to ask nonaggressive questions to elicit more information from the speaker.
- Summarize what the person said and check to make sure you understand correctly.

In addition to these suggestions, Bob Gunn (2001), president of a consulting firm for many Fortune 500 companies, notes the importance of empathic listening in professional situations:

> Feelings are to the quality of hearing as our sense of smell is to the enjoyment of a great meal or our sense of touch is to the expression of love. You are listening deeply when you become "lost in the words" and find yourself experiencing deep feelings of joy, gratitude, surprise, curiosity, warmth, closeness, wonder, beauty, or appreciation. You are hearing at a more profound level. The stronger the feeling, the more profound the understanding. And the more profound the understanding, the clearer the subsequent course of action. (p. 12)

The point made by Gunn is that effective listeners must understand not only what their customers are saying, but also what they are feeling. Those who do this effectively are able to build stronger relationships with customers and clients.

Effective Listening in Classroom Settings

Take a moment to think about how often, as a student, you find yourself listening to a teacher lecture. If you were to estimate how much of your time is spent listening to lectures, how much would it be? If you said "a lot," you would not be alone. Researchers have estimated that college students spend at least 10 hours per week attending lectures (Anderson & Ambruster, 1986). If you take a typical 15 credit/hour load, that 10 hours per week translates into about 80 percent of your time in class being spent listening to lectures (Armbruster, 2000). The prominence of listening in students' lives led Vinson and Johnson (1990, p. 116) to coin the phrase "**lecture listening,**" which is *the ability to listen to, mentally process, and recall lecture information.*

lecture listening

The ability to listen to, mentally process, and recall lecture information.

What constitutes effective lecture listening? Although a variety of answers have been posed to this question, educational researcher Michael Gilbert (1988) provides the following general suggestions:

- *Find areas of interest in what you are listening to.* Constantly look for how you can use the information.
- *Remain open.* Avoid the temptation to focus only on the lecturer's delivery; withhold evaluative judgments until the lecture has finished; recognize your emotional triggers and avoid letting them distract you.

- *Work at listening.* Capitalize on your mind's ability to think faster than the teacher can talk. Mentally summarize and review what has been said, mentally organize information, and find connections to what you already know or are currently learning.

- *Avoid letting distractions distract.* Monitor your attention and recognize when it is waning. If you are becoming distracted, refocus your attention on the teacher.

- *Listen for and note main ideas.* Focus on the central themes of what is being presented and make notes about those themes. Effective notes outlining the main ideas of a lecture can, in some cases, be more useful than pages of notes containing unorganized details.

In addition to Gilbert's suggestions, communication researcher Dan O'Hair and colleagues (1988) recommend that you practice flexibility in listening. By practicing your listening skills while watching information-packed documentaries or while attending public presentations on your campus you will not only become a more effective lecture listener, but you will also learn valuable information during these experiences!

A final lecture listening strategy, one that we view as essential, is to take effective notes. Our own research has found that effective note taking during lectures can increase scores on exams by more than 20 percent—a difference between receiving a C and an A (Titsworth & Kiewra, 1998). Unfortunately, students typically do not record enough notes during a lecture. Research generally shows that less than 40 percent of the information in a lecture makes it into students' notes. In short, most students are unable to capitalize on the benefits of note taking simply because their notes are incomplete.

Now that we understand why note taking is so important, how can we become more effective note takers? Most universities have study-skills centers where you can find information on different note-taking formats. Although the exact format for note taking might vary from one person to another, the objective is the same. In your notes your goal should be to record both the outline of the lecture (called organizational points) as well as the details accompanying those points. The most effective way to ensure that you record all of these points is to listen for **lecture cues,** which are *verbal or nonverbal signals that stress points or indicate transitions between ideas during a lecture.* Table 5.2 summarizes various types of lecture cues commonly used by teachers. While taking notes you should listen and watch for these types of cues.

lecture cues

Verbal or nonverbal signals that stress points or indicate transitions between ideas during a lecture.

Lecture listening is a common communication behavior for students.

TABLE 5.2   COMMON LECTURE CUES USED BY TEACHERS

Type of Cue	Example	Main Uses
Written cues		
Outlines	Outline of lecture on transparency or PowerPoint slide	Indicate main and subordinate ideas
Words/phrases	Writing a term on the chalkboard	Stress important terms and accompanying definitions
Verbal importance cues	"Now, *and this will be on the exam next week,* we will explore . . ."	Stress important concepts deemed essential for recall/understanding
Semantic cues	"Here is an *example* [*definition, explanation, conclusion, implication,* or *illustration*] of uncertainty reduction theory in action . . ."	Signal common types of details that make up lecture content
Organizational cues	"The *third thing* I want to discuss today is . . ."	Orally provide indications of main and subordinate points in a lecture
Nonverbal cues	Holding up two fingers when saying "I will discuss two concepts today . . ."	Can serve any of the functions of nonverbal behaviors discussed in the chapter on nonverbal communication

Homework Assignment

Have students select their next teacher and tally how often they use each type of lecture cue discussed in Table 5.2. Which cues do students think are most important or effective during lectures?

Our research has examined the importance of cues for students (Titsworth & Kiewra, 1998). We taught a group of students about organizational cues and had them listen for those cues and take notes during a videotaped lecture. Students in another group were not informed about organizational cues but viewed and took notes over the same lecture. Students who were taught about organizational cues recorded four times the number of organizational points and twice the number of details in their notes. These students were able to capitalize on their note-taking effectiveness; they received the equivalent of an A on a quiz over the lecture. Their counterparts, who were unaware of and did not listen for organizational cues, received the equivalent of a C. Our experiment looked at the effects of teaching students about organizational cues only. Imagine what could happen if these students had been taught about all types of lecture cues! Fortunately, you are now equipped with this information.

Effective Listening for Mediated Communication

Think about how much of your time is spent watching television, listening to the radio, reading magazines, newspapers, or books, reading and writing e-mail, chatting online, or just surfing the Web. Many of us might avoid answering that question because the answer might frighten us. The American Academy of Pediatrics (2001) notes that children and adolescents

DIFFERENCES IN ACTIVE LISTENING

The way a person actively listens can vary from culture to culture. College students in Finland, for example, listen carefully and take notes but do not respond overtly while being addressed by the professor. In fact, they remain quite expressionless. In some Native American tribes and in some Hispanic groups, people avert their eyes when listening; but in groups such as northern whites and blacks, people tend to maintain eye contact while actively listening. How would you describe the norms of listening in your culture, community, or school?

spend more than 20 hours per week watching television. This translates into approximately three hours per day viewing TV programming. When including other forms of media, such as listening to music, playing video games, and using the Internet, this daily intake of media jumps to over 6½ hours per day, or over 42 hours per week. By the time you started your first college class (around the age of 18) you had viewed an estimated 200,000 acts of violence on TV alone. This intake of mediated messages does not diminish. By the time you reach age 70 it is estimated that you will have spent the equivalent of 7 to 10 years watching television.

Given the quantity of mediated communication we are exposed to each day, we must become critical consumers of such information. Think how much money you would spend if you "bought in" to every commercial you saw, or think of how much time it would take for you to read every e-mail message you get (including "junk" e-mail). Simply put, good listening behaviors are essential for us because mediated communication is so prevalent.

One way to be an effective listener in a mediated culture is to have information literacy. **Information literacy** is defined by the American Library Association (2001) in the following way: *"To be information literate an individual must recognize when information is needed and have the ability to locate, evaluate and use effectively the information needed."* According to this definition, information-literate individuals are able to think critically, know when and how to find more information, and know how to evaluate information.

Mediated communication is not limited to advertising and television. An estimated 476 million people worldwide currently use the Internet; by the year 2003 that number is expected to nearly double (Global Reach, 2001). How do people use the Internet? Communication scholars at UCLA conducted a comprehensive study of various issues related to

information literacy

The ability to recognize when information is needed and to locate, evaluate, and effectively use the information needed.

E-Note

COMMUNICATING EMOTIONS ONLINE

When people use "chat" services or e-mail they tend to use emoticons and other strategies to display emotion and relational messages. Make a list of strategies that you or your friends use to indicate feelings and emotions when engaging in online mediated communication. ☺

Internet use. They found that nearly 55 percent of Americans use the Internet for e-mail and that people feel the Internet increases their ability to stay in contact with others. Additionally, just over one quarter of Internet users indicated that they have online friends whom they would not have met through other means (UCLA Internet Report, 2000). The implication of these statistics is that the Internet, once a form of mass communication, has become an important tool for interpersonal communication as well.

When communicating online with others, how can you be an effective listener? The principal problem with online communication—whether the mode is e-mail, chat rooms, listservs, or discussion groups—is that nonverbal communication is difficult. Recall that nonverbal communication is a significant clue about another person's emotions and feelings. Without the ability to see and hear the other person, how could you tell what that person is really thinking? To successfully listen for relational messages online you must look for obvious clues such as **emoticons,** or *typographic symbols showing emotional meaning.* An example of an emoticon could be a "☺" at the end of a paragraph or using ALL CAPITAL LETTERS to indicate "shouting." Because nonverbal communication is more difficult online, it is important to check your perceptions before responding to messages.

emoticons

Typographic symbols showing emotional meaning.

Chapter Review

SUMMARY

- Hearing is the physical act of receiving a sound. We hear all of the noises around us. Listening is the active process of receiving, paying attention to, assigning meaning to, and responding to sounds. Listening is an active process whereas hearing is reflexive.

- Understanding listening is important because effective listening behaviors are related to success in our personal relationships, our workplace productivity, and even our ability to think clearly.

- Listening is generally divided into active, empathic, critical, and enjoyment listening. Active listening, which is listening with a purpose, includes both empathic and critical listening. Empathic listening is when you are attempting to understand another person. For example, hearing your best friend complain about the behaviors of a significant other involves empathic listening. Critical listening requires evaluating a speaker's message for accuracy, meaningfulness, and usefulness. Listening to a salesperson's pitch requires careful critical listening behaviors. In addition to listening for pragmatic reasons, we also listen to things like music for enjoyment purposes.

- A variety of internal and external barriers prevent many of us from being effective listeners. One barrier is noise, which includes both physical distractions and internal distractions. Physical distractions are any audible noises in the communication environment. Internal distractions can include mental, factual, or semantic distractions. Perceptions of others and your own behaviors can also become barriers to effective listening.

- Critical thinking involves careful analysis of both the communication situation and the message of the speaker. Analyzing the situation requires that you carefully understand the communication situation in which you are involved. Analyzing the message requires you to evaluate the process by which the message was generated, the propositions advanced by the speaker, and proofs offered to support those propositions.

- Verbal and nonverbal communication can be used to help you improve your listening behaviors. Asking questions, inviting additional comments, using descriptive responses, and providing affirming statements are all examples of effective verbal strategies. Being nonverbally responsive, using positive facial expressions, establishing direct eye contact, and providing positive vocal utterances are effective nonverbal strategies. Use of such strategies will encourage the speaker to continue speaking and providing you with information.

- General verbal and nonverbal communication strategies can be adapted to specific listening situations. In personal relationships it is important to listen for and understand both content and relational messages. In professional situations it is important to monitor your listening behaviors and elicit information from others in a nonaggressive way. In classroom situations students should work hard at lecture listening, take notes, and pay attention to lecture cues provided by the teacher. In mediated communication situations it is important to listen and think critically about what is heard.

159

⦿ VIDEO LINK: CRITICALLY LISTENING TO PERSUASIVE MESSAGES

Video Episode 5: "On the Air with Campus-Community Connection"

This chapter notes that critical listening and critical thinking go hand-in-hand. To listen and think critically, you must analyze the communication situation and the message. Analysis of the message includes evaluating the accuracy or presence of factual information, distinguishing between observations and inferences, distinguishing between first- and second-person observations, and analyzing the types of arguments and proofs presented by the speaker. Using the tools of critical thinking, watch "On the Air with Campus-Community Connection" and evaluate the statements of the speakers. Based on your analysis, who do you think won the debate and why?

ISSUES IN COMMUNICATION: ARE YOU LISTENING?

This Issues in Communication narrative is designed to provoke individual thought or discussion about concepts raised in the chapter.

Rachel and Val had been living together for nearly two months. Both had lived in campus housing previously; however, this experience was their first in an apartment. They enjoyed their newfound freedom from campus life. They were able to light candles and listen to mutually favorite artists like Melissa Ethridge while talking until wee hours of the night.

During one such conversation, Val told Rachel about some problems she was having with her supervisor at work: "I have been working at Org-Tec for over a year and have come up with some good ideas on how to make my work more efficient. They are simple things like tying my computer into the phone line, installing contact management software, and so forth," Val said with a somewhat frustrated expression.

"You look like you're upset about something," replied Rachel. Val pondered the issue for a few moments before responding. "I just don't feel like Ali takes my suggestions seriously. I have told her about my ideas a couple of times and she always says they are good, but nothing ever happens." Rachel watched Val and nodded her head. "So Ali is your supervisor?"

"She is, and we were really good friends when I started working there. We spent quite a bit of time together—going to movies, eating lunch, things like that. She became really distant and stopped being friendly a few months ago and has actually been rude at times. I don't know if I want to work there any more. I can get other jobs. . . ." Val became silent and looked at the candle dripping wax on the coffee table.

"Why don't you put together a formal proposal? If you put it on paper, it will be harder for her to ignore and my experience is that people take the ideas more seriously. It will also make it look like you did your homework—Val, are you listening?"

"Oh, I'm sorry Rachel. I was lost in thought! I was just trying to figure out what I did to make Ali upset. What did you say?" The two continued talking, and Rachel described her suggestion in greater detail.

The next afternoon Val tentatively went to work after class. As she walked in the door, she saw Ali talking to another coworker. Val waited until the conversation was over and walked up to Ali saying, "Ali, I wanted to give you a memo I prepared that overviews my proposal for purchasing equipment which will make my workstation more productive. If you want to. . . ." Before Val could finish, Ali cut her off and responded, "I really am in a hurry Val; why don't you just tell me what is on the memo and I. . . ."

Val had reached a boiling point and was ready to blow. This conversation was going like the two previous—Ali was blowing her off. "Ali," Val said, "I don't appreciate being interrupted and I certainly don't appreciate your not even taking time to look over the proposal I drew up. I spent a lot of time on it and would like you to read it before rejecting the idea like you did all of the other times." Val was shocked at her own outburst, and even a little embarrassed about it. "I'm sorry Ali.

I didn't mean to raise my voice. I just have been frustrated with you lately because it seemed like you were blowing my idea off. I thought that given the friendship we used to have, you would at least listen."

"Val, put the memo on my desk, and I promise to read it. I have to run to a meeting with the partners so I won't be able to get to it until this afternoon. From the looks of it, this should be an easy thing to have happen, OK?" As Ali smiled and walked away, Val could only think how ironic it was that she was probably going to get the needed equipment but felt even worse about the situation than before.

Apply what you have learned about listening as you ponder and discuss the following questions: How do people hear and not listen? What factors might have interfered with Val's, Rachel's, or Ali's ability to listen? Explain how active, empathic, or critical listening could have been used to create a more positive scenario. What specific listening strategies could have been used to avoid this particular outcome?

KEY TERMS

Use the *Human Communication* CD-ROM and the *Online Learning Center* at www.mhhe.com/pearson to further your understanding of the following terminology.

Accurate	Feedback	Observations
Active listening	First-person observation	Personal proof
Arguments	Hearing	Positive feedback
Automatic attention	Inductive arguments	Propositions
Bit of information	Inferences	Relational messages
Communication situation	Information literacy	Schema
Content message	Justification	Second-person observation
Critical listening	Lecture cues	Selective attention
Critical thinking	Lecture listening	Short-term memory
Deductive arguments	Listening	Source credibility
Emoticon	Logical proof	Stimulus cues
Emotional proof	Long-term memory	Syllogism
Empathic listening	Message analysis	Valid
Empathy	Mindfulness	Working memory
Enthymemes	Negative feedback	

SELF-QUIZ

Go to the self-quizzes on the *Human Communication* CD-ROM and the *Online Learning Center* at www.mhhe.com/pearson to test your knowledge.

REFERENCES

A dose of music may ease the pain. (2000, December). *Current Health, 27,* 2.

American Academy of Pediatrics. (2001, February). *Policy statement: Children, adolescents, and television* [Internet]. Available: http://www.aap.org/policy/re0043.html.

American Library Association. (2001). *Report of the Presidential Committee on Information Literacy* [Internet]. Available: http://www.ala.org/acrl/nili/ilit1st.html.

Anderson, T. H., & Armbruster, B. B. (1986). *The value of taking notes* (Reading Education Report No. 374). Champaign: University of Illinois at Urbana–Champaign, Center for the Study of Reading.

An ILA definition of listening. (1995). *ILA Listening Post, 53,* 1.

Armbruster, B. B. (2000). Taking notes from lectures. In R. Flippo & D. Caverly (Eds.), *Handbook of college reading and study strategy research* (pp. 175–199). Mahwah, NJ: Lawrence Erlbaum Associates.

Barbara, D. (1957). On listening—The role of the ear in psychic life. *Today's Speech, 5,* 12.

Barker, L. L. (1971). *Listening behavior.* Englewood Cliffs, NJ: Prentice-Hall.

Bochner, A. P., & Kelly, C. W. (1974). Interpersonal competence: Rationale, philosophy, and implementation of a conceptual framework. *Speech Teacher, 23,* 289.

Brooks, W. D., & Heath, R. W. (1989). *Speech Communication* (6th ed.) Dubuque, IA: Wm. C. Brown.

Bureau of Labor Statistics. (2000, January 4). *Bureau of Labor Statistics data* [Internet]. Available: http://146.192.4.24/cgi-bin/surveymost.

Clark, K. B. (1980, February). Empathy: A neglected topic in psychological research. *American Psychologist, 35,* 188.

Di Batista, P. (1997). Deceivers' responses to challenges of their truthfulness: Difference between familiar lies and unfamiliar lies. *Communication Quarterly, 45,* 319–334.

Gilbert, M. B. (1988). Listening in school: I know you can hear me—but are you listening? *Journal of the International Listening Association, 2,* 121–132.

Global Reach. (2001, August 9). *Global internet statistics* [Internet]. Available: http://www.euromktg.com/globstats/.

Goby, V. P. (2000). The key role of listening in business: A study of the Singapore insurance industry. *Business Communication Quarterly, 63,* 41–53.

Gunn, B. (2001, February). Listening as feeling. *Strategic Finance, 82,* 12–15.

Hauser, M. H., & Hughes, M. A. (1988). Defining the cognitive process of listening: A dream or reality? *Journal of the International Listening Association, 2,* 75–88.

Howell, W. S. (1982). *The empathic communicator.* Belmont, CA: Wadsworth.

Miller, G. A. (1994). The magical number seven, plus or minus two: Some limits on our capacity for processing information. *Psychology Review, 101,* 343–352.

O'Hair, M., O'Hair, D., & Wooden, S. (1988). Enhancement of listening skills as a prerequisite to improved study skills. *Journal of the International Listening Association, 2,* 113–120.

Rankin, P. T. (1926). The measure of the ability to understand spoken language. *Dissertation Abstracts, 12,* 847.

Salopek, J. (1999, September). Is anyone listening? Listening skills in the corporate setting. *Training & Development, 53,* 58–59.

Schab, F. R., & Crowder, R. G. (1989). Accuracy of temporal coding: Auditory-visual comparisons. *Memory and Cognition, 17,* 384–397.

Titsworth, B. S., & Kiewra, K. (1998, April). *By the numbers: The effects of organizational lecture cues on notetaking and achievement.* Paper presented at the American Educational Research Association Convention, San Diego, CA.

UCLA Internet Report. (2000). *Surveying the digital future* [Internet]. UCLA Center for Communication Policy. Available: http://www.ccp.ucla.edu.

Vinson, L., & Johnson, C. (1990). The relationship between the use of hesitations and/or hedges and lecture listening: The role of perceived importance and a mediating variable. *Journal of the International Listening Association, 4,* 116–127.

Weinrauch, J., & Swanda, J. (1975). Examining the significance of listening: An exploratory study of contemporary management. *Journal of Business Communication, 13,* 25–32.

Werner, E. K. (1975). *A study of communication time.* Unpublished master's thesis, University of Maryland.

Wood, J. T. (1997). *Communication in our lives.* Belmont, CA: Wadsworth.

Part 2 focuses on people in a variety of communication contexts. This unit will increase your understanding of how people communicate in interpersonal and small group settings, in the workplace, and with the media.

Chapter 6, Interpersonal Communication, explores the nature of interpersonal relationships and how to improve communication within your relationships.

Chapter 7, Intercultural Communication, looks closely at communication between people of different cultures and provides specific strategies for improving intercultural communication.

PART **TWO**

Communication Contexts

Chapter 8, Interviewing, discusses how to succeed in an employment interview and how to compile written credentials.

Chapter 9, The Dynamics of Small Group Communication, explains the processes involved in small group interaction as well as various functions of small groups.

Chapter 10, Communicating at Work, explores different types of organizational structures, communication patterns in organizational networks, and ethical communication practices for the workplace.

Chapter 11, Mediated Communication and Media Literacy, discusses how we can become better consumers and producers of mediated messages.

CHAPTER SIX

It is those who have not really lived—who have left issues unsettled, dreams unfulfilled, hopes shattered and who have let the real things in life . . . pass them by—who are most reluctant to die. It is never too late to start living and growing.

ELISABETH KÜBLER-ROSS

For one human being to love another; that is perhaps the most difficult of all our tasks, the ultimate, the last test and proof, the work for which all other work is but preparation.

RAINER MARIA RILKE

Don't flatter yourself that friendship authorizes you to say disagreeable things to your intimates. The nearer you come into relation with a person, the more necessary do tact and courtesy become. Except in cases of necessity, which are rare, leave your friend to learn unpleasant things from his enemies; they are ready enough to tell them.

OLIVER WENDELL HOLMES JR.

Interpersonal Communication

COUPLES, TEAMS, CULTURES

What will you learn?

When you have read and thought about this chapter, you will be able to:

1. Define interpersonal relationships.
2. Define interpersonal communication.
3. Explain the importance of interpersonal relationships.
4. Describe the dark side of interpersonal relationships.
5. Name and explain the three stages in interpersonal relationships.
6. Identify some of the reasons people begin relationships.
7. Reveal ways to maintain positive relationships over time.
8. List some motivations for terminating relationships
9. Name four essential interpersonal communication behaviors.

Interpersonal relationships can be complicated, and they sometimes require a lot of work. But by expanding your knowledge and learning new skills, you can improve your satisfaction within interpersonal relationships. In this chapter you will learn about interpersonal relationships and interpersonal communication. You will learn the stages of relational development, maintenance, and deterioration. Why do people initiate relationships, maintain them, and end them? You will learn the motivations for such behavior in this chapter. Self-disclosing, using affectionate and supportive communication, influencing others, and developing a unique relationship are all essential concepts that you will study. Although interpersonal communication is challenging, you will learn how to improve your communication in interpersonal relationships.

Teaching Tip
Interpersonal communication and the term "relationships" typically lead students to think only about romantic relationships. Use examples of friendships, family, and romantic relationships when discussing material. This will make the breadth of interpersonal communication theory more apparent.

Marla and Jess, married for 25 years, were asked the secret to a lasting relationship. They hesitate a little before answering. Both say that they don't think there's a magical formula to a successful relationship but, rather, that a deep, lasting relationship requires good communication and a lot of hard work. They talk about how they thought their first date would be their last, but they're thankful that it wasn't. Marla and Jess think one reason they've stayed together so long is the rituals they've established through the years. For example, they dubbed Saturday nights their night out together, when they're both at work they talk to each other on the phone at least once during the day, and each year they celebrate their wedding anniversary by going away together for a weekend. Another factor has been their ability to adapt to changing roles within the family. For example, when Marla got a big promotion at work, Jess took on more responsibilities at home. But the most important factor has been their ability to communicate effectively with each other. The result is a more meaningful relationship than either could have imagined back on their first date.

The Nature of Communication in Interpersonal Relationships

The Definition of Interpersonal Relationships

interpersonal relationship

The association of two people who are interdependent, who use some consistent patterns of interaction, and who have interacted for an extended period of time.

Before we define interpersonal communication, we need to consider the context in which it occurs—within our interpersonal relationships. On the simplest level, relationships are associations or connections. Interpersonal relationships, however, are far more complex. **Interpersonal relationships** may be defined as *associations between two people who are interdependent, who use some consistent patterns of interaction, and who have interacted for an extended period of time.* Consider the different elements of this definition in more detail.

First, *interpersonal relationships include two or more people.* Often, interpersonal relationships consist of just two people—a dating couple, a single parent and a child, a married couple, two close friends, or two coworkers. Interpersonal relationships can also involve more than two people—a family unit, a group of friends, or a social group.

Second, *interpersonal relationships involve people who are interdependent.* Interdependence refers to people's being mutually dependent on each other and having an impact on each other. Friendship easily illustrates this concept. Your best friend, for example, may be dependent on you for acceptance and guidance. You, on the other hand, might require support and admiration. When individuals are independent of each other, or when dependence occurs only in one direction, we do not define the resulting association as an interpersonal relationship.

Third, *individuals in interpersonal relationships use some consistent patterns of interaction.* These patterns may include behaviors generally understood across a variety of situations, as well as behaviors unique to the relationship. For example, a husband may always greet his wife with a kiss. This kiss is generally understood as a sign of warmth and affection. On the other hand, the husband may have unique nicknames for his wife that are not understood outside the relationship.

Fourth, *individuals in interpersonal relationships generally have interacted for some time.* When you nod and smile at someone as you leave the classroom, when you meet a girlfriend's siblings for the first time, or when you place an order at a fast-food counter, you do not have an interpersonal relationship. Although participants use interpersonal communication to accomplish these activities, one-time interactions do not constitute interpersonal relationships. We should note, however, that interpersonal relationships might last for varying lengths of time—some are relatively short, and others continue for a lifetime.

The Definition of Interpersonal Communication

At first, communication professionals defined interpersonal communication by the context, or the situation. In other words, they viewed interpersonal communication as communication that occurred between, or among, a small group of communicators (usually two) in a face-to-face setting, with the opportunity for immediate feedback (Miller, 1978). When defined in this manner, interpersonal communication would include our interactions with strangers, with salespeople in retail stores, and with waiters in restaurants as well as with our close friends, our lovers, and our family members. This very broad definition is generally no longer accepted as useful.

Interpersonal communication is now defined qualitatively as *communication that occurs within interpersonal relationships* (Miller & Steinberg, 1975). This definition suggests a developmental perspective. Interpersonal communication is limited to those situations in which we have knowledge of the personal characteristics, qualities, or behaviors of the other person. Indeed, Miller and Steinberg assert that when we make guesses about the outcomes of conversations based on sociological or cultural information, we are communicating in a noninterpersonal way. When we make predictions based on more discriminating information about the other specific person, we are communicating interpersonally. When we communicate with others on the basis of general social interaction rules such as engaging in turn-taking, making pleasantries, and discussing nonpersonal matters, we are engaging in impersonal or nonpersonal communication. When we communicate with others based on some knowledge of their uniqueness as a person and a shared history, we are communicating interpersonally.

Discussion Topic

In groups or as a class have students identify examples of behavior patterns that define friendships. What are examples of commonly understood patterns of behavior as well as relationship-specific patterns of behavior that define some of their friendships?

interpersonal communication

Communication that occurs within interpersonal relationships.

None of our interpersonal relationships are quite like any of our other interpersonal relationships. A friendship that you might have had with a high school friend is not the same as your new friendships in college. Your relationship to your mother is not the same as your relationship to your father. Even if you have several intimate relationships with people, you will find that none of them is quite the same. On the one hand, our interpersonal relationships are mundane; on the other, they can also be the "sites for spiritual practice and mystical experience" (Crawford, 1996, p. 25).

Nonetheless, we have accumulated a great deal of knowledge on how to communicate more successfully in our interpersonal relationships. This chapter will explore that knowledge. We will consider those abilities that are essential in developing and developed relationships. Before we consider this information, let us consider why we engage in interpersonal relationships.

The Importance of Interpersonal Relationships

According to William Schutz (1976), we have three basic interpersonal needs that are satisfied through interaction with others. These are

1. The need for **inclusion,** or *becoming involved with others.*
2. The need for affection, or *holding fond or tender feeling toward another person.*
3. The need for **control,** or *the ability to influence others, our environment, and ourselves.*

Although we may be able to fulfill some of our physical, safety, and security needs through interactions with relative strangers, we can fulfill the other needs only through our interpersonal relationships.

The interdependent nature of interpersonal relationships suggests that people mutually satisfy their needs in this type of association. Interdependence suggests that one person is dependent on another to have some need fulfilled and that the other person (or persons) is dependent on the first to have the same or other needs fulfilled. For example, a child who is dependent on a parent may satisfy that parent's need for control. The parent, on the other hand, may supply the child's need for affection in hugging, kissing, or listening to the child.

Complementary relationships—*those in which each person supplies something the other lacks*—provide good examples of the manner in which we have our needs fulfilled in interpersonal relationships. A romantic involvement between a popular male and an intelligent female is an example of a complementary relationship, since the woman may find herself involved in the social events she desires and the man may find himself increasingly successful in his classes. Another example of a complementary relationship is a friendship between an introverted individual and an extroverted one. The introvert may teach her friend to be more self-reflective

Discussion Topic

Have students break into groups and discuss examples of personal relationships meeting the needs of affection, inclusion, and control.

inclusion

The state of being involved with others.

control

The ability to influence others, our environment, and ourselves.

Writing Assignment

Have students write a short essay describing an example of a complementary and symmetrical relationship from their own lives.

complementary relationships

Relationships in which each person supplies something the other person or persons lack.

Interpersonal relationships fulfill basic needs.

or to listen to others more carefully, while the extrovert might, in exchange, encourage her to be more outspoken or assertive.

Our needs also may be fulfilled in **symmetrical relationships**—*those in which the participants mirror each other or are highly similar.* A relationship between two intelligent persons may reflect their need for intellectual stimulation. Two people of similar ancestry might marry in part to preserve their heritage.

Whether the other person or persons are similar to us or highly different, our needs are generally fulfilled through our relationships with them.

symmetrical relationships

Relationships between people who mirror each other or who are highly similar.

TRY ◄ ► THIS

Think about your friendship and dating relationships and determine whether they are symmetrical or complementary.

The Dark Side of Interpersonal Relationships

Interpersonal relationships are often pleasurable and positive experiences. However, we also know that they may be painful and negative. Spitzberg and Cupach (1998) have provided the most comprehensive treatment of the shadowy side of relationships. What are some of the

Video Activity

Ask students to view the video segment "Reporting for KTNT: Susan Elliott." In this segment we see a relationship between Susan and Ricky. Based on the segment, would students describe Susan and Ricky's relationship as complementary or symmetrical.

Discussion Topic

The textbook states that the presence of abusive relationships seems more visible today. Why is that? Are there cultural factors that could contribute to the occurrence or visibility of abusive relationships?

Video Activity

Watch a sitcom like *Frasier* to analyze relationship development. Select an episode depicting the development of a new relationship. Have students discuss whether the relationship followed the stages identified by Knapp.

social penetration theory

A theory that explains how relationships develop and deteriorate through the exchange of intimate information.

CD-ROM Activity

Ask students to view the animation titled "Relationship Development" on the student CD-ROM. The animation explains and provides an example of Knapp's stages of relationship development.

qualities of negative relationships? Obsession that includes fatal attraction and jealousy creates negative outcomes. Similarly, misunderstanding, gossip, conflict, and codependency create harmful results. Abuse, which can include sexual, physical, mental, and emotional abuse, is truly harmful to individuals and destructive of relationships. Abusive relationships have probably always existed, but their presence seems more visible today as television programs including talk shows focus on the multiple kinds of abuse that occur in both marital and nonmarital relationships.

This chapter focuses primarily on positive interpersonal relationships and on how to improve interpersonal relationships. We will consider factors that seem to lead to more positive outcomes. However, note that interpersonal relationships can take a decidedly negative turn. In addition, some of the qualities that we associate with healthy relationships— self-disclosure, affectionate communication, influencing others, and developing the unique relationship—can all become extreme and, therefore, unhealthy.

Too often textbooks speak exclusively about the positive aspects of interpersonal relationships. Readers are mistakenly led to believe that by practicing skills of openness and empathy and learning problem-solving and conflict resolution techniques, they will have successful and satisfying relationships. This unrealistic perspective leads to disillusionment when the person puts these ideas into action and does not find satisfying and successful interpersonal relationships. Effective communication, as you have been learning, is very challenging and interpersonal communication may be the most stimulating context of all.

The Stages in Interpersonal Relationships

Communication and relationship development are symbiotic; that is, communication affects the growth of relationships, and the growth of relationships affects communicative behavior (Miller, 1976). Current theories on the growth of relationships rest on the original work of researchers Altman and Taylor (1973). These authors' **social penetration theory** explains the development and deterioration of interpersonal relationships through the exchange of intimate information. The theory states that *interpersonal exchanges move from superficial, nonintimate information transfers to more intimate information exchanges through the process of revealing personal information.* The amount of interaction increases as the relationship develops. Further, cost–reward considerations determine how quickly or slowly relationships develop. Dissolution, or depenetration, is the reverse process of development, or penetration.

Relational Development

Knapp and Vangelisti (2000) expanded on Altman and Taylor's social penetration theory by identifying 10 interaction stages of interpersonal relationships. Baxter (1979, 1982, 1983, 1984) and others have experimentally attempted to validate these stages. The model that Knapp and Vangelisti presented generally appears valid. Furthermore, this developmental model helps organize and explain relational changes. The first five stages cover **relational development,** *the process by which relationships grow* (see Fig. 6.1):

1. **Initiating** is stage 1, *the short beginning period of an interaction.* This stage involves first impressions, the sizing up of the other person, and attempting to find commonality. An example is "scouting" at a party, where you might break off the initiating stage when you don't find what you are seeking in the person you have just met. If this first stage goes well, you might move to stage 2 in a first meeting.

2. **Experimenting** occurs when *the two people have clearly decided to find out more about each other, to quit scouting, and to start getting serious about each other.* This stage includes sharing personal information at a safe level: what music, people, classes, professors, and food you like or dislike. In a situation where you are "captive" in an airplane seat, are waiting for a concert to begin, or sit next to someone in a classroom for three or four months, this stage could start early and last for weeks.

3. **Intensifying** involves *active participation, mutual concern, and an awareness that the relationship is developing* because neither party has quit and both people are encouraging its development. The information exchanges become more personal and more intimate. Both are comfortable with each other, use private jokes and language, and express commitment.

4. **Integrating** means *the two start mirroring each other's behavior in manner, dress, and language.* They merge their social circles, designate common property, and share interests and values. They know more about each other than does anyone else, except long-term best friends, and others see them as a pair.

5. **Bonding** is *the final stage in relational development—the people in the relationship commit to each other.* They may exchange personal items as a symbol of commitment; they may participate in a public ritual that bonds them, as in the case of marriage; or they may vow to be friends for life and demonstrate that commitment by always being present at important points in each other's life. Living together, marrying, having children, buying a home, or moving together to another place are examples of bonding.

relational development

In Knapp's model, the process by which relationships grow.

initiating

In Knapp's stages of relational development, the short beginning period of a relationship.

experimenting

In Knapp's relational development model, the stage in which partners attempt to discover information about each other.

intensifying

In Knapp's relational development model, the stage in which partners become more aware of each other and actively participate in the relationship.

integrating

In Knapp's relational development model, the stage in which partners start mirroring each other's behavior.

bonding

In Knapp's relational development model, the stage in which partners commit to each other.

Active Art

Class Discussion

The images and dialogue in Figure 6.1 represent a very traditional and perhaps stereotypical view of relationships. Discuss ways in which the relationship development model can be used to understand other types of relationships including friendships, family relationships, and romantic relationships that do not follow traditional patterns.

Writing Assignment

Have students select one of their relationships and write an essay identifying the primary dialectic characteristic in that relationship. What are some strategies used by the participants in the relationship to manage the tension created by the opposing forces of the dialectic?

relational maintenance

In Knapp's model, the process of keeping a relationship together.

Figure 6.1   Relationship development.

Relational Maintenance

Once individuals have bonded in a relationship, they enter a stage of **relational maintenance** in which they begin establishing *strategies for keeping the relationship together.* Although Altman and Taylor, as well as Knapp and Vangelisti, briefly considered relational maintenance, they did not do so in much detail. Wilmot (1980) suggested that relationships stabilize when the partners reach a basic level of agreement about what they want from the relationship. In addition, relationships can stabilize at any level of intimacy, and even "stabilized" relationships may have internal movement.

While the developmental model created by Altman and Taylor and extended by others would suggest that relational maintenance is a plateau or leveling-off of the relationship, most evidence suggests that the maintenance phase of a relationship is not best represented by a flat line. Instead, people become more intimate or closer at some periods and more distant and less close at other times. The maintenance phase of a relationship might be more appropriately depicted as a jagged, rather than a straight, line.

Indeed, Baxter and her colleagues (Baxter, 1987, 1988, 1990, 1992, 1993; Baxter & Montgomery, 1996; Dindia & Baxter, 1987) and other researchers (Hause & Pearson, 1994; Lowrey-Hart & Pearson, 1997; Pawlowski, 1998) have developed and demonstrated the importance of dialectical theory in interpersonal relationships. **Dialectic** refers to *the tension that exists between two conflicting or interacting forces, elements, or ideas.* When dialectic theory is applied to interpersonal relationships, we acknowledge that relationships often incorporate contradictions or contrasts within them, and they are always in process. By **contradictions,** we mean that *each person might have two opposing desires for maintaining the relationship*—you want to be with your partner, but you also have a need for space and time away from him. By **process** we recognize that *relationships are always changing.* Thus relational maintenance cannot be depicted as a flat line, but rather one that has peaks and valleys.

What are some of the primary dialectics identified by Baxter? Three emerged in the early work. The **dialectic of integration/ separation** means that we feel a *tension between wanting to be separate entities and wanting to be integrated with another person.* The **dialectic of stability/change** suggests *the tension between wanting events, conversations, and behavior to be the same, but also desiring change.* The **dialectic of expression/privacy** suggests *the tension between wanting to self-disclose and be completely open but also wanting to be private and closed.*

dialectic

Tension that exists between two conflicting or interacting forces, elements, or ideas.

contradictions

In dialectic theory, each person in a relationship has two opposing desires for maintaining the relationship.

process

In dialectic theory, relationships are always in change.

dialectic of integration/ separation

Tension between wanting to be separate entities and wanting to be integrated with another person.

dialectic of stability/change

Tension between wanting events, conversations, and behavior to be the same, while also desiring change.

dialectic of expression/ privacy

Tension between wanting to self-disclose and be completely open while also wanting to be private and closed.

Think, Pair, Share

How do people manage the dialectics they find in their interpersonal relationships? Baxter (1990) studied people like you to learn that relational couples generally rely on four strategies:

selection

Managing dialectics by choosing one need over the other.

1. **Selection**—*couples choose one of their needs over the other.* They decide that their time together is far more important than time they spend alone and try to spend every waking moment together, for example. Or they decide that predictability is more important than novelty and enjoy dinner at the same restaurant every Friday evening.

separation

Managing dialectics by fulfilling one need in some situations and the other in different situations.

2. **Separation**—*contradictory needs are met by fulfilling one in some situations and the other in different situations.* For instance, the couple decides that during the workday, they will interact with others and maintain their independence. However, every evening must be spent together. Or they decide that the quick meals they catch together will be at a multitude of different fast-food restaurants, but that celebratory meals are always at one favorite restaurant.

neutralization

Managing dialectics by compromise.

3. **Neutralization**—*contradictory needs are not met completely, but a compromise is struck.* The couple provides private information about some matters, but not about others. Or they spend about half of their free time with each other and about half of it with others.

reframing

Managing dialectics by transformation of needs so they are no longer regarded as opposites.

4. **Reframing**—*contradictory needs are transformed so they no longer are regarded as opposites.* Commuting couples sometimes explain that being apart so much leads to greater intimacy and closeness. The couple who is always living on the edge and exploring new personal ground describe their behavior as predictable or routine.

Consider one of your personal relationships—with a family member, close friend, or intimate partner. Which of these strategies do you use? Think of examples that illustrate what you do. After you have spent a few minutes identifying some of the strategies to manage contradictions in your relationship, share them with a partner in class. How do you differ? How are you similar in relational management? What have you learned from sharing your ideas with a classmate?

Relational Deterioration

The last five stages identified by Knapp and Vangelisti (2000) occur during **relational deterioration,** *the process by which relationships disintegrate:*

1. **Differentiating** occurs when *the two partners start emphasizing their individual differences instead of their similarities.* Instead of going to movies together, he plays basketball with his friends and she golfs with her friends. Some separate activities are healthy in a relationship, but in differentiation the pulling apart is to get away from each other.

2. **Circumscribing** is characterized by *decreased interaction, shorter times together, and less depth to sharing.* The two people might go to public events together but do little together in private. Each person figuratively draws a circle around himself or herself, a circle that does not include the other person. The exchange of feelings, the demonstrations of commitment, and the obvious pairing are disappearing.

3. **Stagnating** suggests a *lack of activity, especially activity together.* Interactions are minimal, functional, and only for convenience. The two people now find conversation and sharing awkward instead of stimulating. During this stage, each individual may be finding an outlet elsewhere for developmental stages.

4. **Avoiding** brings *reluctance to interact, active avoidance, and even hostility.* The two former partners are now getting in each other's way, each seeing the other as an obstacle or a limitation. The amount of their talk may actually increase, but the content and intent are negative. Arguing, fighting, disagreeing, and flight mark their interactions.

5. **Terminating** occurs when *the two people are no longer seen by others or themselves as a pair.* They increasingly dissociate, share nothing, claim common goods as individual property, and give back or get rid of the symbols of togetherness. Divorce, annulment, and dissolution are manifestations of this stage, as are people who no longer live together, former friends who have nothing to do with each other, and roommates who take separate and distant quarters.

Knapp and Vangelisti (2000) acknowledged that individuals do not progress in a linear way through the stages of development and deterioration (summarized in Table 6.1). They proposed that people move within stages to maintain their equilibrium or stability. In other words, people might behave in a way that is more characteristic of one stage even though they are generally maintaining the interaction patterns of another stage.

relational deterioration

In Knapp's model, the process by which relationships disintegrate.

differentiating

In Knapp's relational development model, the stage in which partners emphasize their individual differences rather than their similarities.

circumscribing

In Knapp's relational development model, the stage marked by a decrease in partners' interaction, time spent together, and depth of sharing.

stagnating

In Knapp's relational development model, the stage of deterioration marked by the partner's lack of activity, especially together.

avoiding

In Knapp's relational development model, the stage characterized by partners' reluctance to interact, active avoidance, and hostility.

terminating

In Knapp's relational development model, the stage of deterioration in which the partners are no longer seen as a pair by themselves or others.

TABLE 6.1   AN OVERVIEW OF INTERACTION STAGES

Process	Stage	Representative Dialogue
Coming Apart	1. Differentiating	"I Just don't like big social gatherings." "Sometimes I don't understand you. This is one area where I'm certainly not like you at all."
	2. Circumscribing	"Did you have a good time on your trip?" "What time will dinner be ready?"
	3. Stagnating	"What's there to talk about?" "Right. I know what you're going to say, and you know what I'm going to say."
	4. Avoiding	"I'm so busy, I just don't know when I'll be able to see you." "If I'm not around when you try, you'll understand."
	5. Terminating	"I'm leaving you . . . and don't bother trying to contact me." "Don't worry."

SOURCE: From *Interpersonal Communication and Human Relationships,* 3rd ed. by Mark L. Knapp and Anita L. Vangelisti, 1996, Boston: Allyn and Bacon. Copyright © 1996 by Allyn and Bacon. Reprinted by permission.

Discussion Topic

Knapp's theory of relationship development and dissolution suggests that people do not move through the stages in a linear fashion. Do students agree or disagree with this viewpoint based on their own experiences?

In addition, communication skills can alter the relational trajectory. In relationships that are dysfunctional or deteriorated, communication can help to heal or remedy problems. In new relationships, communication may stimulate relational development and growth. Aging relationships may be functional or dysfunctional. Communication skills allow us to subscribe to realistic hope in our relationships.

Finally, individuals do not move through each of these stages with everyone they meet. Research shows that people base decisions to develop relationships on such factors as physical attractiveness, personal charisma, and communication behaviors (Friedman, Riggio, & Casella, 1988; Sabatelli & Rubin, 1986). In general, we are more likely to attempt to develop relationships with people who are attractive, emotionally expressive, extroverted, and spontaneous. In the next section of this chapter we will consider some of the theories that suggest why we select some people with whom to relate and why we neglect, or even reject, other people.

Motivations for Initiating, Maintaining, and Terminating Relationships

Motivations for Initiating Relationships

What happens in initial interactions with people? The **uncertainty reduction theory** developed by Charles R. Berger and Richard J. Calabrese (1975) states that *upon first meeting, strangers seek to reduce the uncertainty that they have about the other person.* They write, "When strangers meet, their primary concern is one of uncertainty reduction or increasing predictability about the behavior of both themselves and others in the interaction" (p. 100).

These researchers also identified three basic strategies by which people seek information about another person. *Passive strategies* occur when people simply observe the second person. You might watch a classmate in the course that you have together, for instance. *Interactive strategies* mean simply that the first person communicates directly with the second person. For instance, you strike up a conversation about mundane events and then begin to ask the person questions about himself or herself. *Active strategies* involve the first person making a request to someone to set up a situation where the second person can be observed (passive strategy) or you can talk with him or her (interactive strategy). For example, you ask a friend to bring someone to a restaurant where you can choose to observe and/or speak with her or him.

Berger and Calabrese identified several **axioms,** or *statements held to be true without proof,* that solidify the theory. To summarize, they posit that as verbal communication increases and nonverbal expressiveness increases, uncertainty will decrease in an initial interaction. They note that high levels of uncertainty can cause an increase in information-seeking behavior, a decrease in the intimacy level of the communication content, high rates of reciprocity, and a decrease in liking. They predict that when similarities between people exist, the level of uncertainty is reduced. Finally, they claim that shared communication networks reduce uncertainty while a lack of shared networks increases uncertainty.

Knobloch and Solomon (1999) note that uncertainty can arise around the self, the partner, and the relationship but that most research focuses on uncertainty about the partner. They further developed the theory and learned that people in dating relationships identify three issues of uncertainty about the self or the partner: the individual desire for the relationship, the evaluation of the relationship, and the goals for the relationship. In other words, people may be uncertain about their own or their partner's desire, evaluation, and goals for the relationship. They identified four issues of uncertainty around the relationship itself: behavioral norms for the relationship, mutuality of feelings between the partners, current definition of the relationship, and future of the relationship. With the relationship as the focus, individuals may be uncertain about the norms, the shared feelings of the partners, and the definition and future of the relationship. Apprehension may also affect levels of uncertainty (Schumacher & Wheeless, 1997).

William Gudykunst and his colleagues (Gudykunst, 1983; Gudykunst & Nishida, 1984, 1989; Gudykunst, Yang, & Nishida, 1985) identified cross-cultural differences in uncertainty reduction. People from Western individualized cultures such as the United States are more likely to use interactive strategies and ask direction questions. Those from Eastern collectivistic cultures including Korea are more likely to use passive strategies such as observing the second person.

---

uncertainty reduction theory

A theory that upon first meeting, strangers seek to reduce the uncertainty that they have about the other person.

axioms

Statements accepted as true without proof.

Group Discussion

Uncertainty reduction theory assumes that people strive to reduce uncertainty in their personal lives, including their personal relationships. Are there situations where uncertainty is wanted? Can the groups think of examples where the communicator would want to maintain some degree of uncertainty?

anxiety uncertainty management

A theory that suggests that people who find themselves in unfamiliar cultures feel uncertainty, which leads to anxiety.

Gudykunst extended his early research into a theory that is known as **anxiety uncertainty management** (Gudykunst, 1985, 1991, 1993, 1995; Kim & Gudykunst, 1988). This theory suggests that *people who find themselves in unfamiliar cultures feel uncertainty, which leads to anxiety.* Gudykunst observes that feelings of uncertainty are cognitive in nature: The person considers questions such as "What does this mean?" "What should I do?" "What is expected of me?" On the other hand, anxiety is affective, or emotional, in nature. The person feels overwhelmed, frightened, and unsure of himself or herself. Building on this work, Young Yun Kim (1988, 1995) determined that communication provides the vehicle by which people adapt to new and different cultural contexts.

The uncertainty reduction theory, and its related axioms, has received criticism since its inception (Bradac, 2001). Sunnafrank (1986, 1990) argues that uncertainty is not the primary issue in the early stages of a relationship. He and others suggest that factors like attraction and similarity are at least equally important factors for motivating a developing relationship (Duck, 1994). Kellerman and Reynolds (1990) also maintain that liking is more important than uncertainty in inspiring a relationship. They argue that we frequently meet people about whom we are uncertain, but we have no curiosity about learning more about them. Brashers (2001) notes that uncertainty does not always produce anxiety. He observes that we can best understand communication and uncertainty management as we answer questions about "the experience and meaning of uncertainty, the role of appraisal and emotion in uncertainty management, and the range of behavioral and psychological responses to uncertainty" (p. 477).

Let us consider some of the factors beyond uncertainty reduction that encourage relational initiation. While millions of people exist in this world, we have interpersonal relationships with a relatively small number of them. How do you determine which people you will select to be your friends, lovers, or family members? How are you attracted to them? Why do you cultivate relationships with them? How does communication figure into the equation?

proximity

Term referring to location, distance, and range between persons and things.

First, **proximity,** or *location,* is obvious but important. You are probably not going to have relationships with people from places you have never been. You are most likely to find others where you spend most of your time. For this reason, a roommate can easily become a friend. Coworkers, too, often become friends (Sias & Cahill, 1998). People who go to the same religious services, belong to the same social clubs, or are members of the same gang are most likely to become friends. People who share a major or a dormitory, cafeteria, car pool, or part of the seating chart in a class are also likely candidates. To underline the potency of proximity, consider that changes in location (high school to college and college to job) often change relationship patterns.

Second, we select, from all the people we see, the ones we find high in **attractiveness,** *a feature that takes three forms: task, social, and physical* (McCroskey & McCain, 1974). In other words, a person who is desirable to work with, who seems to have "social value" in that others also show interest in him or her, and who physically looks good to us is attractive (Pearson & Spitzberg, 1990). Attractiveness is not universal. The attractiveness and the importance of particular physical features vary from culture to culture (Hetsroni & Bloch, 1999) and from person to person. Because of perceptual differences, you will not be looking for the same person as everyone else.

attractiveness

A concept that includes physical attractiveness, how desirable a person is to work with, and how much "social value" the person has for others.

TRY ◀ ▶ THIS

List the features of attractiveness of your best friend, your boyfriend or girlfriend, or your lover or spouse.

Responsiveness, *the idea that we tend to select our friends and loved ones from people who demonstrate positive interest in us,* is another feature of attraction. Not everyone responds positively to us, but someone who does is likely to get our attention. Few characteristics are more attractive than someone who actively listens to us, thinks our jokes are funny, finds our vulnerabilities wonderful, and sees our faults as amusing. In short, we practically never select our friends from among those who dislike us.

responsiveness

The idea that we tend to select our friends from people who demonstrate positive interest in us.

Similarity, *the idea that our friends and loved ones are usually people who like or dislike the same things we do,* is another feature of attractiveness. People in interpersonal relationships often look, act, or think similarly. Whatever we consider most important is the similarity we seek, so some friends or people in loving relationships are bound by their interests, others by their ideology, and still others by their mutual likes and dislikes. A hard-core environmentalist is unlikely to be close personal friends with a developer, whereas the developer is likely to select friends from people in the same business, country club, and suburb. Thousands of people find their friends in the same circle where they work: clerical workers with clerical workers, managers with managers, and bosses with bosses. Similarity is a powerful form of attraction.

similarity

The idea that our friends are usually people who like or dislike the same things we do.

Complementarity is *the idea that we sometimes bond with people whose strengths are our weaknesses.* Whereas you may be slightly shy, your friend may be assertive. In situations that call for assertiveness, she may play that role for you. A math-loving engineer may find friendship with a people-loving communication major, who takes care of the engineer's social life while the engineer helps his friend with math courses.

complementarity

The idea that we sometimes bond with people whose strengths are our weaknesses.

social exchange theory

Economic model that suggests that we develop relationships on the basis of their rewards and costs.

Discussion Topic

Is the economic perspective of social exchange theory a productive view of why relationships are formed? Are there instances where this profit/loss model does not guide our motives for developing relationships with others?

Having a friend or loved one who is too much like you can result in competitiveness that destroys the friendship.

Social exchange theory is an economic model which suggests that *we develop relationships on the basis of their rewards and costs.* In other words, we are looking for maximum profits and minimal losses. Every relationship we have has inherent costs—time provided to each other, money that is spent, and decisions that are made that sometimes benefit the partner but not the self. Each relationship also has rewards—status, increased income, or love. Following social exchange theory, you make an assessment of your relative "worth," or your rewards minus your cost. You attempt—perhaps unconsciously—to find others with whom to relate who have the same or greater worth. When others do not measure up, you feel dissatisfied with the relationship; when they do, you feel a level of contentment.

Motivations for Maintaining Relationships

After you have gotten to know someone, why do you continue to relate to him or her? You may begin to relate to dozens of people, but you do not continue friendships, family relationships, or love relationships with everyone with whom you start a relationship. Consider friends that you had in elementary school or high school. Do you maintain any of those friendships now? Have you established an intimate relationship with someone, but broken up with her or him? Do you have family members with whom you are close and others with whom you hardly speak? Let us consider some of the motivators that encourage continuing a relationship.

Although we initially develop a relationship on the basis of such factors as attractiveness and personal charisma, we maintain relationships for different reasons. Maintained relationships invite certain levels of predictability, or certainty (Perse & Rubin, 1989). Indeed, we attempt to create strategies that will provide us with additional personal information about our relational partners (Berger & Kellermann, 1989). We are also less concerned with partners' expressive traits (e.g., being extroverted and spontaneous) and more concerned with their ability to focus on us through empathic, caring, and concerned involvement (Davis & Oathout, 1987). Indeed, as relationships are maintained, partners not only become more empathic but also begin to mirror each other's behavior.

Co-cultural Differences

Motivations for maintaining relationships are not simple. Many co-cultural differences affect our maintenance behaviors. For example, women use more maintenance strategies than do men (Ragsdale, 1996). People with different ethnicities express different primary needs in their interpersonal relationships. Collier (1996) demonstrated that "Latinos emphasized relational support, Asian Americans emphasized a caring, positive exchange of ideas, African Americans emphasized respect and acceptance, and Anglo Americans emphasized recognizing the needs of the individual" (p. i). People from different generations view intergenerational communication differently (Harwood, McKee, & Lin, 2000). In addition, people display different levels of nonverbal involvement and intimacy with their romantic partners (Guerrero, 1996).

Conversational Difficulties

Communication in interpersonal relationships, as we noted earlier, is not always easy. Conversations among people can be difficult. Stone, Patton, and Heen (1999) suggest that difficult conversations may be subdivided into the components of "what happened," "feelings," and "identity." The "what happened" part of the conversation centers on differences in perception, interpretations, and values. This part of the conversation is not about facts or the truth, but about perceptions. We verbalize what we believe really was said and done. In the "feelings" portion, we communicate and acknowledge the emotional impact that each person holds. Finally, in "identity," the communicators express the situation's underlying personal meaning.

An example may clarify these three components of difficult conversations. Imagine that your intimate partner, after a long night of partying, tells you that she would really like to be free to date others. You are very troubled by the statement and plan on a conversation in which you talk about the comment and the events of the entire evening. You decide that you will share that you believe that she was drinking too much and flirting with everyone at the club. You also are not sure if she remembers her comments after the long evening. Your verbalization of what you believe was said and done forms the "what happened" part of the conversation. When you add your acknowledgment of how you felt, you are adding the "feelings" part of the conversation. Finally, when you express your perception of the underlying meaning of her behavior for you, you are engaged in the "identity" portion of the conversation. Of course, conversations are not monologues and your partner may have different perceptions about each of the three elements in this difficult conversation.

What should a communicator know about errors that people make in conversations? Stone, Patton, and Heen (1999) suggest that the greatest mistake that people make in conversations is assuming that they are right and the other person is wrong. The second error that many people make is that they do not ask enough questions; they advocate instead of inquire. Third, people assume that rationality is essential and that feelings are irrelevant. How can we improve difficult conversations? The authors recommend that people know their purpose and that that purpose should be forward-looking. What is the solution or action that you wish to see? Having a conversation because you want to vent, because you are upset, or because you simply think you should talk is not a sufficient or futuristic goal. Second, conversationalists should also consider the reaction the other person might have so they are not thrown off balance. Finally, people should recognize that conversations are often difficult, but that difficult conversations are inevitable.

People experience many conversational challenges every day. For example, how can you give advice to someone without threatening him or her? Recent research suggests that the sequencing of giving advice is critical (Goldsmith, 2000). Communication cannot be viewed as individual isolable comments but as a sequence of interactions.

How explicit, or clear and obvious, should you be in interpersonal relationships? Factors like affection and social closeness affect the perception of explicitness. Solomon (1997) found a curvilinear relationship between intimacy and explicitness. In other words, when you are in earlier stages of an interpersonal relationship or in later stages, explicitness is more frequent. During the middle stages of a relationship, you are less explicit.

dependence power

Control over a relationship held by a person who is committed to the relationship but perceives the partner to be less committed and who has a number of viable relationship alternatives.

In addition, people are not always equally committed to a relationship, and some partners have more relational alternatives than do others. Indeed *when one person is committed to the relationship but perceives the partner to be less committed and to have a number of viable relationship alternatives,* we identify the partner, or second person, as having **dependence power.** In couples in which one person has dependence power, differences in communication and perceptions occur between the two partners (Samp, 2001).

Another problem in interpersonal communication is that people in interpersonal relationships do not always agree, and they may have different goals. Consequently, they sometimes use strategies to achieve particular goals. The choices of negotiation strategies are many and vary based on differences in power, liking, and the importance of the context (Pavitt & Kempt 1999).

Partners sometimes desire change in their relationship. One may want to be less or more intimate with the other. How is this desire for change shown? A demand—withdraw pattern is one pattern of interaction that occurs when partners wish for change. One partner makes increasing demands while the second person increasingly withdraws from the relationship (Caughlin & Vangelisti, 1999).

Satisfying Relationships

Couples can achieve satisfying and long-term relationships, however. Pearson (1996) looked at couples who had been happily married for more than 40 years. She found that many of these marriages were characterized by stubbornness ("This marriage will succeed no matter what"), distortion ("She is the most beautiful woman in the world"), unconditional acceptance (regardless of faults), and the continuous push and pull of autonomy or independence versus unity or interdependence. Maintaining positive, satisfying relationships is not easy, but the people who are the most satisfied with their relationships are probably those who have worked hardest at maintaining them. Communicatively, people in long-term and satisfied relationships are distinctive from those in short-term or unhappy relationships. Sillars, Shellen, McIntosh, and Pomegranate (1997) found that people in long-term and satisfied relationships are more likely to use joint rather than individual identity pronouns (e.g., "we" and "us" rather than "I" or "me").

Motivations for Terminating Relationships

Although our goal may be to maintain satisfying relationships, this outcome is not always possible. Relationships do not last. About half of all marriages end in divorce. In second and third marriages, the failure rate is even higher. In this section we will discuss factors that lead to relational termination. Why do interpersonal relationships end? What factors encourage people to seek the conclusion, rather than the continuation, of a relationship? We can organize our discussion around individual characteristics and message characteristics.

TRY◄►THIS

All of us have terminated relationships. Consider one of the relationships that you have terminated within the last year or two. What factors caused you to terminate it?

Individual Characteristics

While we cannot discuss all of the individual characteristics that a person might possess that will lead to relational termination, we should recall the discussion earlier in this chapter that focused on the dark side of relationships. We noted that obsession, codependency, and abuse were destructive individual characteristics. Although a complete discussion of these topics does not fit the scope or nature of this text, we will focus on one form of obsession here. Jealousy, common in relationships, has a number of associated communicative behaviors.

Jealousy, or *being possessively watchful of the partner or feeling suspicious about potential rivals for the partner's affections,* is one characteristic that can be damaging to a relationship (Guerrero & Eloy, 1992). If jealousy is communicated through avoidance or anger, its effects can be especially harmful (Andersen, Eloy, Guerrero, & Spitzberg, 1995). At the same time, the responses to jealousy may serve six different important functions within romantic relationships. Responses to jealousy "can help maintain one's relationship, preserve one's self-esteem, reduce uncertainty about the

jealousy

Possessive watchfulness of the partner or suspicion about potential rivals for the partner's affections.

primary relationship, reduce uncertainty about the rival relationship, re-assess the relationship, and restore equity through retaliation" (Guerrero & Afifi, 1999, p. 216). The communication of jealousy may serve to initiate essential communication about the relationship. However, jealousy often invites deterioration.

Message Characteristics

hurtful messages

Messages that create emotional pain or upset.

Hurtful messages, or *messages that create emotional pain or upset,* can end a relationship. Hurtful messages occur in most relationships, even those where couples are very satisfied, and do not always end in disruption of the relationship. However, if hurtful messages become a pattern or are so intense that one partner cannot forget them, they can be disruptive. Why do some hurtful messages create significant relational problems and others do not? Duck and Pond (1989) suggest that the history, closeness of the couple, and satisfaction with the relationship all affect how people perceive and respond to their own interaction.

Hurtful messages may be more or less harmful to the relationship depending on the reaction of the second person. Vangelisti and Crumley (1998) determined that people responded in one of three ways: active verbal responses (for example, attacking the other, defending oneself, or asking for an explanation), acquiescent responses (for example, apologizing or crying), and invulnerable responses (for instance, laughing or ignoring the message). People who felt extremely hurt were more likely to use acquiescing responses than were those who were less hurt. People who were less hurt more often used invulnerability than did those who felt the hurt was extreme. They also found that relational satisfaction was positively related with active verbal responses.

deceptive communication

The practice of deliberately making somebody believe things that are not true.

Deceptive communication, or *the practice of deliberately making somebody believe things that are untrue,* can also lead to relational dissatisfaction and termination. Probably all relational partners engage in some level of deception from time to time. The "little white lie," the lack of revealing the "whole truth," and the omission of some details are commonplace. However, deliberate and regular deception can lead to the destruction of trust and the end of the relationship.

veracity effect

The assumption that messages are truthful.

At the same time, people do not appear to be very accurate in their detection of dishonest communication. Most research suggests that the accuracy rate of determining deception is just over 50 percent. However, when honest information and deceptive communication are separated, different results occur. When people are responding to truthful messages, they are much better than chance at determining the truthfulness of the messages. However, when they are presented with deceptive messages, they are less likely to make accurate judgments of the deception. The **veracity effect** suggests that *people assume that messages that they receive are truthful* (Levine, Park, & McCornack, 1999). Consequently, they make more errors in judging truthfulness when the message is deceptive.

People who tell familiar and unfamiliar lies actually vary in their behavior when they are telling the lie and when they are asked questions about the lie. The length of their pauses and their eye gaze as well as the amount of laughing and smiling they provide varies. However, observers do not notice these differences and cannot distinguish between familiar and unfamiliar lies that are told to them (di Battista, 1997). In short, we do not seem to be very accurate in determining deceptive behaviors.

Aggressiveness occurs when *people stand up for their rights at the expense of others and care about their own needs but no one else's.* Aggressiveness might help you get your way a few times, but ultimately others will avoid you and let their resentment show. People who engage in aggressive behavior may do so because of negative self-concepts or because they have learned this pattern of behavior in their original homes. Martin and Anderson (1997) show that both sons and daughters have patterns of verbal aggression that are similar to their mothers.

Aggressiveness is not the same as argumentativeness. **Argumentativeness,** defined as *the quality or state of being argumentative,* is synonymous with being contentious or combative. People who are argumentative are not verbally aggressive (Semic & Canary, 1997). Indeed, argumentative people may value argument as a normal social communicative activity. Argumentativeness patterns are shown to be similar between mothers and their children (Martin & Anderson, 1997).

aggressiveness

Assertion of one's rights at the expense of others and care about one's own needs but no one else's.

argumentativeness

The quality or state of being argumentative; synonymous with contentiousness or combativeness.

Essential Interpersonal Communication Behaviors

Many of the communication behaviors that we have discussed in this text are important in interpersonal communication. You need to be aware of factors like perception, have a good self-concept, provide clear verbal and nonverbal cues to others, and be able to listen and empathize as others provide messages to you. Moreover, some additional communication behaviors are associated with effective interpersonal communication. In an interpersonal relationship, you reveal yourself to others, you show affection and support, you influence others, and you develop the unique nature of the interpersonal relationship. In this section of the chapter we consider these four interpersonal communication areas: self-disclosure; affectionate communication; influence, which includes compliance-gaining and interpersonal dominance; and the development of the exclusive relationship.

Self-Disclosure

One change that occurs as relationships become deeper and closer lies in the intentional revealing of personal information. **Self-disclosure** is *the process of making intentional revelations about oneself that others would be*

self-disclosure

The process of making intentional revelations about oneself that others would be unlikely to know and that generally constitute private, sensitive, or confidential information.

Video Activity

Ask students to view the video segment "The Hospital." How did self-disclosure play a role in the conversation between Susan and her mother?

unlikely to know and that generally constitute private, sensitive, or confidential information. Self-disclosure consists of information that is intentionally provided. Pearce and Sharp (1973) distinguish among self-disclosure, confession, and revelation. They define self-disclosure as voluntary while they view a confession as being forced or coerced information and revelation as unintentional or inadvertent communication.

Jourard (1964) suggests that self-disclosure makes one "transparent" to others, that disclosure helps others to see a person as a distinctive human being. Self-disclosure goes beyond self-description. Self-description generally involves more public information. Self-disclosure does not include telling someone that you are petite or bald because those physical features are obvious; self-disclosure also does not comprise statements about your student status, a professor's discipline, or information about where you were born because this information is generally public knowledge. Your position on abortion, your strong and close relationship with your grandfather, your sexual history, your deepest fears, one of your proudest moments, and problems with drugs or alcohol would be considered self-disclosure by most definitions. Self-disclosure, not always negative, is generally private information.

Why Is Self-Disclosure Important?

Self-disclosure is important for two reasons: Disclosure allows you to develop a more positive attitude about yourself and others and disclosure allows you to establish more meaningful relationships with others. Have you ever experienced a problem or faced a difficult situation? Most of us have, and we know that sharing our fears or telling others about our anguish provides comfort. Self-disclosure allows us to share our humanness with others. Hastings (2000) found that self-disclosure is a powerful form of communication in grief and in healing a fractured identity.

Through self-disclosure, relationships grow in depth and meaning. If you use self-disclosure appropriately, your relationships will move from being fairly superficial to being deeper and more meaningful. Partners in romantic relationships, for example, report greater security when self-disclosure between them is intentional and honest (Le Poire et al., 1997). When you self-disclose more to others, they will most likely disclose more to you. On the other hand, the inability to self-disclose can result in the end of a relationship. Without the opportunity for self-disclosure and active listening, relationships appear to be doomed to shallowness, superficiality, or termination.

At the same time, self-disclosure can be used inappropriately. Have you ever sat on an airplane next to a stranger and had the stranger reveal highly personal information to you? Have you ever dated someone who insisted on sharing private information too early in the relationship? Have you had friends who told you negative information about themselves long before you knew virtually anything else about them? Self-disclosure is not always appropriate. In the next section we will consider some of the findings about self-disclosure that may provide guidelines for your self-disclosing behavior.

What Factors Affect Appropriate Self-Disclosure?

Disclosure generally increases as relational intimacy increases. We do not provide our life story to people we have just met. Instead, in the developing relationship, we reveal an increasing amount of information. We might begin with positive information that is not highly intimate and then begin to share more personal information as we learn to trust the other person. In this way, our disclosure tends to be incremental, or to increase over time.

Disclosure increases when people wish to reduce uncertainty in their relationships. Earlier in this chapter we discussed uncertainty reduction theory. Although the theory is not without its critics, sometimes our motive in interaction is to reduce uncertainty. We know that if we disclose information about ourselves, others will generally do the same. When we seek information about others, we find that one strategy in gleaning information is to first disclose to others.

Disclosure tends to be reciprocal. This conclusion is related to the last. When people offer us information about themselves, we tend to return the behavior in kind. Indeed, when people reciprocate self-disclosure, we tend to view them positively; when they do not, we tend to view them as incompetent (Cozby, 1972, 1973; Hosman & Tardy, 1980). Dindia, Fitzpatrick, and Kenny (1997) studied dyadic interaction between women and men and strangers and spouses. They concluded that in conversations, disclosure of highly intimate feelings was reciprocal. Reciprocity is also shown in nonverbal behaviors. Guerrero, Jones, and Burgoon (2000) showed that romantic partners in high-intimacy conditions reciprocated their partners' intimacy change by appearing more nonverbally involved and pleasant and engaging in more verbal intimacy. Those who engaged in low intimacy conditions also reciprocated by becoming less nonverbally pleasant and fluent as well as more verbally hostile. They also became more vocally anxious and less composed after their partners decreased intimacy.

Negative disclosure is directly related to the intimacy of the relationship; however, positive disclosure does not necessarily increase as the relationship becomes more intimate. What does this mean? As we become closer to another person, we are more likely to reveal negative information about ourselves. Positive information, on the other hand, flows through conversations from the earliest developmental stages throughout the lifetime of the relationship. Hence, negative information increases over time, but positive disclosure does not necessarily increase.

Self-disclosure may be avoided for a variety of reasons. Self-disclosure does not flow freely on all topics. Indeed, relational partners

Writing Assignment

Have students write a short essay describing a situation where they self-disclosed and it resulted in a more fulfilling relationship or where they were hurt by it. Ask them to analyze the outcome of the situation by discussing how the self-disclosure process positively or negatively influenced the relationship.

Team Challenge

SAFE SEX AND COMMUNICATION

Lucchetti (1999) studied college students who were in close relationships to determine if they honestly disclosed their sexual histories before engaging in sex. She reasoned that although safe sex is a goal for most relational partners, openness and honesty about one's past could hurt a developing relationship. She found that although the vast majority of the students (99.7 percent) surveyed felt knowledgeable about safe-sex activities, over 40 percent did not realize that revealing one's sexual history was a safe-sex practice. In addition, one-third of those who were sexually active had not disclosed their past sexual history with at least one partner prior to becoming sexually involved, and at least one-fifth of the sexually active students purposefully misrepresented their sexual history to their sexual partners. Finally, those who believed disclosure of their sexual history is a requirement before becoming sexually intimate were less likely to change their sexual history in their disclosures to their partners.

With a group of your classmates, consider ways that you could create a campaign to encourage safe sex and honest disclosure about one's sexual history. What kinds of messages would influence students on your campus? What kinds of messages would not? How would you persuade them that the honest disclosure of one's sexual history is one part of safe-sex activities? If you were to launch such a campaign, how would you convince the various stakeholders (college administrators, faculty, students, taxpayers, and people in the community) that this goal is reasonable? What resistance might you find? What barriers would you need to overcome to successfully launch your campaign?

---

may avoid self-disclosure for reasons of self-protection, relationship protection, partner unresponsiveness, and social appropriateness. As Afifi and Guerrero observed, "Some things are better left unsaid" (1998, p. 231). At the same time, topics that are taboo under some conditions may be appropriate later when conditions change (Roloff & Johnson, 2001).

Relational satisfaction and disclosure are curvilinearly related. Satisfaction is lowest with no disclosure and with excessive disclosure; it is highest when self-disclosure is provided at moderate levels. Consider your own personal relationships. Does this conclusion appear to be accurate?

Affectionate and Supportive Communication

Affection, the holding of *fond or tender feelings toward another person*, is essential in interpersonal relationships. You express your affectionate feelings for others in interpersonal relationships in a variety of ways. Often these expressions are nonverbal as you touch, hug, kiss, or caress another person. You also engage in verbal statements of affection such as "I care about you," "I really like being with you," or "I love you."

affection

Holding fond or tender feelings toward another person.

We learn about affectionate communication in our original families. Do people simply model the affection they received from parents? Or do they compensate for negative patterns later on? Floyd and Morman (2000) show that both of these factors occur. In a study of fathers and sons, they determined that the fathers both use their own fathers and a model of compensation in their affectionate fathering behaviors of their own sons.

You know that a number of variables affect the appropriateness of statements of affection. Therefore, affectionate communication may be viewed as risk-laden. Among the factors that you will consider when you choose to offer affectionate statements to a relational partner are your own biological sex, the partner's biological sex, the kind of relationship you have (platonic or romantic), the privacy and emotional intensity of the situation, and the predispositions of the communicators (Floyd, 1997a; 1997b; Floyd & Morman, 1998, 2000). Telling another person that you love him or her may hold significantly different meanings depending on your sex, your partner's sex, how you have defined your relationship in the past, the degree of privacy of the situation in which you choose to share your feelings, and how the other person feels about you.

Although generally positive, the expression of affection may not always be so. If the receiver of the affectionate message does not reciprocate, the sender of the message may feel embarrassed or feel that he has lost face. Floyd and Burgoon (1999) found that, indeed, expressions of liking do not always result in positive relational outcomes. Recall a time when you expressed affection toward another person and she or he did not return the same warmth. How did you feel? In general, when people have particular expectancies about communicative behavior and those expectancies are not met, both disruption and adaptation follow (LePoire & Yoshimura, 1999).

One specialized form of affection is forgiveness. In virtually every interpersonal relationship, errors are made and people have the opportunity to allow the event to destroy the relationship or to forgive the other person and maintain the relationship. Kelley's (1998) extensive research on forgiveness shows that this interpersonal behavior is complex. Forgiveness must be understood in terms of the relationship type, the forgiver and the offender motivations, the forgiver and the offender strategies, and the relational consequences of forgiveness. Making a decision to forgive another person requires the consideration of all these factors.

Discussion Question

What factors do you consider when trying to determine whether to forgive someone? Are there specific criteria you use to make that decision?

Supportive communication is also important in interpersonal communication. Support may include giving advice, expressing concern, and offering assistance. Although people generally respond well to supportive communication, the type of support preferred may vary as a result of the receiver's age (Caplan & Samter, 1999) and the support providers' goals (MacGeorge, 2001). In times of distress, comforting messages (suggesting a diversion, offering assistance, and expressing optimism, for example) encourage people to feel less upset. At the same time, the recipients of such messages may also feel demeaned. The distressed person is most likely to feel less upset when the comforting message is offered from a close friend rather than an acquaintance (Clark, Pierce, Finn, Hsu, Toosley, & Williams, 1998). Comfort, then, is viewed as most positive in close interpersonal relationships rather than in more distant ones.

Influencing Others

Later in this book we will discuss influencing others in public communication settings. For now, we consider the notion of influencing others in interpersonal settings. In general, **influence** is *the power that a person has to affect other people's thinking or actions.* In interpersonal communication, influence has been studied widely. One body of research has focused on compliance-gaining and compliance-resisting. **Compliance-gaining** may be defined as *those attempts made by a source of messages to influence a target "to perform some desired behavior that the target otherwise might not perform"* (Wilson, 1998, p. 273). Compliance-gaining occurs frequently in interpersonal communication. We ask a friend for advice, we ask a parent for financial assistance, or we encourage a relational partner to feel more committed. Children become more skillful at identifying situational and personal cues in possible compliance-gaining as they develop, with girls showing more sensitivity than boys (Marshall & Levy, 1998).

Although research has been conducted on compliance-gaining, many of the findings have confused rather than clarified because of the multiple considerations that are involved (Hullett & Tamborini, 2001; Levine & Boster, 2001; Ma & Chuang, 2001; Miller, 1998; Richmond, McCroskey, & Roach, 1997; Schraeder, 1999). We do know that people generally prefer socially acceptable, reward-oriented strategies (Miller, Boster, Roloff, & Seibold, 1977). They do not favor negative, threatening, or punishing strategies. In early interactions, too, people prefer "prosocial" appeals, but after they have encountered resistance to their appeals, they become far less polite. This behavior, known as the "rebuff phenomenon," occurs across several relationships, cultures, and settings. Hample and Dallinger (1998) have shown that once message sources are rebuffed, they are less concerned about harming their relationship with the other person and more concerned with gaining compliance.

---

influence

The power to affect other people's thinking or actions.

compliance-gaining

Those attempts made by a source of messages to influence a target to perform some desired behavior that the target otherwise might not perform.

Group Discussion

Teachers use a variety of compliance-gaining tactics. How do teachers try to get students to behave in a classroom? What are some strategies students use to resist teachers' compliance-gaining attempts?

Compliance-resisting occurs when *targets of influence messages refuse to comply to requests.* When resisting requests, people often offer reasons for their refusal (Saeki & O'Keefe, 1994). People who are more sensitive to others and who are more adaptive are more likely to engage in further attempts to influence (Ifert & Roloff, 1997). Indeed, they may address some of the obstacles they expect when they initiate their original request and they may adapt later attempts to influence by offering counterarguments.

For example, if you are asking a friend to borrow his car, you might consider some of the reasons he might refuse. He might state that he needs his car at the same time, that the last time you borrowed his car you returned it with no gas, or that the only time he ever hears from you is when you want something from him. In your initial message, you might suggest to him that you have felt that you have been neglecting him and that you want to spend some time together and, in addition, that you have not been as considerate as you could be with him. When he suggests that he needs his car at the same time that you do, you might offer to use his car at a different time.

Closely related to compliance-gaining is interpersonal dominance, which allows us to gain compliance in interpersonal settings. Burgoon and her associates (Burgoon, Johnson, & Koch, 1998) offer a definition of **interpersonal dominance** as *"a relational, behavioral, and interactional state that reflects the actual achievement of influence or control over another via communicative actions"* (p. 315). They view the concept as one that occurs between, or among, people, not a personality characteristic that is separate from an interaction. They differentiate dominance from power in that power is a perceived quality of a person, whereas dominance is both behavioral and interactional. Burgoon and Dunbar (2000) suggest that interpersonal dominance is most likely a combination of person, situation, and relationship factors. As such, interpersonal dominance is most likely related to specific verbal and nonverbal behaviors (Burgoon & LePoire, 1999).

Dominance, often viewed negatively, has been viewed in ambiguous ways (sometimes being equated with power, status, or aggression). Burgoon's recent research suggests that a better use of the term is to refer to dominance more comprehensively and to include positive qualities that embody social competence. Burgoon, Johnson, and Koch (1998) determined that interpersonal dominance has four dimensions. *Persuasiveness and poise* suggest that the person is influential and behaves with dignity. *Conversational control and panache* means that the individual has a strong presence and is expressive. *Task focus* suggests that the person remains centered on the task. Finally, *self-assurance* suggests a level of confidence and an avoidance of either arrogance or timidity.

compliance-resisting

Refusal of targets of influence messages to comply to requests.

interpersonal dominance

A relational, behavioral, and interactional state that reflects the actual achievement of influence or control over another via communicative actions.

E-Note

TESTING YOUR INTERPERSONAL SKILLS

www.queendom.com is a site for multiple tests on relationships, personality, health, career, and intelligence. Although the validity and reliability information on the tests is not provided, the tests do provide an interesting starting point to think about how your personality and relationship scores might affect your interpersonal relationships and communication with others. Relevant to this chapter are tests on arguing, assertiveness, commitment readiness, communication skills, conflict management, coping skills, jealousy, relationship attachment, relationship satisfaction, romantic personality, romantic space, and self-disclosure. You might wish to take one or more of these tests with someone with whom you have an interpersonal relationship. Share your responses with each other and determine the perceived accuracy of the test results with your partner. Does your partner see you differently or similarly to how you perceive yourself? How could differences in perception affect your relationship?

Video Activity
Select a movie like *You've Got Mail* or a TV show such as *Friends* about a relationship. Have students analyze personal idioms and rituals that develop in the relationship. This can be discussed in class or written about in reflection papers.

personal idioms
Unique forms of expression and language understood only by individual couples.

rituals
Formalized patterns of actions or words followed regularly.

Developing a Unique Relationship

Interpersonal relationships are defined by their uniqueness. In a sense relational couples create a "culture of two" (Betcher, 1987). They may have unique names for each other and shared experiences that others do not have with them, and they may develop distinctive patterns of interaction. Bruess and Pearson (1993) found that couples who created **personal idioms,** or *unique forms of expression and language understood only by them,* expressed high relational satisfaction. Did your parents have a unique name for you that no one else used? Do you have a way of referring to an event with an intimate that no one else understands? Do you have a way of expressing a thought, idea, or need with a friend that no one else can decipher? All of these are personal idioms.

Through playful interaction and the creation of **rituals,** or *formalized patterns of actions or words followed regularly,* couples create a shared culture. Rituals may become so routine that we do not realize that they comprise the fabric of a relationship. However, if a relational partner does not enact them, uneasiness often follows. For example, can you recall a time when your partner failed to call you, say "I love you," bring you flowers or a gift, or enact another regular behavior? Although the importance of the ritual was perhaps never verbalized, you probably felt hurt or neglected.

Bruess and Pearson (1997) revealed that the following seven rituals are important characteristics of long-term interpersonal relationships:

1. *Couple-time rituals*—for example, exercising together or having dinner together every Saturday night.
2. *Idiosyncratic/symbolic rituals*—for example, calling each other by a special name or celebrating the anniversary of their first date.
3. *Daily routines and tasks*—for example, if living together, one partner might always prepare the evening meal and the other might always clean up afterward.
4. *Intimacy rituals*—for example, giving each other a massage or, when apart, talking on the telephone before going to bed.
5. *Communication rituals*—for example, getting together for lunch with a friend every Friday afternoon or going out to a coffee bar with a significant other.
6. *Patterns, habits, and mannerisms*—for example, meeting her need to be complimented when going out for a fancy evening, and meeting his need to be reassured before family events.
7. *Spiritual rituals*—for example, attending services together or doing yoga together in the evening.

The Possibilities for Improvement

Can you improve your communication in interpersonal relationships? Until relatively recently, many people felt that learning to relate more effectively to others was impossible. Today, most individuals feel such a possibility does exist. Are such changes easy? Generally, they are not. You should not expect that an introductory course in communication will solve all of your relational problems. Self-help books that promise instant success will probably result only in permanent disillusionment. Courses on assertiveness training, relaxation techniques, and marital satisfaction provide only part of the answer. Improving relationships is a lifelong process which nobody perfects but which many people can improve for their own benefit.

Bargaining

Often we engage in bargaining in our interpersonal relationships. **Bargaining** occurs when *two or more parties attempt to reach an agreement on what each should give and receive in a transaction between them.* Bargains may be explicit and formal, such as the kinds of agreements you reach with others to share tasks, to attend a particular event, or to behave in a specified way. Bargains may also be implicit and informal. For example,

bargaining

The process in which two or more parties attempt to reach an agreement on what each should give and receive in a relationship.

Discussion Question

The text mentions no evidence of how gender is related to effective bargaining skills. Do members of the class think males or females tend to be better bargainers in interpersonal relationships?

in exchange for receiving a compliment from him every day, you might agree not to tell embarrassing stories about your boyfriend in public. You may not even be aware of some of the unstated agreements you have with others with whom you communicate.

A study on interpersonal bargaining (Deusch & Kraus, 1962) identified three essential features of a bargaining situation:

1. All parties perceive the possibility of reaching an agreement in which each party would be better off, or no worse off, than if no agreement were reached.
2. All parties perceive more than one such agreement that could be reached.
3. All parties perceive the other to have conflicting preferences or opposed interests.

What are some examples of bargaining situations? You may want to go out with friends when your spouse would prefer a quiet evening at home. A woman might prefer to go hiking, whereas her husband is more eager to take a cruise. One person could use the word *forever* to mean a few days or weeks, whereas another assumes the word refers to a much longer period of time. In each of these instances, the disagreement can be resolved through bargaining.

Thibaut and Kelley (1959) underlined the importance of bargaining in interpersonal communication:

> Whatever the gratifications achieved in dyads, however lofty or fine the motives satisfied may be, the relationship may be viewed as a trading or bargaining one. The basic assumption running throughout our analysis is that every individual voluntarily enters and stays in any relationship only as long as it is adequately satisfactory in terms of rewards and costs.

Learning Communication Skills

If you wish to improve your communication within your interpersonal relationships, you must have a commitment to learning a variety of communication skills. You must understand the importance of perceptual differences among people, the role of self-concept in communication, the nature of verbal language, and the role of nonverbal communication. You must be willing to share yourself with others as you self-disclose, and you must be willing to attempt to understand other people through careful and conscientious listening. In addition, you must recognize that even when you thoroughly understand these concepts and are able to implement them in your behavior, your interactions with others may not be successful. Communication is dependent on the interaction between two communicators, and one person cannot guarantee its success. Others may have conflicting goals, have different perspectives, or communicate incompetently.

Learning individual communication concepts and specific communication skills is essential to effective interaction. You also need to understand the impact of these skills. For example, you do not communicate at home the way you do in the classroom. Self-disclosure, which is especially appropriate and important within the family context, may be out of place in the classroom. Preparation and planning are important in an interview, but they may be seen as manipulative in a conversation between partners.

Behavioral Flexibility

In addition to being improved by an understanding of communication concepts, skills, and settings, our interactions may be greatly enhanced by an underlying approach to communication behavior called behavioral flexibility. **Behavioral flexibility** is defined as *the ability to alter behavior to adapt to new situations and to relate in new ways when necessary* (Pearson, 1983). Behavioral flexibility allows you to relax when you are with friends or to be your formal self while interviewing for a job. The key to behavioral flexibility may be self-monitoring, always being conscious of the effect of your words on the specific audience in a particular context.

TRY ◄►THIS

Define behavioral flexibility and determine to what degree you exhibit this trait.

Flexibility is important in a variety of fields. For example, biologists and botanists have demonstrated that extinction of certain living things occurs because of an organism's inability to adapt to changes in the environment. Psychologists have suggested that women and men who are **androgynous**—*who hold both stereotypically male and stereotypically female traits*—are more successful in their interactions than are people who are unyieldingly masculine or absolutely feminine. Flexibility in psychological gender roles is more useful than a static notion of what being a man or a woman means in our culture. For instance, if you are a single parent, you may be called on to behave in a loving and nurturing way to your child, regardless of your sex. If your goal is to be a successful manager in a large corporation, you may have to exhibit competitiveness, assertiveness, and a task orientation, regardless of your sex. As you move from interactions with coworkers to interactions with family and friends, you may need to change from traditionally "masculine" behaviors to those that have been considered "feminine."

Video Activity

Ask students to view the video segment "The Hospital." To what extent did various characters in the segment demonstrate behavioral flexibility? Discuss how behavioral flexibility was necessary because traditional family roles were becoming blurred. The grandmother was ill, the mother had to assume the role of caregiver, Susan had to "take care" of her mother, etc.

behavioral flexibility

The ability to alter behavior to adapt to new situations and to relate in new ways when necessary.

androgynous

A term used in reference to persons who possess stereotypical female and male characteristics.

Behavioral flexibility is especially important in interpersonal communication because relationships between people are in constant flux. For example, the family structure has gone through sharp changes in recent years. In addition, the United States has an increasing older population. Changes in the labor force also require new skills and different ways of interacting with others. People travel more often and move more frequently. Four million unmarried couples cohabit (Singletary, 1999). As a result of these types of changes, people may interact differently today than in the past.

What kinds of changes might you expect in your own life that will affect your relationships with others? You may change your job 10 or more times. You may move your place of residence even more frequently. You probably will be married at least once, and possibly two or three times. You probably will have one child or more. You will experience loss of family members through death and dissolution of relationships. You may have a spouse whose needs conflict with your needs. Other family members may view the world differently than you and challenge your perceptions. When your life appears to be most stable and calm, unexpected changes will occur.

How can behavioral flexibility assist you through life's changes? A flexible person draws on a large repertoire of behaviors. Such an individual is confident about sharing messages with others and about understanding the messages that others provide. The flexible person is able to self-disclose when appropriate but does not use this ability in inappropriate contexts. The flexible person can demonstrate listening skills but is not always the one who is listening. The flexible person can show concern for a child who needs assistance, can be assertive on the job, can be yielding when another person needs to exercise control, and can be independent when called on to stand alone. The flexible person does not predetermine one set of communication behaviors he or she will always enact. The flexible person is not dogmatic or narrow-minded in interactions with others.

To remember that changes are not always negative is important. In fact, considerable change is positive. For instance, when you graduate from college, the changes that occur are generally perceived as positive. When you enter into new relationships, you generally encounter positive change.

But even positive change can be stressful. Gail Sheehy, author of *Passages: Predictable Crises of Adult Life* (1976), wrote:

> We must be willing to change chairs if we want to grow. There is no permanent compatibility between a chair and a person. And there is no one right chair. What is right at one stage may be restricting at another or too soft.

Class Discussion

What are some examples of situations where a person must demonstrate behavioral flexibility? For example, going to college is a time when we typically become more flexible. What are other examples of instances or situations where behavioral flexibility is critical?

TRY ►THIS

List the major changes you have made in your life, and determine how each has led to changes in your communication.

Chapter Review

SUMMARY

In this chapter you have learned the following:

- Interpersonal relationships provide one context in which people communicate with each other. Interpersonal relationships are associations between two or more people who are interdependent, who use some consistent patterns of interaction, and who have interacted for a period of time. Interpersonal relationships are established for a variety of reasons.

- Most interpersonal relationships are positive, but interpersonal relationships also have a dark side.

- Most relationships go through definable stages of development, maintenance, and deterioration. Why do people initiate relationships?

  - The uncertainty reduction theory suggests that strangers seek to reduce uncertainty.

  - Some researchers suggest that factors like attraction and similarity are at least as important as reducing uncertainty.

  - Other factors that may motivate initiating a relationship include proximity, attractiveness, responsiveness, similarity, complementarity, and social exchange.

- Relationship maintenance is challenging.

  - Although some aspects of maintenance seem to generalize across most relationships, we know that co-cultural differences affect our maintenance behaviors.

  - People can achieve satisfying relationships.

- At the same time, conversational difficulties are challenging to the most competent communicator.

- Why do people terminate relationships?

  - Termination might be motivated by the individual characteristics of the partners, such as jealousy.

  - Message characteristics might also encourage termination: Hurtful messages, deceptive communication, and aggresiveness may have a destructive effect on interpersonal relationships.

- Although interpersonal communication behaviors cannot be prescribed, four communication behaviors are essential to competent interpersonal communication.

  - Self-disclosure is the process of making intentional revelations about oneself that others would be unlikely to know and that generally constitutes private, sensitive, or confidential information. Affectionate communication includes your expression of fond or tender feelings toward another person.

  - One goal that interpersonal communicators hold is to influence others in their interpersonal relationships.

  - We develop our unique relationship through personal idioms and playful interactions.

- We can improve relationships through communication by developing behavioral flexibility.

◉ VIDEO LINK: INTERPERSONAL ROLES DURING FAMILY CRISES

Video Episode 2: "The Hospital"

Interpersonal relationships require us to take on certain roles. By enacting roles we are able to model our behaviors around scripts, which tell us how to behave and communicate. "The Hospital" illustrates the concept of roles in interpersonal relationships. As you view the segment, consider whether Susan Elliott or her mother is acting as the primary caregiver in the relationship. What do you attribute this role definition to? Also, do any of the characters in this segment exhibit tolerance for ambiguity? Does defensiveness play a role in any of the communication interactions in this segment?

ISSUES IN COMMUNICATION: THE CASE OF A FATHER AND A SON

This Issues in Communication narrative is designed to provoke individual thought or discussion about concepts raised in the chapter.

On August 23, 1999, a man identified simply as Stephan posted the following story on www.relationship-talk.com:

A man came home from work late again, tired and irritated, to find his five-year-old son waiting for him at the door.

"Daddy, may I ask you a question?"

"Yeah, sure. What is it?" replied the father.

"Daddy, how much money do you make an hour?"

"That's none of your business! What makes you ask such a thing?" the father said angrily.

"I just wanted to know. Please tell me, how much do you make an hour?" pleaded the little boy.

"If you must know, I make $20 an hour."

"Looking up, he said, "Daddy, may I borrow $9 please?"

The father was furious. "If the only reason you wanted to know how much money I make is just so you can borrow some to buy a silly toy or some other nonsense, then you march yourself straight to your room and go to bed. Think about why you're being so selfish. I work long, hard hours every day and don't have time for such childish games."

"The little boy quietly went to his room and shut the door.

The father sat down and started to get even madder about his little boy's questioning. How dare he ask such questions only to get some money. After an hour or so he calmed down. He started to think he might have been a little hard on his son. Maybe there was something he really needed to buy with that $9, and he didn't ask for money very often. The father went to his son's room and opened the door. "Are you asleep, son?" he asked.

"No daddy, I'm awake," replied the boy.

"I've been thinking, maybe I was too hard on you earlier," said the father. "It's been a long day and I took my aggravations out on you. Here's that $9 you asked for."

"The little boy sat straight up, beaming. "Oh, thank you daddy!" he yelled. Then, reaching under his pillow, he pulled out some more crumpled-up bills.

The father, seeing that the boy already had money, started to get angry again.

The little boy slowly counted out his money, then looked up at his father.

"Why did you want more money if you already had some?" the father grumbled.

"Because I didn't have enough, but now I do," the little boy replied. "Daddy, I have $20 now. Can I buy an hour of your time?"

Although this story might be apocryphal, many of us find ourselves living fast-paced lives with little time to spend in interpersonal communication. Apply what you have learned about interpersonal relationships and interpersonal communication as you ponder and discuss the following questions: What kind of interpersonal communication skills did the son possess? How about the father? If you were the father, how would you respond to the little boy's question? How are the child's needs for inclusion, affection, and control being met by the father? What dialectic tensions are present? How does the concept of bargaining apply to this story? Does behavioral flexibility seem to be important here? If you were a member of this family (the mother, a grandparent, or a sibling of the boy), what would you do upon hearing about this interaction?

KEY TERMS

Use the *Human Communication* CD-ROM and the *Online Learning Center* at www.mhhe.com/pearson to further your understanding of the following terminology.

Affection
Aggressiveness
Androgynous
Anxiety uncertainty
    management
Argumentativeness
Attractiveness
Avoiding
Axioms
Bargaining
Behavioral flexibility
Bonding
Circumscribing
Complementarity
Complementary
    relationships
Compliance-gaining
Compliance-resisting
Contradictions
Control
Deceptive communication

Dependence power
Dialectic
Dialectic of
    expression/privacy
Dialectic of
    integration/separation
Dialectic of stability/change
Differentiating
Experimenting
Hurtful messages
Inclusion
Influence
Initiating
Integrating
Intensifying
Interpersonal
    communication
Interpersonal dominance
Interpersonal relationship
Jealousy
Neutralization

Personal idioms
Process
Proximity
Reframing
Relational deterioration
Relational development
Relational maintenance
Responsiveness
Rituals
Selection
Self-disclosure
Separation
Similarity
Social exchange theory
Social penetration theory
Stagnating
Symmetrical relationships
Terminating
Uncertainty reduction
    theory
Veracity effect

SELF-QUIZ

Go to the self-quizzes on the *Human Communication* CD-ROM and the *Online Learning Center* at www.mhhe.com/pearson to test your knowledge.

REFERENCES

Afifi, W. A., & Guerrero, L. K. (1998). Some things are better left unsaid II: Topic avoidance in friendships. *Communication Quarterly, 46,* 231–249.

Altman, I., & Taylor, D. A. (1973). *Social penetration: The development of interpersonal relationships.* New York: Holt, Rinehart and Winston.

Andersen, P. A., Eloy, S. V., Guerrero, L. K., & Spitzberg, B. H. (1995). Romantic jealousy and relational satisfaction: A look at the impact of jealousy experience and expression. *Communication Reports, 8,* 77–85.

Baxter, L. (1979). Self-disclosure as a relationship disengagement strategy: An exploratory investigation. *Human Communication Research, 5,* 212–222.

Baxter, L. (1982). Strategies for ending relationships: Two studies. *Western Journal of Speech Communication, 46,* 223–241.

Baxter, L. (1983). Relationship disengagement: An examination of the reversal hypothesis. *Western Journal of Speech Communication, 47,* 85–98.

Baxter, L. (1984). Trajectories of relationship disengagement. *Journal of Social and Personal Relationships, 1,* 29–48.

Baxter, L. (1987). Symbols of relationship identity in relationship cultures. *Journal of Social and Personal Relationships, 4,* 261–279.

Baxter, L. (1988). A dialectical perspective on communication strategies in relationship development. In S. W. Duck, D. F. Hay, S. E. Hobfoll, W. Iches, & B. Montgomery (Eds.), *Handbook of personal relationships* (pp. 257–273). London, UK: Wiley.

Baxter, L. (1990). Dialectical contradictions in relationship development. *Journal of Social and Personal Relationships, 7,* 69–88.

Baxter, L. (1992). Forms and functions of intimate play in personal relationships. *Human Communication Research, 18,* 336–363.

Baxter, L. (1993). The social side of personal relationships: A dialectical perspective. In S. Duck (Ed.), *Understanding relationship processes: Vol. 3. Social context and relationships* (pp. 139–165). Newbury Park, CA: Sage.

Baxter, L., & Montgomery, B. (1996). *Relating: Dialogues and dialects.* New York: Guilford Press.

Berger, C. R., & Calabrese, R. J. (1975). Some explorations in initial interactions and beyond: Toward a developmental theory of interpersonal communication. *Human Communication Research, 1,* 98–112.

Berger, C. R., & Kellermann, K. (1989). Personal opacity and social information gathering. *Communication Research, 16,* 314–351.

Betcher, W. (1987). *Intimate play: Creating romance in everyday life.* New York: Viking.

Bradac, J. J. (2001). Theory comparison: Uncertainty reduction, problematic integration, uncertainty management, and other curious constructs. *Journal of Communication, 51,* 456–476.

Brashers, D. E. (2001). Communication and uncertainty management. *Journal of Communication, 51,* 477–497.

Bruess, C. J. S., & Pearson, J. C. (1993). "Sweet pea" and "Pussy cat"? An examination of idiom use and marital satisfaction over the life cycle. *Journal of Social and Personal Relationships, 10,* 609–615.

Bruess, C. J. S., & Pearson, J. C. (1997). Interpersonal rituals in marriage and adult friendship. *Communication Monographs, 64,* 25–46.

Burgoon, J. K., & Dunbar, N. E. (2000). An interactionist perspective on dominance-submission: Interpersonal dominance as a dynamic, situationally contingent social skill. *Communication Monographs, 67,* 96–111.

Burgoon, J. K., Johnson, M. L., & Koch, P. T. (1998). The nature and measurement of interpersonal dominance. *Communication Monographs, 65,* 308–335.

Burgoon, J. K., & LePoire, B. A. (1999). Nonverbal cues and interpersonal judgments: Participant and observer perceptions of intimacy, dominance, composure and formality. *Communication Monographs, 66,* 105–124.

Caplan, S. E., & Samter, W. (1999). The role of facework in younger and older adults' evaluations of social support messages. *Communication Quarterly, 47,* 245–264.

Caughlin, J. P., & Vangelisti, A. L. (1999). Desire for change in one's partner as a predictor of the demand/withdraw pattern of marital communication. *Communication Monographs, 66,* 66–89.

Clark, R. A, Pierce, K. F., Hsu, K., Toosley, A., & Williams, L. (1998). The impact of alternative approaches to comforting, closeness of relationship, and gender on multiple measures of effectiveness. *Communication Studies, 49,* 224–239.

Collier, M. J. (1996). Communication competence problematics in ethnic friendships. *Communication Monographs, 63,* 314–336.

Cozby, P. C. (1972). Self-disclosure, reciprocity, and liking. *Sociometry, 35,* 151–160.

Cozby, P. C. (1973). Self-disclosure: A literature review. *Psychological Bulletin, 79,* 73–91.

Crawford, L. (1996). Everyday Tao: Conversation and contemplation. *Communication Studies, 47,* 25–34.

Davis, M. H., & Oathout, H. A. (1987). Maintenance of satisfaction in romantic relationships: Empathy and relational competence. *Journal of Personality and Social Psychology, 53,* 397–498.

Deusch, M., & Kraus, R. M. (1962). Studies of interpersonal bargaining. *Journal of Conflict Resolution, 6,* 52.

di Battista, P. (1997). Deceivers' responses to challenges of their truthfulness: Difference between familiar lies and unfamiliar lies. *Communication Quarterly, 45,* 319–334.

Dindia, K. (1997). Self-disclosure, self-identity, and relationship development: A transactional/ dialectical perspective. In S. Duck (Ed.), *Handbook of personal relationships* (2nd ed., pp. 411–426). Chichester, England: Wiley.

Dindia, K., & Baxter, L. A. (1987). Strategies for maintaining and repairing marital relationships. *Journal of Social and Personal Relationships, 4,* 143–158.

Dindia, K., Fitzpatrick, M. A., & Kenny, D. A. (1997). Self-disclosure in spouse and stranger interaction. *Human Communication Research, 23,* 388–412.

Duck, S. W. (1994). *Meaningful relationships.* Thousand Oaks, CA: Sage.

Duck, S. (Ed.). (1997). *Handbook of personal relationships: Theory, research and interventions* (2nd ed.). Chichester, England: Wiley.

Duck, S., & Pond, K. (1989). Friends, Romans, countrymen, lend me your retrospections: Rhetoric and reality in personal relationships. In C. Hendrick (Ed.), *Close relationships* (pp. 17–38). Newbury Park, CA: Sage.

Floyd, K. (1997a). Affectionate communication in nonromantic relationships: Influences of communicator, relational, and contextual factors. *Western Journal of Communication, 61,* 279–298.

Floyd, K. (1997b). Communicating affection in dyadic relationships: An assessment of behavior and expectancies. *Communication Quarterly, 45,* 68–80.

Floyd, K., & Burgoon, J. K. (1999). Reacting to nonverbal expressions of liking: A test of interaction adaptation theory. *Communication Monographs, 66,* 219–239.

Floyd, K., & Morman, M. T. (1998). The measurement of affectionate communication. *Communication Quarterly, 46,* 144–162.

Floyd, K., & Morman, M. T. (2000). Reacting to the verbal expression of affection in same-sex interaction. *Southern Communication Journal, 65,* 287–299.

Friedman, H. S., Riggio, J. R. E., & Casella, D. F. (1988). Nonverbal skill, personal charisma, and initial attraction. *Personality and Social Psychology Bulletin, 14,* 203–211.

Goldsmith, D. J. (2000). Soliciting advice: The role of sequential placement in mitigating face threat. *Communication Monographs, 67,* 1–19.

Gudykunst, W. B. (1983). Uncertainty reduction and predictability of behavior in low and high context cultures. *Communication Quarterly, 31,* 49–55.

Gudykunst, W. B. (1985). The influence of cultural similarity, type of relationship and self-monitoring on uncertainty reduction processes. *Communication Monographs, 52,* 203–217.

Gudykunst, W. B. (1991). *Bridging differences: Effective intergroup communication.* Newbury Park, CA: Sage.

Gudykunst, W. B. (1993). Toward a theory of effective interpersonal and intergroup communication: An anxiety/uncertainty management (AUM) theory: Current status. In R. Wiseman (Ed.), *Intercultural communication theory* (pp. 8–58). Newbury Park, CA: Sage.

Gudykunst, W. B. (1995). Theorizing in intercultural communication. In R. L. Wiseman (Ed.), *Intercultural communication theory* (pp. 8–58). Thousand Oaks, CA: Sage.

Gudykunst, W. B., & Nishida, T. (1984). Individual and cultural influences on uncertainty reduction. *Communication Monographs, 51,* 23–36.

Gudykunst, W. B., & Nishida, T. (1989). Theoretical perspectives for studying intercultural communication. In M. Asante & W. Gudykunst (Eds.), *Handbook of international and intercultural communication* (pp. 17–46). Newbury Park, CA: Sage.

Gudykunst, W. B., Yang, S. M., & Nishida, T. (1985). A cross-cultural test of uncertainty reduction theory: Comparisons of acquaintances, friends, and dating relationships in Japan, Korea, and the United States. *Human Communication Research, 11,* 407–454.

Guerrero, L. K. (1996). Attachment-style differences in intimacy and involvement: A test of the four-category model. *Communication Monographs, 63,* 269–292.

Guerrero, L. K., & Afifi, W. A. (1999). Toward a goal-oriented approach for understanding communicative responses to jealousy. *Western Journal of Communication, 63,* 216–248.

Guerrero, L. K., & Eloy, S. V. (1992). Relationship satisfaction and jealousy across marital types. *Communication Reports, 5,* 23–41.

Guerrero, L. K., Jones, S. M., & Burgoon, J. K. (2000). Responses to nonverbal intimacy change in romantic dyads: Effects of behavioral valence and degree of behavioral change on nonverbal and verbal reactions. *Communication Monographs, 67,* 325–346.

Hample, D., & Dallinger, J. M. (1998). On the etiology of the rebuff phenomenon: Why are persuasive messages less polite after rebuffs? *Communication Studies, 49,* 305–321.

Harwood, J., McKee, J., & Lin, M-C. (2000). Younger and older adults' schematic representations of intergenerational communication. *Communication Monographs, 67,* 20–41.

Hastings, S. O. (2000). Self-disclosure and identity management by bereaved parents. *Communication Studies, 51,* 352–371.

Hause, K. S., & Pearson, J. C. (1994, November). *The ebb and flow of marriage: Relational dialectics over the family life cycle.* Paper presented at the meeting of the Speech Communication Association, New Orleans, LA.

Hetsroni, A. & Bloch, L-R. (1999). Choosing the right mate when everyone is watching: Cultural and sex differences in television dating games. *Communication Quarterly, 47,* 315–332.

Homans, G. C. (1961). *Social behavior: Its elementary forms.* New York: Harcourt Brace Jovanovich.

Hosman, L. A., & Tardy, C. H. (1980). Self-disclosure and reciprocity in short- and long-term relationships: An experimental study of evaluational and attributional consequences. *Communication Quarterly, 28,* 20–29.

Hullett, C. R., & Tamborini, R. (2001). When I'm within my rights: An expectancy-based model of actor evaluative and behavioral responses to compliance-resistance strategies. *Communication Studies, 52,* 1–16.

Ifert, D. E., & Roloff, M. E. (1997). Overcoming expressed obstacles to compliance: The role of sensitivity to the expressions of others and ability to modify self-presentation. *Communication Quarterly, 45,* 55–67.

Jourard, S. M. (1964). *The transparent self: Self-disclosure and well-being.* New York: Van Nostrand Reinhold.

Kellerman, K., & Reynolds, R. (1990). When ignorance is bliss: The role of motivation to reduce uncertainty in uncertainty reduction theory. *Human Communication Research, 17,* 5–75.

Kelley, D. L. (1998). The communication of forgiveness. *Communication Studies, 49,* 255–271.

Kim, Y. (1988). *Communication and cross cultural adaptation.* Philadelphia: Multilingual Matters.

Kim, Y. (1995). Cross cultural adaptation: An integrated theory. In R. Wiseman (Ed.), *Intercultural communication theory.* Newbury Park, CA: Sage.

Kim, Y., & Gudykunst, W. (Eds.) (1988). *Cross cultural adaptation: Current approaches.* Newbury Park, CA: Sage.

Knapp, M. L., & Vangelisti, A. L. (2000). Interpersonal communication and human relationships. (4th ed.) Boston: Allyn and Bacon.

Knobloch, L. K., & Solomon, D. H. (1999). Measuring the sources and content of relational uncertainty. *Communication Studies, 50,* 261–278.

Le Poire, B. A., Haynes, J., Driscoll, J., Driver, B. N., Wheelis, T. F., Hyde, M. K., Prochaska, M., & Ramos, L. (1997). Attachment as a function of parental and partner approach-avoidance tendencies. *Human Communication Research, 23,* 413–441.

LePoire, B. A., & Yoshimura, S. M. (1999). The effects of expectancies and actual communication on nonverbal adaptation and communication outcomes: A test of interaction adaptation theory. *Communication Monographs, 66,* 1–30.

Levine, T. R., & Boster, F. J. (2001). The effects of power and message variables on compliance. *Communication Monographs, 68,* 28–48.

Levine, T. R., Park, H. S., & McCornack, S. A. (1999). Accuracy in detecting truths and lies: Documenting the "Veracity Effect." *Communication Monographs, 66,* 125–144.

Lowrey-Hart, R., & Pearson, J. C. (1997, November). *There is a war inside of me between my blackness and your whiteness: Understanding the African American student experience in higher education through a relational dialectic perspective.* Paper presented at the meeting of the National Communication Association, Chicago, IL.

Lucchetti, A. E. (1999). Deception in disclosing one's sexual history: Safe-sex avoidance or ignorance? *Communication Quarterly, 47,* 300–314.

Ma, R., & Chuang, R. (2001). Persuasion strategies of Chinese college students in interpersonal contexts. *Southern Communication Journal, 66,* 267–278.

MacGeorge, E. L. (2001). Support providers' interaction goals: The influence of attributions and emotions. *Communication Monographs, 68,* 72–97.

Marshall, L. J., & Levy, V. M., Jr. (1998). The development of children's perceptions of obstacles in compliance-gaining interactions. *Communication Studies, 49,* 342–357.

Martin, M. M., & Anderson, C. M. (1997). Aggressive communication traits: How similar are young adults and their parents in argumentativeness, assertiveness, and verbal aggressiveness. *Western Journal of Communication, 61,* 299–314.

McCroskey, J. C., & McCain, T. A. (1974). The measurement of interpersonal attraction. *Speech Monographs, 41,* 267–276.

McGee, E. A. (1982). *Too little, too late: Services for teenage parents.* New York: Ford Foundation.

Mead, G. H. (1934). *Mind, self, and society.* Chicago: University of Chicago Press.

Miller, G. R. (1976). *Explorations in interpersonal communication.* Beverly Hills, CA: Sage.

Miller, G. R. (1978). The current status of theory and research in interpersonal communication. *Human Communication Research, 4,* 164–178.

Miller, G. R., Boster, F. J., Roloff, M. E., & Seibold, D. (1977). Compliance-gaining message strategies: A typology and some findings concerning effects of situational differences. *Communication Monographs, 44,* 37–51.

Miller, G. R., & Steinberg, M. (1975). *Between people: A new analysis of interpersonal communication.* Chicago: Science Research Associates.

Miller, M. A. (1998). The social process of drug resistance in a relational context. *Communication Studies, 49,* 358–375.

Montgomery, B. M., & Baxter, L. A. (Eds.). (1998). *Dialogism and relational dialectics.* Mahwah, NJ: Lawrence Erlbaum Associates.

Pavitt, C., & Kempt, B. (1999). Contextual and relational factors in interpersonal negotiation strategy choice. *Communication Quarterly, 47,* 133–150.

Pawlowski, D. R. (1998). Dialectic tensions in marital partners' accounts of their relationships. *Communication Quarterly, 46,* 396–412.

Pearce, W. B., & Sharp, S. M. (1973). Self-disclosing communication. *Journal of Communication, 23,* 409–425.

Pearson, J. C. (1983). *Interpersonal communication: Clarity, confidence, concern.* Glenview, IL: Scott, Foresman.

Pearson, J. C. (1996). Forty-forever years? Primary relationships and senior citizens. In N. Vanzetti & S. Duck (Eds.), *A lifetime of relationships* (pp. 383–405). Pacific Grove, CA: Brooks/Cole.

Pearson, J. C., & Spitzberg, B. H. (1990). *Interpersonal communication: Concepts, components, and contexts.* Dubuque, IA: William C. Brown.

Perse, E. M., & Rubin, R. B. (1989). Attribution in social and parasocial relationships. *Communication Research, 16,* 59–77.

Ragsdale, J. D. (1996). Gender, satisfaction level, and the use of relational maintenance strategies in marriage. *Communication Monographs, 63,* 354–369.

Richmond, V. P., McCroskey, J. C., & Roach, K. D. (1997). Communication and decision-making styles, power base usage, and satisfaction in marital dyads. *Communication Quarterly, 45,* 410–426.

Roloff, M. E., & Johnson, D. I. (2001). Reintroducing taboo topics: Antecedents and consequences of putting topics back on the table. *Communication Studies, 52,* 37–50.

Rosenfeld, L. B. (1979). Self-disclosure avoidance: Why I am afraid to tell you who I am. *Communication Monographs, 46,* 63–74.

Sabatelli, R. M., & Rubin, M. (1986). Nonverbal expressiveness and physical attractiveness as mediators of interpersonal perceptions. *Journal of Nonverbal Behavior, 10,* 120–133.

Saeki, M., & O'Keefe, B. (1994). Refusals and rejections: Designing messages to serve multiple goals. *Human Communication Research, 21,* 67–102.

Samp, J. A. (2001). Dependence power, severity appraisals, and communicative decisions aout problematic events in dating relationships. *Communication Studies, 52,* 17–36.

Schraeder, D. C. (1999). Goal complexity and the perceived competence of interpersonal influence messages. *Communication Studies, 50,* 188–202.

Schumacher, B. K., & Wheeless, L. R. (1997). Relationships of continuing uncertainty and state-receiver apprehension to information-seeking and predictions in dyadic interactions. *Communication Quarterly, 46,* 427–445.

Schutz, W. (1976). *The interpersonal underworld.* Palo Alto, CA: Science and Behavior Books.

Semic, B. A., & Canary, D. J. (1997). Trait argumentativeness, verbal aggressiveness, and minimally rational argument: An observational analysis of friendship discussions. *Communication Quarterly, 45,* 355–378.

Sheehy, G. (1976). *Passages: Predictable crises of adult life.* New York: Dutton.

Sias, P. M., & Cahill, D. J. (1998). From coworkers to friends: The development of peer friendships in the workplace. *Western Journal of Communication, 62,* 273–299.

Sillars, A., Shellen, W., McIntosh, A., & Pomegranate, M. (1997). Relational characteristics of language: Elaboration and differentiation in marital conversations. *Western Journal of Communication, 61,* 403–422.

Silverman, S. L., & Silverman, M. G. (1963). *Theory of relationships.* New York: Philosophical Library.

Singletary, M. (1999, February 21). The color of money. *The Washington Post,* pp. H1, H4.

Solomon, D. H. (1997). A developmental model of intimacy and date request explicitness. *Communication Monographs, 64,* 99–118.

Spitzberg, B. H., & Cupach, W. R. (1998). *The dark side of close relationships.* Mahwah, NJ: Lawrence Erlbaum Associates.

Stokes, J., Fuehrer, A., & Childs, L. (1980). Gender differences in self-disclosure to various target persons. *Journal of Counseling Psychology, 27,* 192–198.

Stone, D., Patton, B., & Heen, S. (1999). *Difficult conversations: How to discuss what matters most.* New York: Viking.

Sunnafrank, M. (1986). Predicted outcome value during initial interactions: A reformulation of uncertainty reduction theory. *Human Communication Research, 13,* 3–33.

Sunnafrank, M. (1990). Predicted outcome value and uncertainty reduction theories: A test of competing perspectives. *Human Communication Research, 17,* 76–103.

Thibaut, J. W., & Kelley, H. H. (1959). *The social psychology of groups.* New York: Wiley.

Vangelisti, A. L., & Crumley, L. P. (1998). Reactions to messages that hurt: The influence of relational contexts. *Communication Monographs, 65,* 173–196.

Vanzetti, N., & Duck, S. (Eds.). (1996). *A lifetime of relationships.* Pacific Grove, CA: Brooks/Cole.

Walster, E., Walster, G. W., & Berscheid, E. (1978). *Equity: Theory and research.* Boston: Allyn and Bacon.

Wilmot, W. W. (1980). *Dyadic communication* (2nd ed.). Reading, MA: Addison-Wesley, 1980.

Wilson, S. R. (1998). Introduction to the special issue on seeking and resisting compliance: The vitality of compliance-gaining research. *Communication Studies, 49,* 273–275.

Human beings draw close to one another by their common nature, but habits and customs keep them apart.

CONFUCIAN SAYING

Human culture without language is unthinkable.

CLYDE KLUCKHOHN

The thing I like most about Brooklyn is all the different people who live there. The thing I like least about Brooklyn is that these people do not get along with each other.

ELDERLY AFRICAN-AMERICAN

BROOKLYN RESIDENT

Intercultural Communication

What will you learn?

When you have read and thought about this chapter, you will be able to:

1. Explain why you should study intercultural communication.
2. Identify cultures and co-cultures.
3. Provide examples of co-cultural strategies.
4. Explain potential intercultural communication problems.
5. Identify broad cultural characteristics.
6. Practice strategies for improving communication with people from other cultures and co-cultures.

This chapter introduces you to communication between cultures and co-cultures. Being an effective communicator means interacting with people from various racial, ethnic, and cultural backgrounds. The goal of this chapter is to increase your confidence in your ability to communicate with people of other cultures and co-cultures. The chapter stresses the importance of communicating in an ever-changing world. The chapter also explains cultures and co-cultures, reveals strategies used by co-cultures to interact with dominant cultures, identifies broad characteristics of several cultures, and provides strategies for improving intercultural communication.

Teaching Tip
Take caution when exercising authority to assign students to study specific cultures or co-cultures. Forcing students to study groups could breed contempt and short-circuit the objective of the chapter. Allow students the opportunity to choose cultures and co-cultures they investigate for homework or class activities.

Anisa Puria's family is originally from India. Anisa was born there, but she lived there only until she was three years old, which is when Anisa and her family moved to the East African country of Tanzania. Now 18, Anisa and her family have lived in Tanzania ever since. Anisa is fluent in Hindi, English, and Swahili, the latter being the language of trade in East Africa. She still wears a sari (the traditional Indian dress) every day. Anisa is currently studying abroad in the United States. She isn't sure if it's the sari, her British accent, or her skin color, but Anisa has noticed that white American students rarely speak to her unless she speaks to them first. They seem unfamiliar with where Tanzania is, and they seem confused that a person of Indian origin would come from an African country.

Chris Johnson grew up in North Dakota, graduated from North Dakota State University and currently works for Midwest Software, a rapidly growing software company. As a technical specialist, Chris is frequently sent to other countries where his company's software is being used. Although he's only 26, he's already been to Austria, Germany, France, and Denmark. While Chris knows his company's software inside and out, communicating with people from a variety of countries isn't always easy for him. The language barrier is one issue, but not knowing a country's customs also puts him at a disadvantage. The next time he has to travel to another country, Chris plans to do some research about that country's customs prior to leaving. He also would like to learn a few basic words of the country's native language—*hello, goodbye,* and *computer* would be a good place to start.

Perhaps you, too, would be reluctant to talk to someone like Anisa. Maybe, like Chris, you will one day find yourself having to communicate with people from other cultures. You may even find communication difficult with co-cultures and social groups whose ways of thinking or behaving are different from your own. If so, this chapter may help you feel more confident communicating with people from different cultures and co-cultures.

Why Is the Study of Intercultural Communication Important?

intercultural communication

The exchange of information between individuals who are unalike culturally.

Rogers and Steinfatt (1999) define **intercultural communication** as *"the exchange of information between individuals who are unalike culturally."* Not long ago, intercultural communication involved only missionaries, jet-setting business executives, foreign correspondents, and some national political figures. Now, however, developments in technology and shifts in demographics have created a world in which intercultural communication is inevitable. Events on September 11, 2001, changed our perceptions of travel and of other cultures. Americans were surprised to find they were hated;

they soon discovered that most Americans knew little about Islamic religion, about predominantly Muslim countries, and about many nations in the area around Afghanistan. Intercultural communication is essential because of *our increasing exposure to people of other cultures and co-cultures.* More people are exposed to different global cultures through vacation travel, global jobs, international conflicts, military and humanitarian service, and the presence of immigrants, refugees, and new citizens. More people are also exposed to different co-cultures from ethnic groups, to neighborhood gangs, to partisan political groups, to gay and lesbian societies. Some of you will work and live every day with people different from yourself. Others of you will only occasionally encounter co-cultures or cultures with which you are unfamiliar. But in our modern world chances are excellent that you will need to know the basics of intercultural communication presented in this chapter.

A second reason for studying intercultural communication is *our economic need to relate to others.* Today we sell our corn, wheat, and cars in Asia, and we buy coffee from Colombia, bananas from Costa Rica, and oil from Africa, the Middle East, and South America. Our clothing comes from developing nations, our shoes are mostly made in third world countries, and your car may have been assembled in Germany, Hungary, Mexico, or Canada. Business that was previously domestic only is now global. The students of today will find themselves working with people from many different cultures because of our global economy.

A third reason to study intercultural communication is, simply, *our curiosity about others.* We are curious about people who don't look like us, sound like us, or live like us. We wonder why one woman always wears a long dress and veil, why another always walks five paces behind her spouse, why a man wears a turban, and why some people don't eat meat. We are curious about arranged marriages, rituals like funerals and weddings, and sports like sumo wrestling, kick boxing, and cricket. We express disbelief that fanatics in an otherwise peace-loving religion promise heaven to suicidal followers as a reward for murdering innocent people. We do not understand fanatics in our own country who stockpile weapons to attack our own government. Intercultural communication includes better understanding of cultural and co-cultural friends and enemies.

A fourth reason for an interest in intercultural communication is the *convergence of technologies.* For most of the twentieth century intercultural activity required an expensive flight or phone call. Now, people can communicate with each other around the world on the Internet. Phone, video, and audio merge into a system that can allow for sight and sound. Cellular phones, pagers, and handheld computers bring communication technology to your fingertips. The new technologies have transformed interpersonal and face-to-face communication.

Discussion Question

Ask students to discuss how the events of September 11, 2001, changed Americans' views on culture. Did we become more accepting of other cultures, more aware of other cultures, or did September 11 not affect our view on world culture?

Discussion Topic

Have students discuss their own experiences interacting with other cultures or co-cultures. Do any students have pen pals from other cultures?

Class Activity

Have students select co-cultures in the United States and present a group symposium on those co-cultures. The symposium should address the characteristics of each co-culture, how it differs from and interacts with the dominant culture, and any rituals or customs unique to the co-culture.

A fifth reason for an interest in intercultural communication is the *influx of foreign-born immigrants, aliens, and refugees that has changed the face of America.* One communication teacher from Los Angeles reported that his public-speaking class had students from 12 countries, and most spoke English as a second language. In metropolitan Washington, D.C., your waiter is from Colombia, South America, your cab driver is from Ethiopia, the porter is from the Sudan, the dry cleaner is from Korea, and the barber is a Vietnamese woman. The story is similar for Miami, New York City, Detroit, Chicago, and many other American cities. If not a melting pot, America is now and always was an exotic salad with many cultures contributing to its overall flavor. You can communicate better with people from other cultures if you know something about theirs.

What Are Cultures and Co-cultures?

culture

A system of shared beliefs, values, customs, behaviors, and artifacts that the members of a society use to cope with one another and with their world.

co-culture

A group whose beliefs or behaviors distinguish it from the larger culture of which it is a part and with which it shares numerous similarities.

Video Activity

Have students view the video segment "Sam's Graduation Party." Ask students to identify probable members of various co-cultures in the segment. Use this as an opportunity to discuss the fact that we all belong to some co-cultures (age groups, gender groups, etc.).

You have just learned that intercultural communication is the exchange of information between people of different cultures, but you may be uncertain about the definitions of culture and co-culture. **Culture** can be defined as *a system of shared beliefs, values, customs, behaviors, and rituals that the members of a society use to cope with one another and with their world.* Transmitted from generation to generation through social learning, culture is the mechanism that allows human beings to make sense of the world around them. Cultures include a wide variety of races, ethnic groups, and nationalities.

In the United States, a number of co-cultures exist based on language, race, religion, economics, age, gender, and sexual orientation. A **co-culture** is *a group that is similar to and part of the larger culture but is distinguished by beliefs and behaviors that differ from the larger culture.* Co-culture is used here because the word *subculture* implies that these groups are somehow inferior to the dominant culture. In the United States, where the dominant culture is white and Christian, examples of co-cultures are African Americans, Muslims, and gay or lesbian groups. These people experience a lifestyle or embrace a belief system that differs from that of the dominant culture. Note that an individual can belong to a number of co-cultures. A person can be, for example, Latino, adolescent, and a Libertarian.

Next we are going to explore some methods used by co-cultures to communication with dominant cultures. An example would be a gay male who works in an office with a dominant culture of straight men and women. What choices does that person have in relating to other workers? The next section explains passive, assertive, and aggressive strategies that lead to goals of separation, accommodation, or assimilation.

Co-cultural Strategies

Kramarae (1981) introduced "**muted group theory,**" the idea that *women were largely silenced by men when women's ideas were unvalued, underestimated, and sometimes unheard.* Since she introduced that idea much has been written about **marginalized groups,** *people who are made to feel like outsiders in the other people's world.* A white person in an African-American church, a gay male in the company of a group of heterosexual men, or a woman in a male-dominated board room are all examples of individuals who might feel transparent, irrelevant, silenced, or unheard.

Co-cultural identity is often indicated with artifacts.

For further insight on how muted, marginalized individuals communicate with people outside their particular group, we turn to a study by Mark Orbe (1996) in which he uncovered the strategies used by "nondominant groups:" "people of color, women, gays/lesbians/bisexuals, people with disabilities, lower/working class, and the young and elderly" (p. 158). Although the entire study cannot be covered here, we will look at some of the strategies used by nondominant, marginalized groups to communicate with the more privileged perspectives of European Americans, males, heterosexuals, able-bodied, youthful, middle/upper class, and/or Christian groups—the dominant culture in the United States (Folb, 1994 as quoted in Orbe, 1996).

TRY ◄►THIS

Think of times when you were a minority voice trying to communicate with a dominant culture (as a kid bargaining with parents, an employee negotiating with bosses, a debtor talking with someone about an unpaid bill, etc.). What strategies did you use in trying to get through to some group that actually had more power than you did?

The Goals of Co-cultural Communication Strategies

When individuals from nondominant groups have to contend with those from dominant groups, they ordinarily seek one or more of three outcomes: assimilation, accommodation, or separation. **Assimilation** in this context means that *the individuals from the nondominant group attempt to "fit in" the dominant group.* Examples would be dressing like others in the workplace,

muted group theory

The idea that women were largely silenced by men when women's ideas were unvalued, underestimated, and sometimes unheard.

marginalized groups

People who are made to feel like outsiders in the other people's world.

Discussion Question

What are examples of co-culture groups that attempt to assimilate, accommodate, and separate from the dominant U.S. culture?

assimilation

Individuals from the non-dominant group attempt to "fit in" the dominant group.

accommodation

The nondominant individual participates with the dominant group without losing his or her cultural identity.

separation

The nondominant individual resists interactions with the dominant group, preferring instead to relate more exclusively with his or her own group.

passive mode

An attempt to separate by having as little to do as possible with the dominant group.

avoidance

A conscious attempt not to engage with people in the dominant group.

assertive mode

Self-enhancing, expressive communiction that takes into account both self and others' needs.

utilization of liaisons

Relating to the dominant group through others with a shared cultural identity or with a trusted individual from the dominant group.

forgoing the earring at the company picnic, or talking about sports when you have no interest in them.

A second goal, **accommodation,** in this context means *not losing your cultural identity in participating with the dominant group.* The marginalized individual tries to maintain positive relationships with the dominant group without denying his or her membership in a nondominant group. The woman who makes no secret of her lesbian relationship brings her partner to the company picnic. The biker who wears his leathers to a community event, the fundamentalist Christian woman who does not cut her hair, and the Sikh who wears a turban and always has a beard are examples of people in American culture who are trying to relate without denying their nondominant cultural or co-cultural membership.

A third goal, **separation,** in this context means that *the nondominant individual resists interactions with the dominant group, preferring instead to relate more exclusively with his or her own group.* Examples are the gang members who relate only to each other, low-income individuals who relate almost exclusively to other low-income people, and individuals from a religious group that chooses to cloister, keep to themselves, and avoid contact with outsiders.

Co-cultural Communication Modes Categorized

Co-cultural communication modes for relating to the dominant culture tend to fall into three categories: passive, assertive, or aggressive. **Passive modes** are *an attempt to separate by having as little to do as possible with the dominant group.* An example of a passive strategy would be the youngest and newest employee who works at her desk all day but resists small talk, refuses to go out to lunch with the others, and keeps her own life as private as possible. This particular strategy, called **avoidance,** is *characterized by a conscious attempt not to engage with others in the dominant group.*

A second category of co-cultural communication is the **assertive mode,** which can be defined as *"self-enhancing, expressive communication that takes into account both self and others' needs"* (Orbe, 1996, p. 170). Just being yourself can be an assertive strategy for someone from a nondominant group. The black male who wears a dashiki to work is being assertive, as is the lesbian who might wear masculine-appearing attire. An example of an assertive strategy is **utilization of liaisons,** which means *relating to the dominant group through others with a shared cultural identity or with a trusted individual from the dominant group* (Orbe, 1996, p. 168). The employer knows that those in the low-paid, predominantly female secretarial pool are unified and bonded with each other through Professional Secretaries International, their organization. To pick on one unfairly could result in a decidedly chilly atmosphere around the office.

MODES	GOALS: SEPARATION	ACCOMMODATION	ASSIMILATION
PASSIVE	Avoidance Strategy		
ASSERTIVE		Utilizing Liaisons Strategy	
AGGRESSIVE			Confrontational Strategy

Figure 7.1   Approaches and goals of co-cultural communication (based on but not the same as Orbe's [1996, p. 171] configuration, which has more strategies and which places confrontation in the accommodation column).

The nondominant secretaries can reveal their needs to their employer in a shared responsibility manner because, in spite of a status difference, the nondominant group has some power by association.

A third category of co-cultural communication is the aggressive mode of relating to the dominant culture. The **aggressive mode** would include *"those behaviors perceived as hurtfully expressive, self-promoting, and assuming control over the choices of others"* (Orbe, 1996, p. 170). Aggressive strategies could be described as "in your face," an attempt to make others acknowledge your disability, your ethnicity, or your sexual preference. An example is **confrontational tactics,** or *belligerent attempts to make the dominant groups hear your position.* A blatant example occurred when the group known as Queer Nation, a radical gay organization, disrupted a formal, black-tie event in Manhattan by disrupting the celebration with their message to the group. They were forcefully ejected from the event. A more modest example would be the Asian woman who defies the stereotype of the passive Asian woman by insisting on answering questions and raising issues in every class. We classify these confrontational tactics under the assimilation goal because they are relatively extreme methods of making the dominant group recognize the voice of the marginalized. Figure 7.1 shows how the three modes—passive, assertive, and aggressive—relate to the three goals of co-cultural communication—separation, accommodation, and assimilation.

Discussion Question

What are some circumstances or examples where a co-culture group would want to engage in passive, assertive, and aggressive mode communication with the dominant culture?

aggressive mode

Those behaviors perceived as hurtfully expressive, self-promoting, and assuming control over the choices of others.

confrontational tactics

Belligerent attempts to make the dominant groups hear your position.

Video Activity

Ask students to view the video segment "The Right Kind of Care." To what extent did students think ethnocentrism played a role in Susan and her grandmother's reaction to Mr. Chamberlin and Ms. Min?

What Are Some Potential Intercultural Communication Problems?

Intercultural communication is subject to all the problems that can hamper effective interpersonal communication. However, several additional problems may occur during intercultural interactions. Becoming aware of these issues can help you avoid them or reduce their effects. Keep in mind that although the barriers identified here can be problematic, they do not occur in every exchange.

Ethnocentrism

The largest problem that occurs during intercultural communication is that people bring an ethnocentric perspective to the interaction. **Ethnocentrism** is *the belief that your own group or culture is superior to all other groups or cultures.* You are ethnocentric if you see and judge the rest of the world only from your own culture's perspective. Some common examples include thinking that everyone should speak English, that people in the United States should not have to learn languages other than English, that the U.S. culture is better than Mexico's, or that the Asian custom of bowing is odd (Dodd, 1998). To some extent, each of us operates from an ethnocentric perspective, but problems arise when we interpret and evaluate other cultures by the norms and standards of our own. Generally, a lack of interaction with another culture fosters high levels of ethnocentrism and encourages the notion that one culture is somehow superior to another. Ethnocentrism can create defensiveness on the part of the person who is being treated as if he or she is somehow deficient or inferior.

In ethnocentrism you use your own culture as the measure that others are expected to meet, whereas in **cultural relativism** you *judge another person's culture by its own context.* Saying that the Asian custom of bowing is odd overlooks the long history of bowing to one another as a sign of respect. To communicate effectively with people from different cultures, you need to accept people whose values and norms may be different from your own.

Stereotyping

Rogers and Steinfatt (1999) define a **stereotype** as *"a generalization about some group of people that oversimplifies their cultures."* In one way stereotyping is unavoidable. When you think of lawyers, physicians, gardeners, and homeless people, generalized images come to mind. Stereotyping becomes troublesome in communication when people make assumptions about an individual on the basis of simplified notions about the group to which he or she belongs. When you meet an attorney, do not assume that she is shady. When you meet an Asian, do not assume that he is good at math. When you meet a beautiful blonde, do not assume that she is empty-headed. Our assumptions get us in trouble when we apply to an individual what we guess to be true of a group. Such stereotypes are injurious to individuals and groups.

Allport (1958) noted that people are more likely to stereotype individuals and groups with whom they have little contact. It's easy to make unwarranted assumptions about people or groups; challenge yourself to learn more about people from cultures and co-cultures other than your own by getting to know them.

---

ethnocentrism

The belief that your own group or culture is superior to other groups or cultures.

cultural relativism

The belief that another culture should be judged by its context rather than measured against your own culture.

stereotype

A generalization about some group of people that oversimplifies their culture.

Discussion Question

Ask students to share stereotypes they have heard about Americans. After developing a list, ask students how these stereotypes make them feel.

Teaching Tip

The discussion of stereotypes can be difficult. Focusing on stereotypes of Americans rather than specific co-cultures can prevent some students from feeling uncomfortable.

What Are Some Characteristics of Different Cultures?

Accepting that your own culture is not superior to another person's culture is one way to improve intercultural communication. Another way is by understanding some of the values and norms of other cultures. For example, say you are an American teaching in Japan (a *collectivist* culture). Your students' first assignment is to give a speech before the class. After you give them the assignment, they automatically form groups and each group selects a spokesperson to give the speech. In the United States (an *individualistic* culture), students would be unlikely to turn a public-speaking assignment into a small-group activity, unless specifically directed to do so. If you didn't know something about the norms and customs of the Japanese culture, you might have been totally baffled by your students' behavior.

In this section you will learn about four characteristics of cultures: individualistic versus collectivist cultures, uncertainty-accepting versus uncertainty-rejecting cultures, implicit-rule versus explicit-rule cultures, and high-context versus low-context cultures. Keep in mind that the characteristics discussed here are general tendencies: They are not always true of a culture, and they are not true of everyone in a culture.

One student comes to mind. An ethnic Korean, his name was Schlumpberger. Adopted by a Minnesota family soon after birth, he had never been to Korea, had never spoken a word of Korean, and did not know much about Korea. He was a suburban American kid. Anyone who assumed that this student was Asian in any respect except appearance would have been incorrect, yet that assumption would have been easy to make based on appearance.

Individualistic versus Collectivist Cultures

Much of what is known about individualistic and collectivist cultures comes from a study by Hofstede (1980) that involved more than 100,000 managers from 40 countries (see Fig. 7.2). Although neither China nor Africa was included, the study is a classic in its comprehensiveness.

Individualistic cultures are *societies that value individual freedom, choice, uniqueness, and independence.* These cultures place "I" before "we" and value competition over cooperation, private property over public or state-owned property, personal behavior over group behavior, and individual opinion over what anyone else might think. In an individualistic society people are likely to leave the family home or the geographic area in which they were raised to pursue their dreams; their loyalty to an organization has qualifications; they move from job to job; and they may change churches that no longer meet their needs. Loyalty to other people has limits: Individualistic

Writing Assignment

Have students write an essay comparing and contrasting a collectivist culture with an individualistic culture. This assignment can be expanded to involve other cultural differences discussed in the text.

Video Activity

Ask students to view the video segment "The Right Kind of Care." Can students identify whether Mr. Chamberlin and Ms. Min likely came from individualistic or collectivist cultures? This same video segment could be analyzed for other elements of culture.

individualistic cultures

Cultures that value individual freedom, choice, uniqueness, and independence.

**CD-ROM
Activity**

Ask students to view
the animation titled
"Cultural Differences"
on the accompanying
student CD-ROM. The
animation explains
general differences
between cultures.

Teaching Tip

Point out that
understanding of
cultural differences
can increase the
awareness that rules
for communication
change from one
culture to the next.
Many students are
tempted to take this
information and
particularize it to
individuals of other
cultures. To point out
that people should be
treated as individuals
is important.

Individualistic cultures vs. Collectivist cultures

Individualistic cultures value individual freedom, choice, uniqueness, and independence, while collectivist cultures value the group, family, tribe, clan, and culture over the individual.

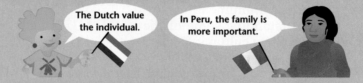

Low context cultures vs. High context cultures

Low context communication styles emphasize the source of communication, with intentions stated overtly. In high context cultures much of the information about the source, intentions, and other information is understood but not explicitly stated.

Uncertainty accepting cultures vs. Uncertainty rejecting cultures

Uncertainty accepting cultures are far more likely to tolerate ambiguity and diversity. Uncertainty rejecting cultures have a more difficult time accepting these things.

Implicit-rule cultures vs. Explicit-rule cultures

Implicit rules are implied rules for behavior in a culture and are "implicitly known" to all members of the culture. Explicit-rule cultures are more likely to openly discuss procedures for action and expectations for behavior.

Monochronic cultures vs. Polychronic cultures.

Monochronic cultures view time as compartmentalized between task, personal and social dimensions. Polychronic time cultures view time as culturally based and relationally oriented.

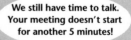

Figure 7.2   Cultural differences.

cultures have high levels of divorce and illegitimacy. According to the Hofstede (1980) study, the top-ranking individualistic cultures are the United States, Australia, Great Britain, Canada, and the Netherlands.

Collectivist cultures, on the other hand, *value the group over the individual.* These cultures place "we" before "I" and value commitment to family, tribe, and clan; their people tend to be loyal to spouse, employer, community, and country. Collectivist cultures place a higher value on cooperation than on competition and on group-defined social norms and duties than on personal opinion (Coleman, 1998). An ancient Confucian saying captures the spirit of collectivist cultures: "If one wants to establish himself, he should help others to establish themselves first." The highest-ranking collectivist cultures are Venezuela, Pakistan, Peru, Taiwan, and Thailand (Hofstede, 1980).

collectivist cultures

Cultures that value the group over the individual.

Low-Context versus High-Context Cultures

Hall (1976, 1983) enriched our understanding of collectivist and individualistic cultures when he defined low-context and high-context systems of communication. In **low-context (LC) cultures,** found most frequently in individualistic countries like the United States and Scandinavia, *communication tends to be centered on the source* ("I"), *with intentions stated overtly* ("I want you to consider buying this . . ."), *and with a direct verbal style* ("Get over here now!"). As Hall explained: "Most of the information must be in the transmitted message in order to make up for what is missing in the context" (1976, p. 101). Individual pride and

low-context (LC) cultures

Cultures like the United States and Scandinavia where communication tends to be centered on the source, with intentions stated overtly, and with a direct verbal style.

self-esteem, personal autonomy and power, and individual ego-based emotions enter the picture in LC communication patterns (Ting-Toomey, 1997).

high-context (HC) cultures

Cultures like those of the Asian Pacific Rim and Central and South America where much of the meaning is "preprogrammed information" understood by the receiver and transmitted also by the context in which the transaction occurs.

High-context (HC) cultures are more common in the Asian countries of the Pacific Rim as well as Central and South America, where *"only minimal information [is] in the transmitted message"* (Hall, 1976, p. 111). Instead, in HC communication much of *the meaning is "preprogrammed information" understood by the receiver and transmitted also by the setting in which the transaction occurs.* Who is invited to the table, where people sit, and what everyone knows is supposed to occur ahead of time are important features in HC communication.

Interestingly, all cultures have some concept of **face,** which reflects *people's need for a sense of self-respect in a communication situation* (Ting-Toomey, 1997). Even Americans use the expression "he lost face." But the concept of face appears to be even more important in collectivist cultures where "we" looms larger than "I." Communicators "lose face" and "gain face" differently in different cultures. In the United States, for example, a teacher would definitely lose face if a student proved the teacher wrong in the classroom in front of the other students. Former New York City mayor Rudolph Giuliani, an unpopular lame-duck politician with a lover and wife bringing him unflattering public attention, gained face in the aftermath of the September 11 terrorism attack with his intense dedication to the city's unprecedented problems. By October 1, 2001, he had "gained face" so much that he was addressing the United Nations, an occurrence that would have been regarded as unthinkable only weeks before.

face

People's need for a sense of self-respect in a communication situation.

Cohen (1991) points out the importance of face in collectivist, HC cultures. He writes: "Given the importance of face, the members of collectivist cultures are highly sensitive to the effect of what they say on others" (p. 26). He adds, "Language is a social instrument—a device for preserving and promoting social interests as much as a means for transmitting information" (p. 26). Americans observe that people from HC cultures are almost excessive in their praise for their receivers; exuberant in their courtesy; devoid of conflict, contradiction, and even directness; and practically never say a direct "no" to even an unreasonable request.

Uncertainty-Accepting versus Uncertainty-Rejecting Cultures

uncertainty-accepting cultures

Cultures that tolerate ambiguity, uncertainty, and diversity.

Uncertainty-accepting cultures *tolerate ambiguity, uncertainty, and diversity.* Some of these cultures already have a mixture of ethnic groups, religions, and races. They are more likely to accept political refugees, immigrants, and new citizens from other places. They are less likely to have a rule for everything and more likely to tolerate general principles. Uncertainty-accepting cultures include the United States, Great Britain,

LOSING FACE

With a group of classmates, consider together ways that people in our culture gain and lose face. What are the consequences of gaining or losing face? What usually happens to the person who has either gained or lost face?

Denmark, Sweden, Singapore, Hong Kong, Ireland, and India (Hofstede, 1980). Interestingly, Singapore is a country that is more tolerant of uncertainty and diversity but has many rules, including one prohibiting chewing gum. This oddity should serve as a reminder that these characteristics are generalizations and therefore are not found consistently in every culture.

Uncertainty-rejecting cultures *have difficulty with ambiguity, uncertainty, and diversity.* These cultures are more likely to have lots of rules; more likely to want to know exactly how to behave; and more likely to reject outsiders such as immigrants, refugees, and migrants who look and act differently than they do. Among the most common uncertainty-rejecting cultures are Japan, France, Spain, Greece, Portugal, Belgium, Peru, Chile, and Argentina (Samovar, Porter, & Stefani, 1998).

uncertainty-rejecting cultures

Cultures that have difficulty with ambiguity, uncertainty, and diversity.

Implicit-Rule versus Explicit-Rule Cultures

An **implicit-rule culture** is one in which *information and cultural rules are implied and already known to the participants.* For example, a traditional Arab woman knows one of the rules of her culture is that she is to walk a few paces behind her husband. People from an implicit-rule culture tend to be more polite, less aggressive, and more accommodating. Some implicit-rule cultures include the Middle East, Africa, and Latin America (Dodd, 1998).

An **explicit-rule culture** is one in which *information and cultural rules are explicit, procedures are explained, and expectations are discussed.* For example, in U.S. families, parents often discuss beforehand with their small children how the children are to act during a visit from someone of importance. People from an explicit-rule culture tend to be more combative, less willing to please, and less concerned about offending others. Some explicit-rule cultures are northern and western Europe and the United States (Dodd, 1998).

You might think about the difference between an implicit-rule culture and an explicit-rule culture in this way: In an implicit-rule culture the

implicit-rule culture

A culture in which information and cultural rules are implied and already known to the participants.

explicit-rule culture

A culture in which information and cultural rules are explicit, procedures are explained, and expectations are discussed.

social rules are part of who and what you are. They are learned over time from others and are no more discussed than washing your hands or brushing your teeth are in America. In an explicit-rule country, rules are often developed, discussed, and negotiated as you go along.

M-Time versus P-Time Cultures

The last intercultural characteristic we will consider here is another of Hall's (1983) concepts for differentiating among cultures of the world. **M-time,** or *monochronic time schedule, compartmentalizes time to meet personal needs, separates task and social dimensions, and points to the future* (Ting-Toomey, 1997). M-time is dominant in Canada, America, Northern Europe, and among German cultures. These cultures see time as something that can be compartmentalized, wasted, or saved. Americans might schedule times to work out, to meet individual appointments, to go to meetings, and to take the family to a fast-food restaurant. Time is segmented, dedicated to work or social experiences (but usually not both), and plotted toward future events and activities. Within this scheme, getting to any appointment on time is treated with considerable importance.

Hall's (1983) concept of **P-time** is an abbreviation for *polychronic time schedule, where a culture views time as "contextually based and relationally oriented"* (Ting-Toomey, 1997, p. 395). For P-time cultures time is not saved or wasted; instead, time is only one factor in a much larger and more complicated context. Why halt a conversation with an old friend to hurry off to an appointment on a relatively unimportant issue? Relationships in some contexts trump time considerations. P-time cultures orchestrate their relational and task obligations with the fluid movements of jazz, whereas M-time cultures strive mainly to stay on schedule, be efficient, and value tasks over relationships. Typical P-time cultures are Latin American, Middle Eastern, Asian, French, African, and Greek. America is predominantly M-time because of the strong European influence, but some co-cultures within the United States exhibit P-time tendencies.

Table 7.1 summarizes the eight concepts we discussed in this section. Most of the information is adapted from Carley Dodd's (1998) book entitled *Dynamics of Intercultural Communication.*

M-time

The monochronic time schedule, which compartmentalizes time to meet personal needs, separates task and social dimensions, and points to the future.

P-time

The polychronic time schedule, where a culture views time as "contextually based and relationally oriented."

Discussion Topic

What do you think happens when an M-time person lives in American culture? How can P-time people and M-time people negotiate this cultural difference in the way time is used?

TABLE 7.1   SUMMARY OF CULTURAL CHARACTERISTICS

INDIVIDUALISTIC VS. COLLECTIVIST CULTURES

INDIVIDUALISTIC CULTURES TEND TO:	COLLECTIVIST CULTURES TEND TO:
Value individual freedom; place "I" before "we."	Value the group over the individual; place "we" before "I."
Value independence.	Value commitment to family, tribe, and clan.
Value competition over cooperation.	Value cooperation over competition.
Value directness and clarity.	Value indirect communication.
Value telling the truth over sparing feelings.	Value "saving face" by not causing embarrassment.
Examples: United States, Australia, Great Britain, Canada, Netherlands	*Examples:* Venezuela, Pakistan, Peru, Taiwan, Thailand

UNCERTAINTY-ACCEPTING VS. UNCERTAINTY-REJECTING CULTURES

UNCERTAINTY-ACCEPTING CULTURES TEND TO:	UNCERTAINTY-REJECTING CULTURES TEND TO:
Be less threatened by ideas and people from outside.	Be threatened by ideas and people from outside.
Be willing to take risks in the face of uncertainty.	See uncertainty as a continuous hazard.
Avoid rules and seek flexibility.	Establish formal rules for behavior.
Dislike structure associated with hierarchy.	Prefer stability, hierarchy, and structure.
Prize initiative and doing things on one's own.	Seek agreement, consensus.
See truth as relative, and question authority.	Believe in absolute truths and expert authority.
Value individual opinion, general principles, and common sense.	Embrace written rules, planning, regulation, rituals, and ceremonies.
Examples: United States, Great Britain, Denmark, Sweden, Singapore, Hong Kong, Ireland, India	*Examples:* Japan, France, Spain, Greece, Portugal, Belgium, Peru, Chile, Argentina

IMPLICIT-RULE VS. EXPLICIT-RULE CULTURES

IMPLICIT-RULE CULTURES TEND TO:	EXPLICIT-RULE CULTURES TEND TO:
See cultural rules as implied, already known to participants.	See cultural rules as explicit; procedures are explained and discussed.
See an attack on an issue as an attack on the person; person and issue are perceived as one.	Person and issue are separate.
Prefer "saving face," the need to soothe an embarrassed or insulted person.	Expect communicators to be straightforward; people have to cope with embarrassment or insult.
Examples: Middle East, Africa, Latin America	*Examples:* Northern and Western Europe, United States

(Continued)

TABLE 7.1   CONCLUDED

Low-Context vs. High-Context Cultures	
Low-Context (LC) Cultures Tend to:	High-Context (HC) Cultures Tend to:
See communication as centered on the source, "I."	See communication as centered on the receiver.
State intentions overtly.	Approach subjects obliquely or even circuitously.
Employ a direct verbal style.	Load much of the meaning into the setting or context.
Load information into the transmitted message.	Treat language as a device for preserving and promoting social interests.
Reduce the importance of context.	Demonstrate considerable respect for the receiver.
	Avoid saying a direct "no" to a request.
Examples: United States, Western Europe, Scandinavia	*Examples:* Asian Pacific Rim, Central America, South America

M-Time vs. P-Time Cultures	
M-Time Cultures Tend to:	P-Time Cultures Tend to:
Compartmentalize time.	Factor in time as one element of a larger context.
Say that they can waste or save time.	Value social relationships and time considerations together.
Separate work and social time, task and relational time.	Orchestrate family and social responsibilities and task dimensions.
Point to the future.	Not see time as a commodity that can be saved, advanced, or wasted.
Examples: North America, Northern Europe, and Germany	*Examples:* Latin America, Middle East, Asia, France, Africa, and Greece

SOURCE: Based on Carley Dodd, *Dynamics of Intercultural Communication*, 4th ed. Copyright © 1998 The McGraw-Hill Companies, Inc. All Rights Reserved. Reprinted by permission.

What Are Some Strategies for Improving Intercultural Communication?

Effective intercultural communication often takes considerable time, energy, and commitment. Although some people would like "10 easy steps" to effective intercultural communication, no foolproof plan is available. However, the strategies presented here should provide you with some ways to improve intercultural communication and, we hope, avoid potential problems. Having some strategies in advance will prepare you for new situations with people from other cultures and co-cultures and will increase your confidence in your ability to communicate effectively with a variety of people.

1. *Conduct a personal self-assessment.* How do your own attitudes toward different cultures and co-cultures influence your communication with them? One of the first steps toward improving your intercultural communication skills is an honest assessment of your own communication style, beliefs, and prejudices.
2. *Practice supportive communication behaviors.* Supportive behaviors, such as empathy, encourage success in intercultural exchanges; defensive behaviors tend to hamper effectiveness.
3. *Develop sensitivity toward diversity.* One healthy communication perspective holds that you can learn something from all people. Diverse populations provide ample opportunity for learning. Take the time to learn about other cultures and co-cultures before a communication situation, but don't forget that you will also learn about others simply by taking a risk and talking to someone who is different from you. Challenge yourself. You may be surprised by what you learn.
4. *Avoid stereotypes.* Cultural generalizations go only so far; avoid making assumptions about another's culture, and get to know individuals for themselves.
5. *Avoid ethnocentrism.* You may know your own culture the best, but that familiarity does not make your culture superior to all others. You will learn more about the strengths and weaknesses of your own culture by learning more about others.
6. *Develop code sensitivity.* Developing **code sensitivity** means learning to *use the verbal and nonverbal language appropriate to the cultural or co-cultural norms of the individual with whom you are communicating.* When communicating with someone, be sensitive to the verbal and nonverbal language of that person's culture or co-culture. The more you know about another's culture, the better you will be at adapting.
7. *Seek shared codes.* A key ingredient in establishing shared codes is **tolerating ambiguity,** or *being open-minded about differences,* while you determine which communication style to adopt during intercultural communication.
8. *Use and encourage descriptive feedback.* Feedback encourages adaptation, and effective feedback is crucial in intercultural communication. During intercultural exchanges, both participants should be willing to

code sensitivity

The ability to use the verbal and nonverbal language appropriate to the cultural or co-cultural norms of the individual with whom you are communicating.

tolerating ambiguity

Being open-minded about differences.

Meeting and greeting is part of code sensitivity.

Writing Assignment

Have students write a short essay describing the top three ways they could improve their own intercultural communication competence. They should share their ideas with the class or group members.

accept feedback and exhibit supportive behaviors. Feedback should be immediate, honest, specific, and clear.

9. *Open communication channels.* Intercultural communication can be frustrating. One important strategy to follow during such interactions is to keep the lines of communication open.

10. *Manage conflicting beliefs and practices.* Think ahead about how you are going to handle minor and major differences from everyday behavior to seriously different practices like punishments (beheading, stoning), realities (starvation, extreme poverty), and beliefs (male superiority, female subjugation). See "Issues in Communication" at the end of this chapter.

TRY ◄►THIS

Try striking up a conversation with someone who is very unlike you by employing some of the strategies for improving intercultural communication. What assumptions did you make about the person before the conversation? What occurred in your conversation that either reinforced or challenged those assumptions?

Chapter Review

SUMMARY

In this chapter you have learned the following:

- The study of intercultural communication is important because
  - We are increasingly exposed to people of other cultures and co-cultures.
  - We have an economic need to relate to others.
  - We are curious about others.

- Co-cultures communicate with the dominant culture with different modes, goals, and strategies.
  - The three modes of communication employed by co-cultures are passive, assertive, and aggressive.
  - The three goals of co-cultural communication with the dominant culture are separation, accommodation, and assimilation.
  - Three strategies co-cultures use when communicating with the dominant culture are the passive/separation strategy called avoidance; the assertive/accommodation strategy called utilizing liaisons, and the aggressive/assimilation strategy called confrontational tactics.

- Ethnocentrism and stereotyping result in communication problems both in intercultural and co-cultural interactions.

- Cultural barriers can be reduced by learning the norms and values of other cultures.

- Cultures can be characterized by variations such as
  - Individualist versus collectivist cultures.
  - Low-context versus high-context cultures.
  - Uncertainty-accepting versus uncertainty-rejecting cultures.
  - Implicit-rule versus explicit-rule cultures.
  - M-time versus P-time cultures.

- You can strive to improve your own communication competence by
  - Conducting a personal self-assessment.
  - Practicing supportive communication behaviors.
  - Developing sensitivity toward diversity.
  - Avoiding stereotypes.
  - Avoiding ethnocentrism.
  - Developing code sensitivity.
  - Seeking shared codes.
  - Using descriptive feedback.
  - Opening communication channels.
  - Managing conflicting beliefs and practices.

⊙ VIDEO LINK: SUSAN ELLIOTT AND GRANDMA GO INTERCULTURAL

Video Episode 3: "The Right Kind of Care"

Culture is defined as a system of shared beliefs, values, customs, behaviors, and rituals that the members of a society use to cope with one another and with their world. This chapter discusses characteristics of world cultures including high versus low context, implicit versus explicit rules, and individual versus collectivist cultures. In "The Right Kind of Care," you meet Donell Chamberlin and Vivian Min. Observe their behaviors and try to characterize the type of culture they come from (note that individuals do not always exhibit all characteristics of their home culture). Do Susan Elliott and her grandmother exhibit intercultural communication competence? Why or why not?

ISSUES IN COMMUNICATION: THE ETHICAL DILEMMAS OF INTERCULTURAL COMMUNICATION

This Issues in Communication narrative is designed to provoke individual thought or discussion about concepts raised in the chapter.

Jo Dahveeto was a world traveler, but she was often troubled by different practices in different cultures. Some practices were positive and probably ought to be adopted by other cultures. The practice of giving gifts to guests, as is done in Thailand, Malaysia, and other Pacific Rim countries, would be an example.

Other practices were irritating but not very important. Chinese people, for example, crowd to the counter instead of lining up in an orderly fashion like Westerners are wont to do. And Caribbean, Central American, and South African drivers seemed to have only a vague sense of the center line on the road. Irritating, but not very important.

What really bothered her the most were practices that were acceptable and even encouraged in one culture but discouraged or even illegal in her own. Afghan women, for example, under the Taliban regime were not allowed to go to school, leave the home without a male escort, converse with an unrelated male, or go outside without being totally covered. An unmarried woman seen with an unrelated male could receive 100 lashes; a married woman with an unrelated male could be stoned to death. Young males were allowed to beat mature women who were thought to have disobeyed one of the many rules of behavior.

In parts of northern Africa and the Middle East women were subjected to female circumcision, a bit of surgery that Jo regarded as mutilation. In China people whose religion bothered the government authorities were punished and sometimes killed for their beliefs. Many countries around the world killed journalists and judges who were courageous enough to reveal damaging information or prosecute crimes.

The question that Jo faced in all her travels around the globe was how to relate—to communicate—with individuals from other cultures when those cultures were violating human rights. Should she visit only Western-style democracies? Should she let her international hosts know her position on human rights? What was her responsibility as a citizen of the world to relate to cultures unlike her own?

Apply what you have learned about intercultural communication as you ponder and discuss what Americans can or should do when faced with practices, major and minor, that violate their sense of fairness, justice, or human rights. What would you do as a visitor to a culture that practiced measures with which you disagreed?

KEY TERMS

Use the *Human Communication* CD-ROM and the *Online Learning Center* at www.mhhe.com/pearson to further your understanding of the following terminology.

Accommodation
Aggressive mode
Assertive mode
Assimilation
Avoidance
Co-culture
Code sensitivity
Collectivist cultures
Confrontational tactics
Cultural relativism
Culture

Ethnocentrism
Explicit-rule culture
Face
High-context (HC) culture
Implicit-rule culture
Individualistic cultures
Intercultural communication
Low-context (LC) culture
Marginalized groups
M-time

Muted group theory
Passive mode
P-time
Separation
Stereotype
Tolerating ambiguity
Uncertainty-accepting cultures
Uncertainty-rejecting cultures
Utilization of liaisons

SELF-QUIZ

Go to the self-quizzes on the *Human Communication* CD-ROM and the *Online Learning Center* at www.mhhe.com/pearson to test your knowledge.

ADDITIONAL RESOURCES

Bradford, L., Meyers, R. A., & Kane, K. (1999). Latino expectations of communicative competence: A focus group interview study. *Communication Quarterly, 47*(1), 98–117.

Martin, J. N., & Davis, O. I. (2001). Conceptual foundations for teaching about whiteness in intercultural communication courses. *Communication Education, 50* (4), 298–313.

Race and Communication in America: On the thirtieth anniversary of the assassination of Rev. Martin Luther King, Jr. (1998). *The Southern Communication Journal, 63*(3), 181–260. Six articles on African-American culture.

Rogers, E. M., & Steinfatt, T. M. (1999). *Intercultural communication*. Prospect Heights, IL: Waveland Press.

REFERENCES

Allport, Gordon W. (1954/1958). *The nature of prejudice.* Cambridge, MA: Addison-Wesley/Garden City, NY: Doubleday.

Bradford, L., Meyers, R. A., & Kane, K. (1999). Latino expectations of communicative competence: A focus group interview study. *Communication Quarterly, 47*(1), 98–117.

Cohen, R. (1991). *Negotiating across cultures: Communication obstacles in international diplomacy.* Washington, DC: U.S. Institute of Peace.

Coleman, D. (1998, December 22). The group and self: New focus on a cultural rift. *The New York Times,* p. 40.

DeVito, J. A. (1986). *The communication handbook: A dictionary.* New York: Harper & Row.

Dodd, C. H. (1998). *Dynamics of intercultural communication* (5th ed.). New York: McGraw-Hill.

Folb, E. (1994). Who's got the room at the top? Issues of dominance and nondominance in intracultural communication. In L. A. Samovar & R. E. Porter (Eds.), *Intercultural communication: A reader* (pp. 119–127). Belmont, CA: Wadsworth.

Hall, E. T. (1976). *Beyond culture.* New York: Doubleday.

Hall, E. T. (1983). *The dance of life.* New York: Doubleday.

Hofstede, G. (1980). *Culture's consequences: International differences in work-related values.* Beverly Hills, CA: Sage.

Kramarae, C. (1981). *Women and men speaking.* Rowley, MA: Newbury House.

Martin, J. N., & Davis, O. I. ((2001). Conceptual foundations for teaching about whiteness in intercultural communication courses. *Communication Education, 50* (4), 298–313.

Orbe, M. P. (1996). Laying the foundation for co-cultural communication theory: An inductive approach to studying "nondominant" communication strategies and the factors that influence them. *Communication Studies, 47,* 157–176.

Race and Communication in America: On the thirtieth anniversary of the assassination of Rev. Martin Luther King, Jr. (1998). *The Southern Communication Journal, 63*(3), 181–260.

Rogers, E. M., & Steinfatt, T. M. (1999). *Intercultural communication.* Prospect Heights, IL: Waveland Press.

Samovar, L. A., Porter, R. E., & Stefani, L. A. (1998). *Communication between cultures* (3rd ed.). Belmont, CA: Wadsworth.

Ting-Toomey, (1997). Managing intercultural conflicts effectively. In L. A. Samovar & R. E. Porter (Eds.), *Intercultural communication: A reader* (8th ed., pp. 392–404). Belmont, CA: Wadsworth.

CHAPTER EIGHT

Chance favors only the mind that is prepared.

LOUIS PASTEUR

What you are stands over you the while, and thunders so that I cannot hear what you say to the contrary.

RALPH WALDO EMERSON

Even in the meanest sorts of Labor, the whole soul of a man is composed into a kind of real harmony the instant he sets himself to work.

THOMAS CARLYLE

Interviewing

What will you learn?

When you have read and thought about this chapter, you will be able to:

1. Distinguish an interview from other communication contexts.
2. Discuss common elements of interviews.
3. Identify the different types of questions used in interviews and how to sequence them.
4. Write credentials for employment interviews.
5. Describe and utilize effective strategies for employment interviews.

Interviews take place in many settings—some of which are not immediately apparent. When was the last time you visited a doctor? Did the appointment begin by the doctor asking you questions? What about the last time you met with your adviser? Did she ask you how your courses were going? Interviews come in many forms. In this chapter we introduce you to general fundamental skills involved in interviewing and also discuss effective strategies for employment selection interviews and informative probing interviews.

Corell had been employed at SuperBuy for one year. Although most new employees moved through several departments during their first year, Corell found his niche in the computer department selling computers and peripheral devices to customers. Although SuperBuy does not pay commission to its sales associates, Corell had quickly become one of the top salespeople in the department.

Because he had been in the store for one year, Corell's performance appraisal interview was due. As part of that process, the assistant manager in charge of sales shadowed Corell for two hours, listening in on conversations he had with customers as well as watching him perform other job duties like merchandizing and completing paperwork. Corell was a little nervous, but he just tried to act natural. Midway through the first hour of his shift he noticed an older couple walk into the computer area; company policy is to greet every customer in your department, so Corell approached the couple.

"Hello folks, my name is Corell. Can I help you find anything?"

The man looked uncomfortable; however, the woman spoke up: "We are thinking about buying a computer for our home and just wanted to look around a little."

Corell sensed from her answer that the two did not know exactly what they were looking for and decided to ask a few questions. "Do the two of you currently own a computer?" This time the man answered.

"No, and I am not sure we can really afford one. These all look so expensive and we'll probably end up putting it in the storage room!"

Corell knew at this point that the couple probably did not know much about computers but that they had a specific reason for looking for one. "Have the two of you thought much about what you want to use the computer for? Are there any things that you specifically want to do with it?"

The woman responded. "Our daughter just had a baby, but they live in Vermont. We won't be able to get out there real often, but she said she could send us pictures every day if we could get e-mail. So, I told William here that we should look into getting one." This answer helped Corell out quite a bit. He knew that the couple could get a great computer for a very reasonable price if all they needed was Internet access for sending e-mail and looking at pictures.

"I think I might have something you would be interested in. This system over here is actually one of our more modest systems—you can see that it is under $800— but it is perfect for Internet because of the modem and it will also let you look at and print out pictures with the packaged software. Even better, the system comes with a color printer so you can print out all of those pictures and put them in frames."

William responded, "Well, that price tag is a lot better! We might be able to do that after all!" Corell figured at this point that he was going to make the sale. More important, he knew that the assistant manager looking over his shoulder would be impressed. Many of the other associates would have tried to take advantage of the couple by showing them a larger computer than they needed. By asking a few simple questions, Corell unearthed all of the information he needed to find a computer matching what the couple needed.

Why Is Interviewing a Context of Communication?

Interviewing is a form of interpersonal communication that involves the sending and receiving of messages. According to *Merriam-Webster's Collegiate Dictionary* (2001), the word *interview* derives from the French *entrevue, entrevoir* ("to see one another," "to meet"). Culturally, we have come to understand an **interview** as *a dyadic communication context with a purpose or goal.* In an interview, two parties—a dyad—communicate in a preplanned situation, primarily by asking and answering questions. We use the term *two parties* to indicate that although interviews may involve two or more *people* (a doctor interviewing a patient, two police officers interviewing a suspect, a landlord interviewing three potential tenants), they never involve more than two *parties*—an interviewer party and an interviewee party. In the story at the beginning of this chapter, Corell was one party involved in an interview and the older couple purchasing the computer were the other party. The story also noted that Corell was soon to take part in an appraisal interview with his supervisor. That example illustrates the pervasiveness of interviews in our lives. The interview context, like other interpersonal interactions, normally involves a face-to-face encounter, although interviewing increasingly occurs through e-mail, videoconferencing, and the telephone.

interview

A dyadic communication context with a purpose or goal.

Discussion Question

Ask students to identify the different types of interviews they have experienced as either an interviewer or interviewee. If ideas reflect a narrow identification of interviews (e.g., job interviews), encourage them to consider health care encounters, collecting evidence for a term paper, and buying a car as examples of interview situations.

How Do Interviews Differ from Other Interpersonal Interactions?

Interviews are different from other interpersonal encounters in several important ways. First, interviews are conducted to achieve specific goals. Other interpersonal interactions may have underlying objectives as well, but in an interview, the purpose is more clearly stated and understood by both parties. In fact, interviews can be classified according to their functions (Goyer, Redding, & Rickey, 1968). This functional perspective highlights the (1) information giving, (2) information seeking, and (3) persuasive objectives of interviews. The primary function of some interviews is to inform, whereas other interviews are intended to elicit facts, attitudes, and feelings. If the goal of an interview is to persuade, the participants attempt to influence the perception of the other party and to induce some sort of change. Obviously, some elements of information giving, information seeking, and persuasion are present in all interviews, but often a primary function predominates.

Second, interviews are often more structured than informal conversations as the interviewer usually has a preestablished agenda that guides the interaction. Thus interviews are more prepared than informal conversations. Typically, both interviewer and interviewee carefully prepare prior to the interview. Finally, the sequence of the interview is more predictable than most interpersonal encounters. The interviewer usually selects topics and asks questions while the interviewee typically provides responses.

Discussion Question

Ask students to discuss how the relationship dimensions of control, inclusion, and affection may differ between interviews conducted face-to-face versus interviews conducted online. Students can also discuss how they might prepare differently for online interviews.

Asking and answering questions is the primary mode of communication in interviews.

The Fundamentals of Interviewing

Whether an interview is for employment selection or for diagnosing an illness, all interviews share certain characteristics. In this section, we describe the basic interview fundamentals by discussing the structure of an interview, the types of questions you can ask, and how you can organize questions.

Video Activity

Ask students to view the video segment "The Right Kind of Care." Did students think Susan and her grandmother used the direct, indirect, or combined approach to interviewing?

Structuring the Interview

Like effective written communication, an interview is structured logically, with (1) an opening, (2) a body, (3) a closing organized in such a way as to establish the overall message and to make sense of the interaction (Fontana & Frey, 1998).

The Opening

The primary function of the opening of an interview is to motivate participation, so what you say and how you say it at the beginning set the tone for the interaction. Interviewers should (1) introduce themselves properly, (2) establish some rapport with the respondent, (3) identify the purpose of the interview, and (4) provide an orientation to the interview. This process reduces what is known as **relational uncertainty,** *a state of suspicion or doubt* (Knapp, 1978). If respondents know what to expect during an interview, they will be more trusting and more likely to relax and concentrate on the process of answering questions. An incomplete interview

relational uncertainty

A state of suspicion or doubt.

opening can create an atmosphere of distrust that may prevail through-out the entire interview. Furthermore, the interviewer will want to establish the purpose of the interview at the outset, as illustrated in these sample openings:

> "Mary, I'm John Smythe from the Citizens' Action Coalition, and I would like 10 minutes of your time to get your input on the proposed utility rate hike."

> "Good evening. I'm John Smythe from the Citizens' Action Coalition. Your next-door neighbor suggested you might be willing to participate in a brief interview about the proposed utility rate hike that is coming up. We could really use your help."

What you state as the purpose for the interview should reflect the appropriate appeal to the particular respondent; otherwise, cooperation may not result. For example, if John Smythe was an executive with the utility company, the "rate hike" topic would have no appeal for him.

The Body

The best method for organizing the body of an interview is to develop *an outline of topics and subtopics to be covered.* This outline then becomes your **interview guide** (Fontana & Frey, 1998). Interview guides remind interviewers to cover all important topics. You will want to arrange your interview guide in a logical fashion that permits you to investigate all critical areas.

After completing an interview guide, the interviewer may choose to develop additional structure for the interview. The outline provided by the guide can be developed into a more elaborate document, an interview schedule. An **interview schedule** *contains major questions and follow-up questions; the schedule is a useful tool in keeping the interview focused on the topic or issue of concern.* The schedule is usually a list of questions that can be developed into a manuscript allowing the interviewer to write out arguments or instructions to be used in the interview.

Both an interview guide and schedule can be used during the interview to record answers and after the interview to recall information. Each interviewer needs to decide what format is necessary and sufficient based on the context of the interview. Interview schedules are typically used when replication across interviews is important, as is the case with research interviews and employment interviews.

The Closing

Effectively closing an interview requires as much thought as does opening and organizing the interview. An abrupt ending can hinder the professional relationships involved. Thus, recognizing the functions of the closing as well as verbal and nonverbal strategies for accomplishing these functions is

---

Video Activity

Ask students to view the video segment "The Right Kind of Care." How could Susan and her grandmother have handled the opening of the interview to further reduce relational uncertainty? Did Mr. Chamberlin or Ms. Min appear to have more uncertainty?

interview guide

An outline of topics and subtopics to be covered.

interview schedule

A list of major questions and follow-up questions; the schedule is a useful tool in keeping the interview focused on the topic or issue of concern.

Classroom Activity

Prior to class, have students develop an interview schedule for the position of resident assistant (RA) for one of the college dormitories. During class, pair students up and have them interview their partners for the position.

important. The functions of interview closings can be described as (1) concluding, (2) summarizing, and (3) supporting (Fontana & Frey, 1998).

First, **closings** *indicate the termination of the interview.* You are probably familiar with some of the more subtle signals that a meeting is concluding. For instance, when someone says "Well. . . ," you may be about to be dismissed. Similarly, if one party looks at a clock on the wall, the other can anticipate that "time is up." Standing up, straightening in your seat, leaning forward, moving away from the other party, breaking eye contact, and offering to shake hands are clearly nonverbal cues that the interaction is coming to a close.

Effective closure to an interview also includes a summary of the interview itself. Summaries repeat key information and agreements and verify the accuracy of information, if necessary. Finally, interviewers should provide support in an interview closing, including an expression of appreciation for participation in the interview as well as an orientation to future decision making or actions. Setting the groundwork for future contacts is important if appropriate.

Expressing appreciation, summarizing the interview, and planning for another meeting are verbal indications that a participant intends to close the interview. In an ideal interview closing, both parties understand the signals and respond appropriately. In the worst-case scenario, one participant feels rushed or offended, and the closing negates any positive, productive results achieved so far. Thus, be aware of the importance of closing an interview effectively.

Types of Questions

Asking and answering questions make up an integral part of an interview. Questions are the instruments that drive the interview process; they help govern the flow of information exchange. The efficiency of that process depends in large measure on the types of questions used in the interview.

Questions can take many forms and be characterized by several dimensions. Basically, questions can be (1) open or closed, (2) primary or secondary, (3) neutral or leading, and (4) hypothetical or behaviorally based.

Open and Closed Questions

Open questions *permit freedom in the length and nature of the response,* whereas **closed questions** *restrict the response, often asking for specific information or supplying answer options from which the respondent chooses.* A subcategory of the closed question is a **bipolar question,** which is *a question that limits answer options to two choices.* The follow-

---

closings

Stage of an interview indicating its termination.

Video Activity

Ask students to view the video segment "The Right Kind of Care." Have students identify various types of question used during the two interviews.

open question

A question worded to permit freedom in the length and nature of the response.

closed question

A question worded to restrict the response, often asking for specific information or supplying answer options from which the respondent chooses.

bipolar question

A question that limits answer options to two choices.

ing examples illustrate how differently you can word questions about a single topic:

> *Open question:* "What do you know about our company?"
>
> *Closed question:* "In your opinion, what word best describes our company?"
>
> *Bipolar question:* "Do you know anything about our company?" (Invites a "yes" or "no" response.)

Primary and Secondary Questions

The second characteristic of a question is whether it is primary or secondary. **Primary questions** are used to *introduce areas of inquiry and are coherent in themselves,* whereas **secondary questions** are used to *pursue the trail of information discovered in the response to a previous primary question.* Think of a secondary question as a device to probe for further information or to clarify what has been said. The value of a secondary question is that, by using follow-up questions, the interviewer is less likely to form false conclusions about a topic and is more likely to find useful, accurate information. The types of secondary questions that can assist an interviewer are the clearinghouse question, nudging question, reflective question, and informational question. The **clearinghouse question** is used to *assure an interviewer that all essential information is provided.* The **nudging question** is used to *motivate further interaction.* The **reflective question** is used to *verify information* when accuracy is a concern, and the **informational question** is used to *clarify an answer that appears to be vague or superficial.* Table 8.1 illustrates these four types of secondary questions.

Some additional tactics that can assist an interviewer in getting information are to rephrase the question in slightly different words, to restate the question, and to use what is known as a silent probe. To use a **silent probe** simply means *to refrain from saying anything for a brief time, letting*

primary question

A question that introduces areas of inquiry and is coherent in itself.

secondary question

A question that pursues the trail of information discovered in the response to a previous question.

clearinghouse question

A question worded to assure an interviewer that all essential information is provided.

nudging question

A question that motivates further interaction.

reflective question

A question that verifies information when accuracy is a concern.

informational question

A question worded to clarify an answer that appears to be vague or superficial.

silent probes

To refrain from saying anything for a brief time, letting the respondent fill in the silence.

TABLE 8.1 EXAMPLES OF SECONDARY QUESTIONS	
TYPES OF SECONDARY QUESTIONS	SAMPLE QUESTIONS
Clearinghouse question	What else do you want me to know?
Nudging question	And then what did you do?
Reflective question	So, you think you'll go to the party after all?
Informational question	Tell me a little about that . . .

the respondent fill in the silence. These tactics, along with the four types of secondary questions, should prove useful to interviewers in many interview contexts.

Neutral and Leading Questions

neutral question

A question that requires an answer consistent with candidates' positions on an issue, with their beliefs, with their attitudes and values, or with the facts as they know them.

Neutral questions *permit respondents to provide an answer consistent with their position on an issue, with their beliefs, with their attitudes and values, or with the facts as they know them.* Interviewers use **leading questions** *to elicit a particular response from an interviewee.* The wording of a question usually suggests the direction of the answer. Obviously, a leading question can be intentional or unintentional, but interviewers and respondents should know that the content of the question has the potential for bias. The examples in Table 8.2 indicate how differences in phrasing can influence the quality of a response.

leading question

A question worded to elicit a particular response from an interviewee.

Hypothetical or Behaviorally Based Questions

hypothetical question

A question that requires the interviewee to describe how he or she would behave in specific situations.

Hypothetical questions *require interviewees to describe how they would behave in specific situations.* In employment interviews, for instance, hypothetical questions are based on the Critical Incident Technique (CIT) of job analysis, which calls for examples of unusually effective or ineffective job behaviors for a particular job (Byars & Rue, 2000). These incidences are converted into interview questions that describe a situation and then require the interviewee to discuss how he or she would handle that hypothetical situation.

behaviorally based question

A question that focuses on an applicant's past actions and behaviors to determine how he or she will perform in the future.

Many companies today use behavioral-style questions. **Behaviorally based questions,** also referred to as targeted-selection questions, *focus on an applicant's past actions and behaviors to determine how he or she will perform in the future* (Byars & Rue, 2000). Rather than relying on an

TABLE 8.2 NEUTRAL AND LEADING QUESTIONS	
NEUTRAL QUESTIONS	LEADING QUESTIONS
What is your opinion of unionized organizations?	Do you agree with other interviewees that unions are beneficial for employees?
What do you think about the new federal budget?	Don't you think senior citizens will be harmed by the new federal budget?
How does this product compare with what you normally purchase?	Surely you would agree that this product is superior to any other, wouldn't you?

interviewee's opinion of how she or he would handle a "what if" situation, behaviorally based questions require interviewees to talk about specific situations they have encountered in the past and how they handled those situations. The following examples illustrate the difference between hypothetical and behaviorally based questions:

> *Hypothetical question:* "A customer comes into the store to pick up a printer she left for repair. The repair was supposed to have been completed a week ago and is still not done. The customer is very angry. How would you handle the situation?"

> *Behaviorally based question:* "Sooner or later we all have to deal with a customer who is angry. Think of a time when you had to handle an unreasonable request. Describe that situation. What did you do?"

Table 8.3 provides examples of targeted-selection questions that are often used in employment interviews. Employers support behaviorally based interviews because they have found that past behaviors predict future behaviors. Hypothetical questions focus on how interviewees would handle a particular situation, whereas behavioral questions focus on how they did handle particular situations.

An understanding of how to structure the interview and develop and organize questions is relevant to a variety of interviews, including persuasive interviews, appraisal interviews, exit interviews, counseling interviews, and health care interviews. The employment interview is probably the most important for college students, and so these are covered in-depth in the remaining sections of this chapter.

Classroom Activity

In groups of four or five, have students come up with a series of bona fide occupational qualifications (BFOQs) for a management position (e.g., time management skills, ability to lead meetings). Next, have students develop both hypothetical and behaviorally based questions that address these BFOQs.

TABLE 8.3   EXAMPLES OF BEHAVIORALLY BASED QUESTIONS

Can you provide me with an example of when you worked extra hard and felt a great sense of accomplishment?

What are some examples of spur-of-the-moment decisions that you have made? Why did you make them so quickly?

Can you think of a change in an organization you were or are a member of which your peers would recognize as resulting principally from an innovation you developed or a change you suggested?

Recall a time when you had to call on others for assistance to resolve a problem. How did you gain their help or cooperation?

Can you give me an example of when you volunteered to help work on some tasks that were not necessarily your regularly assigned responsibilities?

Employment Interviews

Students spend years pursuing a formal education and developing special skills that will enable them to function in their chosen careers. Unfortunately, they often believe that proof of that education and skill is all that is required to get the "ideal job." In fact, getting a job is work in itself. Self-knowledge and the ability to express what you believe to be true about yourself are essential in an interview. You should have a clear understanding of the career field in which you plan to spend your productive years, as well as some insight into the effect that current social and economic conditions may have on that field. Background information about the company or organization for which you would like to work and the position for which you are applying is also a factor to consider before the interview. Next, we will consider these issues as well as how to prepare for and participate in an interview as well as postinterview strategies.

What Is Anticipatory Socialization?

anticipatory socialization

Process through which individuals develop a set of expectations and beliefs concerning how people communicate in particular occupations and in formal and informal work settings.

Before applying for a job or entering a specific organization, most of us undergo the process of **anticipatory socialization** to *develop a set of expectations and beliefs concerning how people communicate in particular occupations and in formal and informal work settings* (Jablin, 2001). In fact, learning how to work in a position begins in early childhood.

An important component of anticipatory socialization is self-concept. The most widely accepted approaches to anticipatory socialization suggest that as individuals mature from childhood to young adulthood, they are gathering occupational information from the environment, comparing this information against their self-concept, and weighing alternatives involved in choosing an occupation and a specific job (Jablin, 2001). Thus a self-inventory is an important component of any job search.

Self-Inventory

What do you really know about yourself? When was the last time you took inventory of your assets and liabilities? Could you express these qualities intelligently? Answers to these questions are essential when you are preparing for a job-seeking interview. One way of approaching this difficult task is to ask yourself what your friends, family, and coworkers would say about you. What words would they use to describe you, and why? What successes and failures would they attribute to you? Why do you need this self-assessment just to get a job? The answer is simply that you cannot talk intelligently about yourself if you do not know much about yourself.

In an employment interview, no one speaks for you but you. No one knows your best features better than you do, and no one will benefit from your description of those assets more than you will. As an intelligent interviewee, you must begin your preparation for a job search with a thorough assessment of your skills, interests, attributes, and achievements. Although not exclusive of other possible areas to explore, consider tallying the following:

1. Your work and educational experiences.
2. Your motivations and goals.
3. Your strengths and weaknesses.
4. Your likes and dislikes.
5. Your skills.
6. Roles you played in campus extracurricular activities.
7. What, if any, professional experience you have had (including co-op programs and internships).
8. Your interests and hobbies.
9. Your talents, aptitudes, and achievements.
10. What is important to you in a position and an organization.

Be thorough in your analysis so that when you get ready to participate in a job-seeking interview, you will be able to define and describe the benefits you can bring to an organization. Ideally, you should then be able to summarize what you know about yourself in a single, detailed answer to the most commonly used first question in an employment interview: "Tell me about yourself."

On your journey to self-awareness, know that resources are available to help you. Most college campuses have career counseling centers dedicated to helping you better understand your passions and skills as well as offering information about potential career paths. The Riley Guide at www.dbm.com/jobguide/jsguides.html has a good summary of career counseling sites available on the Internet.

Discussion Question
Ask students to talk about the various socializing agents that have influenced the development of their understanding of particular professions (e.g., media, family, school). Next, have students identify stereotypes that exist about communication in particular professions (e.g., doctors use jargon that patients often misunderstand).

TRY ◄►THIS

Several online career counseling sites provide numerous resources including interactive tests to give you an idea about possible career directions and articles dealing with various career issues. In his text Job-Hunting on the Internet, Richard Bolles (1999) recommends John Holland's SDS (Self-Directed Search), which can be accessed at www.self-directed-search.com. Go to this link and complete the interactive career test.

Conducting a Job Search

After you have reflected on your career interests and abilities, you can embark on the exciting, sometimes frustrating, journey of a job search. The U.S. job market has more than 16,000,000 employers. How do you get access to those employers who are hiring? According to Richard Bolles (2000) in *What Color Is Your Parachute?*, the conventional job-hunting methods of networking, using placement offices on college campuses, and job agencies have the highest rates of success. Thanks to technological advances, we can now add another job-hunting method: electronic job banks. An aggressive job-hunting approach uses all available methods.

network

An intricate web of contacts and relationships designed to benefit the participants.

A **network** is *an intricate web of contacts and relationships designed to benefit the participants*—including identifying leads and giving referrals (Bolles, 2000). To begin networking, you can conduct information-seeking interviews with people who do what you would like to do, successful people from your chosen field, people who have access to information you need, and people who have access to other people you want to contact. If these interviews go well, you may glean information about the career, job, or specific company in which you are interested; an evaluation of your career goals, résumé, interviewing skills; and names of other people you can contact for further information.

Information about job vacancies is readily available through classified ads, placement offices on college campuses, and job agencies. Additionally, "job listings," also known as "job postings," are available online. Be warned, however, that online searches are most fruitful for those looking for computer-related jobs (Bolles, 1999). In fact, Bolles estimates that for individuals searching for non–computer-related jobs, only 3 out of 100 will find a job using online methods.

Situational Knowledge

To present yourself as a mature candidate for employment for any job, you will want to illustrate your knowledge of your chosen field, the effect of current social and economic conditions, and the trends that are occurring in the field. Beyond your socialization experiences, this information is available in newspapers and periodicals. You will want to keep current on all aspects of the career field. Employers will view you more positively if you are conversant on these issues.

Writing Assignment

Have students write a one-page job description for a position. Students should outline the basic job duties as well as BFOQs for the position.

You should have a comprehensive understanding of the organization to which you are applying. You should be familiar with the current information on company officers, products or services that are offered, geographical locations, and potential mergers, acquisitions, and expansion plans.

It is important for you to be very familiar with the job description for the position for which you are applying. As indicated earlier, through anticipatory socialization we come to understand the general responsibilities associated with occupations in our culture. However, nearly all organizations rely on official documents—job descriptions—to make business-related decisions, including hiring employees. A **job description** *defines the job in terms of its content and scope*. Although the format can vary, job descriptions may include information on job duties and responsibilities; the knowledge, skills, and abilities necessary to accomplish the

job description

A document that defines the job in terms of its content and scope.

ONLINE JOB SEARCHES

One key to success with online searching is using regional job sites that allow you to focus your efforts by geographic location, including international destinations. Job resources by U.S. region are available at **www.wm.edu/csrv/career/stualum/jregion.html**. Job resources organized by international regions are available at the WWW Employment Office, **www.harbornet.com/biz/office/annex.html**; the famous Monster Board, **www.monster.com**; and the Jobspace Database, **www.jobspace.com**.

Another key to success is using online job listings from state employment services offices. America's Job Bank (**www.ajb.dni.us/**) is maintained by the U.S. Public Employment Service and links 1,800 state employment service offices in the United States.

Finally, through various online sites you can access job listings from newspaper classified ads. The following websites allow you to search daily classified ads from newspapers across the country:

www.careerpath.com
www.jobbankusa.com/news1.html
www.gallery.uunet.be/internetpress/link40.htm
www.newslink.org/new.html
www.nationaladsearch.com

duties; working conditions; relationships with coworkers, supervisors, and external stakeholders; and the extent of supervision required.

Because of Equal Employment Opportunity Legislation (EEO laws; see page 257), job descriptions are the cornerstone to employment-related decisions in our culture. Everything that is asked and answered during employment interviews should relate back to the bona fide occupation qualifications (BFOQs; see page 257) necessary to perform the job as outlined in the job description. Therefore, you must have a realistic concept of the duties and responsibilities associated with the position and be able to discuss how your training, experience, and skills are compatible with the requirements for the position. Often you can obtain a copy of the job description for an employment vacancy through the human resource office of the organization. You may also be able to find this background information in annual reports or recruitment literature. If neither is available to you, make use of the library resources in your community or on your university campus or check the organization's website.

Active Art

Self Inventory

- Work and education
- Skills
- Talents and achievements
- Interests and hobbies
- Motivation and goals

Conducting the Job Search

- College career and placement office
- Newspapers and trade journal advertisements
- On-line job searches
- Networking

Gaining Situational Knowledge

- Finding information about your career field
- On-line research about companies
- Job descriptions

Preparing Written Materials

- Cover letter
- Resume
- Professional portfolio

Interviewing for the Job

- Pre-planning
- Demonstrating interpersonal communication competence
- Asking appropriate questions
- Answering questions effectively

Post Interview

- Carefully evaluate job offer
- Send a letter of appreciation

Figure 8.1   The employment interview process.

How Do You Prepare Written Credentials?

The written presentation of your credentials functions to gain the attention of interviewers. As you are creating your résumé and cover letter, remember that the purpose of employment interviews is to make decisions about the degree of fit between people and jobs. Collectively, your credentials should illustrate your ability to successfully do the job.

Résumés

Writing a résumé is a project that takes time and effort. We encourage you to view the process of compiling a résumé as an investment that pays off in numerous ways. The soul-searching involved with creating a résumé functions to focus your life accomplishments and future goals. A résumé puts you into employment databases and, if it is successful, lands you interviews. Résumés also serve employers in numerous ways. Résumés allow employers to predict the future performance of job candidates, simplify the hiring process, and serve as a reference source for the postinterview period (Henricks, 2000). To successfully create a résumé, you must consider style, content, and format.

Style   The **style** of a résumé deals with *the overall tone created by your linguistic and aesthetic choices.* We recommend that the style of your résumé reflect your personality in a concise and professional way, be confident but not arrogant, and accurately highlight your credentials. Next, we provide several stylistic suggestions and illustrate them in the sample résumé provided in Figure 8.2.

style

The overall tone created by your linguistic and aesthetic choices.

First, to write résumés using complete sentences and the pronoun "I" is unnecessary. Descriptive clauses are sufficient as long as they are understandable. Many experts recommend beginning descriptive clauses with action verbs such as *planned, supervised,* and *conducted* (Henricks, 2000). These words catch employers' attention because they are concrete and indicate what you have done. Some commonly used action verbs are listed in Table 8.4. Should you use past- or present-tense verbs? The tense depends on whether you are currently performing the particular job duties. Use present-tense verbs for present employment and activities, and use past-tense verbs for presenting historical information.

Whenever possible, you should quantify information. The following examples illustrate how to quantify information to illustrate the scope of your accomplishments: (1) managed a $30,000 budget for Lambda Chi Alpha, (2) supervised 10 customer service representatives, and (3) increased sales by 200 percent. Employers look for accomplishments like these because they are concrete, measurable, and significant.

Be consistent. Whenever you make stylistic decisions, be consistent. If you are going to use bullets to present your job duties, use bullets throughout your résumé. If you choose to put a period at the end of your

Discussion Topic

Ask students to critique the résumé pictured in Figure 8.2 based on the text's discussion of style, content, and format of résumés.

140014 35th St South   701-236-8769
Fargo, ND 58103   jonesma@umd.edu

Madeliene Clair Jones

Objective   To obtain a position in web design providing quality service to
non-profit organizations.

Experience   1999—Present   Ignus, Inc   Omaha, NE
Web Designer

- Plan and create websites.
- Scan, resize, and optimize all graphics.
- Attend sales meetings with clients and sales representatives.
- Suggest changes for sites of prospective clients

1997–1999   Butler Machinery Company   Omaha, NE
Office Assistant

- Updated and maintained the machine inventory on company website.
- Performed miscellaneous office duties including typing, faxing, and mailing.
- Implemented training course for 20 new employees.

1996–1997   Mail Boxes Etc   Ohama, NE
Senior Sales Representative

- Packaged and shipped out packages for UPS, USPS, and FedEx.
- Sorted mail.
- Facilitated monetary transactions.
- Scanned pictures for company website.

Education   1996–2000   Creighton University   Omaha, NE

- B.A., Business Administration and Computer Science.
- Graduated Summa Cum Laude.
- GPA 3.85.

Skills   Proficient in HTML Language, Microsoft Access, Adobe
Photoshop, Microsoft Outlook, Fireworks, PhotoEditor, Internet
Explorer, C++ Language, Microsoft Excel, PowerPoint, Word,
Dreamweaver, and GoldMine Mktg.

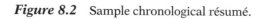

Figure 8.2   Sample chronological résumé.

TABLE 8.4   ACTION VERBS FOR RÉSUMÉS

Accomplished	Formulated	Ordered	Succeeded
Adapted	Generated	Participated	Supervised
Administered	Handled	Performed	Supplied
Analyzed	Headed	Persuaded	Supported
Balanced	Identified	Prepared	Tabulated
Disbursed	Managed	Revised	Uploaded
Examined	Modified	Searched	Verified
Executed	Notified	Selected	Volunteered
Explained	Obtained	Sponsored	Won
Filed	Offered	Streamlined	Wrote

bulleted descriptions, make sure you consistently use periods. If you indent one job title five spaces and underline, make sure all your job titles are indented five spaces and underlined.

Be concise. Remember that you do not have to put everything in a résumé. In fact, view your résumé as an appetizer. You can tell about the main course in the interview. Unless you have more than seven years of work experience, most experts agree that your résumé should not be longer than one page (Henricks, 2000).

Be neat. Given that employers have very limited time to spend reading your résumé, the overall impression it creates is important. Employers judge you and your capabilities based in part on the physical appearance of your résumé. Poorly proofread, sloppy documents are difficult to ignore and will decrease your chances at securing an interview.

Content   The content of résumés for college students typically includes contact information as well as your objectives, education, experience, skills, and campus activities or community involvement. Without contact information, the rest of your résumé is useless. On every résumé you send out, you must include complete information about how to contact you, including an e-mail address.

An **objective statement,** or *an articulation of your goals,* is usually the first information on the résumé, just below your contact information. Objective statements are important because they allow you to tailor your credentials and goals to the needs of a particular organization and job description (Crosby, 1999). In addition to describing your personal goals, you should consider what the organization needs or what types of issues

objective statement

An articulation of your goals.

it faces when you are writing your objective statement. The following are examples of objective statements:

Example 1: To apply programming skills in an environment with short deadlines and demanding customers.

Example 2: To achieve consistent improvement in sales profitability of units under my supervision.

Employers also want to see your educational credentials. They do not necessarily believe that your college professors taught you everything you need to know to succeed at their company. Rather, your credentials show that you had the intellect to go to college, the determination to complete high school, and the capability of learning new things and finishing complex projects. In summarizing your education, you should include degrees awarded, completion dates (or anticipated completion dates), schools attended, majors and minors, and honors or scholarships. Employers always look at your education, but the further along you are in your career, the smaller the role your education plays on your résumé. Instead, experience becomes more important.

With few exceptions, employers will focus much of their attention on your past jobs, whether you are a freshly minted college graduate or an experienced individual changing jobs or careers. Employers look at the types of jobs you have held, job tenure, job duties, and accomplishments. When describing your work experience, make sure you include a job title, name of the organization, dates of employment, and a description of your major responsibilities and achievements. Remember to use action verbs and quantify accomplishments whenever possible.

Most résumés also include a skills section highlighting abilities ranging from being able to use Microsoft Word to fluency in multiple languages. The skills section of your resume should be tailored to the job description of the position for which you are applying.

Many college students end their résumé with a discussion of their campus activities and/or community involvement. When discussing membership in groups, do not stop at merely listing the group. Rather, indicate your level of involvement, including participation on committees and leadership positions. Involvement in campus and community organizations is important because involvement translates, in the mind of many employers, to workplace citizenship.

Format   Now that you are familiar with stylistic and content choices, you need to consider how to organize information on your résumé. College students typically rely on chronological, functional, and/or online formats.

chronological résumé

A document that organizes credentials over time.

The **chronological résumé,** which *organizes your credentials over time,* is what most people envision when they think of a résumé. A résumé based on time has long been the standard and, despite technological advances allowing for electronic résumés, continues to be the most widely accepted format (Henricks, 2000). The core concept of the chronological résumé is accomplishments over time. To refer to a résumé as "reverse chronological" would be more appropriate, because in describing your work experience (and education), you begin with your last or present job and continue back to past jobs. Figure 8.2 is an example of a chronological résumé.

Whereas the chronological format organizes your experience based on "when" you acquired it, the **functional résumé** *organizes your experience by type of function performed.* If you have had a variety of jobs (e.g., teaching, sales, advertising), the functional résumé allows you to group jobs by the skills developed and duties performed. Graduating college students will use a functional résumé to group "professional experience" separately from "other work experience," which may include jobs that do not directly relate to your career goal but nonetheless illustrate your work ethic.

The impact of the Internet is evident in many facets of our lives, including our professional roles. For that reason, you may need to have an **online résumé,** *prepared in plain text (ASCII), hypertext markup language (HTML), or another format and posted on the Web.* Plain text résumés have limited formatting options. For instance, you cannot center, bold, or italicize text. Résumés that use HTML formatting can include all sorts of fancy formatting. As more advanced technologies develop, other ways of transmitting résumés online will emerge. For more information on creating electronic résumés, we suggest that you consult several online sites that describe how to create an electronic résumé as identified in the accompanying e-note.

functional résumé

A document that organizes credentials by type of function performed.

online résumé

A résumé in plain text (ASCII) or in hypertext language (HTML) and posted on the Web.

Cover Letters

A **cover letter** is *a short letter introducing you and your résumé to an interviewer,* and it typically accompanies your résumé. Cover letters are persuasive documents that function as an introduction, sales pitch, and overview of your qualifications as related to the job description. Cover letters are important because they help ensure that your résumé is read and help target your appeal for a particular job. As with any persuasive document, a cover letter has four main sections: (1) attention, (2) interest, (3) desire, and (4) action (Krizan, Merrier, & Jones, 2002).

After headings that contain your address and the interviewer's address, your cover letter should gain the attention of the reader. At this point, you should indicate the position for which you are applying, indicate how you heard about the position, and provide a general overview of your qualifications. In paragraph two, you need to arouse the reader's interest and demonstrate your desire for the job. At this point, you want to describe your major experiences and strengths as they relate to the job. If possible, mention one or two accomplishments that illustrate your proficiency and effectiveness. The main idea is to create interest and show how your skills and qualifications can be of value to the organization.

cover letter

A short letter introducing you and your résumé to an interviewer.

You can refer the reader to the enclosed résumé for more detail on your qualifications and experience. In the third paragraph, you need to suggest action. Restate your interest in the position or organization and your desire for a face-to-face meeting. Finally, express your appreciation for the reader's time and/or consideration.

When writing a résumé, you rarely use full sentences or poetic flair. A cover letter, however, provides an opportunity to demonstrate your writing skills. The design attributes of your cover letter should be consistent with your résumé, including typefaces, font sizes, line spacing, and paper choice. Figure 8.3 provides a conventional outline for generating a cover letter.

What Are Some Interviewing Strategies?

Preplanning

The best way for applicants to prepare for their role in job-seeking interviews is to know what employers seek in applicants and how they find pertinent information. Remember, the major purpose of the interview is to obtain and synthesize information about the abilities of an individual and the requirements of the job. The best way to plan for a successful interview is to review the job description and information about the organization, familiarize yourself with current events affecting the particular industry and/or job, reflect on your experiences and skills as related to the job description, and prepare answers to important questions.

In preparing answers to potential interview questions, remember that questions are tailored to the job description at hand and ascertaining candidates' abilities to accomplish job duties.

HEADING
Name
Address
City, State, Zip Code
Phone
e-mail address

INSIDE ADDRESS   **DATE**
Name, Title
Department, Organization
Address
City, State, Zip Code

SALUTATION: Use title and last name if available (e.g., Dear Dr. Smith or Dear Ms. Jones). Do not use a first name unless you know the person well and are sure this is acceptable. If you do not have a name, use the title (e.g., Dear Employment Manager).

PARAGRAPH I: Gain *attention* and state purpose—indicate the position or type of work for which you are applying. Mention how you heard about the opening or the organization. You may also want to provide a general overview of your qualifications for the position (functions as a preview statement for your letter).

PARAGRAPH II: Arouse *interest* and demonstrate *desire*—summarize qualifications and describe enclosure. Here you want to describe your major strengths as they relate to the position you are seeking. If possible, mention one or two recent accomplishments that illustrate your proficiency and effectiveness. The main idea is to create interest and show how your skills and qualifications can be of value to the organization. Refer the reader to the enclosed résumé for more detail on your qualifications and experience.

PARAGRAPH III: Suggest *action*. Restate your strong interest in the position or organization and your desire for a face-to-face meeting. Include a statement about how the reader may contact you. Finally, express your appreciation for the reader's time and/or consideration.

COMPLIMENTARY CLOSE (Sincerely yours,)

(Leave 3 blank lines)

NAME

POSTSCRIPT (Enclosure; Enc.)

Figure 8.3   Generic format for a cover letter.

Think, Pair, Share

PRACTICING FOR THE INTERVIEW

Practice answering these typical job interview questions with a partner.

Why would you like to work for us?

What do you know about our products or services?

How have your previous work positions prepared you for this experience?

What do you think your previous supervisors would cite as your strengths? Weaknesses?

Describe a typical strategy that you would use in a customer service call.

What criteria do you use when assigning work to others?

How do you follow up on work assigned to others?

Which aspect of your education has prepared you most for this position?

Which course did you like most in college?

If you had your education to do over again, what would you do differently and why?

Why did you choose _____ as your major?

What do you think is the greatest challenge facing your field today?

Which area of your field do you think will expand the most in the next few years?

Practicing competent responses to potential questions is an important method of managing anxiety that is normally experienced by interviewees. Mentally talk to yourself prior to the interview. Build your confidence by telling yourself that you have done all you can to prepare for the interview. You have anticipated questions and have prepared answers; you have learned about the company. You are ready for the interview.

Demonstrate Interpersonal Communication Competence

During the interview, you must present yourself as a potential asset to the organization. Doing so requires using verbal and nonverbal communication to (1) create a good first impression, (2) speak with clarity, and (3) demonstrate interest.

Just as your written credentials should reflect a professional and competent image, so should you. One of the most obvious ways to create a good first impression is by the way you dress. The general rule is that you should match the style of dress of the interviewer. For professional positions, conservative dress is typically appropriate (dark suits, white shirts or blouses, standard ties for men, dark socks or neutral hose, dark shoes).

Be sure to wear clothes that fit and are comfortable but not too casual. Be modest with your use of jewelry and cologne.

Arriving on time and introducing yourself in a courteous manner are also important to impression management. Allow the interviewer to take the lead. If an offer is made to shake hands, do so with a firm grip and a smile. Sit when asked to do so. Keep in mind, we are suggesting impression management techniques as a way to present yourself in a positive yet honest manner—not in a manipulative or dishonest manner.

First impressions occur the instant an interview begins.

Competent communicators speak with clarity. In one study of personnel interviewers' perceptions of applicants' communication skills, a lack of response clarity and poor grammar were among the most often cited communication inadequacies observed during employment interviews (Peterson, 1997). Yet 98 percent of respondents in Peterson's study, as well as other research (Ralston & Kirkwood, 1999; Rosenfeld, 1997) indicated that such skills affect hiring decisions. Even if you have to pause before responding, organize your answer and avoid slurring your words, using potentially offensive language, or using grammatically incorrect sentences. Many applicants do not convey clear messages because their sentences include vocalized pauses (uhs, ums), verbal fillers (you know), and repetitive phrases (things like that). In sum, the employment interview is a context to practice the skills you have been learning about and developing in this course.

To be interpersonally effective in interviews, you must demonstrate interest. One of the most important ways to demonstrate interest is by maintaining strong eye contact with the interviewer. Several studies have indicated that eye contact is one of the most important indicators of interview success (Burnett & Motowidlo, 1998; Peterson, 1997; Stevens & Kristoff, 1995). Although you may be tempted to focus on responding to questions as the central interviewing skills, listening can demonstrate your interest and improve your responses. Also, use body language to show interest. Smile, nod, and give nonverbal feedback to the interviewer. Be sure to thank the interviewer for his or her time and consideration of you as a candidate.

Video Activity

Ask students to view the video segment "The Right Kind of Care." Have students compare the relative effectiveness of Mr. Chamberlin and Ms. Min in terms of their answers to questions. How could either interviewee have been more effective answering questions?

Answer Questions Effectively

Answering questions effectively is critical for interviewees. Research has shown that various strategies are associated with successfully answering questions (Burnett & Motowidlo, 1998; Peterson, 1997; Stevens & Kristoff, 1995). Four key guidelines emerge from that body of research: (1) offer relevant answers, (2) substantiate your claims with evidence, (3) provide accurate answers, and (4) be positive.

Your answers should be relevant to the question asked and to the job description. As an interviewee, you should never evade questions but respond to them thoroughly and directly. In discussing your skills and abilities, try to relate them to the specific position for which you are interviewing. Whenever possible, specify how and why you think you are well suited to this job. By so doing, you demonstrate your knowledge of the position and illustrate the transferability of your knowledge and skills to the job at hand.

Whatever claims you make about your experience, always provide support. Some interviewees give terse, underdeveloped responses, forcing the interviewer to probe endlessly. Do not just say, "I'm really organized." You need to substantiate this self-assertion with examples of when you have demonstrated organizational skills effectively. Presenting claims without evidence can sound self-serving. If you offer evidence to support your assertions, the objective facts and examples will confirm your strengths.

All employers are searching for honest employees, so always provide accurate answers. If an employer finds out you have misrepresented yourself during the interview by exaggerating or lying, everything you do and say will become suspect. Interviews, if they are to be successful, must consist of candid conversation. If you are asked a question that you cannot answer, simply say so and do not act embarrassed. An interviewer has more respect for an interviewee who admits to ignorance than for one who tries to fake an answer.

Accuracy should not be confused as confessing to every self-doubt or shortcoming. In fact, be as positive as possible during interviews as you are "selling" yourself to the employer. To volunteer some limitations or claim personal responsibility for past events is fine, especially in the context of challenges you have met or problems you have encountered. However, avoid being overly critical of others and yourself. You can highlight your strengths and downplay your weaknesses, but always be honest.

Discussion Question

Ask students to come up with questions they would ask an interviewer if applying for internships in their field.

Ask Questions Effectively

Any employer will recognize that you have questions about the job and/or organizational environment. After answering the interviewer's questions, you should be prepared to ask questions. Asking questions provides you with insight necessary to decide if you want this particular job, shows your interest in the job, and demonstrates communication skills.

Recognize that your questions make indirect statements about your priorities, ambitions, and level of commitment. Subsequently, avoid overreliance on questions that focus on financial issues such as salary, vacation time, and benefits. Devise questions that elicit information about the company and/or job that you were unable to obtain through your research. Arrange questions so that the most important ones come first, because you may not get a chance to ask all of your prepared questions. Sample questions to ask employers are provided on the CD-ROM accompanying this text.

Be Prepared for Illegal Questions

Legally, employers must approach the hiring process with reference to the laws that govern employment. These laws are known as *equal employment opportunity (EEO) laws;* they are written and enacted by Congress and by individual state legislatures (Gutman, 2000). The purpose of such laws is to ensure that individuals are selected for employment without bias.

Employers should (1) describe the qualities and skills needed for the position they hope to fill, (2) construct questions that relate to those attributes, and (3) ask the same questions of all candidates for the position. These questions are known as *bona fide occupational qualification (BFOQ) questions.* BFOQ questions should be about skills, training, education, work experience, physical attributes, and personality traits. With rare exceptions, questions should not be about age, gender, race, religion, physical appearance, disabilities, ethnic group, or citizenship.

However, sometimes illegal questions are intentionally or unintentionally posed to interviewees. What should you do when asked an unlawful question? First, determine how important the position is to you. How much do you want and need the job? Second, determine the severity of the EEO violation. If the question is a minor violation and you want the job, consider tactfully refusing to answer or providing a brief answer. If the violation is extreme, consider not only refusing to answer the question but also reporting the interviewer to his superior or to employment agency authorities.

Discussion Topic

Before class, create several illegal job interview questions based on protected characteristics like gender, race, and age. Ask students to describe why these questions are inappropriate for job interviews. Additionally, talk with students about how they should handle illegal questions they may be asked in interviews.

What Is Involved in the Postinterview Stage?

Most interviews end with some plan for future action on the part of both the interviewee and interviewer. When the decision will be reached and how it will be communicated are usually specified by the interviewer. As an interviewee, make certain you carry out appropriate responsibilities, including writing to reconfirm your interest in the position and thanking the interviewer for his or her time. Additionally, you need to be prepared to deal with various interview outcomes.

A letter of appreciation is appropriate after an interview and should be sent within one or two days following the interview. If a company has been corresponding with you using e-mail, then you should send an e-mail thank-you letter. If you are still interested in the position, you should express that interest in the letter. If you are not interested in the position, a letter is still appropriate. In the latter case, in fairness to the employer, you should withdraw your candidacy.

After all employment interviews, you will have to deal with decision outcomes. When you receive an offer that you want to accept, reply within five days. To accept the offer, obtain any essential information about assuming the position, including salary and benefits, and express appreciation. The salary question is an important one. The employer may have set a salary or a salary range for the position. Before negotiating a salary offer, you should research salaries paid for similar jobs in the employer's geographic area (Porot, 2000). Your campus career center or the salary calculator website at www.homefair.com/homefair/cmr/salcalc.html are good sources for salary information. Be aware that a job offer and a written acceptance of that offer constitute a legally binding contract for both you and the employer. So before you write an acceptance letter, be sure you want the job.

You may find yourself in the position of rejecting a job offer. The best approach is to state the reasons for refusing the offer, decline the offer explicitly, and close on a pleasant note by expressing gratitude. By taking the time to write a sincere, tactful letter, you leave the door open for future contact.

One of the attractive features of mastering the employment interview is that its skills transfer nicely to other organizational interactions, including everyday conversations with supervisors and coworkers. Learning how to ask and answer questions during employment interviews is a skill that you can practice in a variety of settings, including probing interviews.

Class Activity

Before class, have students browse a salary calculator website for their chosen profession. During class, have students share information they discovered.

Chapter Review

SUMMARY

In this chapter you have learned the following:

- Interviewing is dyadic communication with a purpose. Unlike many other forms of communication, interviews are conducted to achieve specific goals including information giving, information seeking, and persuasion. Interviews are also more structured than other forms of communication because participants typically must prepare for the interview.

- All interviews, whether they are for employment selection or diagnosing an illness, share common elements. Basic considerations for all interviews include the structure of the interview, the types of questions used in the interview, and the organization of questions.

- Interview questions can be classified as open or closed questions, primary or secondary questions, neutral or leading questions and hypothetical or behaviorally based questions. The interview is structured with an opening, a body, and a closing. Most questions are asked during the body of the interview and are typically organized into an interview sched-

ule. Questions should be organized according to topics and subtopics to be covered during the interview.

- Written credentials for employment interviews include résumés and cover letters. The style of your résumé should reflect your personality and should be concise. The résumé should also quantify information whenever possible. The content of your résumé should identify your contact information, career objective, education and work experience, skills, campus involvement, and community involvement. The cover letter is a short statement introducing yourself and your résumé. The cover letter has four main sections: attention, interest, desire, and action.

- Effective strategies when preparing for employment interviews include preplanning for questions employers are likely to ask, demonstrating good interpersonal competence during the interview, answering questions effectively, asking questions effectively, and being prepared for illegal questions.

● VIDEO LINK: INTERVIEWS FROM BOTH SIDES OF THE DESK

Video Episodes 3 and 6: "The Right Kind of Care" and "Reporting for KTNT: Susan Elliott"

Preparing for and participating in a job interview is something we all do at various points in our work life. This chapter introduces you to several strategies for planning successful interview experiences. Watch "The Right Kind of Care" and "Reporting for KTNT: Susan Elliott." In "Reporting," what strategies does Susan use to prepare for her interview? What tips do you learn from her behaviors? Do the interviewees in "The Right Kind of Care" answer questions effectively? What types of questions do Susan Elliott and her grandmother ask? Are there strategies they could use to answer questions *more* effectively?

ISSUES IN COMMUNICATION: INTERVIEWING FOR A JOB

For many college students, the employment selection interview poses the greatest uncertainty. As noted in the chapter, a little preparation before the interview can ensure greater success. This Issues in Communication narrative is designed to provoke individual thought or discussion about concepts raised in the chapter. In particular, notice the types of questions asked by Kim, the interviewee, as well as the answers provided by Corell.

Corell had worked at SuperBuy for two years now. He enjoyed his job but wanted to find a position that paid more and offered greater opportunity for advancement. His adviser told him about an opening at a company called Creative Computer Solutions, and Corell decided to apply. He found the job listing and was also able to learn about the company by browsing the company's Web page. After sending his résumé and cover letter, Corell was invited for an interview.

Kim walked up to the young man sitting in the lobby. "Hello, my name is Kim Lang and I am the sales manager here. You must be Corell?"

"Hello. Yes, I am Corell Johnson. Thank you for seeing me today." Kim thought Corell seemed a little unsure of himself—he did not look her in the eye when saying hello. "You're welcome, Corell," said Kim: "Let's step into the meeting room and get started." As they walked into the conference room, Kim continued speaking: "Today I will be asking you a few questions about your background and telling you a little about Creative Computer Solutions. Please, have a seat."

Corell was starting to calm down a little now. He had been in interviews before, but this interview seemed more formal. Everyone he saw was wearing suits, and Corell knew that this was a big step from his current job at a retail store.

"Corell, I see that you are currently employed at a local retail store. Does your job involve selling computers?" Corell nodded, "Yes, I have worked as a computer sales associate since I started working there two years ago." Kim jotted some notes down and continued, "Good, as you know, our company does not just sell computers; we try to solve problems for clients. Can you tell me about a time that you helped a customer solve a problem related to his computer needs?"

This question caught Corell a little off guard. He was not sure what she exactly meant by solving problems, but he thought of an example that seemed to fit the question. "Well, the majority of my sales are to customers who really don't know what they are looking for in a computer. I remember one couple—they must have been in their late 60's—who came into the store looking for a computer that they could use for Internet access. I asked them a few questions to find out what they wanted to use the computer for and was able to show them a computer that would let them use it for that purpose—one that was cheaper than what they were initially looking at. I guess it solved their problem—they came back to the store a few weeks later and showed me a picture of their granddaughter that they received through e-mail."

Kim smiled in response to his answer: "Well Corell, that is exactly what we try to do at CCS— sell the right service and save clients money. We might do it on a larger scale, but the idea is the same." The interview went on for several minutes. Kim asked Corell about his education and his technical knowledge. "Well Corell, that about wraps the interview up," Kim concluded: "We will interview three other applicants and let you know our decision on Thursday. Before we end, do you have any questions for me?"

"Yes, I do," said Corell. "I noticed in the job description that this position pays through commission. Is there also a salary associated with the position, or is it entirely based on commission?" Kim looked at the job description and could see that the salary information was not entirely clear. "That is a good question, Corell. We do offer a salary for the first year of the job. During that year you will make your salary plus a 2½ percent commission. After the first year, you will no longer receive a salary, but you will get 7 percent commission. We do that because so much of your first year is spent in training."

Corell asked a few more questions about the training offered by the company. After the interview was completed, Corell went home and prepared a thank-you letter to send to Ms. Long.

As you read the interview, notice the basic format of the interview. Do you see a distinct opening, body, and closing? Also, what types of questions did Kim ask Corell? Did Corell's answers make the best possible case for him during the interview? Were there other things that Corell did effectively or ineffectively based on suggestions offered in the chapter?

KEY TERMS

Use the *Human Communication* CD-ROM and the *Online Learning Center* at www.mhhe.com/pearson to further your understanding of the following terminology.

Anticipatory socialization
Behaviorally based question
Bipolar question
Chronological résumé
Clearinghouse question
Closed question
Closings
Cover letter
Functional résumé
Hypothetical question

Informational question
Interview
Interview guide
Interview schedule
Job description
Leading question
Network
Neutral question
Nudging question
Objective statement

Online résumé
Open question
Primary question
Reflective question
Relational uncertainty
Secondary question
Silent probes
Style

SELF-QUIZ

 Go to the self-quizzes on the *Human Communication* CD-ROM and the *Online Learning Center* at <u>www.mhhe.com/pearson</u> to test your knowledge.

ADDITIONAL RESOURCES

Adams, B. (1999). *The complete resume book for college students.* Holbrook, MA: Adams Media Corporation.

Allen, J. (2000). *The complete Q & A job interview book.* New York: John Wiley & Sons.

Graben, S. (2000). *The everything online job search book.* Holbrook, MA: Adams Media Corporation.

Lester, M.C. (1998). *Real life guide to starting your career: How to get the right job now!* Chapel Hill, NC: Pipeline Press/Associated Publishers Group.

Washington, T. (2000). *Interview power: Selling yourself face to face in the new millennium.* Bellevue, WA: Mount Vernon Press.

Yate, M. (2001). Cover letters that knock 'em dead (4th ed.). Holbrook, MA: Adams Media Corporation.

REFERENCES

Bolles, R. (1999). *Job-hunting on the Internet.* Berkeley, CA: Ten Speed Press.

Bolles, R. (2000). *What color is your parachute?* (30th ed.). Berkeley, CA: Ten Speed Press.

Burnett, J. R., & Motowidlo, S. J. (1998). Relations between different sources of information in the structured selection interview. *Personnel Psychology, 51*(4), 963–1083.

Byars, L., & Rue, L. (2000). *Human resource management* (6th ed.). New York: McGraw-Hill.

Cronshaw, S. F., & Wiesner, W. H. (1989). The validity of the employment interview: Models for esearch and practice. In R. W. Eder & G. R. Ferris (Eds.), *The employment interview* (pp. 269–281). Newbury Park, CA: Sage Publications.

Crosby, O. (1999). Resumes, applications, and cover letters. *Occupational Outlook Quarterly, 43,* 2–14.

Denzin, N. K. (1998). The art and politics of interpretation. In N. K. Denzin & Y. S. Lincoln (Eds.), *Collecting and interpreting qualitative materials* (pp. 313–344). Thousand Oaks, CA: Sage Publications.

Dipboye, R. L. (1989). Threats to the incremental validity of interviewer judgments. In R. W. Eder and G. R. Ferris (Eds.), *The employment interview* (pp. 45–60). Newbury Park, CA: Sage Publications.

Fontana, A., & Frey, J. (1998). Interviewing: The art of science. In N. K. Denzin & Y. S. Lincoln (Eds.), *Collecting and interpreting qualitative materials* (pp. 47–78). Thousand Oaks, CA: Sage Publications.

Goyer, R. S., Redding, W. C., & Rickey, J. T. (1968). *Interviewing principles and techniques: A project text.* Dubuque, IA: William C. Brown.

Gutman, A. (2000). *EEO law and personnel practices* (2nd ed.). Thousand Oaks, CA: Sage Publications.

Henricks, M. (2000). *Kinko's guide to the winning resume.* United States of America: Kinko's.

Jablin, F. M. (2001). Organizational entry, assimilation, and disengagement/exit. In F. M. Jablin & L. L. Putnam (Eds.), *The new handbook of organizational communication* (pp. 732–818). Thousand Oaks, CA: Sage Publications.

Knapp, M. L. (1978). *Social intercourse: From greeting to goodbye.* Boston: Allyn and Bacon.

Krizan, A., Merrier, P., & Jones, C. (2002). Business communication (5th ed.). Cincinnati, OH: South-Western College Publishing.

Lipkin, M., Putnam, S., & Lazare, A. (1995). *The medical interview: Clinical care, education, and research.* New York: Springer.

Merriam-Webster's Collegiate Dictionary (10th ed.). Springfield, MA: Merriam-Webster.

Neher, W., & Waite, D. (1993). *The business and professional communicator.* Boston: Allyn and Bacon.

Peterson, M. S. (1997). Personnel interviewers' perceptions of the importance and adequacy of applicants' communication skills. *Communication Education, 46*(4), 287–291.

Porot, D. (2000). *101 salary secrets: How to negotiate like a pro.* Berkeley, CA: Ten Speed Press.

Ralston, S. M., & Kirkwood, W. G. (1999). The trouble with applicant impression management. *Journal of Business and Technical Communication, 13*(2), 190–208.

Raza, S. M., & Carpenter, B. N. (1987). A model of hiring decisions in real employment interviews. *Journal of Applied Psychology,* pp. 596–603.

Richardson, L. (1998). Writing: A method of inquiry. In N. K. Denzin & Y. S. Lincoln (Eds.), *Collecting and interpreting qualitative materials* (pp. 345–371). Thousand Oaks, CA: Sage Publications.

Rosenfeld, P. (1997). Impression management, fairness and the employment interview. *Journal of Business Ethics, 16,* 801–808.

Schutz, W.C. (1976). *The interpersonal underworld.* Palo Alto, CA: Science and Behavior Books.

Stevens, C. K., & Kristoff, A. L. (1995). Making the right impression: A field study of applicant impression management during job interviews. *Journal of Applied Psychology, 80,* 587–606.

Stewart, C. J., & Cash, W. B., Jr. (2000). *Interviewing principles and practices* (9th ed.). New York: McGraw-Hill.

Wolcott, H. (1990). *Writing up qualitative research.* Newbury Park, CA: Sage Publications.

CHAPTER NINE

Things come in kinds;
people come in groups.

CHINESE PROVERB

To associate with other
like-minded people in
small, purposeful groups is
for the great majority of
men and women a source
of profound psychological
satisfaction.

ALDOUS HUXLEY

Groups don't just get
things done—they
make extraordinary
accomplishments in
the face of overwhelming
obstacles.

**BUD BAUMANN, VICE PRESIDENT,
CIGNA CORPORATION**

The Dynamics of Small-Group Communication

What will you learn?

When you have read and thought about this chapter, you will be able to:

1. Define small-group communication and state why it is important.
2. Recognize different types of groups.
3. Define leadership and explain its relevance to small-group communication.
4. Explain how culture develops in small-groups.
5. Identify steps in the small-group decision-making process.
6. Discuss two examples of how technology can be used to facilitate small-group communication.
7. Utilize skills necessary for effective and ethical group communication.

Small groups permeate nearly all facets of our lives. Our families, our jobs, our courses, and our friends are all invigorated and driven by small groups of people. In this chapter we address several issues related to small-group communication. After discussing generally what small-group communication is we turn to theories explaining concepts like leadership, group culture, and small-group decision making. The chapter concludes by discussing several processes related to small-group effectiveness: cohesiveness, use of technology, and skills used by ethical group communicators.

Sandy, Serena, Zina, and Allison were eating dinner together in Zina and Allison's apartment. The four had been friends since their first year in college when they were on the same dorm floor. Even as they were nearing graduation, the four continued to remain close—their Thursday dinners were a longstanding ritual. Although their conversations used to revolve around current loves in their lives, they now included more "grown-up" conversations about work and school.

"My job is so much fun," exclaimed Serena. "I work with three other people on a project for the hospital administrator. We're in charge of designing a training program for hospital volunteers."

"Why do they have so many people working on the project?" asked Allison.

"I'm not sure," replied Serena, "but I think it's because each of us does different things for the project. I'm in charge of assessing the effectiveness of the program once it is under way. Two of the other people are in charge of designing the training part, and the fourth person is in charge of coordinating resources. We all have other jobs in the hospital, but Mrs. Jackson, the hospital administrator, asked the four of us to be involved in this new project."

The four continued discussing Serena's job; after a while the conversation shifted to the relationship between Rachel and Ross on *Friends*—not all conversation was "grown-up."

The next day Serena and Zina were sitting together in their communication class. The teacher was explaining how small-group communication is different from interpersonal communication, the previous week's topic.

"Does this make any sense to you?" asked Serena. "I just don't get it—I mean, I don't belong to any small groups of '3 to 10 people sharing interdependent goals'—whatever that means!"

Why Should You Learn about Small Groups?

Small groups are the basic building blocks of our society. Families, work teams, support groups, religious circles, and study groups are all examples of the groups on which our society is built. Serena's comments in the preceding example reflect a typical first reaction to small-group communication: "What's the relevance?" In fact, small groups are critical to our lives. In organizations, the higher up you go, the more time you will spend working in groups. For example, one report estimated that executives spend about *half* their time in business meetings (Cole, 1989). Membership in small groups is both common and important. Research has consistently documented teamwork as one of the most important communication skills for personal and professional success (Vice, 2001).

Small groups are important for five reasons (see Table 9.1). These reasons clarify why you will want to learn how to communicate effectively in

TABLE 9.1   WHY YOU SHOULD STUDY SMALL-GROUP COMMUNICATION

1. Humans need groups to meet needs they cannot meet as individuals.

2. Groups are everywhere.

3. Knowing how groups function and how to operate effectively in them will be a highly valued skill.

4. Working effectively in groups requires training.

5. Small groups are a means of participating in the democratic process.

small groups. First, humans need groups; membership in groups meets needs that we cannot meet for ourselves. William Schutz (1958), a psychologist who has studied group interaction, said that humans have needs for inclusion, affection, and control. The need for **inclusion**—*the state of being involved with others*—suggests that people need to belong to, or be included in, groups with others. As humans, we derive much of our identity, our beliefs about who we are, from the groups to which we belong. Starting with our immediate families and including such important groups as our church, mosque, or synagogue; interest groups; work teams; and social groups—all these help us define who we are. The need for **affection**—*the emotion of caring for others and/or being cared for*— means that we humans need to love and be loved, to know that we are important to others who value us as unique human beings. Finally, we have a need for **control,** or *the ability to influence our environment.* We are better able to exercise such control if we work together in groups. One person cannot build a school, bridge, or new business. However, by working together in groups we *can* accomplish these and other complex tasks. We need others to meet our needs.

inclusion

The state of being involved with others; a human need.

affection

The emotion of caring for others and/or being cared for by them; a human need.

control

The ability to influence our environment.

Writing Assignment

Ask students to write a short paper analyzing how groups they belong to meet their needs for inclusion, affection, and control. The paper could be done as homework or in class. Students should be prepared to share their examples with classmates.

TRY ▶ THIS

Make a list of groups that you belong to. When making your list, identify at least one group you belong to for inclusion purposes, one group for affection purposes, and one group for control purposes. Do any of the groups you belong to meet all three of these needs?

Second, groups are everywhere. You will not be able to escape working in them. For a moment, list all of the groups to which you currently belong, including informal groups such as study groups or your "lunch bunch." Students typically list between 8 and 10 groups, but sometimes as many as 20 or more and rarely fewer than 2. Your presence in groups

American companies have come to realize how helpful groups can be in conducting their business.

will not end upon graduation. Numerous companies have discovered how helpful groups can be and have installed groups at *all* levels.

The third reason is related to the second. Because group work is expected to increase in the future, particularly in business and industry, knowing how groups function and having the ability to operate effectively in them will be highly valued skills. If you expect to advance in the America of the future, you will have to know how to work in a group. In a national survey of 750 leading American companies, 71.4 percent of the respondents mentioned "ability to work in teams" as an essential skill for MBA graduates—more important by far than knowledge of quantitative and statistical techniques (DuBois, 1992). Why are companies so committed to groups? As noted by Bud Baumann, Vice President for Information Technology for CIGNA Corporation, "Groups don't just get things done—they make extraordinary accomplishments in the face of overwhelming obstacles" (quoted in Callaway, 1997, p. 99). So, if you plan to advance in your career, or if you just want to get something done, you must learn how to participate as a member of a team.

Fourth, being an effective group or team member cannot be left to chance. Just because you are placed on a team does not mean you know how to work effectively in that team. As helpful as groups can be to any organization, they often fail because group leaders have not thought through exactly what they want the groups to accomplish or because group members have not been trained in how to behave appropriately as part of a team (Drucker, 1992). Effective group participation cannot be taken for granted. Group members need training to understand the dynamics of small-group interaction, which is much more complex than dyadic (two-person) interaction.

Finally, groups can be an important way for Americans to participate in the democratic process; thus they have the potential to help us achieve our ideals as a society. Because we can accomplish so much more in groups than we can as individuals, group participation can be an important vehicle through which we create and govern our society. A lone voice "crying in the wilderness" may have little effect, but a group of people working hard for a cause in which they believe can make great changes. For example, in the wake of the terrorist attacks on the World Trade Center and the Pentagon, several students on our campus formed a coalition to help victims of the tragedy. Activities undertaken by the group included planning a special blood donation drive on campus and selling "Remember 9-11-01" pens and red, white, and blue ribbons to raise money for victim relief. Astoundingly, many of these activities were planned and implemented the day after the tragedy. When speaking with one of us about these activities, one of the student organizers indicated that all of the students involved in the efforts felt like they were able to accomplish something important while working together. Similar efforts were carried out by groups of people in all types of organizations across the country.

Discussion Question

How did groups play a role in your reaction to the September 11, 2001, terrorist attacks on New York and Washington, D.C.? For example, did you take part in religious services? Did you and your friends discuss the events to help make sense of what happened? How did your family play a role in your reaction?

TRY ▶ THIS

Watch the evening news on one of your local TV stations. While watching the news, make note of each civic or political group discussed. What was each group trying to achieve? Did some groups have the power to make decisions (e.g., political groups)? Did some groups advocate a certain position although they had no power to make decisions (e.g., community groups)?

What Is Small-Group Communication?

Small-group communication is *the interaction of a small group of people to achieve an interdependent goal* (Galanes, Brilhart, & Adams, 2000). This definition implies that:

- Groups must be small enough that members are mutually aware that the group of people is a collective entity. Groups typically contain between 3 and 9 people but may be larger if members perceive the group as an entity.

- The substance that creates and holds the group together is the interaction between members.

- Group members are interdependent—they cannot achieve their goals without the help of other group members.

small-group communication

The interaction of a small group of people to achieve an interdependent goal.

Think, Pair, Share

Small-group communication includes a number of elements that make it both similar to and unique from other communication activities. Take 10 minutes to think about each of the small-group communication characteristics listed below. Generate one example to illustrate each characteristic and answer the question posed for each characteristic. After the 10 minutes are up, pair off with a partner and share your answers.

1. Small groups are comprised of a group of individuals who (a) are mutually aware of each other as individuals, and (b) are mutually aware of the collective nature of the group. Why do you think "mutual awareness" is so important to small groups?

2. Small-group interaction means that each person in the group can influence and be influenced by each other person in the group. Think of a small group you belong to. What are some ways that you have influenced that group? How have some of the group members influenced you? Do you think this "mutual influence" is important for small groups to be effective? Why or why not?

3. Small groups are interdependent—no member of the group can achieve the group's goal without other members of the group achieving the goal also. From your own group experiences, what are some examples of interdependence?

Discussion Question

How is communication in small groups different from interpersonal communication and public speaking?

Video Activity

Ask students to view the video segment "Senior Seminar." To what extent did the group in this segment meet the characteristics of small groups identified in the text? For instance, was Susan's group interdependent?

The definition of small-group communication just presented establishes *communication* as the essential process within a small group. Communication creates a group, shapes each group in unique ways, and maintains a group. As with other forms of human communication, small-group communication involves sending verbal and nonverbal signals that are perceived, interpreted, and responded to by other people. Group members pay attention to each other and coordinate their behavior in order to accomplish the group's assignment. Perfect understanding between the person sending the signal and those receiving the signal is never possible; in a group, members strive to have enough understanding to enable the group's purpose to be achieved.

The Types and Functions of Small Groups

Think for a moment about the different groups you belong to. You may regularly study with other students from your accounting class, you may belong to a club on campus, you may be assigned to participate in a student government group, and you likely have a group of friends with whom you socialize. What are the key differences between these groups? We identify four ways to categorize groups:

- **Task-oriented groups (also called secondary groups)** are *formed for the purpose of completing tasks such as solving a problem or making a decision.* A group of students studying for an exam are taking part in a task-oriented group.
- **Relationship-oriented groups (also called primary groups)** are *usually long-term and exist to meet our needs for inclusion and affection.* Your family is an example of a relationship-oriented group.
- **Assigned groups** *evolve out of a hierarchy where individuals are appointed as members of the group.* Being asked to serve on a student union advisory board is an example of an assigned group.
- **Emergent groups** are *the results of environmental conditions leading to the formation of a cohesive group of individuals.* A group of friends who meet at college is an example of an emergent group.

Classifying groups according to whether they are task, relationship, assigned, or emergent risks oversimplifying a more complex process. Because groups are comprised of people and are sustained through communication, groups can go through several metamorphoses. As you probably can tell, primary or secondary groups are not pure. Members of primary groups, such as families, engage in work, make decisions, and must cooperate to complete tasks. Members of secondary groups forge strong personal bonds and provide each other with affection and recognition. In fact, some of the best secondary groups are those with strong primary characteristics, where members feel appreciated and valued. Likewise, emergent groups can be institutionalized and assigned groups can take on the characteristics of an emergent group.

Although understanding general characteristics of different types of groups is valuable, to recognize that groups are not static entities is equally important. We might belong to an assigned group formed for task purposes. As we interact with members of that group, a relationship-oriented social group may emerge. Just as our personal relationships can go through several turning points, our group membership is also constantly in flux.

task-oriented groups

Also called secondary groups, are groups formed for the purpose of completing tasks, such as solving problems or making decisions.

relationship-oriented groups

Also called primary groups, are groups that are usually long-term and exist to meet our needs for inclusion and affection (love, esteem).

assigned groups

Groups that evolve out of a hierarchy where individuals are assigned membership to the group.

emergent groups

Groups resulting from environmental conditions leading to the formation of a cohesive group of individuals.

Video Activity

Ask students to view the video segment "Senior Seminar." Have students classify Susan's group as task or relational and emergent or assigned.

Leadership is about communication, not personality or luck.

Writing Assignment

Ask students to write a short paper identifying task, relationship, assigned, and emergent groups they belong to. Have any of these groups changed from one type of group to another over time? Students should be prepared to share their examples with classmates.

Teaching Tip

The Try This box uses a matrix to help students organize examples and information. Teaching students to use matrices and other visual representations of information can help them learn material more effectively.

TRY ◄▶THIS

Using examples of groups from your own life, try to find an example to illustrate a group in each cell of the following matrix. For example, think of a relationship-oriented assigned group, a task-oriented emergent group, etc.

	ASSIGNED GROUP	EMERGENT GROUP
RELATIONSHIP-ORIENTED GROUP		
TASK-ORIENTED GROUP		

The Role of Leadership in Small Groups

For most groups to work effectively some structure is necessary. A primary task of the group leader is to provide necessary structure and direction for the group. In this section we explain what leadership is as well as several theories discussing the process of effective leadership.

What Is Leadership?

leadership

A process of using communication to influence the behaviors and attitudes of others to meet group goals.

Hackman and Johnson (1991) define **leadership** as *a process of using communication to influence the behaviors and attitudes of others to meet* *group goals.* Leadership, then, is enacted through communication and persuasion, not through physical force or coercion. Furthermore, only influence designed to benefit the group can be termed small-group leadership. One member persuading another to sabotage a group goal is not considered leadership by this definition.

A **leader** is *a person who influences the behavior and attitudes of others through communication.* In small groups, two types of leader are designated and emergent. A **designated leader** is *someone who has been appointed or elected to a leadership position* (e.g., chair, team leader, coordinator, or facilitator). An **emergent leader** is *someone who becomes an informal leader by exerting influence toward achievement of a group's goal but who does not hold the formal position or role of leader.* Groups benefit from having a designated leader because designated leaders add stability and organization to the group's activities. An emergent leader can be any group member who helps the group meet its goals. Groups work best when all members contribute skills and leadership behaviors on behalf of the group.

How do leaders, designated or emergent, gain their ability to influence others? A classic study by French and Raven (1981) identified five types of leadership **power:**

- **Reward power** is the *ability to give followers what they want and need.*
- **Punishment power** is *the ability to withhold from followers what they want and need.*
- **Coercion** is *a form of punishment power that attempts to force compliance with hostile tactics.*
- **Referent power** is *power based on others' admiration and respect.* **Charisma** is *an extreme form of referent power that inspires strong loyalty and devotion from others.*
- **Expert power** occurs *when the other members value a person's knowledge or expertise.*

All members of a group have the ability to influence other members. For instance, all members, not just the designated leader, can reward others, withhold rewards, or have expertise potentially valuable to the group. In addition, a designated leader's influence usually stems from more than just legitimate power. Besides holding the title of leader, that person also has expertise, referent power, and so forth. In fact, if legitimate power is the leader's only source of influence, then someone else in the group with more broadly based power will probably emerge as a more influential informal leader. In short, all group members possess some sources of influence and can lead the group, even if they do not have the title of leader.

leader

A person who influences the behavior and attitudes of others through communication.

designated leader

Someone who has been appointed or elected to a leadership position.

emergent leader

Someone who becomes an informal leader by exerting influence toward achievement of a group's goal but who does not hold the formal position or role of leader.

power

Interpersonal influence that forms the basis for group leadership.

Discussion Question

In what situations would a designated leader be most effective for facilitating group communication? In what situations would an emergent leader be most effective?

Video Activity

Have students view the video segment "Senior Seminar." Ask students to determine who the leader was. Was there a designated leader? Was there an emergent leader?

reward power

A form of power where the leader gives followers resources they want and need.

punishment power

A form of power where the leader withholds something followers want and need.

coercion

A form of punishment that attempts to force compliance with hostile tactics.

referent power

Power based on others' admiration or respect.

charisma

An extreme type of referent power that inspires strong loyalty and devotion from others.

expert power

Power based on the value other members place on the leader's knowledge or expertise.

Theoretical Approaches to Group Leadership

Since Aristotle's time, people have been interested in what makes a good leader. Is leadership something you are born with? Can you learn to be a leader? In this section, several approaches to understanding leadership are presented. The most useful current theories about leadership focus on the communication behaviors of individuals.

Style Approaches

Style approaches to studying leadership *focus on the pattern of behaviors leaders exhibit in groups.* Considerable research has examined three major styles of designated leader: democratic, laissez-faire, and autocratic. **Democratic leaders** *encourage members to participate in group decisions,* even major ones: "What suggestions do you have for solving our problem?" **Laissez-faire leaders** *take almost no initiative for structuring a group discussion;* they are nonleaders whose typical response is: "I don't care; whatever you want to do is fine with me." **Autocratic leaders** *maintain strict control over their group,* including making assignments and giving orders: "Here's how we'll solve the problem. First, you will . . ." Autocratic leaders ask fewer questions but answer more than democratic leaders; they make more attempts to coerce and fewer attempts to get others to participate (Rosenfeld & Plax, 1975).

TRY ◄►THIS

You have learned that there are different types of leadership style and that leaders base their ability to influence others on the exercise of power. What relationship do you think exists between leadership style and power? In the matrix below, check cells where you think the leadership style matches the base of power. Why do you think these relationships exist?

	DEMOCRATIC LEADER	AUTOCRATIC LEADER	LAISSEZ-FAIRE LEADER
REWARD POWER			
PUNISHMENT POWER			
LEGITIMATE POWER			
REFERENT POWER			
EXPERT POWER			

Discussion Question

Is one type of leadership power best or do effective leaders use all five types of power?

Groups vary in the amount of structure and control their members want and need, but research findings about style have been consistent (Graen, Dansereau, & Minami, 1972; Jurma, 1978, 1979; Maier & Maier, 1957; Preston & Heintz, 1949; White & Lippett, 1960). Most people in the United States prefer democratic groups and are more satisfied in democratically rather than autocratically led groups.

The style approaches imply a single leadership style good for all situations. However, most scholars believe that the style should match the needs of the situation. For example, if you are in a group working on a class project and the deadline is tomorrow, a democratic leadership style might be ineffective because it takes longer to make decisions.

Contingency Approaches

Contingency approaches to studying leadership *assume that group situations vary, with different situations (contingencies) requiring different leadership styles.* In addition, a single group's situation will vary over time. Factors such as the type of task, the time available, and the skill of the members determine what type of leadership is most appropriate for a given situation. Contingency approaches to leadership assume that effective leaders must adapt their leadership style to the situation. For example, newly formed groups may need a more directive leader—someone who will launch the group. As the group begins to mature, a more democratic leadership style may be more appropriate. Thus the choice of leadership style—in this example autocratic or democratic—depends on the contingencies of the situation.

The Communication Competencies Approach

Communication scholars who adopt the **communicative competencies approach** have tried to *focus on the communicative behaviors of leaders as they exercise interpersonal influence* to accomplish group goals. They ask such questions as "What do effective leaders do?" The Communication Competency Model of Group Leadership, developed by Barge and Hirokawa (1989), is one of the most comprehensive models to address this question. This model assumes that leaders help a group achieve its goals through communication skills (competencies). Two competencies include the task and interpersonal, or relationship, distinctions discussed earlier. Leaders must be flexible to draw from a personal repertoire of such competencies. Some of the most important leader competencies are described briefly here:

1. Effective leaders are able to clearly and appropriately communicate ideas to the group without dominating conversation.
2. Effective leaders communicate a clear grasp of the task facing the group.

style approaches

A leadership theory focusing on the pattern of behaviors leaders exhibit in groups.

democratic leaders

Leaders who encourage members to participate in group decisions.

laissez-faire leaders

Leaders who take almost no initiative for structuring a group discussion.

autocratic leaders

Leaders who maintain strict control over their group.

contingency approach

An approach to studying leadership that assumes group situations vary, with different situations (contingencies) requiring different leadership styles.

communicative competencies approach

A leadership theory focusing on the communicative behaviors of leaders as they exercise interpersonal influence to accomplish group goals.

Group Discussion

Identify examples of democratic, laissez-faire, and autocratic leaders. After thinking of examples, individually or as a group complete the Try This activity on p. 274 analyzing relationships between leadership power and leadership style.

distributed leadership

A leadership theory explicitly acknowledging that each member is expected to perform the communication behaviors needed to move the group toward its goal.

Video Activity

Ask students to view the video segment "Senior Seminar." Have students characterize the leadership styles of Mike and Claire.

Discussion Question

People often assume that the distributed leadership approach is ideal in most circumstances. What are situations where this approach may not be the most effective?

3. Effective leaders are skilled at facilitating discussion.
4. Effective group leaders encourage open dialogue and do not force their own ideas on a group.
5. Effective leaders place group needs over personal concerns.
6. Effective leaders display respect for others during interaction.
7. Effective leaders share in the successes and failures of the group.

The Distributed Leadership Approach

All members of a group are responsible for effective group leadership. **Distributed leadership** explicitly acknowledges that *each member is expected to perform the communication behaviors needed to move the group toward its goal.* Although rare, groups may even survive without a designated leader, like the long-term group studied by Counselman (1991), which functioned without a designated leader but was not without leadership. Various members perform leadership functions, such as providing structure, setting group norms, and keeping the group on task. Although unusual, this group supports an important point made earlier: Leadership is a property of the group, not of a single individual.

In fact, groups seem to be more productive when leadership behaviors are distributed. When Barge (1989) compared a leadership model in which the group leader was an active, directive influence to one in which all members engaged in the leadership process, he found that overall leadership activity, not the designated leader's activity alone, predicted overall group productivity.

With distributed leadership all group members enact leadership behaviors.

Establishing Culture in Small Groups

In chapter 7 you learned that national origin, ethnic differences, and language strategies define culture. Small groups are a microcosm of the cultural principles discussed in chapter 7. When small groups are created, they immediately begin developing a unique group culture. Some group cultures are pleasant, whereas others are aggressive, hostile, and demeaning. In this section we discuss how diversity affects group culture, the development of group norms, role structures enacted by group members, and group cohesiveness.

The Effect of Diversity on Group Culture

Within-group diversity is *the presence of observable and/or implicit differences between group members.* We observe within-group diversity when group members differ based on visible characteristics. For example, to visually distinguish between males and females or between members of certain ethnic groups is easy. Group diversity can be implicit when members of a group have differing values, attitudes, and perspectives—personal characteristics that cannot be seen. Collectively, observable and implicit differences between group members can influence the culture of a group.

Group culture is *the socially negotiated system of rules that guide group behavior.* Group culture differs from national and ethnic cultures because a group culture is a relatively unstable and short-term phenomenon. That is, group cultures are constantly in flux and they disappear when the group dissolves. National and ethnic cultures change slowly and are relatively persistent. If you compare two groups from your own life, you can easily understand the concept of group culture. Your group of friends has implicit rules for behavior—inside jokes, slang, norms for touching, and shared objectives. That group likely has a different culture than an assigned group of students you work with in one of your classes. Classroom groups are typically more formal, less cohesive, and more task oriented.

Observable Characteristics and Group Culture

Although many observable characteristics exist in groups, research has generally focused on sex and ethnicity. **Sex** refers to *the biological characteristics we are born with.* This is contrasted with **gender,** which are *the learned characteristics associated with masculinity and femininity.*

Research examining male–female behavior in small groups suggests that differences exist between the sexes. For example, women pay more attention to the relationships among group members whereas men are more instrumental, or task focused (Baird, 1986). Similarly, Smith-Lovin

Video Activity

Ask students to view the video segment "Senior Seminar." Have students identify observable and implicit elements of within-group diversity in Susan's group.

within-group diversity

The presence of observable and/or implicit differences among group members.

group culture

The socially negotiated system of rules that guide group behavior.

sex

The biological reproductive characteristics with which we are born.

gender

The learned characteristics associated with masculinity and femininity.

Cultural Note

CULTURAL DIFFERENCES IN SMALL-GROUP COMMUNICATION

- Conformity in small-group communication is more common in collectivist cultures (which value the group over the individual), such as Venezuela, Pakistan, Peru, and Taiwan.
- Competition and dissent are more common in individualistic cultures (which value freedom, choice, and interdependence), such as the United States, Australia, Great Britain, and Canada.
- A rigid hierarchy with a controlling group leader is preferred in uncertainty-rejecting cultures, such as India, Mexico, and the Philippines.
- Equality among group members, and use of first names, is preferred in uncertainty-accepting cultures, such as Israel, Australia, and New Zealand.
- Clear rules are expected in uncertainty-rejection cultures such as Japan and Greece.
- Flexible rules, high tolerance for ambiguity, and risk taking characterize uncertainty-acceptance cultures like Great Britain.
- Ambiguity and saving face is important in collectivist cultures like China, Korea, and Japan.

Descriptions of various cultures are provided in more detail in chapter 7.

Writing Assignment

Ask students to write a short paper analyzing how cultural diversity will likely impact the use of teams and work groups in the United States. Students should share their ideas with the class.

Teaching Tip

This section as well as the section on gender makes generalizations about how people from various co-cultures tend to behave in small groups. Emphasize to students that research simply reports general trends and that individuals rarely conform to these generalizations.

and Brody (1989) found that women interrupt men and women equally but that men interrupt women more than they interrupt other men. In all-male groups, men interrupt to support each other; but the more women in the group, the less likely this is to occur. Men seem to consider sex to be related to status whereas women do not. Researchers have also found that men are perceived as more controlling than women in groups even when the same behaviors are enacted by both sexes (Burrell, Donohue, & Allen, 1988).

Others researchers have concluded that female–male differences are exaggerated. For example, research has determined that women can dominate group discussion (Mabry, 1989) and that in groups women tend to talk more frequently but for shorter periods of time than men (Duerst-Lahti, 1990).

A noted in chapter 7, communication norms can vary greatly among ethnic cultures. Keep in mind that we carry our cultural learning with us and that our individual cultural rules affect the joint culture we create in small groups. The accompanying culture note summarizes the small-group behaviors valued in different ethnic cultures (Galanes, 1997).

Implicit Characteristics and Group Culture

Physical characteristics like sex and ethnicity are only obvious clues about a person. Although research reviewed in the previous two sections generally demonstrates a connection between observable and implicit characteristics (e.g., females tend to pay more attention to the relationship function of a group), several implicit characteristics remain invisible to the eye—they must be discovered through conversation and dialogue. For example, socioeconomic status, prior work experience, education, area of specialty, personal values, and prior experiences are all important aspects of diversity which are largely unrelated to observable characteristics like sex or ethnicity (Shaw & Barrett-Power, 1998).

Implicit attributes of diversity also affect the ways group members communicate. Shaw and Barrett-Power (1998) note that socioeconomic differences, value differences, and other implicit differences between group members result in different **cognitive paradigms,** or *ways of looking at the world*. Think for a moment about groups in which you have been involved. Although many of the group members may have had similar observable characteristics (mostly from the same ethnic background, for example), they likely had different opinions, attitudes, and values. Such differences in cognitive paradigms have the potential to dramatically affect the ability of the group to achieve consensus or even common ground for dialogue.

Shaw and Barrett-Power (1998) further note that implicit and observable diversity characteristics can interact to create psychological tension for group members. As you initially talk in a group you may feel comfortable because many of the group members appear similar to yourself. In such groups, Shaw and Barrett-Power argue that the group will initially have a high degree of cohesion. As dialogue progresses, group members may begin to realize that substantial differences exist between people based on implicit characteristics—thus creating psychological discomfort. Differences in perspective between people can have important benefits for the group. Diversity of opinions can help ensure that group discussions adequately consider multiple viewpoints on an issue.

Class Activity

Ask students to participate in one of the activities provided in the instructor's manual. After completing the activity, ask students to discuss how group members' cognitive paradigms influenced their statements and behaviors during the activity.

cognitive paradigms

Ways of looking at the world based on individuals' attitudes, beliefs, values, and perceptions.

TRY ► THIS

Define your own implicit characteristics. What attitudes, beliefs, values, or "ways of looking at the world" do you think influence your own communication behaviors? Have any of those implicit characteristics been different from other people who are similar to you in observable characteristics? Have your implicit characteristics been similar to those of another person who is dissimilar from you based on observable characteristics?

Group Activity

Have students form groups. Ask students to identify observable and implicit elements of within-group diversity represented in their small group.

TABLE 9.2 OBSERVABLE AND IMPLICIT WITHIN-GROUP DIVERSITY		
	OBSERVABLE	IMPLICIT
DEFINITION	Within-group diversity based on physical characteristics that can be seen.	Within-group diversity based on individuals' worldview, perspectives, and other personality characteristics.
EXAMPLE	Ethnicity, sex	Religious orientation, educational background

In summary, within-group diversity exists because of observable and implicit group characteristics. Although observable characteristics provide rough guides for first impressions, implicit characteristics may have a greater impact on long-term group dynamics and culture. Table 9.2 summarizes the characteristics of within-group diversity.

The Development of Group Norms

norms

Informal rules for group interaction created and sustained through communication.

The first time members meet as a group, they begin to establish the **norms,** or *informal rules for interaction,* that will eventually guide the members' behaviors. George Homans (1950) called a norm "an idea in the minds of the members of a group, an idea that can be put in the form of a statement specifying what the members . . . ought to do, are expected to do, under given circumstances" (p. 73). At first, the full range of human behavior is available to members. For example, they may greet each other formally ("Ms.," "Dr.," "Professor," etc.) or they may speak informally and use first names. The initial pattern of behavior tends to set the tone for subsequent meetings and to establish the general norms that members will follow. Communication among members establishes the norms.

Most norms are not established directly. For example, if Ali comes late to a meeting and no one seems bothered, other members may get the message that coming on time to meetings is unnecessary. By saying nothing to Ali, the group, without consciously thinking about or formally "deciding," has begun to establish a norm that members need not be on time.

Group Activity

Most group norms are established in and through the communication of the group. Given the opportunity, what norms should be present in a group? Have each group make a list of norms that would guide the behaviors of that group. Groups will discuss their group credo with the class.

The norms of any group tend to mirror the norms of the general culture or co-culture in which the group exists. For example, compare a small group of your college friends with a small group of your grandparents' friends. You and your friends use different language, dress differently, and act differently from the way your grandparents interact with their friends. Differences of age, class, status, and physical condition between these two co-cultures produce slightly different norms in groups formed from these co-cultures. As Shimanoff (1992) stated,

When group members come together for the first time, they bring with them past experiences and expectations regarding cultural and social rules and rules for specific groups they assume may be similar to this new group. It is out of these experiences and expectations as well as its unique interaction . . . that a particular group formulates its rules. (p. 225)

Norms often develop rapidly, without members consciously realizing what is occurring. They can be inferred by observing what members say and do. For example, repeated behaviors (e.g., members always sit in the same seats) provide evidence of a norm. In addition, behaviors that are punished (e.g., one group member chastises another by saying, "It's about time you got here") indicate that a norm has been violated.

Members should pay attention to group norms to ensure that they are appropriate to the group task. As teachers we often observe students working in groups. As we walk around the classroom, groups seem to notice we are standing near them and quickly STOP talking about the band playing at a local club and turn to the topic we asked them to discuss. As we walk away, discussion soon returns to music and fun. Such norms for playfulness, while important for relationship development, may begin to distract the group from assigned tasks. We certainly do not advocate "no fun time" in groups. In fact, we like to talk to our students about music and sports. Nevertheless, a norm that emphasizes all "fun time" and no "work time" can prevent the group from reaching its goal.

The Development of Role Structure

A **role** is *a position in a group that is part of an interlocking structure of other parts.* For example, plays and movies contain interlocking roles, each of which is a different character in the cast. Each character's role must fit within the play or movie structure. The same is true for groups. However, whereas in a movie the actor learns lines that are highly scripted, in a small group the "actor" (the group member) creates the role spontaneously, in concert with the other members. Just as an actor plays different roles in different scripts, individuals enact many diverse roles in the numerous groups to which they belong.

role

A position in a group that is part of an interlocking structure of communicative behaviors.

The Types of Group Roles

Two major types of group roles are formal and informal. A **formal role,** sometimes called a *positional role,* is *an assigned role based on an individual's position or title within a group.* For example, Indira may be her service club's treasurer. As treasurer, she is expected to perform certain duties, such as paying the club's bills, balancing the checkbook, and making regular reports to the club about its financial status. These duties may even be specified in a job description for the position of treasurer. We also expect the person in a particular position to behave in certain ways. For example, what do you think Indira's fellow group members expect of her in addition to her assigned duties? Very likely they expect her to be well

formal role

Also called positional role, is an assigned role based on an individual's position or title within a group.

organized and to present her report clearly and concisely without wandering into topics irrelevant to the treasury.

informal role

Also called a behavioral role, is a role that is developed spontaneously within a group.

An **informal role,** sometimes called a *behavioral role,* is *a role that is developed spontaneously within a group.* The role of each group member is worked out by the interaction between the member and the rest of the group and continues to evolve as the group evolves. Informal roles strongly reflect members' personality characteristics, habits, and typical ways of interacting within a group. For example, Rich jokes around during fraternity meetings. He refuses to take anything seriously, cracks jokes that interrupt others, and calls members who work hard for the fraternity "overachievers." Rich's constant failure to take the group's job seriously has earned him the informal role of playboy in his group. In contrast, Jeff, one of the "overachievers," constantly reminds members about upcoming deadlines. His fraternity brothers have started calling him the group's timekeeper.

The Categories of Behavioral Functions

Roles enacted by group members comprise a set of behaviors that perform a function for the group. For formal roles, the set of behaviors is often specified in writing. For informal roles, the member performs the set of behaviors so regularly that others begin to expect it. Jeff's fraternity relies heavily on his timekeeping duties and would be lost (at least temporarily) if he did not perform them.

A number of classification schemes describe typical group functions that members' behaviors serve. One common scheme classifies behaviors by whether they perform task, maintenance, or self-centered functions. **Task functions** are *behaviors that are directly relevant to the group's purpose and that affect the group's productivity.* Their purpose is to focus group members productively on their assignment. **Maintenance functions** are *behaviors that focus on the interpersonal relationships among members;* they are aimed at supporting cooperative and harmonious relationships. Both task and maintenance functions are considered essential to effective group communication. On the other hand, **self-centered functions** are *behaviors that serve the needs of the individual at the expense of the group.* The person performing a self-centered behavior implies, "I don't care what the group needs or wants. *I* want . . ." Self-centered functions manipulate other members for selfish goals that compete with group goals. Examples of statements that support task, maintenance, and self-centered functions are shown in Figure 9.1. The list is not exhaustive; many more functions could be added.

These behavioral functions combine to create a member's informal role, which is a comprehensive, general picture of how a particular member typically acts in a group. An example of how individual functions combine to create a role is shown in Figure 9.2. As you can see, information-giving and opinion-giving behaviors primarily characterize the information

task functions

Behaviors that are directly relevant to the group's task and that affect the group's productivity.

maintenance functions

Behaviors that focus on the interpersonal relationships among members.

self-centered functions

Behaviors that serve the needs of the individual at the expense of the group.

TASK FUNCTIONS AND STATEMENTS

Initiating and orienting: "Let's make a list of what we still need to do."

Information giving: "Last year, the committee spent $150 on publicity."

Information seeking: "John, how many campus muggings were reported last year?"

Opinion giving: "I don't think the cost of parking stickers is the worst parking problem students have."

Clarifying: "Martina, are you saying that you couldn't support a proposal that increased student fees?"

Extending: "Another thing that Toby's proposal would let us do is . . ."

Evaluating: "One problem I see with Cindy's idea is . . ."

Summarizing: "So we've decided that we'll add two sections to the report, and Terrell and Candy will write them."

Coordinating: "If Carol interviews the mayor by Monday, then Jim and I can prepare a response by Tuesday's meeting."

Consensus testing: "We seem to be agreed that we prefer the second option."

Recording: "I think we decided at our last meeting. Let me check the minutes."

MAINTENANCE (RELATIONSHIP-ORIENTED) FUNCTIONS AND STATEMENTS

Establishing norms: "It doesn't help to call each other names. Let's stick to the issues."

Gatekeeping: "Pat, you look like you want to say something about the proposal."

Supporting: "I think Tara's point is well made, and we should look at it more closely."

Harmonizing: "Jared and Sally, I think there are areas where you are in agreement, and I would like to suggest a compromise that might work for you both."

Tension relieving: "We're getting tired and cranky. Let's take a 10-minute break."

Dramatizing: "That reminds me of a story about what happened last year when . . ."

Showing solidarity: "We've really done good work here!" or "We're all in this together."

SELF-CENTERED FUNCTIONS AND STATEMENTS

Withdrawing: "Do whatever you want; I don't care," or not speaking at all.

Blocking: "I don't care if we've already voted; I want to discuss it again!"

Status and recognition seeking: "I have a lot more expertise than the rest of you, and I think we should do it the way I know works."

Video Activity

Ask students to view the video segment "Senior Seminar." Have students identify examples of various task, maintenance, and self-centered statements made during the discussion by Susan's group.

Figure 9.1   Examples of task, maintenance, and self-centered statements.

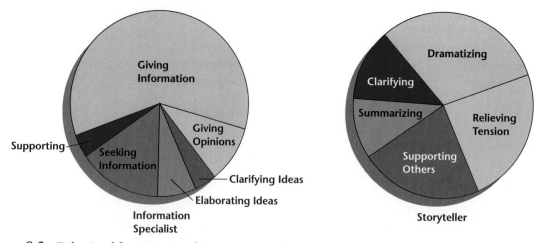

Figure 9.2   Behavioral functions combine to create roles.

Video Activity

Watch a group-oriented film like *The Breakfast Club, Ocean's Eleven,* or *Lord of the Rings.* Have students analyze how different characters enacted various behavioral functions listed in Figure 9.2.

specialist role. The storyteller role is comprised of several behaviors including dramatizing, relieving tension, supporting, summarizing, and clarifying. Numerous other informal roles can be created through combinations of behavioral functions.

TRY ► THIS

Figure 9.2 illustrates how individual behavioral functions combine to create a role. How would you draw your own role in a group you belong to? Pick a group from your own life and draw a pie diagram of behavioral functions of the group showing your role.

Group Cohesiveness

Establishing a Cohesive Climate

group climate

The emotional tone or atmosphere members create within the group.

trust

A group climate characteristic where members believe they can rely on each other.

Another important element that helps shape a group's culture is the **group climate,** which is *the emotional tone or atmosphere members create within the group.* For example, you have probably attended a group meeting where the tension silenced everyone. That atmosphere of tension describes the group's climate. Three factors that contribute heavily to group climate are trust, cohesiveness, and supportiveness.

- **Trust.** Trust means that *members believe they can rely on each other.* Two types of trust relevant to groupwork are task trust and interpersonal trust. Task trust can be violated when group mem-

Defensive Behaviors and Statements

Evaluation:	Judging another person: "That's a completely ridiculous ideal."
Control:	Dominating or insisting on your own way: "I've decided what we need to do."
Manipulating:	"Don't you think you should try it my way?"
Neutrality:	Not caring about how others feel: "It doesn't matter to me what you decide."
Superiority:	Pulling rank, maximizing status differences: "As group leader, I think we should . . ."
Certainty:	Being a "know-it-all": "You guys are completely off base. I know exactly how to handle this."

Supportive Behaviors and Statements

Description:	Describing your own feelings without making those of others wrong: "I prefer the first option because . . ."
Problem orientation:	Searching for the best solution without predetermining what that should be: "We want to produce the best results, and that may mean some extra time from all of us."
Spontaneity:	Reacting honestly and openly: "Wow, that sounds like a great idea!"
Empathy:	Showing you care about the other members: "Jan, originally you were skeptical. How comfortable will you be if the group favors that option?"
Equality:	Minimizing status differences by treating members as equals: "I don't have all the answers. What do the rest of you think?"
Provisionalism:	Expressing opinions tentatively and being open to others' suggestions: "Maybe we should try a different approach . . ."

Figure 9.3   Examples of defensive and supportive statements.

bers do not contribute their share of the work (known as a "hitch-hiker"). Interpersonal trust means that others are working with the best interest of the group in mind rather than advancing hidden agendas.

- **Supportiveness.** Supportiveness refers to *an atmosphere of openness where members care about each other and create cohesiveness* (Gibb, 1961). Examples of both supportive and defensive statements are found in Figure 9.3.

- **Cohesiveness.** Cohesiveness is *the attachment members feel toward each other and the group.* Highly cohesive groups are more open, handle disagreement more effectively, and typically perform better than noncohesive groups (Barker, 1991; Kelly & Duran, 1985).

supportiveness

An atmosphere of openness created when members care about each other and treat each other with respect.

cohesiveness

The attachment members feel toward each other and the group.

Team Challenge

HOW EVIDENCE AFFECTS GROUP DISCUSSION

You and a group of students selected by your teacher are to discuss the truthfulness of the following statement: "Technology has overshadowed critical thinking in higher education." This discussion will take place during parts of two class periods. In the first class period your group is to discuss the statement and arrive at a consensus indicating whether the group thinks the statement is true or false. As homework, each group member is to find one article, book, or credible website that has evidence related to the statement. During the second class period your group will reassess the statement in light of the evidence found by each of the group members. Did the addition of evidence change your group's opinion? What effect do you think the addition of evidence had on the group's discussion?

Groupthink: An Unintended Outcome of Group Cohesiveness

Although cohesiveness is generally desirable for groups, dangers arise from too much cohesion. Groupthink is "a mode of thinking people engage in when they are deeply involved in a cohesive in-group . . . members' striving for unanimity overrides their motivation to realistically appraise alternative courses of action [leading to] a deterioration of mental efficiency, reality testing, and moral judgment" (Janis quoted in Neck, 1996). More simply, **groupthink** happens when *the desire for cohesion and agreement takes precedence over critical analysis and discussion.*

Groupthink can destroy effective decision making. Several historical decision-making blunders have been attributed to groupthink, including the failed Iranian hostage rescue mission, the space shuttle *Challenger* disaster, and the failure of American forces to foresee the attack on Pearl Harbor (Neck, 1996). Although groupthink may be difficult to detect when you are in a group, researchers have identified the following observable signs of groupthink:

groupthink

An unintended outcome of cohesion where the desire for agreement takes precedence over critical analysis and discussion.

Teaching Tip

One way to combat groupthink is to ensure that the group is open to outside information. Point out that the addition of new information often makes seemingly "obvious" decisions less obvious.

- An illusion of invulnerability by the group.
- An unquestioned belief in the morality of the group.
- Collective efforts by group members to rationalize faulty decisions.
- Stereotypical views of enemy leaders as evil, weak, or ineffective.
- Self-censorship of alternative viewpoints.
- A shared illusion that all group members think the same thing.
- Direct pressure on group members expressing divergent opinions.
- The emergence of "mind guards" to screen the group from information contradictory to the prevailing opinion.

The general problem is that group cohesiveness, a desirable characteristic of groups, can lead to groupthink. To protect the group from groupthink while still maintaining cohesiveness, groups are encouraged to appoint a "devil's advocate." The role of that person (or persons) is to raise reasoned objections, to express countering viewpoints, and to provide a "reality check." Groupthink may be avoided if groups stress the importance of supporting opinions with evidence. Furthermore, Bernthal and Insko (1993) recommend that emphasizing commitment to the task rather than just commitment to the group can help members overcome the tendency to hold back differing opinions.

Problem Solving and Decision Making

A primary task facing many groups is solving problems: Student clubs need to raise money, church groups need to plan activities, and social groups must find fun things to do. Group members must be both creative and critical to arrive at the best solutions to these problems. Groups are usually (but not always) better problem solvers than individuals, because several people can provide more information than one person. Groups also can supply more resources and collectively have a broader perspective. Group members can also spot flaws in each other's reasoning. However, trade-offs occur. Group problem solving takes longer, and sometimes personality, procedural, or social problems in a group make work as a team difficult for members. Group problem solving is superior under certain conditions, such as when multiple solutions are equally appropriate, decisions must be acceptable to all the members, and the group has ample time to meet and discuss (Vroom, 1973). Groups are particularly well suited for **conjunctive tasks,** *for which no one member has all the necessary information but each member has some information to contribute.* Individuals are often better at **disjunctive tasks,** *which require little coordination and which can be completed by the most skilled member working alone* (Smith, 1989). Group problem solving is usually more effective when the process is systematic and organized because a group that does not have an overall plan for decision making is more likely to make a poor decision (Gouran & Hirokawa, 1986).

Effective Group Problem Solving

Groups using systematic procedures solve problems more effectively and have higher-quality discussions than do groups that do not use systematic procedures (Gouran, Brown, & Henry, 1978). Following a structured procedure often reminds discussants of something they forgot to do (such as analyze the problem thoroughly) in an earlier stage of problem solving and suggests logical priorities (Poole, 1983a, 1983b). An effective problem-solving process starts with an appropriate discussion question, includes

conjunctive task

A task for which no one member has all the necessary information, but each member has some information to contribute.

disjunctive tasks

Tasks which require little coordination and which can be completed by the most skilled member working alone.

CD-ROM Activity

Ask students to view the animation title "Solving Problems Through Small-Group Discussion" on the accompanying student CD-ROM. The animation illustrates the group decision-making model discussed in this chapter.

A small group has formed to solve a problem related to the construction of a new student union. Through communication the group can establish norms, negotiate conflict and solve problems. Below are four stages or steps that the group must work through in order to reach a solution.

COMMUNICATION

STEP 1:   Wording the discussion question

How should the new union be built so that it will be most useful for the campus community?

STEP 2:   Discussing Criteria

The new union must be wheelchair accessible

It should be centrally located

STEP 3:   Identifying Alternatives

STEP 4:   Evaluating Alternatives

The Solution

Video Activity

Ask students to view the video segment "Senior Seminar." To what extent did the group in this segment follow the recommended steps in problem solving? Have students identify examples illustrating each step in the problem-solving process.

Figure 9.4   Solving problems through small-group discussion.

an explicit discussion of the criteria the group will use to judge potential solutions, and follows a systematic problem-solving procedure.

Wording the Discussion Question

Problem-solving groups typically handle three basic types of discussion questions. *Questions of fact* deal with whether something is true or can be verified. *Questions of value* ask whether something is good or bad, better or worse. Cultural and individual values and beliefs are central to the questions of value. *Questions of policy* ask what action should be taken. The key word *should* is either stated or implied in questions of policy. Examples of each type of question are presented in Figure 9.5.

Regardless of the type of discussion question guiding a problem-solving group, the leader must state the question appropriately. Well-stated questions are clear, are measurable, and focus on the problem rather than on a solution. First, the language and terminology should be concrete rather than abstract. If ambiguous terms such as *effective, good,* or *fair* are used, providing examples helps each group member have as close to the same meaning as possible. Figure 9.6 gives examples of how

Group Activity

Ask groups to pick a current event topic and to write discussion questions of fact, value, and policy related to the topic.

FACT

How has the divorce rate changed in the past 15 years?
How many Hispanic students graduate from high school each year?
What percentage of college students graduate in four years?
How often, on average, does a person speak each day?
What occupations earn the highest annual incomes?

VALUE

Why should people seek higher education?
How should Americans treat international students?
Does our legal system provide "justice for all"?
How should young people be educated about AIDS?
What is the value of standardized tests for college admission?

POLICY

What courses should students be required to take?
Should the state's drunk driving laws be changed?
What are the arguments for and against mandatory retirement?
Should the United States intervene in foreign disputes for humanitarian reasons?
What advantages should government provide for businesses willing to develop in high-risk areas of a city?

Figure 9.5 Questions of fact, value, and policy.

> "I think Ms. Brown is **a good lawyer** because she is *very credible*. She *knows the law* and always comes up with novel arguments that her opposing lawyers can't counter."
>
> "Our solution for the parking problem has to be **effective.** I mean, it has to *reduce parking complaints, eliminate the amount of driving around looking for a space that happens now,* and *not cost the university any money."*
>
> "I think **weapons** should be made illegal. I mean, *guns* are really dangerous in the wrong hands, and you can't tell me that people need *semiautomatic assault rifles* to hunt with."

Figure 9.6   Making abstract concepts more concrete.

PROBLEM QUESTIONS	SOLUTION QUESTIONS
How can we reduce complaints about parking on campus?	How can we increase the number of parking spaces in the campus lots?
What can we do to increase attendance at our club's activities?	How can we improve publicity for our club's activities?
How can we make Ginny Avenue safer to cross?	How can we get the city council to reduce the speed limit on Ginny Avenue?

Figure 9.7   Problem questions versus solution questions.

abstract terms can be made more concrete. Second, a well-stated discussion question helps group members know when the solution has been achieved. For example, a task force charged with "completing a report by May 15 on why membership has dropped from 100 to 50 members" knows exactly what to do by what deadline. Finally, a group should start its problem solving with a problem question rather than a solution question. **Problem questions** *focus on the undesirable present state and imply that many solutions are possible.* They do not bias a group toward one particular option. **Solution questions,** on the other hand, *slant the group's discussion toward one particular option.* They may inadvertently cause a group to ignore creative or unusual options because they blind members to some alternatives. Examples of problem and solution questions appear in Figure 9.7.

Discussing Criteria

Criteria are *the standards by which a group must judge potential solutions.* For example, a solution's likely effectiveness ("Will it work?"), acceptability ("Will people vote for our proposal?"), and cost ("Does this option keep us within the budget?") are common criteria. Group members should discuss and agree on criteria before adopting a solution. Because criteria are based on the values of group members, two members, each using rational tools of decision making, can arrive at different conclusions. The more similar group members are in age, gender, ethnicity, background, attitudes, values, and beliefs, the easier they can agree on criteria.

problem questions

Group questions which focus on the undesirable present state and imply that many solutions are possible.

solution questions

Group questions which slant the group's discussion toward one particular option.

criteria

The standards by which a group must judge potential solutions.

ABSOLUTE CRITERIA (*Must* be met)	IMPORTANT CRITERIA (*Should* be met)
• Must not cost more than $2 million. • Must be wheelchair accessible. • Must include flexible space that can be arranged in different ways.	• Should be centrally located. • Should have stage space for concerts. • Should be attractive to all campus constituencies, including traditional and nontraditional students, faculty, and staff.

Figure 9.8   Absolute criteria versus important criteria for a new student union.

Two kinds of criteria are common. **Absolute criteria** are *those that must be met; the group has no leeway.* **Important criteria** are *those that should be met, but the group has some flexibility.* Group members should give the highest priority to criteria that *must* be met. Ideas that do not meet absolute criteria should be rejected, and the rest should be ranked on how well they meet important criteria. Examples of absolute and important criteria are presented in Figure 9.8.

absolute criteria

Criteria for selecting alternatives that must be met; giving the group no leeway.

Identifying Alternatives

One of the most important jobs a leader has is to encourage group creativity. *One procedure that encourages creativity* is **brainstorming,** a technique that originated in the advertising industry to help develop imaginative advertising campaigns (Osborn, 1975). Group brainstorming is generally enhanced when groups are highly cohesive, when leaders are chosen democratically, and when group members have substantial knowledge related to the problem being addressed (Moore, 2000). In fact, Moore's research suggests that any two of these factors allow groups to outperform individuals when brainstorming.

Critical evaluation kills creativity, so the main rule of brainstorming is "no evaluation," at least during the brainstorming process. Evaluation of the ideas takes place *after* the group has exhausted its options.

important criteria

Criteria for evaluating alternatives that should be met, but the group has some flexibility.

brainstorming

A creative procedure for generating ideas and potential solutions to problems.

Evaluating Alternatives

After group members have adequately brainstormed alternatives, the final task is to evaluate alternatives. At this stage in the discussion, criteria identified by the group in step two are used to judge the efficacy of each solution. Solutions failing to meet absolute criteria are quickly eliminated. Once the nonviable alternatives are eliminated, group members must evaluate each alternative based on remaining important criteria. Eventually, the group must determine which alternative best meets the set of important criteria identified in step two.

Beyond Problem Solving: Group Work in a New Era

Earlier in the chapter we shared the story of a group of students working to raise funds to support victims of the September 11 terrorist attacks in New York and Washington. Certainly, one objective for those students was to solve a problem—raising money. However, we question whether problem solving was the primary function of that group. Groups perform a variety of functions related to but not necessarily focused on problem solving. We offer several additional functions of groups that do not necessarily fit the traditional problem-solving model:

1. *Making decisions.* Many groups exist to make decisions that are unrelated to specific problems. For example, student groups like fraternities and sororities make daily decisions like planning social engagements, community outreach projects, and maintaining facilities. These decisions do not necessarily happen to solve problems, but rather, they happen to sustain the day-to-day functions of the groups.

2. *Effecting change.* Some groups want to influence society but do not have the power to make decisions. At the time of writing this chapter, staff members at one of our universities are on strike. This group of workers has little power to make decisions—they cannot force the state to provide a better offer. However, their actions as a group are intended to raise awareness and plead a case. They want to promote change.

3. *Negotiating conflict.* Groups are often created to resolve conflict. In Los Angeles, small groups were used to bring Latino-American and Armenian-American high school students together to resolve racial tensions. In fact, the National Communication Association in partnership with the Southern Poverty Law Center has used this strategy across the nation to promote intercultural understanding and to help resolve racial conflict.

4. *Fostering creativity.* Groups help us achieve a level of creativity not possible when working alone. The idea that "two heads are better than one" is magnified in groups. People working together to identify creative ideas will likely be more successful than one person acting alone.

5. *Maintaining ties between stakeholders.* A final function for small groups is to bring together stakeholders. **Stakeholders** are *groups of people who have an interest in the actions of an organization.* For example, most schools have parent organizations. The principal of a school might bring together selected teachers and parents to discuss issues facing the school so that open lines of communication between various stakeholders (parents, teachers, and administrators) can be maintained. Various organizations, including businesses, government agencies, and nonprofit organizations, use groups to establish and maintain communication between multiple groups of stakeholders.

stakeholders

Groups of people who have an interest in the actions of an organization.

As you can see, groups exist for many reasons. Although the heart of group activity may indeed be problem solving, not all groups exist solely for that purpose.

Technology and Group Communication Processes

Throughout this book we have explored how various forms of technology impact human communication. In small-group communication, technology can be used for facilitating communication as well as for sharing strategic information necessary for decision making. One form of group technology is decision support systems.

A **group decision support system (GDSS)** is *an interactive network of computers with specialized software allowing users to generate solutions for unstructured problems* (Sosik, Avolio, & Kahai, 1997). Although the exact nature of the GDSS environment can be tailored to specific situations, most GDSS-based group interactions are used to facilitate brainstorming and evaluation of alternatives. In a typical GDSS session members anonymously post ideas using a personal computer. Although postings are anonymous, each member of the group can see ideas posted by other members. By doing this, ideas generated by one person may generate additional ideas by someone else. After a predetermined length of time for brainstorming, members can anonymously rank and/or rate each idea. The software summarizes the results of members' ranking and/or ratings. Most GDSSs also allow members to anonymously vote to indicate their choice for the best alternative. Some GDSSs also allow for anonymous text-based discussions using the computer.

Computers can be used to facilitate group communication.

The key characteristics of GDSSs are anonymity and efficiency. Because individuals' ideas are anonymous, discussions using GDSSs tend to result in better information sharing and critical analysis of ideas than face-to-face interactions (Lam & Schaubroek, 2000). Although GDSSs tend to encourage minority viewpoints to be expressed more frequently, those viewpoints may have less impact on others' opinions in GDSS environments than in face-to-face environments (McLeod, Baron, Weighner, & Yoon, 1997). In addition to being anonymous, GDSSs are also efficient. In reviewing more than 28 experimental studies comparing GDSS discussion groups to face-to-face groups, Hwang (1998) concluded that GDSSs resulted in significantly more ideas generated than traditional face-to-face groups. Thus in the same amount of time the efficiency of brainstorming is significantly improved by GDSS-based discussions. Aiken and Martin (1994) also suggested that GDSSs have the potential to reduce the likelihood of groupthink because alternative opinions can be presented anonymously.

group decision support systems (GDSS)

Interactive network of computers with specialized software allowing users to generate solutions for unstructured problems.

E-Note

SMALL-GROUP SKILLS ON THE WEB

Because small-group communication is becoming such a vital component of nearly every organization, many consulting firms now offer professional workshops aimed at helping organizations implement effective small-group practices. 3M corporation has a website containing several online resources that can help you improve your skills in small groups. Go to the website, **www.3M.com/meetingnetwork/readingroom/facilitation.html**. On this website you will find several activities devoted to improving small-group communication skills. Find and print an activity that looks interesting to you. Each activity begins with a section labeled "theory" explaining the concept being taught. After reading that section, note how you think the activity connects to the chapter. In other words, does the activity relate to one of the concepts or skills discussed in this chapter? If so, how?

Discussion Question

How effective do you think computer-mediated group communication would be? Do you think computer technology would generally help or hinder group communication?

Although GDSSs are gaining wide popularity in the private sector, the cost of such systems makes them unaffordable for most colleges and universities. With effort, many of the GDSS advantages can be gained through setting up private chat rooms where users can log in under anonymous names. Many online services like AOL and Lycos offer chat rooms as a free service. By using nonidentifiable nicknames members of the group can post ideas for viewing by other group members. Entire discussions can take place in such chat rooms where each person remains anonymous.

How Should You Communicate in Small Groups?

If you, as a group member, are responsible, with the other members, for the outcomes of the groups to which you belong, what can you do to help achieve productive outcomes? The ability to speak fluently and with polish is not essential, but the ability to speak clearly is. You will help fellow group members understand you better by organizing your comments during small-group discussions.

1. *Relate your statements to preceding remarks.* Public speakers do not always have the opportunity to respond to remarks by others, but small-group members do. Your statement should not appear irrelevant. Clarify the relevance of your remark to the topic under discussion by linking your remark to the immediately preceding remark.

2. *Use conventional word arrangement.* When you speak, you should use conventional sentences so that people can understand you bet-

ter. You have more latitude in written English, in which punctuation helps readers follow the thought and readers have time to think about what you have written.

3. *Speak concisely.* Don't be long-winded. During a speech, the audience expects the speaker to monopolize the floor, but during a small-group discussion, every member wants and deserves a turn.

4. *State one point at a time.* Sometimes this rule is violated appropriately, such as when one group member presents a report to the rest of the group. However, during give-and-take discussion, stating one idea at a time promotes efficiency and responsiveness.

Being an Ethical Group Member

Ethics are *"a set of principles of right conduct"* (*American Heritage Dictionary of the English Language* [online edition], 2000, np). The unique nature of small groups requires attention to special ethical concerns regarding the treatment of speech, of people, and of information.

First, as noted in the NCA Credo of Ethics discussed earlier in the book, the field of communication strongly supports the value of free speech. Many secondary groups are formed because several heads perform better than one, but that advantage will not be realized if group members are unwilling or afraid to speak freely in the group. An important ethical principle for small groups is that group members should be willing to share their unique perspectives. They should also refrain from saying or doing things that prevent others from speaking freely. Members who are trustworthy and supportive are behaving ethically.

Second, group members must be honest and truthful. In a small group, they should not intentionally deceive one another or manufacture information or evidence to persuade other members to adopt their point of view.

Third, group members must be thorough and unbiased when they evaluate information. Many decisions made in groups, from where to locate a mall to whether it is safe to launch a space shuttle in cold weather, affect people's lives. Such decisions will be only as good as the information on which they are based and the reasoning the members use to assess the information. Group members must consider *all* relevant information in an open-minded, unbiased way by using the best critical thinking skills they can; otherwise, tragedies can result.

Finally, group members must behave with integrity. Members must be willing to place the good of the group ahead of their own goals. Some individuals cannot be team players because they are unable or unwilling to merge their personal agendas with those of the group. Groups are better off without such individuals. If you make a commitment to join a group, you should be the kind of team member who will benefit rather than harm the group. If you cannot in good conscience give a group your support, you should leave the group rather than to pretend to support the group while sabotaging it.

ethics

Rules and standards for the conduct and practices of group members.

Chapter Review

SUMMARY

In this chapter you have learned the following:

- Small-group communication is the interaction of a small group of people working together to achieve a common goal. Small-group communication is relevant to our lives because
  - Humans need groups to meet needs they cannot meet for themselves.
  - Groups are everywhere.
  - Group communication is a highly valued skill.
  - Working effectively in groups requires training.
- Small groups provide a way of participating in society.
- Small groups can be classified as task related, relationship related, assigned, or emergent. Many groups can blur boundaries among these types of groups.
- Leadership is the process of using communication to influence the behaviors and attitudes of people to meet group goals. Various theories discuss how leadership affects small-group communication. The most effective leaders are able to adapt their leadership skills to the needs of the group. Additionally, all members of the group can potentially share leadership responsibilities.
- Group culture is created from several factors including within-group diversity, group norms, individuals' role structures, and group cohesiveness. Although group cohesiveness is generally viewed as a positive element of group culture, highly cohesive groups must take care to prevent groupthink from occurring.
- Group decision making involves four steps
  - Wording the discussion question.
  - Discussing criteria for evaluating potential solutions.
  - Brainstorming alternatives.
  - Evaluating alternatives.
- The group leader(s) can play an important role in helping the group maintain structure and creativity throughout this process.
- Small-group communication can utilize technology to help facilitate communication and decision making.
  - Computer networking, either through traditional or peer-to-peer networking, allows members of a group to communicate electronically and share information.
  - Group Decision Support Systems use special software to facilitate brainstorming and decision making. Group members are able to anonymously present ideas to other members and are also able to anonymously rate and vote for specific alternatives.
- To effectively communicate in small groups you must use clear language and make concise comments that are related to the comments of other group members. You should try to keep your comments limited to one issue at a time.
- Ethical behaviors in group contexts include allowing others to speak without fear, being honest and truthful, carefully evaluating alternatives, and acting with integrity.

◉ VIDEO LINK: SUSAN CLAIRE, ENRIQUE, AND MIKE: A GROUP IN ACTION

Video Episode 4: "Senior Seminar"

Small groups exist for a variety of purposes, not the least of which is to make decisions and get things done. Watch "Senior Seminar" and consider how Susan Elliott's small group performs. Is there an emergent leader in the group? Is the emergent leader the same person as the assigned leader? What leadership styles do the various leaders use? Do you see evidence that the group followed the group problem-solving model discussed in this chapter? What behavioral roles do the various members of the group enact? Finally, do you see evidence that the group was at risk of groupthink?

ISSUES IN COMMUNICATION: REAL WORLD GROUPS

Are small groups relevant to the real world? Certainly the contemporary image of corporate America—particularly corporate giants like Microsoft and General Motors—is that work groups get the job done. But for those of us who work in small businesses with only a handful of employees, how can we use small groups when our staff may itself be a small group?

Allison McLean (2001) reports on the use of peer groups by owners of small printing businesses across the United States. Peer groups vary in size; however, the largest peer group coordinated by the Printing Executive Network (PEN) is about 15 people. Peer groups have been used in the small printing industry for nearly 20 years and there are currently about 11 active groups working under the auspices of the PEN and several others operating independently. Groups are typically comprised of people from businesses with similar financial resources.

Each group has its own norms for meetings. For example, some groups combine social and business activities by meeting in the city of one of the group members, playing golf, and spending two days discussing strategies for marketing and business operations. Other groups meet for shorter durations and limit their activities to discussing business matters. Thus, some peer groups have characteristics of both task-oriented and relationship-oriented groups; others are primarily task-oriented groups. Additionally, some groups bring in outside facilitators, whereas others structure their own meetings.

Two rules guide the behaviors of peer groups. First, no two members of any peer group can be in direct competition with one another. Because of this rule, members of the group can freely give advice without worrying that they will be placed at a competitive disadvantage. Second, peer groups must "hold feet to the fire." McLean explains that the groups act as a sort of "Board of Directors" for individual firms. If the group gives a member suggestions for improvement, the owner of the firm must demonstrate progress toward meeting those suggestions at the next meeting. The groups provide a sense of external accountability not normally felt in small-business environments. To further create this sense of accountability, members normally share financial data for their individual firms with other members of the group.

Although the use of peer groups does pose some expense—mainly for travel—for individual firms, owners acknowledge that receiving recommendations from objective peers more than makes up for any financial loss. In addition, peer groups can provide each other with quick advice or just encouragement. Some groups even pool resources to create advertising campaigns that can be used by each business—thus resulting in a higher quality campaign without higher cost to each firm.

All of the professionals interviewed by McLean indirectly point to the importance of synergy, or the collaborative fit between members of the group. John Stewart, a coordinator for several peer groups, reported that as many as 10 percent to 15 percent of new members of a group elect or are asked to resign their membership within the first four meetings because they are unable to effectively collaborate with other members. Those collaborators who are able to work effectively with the group quickly see advantages from the synergy and collaboration.

Although the term "work groups" typically conjures up images of large corporations, peer groups in the printing industry illustrate how small businesses can also capitalize on the benefits of groups.

Based on this description of peer groups, how would you classify these groups? Are they primary or secondary groups? Are they assigned or emergent? How do you think leadership would be established in these types of groups? How susceptible do you think these groups would be to groupthink? Given the nature of these groups, what types of ethical norms do you think would be necessary for the groups to function effectively?

KEY TERMS

Use the *Human Communication* CD-ROM and the *Online Learning Center* at www.mhhe.com/pearson to further your understanding of the following terminology.

Absolute criteria	Control	Group culture
Affection	Criteria	Group Decision Support
Assigned groups	Democratic leaders	System (GDSS)
Autocratic leaders	Designated leaders	Groupthink
Brainstorming	Disjunctive task	Important criteria
Charisma	Distributed leadership	Inclusion
Coercion	Emergent groups	Informal role
Cognitive paradigms	Emergent leader	Laissez-faire leaders
Cohesiveness	Ethics	Leader
Communicative	Expert power	Leadership
competencies approach	Formal role	Maintenance functions
Conjunctive task	Gender	Norms
Contingency approaches	Group climate	Power

Problem questions
Punishment power
Referent power
Relationship-oriented
   groups
Reward power
Role

Self-centered functions
Sex
Small-group
   communication
Solution questions
Stakeholders

Style approaches
Supportive climate
Task functions
Task-oriented groups
Trust
Within-group diversity

SELF-QUIZ

Go to the self-quizzes on the *Human Communication* CD-ROM and the *Online Learning Center* at www.mhhe.com/pearson to test your knowledge.

REFERENCES

Aiken, M., & Martin, J. (1994, September). Enhancing business communication with group decision support systems. *Bulletin of the Association for Business Communication, 57,* 24–27.

Baird, J. E. (1986). Sex differences in group communication: A review of relevant research. *Quarterly Journal of Speech, 62,* 179–192.

Barge, J. K. (1989, Fall). Leadership as medium: A leaderless group discussion model. *Communication Quarterly, 37,* 237–247.

Barge, J. K., & Hirokawa, R. Y. (1989). Toward a communication competency model of group leadership. *Small Group Behavior, 20,* 167–189.

Barker, D. B. (1991, February). The behavioral analysis of interpersonal intimacy in group development. *Small Group Research, 22,* 76–91.

Bernthal, P., & Insko, C. (1993). Cohesiveness without groupthink: The interactive effects of social and task cohesion. *Group & Organizational Management, 18,* 66–87.

Burrell, N. A., Donohue, W. A., & Allen, M. (1988). Gender-based perceptual biases in mediation. *Communication Research, 15,* 447–469.

Callaway, E. (1997, September 15). That team mystique. *PC Week, 14,* 99–101.

Carlson, J., Carlson, D., & Wadsworth, L. (2000, September 30). The relationship between individual power moves and group agreement type: An examination and model. *SAM Advanced Management Journal, 65,* 44–50.

Cole, D. (1989, May). Meetings that make sense. *Psychology Today, 23,* 14.

Counselman, E. F. (1991, May). Leadership in a long term leaderless group. *Small Group Research, 22,* 240–257.

Drucker, P. (1992). *Managing for the future: The 1990s and beyond.* New York: Truman Talley Books/Dutton.

DuBois, C. C. (1992, September–October). Portrait of the ideal MBA. *The Penn Stater, 31.*

Duerst-Lahti, G. (1990, August). But women play the game too: Communication control and influence in administrative decision making. *Administration and Society, 22,* 182–205.

Foeman, A. K., & Pressley, G. (1987, Fall). Ethnic culture and corporate culture: Using black styles in organizations. *Communication Quarterly, 35,* 293–307.

French, J. R. P., & Raven, B. (1981). The bases of social power. In D. Cartwright & A. Zander (Eds.), *Group dynamics: Research and theory* (3rd ed.). New York: McGraw-Hill.

Galanes, G. J. (1997). The dynamic of small group discussion. In J. C. Pearson & P. E. Nelson (Eds.), *An introduction to human communication* (7th ed.). Dubuque, IA: Brown & Benchmark.

Galanes, G., Brilhart, J., & Adams, K. (2000). *Communicating in groups: Applications and skills.* New York: McGraw-Hill.

Gibb, J. R. (1961). Defensive communication. *Journal of Communication, 11,* 141–148.

Gouran, D. S., Brown, C., & Henry, D. R. (1978). Behavioral correlates of perceptions of quality in decision-making discussions. *Communication Monographs, 45,* 62.

Gouran, D. S., & Hirokawa, R. Y. (1986). Counteractive functions of communication in effective group decision-making. In R. Y. Hirokawa & M. S. Poole (Eds.), *Communication and group decision-making.* Beverly Hills, CA: Sage.

Graen, G., Dansereau, G., & Minami, T. (1972). Dysfunctional leadership styles. *Organizational Behavior and Human Performance, 7,* 216–236.

Hackman, M. Z., & Johnson, C. E. (1991). *Leadership: A communication perspective.* Prospect Heights, IL: Waveland Press.

Homans, G. C. (1950). *The human group.* New York: Harcourt Brace Jovanovich.

Hwang, M. (1998, February). Did task type matter in the use of decision room GSS? A critical review and a meta-analysis. *Omega, 26,* 1–15.

Jurma, W. E. (1978). Leadership structuring style, task ambiguity and group members' satisfaction. *Small Group Behavior, 9,* 124–134.

Jurma, W. E. (1979). Effects of leader structuring style and task-orientation characteristics of group members. *Communication Monographs, 46,* 282.

Kelly, L., & Duran, R. L. (1985). Interaction and performance in small groups: A descriptive report. *International Journal of Small Group Research, 1,* 182–192.

Lam, S., & Schaubroeck, J. (2000). Improving group decisions by better pooling information: A comparative advantage of Group Decision Support Systems. *Journal of Applied Psychology, 85,* 565–588.

Mabry, E. A. (1989). Some theoretical implications of female and male interaction in unstructured small groups. *Small Group Behavior, 20,* 536–550.

Maier, N. R. F., & Maier, R. A. (1957). An experimental test of the effects of "developmental" vs. "free" discussions on the quality of group decisions. *Journal of Applied Psychology, 41,* 320–323.

McLean, A. (2001, April). Peering in to better business: Peer groups in the business industry. *American Printer, 227,* 50–52.

McLeod, P., Baron, R., Weighner, M., & Yoon, K. (1997). The eyes have it: Minority influence in face-to-face and computer-mediated group discussion. *Journal of Applied Psychology, 82,* 706–719.

Moore, R. (2000). Creativity of small groups and of persons working alone. *Journal of Social Psychology, 140,* 142–144.

Neck, C. (1996, November). Letterman or Leno: A groupthink analysis of successive decisions made by the National Broadcasting Company. *Journal of Managerial Psychology, 11,* 3–18.

Osborn, A. (1975). *Applied imagination.* New York: Scribner's.

Poole, M. S. (1983a). Decision development in small groups: II. A study of multiple sequences in decision making. *Communication Monographs, 50,* 224–225.

Poole, M. S. (1983b). Decision development in small groups: III. A multiple sequence model of group decision development. *Communication Monographs, 50,* 321–341.

Preston, M. G., & Heintz, R. K. (1949). Effectiveness of participatory versus supervisory leadership in group judgment. *Journal of Abnormal and Social Psychology, 44,* 344–345.

Rosenfeld, L. B., & Plax, T. B. (1975). Personality determinants of autocratic and democratic leadership. *Speech Monographs, 42,* 203–208.

Schutz, W. C. (1958). *FIRO: A three-dimensional theory of interpersonal behavior.* New York: Rinehart.

Shaw, J., & Barrett-Power, E. (1998). The effects of diversity on small work group processes and performance. *Human Relations, 51,* 1307–1326.

Shimanoff, S. B. (1992). Coordinating group interaction via communication rules. In R. S. Cathcart & L. A. Samovar (Eds.), *Small group communication: A reader* (6th ed., p. 225). Dubuque, IA: William C. Brown.

Smith, H. W. (1989). Group versus individual problem solving and type of problem solved. *Small Group Behavior, 20,* 357–366.

Smith-Lovin, L., & Brody, C. (1989, June). Interruptions in group discussions: The effects of gender and group composition. *American Sociological Review, 54,* 424–435.

Sosik, J., Avolio, B., & Kahai, S. (1997). Effects of leadership style and anonymity on group potency and effectiveness in a group decision support system environment. *Journal of Applied Psychology, 82,* 90–104.

Stroud, L. (1988, November 15). No CEO is an island. *American,* pp. 94–97, 140–141.

Vice, J. (2001). Developing communication and professional skills through analytical reports. *Business Communication Quarterly, 64,* 84–93.

Vroom, V. H. (1973). A new look at management decision-making. *Organizational Dynamics,* pp. 66–80.

White, R. K., & Lippett, R. (1960). Leader behavior and member ration in three "social climates." In D. Cartwright & A. Zander (Eds.), *Group dynamics: Research and theory* (2nd ed.). Evanston, IL: Row, Peterson.

Wood, C. J. (1989). Challenging the assumptions underlying the use of participatory decision-making strategies: A longitudinal case study. *Small Group Behavior, 20,* 428–448.

CHAPTER TEN

Work ought to dignify rather than diminish the human spirit.

GEORGE CHENEY

Meaningful democratic participation in organizations creates better citizens and better social choices, and provides important economic benefits.

STANLEY DEETZ

As is true of all instances when humans band together to amplify their individual efforts, communication is essential in the endeavor of managers to create, produce, and sell products or provide services.

ROBERT HEATH

Communicating at Work

What will you learn?

When you have read and thought about this chapter, you will be able to:

1. Define organizational communication.
2. Recognize different organization types.
3. Explain how structures develop in organizations.
4. Identify different types of organizational structure.
5. Identify types of communication in organizational networks.
6. Describe the process of organizational socialization.
7. Explain how organizational images are created through public relations and crisis management efforts.
8. Utilize communication skills necessary for effective customer service.
9. Recognize and avoid aggressive communication in the workplace, including sexual harassment.

The very fabric of our social, cultural, and economic worlds is **organizationally based,** thus the need for us to be competent communicators in organizational settings is undeniable. Organizational communication practices can enhance, or diminish, our role in inventing a better future and maintaining some degree of control over our work environment. In this chapter we introduce you to the study of organizational communication, including internal and external organizational communication, the dark side of communication in organizations, and ethical approaches to competent communication in organizational settings.

Kisha, a 36-year-old mother of three, decided to finish her degree in graphic arts at the university. Because her youngest two children were still in middle school, Kisha continued to work part time while taking classes. The prospect of two college educations—one for Mattie and another for Serena—loomed on Kisha and William's mind.

While at the university, Kisha developed a solid relationship with her adviser, Dr. Morgan. One afternoon Kisha, nearly in tears, approached Dr. Morgan to talk about problems she was having managing her multiple responsibilities.

"Dr. Morgan, I am having a problem with my supervisor, Tom. He wants me to work more hours next month because it is a crunch time for the firm. They are trying to get a big project done and they need me to be in charge of the artwork for the materials we are producing. I just don't know what to do. I am having a hard time already working and going to school. I won't even mention my poor husband and daughters."

"Kisha, I know exactly what you're saying. I dealt with that same problem when I was trying to get tenure—it seemed like I had to work all day, every day. Sometimes I wonder if it was worth the time I spent in this office rather than with Calvin and Jesse."

"How did you manage? I mean, you got tenure and your family is great. I need help!"

"I just don't have an answer for you, Kisha," replied Dr. Morgan. "Our lives are so complex, and we are not just mothers and wives any more. We belong to several organizations, and they all want our undivided attention. I know I'm guilty of that. I am your teacher, and, of course, the world revolves around my class!"

"I get what you're saying. I mean, I feel like my family, school, and work are all pulling me in different directions. I just need to find ways to cope with it, I guess."

Kisha is not alone in her struggle to manage the multiple responsibilities of belonging to several organizations. In fact, the various organizations we affiliate with create a variety of tensions in our lives. Studying organizational communication helps all of us understand the essential processes of organizing, processes that simultaneously liberate and constrain us.

What Is the Study of Organizational Communication?

Organizations are everywhere. Each of us has many organizational affiliations. Not only do we belong to numerous organizations; we also interact with and seek the services of an even broader range of organizations on a daily basis. For example, you may belong to one or more business organizations, perhaps as employees, supervisors, or investors. Since you are reading this book, you are most likely a student in college. You may also belong to organizations that operate within the boundaries of this broader academic organization—sports teams, governing bodies, sororities or fraternities, academic departments, and maybe more. You are also members of national, state, and local government organizations.

As you begin to reflect on the different organizations to which you belong, you will realize that to escape organizational membership in modern society is virtually impossible. Very few persons have the skills, experiences, or opportunities to personally do everything that is necessary to live a productive life. The vast majority of us actually can do very little; we are constantly at the mercy of electricians, auto mechanics, farmers, and so on. Organizations exist because people's lives have become sufficiently complex that they must cooperate with one another. In other words, **organizations** are *social collectives, or groups of people, in which activities are coordinated to achieve both individual and collective goals.*

Organization is an important term that refers to both a process that people engage in and the successful outcome of the activity. To *organize* is to engage in the process of developing coordinated activities. The term *organization* is also used to describe a specific context. As such, the word identifies structural entities, such as businesses, industries, hospitals, and government agencies. Organizations are typically viewed as "containers," or contexts, buildings, or places where people work, such as Microsoft, the Pentagon, and Philip Morris Industries. Organizations appear to be stable structural entities; yet, when viewing organizations as static structures, we fail to notice the ongoing organizational processes. Weick (1995) reminds us that we can recognize the outcome of *organization* (noun) only when the process of *organizing* (verb) is being accomplished.

The fundamental way in which people organize is through the process of communication. Indeed, our very survival depends on the extent to which we can effectively negotiate and persuade one another within culturally diverse and complex organizational settings. To reflect on organizational life without considering the innumerable ways we interact with others, in one or more languages, through one or more channels, is impossible. The very foundation of any organization is the communication process occurring between people. As discussed in chapter 9, interactions among people are the primary ways in which people move from a disorganized state of individuals to an organized, coordinated group of individuals capable of collectively accomplishing tasks and adapting to environments. In sum, communication is the substance of organizational life.

The study of organizational communication involves understanding how the context of the organization influences communication processes and how the symbolic nature of communication differentiates it from other forms of organizational behavior. We define **organizational communication** as *the ways in which groups of people both maintain structure and order through their symbolic interactions and allow individual actors*

organizations

Social collectives, or groups of people, in which activities are coordinated to achieve both individual and collective goals.

organizational communication

The ways in which groups of people both maintain structure and order through their symbolic interactions and allow individual actors the freedom to accomplish their goals.

structuration

The process of forming and maintaining structures through verbal and nonverbal communication, which establishes norms and rules governing members' behaviors.

the freedom to accomplish their goals. This definition recognizes that communication is the primary tool to influence organizations and gain access to organizational resources. However, communication is not simply a process of exchanging information with one another, although information exchange is an important part of communicating. Communication is a process through which we make sense out of our experiences, a complex system through which we manage meanings that ultimately create and maintain organizational structures. This concept is known as **structuration,** *the process of forming and maintaining structures through verbal and nonverbal communication, which establishes norms and rules governing members' behaviors* (Giddens, 1979, 1984).

Video Activity

Ask students to view the video segment "Senior Seminar." Have students analyze the structuration process in the group dialogue shown in the segment.

Applications of Giddens's (1979, 1984) structuration theory in the study of organizational communication are complex. However, the main point is this: Communication among members is what creates organizational rules and operating procedures in the first place, and once they are established, communication tends to keep the rules and procedures in place.

functional classification system

A classification of organizational types based on the primary purposes for organizing and developing organization within society.

Knowledge about organizational communication allows us to ask informed questions about everyday business practices, develop communication skills that can improve our ability to promote organizational and individual effectiveness, and improve the quality of our work life. We begin our exploration of organizational communication by discussing types of organizations and organizational structures. Next, we highlight processes of internal and external organizational communication. Finally, we explore the "dark side" of organizational communication and ethical approaches to workplace communication.

Types of Organization

Parsons (1963) provides a **functional classification system** of organizational types *based on the primary purposes for organizing and developing organization within society.* Parsons identifies four primary functions that organizations are constructed to perform. Some organizations may seem to perform more than one of these functions. Yet we usually can classify an organization based on the organization's most basic and primary social service.

economic production orientation

Organizations that manufacture products and/or other services for consumers.

Organizations with an **economic production orientation** *manufacture products and/or other services for consumers.* Most profit-making businesses are oriented to economic production. Target and Wal-Mart represent organizations oriented to economic production. These organizations are typically self-sufficient, surviving or failing to survive based on the organizations' abilities to cover expenses through the sale of products and/or services.

Complex organizations require members to perform specialized roles. Such specialization is often reflected by organizational structure.

political-goals orientation

Organizations that generate and distribute power and control within society.

integration-goals orientation

Organizations that help to mediate and resolve discord among members of society.

pattern-maintenance goal orientation

Organizations that promote cultural and educational regularity and development within society.

Organizations oriented to **political goals** *generate and distribute power and control within society.* Federal and local governments generally fund these organizations. Government offices, legislative bodies, police and military forces, and even financial institutions are oriented to political goals given that banking systems create and allocate power in a business economy.

Organizations oriented to **integration goals** *help to mediate and resolve discord among members of society.* Organizations that are created to help solve social problems, including legal offices, the court system, and public-interest groups, are integration oriented.

Organizations oriented to **pattern-maintenance goals** *promote cultural and educational regularity and development within society.* Organizations that function to teach individuals how to participate effectively in society, including families, schools, and religious organizations, promote pattern maintenance. To the extent that they help preserve society by reducing health problems and help the ill to return to their normal functioning within society, health care organizations are oriented toward pattern maintenance.

Not only are organizations an inescapable part of modern life, but organizational life has become exceedingly complex. We are expected to perform unique roles in a variety of organizational structures. Different goals, rules, responsibilities, and communication networks are associated with membership in different organizational structures.

Think, Pair, Share

Organizations can be classified according to the function that they serve for society and us. For each type of organization listed below, think of an example from your own life. You might think of organizations to which you belong (e.g., your school, your work, your church, clubs) or organizations that you are indirectly affected by (e.g., student government, state legislature). Spend about five minutes identifying your own examples and then share your examples with your discussion partner.

- An organization oriented to *economic production*.
- An organization oriented to *political goals*.
- An organization oriented to *integration goals*.
- An organization oriented to *pattern-maintenance goals*.

What are the similarities and differences between your list and your partner's?

Organizational Structures

organizational structure

Patterns of relations and practices created through the coordinated activities of organizational members.

productivity

The ratio of input to output.

quality

Levels of performance outcome measured in ability to meet or exceed stakeholders' expectations.

The patterns of relations and practices created through the coordinated activities of organizational members can be conceptualized as the **organizational structure** (McPhee & Poole, 2001). Most members of organizations know what their jobs are, how they are related to other jobs, who the boss is, and who has what organizational power. Communication practices often depend on knowledge of these facts. In other words, organizational structures assist individuals in dealing with each other and with others in the larger organizational environment.

Ideally, organizational structures allow people who manage and work in companies to be productive and achieve high-quality outcomes. **Productivity** entails *the ratio of input to output;* as material and human resources expended to achieve individual and organizational output decline, productivity increases. **Quality** deals with *levels of performance outcome measured in ability to meet or exceed customer or other stakeholder expectations.*

Understanding structure as patterns that emerge from coordinated activities assumes that organizational structure can take a wide variety of forms, depending on the goals and coordinating activities of organizational members. Organizational structures are often classified as one of two broad types: (1) traditional or bureaucratic structures, and (2) alternative or participatory structures (Harrison, 1994).

Bureaucratic Structures

What is a bureaucracy? The word has come to symbolize red tape, inefficiency, and insensitivity. Though the term is widely used and humans have worked in bureaucratic organizations for the past century, seldom do we reflect on the meaning of a bureaucracy. **Bureaucracy** is a term coined in the 1940s by Max Weber, a German sociologist, and is used to describe *organizational structures characterized by a division of labor, rigid hierarchy of authority, and downward communication that enforces formalized rules and procedures for behavior.*

Division of labor refers to *how a given amount of work is divided among the available human resources.* Bureaucratic structures assume that work can best be accomplished if employees are assigned to a limited number of specialized tasks. By breaking down complex tasks into specialized activities, worker productivity can be increased. One person or twenty sort all the mail; another delivers the mail. Formal positions in a division of labor are thus defined by a group of specialized duties which people are selected to perform based on their technical expertise. The chemists are all located in research and development. Even in very small organizations such as law firms, divisions of labor are present among secretarial staff, paralegals, and attorneys.

Divisions of labor work best when the organization has *clear lines of authority,* or a **chain of command.** In bureaucratic structures, jobs are arranged in a clearly defined **hierarchy** of *formal organizational authority based on the office held and the expertise of individual officeholders.* Hierarchies help to direct interpersonal relationships between organization members toward the accomplishment of organizational tasks. Such structure is clearly represented in the military, the police, the firefighters, and some churches and government offices. Bureaucratic structure can also be seen in manufacturing and service organizations in which various departments are responsible for specific tasks and in which these functional units are linked through a hierarchy.

Managers (i.e., superiors) are *responsible for making decisions and directing activities to accomplish primary organizational goals.* One hallmark of bureaucratic structures is an emphasis on **downward communication,** which occurs *whenever superiors initiate messages to subordinates.* Typically, downward communication focuses on enforcing formalized rules and procedures to guide behavior and accomplish tasks.

An examination of most contemporary organizations should reveal the presence of bureaucratic structure. Consider, for example, registering for the introduction to communication course in which you are currently enrolled. Undoubtedly this process involved following rules for who can take a class and when, standardized procedures created by administrators to organize the process of registration, a hierarchy of university employees coordinating the process including the registrar and support staff, and so on. You may go to the campus union for lunch and observe

bureaucracy

An organizational structure characterized by a division of labor, rigid hierarchy of authority, and downward communication that enforces formalized rules and procedures for behavior.

division of labor

How a given amount of work is divided among the available human resources.

chain of command

Clear lines of authority.

hierarchy

Formal organizational authority based on the office held and the expertise of individual officeholders.

managers

Persons responsible for making decisions and directing activities to accomplish primary organizational goals.

downward communication

Communication in which superiors initiate messages to subordinates.

a division of labor among cooks, wait staff, and janitors, whose work is managed by one or more supervisors.

Although the presence of bureaucracy is undeniable, bureaucratic structures are often criticized for stifling employees through their rigid hierarchies and rules, overemphasizing organizational goals, and limiting participation of individuals in organizational decision making. Scholars and practitioners alike agree that an evolutionary force in our society presently is moving us away from traditional bureaucratic structures toward "participatory" forms of coordinating work activities (Ashcraft, 2000; Cheney, Mumby, Stohl, & Harrison, 1997; Harter & Krone, 2001).

Participatory Organizational Structures

Participatory organizations are structured to *value workplace democracy*. Providing a definition of workplace democracy is complex, with very few individuals agreeing on a single definition. Some scholars frame workplace democracy on a philosophical level as an expression of the fundamental human tendency toward freedom and equality while others focus on methods by which people work together in pursuit of their individual and collective goals. We embrace the following definition of **workplace democracy:**

> *A system of governance which truly values individual goals and feelings [e.g., equitable remuneration, the pursuit of enriching work, and the right to express oneself] as well as typical organizational objectives [e.g., effectiveness and efficiency], and actively fosters the connection between those two sets of concerns by encouraging individual contributions to important organizational choices.* (Cheney, 1995, p. 17)

Democratic organizations can be classified in two groups: (1) participation programs in existing bureaucratic structures, and (2) alternative organizational structures (e.g, cooperatives, feminist organizations). Both types of workplace democracy promote the participation of diverse voices in open dialogue.

Within existing bureaucratic structures, small groups are often used to promote employee participation in decision making. Quality circles and self-managed work teams illustrate this approach to workplace democracy. A **quality circle** is *a small group of employees that meets regularly on company time to recommend improvements to products and work procedures.* Many U.S. companies have used quality circles to improve worker safety, create new products, save production costs, improve current products, and improve the quality of the work environment (Barker, 1999).

Margin glossary

participatory organizations

Organizations that value workplace democracy.

workplace democracy

A system of governance that values individual goals and feelings (e.g., feelings of equitable remuneration, the pursuit of enriching work and the right to express oneself) as well as typical organizational objectives (e.g., effectiveness and efficiency) and actively fosters the connection between those two sets of concerns by encouraging individual contributions to important organizational choices.

quality circle

A small group of employees that meets regularly on company time to recommend improvements to products and work procedures.

TRY ◄ THIS

Identify factors that would facilitate or hinder workplace democracy. For instance, what types of superior–subordinate relationships would promote more democratic practices?

THE CULTURE OF QUALITY CIRCLES

Quality circles were developed after World War II through American and Japanese collaboration (Ruch, 1984). They took hold readily in Japan, which has a small-group-oriented culture. Japanese industry made extensive use of quality circles to improve the quality of Japanese goods. As a result, a Japanese label represents high quality. Quality circles were slower to be adopted in the United States, where managers feared that they would reduce management's power and labor union members feared that they were a ploy to increase production without compensating workers (Lawler & Mohrman, 1985).

Self-managed work teams are autonomous working groups used to accomplish a variety of organizational tasks.

Video Activity

Ask students to view the video segment "Senior Seminar." This segment illustrates the function of self-managed work teams. The students were in charge of producing a package for the campus TV station.

Self-managed work teams, also called autonomous work groups, are *groups of workers who are given the freedom to manage their own work.* For example, an automobile assembly team may be responsible for assembling a car from start to finish, as is done at Volvo and Saturn plants (Deetz, 1995). Workers are free to select their own team leaders and sometimes to hire and fire their own members. They determine who will do what job and in what order. Members of self-managed work teams are often cross-trained so that each member can perform several tasks

self-managed work teams

Groups of workers who are given the freedom to manage their own work.

311

alternative organizations

Employing organizations that define themselves at least somewhat in opposition to the mainstream and are established and maintained with the principle of worker control.

cooperative

A business owned and democratically controlled by its users.

feminist organization

An organization that embraces collectivist decision-making, member empowerment, and a political agenda of ending women's oppression.

Discussion Question

We have witnessed a resurgence in growth of alternative organizations in our country. Ask students to identify possible factors related to this growth.

competently. This arrangement gives the team tremendous flexibility to use workers' skills most efficiently.

Alternative organizations also represent participatory structures. Cheney (1995) defined **alternative organizations** as *"employing organizations that define themselves at least somewhat in opposition to the mainstream and are established and maintained with the principle of worker control"* (p. 171). At the heart of alternative organizational structures is the priority of workplace democracy. Cooperatives and feminist organizations are examples of alternative organizations.

A **cooperative** is *a business that is owned and democratically controlled by its users.* Sugar beet farmers cooperate by limiting production; owning the trucks, planting, and harvesting equipment; and owning and operating the processing plant. By the very nature of their organizational structure, cooperatives have greater formal or legal rights to individual participation. In agricultural cooperatives, every farmer-owner has a voice and a vote in decision making concerning the production, marketing, and selling of products.

Feminist organizations also illustrate participatory organizational structures. Ferree and Martin (1995) defined a **feminist organization** as *one that "embraces collectivist decision-making (i.e., decisions made by the group), member empowerment, and a political agenda of ending women's oppression"* (p. 5). Thousands of organizations, including rape and abuse crisis centers, women's health clinics, women's bookstores, restaurants, theater groups, and credit unions operate from a feminist standpoint. These organizations are usually staffed by women and for women.

TRY ▶ THIS

Most organizational communication research has focused on corporations that have bureaucratic structures. Why do you think scholars and practitioners have studied traditional rather than participatory structures?

Harrison (1994) describes cooperatives and feminist organizations as created by individuals who seek to construct economic and political "alternatives to traditional bureaucratic organization" (p. 261). Alternative organizations have flattened structures with few hierarchical levels. A large number of employees are placed at the same level and their jobs are not ranked as being "above" or "below" other jobs in the organization. The short chain of command allows a relatively rapid movement of messages throughout the organization. By the very nature of their structure, alternative organizations promote horizontal communication among peers and provide space for employees to have an important voice in organizational decision making.

VIRTUAL ORGANIZATIONS

Virtual organizations have unique organizational structures. They are labeled "virtual" because a "physical" structure does not exist; the organization is structured through communication occurring through computer connections. People in an organization can do their work from a remote place (e.g., home, hotel room, car, airplane) through a computer that is linked to other people's computers via telephone lines or cellular connections. Virtual organizations often represent temporary ventures between several companies, each with special expertise. For example, in 1994, three companies—Motorola, IBM, and Apple—created a virtual organization to develop the PowerPC chip, a new computer memory chip. Once the task was completed successfully, they dissolved the temporary structure (Hof, Gross, & Sager, 1994). This book was written primarily through a virtual structure. Two of the authors reside in North Dakota, two authors reside in Minnesota, the executive editor resides in New York City, also the location of the publishing company. Communication among these organizational members was conducted primarily by telephone, e-mail, and surface mail. Some members of this virtual organization never even met each other, much less worked in the same building. However, their communication patterns still provided and maintained a "structure" to guide their work tasks.

Information Management

Regardless of organizational structure, **information** is *a product (outcome) of communication that serves to help people understand and predict the world around them.* Information helps direct organizational behaviors by indicating the most fruitful way to interpret and accomplish tasks. Assume that you are a sales representative for an insurance company, and your supervisor requests that you make a sales call on a potential client. You will use available information to accomplish this task. If you have detailed information about the types of insurance your company offers, rates available, and needs of the potential client, you possess relevant information. Lack of job-related information can lead to disastrous results.

Information is the resource that directs decision making, and communication is the process through which information is created and understood. Deetz, Tracy, and Simpson (2000) encourage large organizations to rely on **management information systems (MISs)** that are *designed and implemented to help manage organizations' varied information needs.* For example, computer-based management information systems can be used to help coordinate activities by organizing, storing, and

information

A product (outcome) of communication that serves to help people understand and predict the world around them.

management information system (MIS)

A system designed and implemented to help manage organizations' varied information needs.

313

providing information. To accomplish their goals, employees depend on communication and on modern information storage and retrieval technologies to collect, interpret, and evaluate relevant information.

Many different sources of communication provide organization members with pertinent information. Research on organizational communication typically focuses on two sources: internal communication and external communication. Internal and external communications perform distinct yet interrelated functions in the process of organizing. Internal communications are used to direct organizational activities to accomplish goals based on information gathered from the organization's environment.

Internal Organizational Communication

Internal organizational communication is *the symbolic interaction that occurs within organizations and among organization members.* Regardless of our organizational role, position, or level of authority, the quality of our organizational experience is based in part on the quality of internal communication. Table 10.1 identifies several different managerial functions served by internal communication. Our discussion of internal communication focuses on communication networks and socialization processes.

internal organizational communication

The symbolic interaction that occurs within organizations and among organizational members.

Classroom Activity

Have students discuss the division of labor and chain of command at the university. Ask students to draw a visual representation of the organization. Afterward, present students with the formal organizational chart of the university and compare it to their visual representations. Finally, have students talk about the advantages and limitations of the university's division of labor.

TABLE 10.1   MANAGERIAL FUNCTIONS OF INTERNAL COMMUNICATION

Describe specific organizational tasks that organizational members are to accomplish

Identify specific job responsibilities of organization members and train them to accomplish duties

Develop and maintain an organizational climate in which internal channels of communication are optimally used

Enforce members' adherence to organizational rules, regulations, and guidelines

Inform organization members of organizational goals, purpose, and directives

Identify members' mutual interests in the success of the organization

Evaluate members' work performance and identify future goals

Coordinate members' accomplishment of tasks

Seek feedback from organization members to solve internal problems and promote ethical conflict

Maintain high-quality organizational output

Source: G. Kreps, *Organizational Communication: Theory and Practice,* 2nd ed. New York: Longman, 1990.

Communication Networks

Communication networks are *patterns of relationships through which information flows in an organization.* Stohl (1995) describes communication networks as capturing "the tapestry of *relationships—*the complex web of *affiliations* among individuals and organizations as they are woven through the collaborative threads of communication" (p. 18). Communication networks emerge in organizations based on formal and informal communication (Monge & Contractor, 2001).

Formal communication consists of *messages that follow prescribed channels of communication throughout the organization.* The most common way of *depicting formal communication networks* is with **organizational charts** like the one in Figure 10.1. Organizational charts provide clear guidelines of who is responsible for a given task and which employees are responsible for others' performance. Figure 10.1 is a typical organizational chart for a bureaucratic structure. It shows that Alexi reports to her boss, Cliff, and Julie reports to Sue.

communication networks

Patterns of relationships through which information flows in an organization.

formal communication

Messages that follow prescribed channels of communication throughout the organization.

organizational chart

A visual depiction of formal communication networks.

Active Art

CD-ROM Activity

Ask students to view the animation titled "Formal Communication Flow" on the accompanying student CD-ROM. The animation illustrates hierarchy, subordination, specialization, downward communication, upward communication, and horizontal communication.

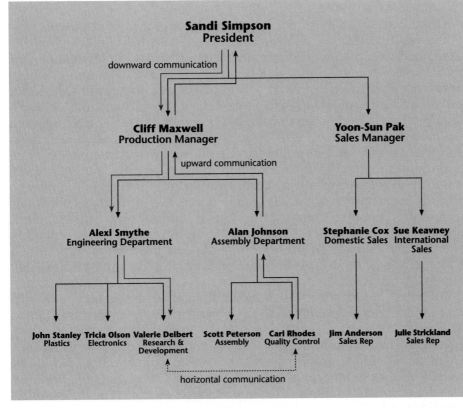

Figure 10.1   Formal communication flow.

Team Challenge

THE IDEAL ORGANIZATIONAL STRUCTURE

The discussion of formal communication networks (downward communication, upward communication, and horizontal communication) points out that such networks are typically depicted using an organizational chart. One criticism of charts like the one provided in Figure 10.1 is that they require a hierarchical structure. Many alternative organizations do not embrace such structures—in fact, they resist them. As a group, discuss two issues. First, how would you organize an ideal organization? Based on your discussion of the first question, your second task is to create an organizational chart or diagram for your ideal organization. How can you draw a picture depicting what you think is an ideal organization?

upward communication

Messages flowing from subordinates to superiors.

horizontal communication

Messages between members of an organization with equal power.

informal communication

Any interaction that does not generally follow the formal structure of the organization but emerges out of natural social interaction among organization members.

Organizational charts demonstrate that communication can flow in several directions: downward, upward, and horizontally. As discussed earlier, downward communication occurs whenever superiors initiate messages to subordinates. Ideally, downward communication should include such things as job instructions, job rationale, policy and procedures, performance feedback, and motivational appeals. *Messages flowing from subordinates to superiors* are labeled **upward communication.** Obviously, effective decision making depends on timely, accurate, and complete information traveling upward from subordinates. *Messages between members of an organization with equal power* are labeled **horizontal communication.** Horizontal communication is important to organizational success when used to coordinate tasks, solve problems, share information, and resolve conflict. Horizontal communication receives much more attention in participatory organizational structures in which employees have more opportunity to formally participate in decision making (e.g., quality circles, self-managed work teams).

Informal communication is generally considered to be *any interaction that does not generally follow the formal structure of the organization but emerges out of natural social interaction among organization members.* Whereas formal communication consists of messages the organization recognizes as official, informal messages do not follow official lines. The concept of **emergent organizational networks** represents *the informal, naturally occurring patterns of communication relationships in organizations* (Monge & Contractor, 2001).

Informal networks often develop through accidents of spatial arrangement, similarity of personalities, or compatibilities of personal skills. Additionally, Conrad and Poole (1998) argue:

> Formal communication networks allow people to handle predictable, routine situations but they are inefficient means of meeting unanticipated communication needs, for managing crises, for dealing with complex or detailed problems, sharing personal information, or exchanging information rapidly. (p. 91)

To summarize, organizational members create emergent networks because insufficient opportunities exist for formal communication and because formal communication networks fail to do the job.

To hear people refer to *informal interactions* as **grapevine communication** is not uncommon. Information introduced into the grapevine travels quickly because messages are uninhibited by structural constraints. Although we publicly tend to discredit the grapevine, research has consistently shown that grapevine communication is amazingly accurate. Scholars have consistently reported 78 to 90 percent accuracy figures in their studies of grapevine communication in organizational settings (e.g., Caudron, 1998).

Traditionally, many companies have viewed grapevine communication as a "time waster" and an activity to be discouraged. Now, however, many companies recognize that casual communication can do even more than formal communication to build organizational success. Managers who listen carefully to informal communication discover it is a useful source of information about employee attitudes and concerns. In one study, managers reported that they often found informal communication to be a better source of organizational information than formal communication (Harcourt, Richerson, & Waitterk, 1991). Some managers actually leak new ideas or proposals to the grapevine to test worker response. Businesses have also been known to leak secret information in hopes that a competitor would react and waste both time and money (Hitt, Ireland, & Hoskinson, 1999).

Organizational Assimilation

In chapter 8, we discussed the process of **anticipatory socialization** through which *individuals develop a set of expectations and beliefs concerning how people communicate in particular occupations and in formal and informal work settings* (Jablin, 2001). However, the process of socialization does not end when individuals select and start positions. Jablin uses the term **organizational assimilation** to describe *the processes through which individuals become integrated into the culture of an organization*. To understand organizational assimilation we must first understand organizational cultures.

When we think about cultures of nations, many things come to mind. For instance, what do you think of when you reflect on American culture?

---

emergent organizational networks

The informal, naturally occurring patterns of communication relationships in organizations.

grapevine communication

Informal interactions.

Video Activity

Ask students to view the video segment "Reporting for KTNT: Susan Elliott." Ask students to consider the process of anticipatory socialization in Susan's career of broadcast journalism. Previous viewing of other segments, particularly the segment "Senior Seminar," may be helpful.

anticipatory socialization

Process through which individuals develop a set of expectations and beliefs concerning how people communicate in particular occupations and in formal and informal work settings.

organizational assimilation

Processes through which individuals become integrated into the culture of an organization.

**Discussion
Question**
Have students talk
about the values,
norms, and practices
of an organization
that they work for or
worked for in the past.
Ask students to
identify how they
learned about the key
values of the
organization. What
happens when a norm
is violated?

**organizational
culture**

A pattern of beliefs,
values, and practices
shared by the
members of an
organization.

norms

Informal rules for
group interaction
created and
sustained through
communication.

**organizational
politics**

The exercise or
negotiation of
power.

You might think about key values that Americans hold, including free-dom, independence, and material goods. You might think of some of the symbols of our culture, including the flag and apple pie. You might con-sider day-to-day behaviors of Americans, including commutes to work, long days balancing the demands of work and family, and watching sport-ing events. Organizations, like countries, have cultures. **Organizational culture** is *a pattern of beliefs, values, and practices shared by the members of an organization.* During the 1980s, the concept of organizational cul-ture exploded in the popular press (e.g., Deal & Kennedy, 1982; Peters & Waterman, 1982).

Practitioners and scholars recognize that cultures arise and are main-tained through communication, and the ways in which we communicate are guided and constrained by the taken-for-granted assumptions of our cul-tures (e.g., Eisenberg & Riley, 2001). In other words, the communication-based process of organizational assimilation allows the new members of an organization to learn the meanings of the group's symbols and the set of attitudes, values, and beliefs common to members.

Through formal socialization efforts, the organization presents its value system to the newcomer. Organizations put a lot of effort into social-ization strategies and programs to create stable, consistent work forces that adhere to **norms**, *informal rules for group interaction created and sus-tained through communication*, consistent with organizational expecta-tions. Training programs have become one of the primary processes by which organizations socialize employees. By completing training pro-grams, employees learn about job duties and how to complete tasks as well as formal and informal rules of communicating in work relationships.

New employees can also gain knowledge through informal meetings with supervisors, handbooks, or conversations with coworkers. Organiza-tional members often rely on observation of behaviors and artifacts in order to draw inferences about cultural values and assumptions. Even the informal grapevine provides a forum through which you can gain knowl-edge of **organizational politics,** or *the exercise or negotiation of power.* Knowledge of an organization is incomplete without awareness of the or-ganization as a political entity.

External Organizational Communication

Organizations exist within broader envi-ronments in which they are linked to the activities of a wide range of other organi-zations and individuals. For instance, a production company probably depends on communication with many related organi-zations, including suppliers of raw materials (e.g., lumber, steel), orga-nizations that distribute and market its products (e.g., department

THE WEB AS AN INFORMATION RESOURCE

An excellent method for organizational members to learn about the external environment is through the Internet and the World Wide Web. Thousands of organizations are now advertising their services and products on Web pages, and within these Internet sites you can learn about organizational innovations. Besides "browsing" these resources for information about customers, competitors, and current trends, you can also use a search engine that will direct you to places on the superhighway that interest you. One such place is www.brint.com, a search engine or index of websites that are specific to business. This resource can help you find the information you need when you type in key words such as "economic trends," "profitable companies," or "business technology."

stores), competitors who produce similar products, and government organizations that license and regulate its industry (e.g., state regulatory boards). *Organizations and individuals with whom organization representatives have direct contact* are known as the organization's **environment** (Sutcliffe, 2001). Members of organizational environments are important because they can exert significant influence on the organization. **External communication** consists of *verbal and nonverbal messages enabling members of an organization to coordinate its activities with those in its environment.*

The organization's environment both sends and receives messages. External messages influence the way people in the environment behave toward the organization. For example, marketing and advertising campaigns are designed to influence the buying patterns of consumers. Messages received from the organization's environment can be used to direct the goals of the organization and how members accomplish their tasks. For example, messages from government sources might inform members of new federal regulations for their industry. By understanding these regulations before they are enforced, employees may have time to design the most effective ways to adapt to these new constraints. Messages from the organizational environment can also be used to assess the relevance of internal organizational activities to current environmental conditions.

Our discussion of external communication will focus on two general functions served by external communication: (1) creating and maintaining organizational images, and (2) providing customer service.

environment

Organizations and individuals with whom organizational representatives have direct contact.

external communication

Verbal and nonverbal messages enabling members of an organization to coordinate its activities with those in its environment.

organizational stakeholder

Any person or group that has an interest, right, claim, or ownership in an organization.

organizational image

Mental picture of an organization that is descriptive and evaluative.

Classroom Activity

Before class, have students find an example of a public relations artifact. Have students write a paper analyzing the rhetorical strategies evident in the artifact. Students can also write about the overall effectiveness of the tool in communicating with organizational stakeholders.

public relations (PR)

The management of communication between an organization and its publics.

crisis management

The use of public relations to minimize harm to the organization in emergency situations that could cause the organization irreparable damage.

Creating and Maintaining Organizational Images

Organizations depend on the existence of key external stakeholders. **Organizational stakeholders** include *any person or group that has an interest, right, claim, or ownership in an organization* (Deetz, 1995). Common stakeholders include the government, customers, investors, suppliers, and the community. Through actions, words, and graphics, organizations seek to have stakeholders identify with them in ways that foster relationships.

As Heath (1994) noted, "Companies try to impose themselves on their environments, rather than merely adapt to them. They attempt to shape their environment by their presence in it, by what they do and say" (p. 228). Just as individuals rely on communication to create, reinforce, and redefine their personal images, so must organizations use external communication to create or redefine images about their services and products. **Organizational images** are *mental pictures of organizations that are descriptive and evaluative.* For instance, Microsoft–Great Plains has an image of being a family-friendly environment, and Ben and Jerry's has an image of valuing employee innovation.

TRY ▸THIS

You are probably familiar with the World Wide Web (WWW). The Web is the graphic part of the Internet. Organizations use websites to communicate with vendors and customers. You can learn a great deal about the "image" a company is trying to create by looking at its website. Find a company website and print out one or more pages. After reading through the website, how would you characterize the organization?

Organizations seek to create and maintain positive images in order to achieve organizational objectives. The term **public relations (PR)** is used to describe *the management of communication between an organization and its publics.* Public relations activities are the formal means by which external communication activities are used to help organization members coordinate actions with external stakeholders (Ledingham & Bruning, 2000). Public relations is not merely designing and sending organizational messages to the environment; PR also involves gathering relevant environmental information for organization members.

Image becomes particularly important during times of organizational crisis. In fact, nowhere in organizational life is the careful analysis of strategies of public relations messages more important than in crisis management. **Crisis management** is *the use of public relations to minimize harm to the organization in emergency situations that could cause the* *organization irreparable damage.* Classic examples include Exxon after the Valdez oil spill, Johnson and Johnson after the discovery of tainted Tylenol tablets, and NASA after the explosion of the *Challenger* space shuttle. More recently, Nike engaged in crisis management after allegations of abuse of child labor (Sellnow & Brand, 2001), as did Ford and Firestone after safety concerns surfaced about the tires on Ford Explorers. Messages crafted and delivered by organizational representatives in the face of such events are related to both short-term image and long-term survival of the organization (Coombs, 2000).

Providing Customer Service

We have often heard that we now live in a "service economy" in which American companies increasingly make money by providing services. In this kind of business environment, one of the most important forms of external communication is that which occurs in providing service to organizational customers. Bitner, Booms, and Tetreault (1990) define the **customer service encounter** as *"the moment of interaction between the customer and the firm"* (p. 71). During this moment, the organizational representative provides professional assistance in exchange for the customer's money or attention.

Customer service became a business buzzword during the 1990s, yet it means different things to different people. For some individuals, customer service means being friendly, shaking hands warmly, and initiating pleasant conversations with clients. For others, customer service means processing customers efficiently and quickly. Still others view customer service as listening intently to identify individual needs and providing sufficient information and/or support to meet those needs. All perspectives are legitimate; however, we must remember that the customer is the ultimate judge of whether customer service interactions are satisfying.

Regardless of how employees understand the concept of customer service, most providers have the goal of influencing their customers' behaviors. An extensive body of research covers communication techniques for compliance gaining. In her book *Communicating with Customers: Service Approaches, Ethics, and Impact,* Ford (1998) reviews compliance-gaining strategies used by customer service representatives. Her work in summarized in Table 10.2.

A wide range of occupations require interactions between employees and clients or customers. In many of these, the provision of service often involves some degree of emotional content (Waldron, 1994). Nurses interact with dying patients in a hospice, ministers counsel troubled parishioners, and social workers help physically abused women. Emotional communication also characterizes other less obvious occupations. Flight attendants must appear happy and attentive during international flights (Murphy, 2001) while bill collectors must remain stern and avoid any trace of sympathy in interactions (Rafeili & Sutton, 1990).

Video Activity

Ask students to view the video segment "The Hospital." Have students critique the interaction between the Elliott family and Hector Lobos. Did Mr. Lobos display effective customer service skills?

customer service encounter

The moment of interaction between the customer and the firm.

Discussion Topic

There is a movement in the health care industry to relabel "patients" as "customers." Similarly, some individuals believe that educators should view "students" as "customers." Ask students to reflect on traditional provider–patient relationships and teacher–student relationships from the standpoint of customer service encounters. Have students discuss how communication patterns in such relationships might be different if viewed from a customer service standpoint. What are the advantages and disadvantages of the customer metaphor in health care and education?

Discussion Question

Ask students to discuss which of these questions they most often rely on when in the position of organizational newcomer. Have them reflect on the appropriateness and usefulness of the different strategies for different contexts.

Discussion Question

Ask students to discuss how both teachers and students engage in emotional work inside and outside the classroom.

emotional labor

Jobs in which employees are expected to display certain feelings in order to satisfy organizational role expectations.

TABLE 10.2 COMPLIANCE-GAINING STRATEGIES USED BY CUSTOMER SERVICE REPRESENTATIVES

Promise: Promising a reward for compliance (e.g., "If you buy this car, I'll throw in a free stereo.")

Threat: Threatening to punish for noncompliance (e.g., "If you don't buy the car before the end of the week, I cannot guarantee the 6 percent interest rate.")

Pre-giving: Rewarding the customer before requesting compliance (e.g., "I will give you $50 just for test-driving this new car.")

Moral appeal: Implying that it is immoral not to comply (e.g., "Since you have small children, you should be looking at our larger models, with more safety features.")

Liking: Being friendly and helpful to get the customer in a good frame of mind to ensure compliance (e.g., "Good afternoon, my how you look nice today. How can I help you?")

SOURCE: W. Z. Ford, *Communicating with Customers: Service Approaches, Ethics, and Impact.* Cresskill, NJ: Hampton Press, 1998.

Arlie Hochschild was the first scholar to deal with this phenomenon in her book *The Managed Heart* (1983). She uses the term **emotional labor** to refer to *jobs in which employees are expected to display certain feelings in order to satisfy organizational role expectations.* Research has indicated that while emotional labor may be fiscally rewarding for the organization and the client, it can be dangerous for the service provider and lead to negative consequences such as burnout, job dissatisfaction, and turnover (e.g., Miller, Ellis, Zook, & Lyles, 1990; Tracy & Tracy, 1998).

The Dark Side of Organizational Communication

Communicating in organizations is not an easy task. In fact, a pervasive part of organizational life is conflict. Conflict can be both destructive and productive. What exactly is conflict? Putnam and Poole's (1987) definition highlights several critical components of conflict: "The interaction of interdependent people who perceive opposition of goals, aims, and values, and who see the other party as potentially interfering with the realization of these goals" (p. 552). Conflict can destroy work relationships or create a needed impetus for organizational change and development. Chapter 9 provided suggestions for how to engage in effective problem solving. In this chapter, we are concerned with the dark side of organizational conflict and environmental stress. In particular, we focus our attention on aggressive communication in the workplace and sexual harassment.

Aggressive Communication in the Workplace

Verbal aggressiveness is understood by communication scholars as *an individual's communication that attacks the self-concepts of other people in order to inflict psychological pain* (e.g., Infante, Riddle, Horvath, & Tulmin, 1992). Verbal aggression is on the rise in organizational settings, with a lot of aggression unrecognized by management. **Workplace aggression** includes *all communication by which individuals attempt to harm others at work.*

Neuman (1998) argues that workplace aggression occurs at three levels: (1) the withholding of cooperation, spreading rumors or gossip, consistent arguing, belligerency, and the use of offensive language; (2) intense arguments with supervisors, coworkers, and customers, sabotage, verbal threats and feelings of persecution; and (3) frequent displays of intense anger resulting in recurrent suicidal threats, physical fights, destruction of property, use of weapons, and the commission of murder, rape, and/or arson. *Instances involving direct physical assaults* constitute **workplace violence;** typically, this is a result of the escalation of workplace aggression.

Most of us are familiar with the term "going postal," originating from an incident in which a postal worker walked up to his boss, pulled a gun from a paper bag, and shot him dead (*Los Angeles Times*, July 18, 1995). Or perhaps we are familiar with the Fort Lauderdale man who opened fire on his former colleagues after being dismissed from his city job cleaning the beaches (*New York Times*, February 10, 1996). Although mediated accounts of workplace violence typically focus on homicides, most workplace aggression involves less dramatic forms of verbal abuse. Studies of verbal aggression in the workplace suggest that 50 percent of workers admit to arguing and criticizing coworkers (Bennett & Lehman, 1996) and over 65 percent of managers reported experiencing verbal aggression—including use of profanity, threats of retaliation, silent treatment, and spreading rumors—in response to negative performance evaluations (Geddes & Baron, 1997).

Cost-cutting in the form of downsizing, layoffs, budget cuts, and pay freezes as well as organizational change engender workplace aggression (Baron, 1999). Organizational communication research has detected negative effects of verbal aggression in superior–subordinate relationships and peer relationships (e.g., Gordon, Infante, & Graham, 1988). The psychological pain produced by verbal aggression includes a range of negative emotions: embarrassment, feelings of inadequacy, humiliation, hopelessness, despair, depression, and so on.

Sexual Harassment

Sexual harassment includes a set of behaviors that constitute workplace aggression. The 1991 Senate confirmation hearings of Supreme Court Justice Clarence Thomas made the issue of sexual harassment a topic of reflection

verbal aggressiveness

An individual's communication that attacks the self-concepts of other people in order to inflict psychological pain.

workplace aggression

All communication by which individuals attempt to harm others at work.

workplace violence

Instances involving direct physical assaults.

Touch can be inappropriate communication in the workplace.

Classroom Activity

Take in a popular culture artifact that deals with sexual harassment (e.g., an episode of *Ally McBeal*, the movie *Disclosure*). Ask students to talk about the mediated depiction of sexual harassment. What underlying values are evident in the portrayal? How are victims and harassers portrayed?

and discussion in corporate boardrooms, schools, and at family dinner tables. Accusations against Bill Clinton, then president of the United States, were lodged by Paula Jones, claiming that he sexually harassed her when he was governor of Arkansas. While sexual harassment has been a pervasive problem in the workplace for decades, these accusations against prominent public officials caused employees and employers alike to recognize the magnitude of the issue (Kreps, 1993).

What is sexual harassment? The Equal Employment Opportunity Communication (EEOC) defines **sexual harassment** as

sexual harassment

Unwelcome, unsolicited, repeated behavior of a sexual nature.

> Unwelcome sexual advances, requests for sexual favors, and other verbal or physical conduct of a sexual nature if (1) submission to the conduct is made a condition of employment, (2) submission to or rejection of the conduct is made the basis for an employment decision, or (3) the conduct seriously affects an employee's work performance or creates an intimidating, hostile, or offensive working environment.

Simply put, sexual harassment is *unwelcome, unsolicited, repeated behavior of a sexual nature.*

The EEOC definition of sexual harassment outlines two different, although sometimes overlapping, types of sexual harassment. The first type, termed **quid pro quo,** involves *a situation in which an employee is offered a reward or is threatened with punishment based on his or her participation in a sexual activity.* For example, a supervisor might tell her employee "I will give you Friday off if you will meet me at my place tonight." The second type of sexual harassment creates a **hostile work environment**, or *conditions in the workplace that are sexually offensive, intimidating, or hostile and that affect an individual's ability to perform his or her job.* For example, if two males talk explicitly about the physical features of a female colleague in her presence, she asks them to stop, and they repeat the offense, sexual harassment has occurred.

A major obstacle to ending sexual harassment is the tendency of victims to avoid confronting the harasser. Most instances of sexual harassment are not confronted, exposed, or reported. Instead, the victim usually avoids the situation by taking time off, transferring to another area, or changing jobs. One of the primary reasons for avoidance is that the perpetrator is usually someone in the organization with authority and status—power over the victim—and the victim feels that exposure or confrontation will backfire.

Clearly, the EEOC's definition indicates that a wide range of communication behaviors can constitute sexual harassment, although many men and women see only serious offenses (e.g., career benefits in exchange for sexual favors) as harassment. However, a person need not suffer severe psychological damage or extensive adverse work outcomes to be a victim of sexual harassment. Additionally, harassment is judged by its effects on the recipient, not by the intentions of the harasser. Because some people may regard any particular behavior as offensive and others not, the courts use what is called the **reasonable person rule** *to determine whether a "reasonable person" would find the behavior in question offensive.* One limitation of this rule is evidence that men and women view sexual harassment differently (Solomon & Williams, 1997). In particular, sexual overtures that women typically view as insulting are viewed by men, in general, as flattering.

Sexual harassment is a serious and pervasive communication problem in modern organizational life, with both the targets of sexual harassment and those accused of sexual harassment (falsely or not) suffering personal and professional anguish and conflict. Note that even though a majority of sexual harassment cases involve women as victims, the EEOC guidelines apply equally to men.

quid pro quo sexual harassment

A situation in which an employee is offered a reward or is threatened with punishment based on his or her participation in a sexual activity.

hostile work environment sexual harassment

Conditions in the workplace that are sexually offensive, intimidating, or hostile and that affect an individual's ability to perform his or her job.

reasonable person rule

Legal concept used by courts to determine whether a "reasonable person" would find behavior in question offensive.

Chapter Review

In this chapter you have learned the following:

- Organizational communication refers to symbolic processes that help organizational members maintain structure and order and accomplish their goals within organizations.

- Organizations can be classified into four general types. Many organizations serve more than one of these functions; however, each organization has a primary role.

  - Economic production organizations manufacture products or services.

  - Political organizations generate and distribute power and control in society.

  - Integrative organizations mediate and resolve conflict in society.

  - Pattern maintenance organizations promote cultural and educational regularity in society.

- Organizational structures emerge out of communication, a process called structuration. The symbolic interaction of organizational members can result in bureaucratic organizations or alternative/participatory organizations.

- Bureaucratic structures in organizations emphasize hierarchy and chains of command.

  - A hallmark of bureaucratic structures is a reliance on downward communication from managers to subordinates.

  - Alternative and participatory organizations embrace the concept of workplace democracy, which emphasizes both individualism and collectivity to achieve organizational objectives.

- Organizational communication networks consist of formal communication, which includes downward, upward, and horizontal communication, and informal communication, which consists of emergent networks and the grapevine.

- Organizational assimilation involves processes through which individuals become integrated into the culture of an organization.

  - Organizational cultures consist of patterns of beliefs, values, and practices shared by the members of an organization.

  - Assimilation into a culture involves the organization's attempts to socialize employees as well as employees' attempts to change their roles and work environments to meet their needs.

- External communication consists of messages enabling members of an organization to coordinate its activities with those in its environment. Public relations efforts are dedicated to creating particular organizational images, or mental pictures of organizations that are descriptive and evaluative.

- Customer service encounters represent moments of interactions between the customer and the firm. Compliance-gaining strategies used by customer service representatives include promises, threats, pregiving, moral appeals, and liking tactics. At times, employees engage in emotional labor in their service roles.

- Workplace aggression includes all communication by which individuals attempt to harm others at work. Sexual harassment is one form of workplace aggression.

- Ethical guidelines for communication and work involve maintaining candor, keeping messages accurate, avoiding deception, maintaining consistent behavior, ensuring timeliness of communication, and confronting unethical behavior.

VIDEO LINK: THE ELLIOTTS ENCOUNTER AN ORGANIZATION

Video Episode 2: "The Hospital"

This chapter introduces you to the concept of organizing. In general, the chapter discusses the various ways we interact with organizations to help us exert control over our lives. In "The Hospital," Susan Elliott, her mother, and her grandmother interact with one such organization, the local hospital. In this scene, do you see evidence of organizational characteristics discussed in this chapter? For example, do you see evidence of division of labor and hierarchy? Does the patient care coordinator, Hector Lobos, display professional communication behaviors when interacting with Susan, Mrs. Elliott, and Grandma? Why or why not?

ISSUES IN COMMUNICATION: MISSION STATEMENTS AND ORGANIZATIONAL COMMUNICATION

This chapter discussed the concepts of external and internal communication. One strategy for defining the focus of internal and external communication is to create an organizational mission statement. Below is a mission statement from one of our universities.

> The University strives to provide an educational environment that supports intellectual development, that welcomes diversity, and that develops the skills and talents of women and men so that they have the capacity to live usefully, act responsibly, and be learners all their lives. The academic programs at the University are founded upon a common liberal studies experience and emphasize developing the unique talents of each person. The University provides baccalaureate-level programs in the liberal arts, natural and social sciences, teacher education, business and technology, the fine arts, and professional areas. It provides selected graduate programs in response to regional needs.
>
> The University encourages scholarly and creative endeavors that promote a commitment by faculty and students to their disciplines, to continuing professional development, and to excellence in learning.
>
> The University enhances the quality of life in the region with the professional, cultural, and recreational services offered by its students, faculty, and staff.

Apply what you have learned about organizational communication as you ponder and discuss the following questions: What stakeholders are highlighted in this mission statement? Based on this mission statement, what core values does this university adhere to? Can you visualize an organizational image of this university based on the mission statement? If you were creating a mission statement for your university, what issues would you emphasize?

KEY TERMS

 Use the *Human Communication* CD-ROM and the *Online Learning Center* at
www.mhhe.com/pearson to further your understanding of the following terminology.

Alternative organizations
Anticipatory socialization
Bureaucracy
Chain of command
Communication networks
Cooperative
Crisis management
Customer service encounter
Division of labor
Downward communication
Economic production
    orientation
Emergent organizational
    networks
Emotional labor
Environment
External communication
Feminist organization
Formal communication
Functional classification
    system
Grapevine communication

Hierarchy
Horizontal communication
Hostile work environment
    sexual harassment
Informal communication
Information
Integration-goals
    orientation
Internal organizational
    communication
Management information
    system (MIS)
Managers
Norms
Organizational assimilation
Organizational chart
Organizational
    communication
Organizational culture
Organizational image
Organizational politics
Organizational stakeholder

Organizational structure
Organizations
Participatory organizations
Pattern-maintenance
    goal orientation
Political-goals orientation
Productivity
Public relations (PR)
Quality
Quality circle
Quid pro quo sexual
    harassment
Reasonable person rule
Self-managed work teams
Sexual harassment
Structuration
Upward communication
Verbal aggressiveness
Workplace aggression
Workplace democracy
Workplace violence

SELF-QUIZ

Go to the self-quizzes on the *Human Communication* CD-ROM and the *Online
Learning Center* at www.mhhe.com/pearson to test your knowledge.

REFERENCES

Aguilar, F. J. (1994). *Managing corporate ethics*. New
    York: Oxford University Press.
Ashcraft, K. (2000). Empowering professional
    relationships: Organizational communication
    meets feminist practice. *Management
    Communication Quarterly 13*(3), 347–392.
Barker, J. R. (1999). *The discipline of teamwork*.
    Thousand Oaks, CA: Sage.
Baron, R. A. (1999). Social and personal
    determinants of workplace aggression: Evidence

for the impact of perceived injustice and the type
    a behavior pattern. *Aggressive Behavior, 25,*
    281–296.
Bennett, J. B., & Lehman, W. E. (1996). Alcohol,
    antagonism, and witnessing violence in the
    workplace: Drinking climates and social
    alienation-integration. In G. R. VandenBos &
    E. Q. Bulatao (Eds.), *Workplace violence*
    (pp. 105–152). Washington, DC: American
    Psychological Association.

Bittner, M. J., Booms, B. H., & Tetreault, M. S. (1990). The service encounter: Diagnosing favorable and unfavorable incidents. *Journal of Marketing, 54,* 71–84.

Caudron, S. (1998). They hear it through the grapevine. *Workforce, 77,* 25–27.

Cheney, G. (1995). Democracy in the workplace: Theory and practice from the perspective of communication. *Journal of Applied Communication Research, 23,* 167–200.

Cheney, G., Mumby, D., Stohl, C., & Harrison, T. (1997). Communication and organizational democracy. *Communication Studies, 48,* 277–279.

Conrad, C., & Poole, M. S. (1998). *Strategic organizational communication: Into the 21st century* (4th ed.). Fort Worth, TX: Harcourt Brace.

Coombs, W. T. (2000). Crisis management: Advantages of a relational perspective. In J. A. Ledingham & S. D. Bruning (Eds.), *Public relations as relationship management* (pp. 73–94). Mahwah, NJ: Lawrence Erlbaum Associates.

Daft, R. L. (1995). *Organization theory and design* (5th ed.). Minneapolis, MN: West.

Deal, T., & Kennedy, A. (1982). *Corporate cultures.* Reading, MA: Addison-Wesley.

Deetz, S. (1995). *Transforming communication transforming business.* Cresskill, NJ: Hampton Press.

Deetz, S., Tracy, S., & Simpson, J. (2000). *Leading organizations through cultural transition: Communication and cultural change.* Thousand Oaks, CA: Sage.

Eisenberg, E., & Goodall, H. L. (2001). *Organizational communication: Balancing creativity and constraint* (3rd ed.). Boston: Bedford/St.Martin's Press.

Eisenberg, E., & Riley, P. (2001). Organizational culture. In F. Jablin & L. Putnam (Eds.), *The new handbook of organizational communication* (pp. 291–322). Thousand Oaks, CA: Sage.

Ferree, M. M., & Martin, P. Y. (1995). *Feminist organizations: Harvest of the new women's movement.* Philadelphia: Temple University Press.

Ford, W. Z. (1998). *Communicating with customers: Service approaches, ethics, and impact.* Cresskill, NJ: Hampton Press.

Geddes, D., & Baron, R. (1997). Workplace aggression as a consequence of negative performance feedback. *Management Communications Quarterly, 10,* 433–454.

Giddens, A. (1979). *Central problems in social theory: Action, structure, and contradiction in social analysis.* Berkeley: University of California Press.

Giddens, A. (1984). *Modernity and self-identity: Self and society in the late modern age.* Stanford, CA: Stanford University Press.

Gordon, W. I., Infante, D. A., & Graham, E. E. (1988). Corporate conditions conducive to employee voice: A subordinate perspective. *Employee Responsibilities and Rights Journal, 1,* 100–111.

Hamilton, C. (2001). *Communicating for results: A guide for business and the professions* (6th ed.). Stamford, CT: Thomson Learning/Wadsworth Publishing.

Harcourt, J., Richerson, V., & Waitterk, M. (1991). A national study of middle managers' assessment of organization communication quality. *Journal of Business Communication, 28,* 348–365.

Harrison, T. (1994). Communication and interdependence in democratic organizations. In S. A. Deetz (Ed.), *Communication yearbook 17* (pp. 247–274). Thousand Oaks, CA: Sage.

Harter, L. M., & Krone, K. (2001). The boundary-spanning role of a cooperative support organization: Managing the paradox of stability and change among non-traditional organizations. *Journal of Applied Communication Research, 29,* 248–277.

Heath, R. (1994). *Management of corporate communication: From interpersonal contacts to external affairs.* Hillsdale, NJ: Lawrence Erlbaum Associates.

Hitt, M., Ireland, R., & Hoskinson, R. (1999). *Strategic management: Competitiveness and globalization* (3rd ed.). Cincinnati, OH: Southwestern College (ITP).

Hochschild, A. (1983). *The managed heart: Commercialization of human feeling.* Berkeley, CA: University of California Press.

Hof, R. D., Gross, N., & Sager, I. (1994, March 7). A computer maker's power move. *Business Week,* 48.

Infante, D., Riddle, B., Horvath, G., & Tumlin, S. (1992). Verbal aggressiveness: Messages and reasons. *Communication Quarterly, 40,* 116–126.

Jablin, F. (2001). Organizational entry, assimilation, and disengagement/exit. In F. Jablin & L. Putnam (Eds.), *The new handbook of organizational communication* (pp. 732–818). Thousand Oaks, CA: Sage.

Kreps, G. (1990). *Organizational communication: Theory and practice* (2nd ed.). New York: Longman.

Kreps, G. (1993). *Sexual harassment: Communication implications.* Cresskill, NJ: Hampton Press.

Lawler, E., & Mohrman, S. (1985, January–February). Quality circles after the fad. *Harvard Business Review*, 65–71.

Ledingham, J. A., & Bruning, S. D. (2000). A longitudinal study of organization-public relationship dimensions: Defining the role of communication in the practice of relationship management. In J. A. Ledingham & S. D. Bruning (Eds.), *Public relations as relationship management* (pp. 55–70). Mahwah, NJ: Lawrence Erlbaum Associates.

McAneny, L. (1997, January). Pharmacists again most trusted: Police, federal lawmakers' images improve. *Gallup Poll Monthly, 376*, 27.

McPhee, R. D., & Poole, M. S. (2001). Organizational structures and configurations. In F. M. Jablin & L. L Putnam (Eds.), *The new handbook of organizational communication: Advances in theory, research, and methods* (pp. 503–543). Thousand Oaks, CA: Sage.

Miller, K. (1999). *Organizational communication: Approaches and processes* (2nd ed.). Belmont, CA: Wadsworth.

Miller, K. I., Ellis, B., Zook, E. G., & Lyles, J. S. (1990). Occupational differences in the influence of communication on stress and burnout in the workplace. *Management Communication Quarterly, 3*, 166–190.

Miller, V., & Jablin, F. (1991). Information seeking during organizational entry: Influences, tactics, and a model of the process. *Academy of Management Review, 16*, 92–120.

Monge, P., & Contractor, N. (2001). Emergence of communication networks. In F. Jablin & L. Putnam (Eds.), *The new handbook of organizational communication: Advances in theory, research, and methods* (pp. 440–502). Thousand Oaks, CA: Sage.

Murphy, A. (2001). The flight attendant dilemma: An analysis of communication and sensemaking during in-flight emergencies. *Journal of Applied Communication Research, 29*, 30–53.

Neuman, J. (1998). Workplace violence and workplace aggression: Evidence concerning specific forms, potential causes, and preferred targets. *Journal of Management, 24*, 391–420.

O'Hair, D., Friedrich, G., & Dixon, L. (2002). *Strategic communication in business and the professions* (4th ed.). Boston: Houghton Mifflin.

Parsons, T. (1963). *Structure and process in modern societies.* New York: Free Press.

Peters, T., & Waterman, R. (1982). *In search of excellence.* New York: Harper & Row.

Pusic, E. (1984). The political impact of organizational democracy. In B. Wilpert & A. Sorge (Eds.), *International perspectives on organizational democracy* (pp. 23–48). Chichester: John Wiley & Sons.

Putnam, L., & Poole, S. (1987). Conflict and negotiation. In F. Jablin (Ed.), *Handbook of organizational communication* (pp. 549–599). Newbury Park, CA: Sage.

Rafeili, A., & Sutton, R. I. (1990). Busy stores and demanding customers: How do they affect the display of positive emotion? *Academy of Management Journal, 33*, 623–637.

Ruch, W. V. (1984). *Corporate communications: A comparison of Japanese and American practices.* Westport, CT: Quorum Books.

Sass, J. (2000). Emotional labor as cultural performance: The communication of caregiving in a nonprofit nursing home. *Western Journal of Communication, 64*, 330–358.

Sellnow, T., & Brand, J. (2001). Establishing the structure of reality for an industry: Model and anti-model arguments as advocacy in Nike's crisis communication. *Journal of Applied Communication Research, 29*, 278–295.

Solomon, D., & Williams, A. (1997). Perceptions of social-sexual communication at work: The effects of message, situation, and observer characteristics on judgments of sexual harassment. *Journal of Applied Communication Research, 25*, 196–216.

Sutcliffe, K. (2001). Organizational environments and organizational information processing. In F. Jablin & L. Putnam (Eds.), *The new handbook of organizational communication* (pp. 197–230). Thousand Oaks, CA: Sage.

Stohl, C. (1995). *Organizational communication: Connectedness in action.* Thousand Oaks, CA: Sage.

Tracy, K., & Tracy, S. (1998). Emotion labor at 911: A case study and theoretical critique. *Journal of Applied Communication Research, 26,* 390–411.

Waldron, V. (1994). Once more, with feeling: Reconsidering the role of emotion in work. In S. A. Deetz (Ed.), *Communication yearbook 17* (pp. 388–416). Thousand Oaks, CA: Sage.

Weick, K. (1995). *Sensemaking in organizations.* Newbury Park, CA: Sage.

Witteman, H. (1993). The interface between sexual harassment and organizational romance. In G. Kreps (Ed.), *Sexual harassment: Communication implications* (pp. 27–62). Cresskill, NJ: Hampton Press.

CHAPTER ELEVEN

Comprehension without critical evaluation is impossible.

FRIEDRICH HEGEL

After 50 years of controversy over the impact of television on children, a new world of online media is emerging that may have even greater impact on them.

KATHRYN C. MONTGOMERY

I find television very educating. Every time somebody turns on the set, I go into the other room and read a book.

GROUCHO MARX

Mediated Communication and Media Literacy

What will you learn?

When you have read and thought about this chapter, you will be able to:

1. Explain the importance of studying mediated communication.
2. Define mediated communication and explain the differences between mass communication and computer-mediated communication.
3. Identify types of mass communication.
4. Discuss ways in which the mass media affect our culture and us.
5. Identify types of computer-mediated communication.
6. Explain the difference between synchronous and asynchronous communication.
7. Discuss how CMC affects the communication process.
8. Understand strategies for becoming a critical consumer of mediated messages.

e all participate in mediated communication, which is *any communication interaction using technology as the primary channel.* The two predominant types of mediated communication—mass communication and computer-mediated communication—inform, entertain, persuade, and provide a means for connecting people. In this chapter you will learn the importance of mediated communication, how mediated communication affects us through the communication process, and how to be a more critical consumer of mediated messages.

Ted, like many other Americans, was glued to the television for the entire day—September 11, 2001. As images of disaster and reports of tragedy permeated Ted's thoughts, he felt strangely connected to the people slowly making their way out of what was soon to be called, simply, "Ground Zero." On one hand, Ted knew that he was thousands of miles away from the tragedy. At the same time, the instantaneous broadcasts of news made Ted feel like he was personally embroiled in what was happening.

Ted's morning had been a roller coaster of anxiety and fear. Initial reports after the tragedy indicated that several additional planes were "unaccounted for" and potentially hijacked. He heard reports of suspected car bombs in Washington; both reports later proved false. As the days slowly crept by, Ted tried to process the events of September 11. When he was not in class or at work, he was mesmerized by the television screen.

Unlike some Americans, Ted did not feel hatred or fear as a result of the tragedy. His best friend, Sharif Azizinamini, was Muslim and Ted knew that the terrorist actions were no more representative of Islam than actions of white supremacists were of Christianity. News reports attempted to make distinctions between militant fundamentalists and other members of Islam; however, such reports also implicitly linked terrorism with Islam. Ted was not surprised to hear that members of the American-Muslim community feared persecution.

Ted continued watching news reports for months. News reports of what happened on September 11 soon gave way to reports of anthrax, FBI warnings, and the "new war on terrorism" taking place in Afghanistan. Ted was still fearful, but he was thankful that the news media provided him with important information.

Teaching Tip

This chapter emphasizes both mass media and computer-mediated communication. Begin this unit with examples showing why it is necessary to be critical consumers of mediated communication. Examples might include sensationalized news stories and dubious Web pages.

Why Should You Study Mediated Communication?

Many of the reasons for studying interpersonal forms of communication are also relevant to the study of mediated communication. Perhaps the most important reason is that by understanding the process of mediated communication, you will learn to think critically about the messages the media send us. You will become a more thoughtful media consumer. As a consumer of the media and as a citizen of a world in which technology seems to be bringing people closer together, your responsibility is to understand how the media function and to develop the skills to interpret their significance. By understanding the nature and function of mediated communication, you can begin to recognize the significance of the media and the role they play in shaping your understanding of the world.

In the introductory story we learned that Ted, like many Americans following the tragedy of September 11, watched the news and accepted on blind faith that those reports were accurate. Because Ted's knowledge of the attacks was not firsthand, the media shaped a large portion of Ted's

Discussion Question

How did the media shape your perception of the September 11 tragedy? Did the way the story was covered make you feel a certain way? What was most significant about the media coverage of the terrorist attacks in your mind?

perceptions about the events. Unlike some Americans, however, Ted was a critical consumer of the media. He knew that terrorists like Osama bin Laden were not representative of the Muslim faith. Ted was able to objectively process mediated messages based on his personal knowledge of Islam. He was a critical consumer of the media, a goal we should all strive for.

TRY ◄ ▶ THIS

How did you use the media on September 11? Did you watch television? How do you think the news reports of September 11 and subsequent issues influenced you?

Beyond becoming a critical consumer of mediated messages, we also produce mediated communication. Sending an e-mail message, creating a Web page, and posting to an online chat room or discussion board are all examples of mediated communication. For decades, textbooks used in introductory communication courses have treated mediated communication as something we listen to, watch, or read—all messages produced by other people. The Internet has forced all of us to change our assumptions about mediated communication. In today's society each of us has the potential to be simultaneous consumers and producers of mediated messages. Thus a second reason to study mediated communication is to become a more thoughtful producer of mediated messages.

Discussion Question

How has mediated communication changed the way you communicate? How do you use e-mail in your daily communication activities? Do you have a personal Web page? What do you use your Web page for?

What Is Mediated Communication?

As mentioned in the previous section, mediated communication is more than just radio, television, and newspapers. **Mediated communication** is *any form of communication that employs electronic means.* Within mediated communication we make the distinction between mass communication and computer-mediated communication.

Wilson and Wilson (1998) define **mass communication** as *a process in which professional communicators using technological devices share messages over great distances to influence large audiences.* You can look at this definition in the context of the communication process, which involves a source, a channel, a message, a receiver, and feedback (Figure 11.1).

In mass communication, a professional communicator is the **source,** *someone who shares information, ideas, or attitudes with someone else.* The source might be a television or newspaper reporter, an

mediated communication

Any form of communication that takes place using electronic means.

Radio is a common form of mass communication.

mass communication

A process in which professional communicators using technological devices share messages over great distances to influence large audiences.

source

Someone who shares information, ideas, or attitudes with someone else.

channel

The means by which a message is sent.

message

Whatever the source attempts to share with another person.

feedback

A response that allows the source to determine if the message was correctly understood.

linear communication

Communication that flows primarily from the sender to the receiver with little or no feedback from the receiver to the sender.

author, or an announcer. The technological devices are the **channels,** or *the means by which a message is sent.* For example, radio and television messages are transmitted via cable and satellite systems, and printed messages are transmitted via printing presses, computers, and, increasingly, satellite. The **message** is *the meaning the source attempts to share with another person.* In mass communication, the large audience comprises the receivers, the people who are the intended recipients of the message. Occasionally a receiver of the message will send **feedback** to the source, that is, *a response that allows the source to determine if the message was correctly understood.* In mass communication feedback can be conveyed through a letter to the editor, an e-mail to your cable provider, or a telephone call to a television station.

As you can surmise from this description of mass communication, this form of mediated communication is **linear** in nature. That is, *communication flows primarily from the sender to the receiver with little or no feedback from the receiver to the sender.* Here we make a distinction between mass communication and computer-mediated communication.

Computer-mediated communication, often referred to as **CMC,** is *human-to-human communication using networked computer environments to facilitate interaction* (Shaff, Martin, & Gay, 2001). CMC is different from mediated communication because the human-to-human interaction is interactive. When you e-mail another person, that person can respond to your message; when you engage in an online chat, other people can interact with you by asking questions or responding to your statements; more advanced programs like Microsoft Netmeeting can even be used to facilitate face-to-face discussions over the Internet. In each of these situations the communication is interactive: You are both a sender and receiver of communication. Figure 11.1 illustrates the communication process in the context of CMC.

Individuals involved in the computer-mediated interaction serve simultaneously as source and receiver. Computers, connected via the Internet or a computer network, act as the channel of communication. Because the interaction is personal, the message can consist of anything the

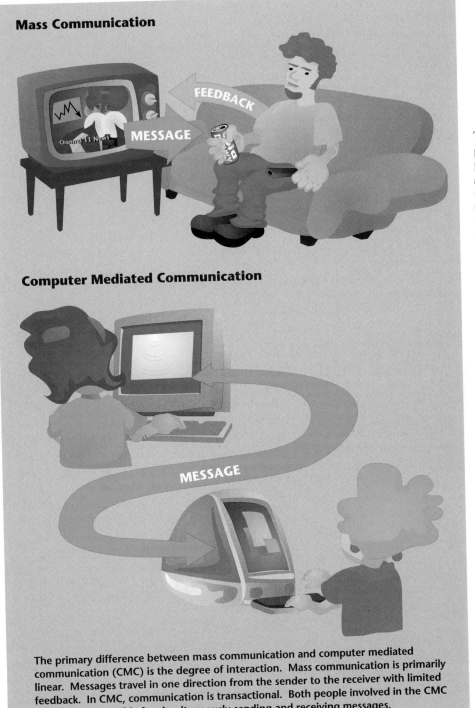

Mass Communication

FEEDBACK

MESSAGE

Channel 11 News

Computer Mediated Communication

MESSAGE

The primary difference between mass communication and computer mediated communication (CMC) is the degree of interaction. Mass communication is primarily linear. Messages travel in one direction from the sender to the receiver with limited feedback. In CMC, communication is transactional. Both people involved in the CMC event are responsible for simultaneously sending and receiving messages.

Teaching Tip

Point out that Figure 11.1 is an adapted version of the transmission model of communication. The transaction model was discussed in chapter 1. Point out that the mass media model emphasizes the roles of the sender (professional media sources) and the channel (the medium).

CD-ROM Activity

Ask students to watch the animation titled "The Mediated Communication Process" on the accompanying student CD-ROM. The animation illustrates basic models for mass communication and computer-mediated communication.

Video Activity

Ask students to view the video segment "On the Air with Campus-Community Connection." Have students analyze elements of the mass communication process model apparent in the segment. Who was the source, who was the intended audience, etc.

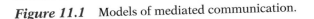

Figure 11.1   Models of mediated communication.

computer-mediated communication (CMC)

Human-to-human communication using networked computer environments to facilitate interaction.

two people wish to discuss: a movie, politics, or even plans for a date. And because CMC is interactive, feedback naturally occurs through the exchange of interactive messages.

TRY ▶ THIS

List all of the ways that you use electronic forms of communication. How frequently do you use e-mail, chat, or instant messaging? How do you use these electronic tools? Do you use them to keep in touch with friends/relatives? Do you use them for business purposes?

Teaching Tip
The key difference between mass media and CMC is the degree of interactivity. Point out that many CMC technologies allow interactivity between communicators, whereas mass-mediated messages generally do not.

Although we view mass communication and CMC as different forms of mediated communication, they share the common element of using electronic channels to facilitate communication. Mediated communication, prevalent in our lives already, will only increase in the future. For that reason, we must become effective consumers and producers of mediated messages.

The Mass Media

The mass media permeate our lives, often without our realization. Instead of listing all of the ways that you are exposed to the media, try to think of a place you can go to escape mediated messages. Such places exist, to be sure. You can turn off your car radio and go for a drive in the country (be careful to avoid billboards). You could lock yourself in your room (be sure to cover those posters and stay off the Internet). Of course, you can also try to find a nice cave in which to spend time (but if the cave has hieroglyphics, you will have to find a new one since hieroglyphics were perhaps the first form of mass communication). As you can see, to escape the influence of the mass media is possible but takes some forethought and planning.

In this section we introduce you to several forms of mass media and discuss how the mass media may affect us.

Discussion Question
Have students list and discuss the ways in which they use computers to communicate. How do they think computer technology will change communication in the future? Will a greater reliance on CMC change how we think about and engage in traditional forms of communication like interpersonal and small-group encounters?

What Are the Mass Media?

The mass media serve a variety of purposes in our lives. We are informed, persuaded, and entertained by the mass media; sometimes all three happen at the same time. In this section we pay particular attention to how we use the mass media as sources of information. For each medium we address its major advantage and disadvantage as a source of information. Critical listeners and consumers keep these advantages and disadvantages in mind as they review information from mediated sources. The suggestions we provide in this section will also be relevant when you conduct research for speeches and papers in this class or other classes.

- *Newspapers.* Freedom of the press has long been America's chief defense against government abuses of its citizens. Our oldest mass medium, newspapers, are one of our most reliable sources of information. Even highly credible newspapers make mistakes, so do not consider everything you read in the paper 100 percent reliable. Among the most reliable newspapers are national publications such as *The Los Angeles Times, The New York Times,* and *The Washington Post.* Some good regional papers include *The Atlanta Constitution, The Miami Herald,* and *The St. Louis Post Dispatch.* Make sure you know which newspapers in your area are considered the most reliable and trustworthy.

TRY ▶ THIS

Compare the front page of a daily newspaper like the New York Times or your local newspaper with the website for that newspaper. How are they similar and different? Do you think the newspaper is trying to reach a different audience with its website? What does the website have that the actual newspaper does not?

- *Television.* Television news is currently the most widely used source of information about current events. When you are watching broadcast news, you should recognize that the immediacy of the news is much more a factor with television than with newspapers and magazines, so skepticism regarding breaking news is particularly important. Broadcast news stations will often go immediately on the air with a breaking news story to "beat" competing stations. Often, however, initial statements and inferences regarding events are unclear or even incorrect.

- *News Magazines.* News magazines are better for in-depth treatment of recent events than are newspapers and television. Information in news magazines is

Today's TV news is immediate and continuous.

Cultural Note

THE INTERNET CULTURE

Later in the chapter we discuss how the mass media affect our culture through gatekeeping, agenda setting, and other processes. For now, think about how the Internet has affected our culture. Dubin (2001) notes that the Internet is now influencing the language we speak. Terms like "mouse" and "virus" have taken on new meanings; new terms like "firewall" and "RAM" now enter our vocabulary when talking about topics other than computers. Noted cultural critic Neil Postman goes so far as to argue that the digital culture perpetuated through the Internet and television has caused our society to emphasize glitz and entertainment rather than rational thought. Such an effect, according to Postman, influences everything from the way we learn to political elections.

Beyond the influence of the Internet in our own culture, other societies must adapt to the rapid worldwide rise in Internet usage. Iran, once a very closed society, is seeing a rapid growth in Internet use among its youth (Moore, 2001). Because the Internet is so "foreign" to the Iranian culture, religious and political leaders are now scrambling to deal with the issue. Religious leaders, called Clerics, are creating Web pages at the same time that government officials are shutting down Internet cafes in Tehran. How do you think access to the Internet could potentially change a culture like Iran? Do you think the Internet has the potential to bring the world together or will it be just another medium of communication like television?

not as immediate as newspapers or television. National news magazines like *Time, Newsweek,* and *US News & World Report* are regarded as reliable sources. Other sources tend to be more liberal—or conservative—leaning and are not as objective.

- *The Internet.* Some of the most outrageous news comes from the **Internet,** *a global network of interconnected computer networks.* Because many Internet sites lack editorial control, rumors and speculative gossip run rampant. Although the Internet makes large quantities of information accessible to remote areas, you should always be skeptical of the quality of information found on the Internet.

‐‐‐‐‐‐‐‐‐‐ TRY ◀▶ THIS ‐‐‐‐‐‐‐‐‐‐

The Internet is a valuable tool for finding information on any number of topics. Select your favorite hobby. Go to <u>www.yahoo.com</u> and search for websites about your hobby. Which sites were most interesting? Were some sites geared to sell you something? Were those sites as useful as other sites for learning information about your hobby?

Teaching Tip

Select an article from a professional journal like *Science* or the *New England Journal of Medicine* that has received attention in popular press. Show students articles from both types of sources and use this as an opportunity to discuss the differences between primary and secondary source material.

- *Professional Journals.* Every academic discipline has professional journals, as do professions such as law and medicine. Generally, professional journals are good sources of information because editorial boards carefully review articles prior to publication. For example, most journals use what is called **blind peer review,** which means that *an article submitted for publication is anonymously reviewed by other professionals in the discipline before being accepted for publication.* The downside of professional journals is that they are written for specialized audiences and often use jargon that is difficult for an ordinary person to understand.

blind peer review

Anonymous review of articles submitted for publication in professional journals by other professionals in the discipline.

What Are the Effects of the Mass Media?

The term "couch potato" has become common in our culture. At one time or another we have all curled up on the couch (or in the lounger) with a bag of chips, big soda, and candy in preparation for our favorite program or to watch a big game. Besides these self-indulging behaviors, the media affect us in numerous other ways. In this section we discuss how the mass media influence our behaviors and shape the culture in which we live.

Video Activity

Ask students to view the video segment "On the Air with Campus-Community Connection." Have students discuss the potential effects of viewing "political talk/debate shows" like the one seen in this segment. Can shows like these cultivate attitudes?

Influencing Behavior

No issue better illustrates the influence of mass media on our actions than the issue of violence. Most people agree that violence is more prevalent in the United States than in most other countries, and many experts think they have proof that mass media are implicated in the burgeoning violence. A look at the research tells part of the story.

The Surgeon General of the United States released a report in 2001 addressing the link between media violence and youth violence (*Youth Violence*, 2001). The overall conclusion of the Surgeon General's report is that hundreds of research studies, spanning several decades, demonstrate a statistically significant relationship between exposure to mediated violence and violent behavior. Violence in the media occurs on television, in movies, music videos, video games, and potentially the Internet. The data summarized by the Surgeon General were collected largely by communication researchers at UCLA and published in the National Television Violence Study Report (Federman, 1998). Consider the following statistics highlighted in the UCLA study:

- 61 percent of television programs contain some violence; only 4 percent feature "nonviolence" themes.
- 44 percent of violent episodes on television involve characters with some qualities worthy of emulation.
- Nearly 75 percent of violent episodes on television feature no immediate punishment or negative reaction to the violent behavior.
- Only 16 percent of violent programs feature long-term, realistic consequences of violence.

Other studies suggest that violence is not limited to television programming. Nearly one-fourth of music videos portray violence (DuRant, Rich, Emans, Rome, Allred, & Woods, 1997).

What is the result of such mediated violence? Statistics reviewed by the American Academy of Pediatrics suggest that as much as 10–20 percent of real-life violence may be attributed to mediated violence (American Academy of Pediatrics, 2001). Real-life examples illustrate these statistics. The 1999 shooting at Columbine High School in Littleton, Colorado, underscored the violence contained in "first-person shooter" video games (Cimons, 2000); listening to "death metal" music was implicated as a possible reason for two boys in San Luis Obispo, California, killing a female classmate as part of a satanic ritual (Waxman, 2001); after several young men died imitating the scene, Touchstone Films removed a video scene in which football players demonstrated their "courage" by lying in the middle of a highway at night (Wilson & Wilson, 1998).

Why does viewing violent imagery lead to violent behavior? Researchers in the field of communication claim that violent programming can desensitize us to violence. In one study, groups of people were shown violent programming or exciting, yet nonviolent programming. After watching the programs for two hours the participants then watched an additional 90-second clip of violent programming. Participants who had previously viewed two hours of violent programming showed very little reaction in heart rate, feelings of anxiety, or changes in mood. Participants who viewed two hours of nonviolent programming had the opposite reaction. They had higher heart rates and experienced increased anxiety, hostility, and depression (Linz, Donnerstein, & Adams, 1989). The implication of this study is that violent programming psychologically affects us. Watching violence makes us desensitized to additional violence.

The influence of television is not entirely negative. Viewers around the world have never known so much about political candidates, accidents, crime, crises, and weather as they do today. With the advent of 24-hour news and weather programs, you can find out the latest news, weather, and road reports whenever you wish.

Shaping Culture

Because people depend on the mass media to inform them, the media play a major role in shaping our culture. **Culture,** in this context, is *a set of beliefs and understandings a society has about the world, its place in it, and the various activities used to celebrate and reinforce those beliefs.* How do media decisions about what is important influence our culture? Consider the influence of televised football on the American culture. The

Mass communication can be delivered electronically.

culture

A set of beliefs and understandings a society has about the world, its place in it, and the various activities used to celebrate and reinforce those beliefs.

sense of "maleness" and competition that surrounds football supports the belief that men are supposed to be big, tough, and macho. The game subtly reinforces the notion that people can be anything they want if only they try hard enough, a distinct belief of the American culture. Indeed, as early as the nineteenth century, cheap paperback novels promoted the American virtues of hard work, education, and rugged individualism. Such values have been repeated in radio programs, magazine stories, and television situation comedies so often they have become a part of our social fabric.

Once you start to think this way, the significance of the mass media as "culture industries" becomes apparent. This viewpoint assumes two important concepts. First, the media are an arena for working out competing definitions of reality. Thus the media become a debating ground for our system of values and beliefs. Second, the effects of the media are not simple, direct results but complex consequences interwoven in the cultural fabric. When you see the media as contributing to the culture, you can ask how they affect that culture on a societal level. In this section we tackle that issue by discussing five cultural functions of the media: gatekeeping, agenda setting, perpetuating stereotypes, and cultivating perceptions.

Gatekeeping   **Gatekeeping** is *the process of determining what news, information, or entertainment will reach a mass audience.* The term *gatekeeping,* coined by Kurt Lewin in 1947, describes news traveling through a series of checkpoints before reaching the public (Wilson & Wilson, 1998). To see how gatekeeping works, consider what happens with a freeway accident involving a large truck and two cars. Gatekeeping first occurs when newspapers, for example, determine if the accident is serious

gatekeeping

The process of determining what news, information, or entertainment will reach a mass audience.

enough to justify sending reporters to the scene. If editors send reporters to the scene, they will act as gatekeepers when they decide if a story should be published. If written, the story goes to a copy editor, who edits the story on the way to the city editor, who judges its importance and placement. A news director at a television station, an acquisitions editor at a book publishing company, and other gatekeepers make such decisions every day. Thus each day, a number of people control what you will see.

agenda setting

The determination of the topics discussed by individuals and society on the basis of the media attention.

Agenda Setting   **Agenda setting** simply means that *when the media pays attention to certain topics, they determine, or set the agenda, for what topics are discussed by individuals and society* (Campbell, 1998). Although journalists attempt to serve as watchdogs of the political process, other forces also shape such agendas. Political and social agendas are both challenged and validated through the information and entertainment media. If the media deem a story or issue important, the story will get media attention; if they perceive the story as unimportant, the story will receive very little attention. Issues deemed important by the media become significant issues in the minds of the public.

To illustrate the agenda-setting function of the media we return to the topic of teen violence. In the wake of the Columbine High School shooting the topic of youth violence has become a significant issue for the media. As media coverage of the topic increased, the nation's attention to the topic also increased. Are people's perceptions of youth violence accurate? According to a study comparing national statistics with the public's views on crime, those perceptions are not accurate. As explained by Dorfman and Schiraldi (2001):

- Although most people believe youth crime is increasing, homicides by juveniles dropped 68 percent from 1993 to 1999.

- In a 1998 poll, nearly two-thirds of the respondents indicated they believed juvenile crime was increasing. In 1998 juvenile crime reached a 25-year low.

- On network television, news about homicides increased by 473 percent from 1990 to 1998; the national homicide arrests dropped by 33 percent over that same time period.

As explained by Dorfman, one of the authors of the report and a researcher with the Berkeley Media Studies Institute, "The majority of Americans who get their information on which to base decisions—whether it's voting decisions or what policies to support or what to be afraid of in the world—get that information from the news. . . . When the news limits the information that people get, that leads to distortion" (quoted in Texeira, 2001). Thus the agenda set by the media not only shapes what we talk about, but it can potentially distort our perceptions of issues.

Team Challenge

HOW ENTERTAINMENT PROGRAMS FRAME ISSUES

Much of our discussion of the mass media focused on news shows. However, the mass media also entertain through sitcoms and dramas. Your group should pick one "entertainment" show to watch (even better if you can watch the show together). After watching the show, your group should discuss the implicit ways that the show frames issues. For instance, if you watch *Everybody Loves Raymond,* how does that show frame family life? How does *ER* frame medical issues? How do you think the framing that occurs on the show you watched could potentially shape the attitudes of viewers?

TRY ► THIS

Watch the evening and nightly news on two of your local or regional TV stations. What issues or stories did the broadcasts emphasize? For instance, what was the "lead story"? Did both stations emphasize the same issues? If you do not have time to watch two TV broadcasts, you can do the same activity with two newspapers from the same day or two news magazines from the same week.

Video Activity

Bring in tapes of the first 10 minutes of several local news broadcasts from the same day. After viewing the tapes, discuss the "agenda" set by the media.

Perpetuating Stereotypes Julia Wood (1994), a communication professor at the University of North Carolina, provides an interesting picture of the world as depicted by the media: It is a world in which white males make up two-thirds of the population. The women are fewer in number perhaps because less than 10 percent live beyond 35. Those who do, like their male counterparts and the younger females, are nearly all white and heterosexual. In addition to being young, the majority of women are beautiful, very thin, passive, and primarily concerned with relationships and getting rings out of collars and commodes. There are a few bad, bitchy women, and they are not so blandly pretty, not so subordinate, and not so caring as the good women. Most of the bad ones work outside the home, which is why they are hardened and undesirable. The more powerful, ambitious men occupy themselves with important business deals, exciting adventures, and rescues of dependent females, whom they often assault sexually.

What Wood is talking about is the stereotypes that mass media perpetuate. Stereotypes often depict people who are not from the dominant culture, which, as you learned in chapter 7, is white, middle-class men.

Video Activity

Ask students to view the video segment "Reporting for KTNT: Susan Elliott." Have students discuss whether Susan's story on homelessness could perpetuate or challenge dominant stereotypes about homelessness.

When the media portray women, the women tend to fit cultural views of gender. Wood (1994) says women are depicted "as sex objects who are usually young, thin, beautiful, passive, dependent, and often incompetent and dumb. Female characters devote their primary energies to improving their appearances and taking care of homes and people" (p. 233). The good women, like Snow White and Sleeping Beauty, tend to be soft, tender, pretty, and passive. The bad women, like the wicked witch in *The Wizard of Oz* and Alex in the movie *Fatal Attraction*, are hard, cold, and aggressive. In films and in TV movies, a man who is tender and cooks for the family or a woman who is a CEO is rarely seen. Instead, people are regularly portrayed in gender roles that are traditional, limiting, and unrealistic. The point is that media portrayals do not necessarily reflect reality. Like the gatekeepers of the news, the movie moguls have an unwritten rule about how women and men must behave. Wood says, "The rule seems to be that a woman may be strong and successful if and only if she also exemplifies traditional stereotypes of femininity—subservience, passivity, beauty, and an identity linked to one or more men" (p. 241).

Unfortunately, the media create numerous other stereotypes. Consider these additional examples:

- The media generally do not represent older adults. In a content analysis of more than 750 advertisements appearing in national news magazines over a one-year period, McConatha, Schnell, and McKenna (1999) found that when older adults were depicted, they were often in passive or dependent roles.

- Native Americans are also relatively invisible in the media. When depicted at all, male Native Americans are depicted as aggressive, and female Native Americans are sexualized (Bird, 1999).

- Latino Americans are often depicted in films and television as servants, "illegal" aliens, and drug dealers (Pachon, 2001).

Although the media perpetuate some stereotypes, positive images can also be presented. A recent article in *Television Quarterly* (Prime Time's Disabled Images, 2001) points out that disabled individuals, once invisible to the media, are now being portrayed in strong, self-reliant roles. For example, Dr. Weaver on *ER* as well as other disabled characters are equal to or higher in status than other characters in the same show.

cultivation effect

Heavy television and media use leads people to perceive reality as consistent with the portrayals they see on television.

Cultivating Perceptions   A final issue illustrating the effects of the mass media is the cultivation of perceptions. The **cultivation effect** suggests that *heavy television and media use leads people to perceive reality as consistent with the portrayals they see on television* (Campbell, 1998). Gerbner (1998), the person credited with defining cultivation theory, notes that widely seen images promote attitudes and values on the part of viewers. Take the issue of violence. Other theories discussed in this chapter sug-

STEREOTYPES IN YOUR LOCAL PAPER

Pick up a copy of your local newspaper. Using only the stories on the front page, make a list of the people quoted, described, or mentioned in the stories. How many of the people were of recognizably ethnic backgrounds? Were certain ethnic groups represented in certain ways (victims of crime, impoverished, etc.)? To what extent did news coverage in the paper play into common societal stereotypes? After you consider these questions individually, discuss within your group the extent to which the media have a responsibility to challenge societal stereotypes. Is social consciousness the responsibility of the media? Why do you think stereotyping is so common in the media? Are the media to blame for stereotyping or are the media simply reflecting something that already exists in our culture?

gest that mediated violence leads to real violence. Gerbner and his colleagues take a less direct route and suggest that heavy television viewing causes one to feel that the world is a dangerous place. Consider the following findings:

- Frequent television viewers perceive their risk of being a victim of violence much greater than less frequent viewers.
- Fear of walking alone at night is much higher for heavy television viewers than for low television viewers.
- Heavy television viewers are more skeptical and predict the worst from other people. Low television viewers are more optimistic.

In addition to explaining how the media affect our perceptions, Gerbner and his colleagues claim that the media normalize violence. That is, repeated exposure to violence leads viewers to believe that violent actions are normal responses to stressful situations. Such normalization of violence has the potential to make a person more predisposed to act violently toward others.

Cultivation theory provides a potentially powerful analysis of how the media affect us. Although a link between mediated violence and real violence is difficult to prove, Gerbner's theory has intuitive appeal. Viewing continual violence and seeing minorities misrepresented are bound to have some long-term effects on our perceptions of the world.

Computer-Mediated Communication

During the 1990s CMC became a common communication tool on most universities and in many businesses. A former graduate school colleague, now a human resources director for a technology firm in Phoenix, told us that her company moved entirely to e-mail as a form of communication. The company actually encourages e-mail rather than face-to-face interactions for internal communication because e-mail is more efficient: People spend less time talking about sports and gossip. We are not ready to advocate the "only e-mail" approach to improving productivity; however, our friend's company illustrates the importance of computer-mediated communication in 21st-century communication practices.

Computer-mediated communication is more than simply using e-mail. In fact, CMC comes in numerous forms. In this section we identify several examples of CMC and discuss research exploring communication processes within a CMC environment.

Types of CMC

Nearly every form of CMC utilizes the Internet or networked computers to facilitate human-to-human interaction. E-mail, for example, can travel around the world using the Internet or across the building using a company's network. Although all CMC shares the concept of networking, the similarities in types of CMC end there. Just as mass media have several varieties, several varieties of CMC also exist. And, like mass media, each variety of CMC has certain advantages and disadvantages.

One way to classify types of CMC is to determine whether the communication is synchronous or asynchronous. **Synchronous communication** occurs when *members of the communication interaction are able to interact in real time and each participant is simultaneously a sender and receiver.* For example, a face-to-face conversation or telephone call is synchronous communication. **Asynchronous communication** occurs when *the communication interaction has delays and each participant must take turns being the sender and receiver.* If you have ever had a pen pal or kept in touch with a friend or family member by mail, you have engaged in asynchronous communication.

Teaching Tip

While discussing CMC, set up "virtual office hours" where students can contact you via e-mail, instant messaging, or chat. Ask students to contact you during your virtual office hours to ask a question or just say hello. Discuss reactions to the use of virtual office hours in class. What are the benefits and drawbacks of this approach?

synchronous communication

Members of the communication interaction interact in real time, and each participant is simultaneously a sender and receiver.

asynchronous communication

Delays occur in the communication interaction and each participant must take turns being the sender and receiver.

TRY ◀▶ THIS

List examples of both synchronous and asynchronous communication that you use to keep in touch with friends, relatives, or coworkers. What are some examples of situations where synchronous communication is most effective for you? What are some examples of situations where asynchronous communication is most effective?

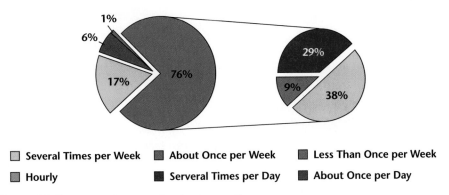

- ☐ Several Times per Week   ■ About Once per Week   ■ Less Than Once per Week
- ☐ Hourly   ■ Serveral Times per Day   ■ About Once per Day

Figure 11.2   How often people check e-mail.

In this section we highlight five of the most common types of CMC: e-mail bulletin board systems, instant messaging/chat, audio-video conferencing, and multi-user environments.

- *Electronic mail.* **Electronic mail** or e-mail *uses the Internet or a computer network to send addressable messages to another person connected to the Internet or network.* E-mail is a popular method of communication for both organizations and individuals (McDermott, 2001; Walker, 2001). The graph in Figure 11.2, based on statistics reported in the UCLA Internet report (2001), illustrates the percentage breakdown for how often people check their e-mail. As you can see, e-mail is quickly becoming a popular form of asynchronous CMC.

- *Bulletin board systems.* **Bulletin board systems (BBS)** are *text-based asynchronous communication tools that allow you to disseminate information to a large number of people.* BBS discussions housed on websites are focused on a particular topic of interest. BBS-like discussions can also take place using a **listserv,** which is an *e-mail–based discussion.* Both Web-based and e-mail–based discussions allow one person to asynchronously post a message to any number of people who have access to the discussion.

- *Instant messaging and chat.* **Instant messaging (IM)** is a *text-based form of synchronous communication that allows users to connect two computers over the Internet and have a "conversation" through their computers.* Instant messaging requires specialized software, often free, that allows you to contact other people and establish instant messaging. **Internet relay chat (IRC)** is a *text-based synchronous communication system that allows multiple users to interact in real time via the Internet.* Various websites host chatrooms that allow multiple users to log on, often with anonymous nicknames, and interact with other users.

electronic mail

Use of the Internet or a computer network to send addressable messages to another person connected to the Internet or network.

bulletin board system (BBS)

Text-based asynchronous communication tool that allows users to disseminate information to a large number of people.

listserv

E-mail–based discussion groups.

instant messaging (IM)

A text-based form of synchronous communication which allows users to connect two computers over the Internet and have a "conversation" through their computers.

Internet relay chat (IRC)

A text-based synchronous communication system that allows multiple users to interact in real time via the Internet.

E-Note

OBSERVING A CHAT ROOM

Go to **yahoo.com** and search for the phrase "chat rooms." The returned results will list several different chat rooms. All chat rooms may require some sort of free registration where you select a user name. Enter one of the rooms and observe the discussion. What issues did participants discuss? How would you characterize chat discussions as similar to and/or different from face-to-face conversations?

audio-video conferencing

Use of the Internet or a network to connect two or more multimedia-capable computers for live, interactive conversations using visual and auditory channels of communication.

multiuser environments

Web-based virtual worlds where participants can interact and engage in fantasy role-playing.

Teaching Tip

Many colleges and universities have on-campus listservs. Create a listserv for your class where students can pose questions, make comments, or engage in discussion. Contact your computer center for assistance in creating a class listserv.

- *Audio-video conferencing.* **Audio-video conferencing** *uses the Internet or a network to connect two or more multimedia-capable computers for live, interactive conversations using visual and auditory channels of communication.* By using computer microphones and inexpensive cameras, it is possible to conduct inexpensive conversations with video over the Internet.

- *Multiuser environments.* **Multiuser environments (MUDs)** *are Web-based virtual worlds where participants can interact and engage in fantasy role-playing.* As you can tell from our description of MUDs, this type of synchronous CMC is far less functional than e-mail, video conferencing, and even instant messaging. Although we can envision ways that multiuser environments could be used in organizational settings, they primarily serve our need for entertainment.

CMC and the Communication Process

Unlike mass media, CMC allows individuals to communicate on a personal level. Because of the personalized nature of CMC, the Internet is quickly becoming a tool for creating, enacting, and maintaining personal relationships not feasible through "snail mail" or long-distance telephone calls. Now, romantic partners in "long-distance relationships" can easily remain in contact; members of the U.S. armed forces stationed overseas can easily communicate with family and friends; you can even create and sustain relationships entirely on line. But can the Internet truly support the warmth of personal interaction that we all seek? Communication scholars have explored the processes and effects of CMC to address this question.

The UCLA Internet Report (2000) provides evidence that CMC is quickly becoming a viable tool for sustaining communication in personal relationships. Participants in the UCLA survey indicated that the Internet has increased their contact with family and friends, professional colleagues, and people sharing their hobbies or personal recreational activities. Furthermore, 26.2 percent of the participants indicated that they have "online friends" whom they have not met in person, and 12.4 percent indicated that they have met someone online and eventually met in person.

In this section we highlight research related to three general areas of CMC research: the nature of CMC interactions, the role of CMC in community formation, and the notion of gender in CMC.

The Nature of CMC Interactions

Based on your knowledge of communication, fundamental differences between CMC and face-to-face communication should be obvious. Primarily, CMC does not allow a full array of nonverbal behaviors to be utilized. Moreover, CMC is more dependent on interpretation of the written word, which has the potential to reduce both the depth and breadth of communication. Thus the question addressed by communication scholars is not so much "How is CMC different from face-to-face communication?" Rather, they ask "How do users of CMC adapt to make CMC more similar to face-to-face communication?"

In chapter 6 you learned about the **uncertainty reduction theory**— *when we meet someone new or encounter new or ambiguous situations we seek to reduce our uncertainty.* Does the process of uncertainty reduction in CMC relationships correspond to uncertainty reduction behaviors in face-to-face relationships? Pratt, Wiseman, Cody, and Wendt (1999) addressed this question by analyzing the content of asynchronous CMC interactions between youngsters and senior citizens who became e-mail "pen pals." A natural strategy for reducing uncertainty, both in CMC and face-to-face communication, is to ask questions. Pratt and colleagues found that, when compared to research on face-to-face relationships, CMC participants asked roughly the same number and same types of questions during their interactions even though the CMC interactions were asynchronous and took longer to develop. One difference between CMC and face-to-face interaction was that CMC participants asked more questions aimed at getting at the "inner self" of the other person. The researchers speculate that this difference could be because CMC participants were not distracted by superficial characteristics like ethnicity or attractiveness.

In addition to uncertainty reduction, researchers have explored similarities and differences in impression formation between face-to-face communication and CMC. **Impression formation** involves *making inferences about another person's personality, values, and traits.* Following either a face-to-face interaction or a CMC interaction, Hancock and Dunham (2001) wanted to determine if impression formations were the same for both types of communication. Results of their study indicated that impressions formed in the CMC communication environments were less detailed but stronger than those formed as a result of face-to-face interactions. We might say that we develop stronger reactions to others during CMC interactions; however, those reactions may be based on a relatively small amount of information.

Homework Activity

Ask students to keep a log of how often they check e-mail during a 24-hour period. How does their usage compare to reported use in the UCLA study?

Teaching Tip

Although many students are familiar with the concept of multiuser domains, not all students are active participants. Using an Internet-capable computer and a computer projector, log into a multiuser domain as a class. Use this as an opportunity to introduce students to what multiuser domains are as well as a launchpad for discussions about the type of communication found in MUDs.

uncertainty reduction theory

A theory explaining the process of reducing psychological uncertainty that arises when we meet someone new or encounter new or ambiguous situations.

impression formation

Making inferences about another person's personality, values, and traits.

Discussion Question

Ask students how they feel CMC "stacks up" against face-to-face communication. Do they see it as a viable alternative? How do they adapt their own CMC behaviors to make CMC more similar to face-to-face communication?

What can we learn from this research? Taken together, the results of these studies teach us a great deal about the nature of CMC interactions. As Flaherty, Pearce, and Rubin (1998) noted, "CMC is not a functional alternative to face-to-face communication" (p. 250). Rather, evidence suggests that CMC users adapt their behaviors to the unique nature of the CMC environment. Rather than relying on visual cues, like pictures, for information, CMC participants are content with visual anonymity. And CMC users may be more likely to discuss core issues about themselves rather than focusing on more superficial cues. Consequently, the question of whether CMC is similar to face-to-face communication is largely irrelevant. CMC is a unique channel of communication to which people can naturally adapt their communication behaviors.

The Role of CMC in Community Formation

Take a moment to think about the communities to which you have belonged. While growing up, you lived in a neighborhood that was part of a larger community. We typically think of communities as physical entities: A map defines the outward boundaries of our towns; towns are made up of discernible neighborhoods; neighborhoods are made up of people's dwellings. Each member of a community has a personal stake in collaborative success of people in the community. If you and your neighbor engage in constant battles, the entire neighborhood feels the tension; if your city has tensions between different groups of people, the entire community is on edge. Thus real communities force us to work together to solve problems and promote a civic commitment to success. Can virtual communities, such as those found on BBS sites or in multiuser domains, achieve the same sense of community as the ones in which we physically live?

A key difference between virtual and physical communities is how they are formed (Byam, 1998). **Physical communities** *form out of geographic pragmatism.* Many towns were established because they were situated on a river or transportation route. People who are part of physical communities are tied together because of geography—they live near each other. **Virtual communities,** however, *are formed out of mutual interest among members*—the connection is psychological similarity rather than geographic proximity. On a basic level, people who live in physical communities often do so because they have to, whereas people who interact in virtual communities do so because they want to. Communication scholars hypothesize that differences between physical and virtual communities potentially have profound implications.

Virtual communities hold a great deal of promise. Because of CMC, people can come together and discuss issues of great personal relevance. For example, Wright (1999) explains that CMC can be used to facilitate support groups. In fact, one of our fathers has a rare form of cancer and belongs to a listserv "community" where he shares advice with others. Without CMC this support network would not be possible. Virtual com-

physical communities

The actual communities we live in—our neighborhoods and cities.

virtual communities

Collections of people who populate discussion boards and/or multiuser environments on the Internet.

Virtual communities allow imaginations to run wild. If you were creating your own virtual community, what rules or norms would you like to see established? Would you base your virtual world on a real-life community? A fantasy community in the past or present? How do you think the text-based medium of most chat rooms would help or hinder the creation of "community spirit" in your virtual world? Think about these issues, and then share your thoughts with your discussion partner.

munities can also serve as a safety valve of sorts. People who feel voiceless and disenfranchised in their own communities may be able to find a secure "home" in a virtual community.

Experts raise several criticisms about virtual communities. As noted by Byam (1998), because virtual communities are not "real" in the traditional sense of the word, members can choose to freely come and go without developing the civic commitment necessary for real communities to function. Moreover, the use of virtual communities as a safety valve allows us to ignore our moral responsibility to those in our physical world. In other words, we risk ignoring real-world problems because a simple click of the mouse can place us in a virtual world that is problem-free. The issue of virtual communities makes salient the point that culture, communication, and ethics are intertwined.

The Relationship among CMC, Gender, and Culture

The final area of research involves the ways in which gender and culture are related to computer-mediated communication. We specifically address research related to two questions. First, are differences in CMC attitudes or behaviors based on gender or ethnicity? Second, can CMC be used as a tool for social change in the areas of gender and ethnicity?

In theory the virtual world of the Internet conceals both gender and ethnicity; the medium is both gender-neutral and color-blind. Of course, this "theory" makes two assumptions, both of which are not necessarily true. The first assumption is that CMC filters out all markers of gender and ethnic heritage. As noted throughout this book, we learn our own personal gender norms and cultural history throughout our lives. To assume that we could "turn off" our gender and cultural background when we turn on the computer would be incorrect. The second assumption is that the virtual world is an egalitarian place where equality and nondiscrimination can reign. This point may be somewhat true but only with equal access to the medium. Unfortunately, this equal access may not be the case.

Research reveals two fundamental points about gender and culture in CMC. First, some differences do appear between men and women in terms of how they are able to adapt to the CMC medium. For example, Adrianson (2001) found that women are able to produce more messages, greater opinion change, more opinions, and higher agreement in face-to-face communication compared to CMC. Thus some evidence shows that men are able to adapt more quickly to the CMC environment. Kramarae (1998) suggests that any gender differences could be attributed to the fact that males dominate the technology arena.

digital divide

A growing gap between those who have access to technology and those who do not.

The second general point made by researchers is that not everyone has access to CMC. The **digital divide** is *a growing gap between those who have access to technology and those who do not.* Or, as explained on the U.S. Commerce Department (2001) Web page titled "Falling through the Net,"

> In just about every country, a certain percentage of people has the best information technology that society has to offer. These people have the most powerful computers, the best telephone service and fastest Internet service, as well as a wealth of content and training relevant to their lives.
>
> There is another group of people. They are the people who for one reason or another don't have access to the newest or best computers, the most reliable telephone service or the fastest or most convenient Internet services. The difference between these two groups of people is what has been called the "Digital Divide."

Statistics reported in the Department of Commerce website indicate that although the number of "connected" individuals has greatly increased, a disproportionate number of ethnic minorities and rural Americans still lack full access to the Internet. Until access is equal, can we claim that the Internet is a color-blind world?

The second general question addressed by CMC researchers on gender and culture issues is whether CMC can be used as an agent of social change. One benefit of CMC is that the connection allows users to come together and discuss important social issues. Although many people may not go to city council meetings or participate in state and national politics, online bulletin boards and other forms of virtual communities provide an outlet for discussion and deliberation. Additionally, Danet (1998) suggests that the CMC environment allows users to "experiment and play" with different personas. As she explains, "Some people are leading double or multiple lives in cyberspace, even with different gender identities. Others are trying out what it might mean to be gender-free, neither male nor female" (p. 130). Through such behaviors, Danet argues, individual users can raise their awareness by being someone other than who they actually are. The long-term consequences of Internet discussions and playful experimentation with different personas could raise social awareness.

Throughout this chapter we have stressed the advantages and disadvantages of various media as we discussed several theories explaining how the media affect us. Attaining an understanding of these issues is the first step in becoming a more literate consumer of mediated information. In this final section we present additional strategies that you can use to critically assess information obtained through mass media or CMC.

Becoming a Literate Consumer of Mediated Communication

Chapter 5 on listening and chapter 14 on finding information present specific strategies you can use to critically listen to and evaluate sources. We encourage you to use those strategies when "listening" to another person's computer-mediated communication or evaluating a Web page or news program.

Media Literacy

The mass media blur the distinction between news and entertainment. As viewers watch the television show *The West Wing*, the all-star cast not only entertains but also provides a lesson on national politics. Likewise, the nightly news must present information on current events in a way that attracts and captivates viewers. Because the mass media both entertain and inform, viewers must understand how to interpret mediated messages critically.

Gerbner (2000), the media critic credited with developing cultivation theory, suggests that viewers keep in mind the following:

- Develop an understanding of how mediated messages are created. Be aware of how different camera angles, lighting designs, editing techniques, and camera movements are used to create certain impressions. Knowledge and awareness of the technical steps involved in producing a mediated message are the first steps in understanding how mediated messages can manipulate us.

- Recognize the motives behind what the media do. The media and entertainment business is just that—a business. All decisions occur within the context of a money-making environment. Even news programs are affected by this reality. During the early stages of the new war on terrorism a prominent reporter "on the ground" in Afghanistan had his contract expire with a prominent news organization. Rather than working on blind faith that a contract would be rewritten, the reporter changed networks and increased his salary. In this situation the ability of two different networks to report important news was dramatically altered because of an economic decision. Literate consumers of mediated messages are aware of this economic reality and interpret meanings accordingly.

- Understand that images found in the media contain values and ideologies. Literate consumers of the media question the foundation of those ideologies and also understand that such implicit messages have a potentially significant impact on viewers.

TRY◄►THIS

A new genre of television show that has emerged over the last several years is "reality TV." Shows like Survivor, Big Brother, *and* Fear Factor *attempt to depict real people in stressful situations. What ideologies do these shows represent? If an alien from another world watched one of these shows, what would the alien learn about our culture?*

CMC Literacy

Like the mass media, CMC must be critically analyzed and evaluated. The issue of critical literacy is compounded when one realizes that the Internet is both a mass medium and a tool for personal communication. Are Web pages with discussion boards a personal communication tool or a mass-mediated message? Because the Internet blurs these forms of mediated communication, being a literate consumer is imperative. In chapter 14 we discuss several criteria that can be used to analyze sources of information. Those criteria should be used when assessing the quality of information-based Web pages. In chapter 5 we discuss tips for effective listening. Those tips should be used when engaging in CMC with another person.

Perhaps the most important point for becoming a literate consumer of CMC is being aware that the Internet is like a large city. In that city, some people will be experts and very credible sources of information; others will present the illusion of expertise but are actually con artists. In cities, companies advertise, students learn, and people engage in the great conversations of life. As you grow up in a city you must learn how to judge the people you talk to. The same is true in the Internet community. Companies sell things, people profess and learn, conversations are carried out, and crimes are committed. Just as you would not walk down a dark street in a city without being aware of potential dangers, you should not travel the information superhighway without heightened awareness.

Chapter Review

SUMMARY

In this chapter you have learned the following:

- Studying mediated communication is important because each of us needs to be a critical consumer of information. Additionally, the popularity of the Internet means that all of us are becoming producers of mediated communication through e-mail, chat, and even the construction of personal Web pages. Knowledge of mediated communication will help you utilize this technology.

- Mediated communication is any form of communication that occurs using electronic means. There are two types of mediated communication:
  - Mass communication occurs when professional communicators use technology like radio and television to share messages to large audiences.
  - Computer-mediated communication (CMC) occurs when a human-to-human interaction takes place using networked computers.
  - Mass communication is primarily linear—messages are sent to audiences with little or no feedback. Computer-mediated communication is more interactive.

- Examples of mass communication include newspapers, television, news magazines, the Internet, and professional journals. Each type of mass communication has several benefits and drawbacks. Knowledge of the different types of mass media and their characteristics will help you become a more effective consumer of the media.

- The mass media affect both people and the culture.
  - Some messages in the mass media affect peoples' behaviors.
  - The mass media have the potential to shape culture by acting as a gatekeeper of information, setting the agenda for issues, shaping attitudes, perpetuating stereotypes, and cultivating perceptions.

- Computer-mediated communication consists of electronic mail, bulletin board systems, instant messaging, chat rooms, audio-video conferencing, and multiuser environments.

- Various forms of CMC are characterized as synchronous or asynchronous communication.
  - Synchronous communication occurs when members of the communication interaction are able to communicate in real time and each participant acts simultaneously as the sender and receiver of messages.
  - Asynchronous communication occurs when the communication interaction is delayed and participants must take turns being the sender and receiver.

- CMC affects the communication process in many ways.
  - To use CMC effectively, users must adapt their communication to the CMC environment. For example, research suggests that CMC users are more likely to discuss deep personal issues rather than focusing on superficial characteristics.

357

- CMC can be studied to shed light on the role of communication in forming virtual communities.

  - CMC has the potential for shaping our culture: It can create social problems like the digital divide, but virtual worlds allow people to express opinions and discuss issues of personal relevance.

- Effective consumers of mediated messages must understand how to critically evaluate messages of the mass media, beginning with an awareness of the media and how technology can be used to shape opinions.

  - Users of CMC must become effective "listeners" during CMC interactions.

⊙ VIDEO LINK: IN FRONT OF THE CAMERA

Video Episode 5: "On the Air with Campus-Community Connection"

Mass-mediated communication usually involves professional broadcasters creating a message and sending it to a large, heterogeneous audience. In "On the Air with Campus-Community Connection," we see an example of a mediated talk show covering the topic of cohabitation. In the program two opponents debate the relative merits of cohabitation and the defense of marriage. Using theories discussed in the chapter, how do you think viewing programs like this would affect viewers? Could such programs cultivate certain perceptions or perpetuate stereotypes? Does the surprise ending of the broadcast affect your perception of the show's credibility?

ISSUES IN COMMUNICATION: THE INTERNET CONNECTING FRIENDS

This Issues in Communication narrative synthesizes several of the concepts discussed in the chapter. As you read the narrative reflect on how the media affects the characters' lives.

Sharif Azizinamini was a TV junkie. Unlike his parents, who grew up without television in their home, Sharif thrived on it. Television was his escape from tests, papers, and lectures—it was his way of dealing with the stresses that go along with attending college far away from home.

September 11, 2001, changed Sharif's view on television altogether. He watched with anger as one news report after another told of destruction to his homeland. Just that summer Sharif, his best friend, Ted, and three other graduating classmates had taken a trip to New York City and toured the now destroyed World Trade Center. Sharif was mad and scared. Besides fearing further terrorist incidents, Sharif also feared that he would be blamed, as a Muslim, for what happened.

As the days wore on, Sharif pried himself from the TV. He had missed several days' worth of classes and knew that he needed to get his life somewhat back to normal. On the Friday after the attacks he left his residence hall and went to the campus computer center to check e-mail and do homework.

Before starting his homework, Sharif thought he would check to see if Ted or any of his other friends were on instant messenger. To his relief, Ted and Kim were online. Sharif quickly sent a message to Ted.

SharifAziz: Ted, what's up? Can you believe what's going on?
Ted2001grad: Hey Sharif. This is CRAZY. I have been watching the news nonstop.
SharifAziz: I know. I was scared to death. The pentagon is a short train ride away from me. How is everyone back there holding up?
Ted2001grad: You know. A lot of people were walking around in a daze. State U had a vigil service today and I went. They had speakers from several different faiths talk—it was nice.
SharifAziz: they had one here too but I did not go.
Ted2001grad: hey man, how are you really holding up? This can't be easy for you.
SharifAziz: Thanks for asking. I have just felt afraid. I can't explain it. People have been cool to me, but I have never felt so lonely.
Ted2001grad: I can understand how you would feel like that. Hey, maybe you can fly home in October and we can

hang out for a while. I just got done talking to Kim and she wants to see you too. We can get the gang back together.
SharifAziz: Yes, that would be good. I'll e-mail Mom and Dad. I had better get to my homework.
Ted2001grad: Hey, I'll expect you back online tomorrow. I had not heard from you for a few days and was starting to worry.
SharifAziz: Will do. Thanks Ted — it is good to talk to you.

This conversation between Ted and Sharif illustrates the role that CMC can play in a person's life. Sharif, who mentioned that he felt isolated in his current environment, was able to talk to his friend and receive support. What role did the type of CMC used by Ted and Sharif play in this interaction? Was it asynchronous or synchronous? Could the same type of interaction have taken place on e-mail or a bulletin board? Are there other methods of CMC that would have been more effective?

This story also illustrates the role of the media. What did we learn about the media from this story? Based on your experiences of watching the news after September 11, do you think the news stories could have contributed to Sharif's feelings of isolation and fear? Why or why not?

KEY TERMS

Use the *Human Communication* CD-ROM and the *Online Learning Center* at www.mhhe.com/pearson to further your understanding of the following terminology.

Agenda setting	Channel	Electronic mail
Asynchronous communication	Computer-mediated communication (CMC)	Feedback
		Gatekeeping
Audio-video conferencing	Cultivation effect	Impression formation
Blind peer review	Culture	Instant messaging (IM)
Bulletin board system (BBS)	Digital divide	Internet

Internet relay chat (IRC)
Linear communication
Listserv
Mass communication
Mediated communication

Message
Multiuser environments
Physical communities
Source

Synchronous
  communication
Uncertainty reduction theory
Virtual communities

SELF-QUIZ

Go to the self-quizzes on the *Human Communication* CD-ROM and the *Online Learning Center* at www.mhhe.com/pearson to test your knowledge.

REFERENCES

American Academy of Pediatrics. (2001). Children, adolescents, and television. *Pediatrics, 107,* 423–426.

Bird S. E. (1999). Gendered construction of the American Indian in popular media. *Journal of Communication, 49,* 61–63.

Byam, N. (1998). The emergence of on-line community. In S. Jones (Ed.), *Cybersociety 2.0: Revisiting computer mediated communication and community* (pp. 35–68). Thousand Oaks, CA: Sage.

Campbell, R. (1998). *Media and culture: An introduction to mass communication.* New York: St. Martin's Press.

Cimons, M. (2000, December 13). Health groups link Hollywood fare to youth violence. *The Los Angeles Times,* p. A34.

Danet, B. (1998). Text as mask: Gender, play and performance on the Internet. In S. Jones (Ed.), *Cybersociety 2.0: Revisiting computer mediated communication and community* (pp. 129–158). Thousand Oaks, CA: Sage.

Dorfman, L., & Schiraldi, V. (2001). Off balance: Youth, race, and crime in the news [Internet]. Building Blocks for Youth Organization. Available: http://www.buildingblocksforyouth.org/media/.

Dubin, M. (2001, August 3). Computers, Internet affect language, reflect culture. *Knight-Ridder/Tribune News Service,* K1606.

DuRant, R., Rich, M., Emans, S., Rome, E., Allred, E., & Woods, E. (1997). Violence and weapons carrying in music videos: A content analysis. *Archives of Pediatrics and Adolescent Medicine, 151,* 443–448.

Federman, J. (Ed.) (1998). *National television violence study,* Vol. 3. Thousand Oaks, CA: Sage.

Flaherty, L., Pearce, K., & Rubin, R. (1998). Internet and face-to-face communication: Not functional alternatives. *Communication Quarterly, 46,* 250–268.

Gerbner, G. (1998). Cultivation analysis: An overview. *Mass Communication and Society, 1,* 75–77.

Gerbner, G. (2000). Reclaiming our cultural myth [Internet]. In The Context Institute website. Retrieved from http://www.contexxt.org/ICLIB/IC38/Gerbner.htm.

Hancock, J., & Dunham, P. (2001). Impression formation in computer-mediated communication revisited: An analysis of the breadth and intensity of impressions. *Communication Research, 28,* 325–332.

Kramarae, C. (1998). Feminist fictions of future technology. In S. Jones (Ed.), *Cybersociety 2.0: Revisiting computer mediated communication and community* (pp. 100–128). Thousand Oaks, CA: Sage.

Linz, D., Donnerstein, E., & Adams, S. (1989). Physiological desensitization and judgment about female victims of violence. *Human Communication Research, 15,* 509–523.

McConatha, J., Schnell, F., & McKenna, A. (1999). Description of older adults as depicted in magazine advertisements. *Psychological Reports, 85,* 1051–1057.

McDermott, I. (2001, January). E-mail for everyone. *Searcher, 9,* 59–65.

Moore, M. (2001, July 1). Cybermania takes Iran by surprise. *The Washington Post,* p. A1.

Pachon, H. (2001, March 8). The "typical" Hispanic family. *The Washington Post,* p. A21.

Pratt, L., Weisman, R., Cody, M., & Wendt, P. (1999). Interrogative strategies and information exchange in computer-mediated communication. *Communication Quarterly, 47,* 46–66.

Prime time's disabled images. (2001). *Television Quarterly, 32,* 44–51.

Shaff, J., Martin, W., & Gay, G. (2001). An epistemological framework for analyzing student interactions in computer mediated communication environments. *Journal of Interactive Learning Research, 12,* 41–65.

Texeira, E. (2001, April 10). Coverage of youth crime promotes fear, study says. *The Los Angeles Times,* p. B3.

UCLA Internet Report. (2000). *Surveying the digital future* [Internet]. UCLA Center for Communication Policy. Retrieved from http://www.ccp.ucla.edu.

United States Department of Commerce. (2001). Falling through the net [Internet]. Retrieved from http://www.digitaldivide.gov/.

Walker, R. (2001, February 5). E-mail hasn't totally replaced in-person meetings yet. *Government Computer News, 20,* 18–21.

Walther, J., Slovacek, C., & Tidwell, L. (2001). Is a picture worth a thousand words? Photographic images in long-term and short-term computer-mediated communication. *Communication Research, 28,* 105–118.

Waxman, S. (2001, January 23). Did "death metal" music incite murder?: Lawsuit against band, distributors could overcome First Amendment hurdle. *The Washington Post,* p. E1.

Wilson, J., & Wilson, S. L. (1998). *Mass media/mass culture* (4th ed.). New York: McGraw-Hill.

Wood, J. T. (1994). *Gendered lives: Communication, gender, and culture,* (pp. 231–244). Newbury Park, CA: Wadsworth.

Wright, K. (1999). Computer-mediated support groups: An examination of relationships among social support, perceived stress, and coping strategies. *Communication Quarterly, 47,* 402–414.

Youth violence: A report of the surgeon general. (2001). [Internet]. Surgeon General website. Retrieved from http://www.surgeongeneral.gov.

Part 3 consists of seven chapters dedicated to public communication.

Chapter 12, Communication Apprehension and Source Credibility, offers strategies for overcoming communication anxiety and explains the importance of source credibility in public presentations.

Chapter 13, Topic Selection and Audience Analysis, provides techniques for finding speech topics and for adapting the message to the audience.

Chapter 14, Finding Information, explains how to use the library, the Internet, and even other people to find supporting material for public presentations.

Fundamentals of Public Speaking: Preparation and Delivery

Chapter 15, Organizing Your Presentation, examines the three main parts of a presentation and includes sample outlines.

Chapter 16, Delivery and Visual Resources, explains the four modes of delivery and explains how to use a wide range of visual aids.

Chapter 17, Informative Presentations, and chapter 18, Persuasive Presentations, discuss the techniques for effectively presenting these two types of presentations and include sample presentations.

CHAPTER TWELVE

Courage is grace under pressure.

ERNEST HEMINGWAY

There are very few monsters who warrant the fear we have of them.

ANDRÉ GIDE

Just trust yourself; then you will know how to live.

JOHANN WOLFGANG VON GOETHE

Communication Apprehension and Source Credibility

What will you learn?

When you have read and thought about this chapter, you will be able to:

1. Distinguish between normal and high communication apprehension.
2. Review some of the methods for reducing your fear of public speaking.
3. Utilize a method of anxiety reduction that works for you.
4. Define source credibility and understand its importance in public presentations.
5. Recite five dimensions or aspects of source credibility.
6. Utilize methods of establishing your own credibility as a presenter.

Fear of public presentations is natural for many but can be unnaturally frightening for a few people. This chapter explores communication apprehension and source credibility. You will learn the difference between the normal, healthy anxiety and the more debilitating high communication anxiety. Increasing your comfort in a public presentation is a worthy goal, because nervousness affects your source credibility. You will learn about five dimensions of credibility, and how to increase your own standing as a presenter.

Reggie Washington was a talented quarterback on the university's varsity football team and a tough competitor on the field. But now, sitting in front of an audience of middle school football players and their parents, Reggie was afraid. Reggie's coach had asked him to speak at a middle school awards banquet. Flattered, he had agreed at once, but he quickly came to regret that decision. He thought about the impending speech constantly, and he hadn't slept well either. At the banquet, after being introduced by the middle school coach, Reggie fidgeted with his tie, kept his eyes glued to the words he had written, heard himself saying "ummm" a lot, and saw his hands shaking. After speaking, he sat down—out of breath from talking so fast.

This chapter is dedicated to helping people like Reggie overcome fear of public speaking and to enhance your credibility as a speaker. The two topics—communication apprehension and source credibility—are linked because how you see yourself is often how the audience sees you. See yourself as confident, and your audience is likely to see you the same way. If you follow the advice in this chapter, you will help your audience perceive you as a more competent speaker.

What Is Communication Apprehension?

communication apprehension (CA)

An individual's fear or anxiety associated with either real or anticipated communication with another person or persons.

The fear of speaking in public goes by many names. Once called "stage fright," a fear most often seen in beginning actors, the concept is now called communication apprehension, or CA, and includes fear of talking on the telephone, fear of face-to-face conversations, fear of talking to authority figures or high-status individuals, fear of speaking to another individual, fear of speaking in a small group, and fear of speaking to an audience. McCroskey (1977) called **communication apprehension (CA)** *"an individual's level of fear or anxiety associated with either real or anticipated communication with another person or persons"* (p. 78).

Why should you know about CA? Even the question is controversial. Some teachers of public speaking feel that discussing CA—even in a textbook—is questionable because students who read about the fear of public speaking may see themselves as more apprehensive. However, as more teachers learn about CA, they want the subject discussed in texts. Both students and teachers want to know what to do about the problem.

You should know about CA for two reasons. The first is that you need to be able to see the difference between normal CA, which most people experience before they give a speech, and high communication apprehension, or HCA, which is a more serious problem. The second reason is that if you are highly apprehensive about communication, you should receive treatment for your problem or you will spend a lifetime handicapped by your fear.

Since most people experience a normal, healthy anxiety when public speaking, we will first discuss normal CA, including the signs of normal fear and what you can do to make that fear work for rather than against you.

Teaching Tip

Knowledge of symptoms and causes of a medical condition is the first step toward treatment. Although students should not confuse CA with a medical condition, the rationale for educating them about CA is similar.

Think, Pair, Share

MANAGING ANXIETY

Think for a few minutes on your own about why you do or do not feel anxiety about doing a public presentation. Pair with a classmate and share your feelings about talking in front of the class or any group. Decide together what you think you could do to reduce your fears before and during a presentation. Share your best ideas with the class.

Communication Apprehension

Most human beings feel fear when they speak in public. In fact, more people fear public speaking than fear death (Wallechinsky, Wallace, & Wallace, 1977). Jerry Seinfeld, the comedian, once quipped that because of the widespread fear of public speaking, more people at a funeral would choose to be the person in the casket than the person giving the eulogy. Beginning speakers often feel fear before and during their early speeches, and experienced speakers feel the same anxiety all over again when they face an unfamiliar audience. Nearly all the students in a public-speaking class feel anxiety when they think about giving their speeches and when they deliver them. Anxiety is normal and can even be helpful. Just as an athlete performs better with a bit of adrenaline in the blood-stream, so does a speaker who uses the heightened alertness to help get the message across.

Discussion Question

If given the choice, would students prefer to deliver their speech with or without the use of a lectern or podium? Why or why not? Can any of the reasons be linked to communication apprehension?

TRY ◄ ► THIS

With a spouse, partner, or friend, discuss your own anxieties about giving a speech, and seek the advice of others about how to reduce any fears you might anticipate.

Teaching Tip

Compare symptomatic feelings associated with CA to normal feelings associated with the "fight-or-flight" phenomenon people experience in dangerous situations. Although less pronounced, symptoms of both phenomena are similar.

What are the classic symptoms of CA for the public speaker? Apprehensive students do not prepare for their speeches the same way that other students do. Daly, Vangelisti, and Weber (1995) found that students high in anxiety exhibited "less audience adaptation, less concern for equipment likely to be available when the speech was presented, less concern about the tools available to aid in preparing the speech, more difficulty in coming up with information for speeches, and greater self-doubts about one's capability as a speaker" (p. 394). Sleeplessness, worry, and reluctance to perform are all signs of apprehension that appear before you

Audiences sense your confidence.

state anxiety

Anxiety engendered by a specific situation.

trait anxiety

Anxiety described as persistent behavior of a continuing nature.

communibiological perspective

The idea that communication apprehension represents individuals' expression of inborn, biological functioning.

give the speech. When you give the speech, anxiety seems to produce "interfering, off-task thoughts" that inhibit skill development (Greene, Rucker, Zauss, & Harris, 1998). Examples of "off-task" thoughts would be thinking about your shaking hands and knees, sweaty palms and forehead, and "cotton mouth"—the feeling that your mouth is dry and your tongue is swollen. One wit noted that public speakers suffer so often from dryness of the mouth and wetness of the palms that they should stick their hands in their mouths. For the public speaker, however, fear is no laughing matter. All of the symptoms named so far are normal, with women reporting higher anxiety patterns than men (Behnke & Sawyer, 2000). Let us turn from what the normal speaker *feels* to how the normal speaker *behaves* when afraid.

The speaker who is afraid—even with normal fear—tends to avoid eye contact, speak softly, utter vocalized pauses ("well," "you know," "mmmmm"), speak too slowly or too quickly, fumble with hands or feet or items in the pocket, stand as far away from the audience as possible, and place as many obstacles as possible between the speaker and the audience (distance, lecterns, notes). The speaker who is overcoming fear looks at the audience; speaks so all can hear easily; avoids vocalized pauses; speaks at a normal rate; moves body, arms, and feet in ways that do not appear awkward; stands at the usual distance from the audience; and uses the lectern to hold notes—not as a hiding place. Dwyer (1998) discovered that CA was not correlated with age, sex, or grade-point average, but HCA women tended to prefer different learning styles than did the other women (pp. 137–150).

Normal CA in a public speaking situation is a **state anxiety,** *engendered by a specific situation,* rather than **trait anxiety,** or *persistent behavior of a continuing nature* (Mladenka, Sawyer, & Behnke, 1998). About one in five students have the serious form of trait anxiety. Indeed, the researcher who studied and popularized CA, James McCroskey, now believes that *"communication apprehension represents individuals' expression of inborn, biological functioning"* (Beatty, McCroskey, & Heisel, 1998, pp. 197–219), a condition that is part of one's nature rather than learned behavior. This **communibiological perspective** (McCroskey & Beatty, 2000) appears to render HCA as congenital and highly resistant to change.

Why should you strive to reduce your anxiety as a public speaker? Research on audience responses to public speakers indicates the importance of overcoming fear for improved public-speaking effectiveness. For example, one study showed that speakers who look at their audience are judged as credible and are seen as more persuasive than those who do not (Hemsley & Doob, 1978). Another study showed that CA speakers who use more vocalized pauses or hesitations are less persuasive (Lind & O'Barr, 1979). Speakers who appear unusually slow or powerless are perceived as less knowledgeable about the topic and, therefore, as less credible (Miller et al., 1976). On a more positive note, MacIntyre and MacDonald (1998) found that "the group with the highest anxiety showed the largest improvement in perceived competence and perception of audience pleasantness"(pp. 359–365).

Now that you understand the fear of public speaking and the way a speaker acts when afraid, you need to focus on the more positive topic of what to do about reducing normal CA.

Reducing High Communication Apprehension

Most people demonstrate a willingness to communicate across a variety of situations, a condition so persistent that researchers regard it as a personality trait (MacIntyre, Babin, & Clement, 1999). A much smaller number of people demonstrate an unwillingness to communicate, a reluctance that extends to the public-speaking situation (McCroskey, 1992).

Among the symptoms of HCA, as listed in Table 12.1, is the attempt to avoid communication situations. Pearson and Yoder conducted a study to find out what would happen if HCA students had a choice of an interpersonal communication course or a public-speaking course. HCA students overwhelmingly chose the interpersonal communication course. The researchers suspected that the HCA students perceived the public-speaking course as much more threatening than the interpersonal communication course (1979). Similarly, in small-group communication, HCA students

---

TABLE 12.1   THE CONSEQUENCES OF HIGH COMMUNICATION APPREHENSION (HCA)

PEOPLE WITH **HCA**

May learn to avoid communication situations altogether (Beatty, 1988).

Have lower overall GPAs and lower scores on college entrance exams (McCroskey & Andersen, 1976; McCroskey, Daly, & Sorensen, 1976).

Are considered less competent, composed, and attractive than others (McCroskey & Leppard, 1975).

Are less likely to receive job interviews, and when hired are less likely to seek promotion (Daly & Leth, 1976).

Often experience diminished self-esteem (Adler, 1980).

Tend to prepare poorly for their speech (Daly, Vangelisti, & Weber, 1995).

In a group discuss with classmates the behaviors exhibited by people with high communication anxiety and the consequences of their behavior. Discuss these questions: Do you believe that extreme shyness is biological or learned? Do you think that people can overcome extreme anxiety about public presentations? What do you think can be done for people who are hampered by extreme anxiety about public speaking?

tend to be nonparticipants in the class or to repeatedly register for, and drop, the class. HCA students try to avoid participating in the kind of communication that arouses their fears.

What are some other characteristics of HCA people? They may choose rooms away from other people, such as at the ends of halls in dormitories, or housing away from busy streets and playgrounds in a housing development. HCA people may sit away from others (back rows of classrooms and lecture halls) or in places in which leadership is not expected (far from the boss's seat). When HCA individuals do find themselves in a communication situation, they may talk less, show less interest in the topic, take fewer risks, and say less about themselves than their classmates do. HCA people may be difficult to get to know. Even when stuck in a situation where communication is unavoidable, they discourage talk with signs of disinterest and silence (see Richmond & McCroskey, 1992).

The effects of HCA can be serious. HCA people are rarely perceived as leaders. They are seen as less extroverted, less sociable, less popular, and less competent than their peers (Feingold, 1983). They are not perceived as desirable partners for courtship or marriage. They are viewed as less composed, less attractive socially, and less attractive as coworkers. Because they communicate reluctantly, and seem so uneasy when they do, HCA people are perceived negatively by others. Therefore, they tend to do poorly in interviews and tend not to get the same quality of jobs as nonapprehensive people do. However, they are not less intellectual, mentally healthy, or physically attractive (Feingold, 1983). The consequences of exhibiting HCA seem serious enough to encourage us to look next at solutions.

If you expect to overcome your fear of public speaking, the first thing you need is a strong desire to do so. You need incentive, motivation, and determination. The Dale Carnegie organization and Toastmasters International have taught public-speaking skills to millions of adults who did not believe in the merits of public speaking until they got out of school. An executive from the Dale Carnegie organization once admitted that before he took the Dale Carnegie course, he was so afraid of public speaking and so outraged that his fear limited his life in so many ways that he decided to overcome his fear by sheer determination. Ironically, the man who was so afraid of public speaking devoted his life to teaching others how to become effective public speakers.

Robinson (1997) conducted a national study to determine what sort of remedies for CA were being performed in college classrooms. Most colleges and universities cannot afford a special section for HCAs, even though one in five students may have high anxiety. Also, few graduate students, lecturers, and teachers in the basic course can take the time necessary to work outside of class with high-anxiety students. As a result, Robinson found that almost 20 percent of departments screen public-speaking students for CA and that the most common in-class treatments are skill training (96 percent), cognitive modification (63 percent), visualization (59 percent), and systematic desensitization (25 percent). Only 13 percent of the programs provided a separate course for HCAs.

The Skills Approach

Fortunately, sheer determination is not the only way to overcome normal fears of public speaking. Another possibility is to do what you are doing: Take a basic communication course. Rubin, Rubin, and Jordan (1997) studied the effects of classroom instruction in a basic communication course and found that HCA students experienced greater positive changes in their posttest than did other students. The same study demonstrated that students who had a low opinion of their own communication competence also raised their scores more than did other students. The **skills approach**—*reducing communication apprehension by improving skills*—include but is not limited to the following additional anxiety-reducing aspects:

1. *Know your topic.* Know more than most of your audience about the topic, find information and interview others about the topic, and organize your speech to fit the time allowed.
2. *Know your audience.* Know who is in your audience, what your listeners are interested in, and how they are likely to respond to your topic.
3. *Know yourself.* If you feel good about yourself—your intelligence, talents, and competence—then you will be more secure and less afraid.
4. *Know your speech.* Practice your speech so that you know the ideas, their order of appearance, and the main messages you want to communicate to the audience.

Class Activity

Ask students to imagine the worst possible thing that could happen to them during a speech. Ask volunteers to share their ideas with the class and write them on the board. As a class, discuss strategies for reducing those fears.

Video Activity

Ask students to view the video segment "Reporting for KTNT: Susan Elliott." What strategies did Susan use to manage nervousness in preparation for her interviews? How could those same strategies be adapted to students' public speeches?

skills approach

Reducing communication apprehension by improving skills such as by taking a public speaking course.

5. *Focus on the message, not on yourself.* If you have selected a topic important to you and your audience and you see your purpose as successfully communicating that message, then you will not be thinking about your hands, mouth, or knees—and neither will your audience.

6. *Recognize your value and uniqueness.* You are the only one who can share what you know with audience members—they cannot get exactly the same perspective from anyone else.

Your instructor may be able to suggest some additional ideas for reducing your anxiety about public speaking, and you may be able to think of some ideas yourself. When some students in a beginning public-speaking class were asked what they did to reduce their fears, they mentioned the following ideas:

1. Practice the speech in the room where you will deliver the speech.
2. Walk to the lectern calmly and confidently; acting confident and poised can make you feel confident and poised.
3. Do not start talking until you feel comfortable in front of your audience. Look at the people in your audience before you start talking to them, just as you would in a conversation.
4. Focus on the friendly faces in the audience—the people who nod affirmatively, smile, and look friendly and attentive. They will make you feel good about yourself and your speech.
5. Have your introduction, main points, and conclusion clear in your head and practiced. The examples and supporting materials will come to mind easily when you remember the important items.

Perhaps you will not find this information startling, but one cure for normal fear of public speaking is exactly what you are doing: taking a course in which you are invited to deliver a number of supervised public speeches to a sympathetic audience. In other words, the speech classroom is a laboratory in which you can work systematically to reduce your fears. Your instructor's comments and those of your classmates can help you discover your strengths and weaknesses. Repeated experiences in front of an audience tend to reduce fear and permit the learning of communication skills that have application both inside and outside the classroom. In short, you are now in the process of reducing your normal fear of public speaking. Table 12.2 presents a checklist that should help you before you give a speech.

cognitive modification

An anxiety-reducing technique designed to bolster the novice speaker's confidence by positive thinking.

Cognitive Modification

The second most popular in-class therapy for HCA is **cognitive modification,** *a technique designed to bolster the novice speaker's confidence by positive thinking* (see, for example, Motley, 1995). This technique attempts to stanch a person's negative thoughts by having him or her substitute a pos-

TABLE 12.2   **REDUCING YOUR FEAR DURING YOUR SPEECH: A CHECKLIST**

Check each of the following items to ensure you have thought about them before your speech and to improve the chances you will do them during your speech.

___ 1. I will look at the audience members during my speech.

___ 2. I will speak loudly enough for people in the back row to hear me with ease.

___ 3. I will have my thoughts ready to avoid hesitations.

___ 4. I will avoid vocalized pauses.

___ 5. I will try to move and gesture naturally.

___ 6. I will not avoid my audience with distance or obstacles.

___ 7. I will speak calmly at a conversational pace.

___ 8. I will look my best to feel my best.

___ 9. I will sleep and eat before I speak.

___ 10. I will practice my speech in the actual setting if possible.

___ 11. I will imagine facing my audience until public speaking worries me less.

___ 12. Most important: I will reduce my fear by focusing on communicating my message to my audience.

itive statement for a negative one. Since a speaker's perceived competence correlates highly with the speaker's level of anxiety (highly confident speakers suffer less anxiety), changing the way one thinks of one's self should increase confidence, which should improve performance. The teacher gets the student to substitute a positive statement "I am intelligent enough to speak in public"—for a negative one "I'm too dumb to speak in public." Students learn to identify negative statements about themselves and to create positive statements about themselves (Robinson, 1997).

Visualization

The third most popular treatment for HCA is **visualization,** *a process of picturing one's self succeeding* (Ayres & Hopf, 1987). In other words, the high-anxiety public-speaking student is asked repeatedly to picture in his or her mind a successful performance (Robinson, 1997). Most students have already practiced this technique. Before a game they have visualized themselves over and over again making the basket, winning the race, or charging through the line. Most of us also rehearse in our minds challenging events: proposing marriage, interviewing for a job, asking for more pay. Most of us have practiced visualization before, so using the technique in a public-speaking class will simply be a new application.

Systematic Desensitization

The fourth most popular method of reducing HCA is called **systematic desensitization.** The method works by having you *combine deep relaxation*

visualization

A process of picturing one's self succeeding to reduce communication apprehension.

systematic desensitization

Combining deep relaxation with fear-inducing thoughts to reduce communication apprehension.

with fear-inducing thoughts (Friedrich & Goss, 1984). Associating the fear with something positive reduces the fear. For example, the person conducting systematic desensitization may ask you to visualize a situation in which you are calm and unafraid to induce deep relaxation. The facilitator may then get you to visualize that scene by linking it to a word like *calm.* After some practice, the facilitator can condition you to think and feel the calm situation by saying the word "calm." Then the facilitator gradually walks you through speech preparation—thinking of a topic, writing the speech, walking to the front of the room, and so on—evoking the word "calm" every time you show signs of anxiety. Working outside of class with HCAs seems to work.

Ayres, Hopf, and Will (2000), concerned that repeated testing was improving apprehension scores, ran a complex test to check on the effects of systematic desensitization. They found "that systematic desensitization produced a significant reduction in communication apprehension that cannot be explained by 'testing effects'" (p. 19).

Self-Managing High Communication Apprehension

self-managed approach

Reducing communication apprehension by self-diagnosis and application of appropriate therapies.

Dwyer (2000) explains that many therapies work to reduce HCA, but no one therapy works for all. Therefore, she promotes a multidimensional model that teaches students a **self-managed approach**—how to *reduce high communication apprehension with self-diagnosis and a variety of therapies.* She matches seven personality dimensions (Lazarus, 1997) with matching techniques. Students can learn how to self-diagnose and how to apply their own therapies. The result? According to Dwyer:

> This research confirms that intervention is possible. High CAs do report change in communication anxiety levels and thus can be helped to manage the CA that negatively affects their lives. This is not to say that introverts will become extroverts or that the shy will become talkaholics or that neurotics will become emotionally stable. It does mean that if they choose to, high trait CAs can be helped to manage their anxiety in many normal communication contexts. (p. 79)

Thus even though the communibiologists have deemed HCA as a temperament that is unlikely to change (Beatty, McCroskey, & Heisel, 1998), the Dwyer study affirms that therapies can be effective in reducing high anxiety in beginning speakers. Table 12.3 lists some relaxation techniques that may help.

TRY◄►THIS

Think of your own anxieties about public speaking and ponder which of the available therapies might be most useful to you.

TABLE 12.3   CALMING NORMAL COMMUNICATION APPREHENSION

To practice the relaxation techniques, do the following:

1. Sit in a comfortable chair or lie down in a comfortable place. As much as possible, rid the area of distracting noises. If possible, play relaxing music or a tape with the sounds of nature.

2. Begin with your face and neck and tense the muscles. Then relax them. Tense again and hold the tensed position for 10 seconds. Relax again.

3. Tense your hands by clenching your fists. Relax. Tense again and hold for 10 seconds. Relax.

4. Tense your arms above your hands and to your shoulders. Relax. Tense again and hold for 10 seconds. Relax.

5. Tense your chest and stomach. Relax. Tense again and hold for 10 seconds. Relax.

6. Tense your feet by pulling the toes under. Relax. Tense again and hold for 10 seconds. Relax.

7. Tense your legs above the feet and up to the hips. Relax. Tense again and hold for 10 seconds. Relax.

8. Tense your entire body and hold for 10 seconds. Relax and breathe slowly.

9. Repeat the word *calm* to yourself. This will help you relate the word to the relaxed feeling you are now experiencing. In the future, when you feel anxious, the word *calm* should help you arrest the apprehension you experience.

SOURCE: Adapted from two exercises from *Communication Works* by Teri Kwal Gamble and Michael Gamble, copyright © 1984 by Random House, Inc. Used by permission of Random House, Inc.

What Is Source Credibility?

More than 2,300 years ago Aristotle (1941) noted that a speaker's "character may almost be called the most effective means of persuasion he possesses." Since that time, scholars have continued to study the importance of the source, or speaker, because they correctly believe that *who* says something determines *who* will listen.

In the public-speaking classroom, you are the source of the message. You need to be concerned about your **source credibility,** *the audience's perception of your effectiveness as a speaker.* You may feel that you do not have the same credibility as a high public official, a great authority on a topic, or an expert in a narrow field. Nonetheless, you can still be a very credible source to your classmates, colleagues, or friends. A lawyer may be credible to her clients, but not to her peers. Source credibility is not something a speaker possesses, like a suit of clothes. Instead, the audience determines credibility. Like beauty, credibility "is in the eye of the beholder" (Rosnow & Robinson, 1967).

source credibility

The audience's perception of a speaker's effectiveness.

A soldier and Secretary of State, Colin Powell earned source credibility with many, but not all, audiences.

A speaker's credibility depends in part on who the speaker is, the subject being discussed, the situation, and the audience. Have you served in the armed forces overseas? You may have earned the right to speak on the pros and cons of supporting yourself. Have you grown up in another country? You may have earned the right to speak on another country's culture, food, or social customs.

Similarly, you might be more credible to some audiences than you are to others—your classmates might find you credible but the local teamsters union might not. The personality characteristics of the audience members also affect their response to your message and to you as a source of that message (Wood & Kallgren, 1988). Some people are more inclined to respond positively to a speaker simply because he or she is attractive, whereas others focus on the content of the speech. Hacker, Zakahi, Giles, and Mc-Quitty (2000) indicate that voters integrate a politician's persona with the politician's position on issues, a blend of attractiveness and content.

How do we gain credibility with an audience? The answer is that you earn the right to speak. You earn the right through your experiences and accomplishments. As one person observed, "Before you express yourself, you need a self worth expressing." You may have earned the right to speak on a number of subjects. Have you worked in a fast-food restaurant? You may have earned the right to comment on the quality of fast food and service. Have you raised children? You may have earned the right to speak on the problems and pleasures of family life. Think about it. What have you experienced, learned, or lived through that has earned you the right to speak?

TRY ► THIS

If you earn the right to speak through your life experiences and life learning, make a list of what you have done or learned that would invite others to see you as credible.

Five Aspects of Credibility

What do audience members perceive that signals speaker credibility? If individuals in the audience base credibility on judgments, what is the basis for those judgments? On what will your classmates be rating you when they judge your credibility? According to research, five of the most important aspects of credibility are competence, trustworthiness, dynamism, common ground, and identification.

Competence

The first aspect of credibility is **competence,** *the degree to which a speaker is perceived as skilled, qualified, experienced, authoritative, reliable, and informed.* A speaker does not have to live up to all these adjectives; any one, or a few, might make the speaker credible. A machinist who displays her metalwork in a speech about junk sculpture as art is as credible as a biblical scholar who is demonstrating his ability to interpret scripture. They have different bases for their competence, but both can demonstrate competence in their own areas of specialization.

Words, use of technology, and an air of authority convey your own competence as a speaker. What can you build into your speech that will help the audience see and understand your competence? What experience have you had that is related to the subject? What training or knowledge do you have? How can you suggest to your audience that you have earned the right to speak about the subject? The most obvious way is to tell the audience of your expertise, but a creative speaker can think of dozens of ways to hint and suggest competence without being explicit, without seeming condescending, and without bragging.

A speaker also signals competence by knowing the substance of the speech so well that he or she can deliver the speech without reading from note cards, without unplanned or vocalized pauses, and without mispronounced words. The speaker who knows the technical language in a specialized field and who can define the terms for the audience is signaling competence. The speaker signals competence who can translate complex ideas into language the audience can understand, who can find ways to illustrate ideas so that the audience can comprehend, and who is familiar with people who know about the subject.

Trustworthiness

The second aspect of credibility is **trustworthiness,** *the degree to which a speaker is perceived as honest, fair, sincere, friendly, honorable, and kind.* These perceptions are also earned. We judge people's honesty by their past behavior. Your classmates will judge your trustworthiness when you deliver your speech. How do you decide whether or not other speakers in

competence

The degree to which the speaker is perceived as skilled, reliable, experienced, qualified, authoritative, and informed; an aspect of credibility.

trustworthiness

The degree to which the speaker is perceived as honest, fair, sincere, honorable, friendly, and kind; an aspect of credibility.

your class are responsible, sincere, dependable, or just? What have you done to earn your audience's trust?

You may have to reveal to your audience why you are trustworthy. Have you held jobs that demanded honesty and responsibility? Have you been a cashier, a bank teller, or a supervisor? Have you given up anything to demonstrate you are sincere? The person who pays his or her own way through college ordinarily has to be very sincere about education, and the person who chooses a lower-paying job because of a sense of public service is displaying sincerity about the job. Being respectful of others' points of view can be a sign of fairness, and being considerate of other people can be a sign of kindness and friendliness. What can you say or do that signals trustworthiness?

Louisiana's David Duke was an unlikely candidate for governor of that state because of his affiliation with some racist organizations. Although he did not win the governorship, the possibility that he might win caused considerable national stir. How did he attempt to demonstrate trustworthiness to a wary audience? He linked his political campaign "to his alleged religious conversion to evangelical Christianity" (McGee, 1998, p. 217). He attempted to signal his trustworthiness by displaying himself as a born-again Christian.

Discussion Question

Are credibility elements like trustworthiness necessary in an informative speech? Why or why not?

Dynamism

dynamism

The extent to which the speaker is perceived as bold, active, energetic, strong, empathic, and assertive; an aspect of credibility.

The third aspect of credibility is **dynamism,** *the extent to which an audience perceives the speaker as bold, active, energetic, strong, empathic, and assertive.* Audiences value behavior described by these adjectives. Perhaps when we consider their opposites—timid, tired, and meek—we can see why dynamism is attractive. People who exude energy and show the passion of their convictions impress others. Watch the television evangelists and note how they look and sound. You can learn to be dynamic. Evidence indicates that the audience's perception of your dynamism will enhance your credibility.

Dynamism is exhibited mainly by voice, movement, facial expression, and gestures. A person who speaks forcefully, rapidly, and with considerable vocal variety; a speaker who moves toward the audience, back behind the lectern, and over to the visual aid; and a speaker who uses facial expression and gestures to make a point are all exhibiting dynamism. What can you do with your voice, movement, facial expressions, and gestures to show the audience you are a dynamic speaker?

Common Ground

common ground

Also known as co-orientation, the degree to which the speaker's values, beliefs, attitudes, and interests are shared with the audience; an aspect of credibility.

Common ground is *the sharing of values, beliefs, attitudes, and interests* (Tuppen, 1974). You tell the audience explicitly how you agree with them. This kind of information sharing is not just demographic—sharing similarities about hometowns, family sizes, and so on—but ideological as well. That is, the speaker tells the audience which ideas he or she has in common with the audience.

For example, Jesse Jackson used common ground when he addressed more than 4,000 mostly white, rural southeastern Ohio students and community members at a campus speech. He persuaded hundreds of students to register to vote by talking about how both the inner-city poor and the rural poor in their area share similar problems of illiteracy, illegitimate births, unemployment, drug dependency, bad schools, and poverty.

An informative speech may require a minimal amount of common ground. However, a persuasive speech requires that the speaker go beyond areas of complete agreement into areas in which the speaker is trying to make a case for acceptance of his or her point of view on the issue.

Examples of student speeches in which the speaker used common ground include speeches about student housing and dormitory food. The student who spoke about student housing complained about the use of three-person rooms in the dormitories. He knew the majority of the students in the class had suffered through a year or two of such living conditions, and he established common ground by simply recounting some of his experiences in trying to study, entertain, and sleep in a three-person room. The student who spoke about the low quality of dormitory food knew most of the audience members had tasted it. She brought in a tray of dormitory food to remind them, and this established common ground. You do not have to be a national figure like Jesse Jackson to establish source credibility with an audience. Some speakers know so much that audiences listen; others are so dynamic that audiences listen; and still others inspire so much trust that audiences listen. You need to determine what you can do or say that will invite the audience to perceive you as credible.

Identification

Another dimension of source credibility seldom requires students' attention in classroom speaking, although it does affect students' behavior. **Identification,** as used here, *refers to young adults' sense of self and self-worth.* Boon and Lomore's (2001) Canadian study of media figures as idols consisted mainly of actors (39 percent), musical artists (31 percent), athletes and dancers (15 percent), a few authors, and a number of celebrities like Bill Gates and Oprah Winfrey. One-fourth of the youth reported that they "engaged in efforts to change aspects of their personality to bring it more in line with that of their favorite idol," nearly 60 percent reported that "their idols had influenced their attitudes and personal values," and nearly half reported "that their

Class Activity

Assume that you are asked to give a speech about college to elderly individuals living at a local retirement facility. How could you establish common ground with that audience?

Class Activity

In groups or as a class ask students to discuss people they most identify with. Use class examples to illustrate the idea of identification. You could also use this as an opportunity to discuss audience analysis. Knowledge of what types of person audience members identify with can provide valuable information about other attitudes and values.

identification

Young adults' sense of self and self-worth as a dimension of source credibility.

favorite idol had inspired them to pursue one or more particular activities or pastimes—generally those in which their idols engaged" (p. 445). Thus identification between media/entertainment stars and youth proves to be a powerful example of source credibility, of influencing the thought and behavior of others.

TRY ◄►THIS

Think of celebrities, sports figures, and entertainers who appear in commercials and print advertisements. Are any of them experts on the products they advertise? Why do you think their endorsement of a product sells merchandise?

Research Findings about Increasing Credibility

Credibility can be achieved before, during, or after a public speech. A speaker can have a reputation before arriving; that judgment can be altered during the presentation; and the evaluation can change again long after the speech has ended. You might think that some speakers are great before you hear them. Then their dull presentation reduces their credibility. In the weeks after the speech, your evaluation of such speakers might rise again because you discover that their message has given you new hope. In other words, credibility is always in flux, always alterable.

Credibility depends on topics, audiences, and situations. This feature makes the concept of source credibility a challenging one to public speakers. These comments about the changing nature of credibility are intended as a caution in interpreting the research findings that follow.

Most of the studies that try to measure the effect of a speaker's message on an audience indicate that highly credible speakers change audience opinions more than speakers whose credibility is poor (Rosnow & Robinson, 1967). At least when the speech is delivered, a person perceived as credible can seek and achieve more changes of opinion (Karlins & Abelson, 1970). However, as time passes, an interesting phenomenon called the **sleeper effect** occurs (Hovland & Weiss, 1967). Apparently, *the source of the speech and the message become separated in the listener's mind*—"I don't remember who said this, but . . ." The result of this separation of source and message is that the message loses impact as audience members later forget they heard the words from a highly credible speaker. The speaker with little credibility benefits from the opposite effect. As time passes, the audience forgets the source of the information, and the message gains impact as illustrated in Figure 12.1. In one study, three or four weeks after a speech, a highly credible speaker and a speaker with little credibility were about even with respect to their ability to change opinions.

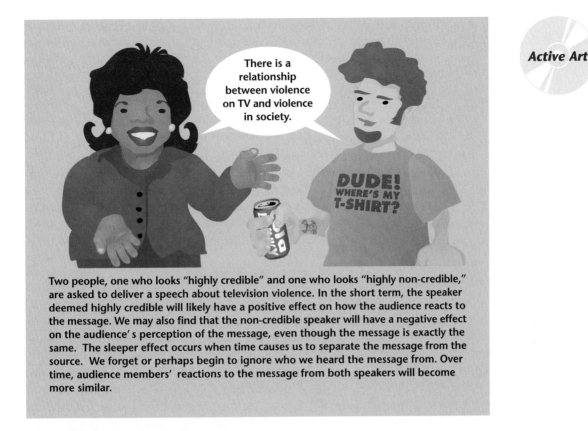

Two people, one who looks "highly credible" and one who looks "highly non-credible," are asked to deliver a speech about television violence. In the short term, the speaker deemed highly credible will likely have a positive effect on how the audience reacts to the message. We may also find that the non-credible speaker will have a negative effect on the audience's perception of the message, even though the message is exactly the same. The sleeper effect occurs when time causes us to separate the message from the source. We forget or perhaps begin to ignore who we heard the message from. Over time, audience members' reactions to the message from both speakers will become more similar.

Figure 12.1   The sleeper effect.

The lesson for the public speaker is that the effect of credibility may be short-lived. In most speech classes, several weeks or more may elapse between your presentations. In between, your classmates are exposed to other speakers and speeches. They need reminders of your credibility. We like to think audiences remember us and our speeches, but students may have difficulty remembering a speech they heard the day before yesterday, much less weeks earlier. Effective speakers remind the audience of their credibility. Remind your audience about your major subject, your special interest in the topic, your special knowledge, or your special experience. Credibility decays over time and must be renewed if you want to have the maximum effect on your audience.

The following generalizations and conclusions are based on a summary of nearly 30 years of credibility studies (Thompson, 1967):

- The introduction of a presenter by another person can increase the speaker's credibility. The credibility of the person making the introduction is as important to the speaker's credibility as what is said in that introduction. Your credibility may also be enhanced if the audience believes your introducer is highly credible. A close friend introducing you can reveal information that could enhance or harm your credibility. To be safe, the presenter should always provide the introducer with information that could potentially increase credibility by showing the speaker's competence, trustworthiness, dynamism, or co-orientation. Your introducer can make evaluative statements about you that might sound self-serving were you to say them.

- The way you are identified by the person introducing you also can affect your credibility. Students who are identified as graduate students are thought to be more competent than those identified as undergraduates. Graduate students are also seen as more fair-minded, likeable, and sincere (Andersen & Clevenger, 1963). Your identification as a sophomore, junior, or senior might affect your credibility with an audience.

- The perceived social status of a presenter can make a difference in credibility. Presenters who are high in status are consistently rated as more credible than speakers of low status. Even more striking is the finding that listeners judge credibility and status during the first 10 or 15 seconds of the speech (Harms, 1961). Probably the audience receives a barrage of clues about the presenter at the very beginning of the speech. They see how the speaker is dressed and make judgments about the speaker's appearance.

- The organization of your presentation can affect your credibility. Students who listen to a disorganized speech think less of a speaker after the speech than they did before the speech (Sharp & McClung, 1966). This judgment by the audience may be based on its expectations. In the public-speaking classroom, students expect good organization; when they perceive a speech as poorly organized, they lower their evaluation of the speaker. The lesson from this study is clear: A speaker should strive for sound organization, lest he or she lose credibility even while speaking.

- A speaker whose delivery is considered effective—whose use of voice, movement, and gesture is effective—can become more credible during a speech (Thompson, 1967). A payoff exists for the student who practices a speech and who learns to be comfortable enough in front of an audience to appear natural, confident, and competent.

- Nonfluencies—breaks in the smooth and fluid delivery of the presentation—are judged negatively. Vocalized pauses, such as "mmh" and "ahh," are nonfluencies. Another kind of nonfluency is the repetitive use of certain words and phrases, such as *well, like,* and *you know* at every transition. These nonfluencies decrease the audience's ratings of competence and dynamism but do not affect the speaker's trustworthiness (Thompson, 1967).

Team Challenge

With a group of classmates see how many of the research findings on source credibility you can recollect. Discuss what each of you can do in your own presentation to take advantage of what you know about source credibility.

Ethical Considerations

As you have learned, credibility is a perceptual variable that is not based on external, objective measures of competence, trustworthiness, dynamism, and co-orientation. However, you retain an ethical obligation to project an honest image of yourself to your audience, to actually be the sort of person you purport to be. The well-known cliché "You can fool all of the people some of the time" may be accurate, but an ethical communicator avoids "fooling" anyone.

To determine if you are behaving ethically, answer the following questions:

1. *Are your speech's immediate purpose and long-range goal sound?* Are you providing information or recommending change that would be determined worthy by current standards? Attempting to sell a substandard product or to encourage people to injure others would clearly not be sound; persuading people to accept new, more useful ideas and to be kinder to each other would be sound.
2. *Does your end justify your means?* This time-honored notion suggests that communicators can have ethical ends but may use unethical means of bringing the audience to a particular conclusion. You want them to join the armed forces, but should you use scare tactics to get them to join?
3. *Are you being honest with your audience?* Are you well informed about the subject instead of being a poseur who only pretends to know? Are you using sound evidence and reasoning to convince your audience? Are your passions about the subject sincere?

Credibility does lie in the audience's perception of you, but you also have an ethical obligation to be the sort of person you project yourself to be. In addition, you must consider the influence of your message on the audience. Persuasive speeches, particularly, may make far-reaching changes in others' behaviors. Are the changes you are recommending sound and consistent with standard ethical and moral guidelines? Have you thoroughly studied your topic so that you are convinced of the accuracy of the information you are presenting? Are you presenting the entire picture? Are you using valid and true arguments? In short, are you treating the listeners in the way you wish to be treated when someone else is speaking and you are the listener? The Golden Rule applies to the communication situation.

Chapter Review

In this chapter you have learned the following:

- Communication apprehension (CA) is a normal anxiety about communicating with others, but high communication apprehension (HCA)—suffered by 20 percent of the population—is a problem for those individuals who experience this fear.
  - HCA individuals tend to avoid communicating with others.
  - HCA individuals choose to live apart from other people.
  - HCA individuals choose to sit apart from other people.
  - HCA individuals speak less than other people.
  - HCA individuals disclose less when they do speak to others.
  - HCA individuals tend to be judged negatively by others.
- In public-speaking situations HCA individuals exhibit signs of fear that tend to make them less effective.
  - HCA individuals prepare poorly for performances.
  - HCA individuals avoid eye contact with the audience.
  - HCA individuals hesitate and pause unexpectedly.
  - HCA individuals appear powerless and slow.
- Remedies for high communication apprehension include but are not limited to
  - Completing a class in public speaking.
  - Working on communication skills to build confidence.
  - Employing cognitive modification.
  - Employing positive visualization.
  - Practicing systematic desensitization.
  - Self-managing anxieties using a variety of therapies.
- The 80 percent of individuals with normal communication anxiety can overcome their fears through self-determination or by
  - Knowing the topic well.
  - Analyzing the audience competently.
  - Knowing the speech content well.
  - Recognizing their own value and uniqueness on the subject.
  - Focusing on communicating with the audience instead of focusing on self.
- Source credibility is the audience's perception of the speaker's worthiness to speak based on five dimensions:
  - Audience perception of the speaker's competence on the topic.
  - Audience perception of the speaker's trustworthiness.
  - Audience perception of the speaker's dynamism.
  - Audience perception of the speaker's common ground with the audience.
  - Audience perception of the speaker's identification or celebrity.
- Among the characteristics that affect source credibility are
  - The status of your introducer and what he or she says about you.
  - Your own status with the particular audience.
  - How well you organized your message.
  - Your skill at delivering the presentation.
  - Your ethical standards.

⊙ VIDEO LINK: SUSAN ELLIOTT'S STRATEGIES FOR MANAGING COMMUNICATION APPREHENSION

Video Episode 6: "Reporting for KTNT: Susan Elliott"

Nearly every human being experiences communication apprehension at some point. Some of us may feel a case of nerves before a speech and many of us will feel butterflies before a job interview. In "Reporting for KTNT: Susan Elliott," we see Susan discuss several strategies for managing her nervousness before important interviews for potential internships. What strategies does Susan discuss? How can you use similar strategies when preparing for a public presentation? Are there other techniques Susan could use to reduce her apprehension? Finally, what effect do you think Susan's preparation will have on her credibility during the interviews?

ISSUES IN COMMUNICATION: SPEAKER CREDIBILITY

This Issues in Communication narrative is designed to provoke individual thought or discussion about concepts raised in the chapter.

Sally Crawford, a sophomore, worked hard on her persuasive speech. She decided her speech topic would be the newly reported dangers of food dyes since she thinks many people use them and are unaware of their danger. She felt she was qualified to talk about the topic because she had recently learned about the possible correlation between cancer and the use of food dye in her introductory nutrition course and because she had recently declared nutrition as her major. Although Sally thought she had already learned enough about the topic from her course, she interviewed her nutrition professor, Dr. Capra, for the speech. Dr. Capra, though very knowledgeable on the topic, also heads a consumer awareness group opposed to the unnecessary use of food additives.

The speech Sally delivered was impassioned and well organized. She felt she accomplished what she had set out to do: to persuade her audi-

ence of the dangers of food dyes through her competence as a speaker, her dynamic delivery, and her ability to convince her listeners that this topic was relevant to their lives. When her instructor asked the class for feedback, Sally was surprised and discouraged to hear that very few of her classmates had been convinced. Many of her classmates said that although she appeared to be competent, they did not consider her very trustworthy because her main source of information was clearly biased. In Sally's effort to be dynamic and persuasive, she had neglected some necessary components of establishing her credibility, and she had not been as thorough as she could have been when she was gathering information.

Apply what you have learned about source credibility as you ponder and discuss the following questions: Do you think Sally's audience was fair? What additional sources could Sally have used for her speech? What could she have done differently to establish herself as a more credible source? What kinds of supporting materials might Sally have used to improve the effectiveness of her speech?

KEY TERMS

 Use the *Human Communication* CD-ROM and the *Online Learning Center* at www.mhhe.com/pearson to further your understanding of the following terminology.

Cognitive modification
Common ground
Communication
  apprehension (CA)
Communibiological
  perspective

Competence
Dynamism
Identification
Self-managed approach
Skills approach
Sleeper effect

Source credibility
State anxiety
Systematic desensitization
Trait anxiety
Trustworthiness
Visualization

SELF-QUIZ

 Go to the self-quizzes on the *Human Communication* CD-ROM and the *Online Learning Center* at www.mhhe.com/pearson to test your knowledge.

REFERENCES

Adler, R. B. (1980). Integrating reticence management into the basic communication curriculum. *Communication Education, 29,* 215–221.

Andersen, K., & Clevenger, T., Jr. (1963). A summary of experimental research in ethos. *Speech Monographs, 30,* 59–78.

Aristotle. (1941). Rhetoric. In R. McKeon (Ed.), *The basic works of Aristotle* (1, 1356a, ll. 12–14) (W. R. Roberts, Trans.). New York: Random House.

Ayres, J., & Hopf, T. S. (1987). Visualization, systematic desensitization, and relational emotive therapy: A comparative evaluation. *Communication Education, 36,* 236–240.

Ayres, J., Hopf, T., & Will, A. (2000). Are reductions in CA an experimental artifact? A Solomon four-group answer. *Communication Quarterly, 48,* 19–26.

Beatty, M. J. (1988). Situational and predispositional correlates of public speaking anxiety. *Communication Education, 37,* 28–39.

Beatty, M. J., McCroskey, J. C., & Heisel, A. D. (1998). Communication apprehension as temperamental expression: A communibiological paradigm. *Communication Monographs, 65,* 197–219.

Behnke, R. R., & Sawyer, C. R. (2000). Anticipatory anxiety patterns for male and female public speakers. *Communication Education, 49,* 187–195.

Beighley, K. C. (1952). An experimental study of the effect of four speech variables on listener comprehension. *Speech Monographs, 19,* 249–258.

Bettinghaus, E. (1961). The operation of congruity in an oral communication situation. *Speech Monographs, 28,* 131–142.

Boon, S. D., & Lomore, C. D. (2001). Admirer–celebrity relationships among young adults: Explaining perceptions of celebrity influence on identity. *Human Communication Research, 27*(3), 432–465.

Daly, J. A., & Leth, S. (1976). *Communication apprehension and the personal selection decision.* Paper presented to the International Communication Association Convention, Portland, OR.

Daly, J. A., & McCrosky, J. C. (Eds.). (1984). *Avoiding communication: Shyness, reticence and communication apprehension.* Beverly Hills, CA: Sage.

Daly, J. A., Vangelisti, A. L., Neel, H. L., & Cavanaugh, P. D. (1989). Pre-performance concerns associated with public speaking anxiety. *Communication Quarterly, 37,* 39–53.

Daly, J. A., Vangelisti, A. L., & Weber, D. J. (1995). Speech anxiety affects how people prepare speeches: A protocol analysis of the preparation processes of speakers. *Communication Monographs, 62,* 383–397.

Dwyer, K. K. (1998). Communication apprehension and learning style preference: Correlations and implications for teaching. *Communication Education, 47,* 137–150.

Dwyer, K. K. (2000). The multidimensional model: Teaching students to self-manage high communication apprehension by self-selecting treatments. *Communication Education, 49,* 72–81.

Feingold, A. (1983). Correlates of public speaking attitude. *Journal of Social Psychology, 120,* 285–286.

Friedrich, G., & Goss, B. (1984). Systematic desensitization. In J. A. Daly & J. C. McCroskey (Eds.), *Avoiding communication: Shyness, reticence and communication apprehension* (pp. 173–188). Beverly Hills, CA: Sage.

Gamble, T. K., & Gamble, M. (1999). *Communication works* (6th ed.). New York: McGraw-Hill.

Gilkinson, H., & Knower, F. H. (1941). Individual differences among students of speech as revealed by psychological test—I. *Journal of Educational Psychology, 32,* 161–175.

Greene, J. O., Rucker, M. P., Zauss, E. S., & Harris, A. A. (1998). Communication anxiety and the acquisition of message-production skill. *Communication Education, 47,* 337–347.

Hacker, K. L., Zakahi, W. R., Giles, M. J., & McQuitty, S. (2000). Components of candidate images: Statistical analysis of the issue-persona dichotomy in the presidential campaign of 1996. *Communication Monographs, 67*(3), 227–238.

Harms, L. S. (1961). Listener judgments of status cues in speech. *Quarterly Journal of Speech, 47,* 168.

Hayworth, D. (1942). A search for facts on the teaching of public speaking. *Quarterly Journal of Speech, 28,* 247–254.

Hebyallah, I. M., & Maloney, W. P. (1977–1978). Content analysis of TV commercials. *International Journal of Instructional Media, 5,* 9–16.

Hemsley, G. D., & Doob, A. M. (1978). The effect of looking behavior on perceptions of a communicator's credibility. *Journal of Applied Social Psychology, 8,* 136–144.

Henrikson, E. H. (1994). An analysis of the characteristics of some "good" and "poor" speakers. *Speech Monographs, 11,* 120–124.

Hovland, C. I., & Weiss, W. (1967). The influence of source credibility on communicator effectiveness. In R. L. Rosnow & E. J. Robinson (Eds.), *Experiments in persuasion* (pp. 9–24). New York: Academic Press.

Karlins, M., & Abelson, H. (1970). *Persuasion.* New York: Springer.

Kramer, E. J. J., & Lewis, T. R. (1931). Comparison of visual and nonvisual listening. *Journal of Communication, 1,* 16–20.

Lazarus, A. (1997). *Brief but comprehensive psychotherapy: The multimodal way.* New York: Springer.

Lind, E. A., & O'Barr, W. M. (1979). The social significance of speech in the classroom. In H. Giles & R. St. Clair (Eds.), *Language and social psychology.* Oxford, England: Blackwell.

MacIntyre, P. D., & MacDonald, J. R. (1998). Public speaking anxiety: Perceived competence and audience congeniality. *Communication Education, 47,* 359–365.

MacIntyre, P. D., Babin, P. A., & Clement, R. (1999). Willingness to communicate: Antecedents & Consequences. *Communication Quarterly 47,* 215–229.

McCroskey, J. C. (1992). Reliability and validity of the Willingness to Communicate scale. *Communication Quarterly, 40,* 16–25.

McCroskey, J. C. (1997). Oral communication apprehension: A summary of recent theory and research. *Human Communication Research, 4,* 78–96.

McCroskey, J. C., & Andersen, J. F. (1976). The relationship between communication apprehension and academic achievement among college students. *Human Communication Research, 3,* 73–81.

McCroskey, J. C., & Beatty, M. J. (2000). The communibiological perspective: Implications for communication in instruction. *Communication Education, 49,* 1–6.

McCroskey, J. C., Daly, J. A., & Sorensen, G. A. (1976). Personality correlates of communication apprehension. *Human Communication Research, 2,* 376–380.

McCroskey, J. C., & Leppard, T. (1975). *The effects of communication apprehension on nonverbal behavior.* Paper presented to the Eastern Communication Association Convention, New York, NY.

McGee, B. R. (1998). Witnessing and *ethos:* The evangelical conversion of David Duke. *Western Journal of Communication, 62*(3), 217–243.

Miller, N., Maruyama, G., Beaber, R. J., & Valone, K. (1976). Speed of speech and persuasion. *Journal of Personality and Social Psychology, 34,* 615–625.

Mladenka, J. D., Sawyer, C. R., & Behnke, R. R. (1998). Anxiety sensitivity and speech trait anxiety as predictors of state anxiety during public speaking. *Communication Quarterly, 46,* 417–429.

Motley, M. T. (1995). *Overcoming your fear of public speaking: A proven method.* New York: McGraw-Hill Custom Series.

Pearson, J. C., & Yoder, D. D. (1979, May). *Public speaking or interpersonal communication: The perspective of the high communication apprehensive student.* East Lansing, MI: National Center for Research on Teacher Learning (ERIC Document Reproduction Service No. ED 173 870).

Petrie, C. R., Jr. (1963). Informative speaking: A summary and bibliography of related research. *Speech Monographs, 30,* 81.

Richmond, V. P., & McCrosky, J. C. (1992). *Communication: Apprehension, avoidance, and effectiveness* (3rd ed.). Scottsdale, AZ: Gorsuch Scarisbrick.

Robinson, T. E., II (1997). Communication apprehension and the basic public speaking course: A national survey of in-class treatment techniques. *Communication Education, 46,* 188–197.

Rosnow, R. L., & Robinson, E. J. (Eds.). (1967). *Experiments in persuasion.* New York: Academic Press.

Rubin, R. B., Rubin, A. M., & Jordan, F. F. (1997). Effects of instruction on communication apprehension and communication competence. *Communication Education, 46,* 104–114.

Sharp, H., Jr., & McClung, T. (1966). Effects of organization on the speaker's ethos. *Speech Monographs, 33,* 182–183.

Thompson, W. N. (1967). *Quantitative research in public address and communication.* New York: Random House.

Tuppen, C. J. (1974). Dimensions of communicator credibility: An oblique solution. *Speech Monographs, 41,* 253–260.

Vohs, J. L. (1964). An empirical approach to the concept of attention. *Speech Monographs, 31,* 355–360.

Wallechinsky, D., Wallace, I., & Wallace, A. (1977). *The people's almanac presents the book of lists.* New York: Morrow.

Wood, W., & Kallgren, C. A. (1988). Communicator attributes and persuasion: Recipients' access to attitude-relevant information in memory. *Personality and Social Psychology Bulletin, 14,* 172–182.

Worthington, E. L., Tipton, R. M., Comley, J. S., Richards, T., & Janke, R. H. (1984). Speech and coping skills training and paradox as treatment for college students anxious about public speaking. *Perceptual and Motor Skills, 59,* 394.

CHAPTER THIRTEEN

There are no uninteresting things; there are only uninteresting people.

G. K. CHESTERTON

One of the finest accomplishments is making a long story short.

KIM HUBBARD

None are so deaf as those who will not hear.

MATTHEW HENRY

Topic Selection and Audience Analysis

What will you learn?

When you have read and thought about this chapter, you will be able to:

1. Brainstorm and do personal inventories to identify speech topics.
2. Evaluate possible topics to determine your involvement.
3. Show how to narrow a topic for a five-minute presentation.
4. Analyze an audience by using all four levels of audience analysis.
5. Provide an example of a belief, an attitude, and a value.
6. Recognize the difficulty of changing beliefs, attitudes, and values.
7. Develop strategies for adapting yourself and your message to an audience.

Often, finding something to speak about seems difficult because you have so many choices. This chapter focuses on topic selection and audience analysis. The overall goal is to teach you techniques that will make you more comfortable with the process of selecting a topic and analyzing your audience, which in turn will start you on a path toward being a more effective and confident public speaker. This chapter will provide you with techniques for quickly determining a speech topic appropriate to both you and your audience, for analyzing and adapting your message to your audience, and for limiting your topic to the appropriate time.

Rosita was worried. Her teacher had assigned her first speech, and she had only one week to prepare. The first two days after the assignment she found herself pondering topic ideas whenever she had a spare moment, but she didn't use any of the techniques her teacher suggested for selecting a topic.

On the third day, she started getting a little nervous about the impending deadline, so she decided to sit down and do some brainstorming. She had some success with that technique but decided to conduct a personal inventory as well. After brainstorming revealed several topic ideas, Rosita decided to sleep on her decision for a night before determining which topic was best for her.

On the fourth day, Rosita decided she would speak about "the health benefits of yoga." Since she had been taking a yoga class for over a year and had read a lot about yoga, Rosita knew it was a topic that she was both interested in and knowledgeable about. She had already narrowed the topic, so she knew her research wouldn't take too much time. Although she got off to a slow start, Rosita managed to get her speech done on time, and it even generated some positive comments from her classmates.

This chapter will help you avoid the worry Rosita experienced when faced with the prospect of selecting a speech topic. Your worries diminish when you learn the process of speech preparation. A first step in that process is selecting your topic.

How Do I Select a Topic?

In this section, you will examine two methods for selecting a speech topic: individual brainstorming and personal inventories. Both methods are designed to make you mindful, thoughtful, and careful about your choice of topic.

Individual Brainstorming

brainstorming

A creative procedure for generating as many ideas as a group or an individual can within a limited period of time.

Brainstorming is *thinking of as many topics as you can in a limited time so that you can select one topic that will be appropriate for you and your audience.* Group brainstorming can be a useful technique for selecting a topic for group discussion; individual brainstorming can be an equally effective way to find a topic for your public speech. Indeed, this technique can help you generate many speech topics. Most students find this method more productive than trying to think of just one topic for their speech.

You'll find individual brainstorming to be relatively quick and easy. First, give yourself a limited time—say, five minutes—and without trying

Team Challenge

BRAINSTORMING FOR TOPICS

Pairs or small groups should give themselves five minutes or less to think of every topic they can as individuals. After selecting their top three, they should share them with each other to determine which might work best with this audience.

to think of titles or even complete thoughts, write down as many topics as you can. When your time is up, you should have a rough list of possible ideas or topics for your speech. This step can be repeated if you want an even larger list from which to choose. Second, select the *three* items from your list that are the most appealing to you as topics for your speech. Third, from those three topics choose the *one* that you think would be most appealing to both you and your audience.

Personal Inventories

Another way to find a topic for your speech is to conduct a **personal inventory,** a *survey of your choices.* You make choices every time you watch a television program, select a video, visit a website, or choose a chat room. You can learn more about your own interests by examining carefully your own choices. In the process of speech preparation, choosing a topic that interests you is a first consideration.

Public speaking starts with the self—with what you know, have experienced, or are willing to learn. Self-analysis, through personal inventories, can help you uncover the areas in which you are qualified to speak.

Your personal inventories of media use are rough indications of your interests. You may also wish to conduct inventories of your hobbies, leisure activities, and talents, the music you listen to, the organizations you belong to, the plays you attend, the jobs you've had, the elective courses you've taken, or the courses you've taken for your major.

Let us look next at how you can size up or evaluate any topics that emerged through brainstorming or personal inventories. Let us look first at your involvement in the topic and then at your knowledge of the topic.

Class Activity

Lead students in an individual brainstorming session. Ask them to spend 5 minutes writing down as many topics as possible. Then students should circle the most appealing topics on their lists.

personal inventory

A speaker's survey of his or her reading and viewing habits and behavior to discover topics of personal interest.

Class Activity

Make copies of the personal inventory sheet found in the instructor's manual. Have students complete the form in class. Ask students to share potential topic ideas with others in a group setting.

TRY ◄►THIS

How does your room, apartment, or home reflect your interest? What equipment, clothing, and other artifacts make this space reflect you and your concerns?

Involvement in the Topic

After you have selected a possible topic area, you should evaluate the topic to see if you have the appropriate involvement in and knowledge of the subject. **Involvement** is simply *a measure of the importance of a topic to the speaker.*

Your brainstorming and personal inventories might have shown that you have an interest in many topics. However, you may not be involved in those particular areas. For example, you could be interested in sports because they allow you a kind of escape from everyday concerns, but you might not be highly involved in sports. How can you tell the difference between mere interest and involvement?

One measure of involvement is how much *time* you put into a topic area. What if you find, through brainstorming and conducting personal inventories, that one of your interests is computers? You could probably consider yourself involved in computers if you spend time around them, learn how they work, read articles about them, and spend time seeking new hardware and software. The amount of time you spend with your topic is, then, one measure of your involvement.

A second measure of involvement is how much *effort* you spend on a particular interest. The person who is really involved in politics is actively involved. That person knows the candidates and politicians, works on campaigns, helps bring out the voters, reads about politics, talks with other interested persons, and joins groups with a similar interest. Involvement, then, is measured by the effort you commit to your subject.

Determining whether or not a speaker is involved in a speech topic is easy. An involved speaker speaks with conviction, passion, and authority. The involved speaker gives many indications of caring about the topic.

The person who is only trying to fulfill an assignment cannot convey the sense of involvement so important in public speaking. Usually, you will find that the speaker who really cares about the topic being discussed is successful at getting you involved in the topic as well.

Knowledge of the Topic

After you have selected a topic area and determined your own involvement in the subject, you need to assess your personal knowledge of the subject. What do you know about the subject that can be communicated to your audience? Your knowledge about the topic comes primarily from three sources: yourself,

Effective speakers know their subject.

Adapting Yourself

In public speaking, the speaker also has to adjust to information about the audience. Just as the college senior preparing for a job interview adapts to the interviewer in dress, manner, and language, the public speaker prepares for an audience by adapting to its expectations. How you look, how you behave, and what you say should be carefully adjusted to an audience you have learned about through observation, experience, and analysis.

Adapting Your Verbal and Nonverbal Codes

The language you use in your speech, as well as your gestures, movements, and even facial expressions, should be adapted to your audience. Does your experience, observation, and analysis of the audience's attitudes indicate your language should be conversational, formal, cynical, or technical? Does your analysis indicate your listeners like numbers and statistics? Do your observations indicate you should pace the stage or stand still behind the lectern? Does your analysis indicate you should not use taboo words in your speech lest you alienate your group, or does the audience like a little lively language?

Adapting Your Topic

Public speakers should be permitted to speak about any topic that fits the assignment. In the classroom, at least, you should select a topic that relates to you. Remember, you will be giving your speech to an audience of classmates; therefore, the topic you select must be adapted to them. Audience analysis is a means of discovering the audience's position on the topic. From information based on observation, description, and inference, you have to decide how you are going to adapt your topic to this audience.

Audience analysis can tell you the challenges you face. If you want to speak in favor of physician-assisted suicide and your audience analysis indicates the majority of your listeners are opposed to that position, you need not conclude the topic is inappropriate. You may, however, adapt to the members of your audience by starting with a position closer to theirs. Your initial step might be to make audience members feel less comfortable about their present position so that they are more prepared to hear your position.

Your analysis might indicate your audience already has considerable information about your topic. You then may have to adapt by locating information the audience does not have. For example, you may want to deliver an informative speech about a controversial local issue, but your analysis may indicate the audience is not only already interested but also has sufficient information of the sort you planned to offer. You can adapt your topic by shifting to the area of the subject about which the audience

Class Activity

Collect several different magazines and take them to class. Have students form groups and give each group a couple of different magazines. Each group should determine who the target market is for each magazine and what the magazine does to appeal to that market (pictures, content, layout, use of color, etc.). Speakers must make similar efforts when adapting to audiences.

is not so well informed: What is the background of the situation? What are the backgrounds of the personalities and the issues? What do the experts think will happen? What are the possible consequences?

Adapting Your Purpose

You should also adapt the purpose of your speech to your audience. Teachers often ask students to state the purpose of a speech—what do you want your audience to know, understand, or do? To think of your speech as one part of a series of informative talks your audience will hear about your topic may help. Your listeners have probably heard something about the topic before, and they are likely to hear about the topic again. Your particular presentation is just one of the audience's exposures to the topic.

Still, the immediate purpose of your speech is linked to a larger goal. The goal is the end you have in mind. Some examples of immediate purposes and long-range goals will illustrate the difference. The following are examples of the immediate purposes and long-range goals of an informative speech:

Immediate Purpose	Long-Range Goal
1. After listening to this speech, the audience should be able to identify three properties of printers.	1. To increase the number of people who will read articles and books about printers.
2. After listening to my talk, the audience should be able to name six expressions that are part of the street language used by urban African-American youth.	2. To help the listeners understand and appreciate the language used by some African-American students.

The following are examples of the immediate purposes and long-range goals of a persuasive speech:

Immediate Purpose	Long-Range Goal
1. After my presentation, the audience should be able to state three positive characteristics of the candidate for mayor.	1. To have some of the audience members vote for the candidate at election time.
2. After my speech, the audience should be able to explain the low nutritional value of two popular junk foods.	2. To dissuade the listeners from eating junk food.

You should note that an immediate purpose has four essential features. First, an immediate purpose is highly specific. Second, it includes the phrase *should be able to.* Third, it uses an action verb such as *state, identify, report, name, list, describe, explain, show,* or *reveal.* Fourth, it is stated from the viewpoint of the audience. You are writing the purpose as an audience objective.

The more specific your immediate purpose, the better you will be able to determine whether you have accomplished that purpose. You should also use audience analysis to help you discover whether your purpose is appropriate. Suppose half the people in your class are going into fields in which a knowledge of food and nutrition is important. They already know more than the average person about nutritional values. Consequently, to deliver a speech about junk food may be inappropriate. To speak to a group of athletes about the importance of exercise may be unwise. You should adapt your purpose to the audience members by considering the level of their information, the novelty of the issue, and the other factors discussed in this chapter.

Adapting Your Supporting Materials

Your personal knowledge, your interviewing, your research, and your Internet search should provide more material for your speech than you can use. Again, audience analysis helps you select materials for your audience. Your analysis might reveal, for example, that your classmates disrespect authority figures. In that case, you might be wasting your time informing them of the surgeon general's opinion on smoking; your personal experience or the experience of some of your classmates might be more important to them than an expert's opinion. On the other hand, if your audience analysis reveals that parents, teachers, pastors, and other authority figures are highly regarded, you may want to quote physicians, research scientists, counselors, and health-service personnel.

As a public speaker, you should always keep in mind that *the choices you make in selecting a topic, choosing an immediate purpose, determining a long-range goal, organizing your speech, selecting supporting materials, and even creating visual aids* are all **strategic choices.** All of these choices are made for the purpose of adapting the speaker and the subject to a particular audience. The larger your supply of supporting arguments, the better your chances of having effective arguments. The larger your supply of supporting materials, the better your chances of providing effective evidence, illustrations, and visual aids. Your choices are strategic in that they are purposeful. The purpose is to choose, from among the available alternatives, the ones that will best achieve your purpose with the audience.

strategic choices

What you choose to do in your speech, from the words to the arguments.

Chapter Review

In this chapter you have learned the following:

- Two methods of topic selection are brainstorming and personal inventories.
  - Involvement in the topic usually results in a better presentation.
  - Knowledge of the topic gives you a head start in speech preparation.
  - Once chosen, the topic needs to be narrowed to fit the time limits, the subject matter, and the audience.
- Four levels of audience analysis can help you determine topic appropriateness.
  - Level 1 distinguishes between voluntary and captive audiences.
  - Level 2, demographic analysis, evaluates the characteristics of audience members.
  - Level 3 analyzes the audience's interest in and knowledge of a topic.
  - Level 4 determines the audiences' attitudes, beliefs, and values.
- Observation, inference, and questionnaires are three methods of audience analysis.
  - Observation involves watching your audience for overt cues about its appearance and behavior.
- Inferences use data about the audience to draw tentative generalizations that can make the audience responses more predictable.
- Questionnaires garner demographic and attitudinal information about the audience.
- Presentations should be adapted to information about the audience gathered through audience analysis.
  - You should adapt your own behavior to audience expectations.
  - You should adapt your verbal and nonverbal codes to this audience.
  - You should adapt your topic to this audience's knowledge and interest levels.
  - You should adapt your purpose to what is possible with this audience.
  - You should adapt your supporting materials to this particular group.

● VIDEO LINK: SELECTING A TOPIC FOR CAMPUS–COMMUNITY CONNECTION

Video Episode 4: "Senior Seminar"

Selecting a topic is one of the most important decisions you will make as a speaker. Rather than simply picking a topic off the Internet, you should use relevant criteria to carefully evaluate several potential topics. In "Senior Seminar," you can observe the process used by members of Susan Elliott's work group to select a topic for their five-minute talk segment. What criteria do they use to select topics? How does the audience play a role in their decision-making process? How could you use a similar process when you select your speech topics?

ISSUES IN COMMUNICATION: WHOOPS! WRONG AUDIENCE

This Issues in Communication narrative is designed to provoke individual thought or discussion about concepts raised in the chapter.

Mary Reich is the new dean of students at Central University. Among her many responsibilities is speaking to student groups on campus. Kerri, a member of one of the sororities on campus, asked Mary if she'd be willing to appear at an event to speak about the university's initiatives to address the drinking epidemic among college students. At the time she was asked, Mary was preoccupied with some other work and she didn't inquire about any of the details. Since the event was a few weeks away, she planned to contact Kerri closer to the event and get the necessary details. Although she penned the event into her daily scheduler, Mary got wrapped up in her many new job responsibilities and forgot about the speech until the day before the event.

Despite her best intentions, Mary hadn't made time to contact Kerri before the event. She re-

called that she was to talk about the university's initiatives to cope with the drinking epidemic on campus, and she had her assistant find out where she needed to be. She wasn't worried about the speech itself because she had public-speaking engagements all the time and was well versed in the subject matter. She was proud of the work the university had done to address the drinking crisis on campus.

When Mary got to the event, she was surprised to see many people she recognized as representatives of student government. She didn't see any of the leaders from the school's sororities and fraternities. Kerri came up to Mary to thank her for coming to speak to the student government. "We're quite interested in hearing what you have to say. We're concerned that the administration has gone too far without seeking the input of student government," Kerri said. Unfortunately, Mary didn't realize that Kerri was also a student government representative. She knew Kerri was in a sorority, so she had made the assumption that she would be speaking to fraternity and sorority members. Now, instead of speaking to an audience who was receptive to the university's initiatives, she had to stand before a hostile group, and she wasn't sure she was prepared for that.

Apply what you have learned about audience analysis as you ponder and discuss the fol-lowing questions: What steps could Mary have taken to better prepare for her speech? How do you think she'll adapt her speech given what she knows about her audience? In what ways would her speech have been different if she really was speaking to frater-nity and sorority members?

KEY TERMS

 Use the *Human Communication* CD-ROM and the *Online Learning Center* at www.mhhe.com/pearson to further your understanding of the following terminology.

Attitude	Captive audience	Observation
Audience analysis	Demographic analysis	Personal inventory
Audience interest	Heterogeneous	Questionnaire
Audience knowledge	Homogeneous	Strategic choice
Belief	Inference	Value
Brainstorming	Involvement	Voluntary audience

SELF-QUIZ

 Go to the self-quizzes on the *Human Communication* CD-ROM and the *Online Learning Center* at www.mhhe.com/pearson to test your knowledge.

ADDITIONAL RESOURCES

ABC News, www.abcradio.com brings news to your ear instead of your eye with newscasts and hourly updates.

On-line magazine, www.slate.com, is a Web-based source of information higher in currency than in accuracy, but attractive as an edgy, less establishment source of information.

Public Broadcasting, www.pbs.org, provides current events, top stories, in-depth coverage, news summaries, and information both from radio and TV.

USNews Online, www.usnews.com, has deeper background information on issues and ideas through its archive search including news and complete articles.

CHAPTER FOURTEEN

Knowledge is the only instrument of production that is not subject to diminishing returns.

J. M. CLARK

You can't build a reputation on what you are going to do.

HENRY FORD

Research is the process of going up alleys to see if they are blind.

MARSTON BATES

Finding Information

What will you learn?

When you have read and thought about this chapter, you will be able to:

1. Explain why research is important.
2. Discuss four types of sources you can use in your speech.
3. Cite information correctly in your speech outline and your oral presentation.
4. Critically evaluate the World Wide Web and other sources.
5. Discuss seven forms of supporting material appropriate for your speech.
6. Explain the difference between evidence and proof.

An effective speech is based on information. This chapter will help you prepare your speech by discussing how you can find information and what types of information to look for. First you will learn about the research process, including why research is important and how to do quality research. Then you will learn how you can use everything from examples to statistics as supporting material in your speech.

Kari wanted to present information on vegetarianism for her informative speech. She had nearly a week before she had to speak, but she wanted to complete her research quickly so that she could get the speech done. She got on the Internet and typed "vegetarianism" into a search engine. The search engine returned links to several thousand Web pages related to her topic—just what she needed.

As Kari explored the various websites she noted something interesting. Several of the websites contained exactly the same information and statistics, yet none of them explained the origins of the information. She was worried about the sources. All of them were obviously biased in favor of vegetarianism, and she was not sure how accurate the information was.

In the library, Kari asked the librarian where she should look for information. After the librarian told Kari to look through the library's electronic databases for articles, Kari mentioned that she had already searched on the Web and was skeptical about some of the sources. The reference librarian explained that although the library databases were accessed though the Web, they were not websites but electronic versions of traditional "hard copy" sources like magazines and journals; the Web interface just made finding things easier.

Kari spent 20 minutes finding sources, many of which she could print out. Kari's new sources, coupled with her Web sources, made the informative speech easy to put together, and her teacher commented that her presentation was "a well-researched speech."

Kari's experience should be typical of the process we all go through when researching a speech. She started early, she carefully evaluated her sources, and she consulted a variety of sources. In this chapter, we give you tips for doing what Kari did: effectively researching your speech.

Why Is Research Important?

Conducting research is a key aspect of the speech preparation process. The information in Table 14.1 illustrates how research helps you at each step in preparing your speech. As you can see, research is not just a part of the speechmaking process; research is a common thread tying together each step of the process.

Finding Information

Effective speakers achieve success through well-crafted presentations that contain compelling evidence and support. In this section we discuss several different types of sources that you can use in your speech, the importance of citing sources of information, and tips for conducting effective research.

TABLE 14.1   RESEARCH AND THE SPEECH PREPARATION PROCESS

PREPARATION STEP	BENEFIT OF RESEARCH
1. Topic selection	Research helps you discover and narrow topics.
2. Organizing ideas	Research helps you identify main and subordinate points.
3. Supporting ideas	Research provides facts, examples, definitions, and other forms of support to give substance to your points.
4. Preparing introduction and conclusion	Research may reveal interesting examples, stories, or quotes to begin or end the speech with.
5. Practice and delivery	Because your speech is well-researched, you will feel more confident and will seem more credible.

Video Activity
Ask students to view the video segment "Senior Seminar." Discuss how research is often necessary before topics can be adequately analyzed. Both Susan and Ricky had done preliminary research on their topics before presenting them to the group.

Active Art

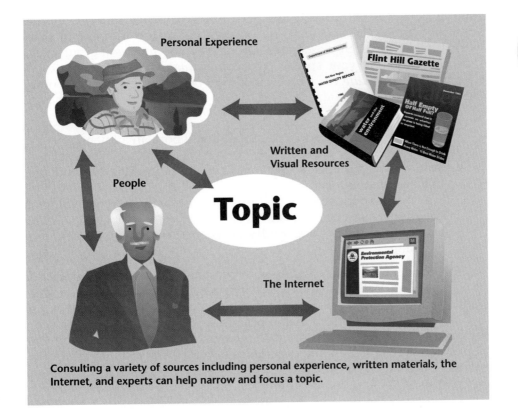

Consulting a variety of sources including personal experience, written materials, the Internet, and experts can help narrow and focus a topic.

Figure 14.1   The research process.

What Information Sources Can You Use?

When preparing your presentation, you can use several different sources of information. We explain four of the most common: personal experience, written and visual resources, the Internet, and other people.

Personal Experience

personal experience

Use of your own life as a source of information.

The first place you should look for materials for the content of your speech is within yourself. Your **personal experience,** *your own life as a source of information,* is something about which you can speak with considerable authority. One student had been a "headhunter," a person who finds employees for employers willing to pay a premium for specific kinds of employees. This student gave a speech from his personal experience concerning what employers particularly value in employees. Another student had a brother who was autistic. In her informative speech she explained what autism is and how autistic children can grow up to be self-reliant and successful in careers. Your special causes, jobs, and family can provide you with firsthand information that you can use in your speech.

However, you should ask yourself critical questions about your personal experience before you use personal experience in your speech. Some of your experiences may be too personal or too intimate to share with strangers or even classmates. Others may be interesting but irrelevant to the topic of your speech. You can evaluate your personal experience as evidence, *data on which proof may be based,* by asking yourself the following questions:

1. Was your experience typical?
2. Was your experience so *typical* that it will bore an audience?
3. Was your experience so *atypical* that it was a chance occurrence?
4. Was your experience so personal and revealing that the audience may feel uncomfortable?
5. Was your experience one that this audience will appreciate or from which this audience can learn a lesson?
6. Does your experience really constitute proof or evidence of anything?

Teaching Tip

Schedule a tour of the library so that students can become acquainted with available resources. On most campuses such tours should be scheduled at least one month in advance.

To consider the ethics of using your personal experience in a speech is also important. Will your message harm others? Is the experience first-hand (your own) or someone else's experience? Experience that is not firsthand is probably questionable because information about others' experiences often becomes distorted as the message is transmitted from one person to another. Unless the experience is your own, you may find yourself passing along a falsehood.

Think, Pair, Share

Written and Visual Resources

A second source of material for your speech is written and visual resources—magazines, journals, newspapers, books, broadcasts, and documentaries that can be consulted for information, arguments, and evidence for your speech. Magazines, journals, and newspapers may be particularly important resources for your speech, as they will provide the most recent information available on your subject. To locate articles on a given topic, you will have to check the periodical indexes in your school's library, which are available in book form and on computerized databases, such as ERIC. Be sure to check with a **reference librarian,** *a librarian specifically trained to help find sources of information,* if you are uncertain about which index will lead you to the articles that are most appropriate for your subject matter.

Most libraries today have a **computer catalog**—*an electronic database containing information about materials in a library.* The computer catalog is similar to the older card catalog because such databases have call numbers and entries arranged by author, subject, and title. When you conduct a search on a topic, the computer helps you narrow your search—something a card catalog cannot do. You begin by typing a word or phrase, such as "mass media and violence"; the computer will then display a list of all the subtopics related to mass media and violence. When you select a subtopic from those displayed, a list of the books related to that specific topic will appear. From this start, you can learn not only the title of the books and where they are located but also whether they are checked out and, if they are, when they are due back. Sometimes the catalog includes a brief summary about the book. Computer catalogs allow you to use Boolean operators to narrow searches. We discuss this concept later when explaining how to narrow Internet searches. Many college and university library catalogs allow you to access other electronic resources like newspaper indexes and databases of articles from professional journals.

CD-ROM Activity

Ask students to view the animation titled "The Research Process" contained on the accompanying student CD-ROM. The animation stresses that research is a process and that no single type of information (e.g., the Internet) provides all relevant facts on a topic. Rather, students should consult multiple types of sources.

reference librarian

A librarian specifically trained to help find sources of information.

computer catalog

An electronic database containing information about materials in a library.

423

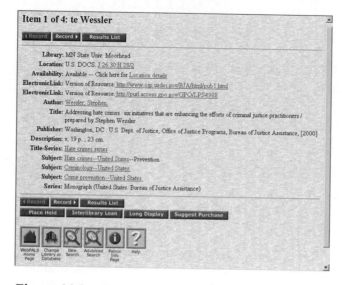

Figure 14.2   Bibliographic information from an electronic catalog.

Internet

A network of interconnected computers and computer networks.

World Wide Web (WWW)

A feature of the Internet that links together all the individual websites.

hyperlink

A link in a WWW document that leads to another website or to another place within the same document.

Regardless of the source you are using, to take good notes, to record the information accurately and precisely, and to credit the author in your speech is important. Most electronic catalogs allow you to print out the bibliographic information for sources (the author, publication date, publisher, title, etc.). A sample printout from an electronic catalog is shown in Figure 14.2.

The Internet

Many students now use the **Internet,** *a network of interconnected computers and computer networks,* to find information for their speeches: The part of the Internet that you are most likely to use in your research is the **World Wide Web (WWW),** which *links together all the individual Web sites.* Called the "Web" because many sites are linked together, this system allows users to travel from one site to another by clicking on hyperlinks. A **hyperlink** is *a link in a WWW document that leads to another website or to another place within the same document.* The Web is like a "multimedia encyclopedia containing over 200 million items" from simple text pages to color pictures, video clips, and audio programs (Gregory, 1999, p. 116). One problem with using the Web is that navigation can be difficult. Dominick (1996) said, "Some have described using the Internet as trying to find your way across a big city without a map. You'll see lots of interesting stuff but you may never get to where you're going" (p. 346). Indeed, to get sidetracked is easy and you may feel somewhat overwhelmed when you are searching for information on the Web, but some suggestions to make your search easier are offered next.

COMMON SEARCH TOOLS ON THE WEB

Search engines and virtual libraries are popular and efficient methods of locating information on the Web.

Some **common search engines** are

Yahoo!: **www.yahoo.com**

Alta Vista: **www.altavista.digital.com**

Encyclopedia Britannica Internet Guide: **www.ebig.com**

Excite: **www.excite.com**

Lycos: **www.lycos.com**

HotBot: **www.hotbot.com**

MetaFind: **www.metafind.com**

Some **virtual libraries** are

The WWW Virtual Library: **lib.org**

Galaxy: **galaxy.com**

Yahoo! Libraries: **dir.yahoo.com/Reference/Libraries/**

Locating Sources on the Web Following are a few basic procedures for locating material on the World Wide Web:

1. Begin by connecting to the Internet and clicking on your **Web browser,** *a tool for viewing pages on the WWW.* Common Web browsers are Netscape and Internet Explorer.

2. If you have the **uniform resource locator (URL),** *an address on the Web where particular information is located,* of the website you are looking for, you can enter the address in the space at the top of your browser. Be careful not to add spaces or capital letters unless they are part of the address.

3. If you do not have an address, you will need to use a **search engine,** *a program on the Internet that allows users to search for information.* One criticism of search engines is that they return links to irrelevant sites. An alternative to using search engines is to use **virtual libraries,** *which provide links to sites that have been reviewed for relevance and usability.* The accompanying e-note provides Web addresses for several popular search engines and virtual libraries.

The Internet invites rapid information searches.

Web browser

A tool for viewing pages on the WWW.

uniform resource locator (URL)

An address on the Web where particular information is located.

search engine

A program on the Internet that allows users to search for information.

425

Class Activity

Copy the Library Scavenger Hunt exercise from the instructor's manual. Have groups of students work on the exercise together. The first group to complete the worksheet or the group with the most correct answers after a specified time gets to pick which day during the first round of speeches their group will speak on.

Class Activity

Have students use a Web browser and key words to search for one Web page that would be effective to use as a resource for their first speech. Ask students to compare the effectiveness of using the Web to an electronic database at your library.

virtual libraries

Websites that provide links to sites that have been reviewed for relevance and usability.

home page

The first page on a website.

bookmarks

A feature of most Web browsers that stores links for immediate retrieval without entering the URL each time you want to access the site.

Figure 14.3 The home page for Yahoo!, a search engine. Notice that each topic area is a hyperlink leading to more detailed information.

Reproduced with permission of Yahoo! Inc. © 2000 by Yahoo! Inc. YAHOO! and the YAHOO! logo are trademarks of Yahoo! Inc.

4. Once you get to a search engine's **home page,** *the first page on a website,* to which supporting materials are linked, you can use a search engine in one of two ways: (1) click on one of the several categories listed, or (2) enter a key word (or words) into the search box, and then click the "search" button. For example, if you were using the first method to look for information on your informative speech topic, the music of Tim McGraw, you would start by clicking on the "Society and Culture" heading on the home page (Figure 14.3). By following links you get progressively more specific information. To find pages about Tim McGraw from the "people" link you must click on "musicians," and then "by genre," and then "country," and then "M" for "McGraw." Eventually, you find a list of websites devoted to the popular country singer (Figure 14.4). This method takes less effort than you might think. If you were using the second method, you would disregard the general subject listings on the home page and start by typing in key words associated with your topic, for example, "Tim McGraw." Of course, you can also use both methods.

5. Although search engines differ, some general tools can be used to narrow your search regardless of the search engine (Table 14.2).

6. If you are using your own computer, you can save your favorite sites as **bookmarks,** a feature of most Web browsers in which *important links can be saved for immediate retrieval without having to look up the URL each time you want to access the site.*

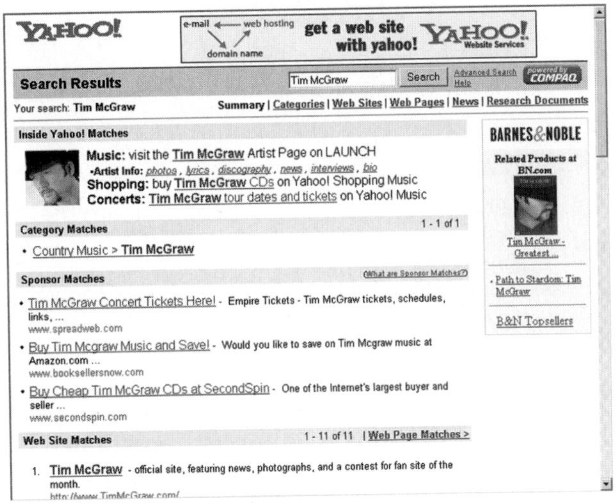

Figure 14.4 List of websites about Tim McGraw from Yahoo!

Reproduced with permission of Yahoo! Inc. © 2000 by Yahoo! Inc. YAHOO! and the YAHOO! logo are trademarks of Yahoo! Inc.

TRY ▶ THIS

Use Yahoo! to find information on your favorite musical artist. Be careful—local artists may not have a "fan page" listed in Yahoo! quite yet. What did you learn from this exercise that could be used to narrow speech topics for your classroom speeches?

TABLE 14.2   TOOLS FOR NARROWING YOUR WWW SEARCH

WORD STEMMING

By default, browsers return any Web page *containing* the word you asked it to search for. For example, if you want to search for the speech acronym *inform,* the search engine would return sites with the words informative, information, informal, informing, and so forth. To prevent this problem, type your search term with a single quote at the end.

Example: Inform'

PHRASE SEARCH

If you are looking for a phrase, put the phrase in quotation marks. For example, simply typing in *public speaking* would return all sites that contain the two words anywhere on the site. Placing the phrase in quote marks will return only sites using the phrase.

Example: "public speaking"

BOOLEAN OPERATORS

Boolean operators allow you to specify logical arguments for what you want returned in a list of matching websites. When multiple terms are typed in a search box (e.g., *tobacco addition*) the default Boolean operator is to place "AND" between the terms. Returned websites will contain both tobacco AND addiction somewhere on the page. Other Boolean operators include NOT (e.g., *PowerPoint NOT Microsoft*), which will return websites with the term before the operator but not sites with the term after the operator. You can also use the operator OR to find sites with one of two possible terms (e.g., *Coke OR Pepsi*).

PARENTHESES

Using parentheses allows you to nest Boolean search arguments. In the following example the search argument will look for websites containing the terms "media" and "violence" but not television.

Example: (media AND violence) NOT television

SOURCE: Adapted from Netscape's net search tips (http://home.netscape.com/escapes/search/tips_0.html).

E-Note

The University of California library has an excellent online exercise illustrating the importance of carefully evaluating Web sources. The address of the exercise is **www.lib.berkeley.edu/TeachingLib/Guides/Internet/Evaluate.html.** Individually, in a group, or as a class, evaluate the various websites listed in the exercise. If you click on the "Tips and Tricks" links, the UC Berkeley librarians provide their own analyses of how effective the various sites are.

Class Activity

Ask students to find one *good* Web page related to their speech topic and one *bad* Web page related to the topic. Ask them to discuss how they made their decision on what is good and bad.

Evaluating Web Sources One problem of using the Internet to gather information is that this medium is unregulated. The information may be biased, or just plain wrong, because no authority monitors the content of the sites. How do you determine what information is accurate and credible? Ultimately, you will have to make that decision. Ask yourself whether someone would have reason to present biased information. If at all possible, verify the information through other sources, such as newspaper or magazine articles. If the source is a scholarly article, check for a list of references, and if a list of references is provided, try to determine if the list is credible by verifying some of the sources. Finally, credible sources often provide the credentials of the person or individuals who wrote the article. If no source is provided, be cautious. Moreover, Web sources should be evaluated like any other source. Later in the chapter we provide rules of thumb for evaluating sources. Those suggestions should be applied to Web sources.

One additional point we like to make about the Internet is that people have different motives for creating Web pages. Some websites are intended to be informative, others are intended to persuade, yet others are out to make money. You should understand that some websites are designed to conceal their true motive: A website might look informative but actually tell only part of a story to persuade you to purchase a service or product. One way to understand the motive of websites is to pay attention to the server extension. Table 14.3 explains the parts of a Web address and the characteristics of Web addresses with different server extensions. No single type of Web address—based on the server extension—is necessarily better than another. Although knowledge of different types of Web address can be valuable, all Web resources require scrutiny.

Class Activity

Divide students into groups and assign them topic areas. Each group should identify a person or type of person who could be interviewed as well as an interview guide with specific questions to ask the interviewee.

People Sources

Speakers often overlook the most obvious sources of information—the people around them. You can get information for your speech from personal experience, written and visual resources, the Internet, *and* from other people. The easiest way to secure information from other people is to ask them in an informational interview.

TABLE 14.3   BREAKING DOWN WEB ADDRESSES

ELEMENTS OF A WEB ADDRESS

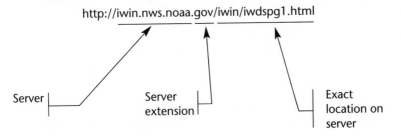

http://iwin.nws.noaa.gov/iwin/iwdspg1.html

Server | Server extension | Exact location on server

COMMON SERVER EXTENSIONS

EXTENSION	DESCRIPTION	EXAMPLE
.edu	Primarily college and university websites	www.ohio.edu Website for Ohio University
.com	Primarily commercial or for-profit websites	www.mhhe.com Website for McGraw-Hill Publishing Company
.gov	Government websites	www.ed.gov Website for the U.S. Department of Education
.net	Primarily Internet service provider public sites, sometimes used as an alternative when a ".com" name has already been taken	www.maui.net Website for Island of Maui Tourism
.org	Primarily not-for-profit organizations	www.helping.org A resource site for volunteerism and nonprofit organizations

Finding People to Interview   As someone who needs information about a particular topic, your first step is to find the person or persons who can help you discover more information. Your instructor might have some suggestions about whom to approach. Among the easier and better sources of information are professors and administrators who are available on campus. They can be contacted during office hours or by appointment. Government officials, too, have an obligation to be responsive to your questions. Even big business and industrial concerns have public relations offices that can answer your questions. Your object is to find

The speaker who uses facial expression, gestures, movements, and voice to make a point exhibits dynamism.

someone, or a few people, who can provide you with the best information in the limited time you have to prepare your speech.

Conducting the Interview   An interview can be an important and impressive source of information for your speech—if you conduct the interview properly. After you have carefully selected the person or persons you wish to interview, you need to observe these proprieties:

1. *On first contact with your interviewee or the interviewee's secretary, be honest about your purpose.* For example, you might say, "I want to interview Dr. Schwartz for 10 minutes about the plans for student aid for next year so that I can share that information with the 20 students in my public-speaking class." It is also wise to tell the interviewee how much time the interview will take.

2. *Prepare specific questions for the interview.* Think ahead of time about exactly what kind of information you will need to satisfy yourself and your audience. Conducting research prior to the interview is often advisable—you will be able to ask better questions. Keep your list of questions short enough to fit the time limit you have suggested to the interviewee.

3. *Be respectful toward the person you interview.* Remember that the person is doing you a favor. You do not need to question aggressively like Mike Wallace on *60 Minutes*. Instead, dress appropriately for the person's status, ask your questions with politeness and concern, and thank your interviewee for granting you an interview.

4. *Tell the interviewee you are going to take notes so you can use the information in your speech.* If you are going to tape-record the interview, you need to ask the interviewee's permission, and you should be prepared to take notes in case the interviewee does not wish to be recorded. Even if you record the interview, to take notes as a backup in case something happens to the tape or tape recorder is a good idea.

TABLE 14.4 EXAMPLES OF VERBAL CITATIONS	
TYPE OF SOURCE	EXAMPLE
Magazine article	"According to Fox Butterfield, a reporter for the *New York Times,* the crime rate is declining in 2001."
Research study	"Elizabeth Graham, a communication researcher, found in a 1997 study that relationships go through different patterns after a divorce."
Web page	"The American Red Cross website, which I visited on October 25, 2001, stated that over 90 million dollars has been raised for the September 11 disaster relief efforts."

5. *When you quote the interviewee or paraphrase the person's ideas in your speech, use oral footnotes to indicate where you got the information.* For example, "According to Dr. Fred Schwartz, the director of financial aid, the amount of student financial aid for next year will be slightly less than it was this year."

Sometimes the person you interview will be a good resource for additional information. For example, one of our students interviewed the director of disability services on our campus for her informative speech about learning disabilities. He not only answered her questions but also gave her an extensive packet of information on the topic. By picking the right source to interview the student was able to obtain all of her research in one stop.

Citing Sources of Information Correctly

Once you find source material, you must provide references for the source both on your outline and in your speech. **Bibliographic references** are *complete citations that appear in the "references" or "works cited" section of your speech outline (or term paper).* Your outline should also contain **internal references,** which are *brief notations of which bibliographic reference contains the details you are using in your speech.* Internal and bibliographic references help readers understand what sources were used to find specific details like statistics, quotations, and examples. Ask your teacher if a particular format should be used for references.

In addition to citing sources in your outline, you must also provide verbal citations during your presentation. Unlike the readers of a paper or speech outline, audience members are less concerned with page numbers and titles of articles. Rather, **verbal citations** tell listeners *who the source is, how recent the information is, and the source's qualifications.* The examples listed in Table 14.4 illustrate how to orally cite different types of sources. Of these sources, students have the most difficult time with Web

Video Activity

Ask students to view the video segment "On the Air with Campus-Community Connection." In this segment the two speakers present several facts and statistics. The casual observer might assume the speakers are using credible evidence. Ask students to identify the actual sources used in the two speeches. Can the evidence be verified based on what was presented?

bibliographic references

Complete citations that appear in the "references" or "works cited" section of your speech outline.

internal reference

Brief notation indicating a bibliographic reference that contains the details you are using in your speech.

verbal citations

Oral explanations of who the source is, how recent the information is, and the source's qualifications.

Team Challenge

Your team should pick a topic that can be researched. As homework, each member of the team should find a different type of source to use. One person should find a Web page, one person a book, one person a magazine article, one person a scientific journal article, etc. In the next class period your team will compare what you found. What types of information were found in the various sources? Were some sources "better" than other sources?

Writing Assignment

Have students complete an annotated bibliography of sources for their first speech (you determine the number of sources required). Be sure to explain which style (APA or MLA) to use.

pages. Remember that the Web address is only that—an address. Although the Web address should be listed in the references or works cited page of your outline, to say the address during your presentation is seldom necessary. The exception would be if you wanted your audience to visit that particular website.

Tips for Effective Research

Learning how to conduct effective research is essential. The Web has streamlined the diversity of information, but this ease necessitates a sound research strategy. In this section we address two issues. First we explain why consulting various types of sources is essential. Second, we discuss key criteria you should use when evaluating sources.

The Importance of Source Variety

Not all sources tell you the same thing. On any given speech topic—global warming, for example—you can obtain information from each type of source: personal experience, visual and written sources, the Internet, and even personal interviews. Each type of source will yield different types of information. Personal experience might tell you how you contribute to global warming by driving your car or using electricity; magazine and newspaper articles might give general background on what global warming is; scientific journals might provide detailed statistics on how much the Earth is heating up; and Web pages might describe groups committed to preventing warming. Our experience suggests that effective speakers consult all types of sources as they progress through the research process.

Criteria for Evaluating Sources

Just finding sources does not ensure that you have effectively researched your speech. You must carefully evaluate the credibility and usefulness of each source. Bourhis, Adams, Titsworth, and Harter (2002) recommend that you use the following criteria when evaluating sources:

1. *Is the supporting material clear?* Sources should help you add clarity to your ideas rather than confusing the issue with jargon and overly technical explanations.
2. *Is the supporting material verifiable?* Listeners and readers should be able to verify the accuracy of your sources. Although verifying information in a book is easy—the book can be checked out and read—information obtained from a personal interview with the uncle of your sister's roommate is not.
3. *Is the source of the supporting material competent?* For each source you should be able to determine qualifications. If your source is a person, what expertise does the person have with the topic? If your source is an organization, what relationship does the organization have with the issue?
4. *Is the source objective?* All sources—even news reports—have some sort of bias. The National Rifle Association has a bias against gun control; Greenpeace has a bias in favor of environmental issues; TV news programs have a bias toward vivid visual imagery. What biases do your sources have, and how might those biases affect the way they frame information?
5. *Is the supporting material relevant?* Loading your speech with irrelevant sources might make the speech seem well researched; however, critical listeners will see through this tactic. Include only sources that directly address the key points you want to make.

These criteria are not "yes or no" questions. Sources will meet some criteria well and fail others miserably. Your job as the speaker is to weigh the benefits and problems of each source and determine whether to include the source in your speech. Indeed, you have a key ethical responsibility to carefully evaluate sources.

Class Activity

Copy a newspaper article or printed Web page and ask students to evaluate the source using the criteria discussed in the book.

Video Activity

Ask students to view the video segment "The Hospital." In this segment Susan's grandmother is concerned about relying on Web-based information to learn about her health issues. Discuss criteria that should be used to evaluate Web sources.

TRY◄►THIS

Find a website and use the questions for evaluating sources to analyze the quality of the website as a source of information. Based on your analysis, would you use the website in a speech?

What Supporting Materials Are Appropriate?

Now that you know where to look for information, the next step is locating **supporting materials,** *information you can use to substantiate your arguments and to clarify your position.* In this section you will examine examples, surveys, testimonial evidence, numbers and statistics, analogies, explanations, and definitions. Some of these supporting materials are used as evidence or proof; others are used mainly for clarification or amplification.

Video Activity

Ask students to view the video segment "On the Air with Campus-Community Connection." Have students analyze the types of supporting material used by the two speakers. Ask what supporting material was used, what was effective, etc.

supporting materials

Information you can use to substantiate your arguments and to clarify your position.

examples

Specific instances used to illustrate your point.

Examples

Examples, *specific instances used to illustrate your point,* are among the most common supporting materials found in speeches. Sometimes a single example helps convince an audience; at other times, a relatively large number of examples may be necessary to achieve your purpose. For instance, the argument that a university gives admission priority to out-of-state students could be supported by showing the difference between the numbers of in-state students and out-of-state students who are accepted, in relation to the number of students who applied in each group. Likewise, in a persuasive speech designed to motivate everyone to vote, you could present cases in which several more votes would have meant a major change in election results.

You should be careful when using examples. Sometimes an example may be so unusual that an audience will not accept the story as evidence or proof of anything. A student who refers to crime in his hometown as an example of the increasing crime problem is unconvincing if his hometown has considerably less crime than the audience is accustomed to. A good example must be plausible, typical, and related to the main point of the speech.

Two types of examples are factual and hypothetical: A *hypothetical* example cannot be verified, whereas a *factual* example can. The length of the example determines whether the example is brief or extended. The following is a brief factual example:

According to the November 2001 issue of *Motor Trend,* "Volkswagen's incredible VW V-8 engine is the first new engine concept in decades" (p. 112).

Here is an extended hypothetical example:

An example of a good excuse for a student missing class is that he or she has a serious auto accident on the way to class, ends up in the hospital, and has a signed medical statement from a physician to prove hospitalization for a week. A poor excuse for a student missing class is that the student, knowing beforehand when the final examination will be held, schedules a flight home for the day before the exam and wants an "excused absence."

The brief factual example is *verifiable*, meaning the example can be supported by a source that the audience can check. The extended hypothetical example is not verifiable and is actually a composite of excuses.

Surveys

Another source of supporting materials commonly used in speeches is **surveys,** *studies in which a limited number of questions are answered by a sample of the population to discover opinions on issues.* Surveys are found most often in magazines or journals and are usually seen as more credible than an example or one person's experience because they synthesize the experience of hundreds or thousands of people. Public opinion polls fall into this category. One person's experience with alcohol can have an impact on an audience, but a survey indicating that one-third of all Americans abstain, one-third drink occasionally, and one-third drink regularly provides better support for an argument. As with personal experience, you should ask some important questions about the evidence found in surveys:

1. *How reliable is the source?* A report in a professional journal of sociology, psychology, or communication is likely to be more thorough and more valid than one found in a local newspaper.
2. *How broad was the sample used in the survey?* Did the survey include the entire nation, the region, the state, the city, the campus, or the class?
3. *Who was included in the survey?* Did everyone in the sample have an equally good chance of being selected, or were volunteers asked to respond to the questions?
4. *How representative was the survey sample?* For example, *Playboy's* readers may not be typical of the population in your state.
5. *Who performed the survey?* Was the survey firm nationally recognized, such as Lou Harris or Gallup, or did the local newspaper editor perform the survey? Did professionals such as professors, researchers, or management consultants administer the survey?
6. *Why was the survey done?* Was the survey performed for any self-serving purpose—for example, to attract more readers—or did the government conduct the study to help establish policy or legislation?

Testimonial Evidence

Testimonial evidence, a third kind of supporting material, is *written or oral statements of others' experience used by a speaker to substantiate or clarify a point.* One assumption behind testimonial evidence is that you are not alone in your beliefs, ideas, and arguments: Other people also support them. Another assumption is that the statements of others should help the audience accept your point of view. The three kinds of testimonial evidence you can use in your speeches are lay, expert, and celebrity.

Class Activity

Copy the report of an opinion poll from a newspaper or magazine. Discuss the usefulness and validity of this type of information as evidence in a speech.

surveys

Studies in which a limited number of questions are answered by a sample of the population to discover opinions on issues.

testimonial evidence

Written or oral statements of others' experience used by a speaker to substantiate or clarify a point.

lay testimony

Statements made by an ordinary person that substantiate or support what you say.

Lay testimony is *statements made by an ordinary person that substantiate or support what you say.* In advertising, this kind of testimony shows ordinary people using or buying products and stating the fine qualities of those products. In a speech, lay testimony might be the words of your relatives, neighbors, or colleagues concerning an issue. Such testimony shows the audience that you and other ordinary people support the idea. Other examples of lay testimony are proclamations of faith by fundamentalist Christians at a church gathering and statements about the wonderful qualities of their college by alumni at a recruiting session.

expert testimony

Statements made by someone who has special knowledge or expertise about an issue or idea.

Expert testimony is *statements made by someone who has special knowledge or expertise about an issue or idea.* In your speech, you might quote a mechanic about problems with an automobile, an interior decorator about the aesthetic qualities of fabrics, or a political pundit about the elections. The idea is to demonstrate that people with specialized experience or education support the positions you advocate in your speech.

celebrity testimony

Statements made by a public figure who is known to the audience.

Celebrity testimony is *statements made by a public figure who is known to the audience.* Celebrity testimony occurs in advertising when someone famous endorses a particular product. In your speech, you might point out that a famous politician, a syndicated columnist, or a well-known entertainer endorses the position you advocate.

Although testimonial evidence may encourage your audience to adopt your ideas, you need to use such evidence with caution. An idea may have little credence even though many laypeople believe in it; an expert may be quoted on topics well outside his or her area of expertise; and a celebrity is often paid for endorsing a product. To protect yourself and your audience, you should ask yourself the following questions before using testimonial evidence in your speeches:

1. Is the person you quote an expert whose opinions or conclusions are worthier than most other people's opinions?
2. Is the quotation about a subject in the person's area of expertise?
3. Is the person's statement based on extensive personal experience, professional study or research, or another form of firsthand proof?
4. Will your audience find the statement more believable because you got the quotation from this outside source?

Numbers and Statistics

A fourth kind of evidence useful for clarification or substantiation is numbers and statistics. Because numbers are easier to understand and digest when they appear in print, the public speaker has to simplify, explain, and translate their meaning in a speech. For example, instead of saying "There were 323,462 high school graduates," say "There were over 300,000 graduates." Other ways to simplify a number like 323,462 would be to write the number on a chalkboard or poster or to use a comparison, such as "Three hundred thousand high school graduates are equivalent to the entire population of Lancaster."

FINDING QUOTATIONS

Go to the website **www.quotationspage.com** and search for quotations on a topic of interest. Were any of the quotations you found effective quotations for a speech? Is this method an effective way to research a speech?

Visual aids can help speakers explain the meaning of statistics and other supporting material. You will learn more about the use of visual aids in chapter 16.

Statistics, *numbers that summarize numerical information or compare quantities,* are also difficult for audiences to interpret. For example, for an audience to interpret a statement such as "Honda sales increased 47 percent" is difficult. Instead, you could round off the figure to "nearly 50 percent," or you could reveal the number of sales this year and last year. You can also help the audience interpret the significance with a comparison such as "That is the biggest increase in sales experienced by any domestic or imported car dealer in our city this year."

You can greatly increase your effectiveness as a speaker if you illustrate your numbers by using visual aids, such as pie charts, line graphs, and bar graphs. You can help your audience by both saying and showing your figures. You also can help your audience visualize statistics by using visual imagery. For example, "That amount of money is greater than all the money in all our local banks," or "That many discarded tires would cover our city 6 feet deep in a single year."

statistics

Numbers that summarize numerical information or compare quantities.

437

analogy

A comparison of things in some respects, especially in position or function, that are otherwise dissimilar.

Analogies

Another kind of supporting material used in public speeches is analogies. An **analogy** is *a comparison of things in some respects, especially in position or function, that are otherwise dissimilar.* For instance, one government official said that trying to find Osama bin Laden is Afghanistan is like trying to find one particular rabbit in the state of West Virginia. Similarly, analogies can be used to show that ancient Roman society is analogous to American society and that a law applied in one state will work the same way in another.

An analogy also provides clarification, but it is not proof because the comparison inevitably breaks down. Therefore, a speaker who argues that American society will fail just as Roman society did can carry the comparison only so far because the form of government and the institutions in the two societies are quite different. Likewise, you can question the rabbit in West Virginia analogy by pointing out the vast differences between the two things being compared. Nonetheless, analogies can be quite successful as a way to illustrate or clarify.

Explanations

Explanations are another important means of clarification and persuasion that you will often find in written and visual sources and in interviews. An **explanation** *clarifies what something is or how it works.* A discussion of psychology would offer explanations and answers, as well as their relation to the field. How does Freud explain our motivations? What is *catharsis,* and how is it related to aggression? What do *id, ego,* and *superego* mean?

explanation

A clarification of what something is or how it works.

A good explanation usually simplifies a concept or an idea by explaining the idea from the audience's point of view. William Safire, once a presidential speechwriter and now a syndicated columnist, provided an explanation in one of his columns about how the spelling of a word gets changed. In his explanation, he pointed out that experts who write dictionaries observe how writers and editors use the language. "When enough citations come in from cultivated writers, passed by trained copy editors," he quotes a lexicographer as saying, "the 'mistake' becomes the spelling" (Safire, 1980). You may find, too, that much of your informative speaking is explanation.

definitions

Determinations of meaning through description, simplification, examples, analysis, comparison, explanation, or illustration.

Definitions

Some of the most contentious arguments in our society center on **definitions,** or *determinations of meaning through description, simplification, examples, analysis, comparison, explanation, or illustration.* Experts and ordinary citizens have argued for years about definitions. For instance, when does art become pornography? Is withdrawal of life-support systems euthanasia or mercy? How you define a concept can make a considerable difference.

Definitions in a public speech are supposed to enlighten the audience by revealing what a term means. Sometimes you can use definitions that appear in standard reference works, such as dictionaries and encyclopedias, but simply trying to explain the word in language the audience will understand is often more effective. For example, say you use the term *subcutaneous hematoma* in your speech. *Subcutaneous hematoma* is jargon used by physicians to explain the blotch on your flesh, but you could explain the term in this way: "*Subcutaneous* means 'under the skin,' and *hematoma* means 'swelled with blood,' so the words mean 'blood swelling under the skin,' or what most of us call a 'bruise.'"

Evidence and Proof

Supporting material in your speech can be nearly anything that provides backing for your argument. Supporting material can be as simple as "I know this works because I did it myself" or as complex as a 50-page report by a government body. Evidence is both stronger and narrower than supporting material. As indicated at the beginning of the chapter, **evidence** is *data or information from which you can draw a conclusion, make a judgment, or establish the probability of something occurring.* In the legal system, strict rules govern what may or may not be used as evidence. In public speaking, the rules are considerably looser, but common sense still applies. For instance, a single example is supporting material and may even be evidence, but a single example is usually insufficient evidence on which to base a claim. Evidence is often described as being strong or weak. The statement "This method works for me" is weak evidence compared with "This method has worked for millions of people."

If supporting material can be considered nearly anything that supports a contention and if evidence is seen as something stronger on which a conclusion or judgment can be based, then proof is the strongest type of support. **Proof** is *evidence that is sufficient to convince your audience of the truth of a claim.* Sufficient evidence could be a single example or hundreds of experiments. Evidence becomes proof when accepted by the audience.

How can you handle evidence in a speech so that it will be regarded as proof? The central concern is knowing what kind of, and how much, evidence will convince an audience that your assertions are true. Some audiences—for example, students grounded in math, business, and economics—are partial to statistics and numerical treatments of a topic. Other audiences are actually repelled by numbers and respond more favorably to long, dramatic stories or examples. The amount of evidence used is also an important consideration. Sometimes, one example proves the point; other times, all the examples in the world would be insufficient to prove your point.

Discussion Question

Have the class discuss what types of evidence they would consider as proof when attempting to prove this claim: "Mandatory attendance in college classes is unfair."

evidence

Data or information from which you can draw a conclusion, make a judgment, or establish the probability of something occurring.

proof

Evidence that is sufficient to convince your audience of the truth of a claim.

No rules govern how much or what kind of evidence should be used in your speech, but standard ways exist for presenting evidence in a speech. First, you need to be highly selective about which evidence you use in your speech to support your claims. You need to choose the evidence that is most important to you and your audience. Second, you need to make a statement—either before or after, or both before and after, the evidence—that reveals what you are trying to prove. Many names for this kind of statement exist: argument, assertion, proposition, claim, and main point. Regardless of the name, the statement is a claim that invites evidence or proof.

The important point to remember about proof is that different people perceive proof differently. The speaker is responsible for demonstrating the truth or probability of a claim. Intelligent analysis of the audience helps the speaker to discover which evidence will be perceived as proof.

Chapter Review

SUMMARY

In this chapter you have learned the following:

- Research is a common thread tying together all aspects of the speech preparation process. Research helps you find and narrow speech topics, identify main points, support your ideas, develop effective introductions and conclusions, and deliver your speech with confidence.

- Students typically use personal experience, written and visual sources, the Internet, and interviews with other people as sources in preparing their speeches.

- Once you have found appropriate sources of information to use in your speech, you must cite the source correctly in your outline and in your verbal presentation.

  - Bibliographic references are complete citations of sources listed in a "references" or "works cited" section of your outline.

  - Internal references are brief notations in the text of the outline indicating which bibliographic reference contains specific information.

  - Verbal citations of sources are given in speeches so listeners can understand the origins of your information.

- All sources, especially WWW sources, must be carefully evaluated by asking the following questions:
  - Is the supporting material clear?
  - Is the supporting material verifiable?
  - Is the source of the supporting material competent?
  - Is the source objective?
  - Is the supporting material relevant?

- To give your speech substance and adequate explanation you must include supporting material—examples, surveys, testimony, numbers or statistics, analogies, explanations, and definitions—obtained from the various sources of information.

- Supporting material is used as evidence for ideas and arguments in your speech.

  - Evidence is data or information from which you can draw a conclusion, make a judgment, or establish the probability of something occurring.

  - Proof is evidence that is sufficient to convince your audience of the truth of a claim.

  - Evidence is something speakers find and use; proof is something audience members accept.

◕ VIDEO LINK: WHY GRANDMA IS WORRIED ABOUT THE WEB

Video Episode 2: "The Hospital"

When searching for information it is tempting to rely exclusively on the most convenient source. Often this means that students rely only on the Internet. In "The Hospital," Hector Lobos advises Susan Elliott and her family about how Susan's grandmother should receive therapy for a mild stroke. Hector recommends several websites and Susan's grandmother raises obvious concerns: How can she trust information on the Web? Mr. Lobos responds that it is easy to evaluate Web sources. If you were asked by Mr. Lobos to help Susan's grandmother learn to evaluate Web resources, what would you tell her?

ISSUES IN COMMUNICATION: FINDING RESOURCES

This Issues in Communication narrative is designed to provoke thought and discussion about topics discussed in the chapter.

Tim, Chris, and Calvin came from the same high school and were excited that they were able to enroll in the same communication class. The teacher, Dr. Matheny, explained the process of putting together a speech and stressed that all students should select a topic and begin researching the speech. Tim, Chris, and Calvin took three very different approaches to implementing Dr. Matheny's suggestion.

Tim's strategy was to start early and get done quickly. He went to the library that evening and asked the reference librarian how to find newspaper articles on the library's electronic database system. After a quick lesson, Tim typed in his speech topic, napster, and hit search. Tim hit a goldmine of hundreds of newspaper articles related to the topic, and he printed five that looked interesting. He was well on the way to being done.

Chris wanted to give a speech about something she already knew. She had worked at a daycare center, KiddiLand, since she was a junior in high school and she felt comfortable talking

about that topic. She was able to use personal examples about how daycare staff were trained at KiddiLand, what activities she conducted with the toddlers, and how the staff had to constantly work to prevent germs from spreading throughout the center. Chris was satisfied. She had plenty of examples from KiddiLand to use in her speech, and she did not have to spend time in the library like Tim.

Calvin wanted to speak on the dangers of using cell phones. Calvin knew of two people who got into car accidents because they were talking on their cell phones and he knew there had to be other things wrong with cell phones. Calvin used the computer in his dorm room to access the Internet. He went to Yahoo! and searched for "cell phone dangers." One site, called "safecell.com," featured several pages worth of information on why cell phones pose extreme risk to users. The site even offered products from the company that could make cell phones safer. Calvin printed out several pages of information from the site—everything from statistics to examples of people who had cancer from using cell phones. Calvin, like his friends, would be done as soon as he typed the outline.

Three days later, Chris, Calvin, and Tim delivered their presentations. Each of the students had excellent delivery, and they all felt that their speeches went well. When Dr. Matheny returned their speech evaluation forms, Tim, Chris, and Calvin were shocked to find that they received low B grades on their speeches. On each speech critique sheet Dr. Matheny had written, "Review notes on how to effectively research your speech."

Apply what you have learned in this chapter as you ponder and discuss the following questions: What advice would you give Tim, Chris, and Calvin for addressing Dr. Matheny's comments in their next speech? What mistakes did each of the speakers make and how could the students have done a better job of researching their speech topics?

KEY TERMS

Use the *Human Communication* CD-ROM and the *Online Learning Center* at www.mhhe.com/pearson to further your understanding of the following terminology.

Analogy
Bibliographic references
Bookmarks
Celebrity testimony
Computer catalog
Definitions
Evidence
Examples
Expert testimony
Explanation

Home page
Hyperlink
Internal reference
Internet
Lay testimony
Personal experience
Proof
Reference librarian
Search engine
Statistics

Supporting materials
Surveys
Testimonial evidence
Uniform resource locator (URL)
Verbal citations
Virtual libraries
Web browser
World Wide Web (WWW)

SELF-QUIZ

Go to the self-quizzes on the *Human Communication* CD-ROM and the *Online Learning Center* at www.mhhe.com/pearson to test your knowledge.

ADDITIONAL RESOURCES

Bourhis, J., Adams, C., Titsworth, S., & Harter, L. (2002). *A style manual for communication studies.* New York: McGraw-Hill.

REFERENCES

Bourhis, J., Adams, C., Titsworth, S., & Harter, L. (2002). *A style manual for communication studies.* New York: McGraw-Hill.
Dominick, J. R. (1996). *The dynamics of mass communication* (5th ed.). New York: McGraw-Hill.
Gregory, H. (1999). *Public speaking for college and career* (5th ed.). New York: McGraw-Hill.

Safire, W. (1980, November 30). When a mistake becomes correct, and vice versa. *Des Moines Sunday Register,* p. 3C.
Senifskey, C. (2001, November). Incredible VW "V-8" engine. *Motor Trend, 53,* 112–114.

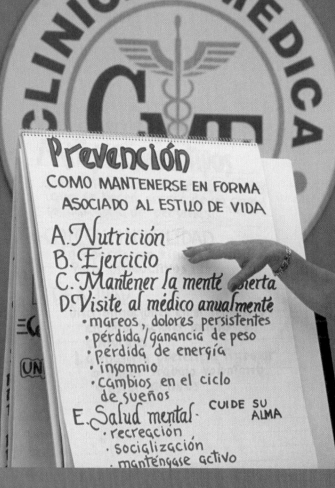

CHAPTER FIFTEEN

Order and simplification are the first steps toward mastery of a subject.

THOMAS MANN

Architecture starts when you carefully put two bricks together.

LUDWIG MIES VAN DER ROHE

Any plan formulated in a hurry is foolish.

RASHI

Organizing
Your Presentation

What will you learn?

When you have read and thought about this chapter, you will be able to:

1. State the functions of an introduction.
2. Reveal some creative ways to fulfill these functions.
3. Identify some outlines useful to a speaker.
4. Apply the principles of outlining.
5. State what is supposed to occur in the body of a speech.
6. Choose an organizational pattern appropriate for your topic.
7. Provide examples of transitions and signposts.
8. Reveal the functions of a speech's conclusion.

In this chapter you will learn how to organize your presentation. You will examine the three main parts of a speech: introduction, body, and conclusion. You will learn the functions of each part and how to effectively organize the content. Understanding the parts of a speech, the functions of each part, and how to organize the entire message is essential to becoming a successful presenter.

Teaching Tip

This chapter discusses several of the "written" elements of the presentation process. Use short writing assignments spaced over several days to ensure that students are working on their first speech in advance rather than the night before. Requiring a preliminary introduction, outline, and conclusion a week before the first speech can dramatically improve the quality of speeches. Various writing assignments are indicated in subsequent annotations.

Jenny was Brian's friend, but even she was having trouble following Brian's presentation. He did not bother to give his speech a title, and he began without even saying what his speech was going to be about. Instead, he just launched into a story about some woman who had lost her job because she tried to unionize the employees at her workplace. Trouble was, Brian followed that story with another one that seemed to have nothing to do with the first. Jenny was tired of listening to him and showed her disdain by looking down at her desk.

After the class was over, Brian asked Jenny why she would not look at him when he was giving his presentation. Jenny was direct: "I didn't know what you were talking about because you were so disorganized. You didn't announce your subject; you didn't tell us what you were going to discuss, and you didn't help us along the way. Maybe you had some good stuff in that presentation, but I couldn't find it because it was such a mess."

Some presenters cannot organize their thoughts, just like some people cannot organize their desktop, their closet, or the trunk of their car. Organization is not difficult, and even the pathologically disorganized person can learn how to organize a presentation. The purpose of this chapter is to walk you through an entire presentation by revealing dozens of ideas for organizing your thoughts.

The Introduction

introduction

The first part of the presentation; its function is to arouse the audience and to lead into the main ideas presented in the body.

The **introduction** is *the opening of your presentation.* The opening is important because audiences use the introduction to "size up" a speaker. In the first few sentences, and certainly in the first few minutes of a speech, audience members decide whether to listen to you—or not. They also decide whether your topic is important enough to warrant their consideration. In those crucial minutes early in the presentation, you can capture your audience's attention and keep their focus, or you can lose their attention—perhaps for the remainder of the presentation. This section of the chapter is devoted to helping you compose the best possible introduction, one that will grab your audience's attention and keep their minds on your topic.

The five functions of an introduction are illustrated in Figure 15.1. These five functions are not necessarily fulfilled in this order. Gaining audience attention often comes at the beginning, but maintaining attention is an important function throughout the speech. Forecasting the speech's organization often comes toward the end of an introduction, but even that function does not have to be last.

To assist you in composing an introduction for your public presentation, this section systematically explores the five functions and presents some examples.

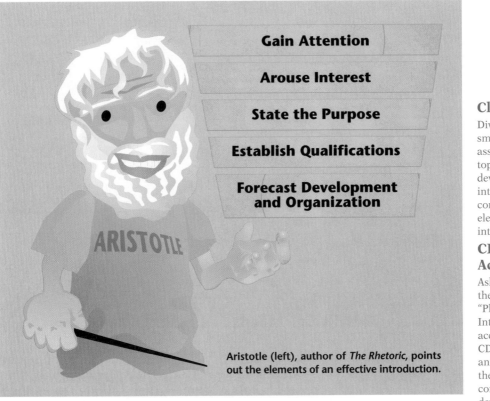

Aristotle (left), author of *The Rhetoric*, points out the elements of an effective introduction.

Figure 15.1   Planning a speech introduction.

TRY ▶ THIS

List the five functions of an introduction. Make sure the introduction of your speech includes these functions.

Gaining and Maintaining Audience Attention

The first function of an introduction is *to gain and maintain attention.* This section suggests many ways to gain and maintain audience attention. Perhaps these suggestions will inspire you to think of even better ideas for your own speech. Remember, these suggestions are not just a bag of tricks you perform for dramatic effect. Instead, you gain and maintain the audience's attention by involving your audience in your topic.

1. *Bring to the presentation the object or person about which you are going to speak.* A student speaking on health foods brings a tray full of health foods, which he shares with the audience after the

Class Activity

Divide the class into small groups and assign each group a topic. Groups should develop an introduction containing the five elements of an introduction.

CD-ROM Activity

Ask students to view the animation titled "Planning a Speech Introduction" on the accompanying student CD-ROM. The animation illustrates the process of constructing a well-developed speech introduction.

Video Activity

Ask students to view the video segment "Reporting for KTNT: Susan Elliott." Ask students to analyze the attention-gaining strategy Susan uses for her application tape. Were her strategies effective?

Writing Activity

Ask students to write an essay describing the attention-gaining strategy they intend to use for their first speech. Collect the essays and provide comments to return to during the next class period.

Ministers often invite the congregation to participate actively in the service.

speech; a student speaking on weightlifting brings her 250-pound friend to demonstrate the moves during the speech; or a student demonstrating the fine points of choreography shows the dancing talents of six friends as a small part of the presentation. Warning: Living things—like people or animals—may or may not behave as you wish when they are the center of attention.

2. *Invite your audience to participate.* Ask questions and invite audience members to raise their hands and answer; teach the audience first-aid techniques by having them do some of the techniques with you; or have everyone stand up and perform the exercise that you are teaching them.

3. *Let your clothing relate to your presentation.* A nurse talking about the dangers of acute hepatitis wears a nurse's uniform; a construction worker dons a hard hat; or a private security officer wears a uniform and badge.

TRY ◄►THIS

See if you can determine how you decide that a presentation is organized. What are the verbal and nonverbal signs of organization? What words signal organization? What are the clues that tell you the speaker is organized? Can you use some of these techniques in your own presentation?

4. *Exercise your audience's imagination.* Have the audience members close their eyes and imagine they are standing on a ski slope, standing before a judge on a driving-while-intoxicated charge, or slipping into a cool Minnesota lake when Miami and Houston are humid and steamy.

5. *Start with sight or sound.* Examples include one minute of music from a speaker, a poster-size picture showing the wonders of Cancun, or the sounds of forest birds chirping in the cool dawn. One student gave a powerful presentation on motorcycle safety. He showed six slides as he talked about the importance of wearing a helmet while driving a motorcycle. Only one item appeared in color on each slide: a crushed or battered helmet that had been worn by someone who lived through a motorcycle accident. His words spoke of safety; the battered helmets reinforced the message.

6. *Arouse audience curiosity.* One student began his speech by saying "A new sport has hit this state, yet it is a national tradition. Held in the spring of the year in some of our most beautiful timbered areas, this sport is open to men and women alike. For responsible adults only, the sport requires common sense and patience. This sport of our grandparents is . . ." Naturally, by this time the audience is very curious about the student's topic and eager to hear more.

7. *Role-play.* A student invites an audience member to pretend to be a choking victim. The speaker then "saves" the victim by using the maneuver she is teaching the audience. Speakers themselves can, for example, play the role of a mechanic fixing a small engine, a nurse showing how to take vital signs, or a salesperson selling a product. Audiences can be asked to play the roles of people whose cars will not start, of paramedics learning what to do in the first few minutes with an accident victim, or customers interested in buying a product.

8. *Show a few slides or a very short film or video.* A football player speaking on violence in that sport shows a short video of punt returns. He points out which players were deliberately trying to maim their opponents with face guards—as they have been taught to do; a Chinese student shows a few slides of her native land; or a student speaking on city slums presents a mind-grabbing sequence of 12 slides showing homeless people in doorways, rats in a child's room, and a family of 10 people living in three rooms. Warning: Do not let the video become your presentation; instead, use film or video to highlight your message.

9. *Present a brief quotation, or have the audience read something you provided.* You can put your audience in the mood for your speech by using a few lines from a popular song, quoting inspiring words from someone the audience admires, or citing a particularly eloquent statement by a pundit, newscaster, or entertainer. One enterprising student handed every class member an official-looking

letter right before his speech. Each letter was a personalized summons to court for a moving violation that was detected by a police-owned spy camera at a busy intersection.

10. *State striking facts or statistics.* Two examples of striking facts: (a) a conservative business magazine reports that prostitutes are among the most successful entrepreneurs on the Internet (Dodes, 2001) and (b) in spite of all the talk about postpartum depression more women may suffer depression *before* childbirth (Samiei, 2001). Three examples of striking statistics:

   a. Fifty states collected a total of over $200 billion from the tobacco companies in 1998, but so far only 5 percent of the money has been used for prevention, while 26 percent has bolstered endowments or state budget reserves ("Five Percent," 2001).

   b. The average American drinks more carbonated soft drinks—56 gallons—than citizens of any other country in the world (What on Earth? 2001).

   c. At Pearl Harbor on December 7, 1941, a total of 2,403 people died; on September 11, 2001, approximately 3,000 died in the World Trade Center; and on April 17, 1862, at the Battle of Antietam, 23,000 Americans—Confederate and Union—were killed, wounded, or missing (Von Drehle, 2001).

11. *Self-disclosure.* Tell audience members something about yourself—related to the topic—that they would not otherwise know: "I took hard drugs for six years"; "I was an eagle scout"; "I earn over $50,000 a year—legally."

12. *Tell a story, a narration.* Example: "I want to tell you about Tiow Tan, a friend of mine. Tan was a big success at South High: He lettered in track and football, and he had the second-highest grades in our senior year. Tan was just as good in college: He had a 3.5 GPA, drove a Corvette, and was selected for a student internship with IBM. But you read about my friend Tan in last week's newspaper. Maybe you didn't know who he was, but he was the one who died in a car wreck with his girlfriend on Route 340. They were killed by a drunken driver." If you choose to use narration, you should indicate to your audience whether the story is hypothetical or an actual account.

Class Discussion

Have students discuss ways that advertisers gain the attention of audiences. Can similar strategies be used in public speeches? Why or why not?

The preceding 12 suggestions for gaining and maintaining audience attention certainly are not the only possibilities, but they have all been used successfully by other students. Your introduction should not simply imitate what you read in this book; instead, think of ideas of your own that will work best for you and your audience.

Some words of caution about gaining and maintaining attention: No matter what method you use for gaining audience attention, *avoid being overly dramatic.* One professor had a harrowing experience in class. She

Think, Pair, Share

was writing down some comments about a speech when the next student rose to deliver his speech. She heard a horrifying groan and looked up to see the student on the floor with his whole leg laid open and bleeding. The other students leaped up and surrounded the injured student while the professor ran to the office to call for emergency assistance. The student had planned to give a speech on first aid and had borrowed a plastic leg wound in living color from the student health center. He had a bag of simulated blood on his stomach, which he squeezed rhythmically so that it would spurt like a severed artery. Unfortunately for the student, his attention-getting action introduction was too realistic. Instead of capturing the audience's attention, he managed to get the participants so upset that they were in no mood to listen to any more speeches that day.

Always *make sure your attention-getting strategy is related to your topic.* Some speakers think every public speech must start with a joke. Starting with a joke is a big mistake if you are not good at telling jokes or if your audience is not interested in hearing them. Jokes can be used in the introduction of a speech if they are topically relevant, but they are just one of hundreds of ways a speaker can gain attention. Another overused device is writing something such as "S-E-X" on the chalkboard and then announcing your speech has nothing to do with sex but that you wanted to get the audience's attention. Again, the problem with this approach is that the attention-getting strategy has nothing to do with the topic.

Arousing Audience Interest

The second function of an introduction is *to arouse audience interest in the subject matter.* The best way to arouse audience interest is to show clearly how the topic is related to the audience. A highly skilled speaker can determine how to adapt almost any topic to an audience. Do you want to talk about collecting coins? Thousands of coins pass through each person's hands every year. Can you tell your audience how to spot a rare one? If you can arouse the audience's interest in currency, you will find it easier to encourage them to listen to your speech about the rare coins you have collected. Similarly, speeches about your life as a mother of four, a camp

Group Activity

Assign each group a different speech topic. Each group should prepare a strategy for arousing audience members' interest in its assigned topic. Discuss results of the activity as a class.

451

counselor, or the manager of a business can be linked to audience interests. The following good example relates the topic to the audience; these words occurred in a student speech on drinking and driving:

> Do you know what the leading cause of death is for people who attend this college? Some of you might think it is a disease that causes the most deaths—cancer, heart attacks, or AIDS. No, the leading cause of death among students at this college is car accidents. Not just ordinary car accidents, but accidents in which the driver has been drinking.

The speaker related her topic to the audience by linking a national problem to her own college. She prepared the audience to receive more information and ideas about this common problem.

Stating the Purpose

The third function of an introduction is *to state the purpose of your speech*. Why state the purpose? Informative speeches invite learning, and learning is more likely to occur if you reveal to the audience what you want them to know. Consider the difficulty of listening to a history professor who spends 50 minutes telling you every detail and date related to the Crusades. Observe how much easier it is to listen to a professor who begins the lecture by stating what you are supposed to learn: "I want you to understand why the Crusades began, who the main participants were, and when the Crusades occurred."

The following are some examples of statements of purpose:

"Today I will tell you three ways to make your car last longer."

"What I want you to remember from my speech is why our national debt is costing a billion dollars per day."

"You will learn in this presentation several methods of protecting your credit card from crooks."

In speaking, as in teaching, audience members are more likely to learn and understand if you are clear about what is expected from them. That goal can be accomplished by stating the purpose in the introduction. However, sometimes in a persuasive speech you may wish to delay giving a statement of purpose until you have set the stage for audience acceptance. Under most circumstances, though—and especially in informative speeches—you should reveal your purpose in your introduction.

Establishing Your Qualifications

The fourth function of an introduction is *to describe any special qualifications you have to enhance your credibility*. You can talk about your experience, your research, the experts you interviewed, and your own education and training in the subject. Although you should be wary about self-praise, you need not be reserved in stating why you can speak about the topic with authority. The following is an example of establishing credibility through self-disclosure:

> I am a Catholic woman and I have a Baptist boyfriend. Our different religions have challenged us both but have strengthened, rather than weakened, our relationship because we have to explain our faiths to each other. With that in mind, I'd like to share with you the similarities between two seemingly different religions.

Forecasting Development and Organization

The fifth function of an introduction is *to forecast the organization and development of the presentation.* The forecast provides a brief outline of your organization, a preview of the main points you plan to cover. Audience members feel more comfortable when they know what to expect. You can help by revealing your plan for the speech. Are you going to discuss a problem and its solution? Are you going to make three main arguments with supporting materials? Are you going to talk for 5 minutes or for 20? Let your audience know what you plan to do early in your speech. Two forecasts follow. Are they adequate in forecasting organization and development?

> Follow my advice this evening and you can earn 10 dollars an hour painting houses, barns, and warehouses. First, I will show you how to locate this kind of work. Next, I will teach you how to bid on a project. And, last, I will give you some tips on how to paint well enough to get invited back.

> My purpose is to help you understand your own checking account. I will help you "read" your check by explaining the numbers and stamps that appear on the face; I will help you manage your checking account by showing you how to avoid overdraw charges; and I will demonstrate how you can prove that your check cleared.

The Body

Most speakers begin composing their presentations with the body rather than the introduction. The order used in composing a presentation differs from the order used in delivering a presentation because the presenter needs to know the content of the presentation to write an effective introduction.

The **body** of a presentation is *the largest portion of the presentation in which you place your arguments and ideas, your substantiation and examples, and your proofs and illustrations.* Since you usually do not have time to state in a presentation everything you know about a subject you need to decide what information to include and what information to exclude. Since the material you will use may not all be of equal importance, you need to decide where in the body to place it—first, last, or in the middle. Selecting, prioritizing, and organizing are three skills that you will use in developing the body of your speech.

body

The largest part of the presentation, which contains the arguments, evidence, and main content.

Just as the introduction of a speech has certain functions to fulfill, so does the body. Following are the main functions of the body:

1. Increase what an audience knows about a topic (informative presentation).
2. Change an audience's attitudes or actions about a topic (persuasive presentation).
3. Present a limited number of arguments and/or ideas.
4. Provide support for your arguments and/or ideas.
5. Indicate the sources of your information, arguments, and supporting materials.

Class Activity

To help students distinguish between main and subordinate points, have the class complete the exercise found in the instructor's manual. This can be done individually or as a group. Review correct answers as a class.

You already know something about organization. Every sentence you utter is organized. The words are arranged according to rules of syntax for the English language. Even when you are in conversation, you organize your speech. The first statement you make is often more general than that which follows. For instance, you might say, "I don't like DeMato for Congress," after which you might say why you don't like DeMato. You probably don't start by stating a specific fact, such as DeMato's voting record, her position on health care, or her torrid love life. Likewise, when we compose a speech, we tend to limit what we say, prioritize our points, and back them as necessary with support—all organized according to principles we have either subconsciously learned (as in the rules of syntax for language) or consciously studied (as in the rules of organization).

TRY ▶ THIS

List the experience, skills, and knowledge that make you qualified to speak on your topic.

The Principles of Outlining

outline

A written plan that uses symbols, margins, and content to reveal the order, importance, and substance of a presentation.

An **outline** is *a written plan that uses symbols, margins, and content to reveal the order, importance, and substance of your speech.* An outline shows the sequence of your arguments or main points, indicates their relative importance, and states the content of your arguments, main points, and subpoints. The outline is a simplified, abstract version of your speech.

Why learn outlining? First, outlining is a skill that can be used to develop written compositions, to write notes in class, and to compose speeches. Second, outlining teaches important skills, such as selecting the information and ideas most important for you and your audience; discriminating between what is more important and less important; and placing arguments, ideas, and support in a structure that will encourage learning and behavioral change. A third advantage is that an outline encourages you to speak conversationally. Some of the best speakers learn how to deliver their presentations from an outline, instead of having every word written out in a manuscript. Useful, important, and readily applicable in a communication class, outlining is an overall organizational plan that you need to understand.

The outline form is versatile and relatively easy to learn as long as you keep a few principles in mind. The first principle of outlining is that *all the items of information in your outline should be directly related to your purpose and long-range goal*. The **immediate purpose** is *what you expect to achieve with your speech today*. You might want the audience to be able to distinguish between a row house and a townhouse, to rent a particular video, to sign a petition, or to talk with others about a topic. All of these purposes can be achieved shortly after the audience hears about the idea. The **long-range goal** is *what you expect to achieve by your message in the days, months, or years ahead*. You may be talking about a candidate two months before the election, but you want your audience to vote a certain way at that future date. You may want to push people to be more tolerant toward persons of your race, gender, sexual preference, or religion, but tolerance is more likely to develop over time than instantly—so it is a long-range goal.

The second principle of outlining is that *the outline should be an abstract of the message you will deliver*. A simplification, the outline should be less than every word you speak but should include all important points and supporting materials. Some instructors say an outline should be about one-third the length of the actual presentation, if the message were in manuscript form. However, you should ask what your instructor expects in an outline, because some instructors like to see a very complete outline, whereas others prefer a brief outline. Nonetheless, the outline is not a manuscript but an abstract of the talk you intend to deliver, a plan that includes the important arguments or information you intend to present.

The third principle of outlining is that *the outline should consist of single units of information*, usually in the form of complete sentences that express a single idea. The following example is incorrect because it expresses more than one idea in more than one sentence:

I. Gun control should be used to reduce the number of deaths in the United States that result from the use of handguns. Half of the deaths from handguns occur because criminals use them to commit murder.

The same ideas can be outlined correctly by presenting a single idea in each sentence:

I. Government regulation of handguns should be implemented to reduce the number of murders in this country.
   A. Half of the murders in the United States are committed by criminals using handguns.
   B. Half of the handgun deaths in the United States are caused by relatives, friends, or acquaintances of the victim.

immediate purpose

What you expect to achieve on the day of your presentation.

long-range goal

What you expect to achieve over a time period longer than the day of your presentation.

main points

The most important points in a presentation; indicated by Roman numerals in an outline.

The fourth principle of outlining is that *the outline should indicate the importance of an item with an outlining symbol.* In the example, the **main points,** or *most important points, are indicated with Roman numerals,* such as I, II, III, IV, and V. The number of main points in a 5- to 10-minute message, or even a longer presentation, should be limited to the number you can reasonably cover, explain, or prove in the time permitted. Most five-minute messages have from one to three main points. Even hour-long presentations must have a limited number of main points because audiences seem unable to remember more than seven main points.

subpoints

The points in a presentation that support the main points; indicated by capital letters in an outline.

Subpoints, *the points supporting the main points, or those of less importance, are indicated with capital letters,* such as A, B, C, D, and E. Ordinarily, two subpoints under a main point are regarded as the minimum if any subpoints are to be presented. As with the main points, the number of subpoints should be limited; otherwise, the audience may lose sight of your main points. A good guideline is to present two or three of your best pieces of supporting material in support of each main point.

The fifth principle of outlining is that *the outline should provide margins that visually indicate the relative importance of the items.* The larger the margin on the left, the less important the item is to your purpose. However, the margins are coordinated with the symbols explained previously; thus the main points have the same left margin, the subpoints have a slightly larger left margin, the sub-subpoints have a still larger left margin, and so on. A correct outline with the appropriate symbols and margins looks like this:

Topic: Conservative speakers & freedom of speech
Immediate purpose: Persuade students to listen to controversial speakers—without heckling.

Conservative Speakers Face "Heckler's Veto"

Introduction

I. The USA's principle of free speech is being threatened today by the very people who should be that principle's greatest supporters—lawyers and students.
   A. Lawyers have assailed Supreme Court Justice Clarence Thomas's address to the National Bar Association.
   B. Boisterous students, aggressive administrators, and an uncharacteristically benign faculty at Columbia University assailed the right of free speech for conservative luminaries.
   C. My purpose is to introduce civility to campus speeches by encouraging my fellow students to understand the true meaning of freedom of speech in the USA.

Body
II. Supreme Court Justice Clarence Thomas has points of view
objectionable to blacks and whites, but he, like all Americans,
has the right to speak and be heard.
   A. The *New York Times* reported that Thomas "accepted the
   invitation [from the ABA] with alacrity even though he knew
   he would confront an audience with many critics" (quoted in
   Yardley, 1998).
   B. According to Jonathan Yardley (1998) of the *Washington
   Post*, Thomas's speech was "angry, bitter and pugnacious."
   C. Nonetheless, Thomas is right about his right to be heard.
      1. Voltaire said, "I disapprove of what you say, but I will
      defend to the death your right to say it," a sentiment
      widely shared by free speech advocates.
      2. Yardley (1998) argues that " 'liberalism' as now defined in
      too many quarters is a synonym for ideological
      conformity and intolerance of dissent."
      3. A cardinal principle among earlier liberals was that
      everyone has a right to be heard, especially those who
      articulate unpopular ideas.

**The First Amendment guarantees
even unpopular speech.**

III. At Columbia University a conference on "Conservative Ideas in
Higher Education" was disrupted by unruly students, closed off
even to those who had paid to attend, and moved outside to Morningside
Park, where at least one speaker was unable to complete his remarks because
of the loud heckling.
   A. According to Nat Hentoff (1998), the dean of students at Columbia
   confined the meeting to Columbia University students only "to ensure the
   safety of our students."
   B. The *Columbia Spectator*, the student newspaper, reported that the rules for
   admission to the conference produced an "effective ban," according to
   Hentoff (1998).
IV. Freedom of speech was not intended to protect the popular, the desired, and
the politically correct; instead, freedom of speech only makes sense as a right
to protect minority opinion, unpopular positions, and even hateful rhetoric.
   A. Communication students should be defenders of the right to free speech
   because that right is the very basis of the communication discipline.
   B. Communication students should recognize that challenging, debating, and
   even vigorous criticism are better armaments in the arena of ideas than are
   room closings, shouting down, and the "Heckler's Veto" (Hentoff, 1998).

Conclusion
   V. While Clarence Thomas and the conservative speakers at Columbia University
   were treated disrespectfully, communication students should remember the two
   examples as reminders that they should be defenders of the right of free speech.

parallel form

The consistent use of complete sentences, clauses, phrases, or words in an outline.

The sixth principle of outlining is that *the items should appear in* **parallel form,** *consisting of complete sentences, clauses, phrases, or words, but not a mixture of these.* Hacker (1995), in her text on writing, says, "Readers expect items in a series to appear in parallel grammatical form" (p. 63). The same could be said of listeners. Most teachers prefer an outline consisting entirely of complete sentences because such an outline reveals more completely the speaker's message. An outline like the one above on free speech is composed entirely of complete sentences; it is an example of parallel form because no dependent clauses, phrases, or single words appear in the outline. To clarify the idea of parallel form, you should note the differences between the following two examples (with the incorrect example shown first):

I. Three measures of educational quality are college entrance exams, teacher–pupil ratios, and expenditures per pupil.
   A. College entrance tests are higher in some states than in others.
      1. Top SAT states—New Hampshire, Oregon, and Vermont
      2. Top ACT states—Minnesota, Wisconsin, and Iowa
   B. Teacher–pupil ratios:
      1. Connecticut and Wyoming are tied for first.
      2. Others in the top 10: New York; Washington, D.C.; New Jersey; Oregon; Delaware; Maryland; Rhode Island; and Massachusetts.
   C. Expenditures per pupil . . .

The example above is incorrect because it mixes sentences (A, B1) and nonsentences (A1, A2, and B2) instead of consistently using one form—complete sentences—as illustrated in the outline below, based on information from the U.S. secretary of education (Bell, 1984):

Topic: Measures of educational quality
Immediate purpose: To inform the audience of criteria used to measure educational quality

Measuring Quality in Our Schools

Introduction
I. An informed electorate and parents in the know need to recognize and understand how the experts are determining the quality of our schools.
   A. Three measures determine quality: college entrance exams, teacher–student ratios, and expenditures per student.
   B. States differ markedly on how they score by these measures.

Body
II. The first measures of educational quality are the two most often used college entrance exams, the ACT (American College Test) and the SAT (Scholastic Aptitude Test).
   A. Minnesota, Wisconsin, and Iowa were the top-scoring states on the ACT.
   B. Oregon, New Hampshire, and Vermont scored highest on the SAT.

CHECK YOUR PRINCIPLES

At the class meeting before a statement of purpose and outline are due, students in groups of five exchange papers and critique each others' work. Pay particular attention to whether or not the outline follows the principles explained in the text.

III. The second measure of educational quality is the teacher–student ratio, or how many students each teacher teaches.
    A. Connecticut and Wyoming tied for first place on this dimension.
    B. Massachusetts, Rhode Island, Maryland, Delaware, Oregon, New Jersey, Washington, D.C., and New York were among the top 10.
IV. The third measure of education quality was the expenditures per student.

This example of correct parallel form uses complete sentences throughout; the outline is parallel because each entry repeats the same or similar forms throughout the composition.

The Development of a Rough Draft

Before you begin composing your outline, you can save time and energy by (1) selecting a topic that is appropriate for you, for your audience, for your purpose, and for the situation; (2) finding arguments, examples, illustrations, quotations, and other supporting materials from your experience, from written and visual resources, and from other people; and (3) narrowing your topic so that you can select the best materials from a large supply of available items.

Once you have gathered materials consistent with your purpose, you can begin by developing a **rough draft** of your outline, *a preliminary organization of the outline.* The most efficient way to develop a rough draft is to choose a limited number of main points important for your purpose and your audience.

Next, you should see what materials you have from your experience, from written and visual resources, and from other people to support these main ideas. You need to find out if you have any materials that support your subpoints—facts, statistics, testimony, and examples. In short, you assemble your main points, your subpoints, and your sub-subpoints for your speech, always with your audience and purpose in mind. What arguments, illustrations, and supporting materials will be most likely to have an impact on the audience? Sometimes speakers get so involved in a topic that they select mainly those items that interest them. In public

rough draft

The preliminary organization of the outline of a presentation.

speaking, you should select the items likely to have the maximum impact on the audience, not on you.

Composing an outline for a speech is not easy. Even professional speechwriters may have to make important changes to their first draft. Some of the questions you need to consider as you revise your rough draft follow:

1. Are my main points consistent with my purpose?
2. Are my subpoints and sub-subpoints subordinate to my main points?
3. Are the items in my outline the best possible ones for this particular audience, for this topic, for me, for the purpose, and for the occasion?
4. Does my outline follow the principles of outlining?

Even after you have rewritten your rough draft, you would be wise to have another person—perhaps a classmate—examine it and provide an opinion about its content.

The next outline (based on a speech by Smith, 1998) is an example of what a rough draft of a speech looks like:

Topic: Sex and persuasion
Statement of purpose: To discourage sexual activity among teenagers

Introduction

    I. Teenagers have sex for the wrong reasons.
       A. Alcohol & sexual activity.
       B. Statistics on sexual activity now and in the past.
       C. Forecast of reasons: peers, family, and school.

Body
    II. Adolescents pushed by peers to have sex.
       A. The influence of friends.
       B. Rewards for having sex.
   III. Family influence on adolescent sex.
       A. Parental power and premarital sex.
       B. Parents talking with teens about sex.
       C. Siblings' influence on adolescent sex.
   IV. Sex education & premarital sex.
       A. Delaying sex for teens.
       B. Clarifying values for teens.

Conclusion
    V. What can reduce teenage sexual-activity level?
       A. Be careful of the friends you choose.
       B. Parent intervention helps.

C. Sex education tends to reduce sexual activity.

D. Abstinence makes the heart grow fonder.

A rough draft of a speech does not necessarily follow parallel form, nor is it as complete as the sentence outline, which often develops out of the rough draft. Mostly, the rough draft provides an overview so that you can see how the parts of the speech, the main points and subpoints, fit together. When you are ready to finalize your outline, you have several options. The sentence outline and key-word outline are two possibilities.

The Sentence Outline

The sentence outline does not have all of the words that will occur in the delivered speech, but it does provide a complete guide to the content. A **sentence outline** *consists entirely of complete sentences.* It shows in sentence form your order of presentation; what kinds of arguments, supporting material, and evidence you plan to use; and where you plan to place them. A look at your outline indicates strengths and weaknesses. You might note, for instance, that you have insufficient information on some main point or a surplus of information on another.

In addition to the sentence outline itself, you may want to make notes on the functions being served by each part of your outline. For example, where are you trying to gain and maintain attention? Where are you trying to back up a major argument with supporting materials such as statistics, testimony, or specific instances? A sentence outline, along with side notes indicating functions, is a blueprint for your speech. The sentence outline can strengthen your speech performance by helping you present evidence or supporting materials that will make sense to audience members and will help you inform or persuade them.

The outline that follows is based on a student's speech (Smith, 1998). The immediate purpose of the speech is to recount the dangers of teenage sexual intercourse, to consider the consequences. The long-term goal was to persuade the audience members to delay or cease having intercourse to reduce the number of young people taking risks with their health and their futures. Notice that the outline consists entirely of sentences.

Sexual Intercourse and Persuasion

Introduction of the Speech

I. Today more and more adolescents are having sex for the wrong reasons.

A. Let me tell you the story of a girl who loses her virginity after drinking alcohol with her boyfriend.

B. In the early 1970s, 35 percent of young women and 55 percent of young men had intercourse by age 18.

C. In this decade 56 percent of young women and 73 percent of young men have intercourse by age 18.

D. My purpose is to encourage reduced sexual activity or abstinence for teenagers by using peer influence, parental influence, and sex education.

sentence outline

An outline consisting entirely of complete sentences.

Writing Assignment

Have students complete a sentence outline for their first speech following the six principles of outlining. Indicate whether a list of references is required and what style guidelines (APA or MLA) should be used for reference formatting.

Functions

Attention—getting information

Statistics to relate topic to audience

Forecast and expectations

Body of the Speech

First main point   II. Adolescents are encouraged to have intercourse by peer pressure.

Supporting material   A. Adolescents with sexually active friends are more likely to be sexually active themselves.

Reasoning   B. Learning theory says rewards such as the approval or acceptance of friends can encourage the early onset of intercourse.

Testimony   C. An interviewed student said that she had intercourse because she felt like she was "the last virgin on earth."

Second main point   III. Family attitudes toward premarital sex can influence adolescent behavior.

         A. Parents, who have legitimate power over teenagers, may not exercise that power against sexual behavior.

Supporting material   B. Parents who talked with adolescent offspring about sex, pregnancy, and contraception were more likely to have teens that used birth control when sexually active.

Direct quotation   C. Older siblings make a difference: Research indicates that second-born adolescents "were more sexually active than firstborns at any age."

Third main point   IV. Sex education in the schools can, in cooperation with the community, churches, and families, discourage adolescent sex.

Direct quotation   A. Several studies demonstrate that "sex education can help delay first
supporting research   intercourse for adolescents who are not sexually active."

Direct quotation   B. Information on reproductive health can "enhance communication and negotiation skills, clarify their values, and change risky behaviors."

Closure on topic   Conclusion of the Speech

Suggested audience   V. To discourage the current trend of adolescents' becoming sexually active, I
response   recommend peer pressure to discourage sexual activity, parental influence to reduce sexual activity, and sex education to persuade teenagers not to become sexually active so early in life.

Summary/review   A. Peer pressure can discourage sexual activity, not just encourage it.
of content   B. Parental influence can reduce the number of early starters.
         C. Sex education seems to reduce sexual activity among teenagers.
Clever ending   D. Absence may make the heart grow fonder, but abstinence certainly does.

References

Barnett, B. (1997, October 15). Education protects health, delays sex. [Online]. Available: www.thi.org/to/tppubs/network/v17–3/nt1734.html [1997, October 15].

Barth, R., et al. (1992). Presenting adolescent pregnancy with social and cognitive skills. *Journal of Adolescent Research, 7,* 208–232.

Parrillo, A. V., Felts, W. M., & Mikow-Porto, V. (1997). Early initiation of sexual intercourse and its co-occurrence with other health-risk behaviors in high school students: The 1993 North Carolina youth risk behavior survey. *Journal of Health Education, 28,* 85–93.

Widmer, E. D. (1997). Influence of older siblings on initiation of sexual intercourse. *Journal of Marriage and the Family, 59,* 928–938.

The Key-Word Outline

Using a manuscript for your entire speech sometimes invites you to become too dependent on the manuscript. Too much attention to notes reduces your eye contact and minimizes your attention to audience responses. Nonetheless, you can become very proficient at reading from a manuscript on which you have highlighted the important words, phrases, and quotations. A complete sentence outline may be superior to a manuscript in that it forces you to extemporize, to maintain eye contact, and to respond to audience feedback. Key words and phrases can also be underlined or highlighted on a sentence outline. An alternative method is to simply use a **key-word outline,** *an outline consisting of important words or phrases to remind you of the content of the speech.*

A key-word outline abstracts the ideas in a speech considerably more than does a sentence outline. A key-word outline ordinarily consists of important words and phrases, but it can also include statistics or quotations that are long or difficult to remember. The outline below came from a student's speech. Notice how the key-word format reduces the content to the bare essentials.

Writing Assignment

Have students prepare a key-word outline prior to their first speech. Specify your desired format for the key-word outline. For instance, do you prefer notecards (how many and what size?) or a one-page typed or handwritten outline?

key-word outline

An outline consisting of important words or phrases to remind the speaker of the content of the presentation.

Why Should You Go to College?

Introduction
  I. What happens if you don't go and if you do?
    A. If you don't
      1. Fewer job opportunities
      2. Less income
      3. More job shifting
    B. If you do
      1. More job opportunities
      2. Higher income
      3. Fewer but better jobs
    C. Education more important, changing market, choices in college

Body
  II. Simpson & Frost on need for more education
    A. Global economy/increased competition
    B. More skills and knowledge
  III. Changing job market
    A. B.S. or B.A. required
    B. Semiskilled, only 10 percent by 2005
  IV. Three college choices
    A. Major
    B. Global perspective
    C. Skills and knowledge

Conclusion
V. Go to college for income, opportunity, & stability
   A. Increased importance of education
   B. Changed job market
   C. College choices
   D. Go to college for a better future

Class Activity

To help students recognize various organizational patterns and the factors that influence the choice of pattern, have the class complete the activity "Which Organizational Pattern Do I Use?" found in the instructor's manual.

A key-word outline fits easily on 3-by-5-inch or 4-by-6-inch note cards or on 8½-by-11-inch paper. If you choose note cards, the following suggestions may be useful.

1. Write instructions to yourself on your note cards. For instance, if you are supposed to write the title of your speech and your name on the chalkboard before your presentation begins, then you can write that instruction on the top of your first card.
2. Write on one side of the cards only. It is better to use more cards with your key-word outline on one side only than to write front and back, which is more likely to result in confusion.
3. Number your note cards on the top so that they will be unlikely to get out of order. If you drop them, you can quickly reassemble them.
4. Write out items that might be difficult to remember. Extended quotations, difficult names, unfamiliar terms, and statistics are items you may want to include on your note cards to reduce the chances of error.
5. Practice delivering your presentation at least two times using your note cards. Effective delivery may be difficult to achieve if you have to fumble with unfamiliar cards.
6. Write clearly and legibly.

Organizational Patterns

organizational patterns

Arrangements of the contents of a presentation.

The body of a presentation can be outlined using a number of **organizational patterns,** *arrangements of the contents of the message.* Exactly which pattern of organization is most appropriate for your presentation depends in part on your purpose and on the nature of your material. For instance, if your purpose is to present a solution to a problem, your purpose lends itself well to the problem/solution organizational pattern. If the nature of your material is something that occurred over a period of time, then your material might be most easily outlined within a time-sequence pattern.

In this section, we will examine five organizational patterns: the time-sequence pattern, the spatial/relations pattern, the cause/effect pattern, the problem/solution pattern, and the topical-sequence pattern. You should keep in mind that these five patterns of organization are prototypes from which a skilled presenter can construct many others. Also, a number of organizational patterns may appear in the same message: An

LINEAR OR CONFIGURAL ORGANIZATION: CULTURE AND COMMUNICATION

Outlining as taught in English composition and communication classes is almost entirely linear. In other words, the outline for a presentation is based on a sequential development of ideas, moving from a beginning to a middle and finally to an end. Many people cannot imagine an outline that is not sequential—for that matter, it's hard to imagine a presentation that is not linear but is still organized and understandable. It's hard to imagine because we live in a linear culture.

What are some of the characteristics of our culture that could be termed "linear"? We like beginnings and endings, points and subpoints. We like text and words, evidence and proof. Sometimes we value objects over people or events—buildings are cooled to preserve the equipment, not the people, inside them. We tend to think directionally. Doing things in a timely fashion is essential to our sense of well-being.

Not all cultures are linear. *Configural* cultures are nonlinear—they tend to see how the arrangement of parts creates a whole object; thus contours or patterns are more important than the sequential development of an idea. Configural cultures tend to think in images. Relationships are valued over objects, and time is seen as flexible. In rural China the professor starts teaching when enough students have gathered; the gathering of the group, not a bell or specific time, determines when class begins.

Can you see how culture affects the way you create an outline for a message? This chapter has introduced you to linear patterns of organization, but how might a person who thinks in configural patterns prepare a presentation? See if you can develop arguments about the merits and limitations of our current instruction on organization in oral communication.

overall problem/solution organization may have within it a time-sequence pattern that explains the history of the problem.

The Time-Sequence Pattern

The **time-sequence pattern** is *a method of organization in which the presenter explains a sequence of events in chronological order.* Most frequently seen in informative presentations, this pattern can be used in presentations

time-sequence pattern

A method of organization in which the presenter explains a sequence of events in chronological order.

that consider the past, present, and future of an idea, an issue, a plan, or a project. It is most useful on such topics as the following:

How the Salvation Army Began	The Future of Space Exploration
The Today Show: A Brief History	Building of the Hearst Castle
The Naming of a Stadium	The Development of Drugs for Treating HIV

Any topic that requires attention to events, incidents, or steps that take place over time is appropriate for this pattern of organization. Following is a brief outline of a composition (Rogers & Hart, 2001) organized in a time-sequence pattern:

History of Technology: The Pioneers

I. Vannevar Bush, an MIT engineering graduate and dean, invented a mechanical computer with rods and gears prior to World War II.
  A. Bush's "differential analyzer" did the math for radar-guided artillery shells in World War II.
  B. Bush had, by 1945, envisioned the "Memex," which he never built but which was remarkably like today's personal computers.
II. J. C. R. Licklider saw computers as a means of human communication, instead of simply computation, in the 1960s.
  A. Licklider challenged the "batch-processing" system in favor of computer time-sharing.
  B. Licklider proposed, for the first time, a concept like the current Internet.
III. Robert W. Taylor created ARPANET at the Pentagon to communicate among contractors.
  A. Taylor brought in Dr. Larry Roberts to develop a wide-area network.
  B. To allow communication among previously incompatible computers, they created the Interface Message Processor.

Notice that the emphasis in this brief outline is on the history of technology—something that occurred over a period of time. A simpler example of a time-sequence pattern of organization is a recipe that depends on the combining of ingredients in the correct order.

The Spatial/Relations Pattern

spatial/relations organization

A method of organization in which the presenter reveals how things relate to each other in space, position, and visual orientation.

Another organizational pattern used mainly in informative presentations is called the **spatial/relations organization.** It is *a pattern that reveals how things relate to each other in space, position, and visual orientation.* Examples are a blueprint, a road map, or a diagram showing furniture arrangements in a room. In a speech, it is more likely to be an explanation of an audio board, how electricity gets from the power plant to your home, or how to best set up your stereo speakers. The following is a more detailed example, describing the parts of the human heart:

Immediate purpose: After listening to my speech, the audience will be able to describe the form and state the function of the human heart.

The Human Heart: Form and Function

Introduction
  I. You should know about the organ that keeps you alive.
      A. The heart fails or falters in more than 1 million people each year.
      B. Learning the form and function of the heart can help you maintain it.
 II. First we will learn about the form and then the function of the heart.

Body
III. The form of the heart includes four chambers.
      A. The right atrium and the left atrium are located on the top of the heart, the top two humps on a valentine.
      B. The right and left ventricles are located on either side of the point at the bottom of a valentine.
 IV. The function of the heart is to receive and to pump blood.
      A. The thin-walled atria are only one-third of the heart and act as receiving chambers for the blood.
      B. The thick-walled ventricles take up two-thirds of the heart and act as two pumping stations for the human heart.

Conclusion
  V. The heart has four chambers with two receivers of blood called atria and two pumpers called ventricles.
      A. This simple organ pumps 18 million gallons of blood during a 70-year lifetime.
      B. Knowing how the heart works can help you understand how to care for it, because when it stops, so do you.

Because the informative presentation about the heart shows how parts relate in space, the pattern is called a spatial/relations organization.

The Cause/Effect Pattern

In using a **cause/effect pattern,** the presenter *first explains the causes of an event, a problem, or an issue and then discusses its consequences, results, or effects.* The presentation may be cause–effect, effect–cause, or even effect–effect. A presentation on inflation that uses the causal-sequence pattern might review the causes of inflation, such as low productivity, and review the effects of inflation, such as high unemployment and high interest rates. The cause/effect pattern is often used in informative presentations that seek to explain an issue. This pattern differs from the problem/solution pattern in that the cause/effect pattern does not necessarily reveal what to do about a problem; instead, the

cause/effect pattern

A method of organization in which the presenter first explains the causes of an event, a problem, or an issue and then discusses its consequences, results, or effects.

organization allows for full explanation of an issue. An example of the cause/effect pattern follows:

Immediate purpose: To inform the class that social drinking can lead to alcoholism

Alcoholism or Abstinence?

Introduction
  I. Most people will never have a problem with alcohol, but for some individuals social drinking will lead to problem drinking and even acute alcoholism.
     A. Social drinking is a cause of alcoholism or chemical dependency on alcohol.
     B. Developmental effects move from social drinking to problem drinking to alcohol dependence.

Body

Cause

 II. Social drinking is a first step toward serious problems with alcohol.
     A. People who drink alcohol at all risk chemical dependence on alcohol.
     B. Nondrinking individuals cannot become alcoholic even if family history indicates a tendency toward alcoholism.

Effect

III. Problem drinking is just another step toward serious problems with alcohol.
     A. A person who cannot seem to stop drinking is already a problem drinker.
     B. A person who passes out or cannot remember what happened has a serious drinking problem.
     C. A person who experiences failure in relationships with others has turned from people to alcohol.
 IV. The problem drinker becomes an alcoholic.
     A. The person who cannot stop drinking has become dependent on alcohol.
     B. The person who is alcoholic can rarely stop without help or intervention.

Conclusion
  V. Social drinking can be seen as a cause for problems with alcohol, including acute alcoholism.

     A. Abstinence or complete avoidance of alcohol can avoid any cause for alcoholism.
     B. Social drinking can lead to undesirable effects like problem drinking and acute alcoholism.
     C. Knowing about the causes and effects of alcohol is important.

The cause/effect pattern of organization is a common pattern in fields as varied as medicine (tobacco causes cancer) and economics (inflation causes recession) and religion (lack of faith results in damnation).

The Problem/Solution Pattern

The fourth pattern of organization, used most often in persuasive presentations, is the **problem/solution pattern.** As the name suggests, *the presenter describes a problem and proposes a solution.* A message based on this pattern can be divided into two distinct parts, with an optional third part in which the presenter meets any anticipated objections to the proposed solution.

problem/solution pattern

A method of organization in which the presenter describes a problem and proposes a solution to that problem.

The problem/solution pattern can envelope other patterns. For example, you might discuss the problem in time-sequence order, and you might discuss the solution using a topical-sequence pattern. Some examples of problem/solution topics follow:

Reducing Fat in Your Diet	Breaking the "Glass Ceiling" for Women
A New Way to Stop Smoking	An Alternative to Welfare
Eliminating Nuclear Waste	Helping the Homeless

Each example implies both a problem and a solution.

The problem/solution pattern of organization requires careful audience analysis because you have to decide how much time and effort to spend on each portion of the speech. Is the audience already familiar with the problem? If so, you might be able to discuss the problem briefly, with a few reminders to the audience of the problem's seriousness or importance. On the other hand, the problem may be so complex that both the problem and the solution cannot be covered in a single presentation. In that case, you may have found a topic that requires a problem presentation and a solution presentation. Your audience analysis is an important first step in determining the ratio of time devoted to the problem and to the solution.

A problem/solution speech in outline form looks like this:

Immediate purpose: Persuade students to choose jogging as a relatively gentle introduction to physical fitness.

Physical Fitness for College Students

Introduction
  I. The fact that many college students are in dreadful physical condition is a problem, but a possible solution is to start jogging.
    A. Students should exercise their bodies as well as their minds.
    B. Jogging is one solution that almost anyone can adopt.

Body
  II. Many students are in poor physical condition.
    A. Americans, including American students, are among the fattest people on Earth.
    B. Colleges and universities no longer require physical education.

III. One solution is jogging, a sport that takes little talent, little expense, and limited effort.
  A. Joggers only have to place one foot in front of the other rapidly to qualify.
  B. Joggers need only jogging shoes and sweat clothes for equipment.
  C. Joggers can run as little or as much as they wish on a regular basis.

Conclusion
IV. If lack of physical conditioning is a problem for students because they are fat and they are no longer required to take physical education, then jogging is one possible solution that demands no talent, little expense, and minimal effort.

The problem/solution pattern has many applications in presentations on contemporary problems and issues. The pattern can be used to discuss price-fixing, poverty, welfare, housing costs, the quality of goods, the quality of services, or the problems of being a student.

The Topical-Sequence Pattern

topical-sequence pattern

A method of organization that emphasizes the major reasons an audience should accept a point of view by addressing the advantages, disadvantages, qualities, and types of person, place, or thing.

The **topical-sequence pattern,** used in both informative and persuasive presentations, *emphasizes the major reasons the audience should accept a point of view by addressing the advantages, disadvantages, qualities, and types of person, place, or thing.* The topical-sequence pattern can be used to explain to audience members why you want them to adopt a certain point of view. This pattern is appropriate when you have three to five points to make, such as three reasons people should buy used cars, four of the main benefits of studying speech, or five characteristics of a good football player. This pattern of organization is among the most versatile. Here is a portion of the topical-sequence outline for a message informing audience members about tarantulas:

Immediate purpose: To inform the audience of the history and characteristics of the world's largest known spider

The Tarantula*

I. The name *tarantula* has an interesting history.
  A. The word *tarantula* is derived from the name of a small town in Italy.
    1. Taranto was a town in Italy where the people experienced a large number of spider bites.
    2. The people of Taranto were bitten so frequently they developed a dance to sweat the spider poison out of their blood.
  B. The name *tarantula* was applied originally to the European wolf spider, the one encountered in Taranto.
  C. The name was transferred to the tropical spider, which is now known as the tarantula.

*Based on an outline composed by Terry Hermiston, Iowa State University.

MATCHING TOPICS WITH PATTERNS

After thinking of three possible topics on which you could speak, pair with a classmate and decide which pattern of organization best fits each of the topics.

II. The tarantula has five unusual characteristics.
   A. The first unusual feature of the tarantula is its size.
      1. Tropical tarantulas are as large as 3 inches in body length and 10 inches in leg span.
      2. Species in the United States range from 1 to 3 inches in body length and up to 5 inches in leg span.
   B. A second unusual feature of the tarantula is that it hunts at night.
   C. A third interesting feature of the tarantula is that it can see only a distance of 2 inches and relies on leg hairs to sense the presence of other things.
   D. A fourth characteristic is that tarantulas are cannibalistic.
   E. A fifth characteristic of the tarantula is that it molts.
      1. Molting decreases with age.
      2. Molting can be accompanied by regeneration of lost parts, such as legs.

The outline could continue to develop main points on why tarantulas make interesting and economical pets and on the myths about their poison. However, the portion of the outline shown here illustrates the main advantage of the topical-sequence outline—it can be used to organize diverse ideas into a commonsense sequence that appeals to an audience.

Transitions and Signposts

So far, you have examined organization in its broadest sense. To look at the presentation as a problem/solution or cause/effect pattern is like looking at a house's first floor and basement. We also need to look more closely at the design of the presentation by examining the elements that connect the parts of a speech together—transitions and signposts.

A **transition** is *a bridge between sections of a message that helps a speaker move smoothly from one idea to another*. Transitions also relax the audience momentarily. A typical transition is a brief flashback and a brief forecast that tells your audience when you are moving from one main point to another.

The most important transitions are between the introduction and the body, between the main points of the body, and between the body and the conclusion of the presentation. Other transitions can appear between the main heading and main points, between main points and subpoints, between subpoints and sub-subpoints, between examples, and between visual aids and the point being illustrated. Transitions can review, preview,

Video Activity

Ask students to view the video segment "On the Air with Campus-Community Connection." Have students pay attention to transitions and signposts used by the two speakers. Were their messages organized clearly?

transition

A bridge between sections of a presentation that helps the presenter move smoothly from one idea to another.

TABLE 15.1 TRANSITIONS

Transition from one main point to another: "Now that we have seen why computers are coming down in cost, let us look next at why software is so expensive."

Transition from a main point to a visual aid: "I have explained that higher education is becoming more and more expensive. This bar graph will show exactly how expensive it has become over the past 5 years."

Transition that includes a review, an internal summary, and a preview: "You have heard that suntanning ages the skin, and I have shown you the pictures of a Buddhist monk and a nighttime bartender who hardly ever exposed themselves to direct sunlight. Now I want to show you a picture of a 35-year-old woman who spent most of her life working in direct sunlight."

TABLE 15.2 SIGNPOSTS

"First, I will illustrate . . ."	"A second idea is . . ."
"Look at this bar graph . . ."	"Another reason for . . ."
"See what you think of this evidence . . ."	"Finally, we will . . ."
"Furthermore, you should consider . . ."	

signposts

Ways in which a presenter signals to an audience where the presentation is going.

Class Activity

Ask students to write transitions and signposts for sentence outlines appearing earlier in the chapter. This can be done in groups where each group is assigned a different outline. Discuss results as a class.

or even be an internal summary, but they always explain the relationship between one idea and another. Transitions are the mortar between the building blocks of the speech. Without them, cracks appear, and the structure is less solid. Table 15.1 gives examples of transitions.

Signposts are *ways in which a presenter signals to an audience where the message is going.* Signposts, as the name implies, are like road signs that tell a driver there is a curve, bump, or rough road ahead; they are a warning, a sign that the presenter is making a move. Whereas transitions are often a sentence or two, signposts can be as brief as a few words. Transitions review, state a relationship, and forecast; signposts just point.

Beginning presenters often are admonished by their instructors for using signposts that are too blatant: "This is my introduction," "This is my third main point," or "This is my conclusion." More experienced presenters choose more subtle but equally clear means of signposting: "Let me begin by showing you . . .," "A third reason for avoiding the sun is . . .," or "The best inference you can draw from what I have told you is. . . ." Table 15.2 gives examples of signposts.

Transitions and signposts help presenters map a message for the audience. Transitions explain the relationships in the message by reflecting backward and forward. Signposts point more briefly to what the presenter is going to do at the moment. Both transitions and signposts help bind the message into a unified whole.

TRY ▶ THIS

How do you know when a speaker is drawing to a close? What signs, cues, or signals occur to prepare you for the end of a presentation? How will you indicate to an audience that your presentation is ending?

The Conclusion

The **conclusion** is *the summary review and challenging final words of a presentation.* Like the introduction, the conclusion fulfills functions. The four functions of a conclusion need not occur in the order shown here, but they are all normally fulfilled in the waning minutes of a presentation:

1. Forewarn the audience that you are about to end the message.
2. Remind the audience of your central idea and the main points of your presentation.
3. Specify what the audience should think or do in response to your speech.
4. End the speech in a manner that makes audience members want to think and do as you recommend.

Let us examine these functions of a conclusion in greater detail.

The first function, the **brakelight function,** *warns the audience that the end of the presentation is near.* Can you tell when a song is about to end? Do you know when someone in a conversation is about to complete a story? Can you tell in a television drama the narrative is drawing to a close? The answer to these questions is usually yes because you get verbal and nonverbal signals that songs, stories, and dramas are about to end. How do you use the brakelight function in a presentation? One student signaled the end of her speech by saying "Five minutes is hardly time to consider all the complications of this issue. . . ." By stating that her time was up, she signaled her conclusion. Another said "Thus, men have the potential for much greater role flexibility than our society encourages. . . ." The word *thus,* like *therefore,* signals the conclusion of a logical argument and indicates the argument is drawing to a close.

The second function of a conclusion—*reminding the audience of your central idea or the main points in your message*—can be fulfilled by restating the main points, summarizing them briefly, or selecting the most important point for special treatment. A woman who was delivering a pro-choice presentation on abortion ended it by reminding her audience of her main point. Her method was to use two quotations

> We need to protect ourselves from closed-minded opinions like that of Senator Jesse Helms, who proposed the following amendment: "The paramount right to life is vested in each human being from the moment of fertilization without

---

conclusion

The last part of the presentation; a summary of the major ideas that is designed to induce mental or behavioral change in an audience.

brakelight function

A forewarning to the audience that the end of the presentation is near.

regard to age, health, or condition of dependency." Instead, let's consider the words of Rhonda Copelon, a staff lawyer with the Center for Constitutional Rights: "To use the Bill of Rights—which also and not incidentally guarantees the separation of church and state—to establish laws as a religious belief on a matter of private moral conduct would be unprecedented. It would transform into a tool of oppression a document which guarantees rights by limiting the power of the state to invade people's lives."

All I ask you to do is to look at the woman's side for a moment. Consider all the implications upon her life. The unborn is not the only one with a right to life. The woman has one too.

Whether you agree with her position on the issue or not, her words were an insightful way to restate the main message and restate the conflicting viewpoints on the issue.

The third function of a conclusion is *to specify what you expect audience members to do as a result of your presentation.* Do you want them to simply remember a few of your important points? Then tell them one last time the points you think are worth remembering. Do you want the audience members to write down the argument they found most convincing, sign a petition, talk to their friends? If so, you should state what you would regard as an appropriate response to your presentation. One student's presentation on unions concluded with the slogan "Buy the union label." Her ending statement specified what she expected of the audience.

Writing Assignment

Ask students to write a conclusion for their first speech and hand it in. Provide feedback on their conclusion and return it during the next class period.

The fourth function of a conclusion is *to end the presentation in a manner that makes audience members want to think and do as you recommend.* You can conclude with a rhetorical question: "Knowing what you know now, will you feel safe riding with a driver who has had a few drinks?"; a quotation: "As John F. Kennedy said, 'Forgive your enemies, but never forget their names' "; a literary passage: "We conclude with the words of Ralph Waldo Emerson, who said, 'It is one light which beams out a thousand stars; it is one soul which animates all men' "; or an action that demonstrates the point of the presentation: The speaker quickly assembles an electric motor for the class and shows that it works, the speaker twirls and does the splits in one graceful motion, or an experiment is completed as the mixture of baking soda and vinegar boils and smokes.

Some cautions about conclusions: In ending a presentation, as in initiating one, you need to avoid being overly dramatic. At one large college in the Midwest, the communication classes were taught on the third floor of the building. In one room, a student was delivering a presentation about insanity. As the speech progressed, the class became increasingly aware that the young man delivering the presentation had a few problems. At first, he was difficult to understand: words were run together, parts of sentences were incoherent, pauses were too long. Near the end of the speech, the young man's eyes were rolling, and his jaw had fallen slack. At the very end of the presentation, he looked wildly at the audience, ran over to the open window, and jumped. The class was shocked. The instructor and students rushed to the window, expecting to see his shattered remains. Far below, on the ground, were 20 fraternity brothers holding a large firefighter's net, with the speaker waving happily from the center. A better idea is to conclude your presentation with an inspirational statement, words that make audience members glad they spent the time and energy listening to you. One student delivered a single line at the end of his talk on automobile accidents that summarized his message and gave his audience a line to remember: "It is not who is right in a traffic accident that really counts," he said, "it is who is left." That conclusion was clever, provided a brief summary, and was an intelligent and safe way to end a presentation.

The Bibliography

When you have completed your outline, you may be asked to provide a **bibliography,** *a list of the sources you used in your presentation.* The main idea behind a bibliography is to inform others of what sources you used for your speech and to enable them to check those sources for themselves. Each entry in your bibliography should be written according to a uniform style. Several accepted style manuals can answer your questions about the correct format for a bibliography: *The Publication Manual of the American Psychological Association* (APA), *The MLA Handbook,* and *The Chicago Manual of Style.* Since some teachers prefer MLA and others prefer APA, you should ask your instructor's preference. This textbook relies on the APA for its bibliography style; therefore, the examples below conform to APA guidelines.

bibliography
A list of sources used in a presentation.

Common sources of bibliographic material for student presentations are newspapers, magazines, journal articles, books, the Internet, and interviews. The correct forms for these sources are as follows:

Newspapers

Murphy, C. (2001, August 12). Young audience redefines church: Casual worship, camaraderie play well at D.C. theater. *The Washington Post,* p. A1.

Magazines

Cottle, M. (2001, August 6). The terrorists next door: House arrest. *The New Republic, 4516,* 18–19.

Journals

Sherry, J. L. (2001, July). The effects of video games on aggression: A meta-analysis. *Human Communication Research, 27(3),* 409–431.

As you can see, the name of the author appears in reverse order so that the list can be easily alphabetized. Notice that the name of the author, the publication date, and the title of the article are followed by periods. Only the first words of the title and subtitle are capitalized. If a volume number is included in your entry, do not write "p." or "pp." before the page numbers. When there is no volume number, you should include "p." for a single page or "pp." for more than one page.

Without an author, the bibliographic entry changes slightly. The title of the article should appear first and the date should follow the title. The entry can then be alphabetized according to the first significant word in the article title. For example:

Asia will surpass U.S. in Internet use (2001, August 13–19). *The Asian Wall Street Journal Weekly Edition,* p. 13.

Books

Pearson, J., West, R., & Turner, L. (1995). *Gender and communication* (3rd ed.). Madison, WI: Brown & Benchmark.

Again, the authors' names are in reverse order for accurate alphabetization; the last author's name, date of publication, and book title are followed by periods. The place of publication is followed by a colon, and the name of the publisher is followed by a period. A bibliographic entry must specify the book pages if the entire book was not used.

For a book with two authors, use an ampersand (&) before the second surname. If a book has more than three authors, use commas to separate all the names and use an ampersand before the final surname.

Internet

Author, I. (date). Title of article. *Name of periodical* [Electronic version], *xx*, pages. Retrieved (date) from (URL).

An example of a citation, from a website would look like this:

Smith, G. (2002). Life in the City. *Journal of Urban Life* [Electronic version], *5*, 110–120. Retrieved from http://jbr.org.

Bibliographic references to material taken from the Internet are fraught with difficulty because of unknowns and possibly missing information. For instance, dates are often difficult to locate in online articles. If one is available, use the listed year of publication. Otherwise, you can use the date of the material's most recent update or, as a last resort, the precise date of your search.

The most important issue to keep in mind is that a reference is designed to enable someone else to locate the material you used in your presentation. Therefore, include as much information in your Internet reference as you can. If possible, conform the reference to the format above. Note that the italicized "*xx*" refers to a volume number when applicable. Also note that the reference does not end in a period because a period in the wrong place renders most Internet addresses unusable.

For more examples of Internet bibliographic entries, refer to the accompanying e-note, which lists websites dealing with this subject.

Interviews

Meister, M. (2001, August 15). [Personal interview].

Pamphlets, handbooks, and manuals may not have complete information about who wrote them, who published them, or when they were published. In that case, you are expected to provide as much information as possible so that others can verify the source.

If you run across sources you do not know how to place in bibliographic form, you can ask your bookstore or a librarian for *The Publication Manual of the American Psychological Association, The MLA Handbook* or *The Chicago Manual of Style*. An excellent reference work designed for communication students is *A Style Manual for Communication Majors* (Bourhis, Adams, & Titsworth, 1999).

College composition texts also include the standard forms for footnote and bibliographic entries.

Chapter Review

In this chapter you have learned the following:

- An effective introduction fulfills five functions, which can occur in any order:
  - To gain and maintain audience attention.
  - To arouse audience interest in the topic.
  - To state the purpose of the presentation.
  - To describe the presenter's qualifications.
  - To forecast the organization and development of the presentation.
- An effective outline for a presentation follows six principles:
  - It relates the information presented to the immediate purpose and long-range goal.
  - It is an abstract of the message you will deliver.
  - It expresses ideas in single units of information.
  - It indicates the importance of items with rank-ordered symbols.
  - It provides margins that indicate the importance of each entry visually.
  - It states entries in parallel form (e.g., complete sentences, as in this list).
- The most frequently used patterns of organization in public presentations are:
  - Time-sequence pattern, or chronology, with items presented serially over time.
  - Topical-sequence pattern, with items listed as a limited number of qualities or characteristics.
  - Problem/solution pattern, which poses a problem followed by a suggested solution.
  - Spatial relations pattern, which shows how items are related in space.
  - Cause/effect pattern, which posits a cause that results in some effect.
- Transitions and signposts link ideas and indicate direction to the audience.
- An effective conclusion fulfills certain functions:
  - It forewarns the listeners that the presentation is about to end.
  - It reminds the audience of the central idea and main points of your presentation.
  - It specifies what you expect from the audience as a result of the presentation.
  - It ends the presentation in a manner that encourages the audience to think and act as you recommend.
- Often a bibliography, a list of sources, accompanies the complete outline.

⊚ VIDEO LINK: A BIG INTRODUCTION

Video Episode 6: "Reporting for KTNT: Susan Elliott"

When organizing your presentation, it is advisable—in fact, necessary—to have a clearly developed introduction, body, and conclusion. Such basic organization is common in other aspects of our lives. Our essays and term papers follow a similar organization. In "Reporting for KTNT: Susan Elliot," Susan prepares her application tape for an internship with two local TV stations. How does Susan's application tape follow the organization process recommended in this chapter? What strategies does Susan use for her attention-gaining strategy and what does this teach you about the role of audience analysis in organizing a speech?

ISSUES IN COMMUNICATION: MAKING A DIFFERENCE

This Issues in Communication narrative is designed to provoke individual thought or discussion about concepts raised in the chapter.

Jim Davis's 13-year-old-son died several years ago when another junior high student opened fire in the school cafeteria. Since that time, Jim has poured his energy and time into researching the possible causes and prevention of violence in schools. He has become an authority on the subject, and people frequently ask him to speak at different events. He recently accepted an invitation to speak on violence to a group of parents at a junior high school in a nearby town.

Violence is a broad topic, so Jim knew he needed to narrow his focus to an area that would be relevant to his audience. He chose to talk about violence in the media, which can lead to more violence in our schools. His immediate goal was to help the parents understand the effect of media violence. His long-term goal was to challenge them to watch television with their children and then discuss the violent content of the programs and how it affects us in reality.

He prepared his presentation carefully and spent several hours examining his final key-word outline to ensure that every point related to his overall goals and to the topic at hand. He decided to start his presentation by showing several clips from television shows and movies that cast violence in a humorous light. He knew he would end up using several different videocassettes throughout the presentation, so he cued each cassette to begin exactly where he wanted it to, labeled them all, and then noted on his outline when he should start the video and what cassette he should use.

After he played the introductory clips, he decided to tell the story of his son's death to raise the question of the connection between fictional and real-life violence. He would then state his thesis: Television and movies find ways to make us laugh at violence, and this leads to a more violent society. He would also explain that he would give them a few simple techniques to use with their own children that would help combat the effects of violence on television.

Throughout the body of his presentation, he used short clips from popular television shows and quoted from well-known sources. He was always careful to use plenty of supporting evidence from respected sources, since he couldn't rely only on his personal experience to persuade others. After working hard to organize and practice his speech, he felt confident that he would do a good job.

Right before the meeting where he was to give his presentation, Jim talked to the person who would be introducing him. Jim asked him to include a few specific notes about himself, especially the articles he had written for several journals and his participation in research on violence at a state university.

His hard work paid off. The speech went smoothly, and as he made eye contact with different members of the audience, he could sense their concentration on what he was saying. When he explained the importance and effectiveness of talking with kids about what they see on TV, several parents nodded in agreement. In conclusion, he showed a last series of video clips and he didn't hear a single chuckle from anyone. He reviewed his main points and encouraged parents to talk with their kids to prevent losing more children to violence.

After the meeting, many parents stayed to talk with Jim and ask him questions. Several people asked if they could get together with him at a later date to continue their discussion. Jim went home that night feeling that he had fulfilled his goals with this speech and had made a difference in some people's lives.

Apply what you have learned about introducing, organizing and concluding a presentation as you ponder and discuss the following questions: Which functions of an introduction did Jim fulfill? How did he do it? How did he use the body of his speech to persuade and inform his audience? How did his choice of a key-word outline help during his presentation? What techniques did he use to hold his audience's attention and increase his own credibility in their eyes?

KEY TERMS

Use the *Human Communication* CD-ROM and the *Online Learning Center* at www.mhhe.com/pearson to further your understanding of the following terminology.

Bibliography	Long-range goal	Signposts
Body	Main points	Spatial/relations
Brakelight function	Organizational patterns	organization
Cause/effect pattern	Outline	Subpoints
Conclusion	Parallel form	Time-sequence pattern
Immediate purpose	Problem/solution pattern	Topical-sequence pattern
Introduction	Rough draft	Transition
Key-word outline	Sentence outline	

SELF-QUIZ

Go to the self-quizzes on the *Human Communication* CD-ROM and the *Online Learning Center* at www.mhhe.com/pearson to test your knowledge.

ADDITIONAL RESOURCES

Adams, T., & Clark, N. (2001). *The Internet: Effective online communication.* Fort Worth, TX: Harcourt.

Bourhis, J., Adams, C., & Titsworth, S. (1999). *A style manual for communication majors* (5th ed.). New York: McGraw-Hill.

Cooren, F., & Taylor, J. R. (1997). Organization as an effect of mediation: Redefining the link between organization and communication. *Communication Theory, 21*(2), 262–264.

Doyle, T., & Gotthoffer, D. (2001). *Speech communication on the Net.* Boston: Allyn & Bacon.

Hager, P. J. (1997). *Designing and delivering scientific, technical, and managerial presentations.* New York: Wiley.

REFERENCES

Adams, T., & Clark, N. (2001). *The Internet: Effective online communication.* Ft. Worth, TX: Harcourt.

American Psychological Association. (1994). *Publication manual of the American Psychological Association* (4th ed.). Washington, DC: Author.

Bell, T. H. (1984, January 6). State school official pleased by Ohio's grade. *Athens Messenger,* p. 13.

Bourhis, J., Adams, C., & Titsworth, S. (1999). *A style manual for communication majors* (5th ed.). New York: McGraw-Hill.

Cooren, F., & Taylor, J. R. (1997). Organization as an effect of mediation: Redefining the link between organization and communication. *Communication Theory, 21*(2), 262–264.

Dodes, R. L. (2001, August). "Free love: The oldest profession is recession proof." *Business Forward,* pp. 28–34.

Doyle, T., & Gotthoffer, D. (2001). *Speech communication on the net.* Boston: Allyn & Bacon.

Five percent of tobacco pact goes to prevention. (2001, August 12). *The Washington Post,* p. A12.

Hacker, D. (1995). *A writer's reference* (3rd ed.). Boston: Bedford Books of St. Martin's Press.

Hager, P. J. (1997). *Designing and delivering scientific, technical, and managerial presentations.* New York: Wiley.

Hentoff, N. (1998, December 26). The hecklers' veto. *The Washington Post,* p. A19.

Rogers, E., & Hart, W. (2001). New communication technology and the changing nature of conversation. In W. Edie & P. E. Nelson (Eds.), *Conversation in America: Changing rules, hidden dimensions.* Newbury Park, CA: Sage.

Samiei, H. V. (2001, August 7). Depression is more common before than after childbirth. *The Washington Post,* p. F7.

Smith, M. (1998). Sexual intercourse and persuasion. Speech presented in Spring Quarter, Interpersonal Communication 342, Communication and Persuasion, Ohio University, Athens.

Von Drehle, D. (2001, September 17–23). Our Pearl Harbor. *The Washington Post* (National Weekly Edition), p. 6.

What on earth? (2001, August 11). *The Washington Post,* p. A14.

Yardley, J. (1998, August 3). For heaven's sake, lawyers, haven't you ever heard of free speech? *The Washington Post,* p. D2.

CHAPTER SIXTEEN

> Courage is grace under pressure.
>
> **ERNEST HEMINGWAY**

> Nothing great was ever achieved without enthusiasm.
>
> **RALPH WALDO EMERSON**

Delivery and Visual Resources

What will you learn?

When you have read and thought about this chapter, you will be able to:

1. State the advantages and disadvantages of each mode of delivery.
2. Name and explain each of the vocal aspects of delivery.
3. Name and explain each of the bodily aspects of delivery.
4. Understand when and why you should use visual aids in your speech.
5. Demonstrate the use of visual aids effectively and correctly in a speech.

any presentations with good content never reach the listener because of poor delivery skills. This chapter explores the delivery of your presentation and the various visual aids you may use in your presentation. You will discover four modes of delivery and the various vocal and bodily aspects of delivery. The final section of this chapter examines some visual aids you can use in your speech—from chalkboards to electronic presentations—and explains how to use them. Read the chapter carefully and you can avoid many problems faced by beginning speakers.

Reggie Washington was a talented quarterback on the university's varsity football team and a tough competitor on the field. But now, sitting in front of an audience of middle school football players and their parents, it was Reggie's turn to be afraid. Reggie's coach had asked him to come to an awards banquet and give a speech—flattered, he had agreed at once, but he quickly came to regret that decision. He thought about the impending speech constantly, and he hadn't slept well either. When it was finally his turn to talk, he fidgeted with his tie, kept his eyes glued to the speech he had written out word for word, heard himself saying "ummm" a lot, and felt his knees weakening. When he finished speaking and sat down, he realized he was out of breath from talking so fast.

Julia Gustaferro was an engineering student who loved technology. Unlike Reggie, who dreaded public speaking, she looked forward to giving her speech because she was already familiar with PowerPoint. She prepared her entire speech on her computer, using snappy graphics, fonts, and fading techniques. She delivered the speech in a dim room, her new super laserpointer piercing the semidarkness. The PowerPoint presentation unfolded without a hitch. Julia was surprised when she received a mediocre grade from her public-speaking teacher for being "overly dependent" on her visual aids, for letting PowerPoint do her speech for her, and for not showing her face during the presentation.

This chapter is dedicated to helping people like Reggie and Julia learn effective vocal and bodily methods of delivery—learn how to strike an appropriate balance between content and personal presentation.

Discussion Question

Have the class discuss the relative importance of delivery style and content. Is content more important or is delivery? Feel free to provide your own reflections.

What Is Delivery?

delivery

The presentation of a speech by using your voice and body to reinforce your message.

Teaching Tip

Stress that students' grades on speeches are not overly dependent on delivery. Students tend to worry most about delivery, which increases apprehension.

Delivery is *the presentation of a speech by using your voice and body to reinforce your message.* People have contradictory ideas about the importance of speech delivery. Some people think "It's not what you say but how you say it that really counts." According to others, "What you say is more important than how you say it." Actually, what you say *and* how you say the message are both important, but some researchers suggest that the influence of delivery on audience comprehension is overrated (Petrie, 1963). Those who challenge the importance of delivery do not say that delivery is unimportant but that, in evaluating the relative importance of delivery and content, content is more important than delivery. That said, the effective public speaker cannot ignore the importance of delivery.

The four modes of delivery—extemporaneous, impromptu, manuscript, and memorized—vary in the amount of preparation required and their degree of spontaneity. Although the four modes are all possible choices, students of public speaking are least likely to use the manuscript and memorized modes. They may be asked to try the impromptu mode at times, but most speech assignments require the extemporaneous mode.

What Are Four Modes of Delivery?

The Extemporaneous Mode

A presentation delivered in the **extemporaneous mode** is *carefully prepared and practiced, but the presenter delivers the message conversationally without heavy dependence on notes.* This mode is message- and audience-centered, with the speaker focused not on the notes but on the ideas being expressed. Considerable eye contact, freedom of movement and gesture, the language and voice of conversation, and the use of an outline or key words to keep the speaker from reading or paying undue attention to the written script characterize this mode.

The word *extemporaneous* literally means "on the spur of the moment" in Latin; however, as practiced in the classroom, this mode of delivery only appears to be spontaneous. The speaker may choose different words as the speech is practiced and as the speaker finally delivers the message, but the focus is on communicating the message to the audience.

You have seen this mode of delivery in the classroom, in some professors' lectures, sometimes in the pulpit, often in political and legal addresses, and usually in speeches by athletes, businesspeople, and community leaders who are experienced speakers. This mode is the one you will learn best in the classroom and the one that has the most utility outside the classroom.

The Impromptu Mode

In the **impromptu mode,** *you deliver a presentation without notes, plans, or formal preparation and with spontaneity and conversational language.* The word *impromptu* comes from Latin and French roots and means "in readiness."

You use the impromptu mode when you answer a question in class, when you say who you are, and when you give people directions on the street. You cannot say much in these situations unless you are "in readiness,"

extemporaneous mode

A carefully prepared and researched speech delivered in a conversational style.

Video Activity

Ask students to view the video segment "On the Air with Campus-Community Connection." What type of delivery mode was used by the two speakers?

Video Activity

Ask students to view the video segment "Senior Seminar." Both Susan and Ricky "present" information on potential topics for the show. What types of presentation style did they use for these short presentations?

impromptu mode

Delivery of a speech without notes, plans, or preparation; characterized by spontaneity and informal language.

unless you know the answers. Ordinarily, this mode of delivery requires no practice, no careful choice of language. The impromptu mode encourages you to "think on your feet" without research, preparation, or practice.

The Manuscript Mode

manuscript mode

Delivery of a speech from a script of the entire speech.

As the name implies, in the **manuscript mode,** *you deliver a presentation from a script of the exact words to be used.* The advantage of this mode is that the presenter knows exactly what to say. The disadvantages of this mode are that the written message invites a speaker to pay more attention to the script than to the audience, discourages eye contact, and prevents response to audience feedback.

Politicians, especially those who are likely to be quoted, as well as clergy and professors, sometimes use this mode of delivery, but students are rarely asked to use this mode except in oral interpretation of literature.

The Memorized Mode

memorized mode

Delivering a speech that has been committed to memory.

Discussion Question

Discuss the four modes of delivery. Have the class identify real speaking situations where they would likely need to use each mode. The extemporaneous mode is most common in speaking situations.

A presentation delivered in the **memorized mode** is *committed to memory.* This mode requires considerable practice and allows ample eye contact, movement, and gestures. However, this mode discourages the speaker from responding to feedback, from adapting to the audience during the speech, and from choosing words that might be appropriate at the moment. In other words, memorization removes spontaneity and increases the danger of forgetting. You have experienced this mode if you ever acted in a play and memorized your part. Politicians, athletes, and businesspeople who speak to the same kind of audience about the same subjects often end up memorizing their speeches. Even professors, when they teach a class for the third time that week, may memorize the lesson for the day.

As a student in the communication classroom, you need to avoid overrehearsing your presentation so much that you memorize the script. Most communication teachers and audiences respond negatively to speeches that sound memorized. As one person put it, "Any presentation that 'sounds memorized'—and most memorized presentations do—never lets the audience get beyond the impression that the speaker's words are not really his or her own, even if they are."

The mode you choose should be appropriate for the message, the audience, and the occasion. Students use the extemporaneous mode most often in learning public speaking because that mode teaches good preparation, adaptation to the audience, and focus on the message. Nonetheless, mode of delivery does not determine effectiveness. Comparing extemporaneous and memorized modes, two researchers concluded that the mode is not what makes the speaker effective. Instead, the speaker's ability is more important. Some speakers are more effective with extemporaneous speeches than with manuscripts, but some speakers use both modes with equal effectiveness (Hildebrandt & Stephens, 1963).

Think, Pair, Share

TRY THIS

Think of places during and after a presentation when you might use the four modes of delivery. Would you ever choose to read a portion of your speech? Would you ever use the impromptu mode? Can you imagine a situation where part of your presentation might be memorized?

Class Activity

Allow student to practice effective vocal delivery by doing the exercise "Poetry in Motion" found in the instructor's manual.

What Are the Vocal and Bodily Aspects of Delivery?

As you have already observed, delivery is how your voice and body affect the meaning of your presentation. They are important parts of the message you communicate to your audience.

Effective speech delivery has many advantages. Research indicates that effective delivery—the appropriate use of voice and body in public speaking—contributes to the credibility of the speaker (Bettinghaus, 1961). Indeed, student audiences characterize the poorest speakers by their voices and the physical aspects of delivery (Henrikson, 1944). Poor speakers are judged to be fidgety, nervous, and monotonous. They also maintain little eye contact and show little animation or facial expression (Gilkinson & Knower, 1941). Good delivery increases the audience's capacity for handling complex information (Vohs, 1964). Thus public speakers' credibility—the audience's evaluation of them as good or poor speakers—and their ability to convey complex information may all be affected by the vocal and bodily aspects of delivery.

Class Activity

To help students become more aware of vocal aspects of delivery, do the exercise "Observing the Vocal Aspects of Delivery" found in the instructor's manual.

Video Activity

Ask students to view the video segment "On the Air with Campus-Community Connection." Have students analyze the vocal and nonvocal aspects of delivery used by the speakers in the segment.

The Vocal Aspects of Speech Delivery

Studying the vocal aspects of speech delivery is like studying music. The words of a speech are like musical notes. As people speak, they create music. Just as different musicians can make the same notes sound quite different, public speakers can say words in different ways to get the

487

audience to respond in various ways. The seven vocal aspects of delivery are pitch, rate, pauses, volume, enunciation, fluency, and vocal variety.

Pitch

pitch

The highness or lowness of a speaker's voice; technically, the frequency of sound made by vocal cords.

Pitch is *the highness or lowness of a speaker's voice*—the voice's upward and downward movement, the melody produced by the voice. Pitch is what makes the difference between the "ohhh" you utter when you earn a poor grade in a class and the "ohhh" you utter when you see something or someone really attractive. The "ohhh" looks the same in print, but when the notes turn to music, the difference between the two expressions is vast. The pitch of your voice can make you sound either lively or listless. As a speaker, you learn to avoid the two extremes: You avoid the lack of change in pitch that results in a monotone, and you avoid repeated changes in pitch that result in a singsong delivery. The best public speakers use the full range of their normal pitch.

Control of pitch does more than make a speech sound pleasing. Changes in pitch can actually help an audience remember information (Woolbert, 1920). Voices perceived as "good" are characterized by a greater range of pitch, more upward inflections, more downward inflections, and more pitch shifts (Black, 1942). Certainly, one of the important features of pitch control is that pitch can alter the way an audience responds to the words. Presenters produce many subtle changes in meaning by changes in pitch. The speaker's pitch tells an audience whether the words are a statement or a question, whether the words mean what they say, and whether the speaker is expressing doubt, determination, irony, or surprise.

Presenters learn pitch control only through regular practice. An actor who is learning to deliver a line has to practice that line many times and in many ways before being sure that most people in the audience will understand the words as intended. The effective presenter practices a speech before friends to discover whether the words are being understood as intended. You may sound angry when you do not intend to, opposed when you intend to sound doubtful, or frightened when you are only surprised. You are not always the best judge of how you sound to others, so you have to seek out and place some trust in other people's evaluations.

Rate

rate

The speed at which speech is delivered, normally between 125 and 190 words per minute.

How fast should you speak when delivering a public presentation? Teachers often caution students to "slow down" because talking fast is a sign of anxiety or nervousness. Debaters speak very rapidly, but usually their opponents understand their message. What is the best way for you to deliver your speech?

Rate is *the speed of delivery*, or how fast you say your words. The normal rate for Americans is between 125 and 190 words per minute, but many variations occur. You need to remember that your rate of delivery depends on you—how fast you normally speak—and on the situation—few people talk fast at a funeral. Rate also depends on the audience and the subject matter. For example, children listening to a story understand better at slower rates, and complex materials may require more patient timing and more repetition.

Pauses

A third vocal characteristic of speech delivery is the **pause**, *an absence of vocal sound used for dramatic effect, transition, or emphasis of ideas.* Presentations are often a steady stream of words, without silences, yet pauses can be used for dramatic effect and to get an audience to consider content. The speaker may begin a speech with rhetorical questions: "Have you had a cigarette today? Have you had two or three? Ten or eleven? Do you know what your habit is costing you in a year? A decade? A lifetime?" After each rhetorical question, a pause allows each member of the audience to answer the question mentally.

On the other hand, **vocalized pauses** are *breaks in fluency that negatively affect an audience's perception of the speaker's competence and dynamism.* The "ahhhs" and "mmhhs" of the beginning speaker are disturbing and distracting. Unfortunately, even some experienced speakers have the habit of filling silences with vocalized pauses. One group teaches public speaking to laypersons by having members of the audience drop a marble into a can every time a speaker uses a vocalized pause. The resulting punishment, the clanging of the cans, breaks the habit. A more humane method might be to rehearse your speech before a friend who signals you every time you vocalize a pause so that you vocalize less often when you deliver your speech to an audience. One speech instructor hit on the idea of rigging a light to the lectern so that every time a student speaker used a vocalized pause, the light went on for a moment. Try not to fear silence when you give your speech. Many audiences would prefer a little silence to vocalized pauses.

One way to learn how to use pauses effectively in public speaking is to listen to how your classmates use them. You should also listen to professional presenters. Watch a talk show host such as Jay Leno or David Letterman during his monologue, watch news anchors and field reporters, listen to radio personalities who do commentary and opinion, and watch and listen to people who give public lectures on campus for ideas on how to use pauses effectively.

Volume

Volume is *the relative loudness of your voice,* but volume is more than just loudness. Variations in volume can convey emotion, importance, suspense, and changes in meaning. You can use a stage whisper in front of

pause

The absence of vocal sound used for dramatic effect, transition, or emphasis of ideas.

vocalized pauses

Breaks in fluency; filling in silences with meaningless words or sounds that negatively affect an audience's perception of the speaker's competence and dynamism.

volume

The loudness or softness of a person's voice.

Electronic devices can enhance projection.

enunciation

The pronunciation and articulation of sounds and words.

an audience, just as you would whisper a secret to a friend. You can speak loudly and strongly on important points and let your voice carry your conviction. Volume can change with the situation. For example, a pep rally may be filled with loud, virtually shouted speeches teeming with enthusiasm, whereas a eulogy may be delivered at a lower, respectful volume. An orchestra never plays so quietly that patrons cannot hear, but the musicians vary their volume. Similarly, a presenter who considers the voice an instrument learns how to speak softly, loudly, and everywhere in between to convey meaning.

Enunciation

Enunciation, the fifth vocal aspect of speech delivery, is *the pronunciation and articulation of sounds and words.* Because people's reading vocabulary is larger than their speaking vocabulary, in speeches they may use words they have rarely or never heard before. To deliver unfamiliar words is risky. One student in a communication class gave a speech about the human reproductive system. During the speech, he managed to mispronounce nearly half the words used to describe the female anatomy. The speaker sounded incompetent to his audience. Rehearsing in front of friends, roommates, or family is a safer way to try out your vocabulary and pronunciation on an audience. Your objective should be to practice unfamiliar words until they are easy for you to pronounce and you are comfortable with them. Also be alert to the names of people you quote, introduce, or cite in your speech.

Audiences are impressed when a student speaker correctly pronounces such names as Goethe, Monet, and de Chardin.

Pronunciation is *the conformity of the speaker's production of words with agreed-upon rules about the sounds of vowels and consonants, and for syllabic emphasis.* The best way to avoid pronunciation errors is to look up unfamiliar words in a dictionary. Every dictionary has a pronunciation key. For instance, the entry for the word *belie* in the *Random House Dictionary of the English Language* looks like this:

> be-lie (bi lī'), v.t.,-lied, -ly-ing. 1. to show to be false; contradict: His trembling hands belied his calm voice . . .*

The entry indicates that the word *belie* has two syllables. The pronunciation key states that the first *e* should be pronounced like the *i* in *if*, the *u* in *busy*, or the *ee* in *been*. The *i*, according to the pronunciation key, should be pronounced like the *ye* in *lye*, the *i* in *ice*, or the *ais* in *aisle*. The accent mark (') indicates which syllable should receive heavier emphasis. You should learn how to use the pronunciation key in a dictionary, but if you still have some misgivings about how to pronounce a word, you should ask your teacher for assistance.

Another way to improve your pronunciation is to prolong syllables. Prolonging the syllables can make even a simple statement dramatic. Prolonging vowel sounds, for instance, gives your voice a resonance attractive to audiences. Prolonging syllables can also make you easier to understand, especially if you are addressing a large audience, an audience assembled outdoors, or an audience in an auditorium without a microphone. The drawing out of syllables can be overdone, however. Some radio and television newspersons hang onto the final syllable so long the practice draws attention to itself.

Articulation—*the production of sounds*—is another important part of enunciation. Poor articulation is so common that people tell articulation jokes. One adult remembers hearing a song about "Willie the Cross-eyed Bear" in Sunday school. The actual song title was "Willing the Cross I Bear." Some children have heard the Lord's Prayer mumbled so many times they think that one of the lines is either "hollow be thy name" or "Howard be thy name."

Articulation problems are less humorous when they occur in your own presentation. They occur because we often articulate carelessly. Among the common articulation problems are the dropping of final consonants and "-ing" sounds ("goin'," "comin'," and "leavin'"), the substitution of "fer" for "for," and the substitution of "ta" for "to." An important objective in public presentations as in all communication is to state words clearly for accurate transmission.

pronunciation

The conformity of the speaker's production of words with agreed-upon rules about the sounds of vowels and consonants, and for syllabic emphasis.

articulation

The production of sounds; a component of enunciation.

---

*From *The Random House Dictionary of the English Language.* Reprinted by permission of Random House, Inc.

Fluency

The sixth vocal characteristic of delivery is **fluency**—*the smoothness of the delivery, the flow of the words, and the absence of vocalized pauses.* Fluency cannot be achieved by looking up words in a dictionary or by any other simple solution. Fluency is not even very noticeable. Listeners are more likely to notice errors than to notice the seemingly effortless flow of words in a well-delivered speech. Also, you can be too fluent. A speaker who seems too glib is sometimes considered dishonest. One study showed the importance of fluency: The audiences tended to perceive the speaker's fluency and smoothness of presentation as a main determinant of effectiveness (Hayworth, 1942).

To achieve fluency, public speakers must be confident about the content of their speeches. If the speakers know what they are going to say and have said it over and over in practice, then they reduce disruptive repetition and vocalized pauses. If speakers master what they are going to say and focus on the overall rhythm of the speech, their fluency improves. Speakers must pace, build, and time the various parts of the speech so they unify in a coherent whole.

Vocal Variety

The seventh vocal aspect of speech delivery—one that summarizes many of the others—is **vocal variety.** This term refers to *voice quality, intonation patterns, inflections of pitch, and syllabic duration.* Public presentations encourage vocal variety because studies show variety improves effectiveness. One of the founders of the National Communication Association, Charles Woolbert, in a very early study of public reading, found that audiences retain more information when there are large variations in rate, force, pitch, and voice quality. More recently, researcher George Glasgow studied an audience's comprehension of prose and poetry and found that comprehension decreased 10 percent when the presenter delivered material in a monotone. Another study proved that audience members understand more when listening to skilled speakers than when listening to unskilled speakers. They also recall more information immediately after the speech and at a later date. The skilled speakers are more effective, whether the material is organized or disorganized, easy or difficult. Good vocalization was also found to include fewer but longer pauses, greater ranges of pitch, and more upward and downward inflections (Beighley, 1952; Black, 1942; Glasgow, 1952; Woolbert, 1920).

Guidelines for Improving Vocal Aspects of Delivery

As you conclude this section on the vocal aspects of speech delivery, the nonverbal aspects of public speaking, you may wonder how you can improve in all these areas. One thing is certainly true: Reading about aspects

FACTS ABOUT DELIVERY

With your classmates in a small group list as many facts as you can about vocal aspects of delivery, without looking at the text. Then try to add to your lists with an open book. Much is known, but most of what is known is based on old studies because few researchers have studied delivery in recent years.

of delivery does little or nothing to improve your performance. Delivery is not something you read about; delivery is something you do. Here are some specific suggestions for improving the vocal aspects of your speech:

1. *Choose one aspect of vocal delivery, and work on it until you are confident enough to move to another.* Do not think that you have to improve in all areas at once. Most likely, you are already competent in some aspects of vocal delivery and need improvement only in a few areas. If you think—and others have told you—that you speak in a monotone, perhaps you ought to start working on vocal variety. You decide what you need to improve and then move to the following step.

2. *Try practicing the skill in your everyday life.* You already use most of the vocal aspects of delivery in conversation: rate, volume, variety, and so on. Often the person who speaks without vocal variety in a public speech talks that way to friends as well. To improve your skill in that area, you can consciously practice making your voice more expressive. Do not think you can work on improving your skills only when you are performing in the classroom. You can improve every time you talk to somebody. Unlike your chemistry, biology, or physics class, where much of what you practice must be done in the laboratory, your communication class has your world as its lab, and you can do your experiments any time you wish.

3. *Be doggedly determined about improvement.* You took many years to become the person you are today, and you will not change your behavior overnight. If you have always been a rapid-fire speaker, a soft-spoken whisperer, or a person who has never used an "-ing" ending, then you are going to have to be determined to achieve any change in your behavior. On the other hand, you should be confident in the knowledge that thousands of people like you learn how to improve their vocal delivery through persistent effort. You are not being asked to do the impossible, but neither should you be deceived into thinking that changing your vocal aspects is easy to achieve.

Next you will move from the vocal aspects of delivery to another non-verbal area—the bodily aspects of delivery.

Teaching Tip

Incorporating peer critiques can be rewarding and informative for students. Some students, however, may feel uncomfortable giving and/or receiving criticism from peers. Take time to discuss appropriate ways to provide meaningful feedback.

Class Activity

To help students become aware of the bodily aspects of delivery, have the class complete the exercise "Observing the Bodily Aspects of Delivery" found in the instructor's manual.

CD-ROM Activity

Ask students to view the animation titled "Effective Delivery Behaviors" found on the accompanying student CD-ROM. The animation explains various nonvocal aspects of effective delivery.

Video Activity

Ask students to view the video segment "On the Air with Campus-Community Connection." Have students analyze the vocal and nonvocal aspects of delivery used by the speakers in the segment.

gestures

Movements of the head, arms, and hands to illustrate, emphasize, or signal ideas in the speech.

TRY ◄►THIS

Try reading a few paragraphs from a story or poem to your spouse, roommate, or friend to test yourself on vocal aspects of delivery. Let your listener give you an opinion and advice about your oral reading skills. What are your strengths? What are your weaknesses? What can you do to improve on the weaknesses and take advantage of the strengths?

The Bodily Aspects of Speech Delivery

The four bodily aspects of speech delivery are gestures, facial expression, eye contact, and movement. These nonverbal indicators of meaning show how speakers relate to audiences, just as they show how individuals relate to each other. When you observe two persons busily engaged in conversation, you judge their interest in the conversation without hearing their words. Similarly, in public speaking, the nonverbal bodily aspects of delivery reinforce what the speaker is saying. Kramer and Lewis (1931) showed that audience members who can see the speaker comprehend more of the speech than do audience members who cannot see the speaker. Apparently, the speaker's bodily movements convey enough meaning to improve the audience's understanding of the message. See Figure 16.1 on the next page for active art on delivery.

Gestures

Gestures are *movements of the head, arms, and hands used to illustrate, emphasize, or signal ideas in a speech.* People rarely worry about gestures in a conversation, but when they give a speech in front of an audience, arms and hands seem to be bothersome. Perhaps people feel unnatural because public speaking is an unfamiliar situation. Do you remember the first time you drove a car, the first time you tried to swim or dive, or the first time you tried to kiss? The first time you give a speech, you might not feel any more natural than you did then. Nonetheless, physically or artistically skilled people make their actions look easy. A skilled golfer, a talented painter, and a graceful dancer all perform with seeming ease. Beginners make a performance look difficult. Apparently, human beings have to work diligently to make physical or artistic feats look easy.

What can you do to help yourself gesture naturally when you deliver your presentation? The answer lies in feelings and practice. When representatives from Mothers Against Drunk Driving (MADD) deliver speeches protesting lax laws on driving while intoxicated, they frequently present with sincerity and strong gestures. They also look very natural. The main reason for their natural delivery may be their feelings about the issue that they are discussing. They are upset, and they show their emotion in their words and movements. They are mainly concerned with getting their message across. You can also deliver a speech more naturally by concentrating on getting the message across. Self-conscious attention to your gestures is often self-defeating—the gestures look studied, rehearsed, or slightly out of rhythm with your message. Selecting a topic you find involving can have the unexpected benefit of improving your delivery, especially if you concentrate on your audience and your message.

Another way of learning to make appropriate gestures is to practice a speech in front of friends who are willing to make positive suggestions. Constructive criticism is also one of the benefits you can receive

Hand gestures reinforce the verbal message.

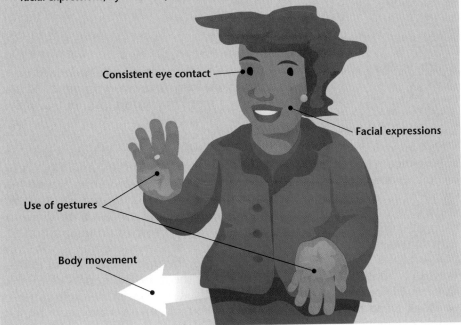

Effective delivery will not make a poorly prepared speech good, but it can make a well-prepared speech great. Effective delivery encompasses a variety of behaviors including variations in pitch and volume. Non-vocal aspects of effective delivery include gestures, facial expressions, eye contact, and movement.

Consistent eye contact

Facial expressions

Use of gestures

Body movement

Figure 16.1   Effective delivery behaviors.

Class Activity

Show students pictures of speaking situations (you can also use video without sound). Based only on observing the speaker's nonverbal behaviors, what inferences can the audience draw about what the speaker is saying?

Active Art

TABLE 16.1   SEVEN SUGGESTIONS FOR GESTURING EFFECTIVELY

1. Keep your hands out of your pockets and at your sides when not gesturing.

2. Do not lean on the lectern.

3. Gesture with the hand not holding your notes.

4. Make your gestures deliberate—big and broad enough so that they do not look accidental or timid.

5. Keep your gestures meaningful by using them sparingly and only when they reinforce something you are saying.

6. Practice your gestures just as you do the rest of your speech so that you become comfortable with the words and gestures.

7. Make your gestures appear natural and spontaneous.

SOURCE: From *Communication Works* by Teri Kwal Gamble and Michael Gamble, copyright © 1984 by Random House, Inc. Used by permission of Random House, Inc.

from your speech instructor and your classmates. Actors spend hours rehearsing lines and gestures so that they will look spontaneous and unrehearsed on stage. In time, and after many practice sessions, public speakers learn which arm, head, and hand movements seem to help and which seem to hinder their message. Through practice, you too can learn to gesture naturally, in a way that reinforces, rather than detracts from, your message (see Table 16.1).

Facial Expression

facial expression

Any nonverbal cue expressed by the speaker's face.

Another physical aspect of delivery is facial expression. Your face is the most expressive part of your body. **Facial expression** consists of *the nonverbal cues expressed by the speaker's face.* Eyebrows rise and fall; eyes twinkle, glare, and cry; lips pout or smile; cheeks can dimple or harden; and a chin can jut out in anger or recede in yielding. Some people's faces are a barometer of their feelings; others' faces seem to maintain the same appearance whether they are happy, sad, or in pain. Because you do not ordinarily see your own face when you are speaking, you may not be fully aware of how you appear when you give a speech. In general, speakers are trying to maintain a warm and positive relationship with the audience, and they signal that intent by smiling as they would in conversation with someone they like. However, the topic, the speaker's intent, the situation, and the audience all help determine the appropriate facial expressions in a public speech. You can discover the appropriateness of your facial expressions by having friends, relatives, or classmates tell you how you look when practicing your speech. You can also observe how famous people use facial expressions to communicate.

Eye Contact

Another physical aspect of delivery important to the public speaker is eye contact. **Eye contact** refers to *sustained and meaningful contact with the eyes with persons in the audience.* Too much eye contact, "staring down the audience," is too much of a good thing, but looking too much at notes—lack of eye contact—is poor delivery.

eye contact

The extent to which a speaker looks directly at the audience.

Audiences prefer maintenance of good eye contact (Cobin, 1962), and good eye contact improves source credibility (Beebe, 1974). Such conclusions are particularly important, since individuals in other cultures may view eye contact differently. A presenter from another country may be viewed less positively by an American audience than she would be in her native country. Similarly, Americans need to recognize and appreciate cultural differences in eye contact as well as other nonverbal cues.

Eye contact is one of the ways people indicate to others how they feel about them. People are wary of others who do not look them in the eye during a conversation. Similarly, in public speaking, eye contact conveys your relationship with your audience. The public speaker who rarely or never looks at the audience may appear disinterested in the audience, and the audience may resent being ignored. The public speaker who looks over the heads of audience members or scans audience members so quickly that eye contact is not established may appear to be afraid of the audience. The proper relationship between audience and speaker is one of purposeful communication. You signal that sense of purpose by treating audience members as individuals with whom you wish to communicate—by looking at them for responses to your message.

How can you learn to maintain eye contact with your audience? One way is to know your speech so well that you have to make only occasional glances at your notes. The speaker who does not know the speech well is manuscript-bound. Delivering an extemporaneous speech from key words or an outline is a way of encouraging yourself to keep an eye on the audience. One of the purposes of extemporaneous delivery is to enable you to adapt to your audience. That adaptation is not possible unless you are continually observing the audience's behavior to see if your listeners appear to understand your message.

Other ways of learning to use eye contact include scanning your entire audience and addressing various sections of the audience as you progress through your speech. Concentrating on the head nodders (not sleepers but affirmers) may also improve your eye contact. In almost every audience, some individuals overtly indicate whether your message is coming across. These individuals usually nod yes or no with their heads, thus the name *nodders*. Some speakers find that friendly faces and positive nodders improve their delivery.

Movement

bodily movement

What the speaker does with his or her entire body during a speech presentation.

A fourth physical aspect of delivery is **bodily movement**—*what the presenter does with his or her entire body during a speech presentation.* Sometimes the situation limits movement. The presence of a fixed microphone, a lectern, a pulpit, or any other physical feature of the environment may limit your activity. The length of the speech can also make a difference. A short speech without movement is less difficult for both speaker and audience than is a very long speech.

Good movement is appropriate and purposeful. The "caged lion" who paces back and forth to work off anxiety is moving inappropriately and purposelessly in relation to the content of the presentation. You should move for a reason, such as walking a few steps when delivering a transition, thereby literally helping your audience to "follow you" to the next idea. Some speakers move forward on the points they regard as most important.

Because of the importance of eye contact, the speaker should always strive to face the audience, even when moving. Some other suggestions on movement relate to the use of visual aids. Speakers who write on the chalkboard during a speech have to turn their backs on the audience. Avoid turning your back either by writing information on the board between classes or by using a poster or an overhead projector.

You can learn through practice and observation. Watch your professors, teaching assistants, and fellow students when they deliver their speeches to determine what works for them. They may provide positive or negative examples. Similarly, you will need to determine what works best for you when you practice your speech. The form in Table 16.2 can be used to evaluate nonverbal delivery.

TRY ◄ ►THIS

Attend a speech, sermon, or other public presentation and take notes on vocal and bodily aspects of the presenter's delivery. Use your observations as a basis for developing your own style of delivery.

What Are Visual Aids?

Do you learn best when you read something, when you watch something, or when you do something? Certainly, some skills are best learned by doing. Reading about how to program a VCR or watching another person perform the task is no substitute for trying to perform the task yourself. However, not everything lends itself to doing. You cannot do economics in the same way you can change a tire. Because so much of public speaking deals with issues and topics that cannot be performed, you must know the most effective methods of communicating in a public presentation.

TABLE 16.2   EVALUATION FORM FOR NONVERBAL ASPECTS OF DELIVERY

To summarize the material on vocal and bodily aspects of delivery, you should examine the sample evaluation form below. Use this scale to evaluate yourself and others on each of the following items: 1 = Excellent, 2 = Good, 3 = Average, 4 = Fair, 5 = Weak

VOCAL ASPECTS OF DELIVERY—THE VOICE

_____ Pitch: Upward and downward inflections

_____ Rate: Speed of delivery

_____ Pause: Appropriate use of silence

_____ Volume: Loudness of the voice

_____ Enunciation: Articulation and pronunciation

_____ Fluency: Smoothness of delivery

_____ Vocal variety: Overall effect of all of the above

BODILY ASPECTS OF DELIVERY

_____ Gestures: Use of arms and hands

_____ Facial expression: Use of the face

_____ Eye contact: Use of eyes

_____ Movement: Use of legs and feet

To determine if people remember best through telling alone, through showing alone, or through both showing and telling, researchers measured retention three hours and three days after a communication attempt. The results follow (Zayas-Boya, 1977–1978).

METHOD	RETENTION 3 HOURS LATER	RETENTION 3 DAYS LATER
TELLING ALONE	70%	10%
SHOWING ALONE	72	20
SHOWING AND TELLING	85	65

Apparently, people retain information longer when they receive the message both through their eyes *and* through their ears. Audiences that remember a message because the visual aids helped their comprehension are more persuaded by the presentation than are audiences that do not see visual aids.

Students sometimes think that public-speaking instructors like them to use visual aids, but they will not use visual aids for public speaking outside the classroom. In fact, the use of visual aids is big business. Can you imagine an architect trying to explain to a board of directors how the new building will look without using models, drawings, and computer graphics? Can you envision a business presentation without PowerPoint?

Class Activity

Divide students into small groups. Ask each student to develop a three-step dance routine to teach the class. Each group should be able to demonstrate and explain how to do the dance routine. Select one group to explain but not demonstrate their dance routine to the class. Ask a second group to demonstrate their dance routine with no verbal explanation. Ask a third group to verbally explain and demonstrate its dance routine. Use this activity to illustrate how visual aids and spoken messages work together to add clarity.

Video Activity

Ask students to view the video segment "Reporting for KTNT: Susan Elliott." How does Susan plan to use visual aids to make her application for the internship more effective?

Class Activity

To help students get practice using visual aids, have the class do the "object impromptu" speaking assignment described in the instructor's manual.

Can you sell most products without showing them? Apparently, the skillful use of visual aids is an expectation in the world of business and industry. The place to learn how to use visual aids is in the classroom.

What are **visual aids?** They are *any items that can be seen by an audience for the purpose of reinforcing a message,* from the way you dress, to words on the chalkboard, to items brought in to show what you are talking about. A student who wears a police uniform when talking about careers in law enforcement, one who provides a handout with an outline of her speech for the class, and yet another who brings in chemistry equipment are all using visual aids.

visual aids

Any items that can be seen by an audience for the purpose of reinforcing a message.

The Uses of Visual Aids

Class Activity

To help students distinguish between appropriate and inappropriate visual aids, have them complete the exercise found in the instructor's manual.

One of the main reasons for using visual aids has already been stated: People tend to learn and retain more when they both see and listen. The effective speaker knows when words alone will be insufficient to carry the message. Some messages are more effectively communicated through sight, touch, smell, and taste. Use visual aids when they reduce complexity for easier understanding (such as when you are explaining many or complex statistics or ideas) and when they support your message better than words (such as when you display a bar graph showing the increasing costs of home ownership). The use of visual aids demands that you become sensitive to what an audience will be unable to understand only through your words.

Visual aids are not appropriate for all speeches at all times. In fact, because they take preparation and planning, they may be impossible to use in many impromptu situations. Also, visual aids should not be used for their own sake. Having visual aids is no virtue unless they help the audience in understanding your message or unless they contribute in another way to your purpose.

Visual aids should be visible to the audience only when needed and should be out of sight during the rest of the presentation. Otherwise, visual aids can become a distraction that steals the focus from you. See Table 16.3 for additional hints on the use of visual aids.

Visual aids, like the facts in your speech, may require documentation. You should either show on the visual aid itself or tell the audience directly where you got the visual aid or the information on it.

TRY ◄►THIS

Are you especially good at something that could enhance your presentation? Can you draw, sing, play an instrument, take photos, or create a PowerPoint presentation? Sometimes your own talents and abilities can greatly strengthen your presentation.

TABLE 16.3   SOME HELPFUL HINTS FOR USING VISUAL AIDS

1. Do not talk to your visual aids. Keep your eyes on your audience.

2. Display visual aids only when you are using them. Before or after they are discussed, they usually become a needless distraction to the audience.

3. Make sure everyone in the room can see your visual aids. Check the visibility of your visual aid before your speech, during practice. If the classroom is 25 feet deep, have a friend or family member determine if the visual aid can be read from 25 feet away. Above all, make sure you are not standing in front of a visual aid.

4. Leave a visual aid in front of the audience long enough for complete assimilation. Few things are more irritating to an audience than to have a half-read visual aid whipped away by a speaker.

5. Use a pointer or your inside arm for pointing to a visual aid. The pointer keeps you from masking the visual, and using your inside arm helps you to avoid closing off your body from the audience.

Types of Visual Resources

What kinds of visual resource can you choose from? They are too numerous to catalog all of them here, but several of the primary sources used by public speakers are chalkboards, posters, opaque or overhead projectors, films and slides, videotapes, photographs, drawings, models and physical objects, handouts, yourself or an assistant, and electronic presentations.

Chalkboards

Chalkboards are the most readily available visual aid. Any statistics, facts, or details difficult to convey orally can be written on the chalkboard. You can write your name and the title of your speech on the chalkboard. You can also write down important or unusual words you use in your speech. You can use the chalkboard to list the items from your speech you want your audience to remember.

The following are some suggestions for using a chalkboard:

1. *Ask your instructor when writing on the chalkboard is appropriate.* Some instructors prefer that you write the information on the chalkboard before class, rather than between speeches.

2. *Practice writing on the chalkboard.* Writing legibly on a chalkboard actually takes some practice. You need to print legibly and large enough so that even people in the last row can read your words. Avoid that tooth-shattering squeal of the chalk on the chalkboard by using used chalk and writing with the chalk at an angle.

Teaching Tip

Forewarn students about which types of visual aid are *not* appropriate in your class (e.g., weapons, live animals, graphic pictures). Also, fully brief students about equipment that may be available for use (e.g., overhead projector, computer with projector, easel, VCR). Be prepared to show students how to use such technology. Indicate whether you deem hand-drawn visuals (e.g., hand-drawn poster or chalkboard renderings) acceptable.

3. *Practice delivering your speech while talking about items written on the chalkboard.* Try to face your audience while you speak, and use a pointer or your hand to direct the audience's attention to the statements or illustrations on the chalkboard.

A skillful presenter knows when to place the information on the chalkboard, how to write the information on the chalkboard, and how to deliver the speech when using the chalkboard. The effective speaker also knows what kinds of information should be placed on the chalkboard and whether telling, showing, or doing both will help the audience the most. Effective speakers use the chalkboard for "point clinchers," as a way to indicate to the audience the most important points in the speech (Haas & Packer, 1955).

Posters

Posters are another way to present your ideas visually. They are handier than the chalkboard because they can be prepared ahead of time. The general directions for creating an effective poster are similar to those listed for the chalkboard. The information on the poster should be information that is difficult to convey or to understand through listening. The information should be drawn or written in large scale so that people at the back of the room are able to see every word or illustration. The presenter should face the audience while working with the information on the poster; and the visual message should highlight important points.

The message on a poster may be a written message showing the number of calories in hamburgers from fast-food restaurants, stating the three primary reasons tuition should be raised, or listing the advantages of co-op bookstores. Remember to round off the numbers for easier understanding.

Three means of illustrating information on posters are bar graphs, pie charts, and line graphs. A *bar graph* helps you show an audience how a number of different items compare. For example, the bar graph in Figure 16.2 compares the amount of after-tax contributions to charity by American millionaires. As the bar graph clearly indicates, millionaires gave progressively less money to charity between 1980 and 1990.

The *pie chart* in Figure 16.3 shows what portion of the family budget goes for shelter, food, transportation, and entertainment. Although pie charts show proportions quite well, people are more likely to understand a bar graph than a pie chart. What percentage of the family income in the pie chart in Figure 16.2 is spent on entertainment? Naturally, the speaker could help by showing the percentages in each slice of the pie.

Figure 16.4 is an example of a *line graph,* showing the dramatic decline in the percentage of Americans who earn their living on a farm. The line graph helps the audience visualize the precipitous drop in numbers.

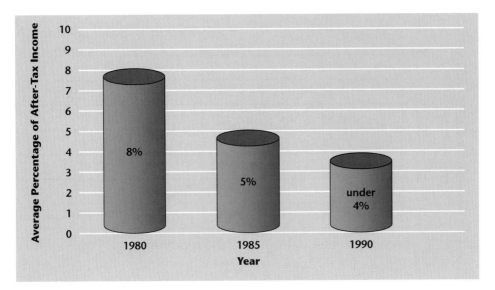

Figure 16.2   How much do millionaires give to charity?

SOURCE: Office of Tax Analysis, U.S. Department of Treasury.

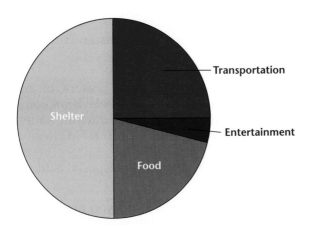

Figure 16.3   A pie chart.

Some suggestions for using posters follow:

1. Keep the message simple. A frequent problem with visual aids is too much clutter. The audience should be able to grasp your point quickly.

2. Use bar graphs rather than pie charts whenever possible because people tend to underestimate the relative area of circles (MacDonald-Ross, 1977).

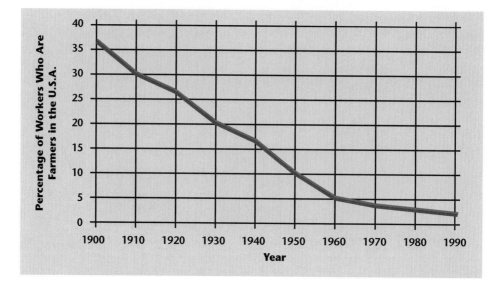

Figure 16.4   The line graph shows the dramatic decline in the number of farmers in the 20th century.

SOURCE: Data from U.S. Census Bureau and U.S. Dept. of Agriculture.

3. Use color and your artistic talents to make the poster attractive and to gain and maintain attention.
4. Be sure the poster is large enough for everyone to see.
5. Use ready-made posters or pictures, such as travel posters, or get hints for your own illustrations from those used on television commercials. Television advertisers tend to use outdoor, daytime shots, with one person but not crowds (Hebyallah & Maloney, 1977–1978).
6. Learn to use a flip chart—a series of posters. For special effects, uncover each item as you come to it.

Keep your poster in front of the audience as long as you are talking about the subject portrayed. In some cases, place the used poster on the chalk tray so that you can refer to your illustration again in your conclusion as you review the content of your speech.

Opaque or Overhead Projectors

Opaque and overhead projectors demand special equipment and practice, but they, too, have advantages in a speech. An opaque projector or Elmo, a small-object projector, can project a picture or print from a magazine or book or relatively small objects. Opaque projectors require dim lights and an empty wall or screen. An overhead projector can project transparencies or sheets of clear plastic on which the speaker can write with a special pencil or marker. Transparencies are best prepared ahead of time, but short messages can be printed on them as the speaker talks.

Films and Slides

Films and slides are good visual supplements to your speech as long as they do not become the speech. Both have the disadvantage of placing the audience and the speaker in the dark, where audience response is hidden. Even so, a one-minute film showing violence on the basketball court or five or six slides showing alternative energy sources can strengthen your presentation. When you use slides and films, you should check the equipment and rehearse. An upside-down slide or a jittery film can ruin your speech. You should also arrange for a classmate to turn off the lights so that you do not have to interrupt your speech by asking someone to turn off the lights or by doing it yourself.

Videotapes

Videotapes of movies, homemade videos, and portions of cable and network television offer the speaker another opportunity to fortify a speech. The downside of videos is that the speaker must supply and set up equipment, prepare the video carefully before presentation, and ensure that the equipment works properly. Resist the temptation to show too much. You should not let the video become the speech; instead, the video gains attention, provides support, or shows evidence that should not overshadow your personal contributions to the presentation. The shorter the speech, the shorter the video should be.

Photographs

Another kind of visual aid is photographs. A student who is speaking about Spanish architecture can use photographs of homes and public buildings. A student who is talking about identifying types of trees can have pictures of each type. And a student who is demonstrating how to assemble a bicycle can have a series of photographs to illustrate and clarify the point.

A word of warning about photographs: Ordinary-size photographs are too small to be seen easily by a classroom full of students. You should consider using enlarged, poster-size photographs for all to see. Passing around individual photographs is also a questionable practice because the audience will be distracted from your speech as they view the pictures individually. If you have a number of photos, the audience will still be looking at them when the next speaker gets up to speak.

Figure 16.5   A drawing used as a visual aid.

Drawings

Drawings are another type of visual aid useful in public speaking. Most line drawings are simple and are used to clarify. When you draw a map to show your audience how to get to a specific place, when you draw the human foot and name the bones, or when you draw a cartoon character, you are using drawings as visual aids. Figure 16.5 shows a drawing used by a student speaker to illustrate a healthy lifestyle.

Models, Physical Objects, and Animals

Living models and physical objects can also be used as visual aids. For a speech on fashion design, you can have people model the clothes. For a speech on exercise machines, you can have someone demonstrate the machine.

Physical objects might be the best visual aid if your presentation is about something small enough or controllable enough to show but large enough to be seen by everyone without being passed around. Students have brought in model cars, chemistry sets, musical instruments, mountain climbing equipment, weights, and volcanic lava. Live pets, however, can pose special problems for the speaker. Snakes, dogs, cats, hamsters, and monkeys have a unique ability to make fools of their owners. They also are often highly distracting before and during the speech. Finally, some public-speaking teachers or college or university rules prohibit animals in the classroom.

Handouts

Handouts are an especially effective way to communicate messages difficult to convey orally. One student passed out the American Cancer Society's list of cancer danger signs. Another distributed a handout with the names and call numbers of all the country-and-western music stations because he knew the audience was unlikely to remember all the names and numbers. Still another student distributed the contract used when people bequeath parts of their body to a medical center. Such handouts carry the impact of your speech beyond the classroom. They are usually kept, sometimes taken home where they are seen by others, and often discussed later by roommates and spouses.

Handouts have many advantages, but they also have some shortcomings. One shortcoming is that they can be very distracting to the audience and disturbing to the speaker. When distributed during your speech, the handout gets the focus of attention instead of you. The problem is not entirely solved when you distribute handouts at the end of your speech because then they steal the focus from the next speaker.

A second disadvantage is that handouts sometimes carry too much of the content of the speech and may become a substitute for the speech. The audience does not have to listen to the speech because they already have the message in print.

Yourself or an Assistant

Sometimes you or a friend or an acquaintance might be the best visual aid for your speech. You or your assistant can demonstrate karate, show some dance steps, or wear a lead apron. One of you can wear clothing appropriate for your speech: a suit when telling how to succeed in an interview for a white-collar job, a lab coat when demonstrating chemical reactions, or a uniform when telling why other students should join the ROTC program. One student wore an old flannel shirt, tattered jeans, and a rag tied around his head. He carried a lantern. His speech was about "steam tunneling," an unauthorized sport in which students explored the university's steam tunnels. He was faulted for encouraging his audience to participate in an activity strongly discouraged by the university administration, but he certainly was appropriately dressed for his speech.

Electronic Presentations

Finally, you may wish to use an electronic presentational software program as a visual aid. The use of such programs has become increasingly common in education and business. Many presentational software programs are available, but Microsoft's PowerPoint is one of the more popular ones. Most presentational software programs allow speakers to develop on-screen slide shows; use printed slides (including 35 millimeter);

TABLE 16.4   HELPFUL HINTS FOR SPEECH DELIVERY

1. Practice your speech so that you can deliver your message with only occasional glances at your notes.

2. Keep your eyes on your audience so that you can sense whether you are communicating your message.

3. Use facial expression, gestures, and movements to help communicate your message.

4. Use your voice like a musical instrument to keep the sounds interesting and to affect the audience's response.

5. Speak loudly enough for audience members to hear, slowly enough so that they can listen with understanding, and smoothy enough so that they do not focus on your faults.

6. Use visual images to communicate material not easily understood through listening.

7. Make your writing on the chalkboard or on posters large enough for all to see and simple enough for all to understand.

8. Consider using photographs, drawings, live models, objects, slides, films, handouts, videotapes, and yourself to help communicate your message.

9. Sound conversational, look natural, and strive to communicate your message to your listeners.

10. Observe how your classmates, professors, and other speakers deliver their speeches so you can learn from them.

Teaching Tip

Many students are very adept at using PowerPoint and other computer presentation software. If students have access to such technology in your classroom, it is wise to provide suggestions on how many slides are appropriate for their speeches. Though this guideline may vary greatly, one slide per minute is a good rule of thumb. Thus, if your maximum time limit for speeches is 7 minutes, students should attempt to have no more than seven PowerPoint slides.

make black-and-white or color transparencies; produce slide shows with customized transitions; create charts and graphs using graphic files; and make speaker notes, audience handouts, and speech outlines. You can also insert clip art on a slide; use dissolves as transitions; create builds (a bulleted list that begins with the first bullet on the first slide, then adds the second bullet onto the second slide, and so on); or scan in pictures, text, or other visuals. Presentational software also allows you to customize your presentation for different audiences.

As with other visual aids, you should note the helpful hints in Table 16.4 and you must follow certain guidelines when using presentational software in your speech:

1. *Don't rely too heavily on an electronic presentational tool.* As with any visual aid, your electronic presentation should enhance your speech, not become the speech. Your instructor needs to assess your delivery skills, not just your technical prowess.

2. *Avoid cluttered screens by minimizing words and images.* Stick to only a few words per slide and only a few words per line; then elaborate as needed when you give your speech. Graphic images can enhance your presentation, but too many graphics can distract your audience from your speech.

3. *Use an appropriate font, and don't use too many different typefaces.* The font is the size of your letters, and the typeface is the style of the letters. Don't use a font smaller than 48 points in your presentation. In a large lecture, use 60 to 72 points for headings and no less than 48 points for subtopics or additional explanations. As far as typefaces are concerned, stick with one or two typefaces in the same presentation.

4. *Practice your speech using your electronic presentational aid.* If possible, practice in the classroom in which you will give the speech with the equipment that you will use during your actual speech.

5. *Make sure everything is arranged in advance.* Before your presentation, check to make sure a room with the proper equipment is available and reserved for your presentation.

6. *Be prepared to abandon your electronic presentation.* In case of a power outage or faulty equipment, be prepared with handouts you can use instead.

Most presentational software packages are user-friendly, and often the software itself will lead you through the program. However, to learn about all the options that are available to you within a given software package, you may wish to take a short workshop, many of which are offered by college or university technology departments.

Chapter Review

SUMMARY

In this chapter you have learned the following:

- Four modes of delivery are
  - The extemporaneous mode, where the speech is carefully prepared but appears relatively spontaneous and conversational.
  - The impromptu mode, which actually is spontaneous and without specific preparation.
  - The manuscript mode, where the presenter uses a script throughout delivery.
  - The memorized mode, which employs a script committed to memory.
- Vocal aspects of delivery include
  - Pitch—the highness or lowness of the presenter's voice.
  - Rate—the speed of delivery.
  - Pauses—the purposeful silence to invite thought or response.
  - Volume—the loudness of the presenter's voice.
  - Enunciation—the pronunciation and articulation of words.
  - Fluency—the smoothness of delivery.
  - Vocal variety—voice quality, intonation patterns, inflections, and syllabic duration.
- Bodily aspect of delivery include
  - Gestures—movement of the head, arms, and hands.
  - Eye contact—sustained and meaningful attention to eyes and faces of audience members.
  - Facial expression—the variety of messages the face can convey.
  - Movement—the motion by the entire body but especially purposeful movement by the feet.
- Visual aids to reinforce or clarify the message include
  - Chalkboards
  - Posters
  - Projectors
  - Films
  - Slides
  - Videotapes
  - Photos
  - Drawings
  - Models and objects
  - Handouts
  - Yourself
  - Electronic software

◉ VIDEO LINK: DELIVERY WITH A PUNCH

Video Episodes 5 and 6: "On the Air with Campus-Community Connection" and "Reporting for KTNT: Susan Elliott"

Effective delivery is the process of using your voice and your body to reinforce your message. Watch "On the Air with Campus-Community Connection" and critique the two speakers' delivery styles. What aspects of their delivery are effective and what aspects need improvement? This chapter also discusses the role of visual aids in presentations. View "Reporting for KTNT: Susan Elliott" and consider the decisions Susan makes concerning visual materials she can include in her application tape. If you were advising her, what would you suggest including in her tape to give it the most impact?

ISSUES IN COMMUNICATION: STYLE AND SUBSTANCE

This Issues in Communication narrative is designed to provoke individual thought or discussion about concepts raised in the chapter.

Danny O'Neill was an assistant sales manager at a Buick dealership by day and a college student by night. He worked hard on his speech, "How to Buy a Used Car without Losing Your Shirt." Drawing on personal knowledge and experience he developed a carefully crafted, three-point outline with supporting materials under each point. He even found additional sources, more than were required for the assignment. Because he was so familiar with his topic, he practiced the speech only once.

But as soon as Danny began speaking, he knew he was in trouble. To ease his nervousness, he read his notes and avoided eye contact when he looked up. He heard his own voice racing through the speech in a monotone. Remember-

ing past speech evaluations, Danny slowed his pace and gripped the lectern tightly to keep from fidgeting.

Danny's instructor complimented him on the solid content and organization of the speech but noted his weak delivery skills, especially since this was his third speech in the class. The instructor gave Danny a C+. Danny felt this grade was unfair and decided to talk to the teacher about his performance and his grade.

Apply what you have learned about delivery and visual resources as you ponder and discuss the following questions: In what specific ways could Danny work to improve his vocal and bodily delivery skills? What visual resources would have been appropriate for this type of speech? Does Danny have a basis for requesting a higher grade? Which is more important in your mind, delivery or content?

KEY TERMS

 Use the *Human Communication* CD-ROM and the *Online Learning Center* at www.mhhe.com/pearson to further your understanding of the following terminology.

Articulation	Fluency	Pronunciation
Bodily movement	Gestures	Rate
Delivery	Impromptu mode	Visual aids
Enunciation	Manuscript mode	Vocal variety
Extemporaneous mode	Memorized mode	Vocalized pauses
Eye contact	Pause	Volume
Facial expression	Pitch	

SELF-QUIZ

 Go to the self-quizzes on the *Human Communication* CD-ROM and the *Online Learning Center* at www.mhhe.com/pearson to test your knowledge.

ADDITIONAL RESOURCES

Edwards, M. (1992). "Now presenting . . . (use of visual aids during sales presentations)." *Sales & Marketing Management, 14,* 23–24.

Pierson, W. S. (1993). Talking through your eyes. *American Salesman, 10,* 21–24.

Pogatos, F. (Ed.). (1992). *Advances in nonverbal communication: Sociocultural, clinical, esthetic, and literary perspectives.* Philadelphia: Benjamin.

Rader, S. (1997). www.nvgc.vt.edu/support/fall97.html.

REFERENCES

Beebe, S. A. (1974). Eye contact: A nonverbal determinant of speaker credibility. *Speech Teacher, 23,* 21–25.

Beighley, K. C. (1952). An experimental study of the effect of four speech variables on listener comprehension. *Speech Monographs, 19,* 249–258.

Bettinghaus, E. (1961). The operation of congruity in an oral communication situation. *Speech Monographs, 28,* 131–142.

Black, J. W. (1942). A study of voice merit. *Quarterly Journal of Speech, 28,* 67–74.

Bruskin, & Goldring, (1973). What are Americans afraid of? *Bruskin Report, 53.*

Cobin, M. (1962). Response to eye contact. *Quarterly Journal of Speech, 48,* 415–418.

Daly, J. A., Vangelisti, A. L., Neel, H. L., & Cavanaugh, P. D. (1989). Pre-performance concerns associated with public speaking anxiety. *Communication Quarterly, 37,* 39–53.

Feingold, A. (1983). Correlates of public speaking attitude. *Journal of Social Psychology, 120,* 285–286.

Gamble, T. K., & Gamble, M. (1999). *Communication works* (6th ed.). New York: McGraw-Hill.

Gilkinson, H., & Knower, F. H. (1941). Individual differences among students of speech as revealed by psychological test—I. *Journal of Educational Psychology, 32,* 161–175.

Glasgow, G. M. (1952). A semantic index of vocal pitch. *Speech Monographs, 19,* 64–68.

Haas, K. B., & Packer, H. Q. (1955). *Preparation and use of audiovisual aids.* New York: Prentice-Hall.

Hayworth, D. (1942). A search for facts on the teaching of public speaking. *Quarterly Journal of Speech, 28,* 247–254.

Hebyallah, I. M., & Maloney, W. P. (1977–1978). Content analysis of TV commercials. *International Journal of Instructional Media, 5,* 9–16.

Hemsley, G. D., & Doob, A. M. (1978). The effect of looking behavior on perceptions of a communicator's credibility. *Journal of Applied Social Psychology, 8,* 136–144.

Henrikson, E. H. (1944). An analysis of the characteristics of some "good" and "poor" speakers. *Speech Monographs, 11,* 120–124.

Hildebrandt, H. W., & Stephens, W. (1963). Manuscript and extemporaneous delivery in communicating information. *Speech Monographs, 30,* 369–372.

Kramer, E. J. J., & Lewis, T. R. (1931). Comparison of visual and nonvisual listening. *Journal of Communication, 1,* 16–20.

Lind, E. A., & O'Barr, W. M. (1979). The social significance of speech in the classroom. In H. Giles & R. St. Clair (Eds.), *Language and social psychology.* Oxford, England: Blackwell.

MacDonald-Ross, M. (1977, Winter). How numbers are shown: A review of research on the presentation of quantitative data in texts. *AV Communication Review, 25,* 359–409.

Miller, N., Maruyama, G., Beaber, R. J., & Valone, K. (1976). Speed of speech and persuasion. *Journal of Personality and Social Psychology, 34,* 615–625.

Pearson, J. C., & Yoder, D. D. (1979, May). *Public speaking or interpersonal communication: The perspective of the high communication apprehensive student.* East Lansing, MI: National Center for Research on Teacher Learning (ERIC Document Reproduction Service No. ED 173 870).

Petrie, C. R., Jr. (1963). Informative speaking: A summary and bibliography of related research. *Speech Monographs, 30,* 81.

Vohs, J. L. (1964). An empirical approach to the concept of attention. *Speech Monographs, 31,* 355–360.

Woolbert, C. (1920). The effects of various modes of public reading. *Journal of Applied Psychology, 4,* 162–185.

Worthington, E. L., Tipton, R. M., Comley, J. S., Richards, T., & Janke, R. H. (1984). Speech and coping skills training and paradox as treatment for college students anxious about public speaking. *Perceptual and Motor Skills, 59,* 394.

Zayas-Boya, E. P. (1977–1978). Instructional media in the total language picture. *International Journal of Instructional Media, 5,* 145–150.

CHAPTER SEVENTEEN

Nothing is so firmly believed as what we least know.

MICHEL DE MONTAIGNE

Everything has been thought of before; the challenge is to think of it again.

JOHANN WOLFGANG VON GOETHE

A word to the wise is not sufficient if it does not make sense.

JAMES THURBER

Informative
Presentations

What will you learn?

When you have read and thought about this chapter, you will be able to:

1. Recognize the goals of informative presentations.
2. Identify topics appropriate for informative speaking.
3. Provide examples of immediate behavioral purposes for an informative presentation.
4. Define concepts related to informative speaking, such as information hunger, information relevance, extrinsic motivation, informative content, and information overload.
5. Use the skills of defining, describing, explaining, and narrating in an informative presentation.

The goal of informative presentations is to enhance an audience's knowledge and understanding of a topic. In this chapter you will learn how to choose topics for an informative speech and how to develop behavioral purposes for them. The chapter discusses techniques that will help you effectively present an informational speech to an audience and explains how to organize your speech. Effective informative speakers demonstrate certain skills that contribute to their effectiveness, so the chapter covers the four skills of defining, describing, explaining, and narrating. Finally, the chapter includes an example of an informative presentation.

Teaching Tip

Provide students with
a copy of the
evaluation form you
intend to use. Take
time in class to
examine elements of
the form and discuss
how points are broken
down and what your
expectations are.
Thorough review of
the evaluation form
can help students
realize that grading
speeches can be
objective rather than
entirely subjective.
Sample evaluation
forms are found in the
instructor's manual.

Class Activity

To help students
assess the relevance of
an informative speech
topic, ask them to
complete the exercise
"Speech Significance"
found in the
instructor's manual.

Anita Byers was the new literature teacher in a suburban middle school; her class included 33 highly energetic teenagers. Anita spent a lot of time preparing her lesson plan for the opening weeks of school. She knew she needed to teach the students how to write without making serious grammatical errors, and she wanted to instill positive attitudes toward literature. But her most immediate goal was to inspire her students to read and enjoy novels, short stories, and poetry. Once Anita had her basic lesson plan outlined, she spent hours brainstorming how she might make the class interesting and relevant. Whenever she could, Anita decided to use music or clips from popular movies to grab her students' interest and to illustrate the concepts she wanted them to understand. She hoped that her students would deepen their interest in reading and writing well and that they would develop a strong sense of how fundamental these skills are for their future success.

Samantha Kuhn was a Seventh Day Adventist. Often, when people at work or school heard of her faith, she ended up explaining—sometimes at great length—what she believes and how her religion works. When she was younger, Samantha found the repeated explanations to be tiresome, but as she matured, she discovered that both she and her conversational partner gained something in the exchange. The other person knew more than he or she had known about Seventh Day Adventists, and Samantha often learned a little more about the other person's system of belief as well. Most of the time the conversations were enjoyable and informative (she had spoken with a Muslim and a Buddhist so far this year), and she looked forward to such exchanges.

Anita and Samantha are involved in similar situations. Both are trying to find ways to effectively communicate information to others so that their respective audiences gain knowledge and understanding about the topic, which is exactly the goal of an informative speech—to increase what an audience knows and understands.

At some time in your life you will probably find yourself informing others through oral reports, instructions, and speeches. The primary vehicle for informing others is the informative presentation intended to increase what an audience knows and understands.

How Do You Prepare an Informative Speech?

To prepare an informative speech, you should know

1. Why you deliver the speech: the intent, purpose, and goal of informative speaking.
2. What kinds of topics best lend themselves to informative speaking.
3. What the immediate behavioral purposes of informative speaking are, and how to determine if you have fulfilled them.

The Goal of an Informative Presentation

Understanding the goal or intent of an informative presentation requires that you understand the "end product" you seek and how to reach that end in ways that enlighten the audience and clarify the topic. The end product of informative speaking is *to increase an audience's knowledge or understanding of a topic.* You accomplish that goal by clarifying your topic in ways that retain the interest of your audience. To *clarify* means "to make clear," from Latin, Middle English, and Old French roots. To clarify a concept for an audience, the presenter assumes the audience does not understand the topic clearly until the speaker has an opportunity to explain the subject. Typically, most audience members have insufficient knowledge or understanding to master or comprehend the informative presentation topic. For example, in early September 2001, few Americas had ever heard of Osama bin Laden or could find Afghanistan on the map. Almost overnight reporters with visuals made bin Laden a household name and image and drilled into people's minds the location, climate, population, and culture of Afghanistan. Informative presentations defined, illustrated, and explained to increase our understanding. See p. 520.

Clarifying a topic for an audience is a primary goal of an informative presentation, but a second concern is to make the topic of an informative presentation interesting and significant to the audience. You arouse an audience's **interest,** *or curiosity about a topic,* by showing how the subject can be of importance, by relating stories of your own experiences with the subject, and by demonstrating gaps in your listeners' knowledge that they will want to fill. In fact, if a bit of persuasion is likely to slip into an informative presentation, the appropriate place is early in the speech, where you relate the topic to the audience. Here you may reveal why the audience should know more about our armed forces, student loans, or housing costs. How to make a topic palatable to the audience is a continuing concern of the informative speaker.

Besides being interesting, the informative speech should meet the standard of *significance.* The **significance** of your message *is its importance and meaningfulness to, or its consequences for, the audience.* The listeners, not the speaker, determine significance. For instance, a speech on fathers who illegally withhold child support is more likely to be both interesting and significant to a roomful of struggling single mothers than to a roomful of sophomore fraternity men. A speech on the history of matches might lack interest and significance, and a speech on tax support for emerging nations might be high in significance but low in audience interest.

Video Activity

Ask students to view the video segment "The Hospital." Hector Lobos presents a brief informative message to the Elliott family. What is the goal of Hector's message?

Writing Assignment

To help provide guidance through the process of putting together an effective informative speech, have students complete the exercise found in the instructor's manual.

interest

Curiosity about a topic.

significance

The importance, meaningfulness, or consequences of a message for an audience.

TRY ◀▶ THIS

Many soft drink cans carry a warning to phenylketonurics, *but very few people know what this warning means. Can you think of other words, concepts, or ideas that seem mysterious? Think of three for possible presentation topics.*

Discussion Question

Pick several of the topics from the list of sample topics and ask students to explain how those topics could be made interesting to the audience.

Topics for Informative Presentations

Chapter 13 already provided you with a general introduction to topic selection, but here we will focus specifically on topics appropriate for the informative presentation. Selecting a topic for informative presentations and narrowing the topic to the length restrictions of the speech are early concerns for the informative presenter. You can brainstorm for topics and conduct personal inventories of your reading and viewing habits to determine your interests. Even with that information, you may not know exactly what kinds of topics are most appropriate for informative presentations.

The main intent of the presenter should be to be informative; that is, most of the content of the speech should focus on increasing audience knowledge and clarifying concepts for greater understanding. Many informative presentations reveal how to do something, what something is, or how something happens—speeches of exposition, definition, and description, respectively. A list of topics for a number of student-delivered informative speeches is presented below.

The informative speaker must arouse the interest of the audience and show the significance of the topic.

Stem cell research
Youth gangs
Genetic cloning
Bioterrorism
Youth suicide
Civil rights
Privacy rights
Terrorism
Electric cars
Alcohol abuse
Bulimia
Holistic health
Stock market
Spirituality
Disaster relief
Investment strategies

New software
Scandals
Greenhouse effect
Nutrition
Diabetes
Mountain climbing
Self-defense
Buddhist beliefs
Computer viruses
Telemarketing
Depression
Athletic injuries
Cocaine/opiates
Child care
Steroids
Illegal drugs

INFORMATION SOURCES FOR AN INFORMATIVE SPEECH

Looking for an insightful quotation? This source includes *Bartlett's Familiar Quotations,* poetry, and quotes by famous men and women: **www.columbia. edu/acis/bartleby**

Want links to thousands of newspaper, magazine, television, and radio web sites? Try this site: **www.mediainfo.com/emedia**

This Stanford University Library site provides links to academic journals like *Science Magazine:* **highwire.stanford.edu**

Want background information on a subject? This site gives you access to the archives of a world-class newspaper: **www.washingtonpost.com**

SOURCE: M. McGuire, L. Stilbourne, M. McAdams, and L. Hyatt, *Internet Handbook for Writers, Researchers, and Journalists* (New York: Guilford, 1997).

Teaching Tip

Have students confer in groups to get feedback on potential topic ideas. Small groups can serve as "focus groups" to determine high-interest topics or ways to focus various issues on a topic.

CD-ROM Activity

Ask students to view the animation titled "Behavioral Purposes and Informative Speaking" found on the accompanying student CD-ROM. The animation discusses how a speaker must keep the purpose of the speech in mind when planning an informative presentation.

The topics, not necessarily the titles of the presentations, are listed. Therefore, many of the topics look broader than they would be if they were delivered as speeches. Nonetheless, this list of topics may give you some ideas for an informative presentation topic.

Another method of finding a topic for a presentation to inform would be to explore what the audience might want to know about topics that fall under broad categories such as sports, leisure activities, competitions, training, and practice. A member of the armed forces might want to inform the audience about recruitment, benefits, opportunities, and hardships. In other words, choose a general area of interest and reduce that area down to a topic that can be covered in the time allotted.

Once you have selected and narrowed a topic in a manner appropriate for you, your audience, and the situation, you are ready to specify the behavioral purposes of your informative speech.

The Behavioral Purposes of Informative Speeches

Two important questions for the informative speakers are

1. What do I want my audience to know or do as a result of my speech?
2. How will I know if I am successful?

Students learn better if they know exactly what the teacher expects them to learn. Similarly, an audience learns more from an informative presentation if the speaker states exactly what the audience is expected to know or do. The effects of an informative presentation, however, are

519

Active Art

Giving an informative presentation is much like teaching a class. Your goal is to teach the audience about some fact, concept, process, or object. To determine whether you have met your goal as a presenter (or teacher), you must follow steps to assess whether your presentation achieved the desired behavioral outcome for your audience.

Step 1: Plan Objectives
The first step in planning your speech should be to determine what objectives you want your audience to meet.

Step 2: Pre-Assessment
The second step is to conduct a pre-assessment of your audience. Pre-assessment could take the form of asking a few classmates questions a few days before your speech or even passing out a short quiz.

Step 3: Deliver Speech
The third step is to actually teach or inform your audience. This is where you plan your speech so that it provides the best opportunity for your audience to meet the objectives you have set for them.

Step 4: Post-Assesment
The final step is post-assessment. Like the pre-assessment, the post-assessment could be informal – asking a few people questions after your presentation is completed – or more formal – handing out a quiz or survey.

Figure 17.1 Behavior purposes and informative speaking.

unknown unless you make the effects behavioral; that is, your speech should result in observable behavioral change. A teacher discovers whether students learned from a lecture by giving a quiz or having the students answer questions in class. In the same way, the informative speaker seeks to discover whether a message was effectively communicated by seeking overt feedback from the audience. The overt feedback you seek concerns the **immediate behavioral purposes** of your presentation, *the actions expected from an audience during and immediately after the speech.*

The most common immediate behavioral purposes in an informative presentation encourage audience members to do the following:

1. *Describe objects, persons, or issues.* For example, after hearing a speech, audience members can *describe* an English setter, a person with Down syndrome, or the Libertarian position on welfare.
2. *Distinguish between different things.* For example, after hearing a speech, audience members can *distinguish* between fool's gold and real gold, between a counterfeit dollar and a real dollar, or between a conservative position and a liberal position.
3. *Compare items.* For example, after hearing a speech, audience members can *compare* prices on automobiles with the same features and options, a poetic song and a sonnet, or diamonds for cut, clarity, and carats.
4. *Define words, objects, or concepts.* For example, after hearing a speech, audience members can *define* what kerogen is, describe an English Tudor house, or explain the concept of macroeconomics.
5. *State what they have learned.* After hearing a speech, audience members can tell you, or can write, the most important points of your speech or are able to tell others what you said.

The common behavioral purposes of an informative speech are to describe, distinguish, compare, define, and state. How does a speaker know whether or not these behavioral purposes were accomplished? One method of discovering whether audience members learned anything from your presentation is to discover what they know both at the beginning and at the end of the speech. For instance, you could ask at the beginning of your speech, "How many of you have ever taken a personality test?" If you get a small but enthusiastic response, you know you will be informing them about something that is unfamiliar but interesting to them. After you explain the different types of tests and the discrepancies between them, you can ask certain students at the end of the speech to contrast the Thematic Apperception Test and the Myers-Briggs Type Indicator.

Similarly, you may ask your classmates to write down something or demonstrate that they understood your message. If you explained how to administer CPR, you could ask a volunteer classmate to show that she understood the steps. Similarly, if your topic was to inform the class about

immediate behavioral purposes

Actions a speaker seeks from an audience during and immediately after a speech.

Class Activity

Divide the class into four groups. Assign each group one of the first four behavioral purposes of informative speaking. Have each group brainstorm topics that would be appropriate for the behavioral purpose assigned. Groups should share their ideas with the class.

Video Activity

Ask students to view the video segment "Senior Seminar." Have students analyze how the group evaluated the potential topics for the show. Did the topics generate information hunger? Was extrinsic motivation involved in the topics?

nutrition, you could ask them to list the foods with the highest or lowest fat content. In each case, the speaker states the purpose in such a way that he or she can determine whether the speaker accomplished his or her purpose.

Once you have decided on specific behavioral purposes for addressing an audience, you must select strategies for achieving those purposes. In other words, you must decide how to adapt your behavioral purposes and the materials of your speech to your particular audience.

How Do You Effectively Present Information to an Audience?

Audience analysis (see chapter 13) should help you determine how much audience members already know and how much you will have to tell them to engender understanding. Then you will have to decide how to generate information hunger, achieve information relevance, use extrinsic motivation, select content, and avoid information overload in your speech.

Information Hunger

information hunger

The audience's need for the information contained in the speech.

rhetorical questions

Questions asked for effect, with no answer expected.

An informative speech is more effective if the presenter can generate **information hunger** in the audience—that is, if the speaker can create *a need for information in the audience*. Information hunger is easiest to create when a speaker has analyzed the audience and believes hunger for the information can be aroused. Arousal of interest during the speech is related to how much the audience will comprehend (Petrie, 1963). The following **rhetorical questions,** *questions asked for effect, with no answer expected,* could be used to introduce an informative speech and to arouse audience interest: "Are you aware of the number of abused children in your hometown?" "Can you identify five warning signs of cancer?" "Do you know how to get the best college education for your money?" Depending on the audience, these rhetorical questions could be of interest.

Class Activity

To illustrate the concept of information hunger, ask students to complete the exercise "Hunger to Speak" found in the instructor's manual.

Rhetorical questions are just one method of arousing information hunger. Another method is to arouse the audience's curiosity. For example, you might state "I have discovered a way to add 10 years to my life," "The adoption of the following plan will ensure world peace," or "I have a secret for achieving marital success." In addition, a brief quiz on your topic early in the speech arouses interest in finding the answers. Unusual clothing is likely to arouse interest in why you are so attired, and an object you created will likely inspire the audience to wonder how you made the object. Rhetorical questions and arousing curiosity are just a few of the many ways the presenter can generate information hunger.

GENERATING INFORMATION HUNGER

Think first on your own of ways—besides rhetorical questions and arousing curiosity—that you could arouse information hunger in an audience. After writing down some ideas of your own, share them with a classmate and see if the two of you can think of still others, the best of which can be shared with the class.

Information Relevance

A second factor relating an informative presentation to an audience is **information relevance,** *the importance, novelty, and usefulness of the information to the audience.* When selecting a topic for an informative presentation, the speaker should carefully consider the relevance of the topic to the particular audience. Skin cancer might be a better topic in the summer, when students are sunbathing, than in the spring, when they are studying for finals. A presentation on taxes could be awfully dull. A speech on how present tax laws cost audience members more than they cost the rich might be more relevant, and a speech on three ways to reduce personal taxes might be even more relevant. However, if your audience happens to be composed of 18- to 21-year-olds who have never paid taxes, none of the three topics might be relevant. Similarly, a speech on raising racehorses, writing a textbook, or living on a pension might be informative but not relevant because of the financial status, occupation, or age of the listeners. The informative speaker, then, should exercise some care in selecting a topic that interests the audience (Cofer, 1961).

People expose themselves first to information that is supportive or that fits in with what they already believe or know, and they reject less supportive information first. Thus your intended listeners' predisposition toward a topic can determine whether they will come to hear your speech and then whether they will listen (Wheeless, 1974).

information relevance

The importance, novelty, and usefulness of the topic and the information.

Extrinsic Motivation

A third factor in relating an informative speech to an audience is **extrinsic motivation,** *reasons outside the speech itself for listening to the content of the speech.* An audience is more likely to listen to, and comprehend, a presentation if reasons exist outside the speech itself for concentrating on the content of the speech (Petrie & Carrel, 1976). A teacher who tells students to listen carefully because they will be tested at the end of the hour is using extrinsic motivation. A student can use extrinsic motivation at the

extrinsic motivation

A method of making information relevant by providing the audience with reasons outside the speech itself for listening to the content of the speech.

beginning of a speech by telling an audience "Attention to this speech will alert you to ways you can increase energy and creativity," or "After hearing this speech, you will never purchase a poor-quality used car again."

Extrinsic motivation is related to the concept of information relevance. The audience member who would ordinarily lack interest in the topic of fashion might find that topic relevant when it is linked to job interviews and the kinds of clothing, jewelry, and shoes that job interviewers seem to prefer. The audience member's interest in getting a job makes the interviewer's preferences an extrinsic motivation for listening carefully to the speech.

Any external reasons for listening need to be mentioned early in the speech, before the message you want the audience to remember. A statement such as "You will need this background material for the report due at the end of this week" provides extrinsic motivation for the managers who hear this message from their employer. Similarly, in an informative speech, you may be able to command more attention, comprehension, and action from audience members if they know some reasons outside the speech itself for attending to your message.

TRY ◀▶ THIS

List the reasons your audience should listen to your speech. Determine how you could motivate your audience to listen.

Informative Content

informative content

The main points and subpoints, illustrations, and examples used to clarify and inform.

A fourth factor in relating an informative presentation to an audience is the selection of **informative content,** *the main points and subpoints, illustrations, and examples used to clarify and inform.* The following are principles of learning and research findings that can guide you in selecting your speech content:

Class Activity

Assign students to groups. Have them discuss how the recommendations for informative content can be reflected in a well-prepared speech outline.

1. **Audiences tend to remember and comprehend generalizations and main ideas better than details and specific facts** (Petrie, 1963). The usual advice to speakers—that content should be limited to a relatively small number of main points and generalizations—seems to be well grounded. Specifically, public speakers are well advised to limit themselves to two to five main points or contentions. Even if the speech is very long, audiences are not likely to remember a larger number of main points.

2. **Relatively simple words and concrete ideas are significantly easier to retain than more complex materials** (Baird, 1974; Ernest, 1968). Long or unusual words may dazzle an audience into thinking you are intellectually gifted or verbally skilled, but

they may also reduce audience understanding of the speech content. Keep the ideas and the words used to express those ideas at an appropriate level.

3. **Humor can make a dull speech more interesting to an audience, but humor does not seem to increase information retention.** The use of humor also improves the audience's perception of the character of the speaker, and it can increase a speaker's authoritativeness when a speech is dull, although not when the speech is interesting (Gruner, 1970).

4. **Early remarks about how the speech will meet the audience's needs can create anticipation and increase the chances that the audience will listen and understand** (Petrie, 1963). Whatever topic you select, you should tell audience members early in your presentation how the topic is related to them. Unless you relate the topic to their needs, they may choose not to listen.

5. **Calling for overt audience response, or actual behavior, increases comprehension more than repetition does.** In a study of this subject, the overt responses invited were specific, "programmed" questions to which the appropriate overt

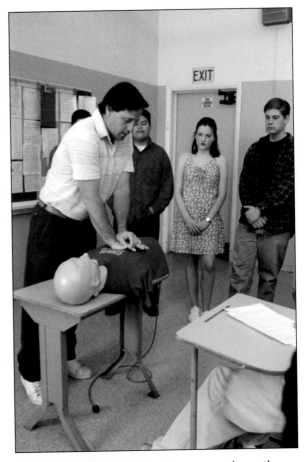

Having the audience practice what you preach greatly increases their comprehension.

responses were anticipated (Tucker, 1964). An informative presenter can ask for overt responses from audience members by having them perform the task being demonstrated (for example, two people dance after you explain the technique of the waltz); by having them stand, raise hands, or move chairs to indicate affirmative understanding of the speaker's statements (for example, "Raise your hand if you are familiar with local building codes"); or by having them write answers that will indicate understanding of the informative speech (for example, "List four ways to lower your blood pressure"). Having an audience go through an overt motion provides feedback to the speaker and can be rewarding and reinforcing for both speaker and listener.

Information Overload

The informative speaker needs to be wary about the amount of information included in a presentation. The danger is **information overload,** providing *much more information than the audience can absorb in amount, complexity, or both.*

Information overload comes in two forms. One is *quantity:* The speaker tells more than audience members ever wanted to know about a subject, even when they are interested in it. The speaker tries to cram as much information as possible into the time allowed. Unfortunately, this cramming of information makes it more difficult to understand.

A second form of information overload is *complexity:* The speaker uses language or ideas that are beyond the capacity of the audience to understand. An engineer or a mathematician who unloads detailed formulas on the audience or a philosopher who soars into the ethereal heights of high ideas may leave the audience feeling frustrated and more confused than before the speech.

The solution to information overload is to speak on a limited number of main points with only the best supporting materials and to keep the message at a level the audience can understand.

Content Organization

The suggestions that follow are based on studies that reveal specific ways the informative speaker can help an audience understand the content of the presentation. In general, the research supports the old saying that you should tell audience members what you are going to tell them, tell them, and then tell them what you told them.

Charles R. Petrie, Jr. (1963), in his studies of informative speaking, found that the use of transitions can increase an audience's comprehension. That finding underlines the importance of building transitions between your introduction and body and between your body and conclusion. You should also use transitions when you move from one main point to another and when you move into and out of the use of visual aids.

In organizing your informative presentation, you should determine which ideas, points, or supporting materials are of greatest importance. Apparently, an audience understands the important points better if the speaker signals their importance by saying, "Now get this," or "This is very important." Some redundancy, or planned repetition, also can increase comprehension (Pence, 1954). Some of that planned repetition can be included in the previews and reviews in your informative speech (Baird, 1974). Advance organizers, or previews in written work, aid retention by providing the reader with key points prior to their presentation in a meaningful, but unfamiliar, passage (Ausubel, 1960). In speaking, as well as in writing, listeners can more easily grasp information when they are invited to anticipate and to review both the organization and the content of a speech.

TABLE 17.1   A CHECKLIST FOR THE INFORMATIVE PRESENTATION

_____1. What have you done to arouse information hunger?

_____2. How have you rendered the topic relevant to this audience?

_____3. Have you proved extrinsic motivation for listening?

_____4. Have you followed the advice about informative content?

_____5. Have you avoided information overload?

When you have completed an outline that includes everything you plan to say, you should check your speech for information overload. Overload is a special problem in the informative presentation because speakers have a tendency to inundate listeners with information. Just as some writers believe a longer paper is a better paper, some speakers think the sheer quantity of information improves a speech. The most effective public speakers know the quantity of material in a speech makes less difference than its quality. They also know listeners pay more attention to carefully selected material that is well adapted to their needs. In a five- to eight-minute informative presentation, the speaker has only four to six minutes to present supporting materials; the remainder of the time is spent introducing the subject, making transitions, and making internal and final summaries. Your organizational plan should show what material you intend to include in your speech and should be your final check on the quantity and quality of the information you intend to present. Finally, use the checklist in Table 17.1 to see if you have related the presentation to the audience.

Skills for Informative Speaking

Public presenters who are highly effective at informative speaking demonstrate certain skills that contribute to their effectiveness. One of these skills is _defining._ Much of what an informative speaker does is reveal to an audience what certain terms, words, and concepts mean. Another skill is _describing;_ the informative speaker often tells an audience how something appears: what it looks, sounds, feels, and even smells like. A third skill is _explaining,_ or trying to say what something is in words the audience can understand. A fourth skill is _narrating,_ an oral interpretation of a story, an event, or a description.

Video Activity

Ask students to view the video segment "On the Air with Campus-Community Connection." How did the speakers attempt to define terms during their presentations? Were the definitions of terms important to their overall point?

Defining

A student who was a model gave a speech in which she talked about _parts modeling;_ a student who made his own butter gave an informative speech in

Writing Assignment

Ask students to pick one term for their speech and find the following types of definitions: comparison, synonym, contrast, antonym, etymology, and operational. The student should use reference materials as well as creativity to generate the definitions.

comparison

A means of defining by pointing out similarities between the known and the less known.

contrast

The comparison of unlike things.

synonym

A word that means approximately the same as another word.

antonym

A word that means the opposite of another word.

etymology

The historical origin of a word.

operational definition

A definition which states the process that results in the thing being defined.

which he talked about the *dasher* and the *clabber, bilky* milk, and butter that *gathered;* an informative speech on aerobics included such terms as *arteriosclerosis, cardiovascular–pulmonary system,* and *cardiorespiratory endurance.* What were these students talking about? In each case, they were using words most persons in the audience did not understand. To use terms audience members do not understand is all right as long as you explain the terms in language they *can* understand. You clarify by defining your terms. Among the most useful methods of defining are the use of comparison, contrast, synonyms, antonyms, etymology, and operational definitions.

The student who told about making butter defined through **comparison,** *pointing out similarities between the known and the less known,* by explaining that "the dasher consists of a stick similar to a broom handle. A cross made of two slats, 4 inches long and 2 inches wide, is nailed to the end of the handle. The dasher is inserted into the churn, and the churn's opening is covered by a tightly fitted wooden lid with a hole in the middle for the dasher." The student defined a dasher by comparing it to the better-known broomstick and by revealing how it was constructed.

Another means of definition is **contrast,** *the comparison of unlike things.* In an informative speech, you can contrast hypochondriasis with psychotic disorders by contrasting the symptoms and effects of each.

A speaker also might define through a **synonym**—*a word that is close or similar in meaning to another word.* For example, in an informative speech, the speaker might say depressive psychosis is characterized by loss of interest, dejection, stupor, and silence—a series of words similar to behaviors exhibited by a depressive psychotic patient.

An **antonym** is *a word that means the opposite of another word.* A hyperactive child is not quiet, immobile, silent, patient, or unexpressive.

Sometimes it is easier to explain a concept or term by revealing its **etymology,** *the historical origin of a word.* A desk dictionary may give a very brief statement on the origin of a word. You can locate more complete origins in such specialized dictionaries as the *Oxford English Dictionary* or the *Etymological Dictionary of Modern English.* A speaker talking about sexual variations might use the term *lesbianism* and could define the term by explaining that the Greek poet Sappho wrote poetry about sexual love between women about 600 years before Christ. Because Sappho lived on the island of Lesbos, "followers of Sappho," or female homosexuals, became known as lesbians. The story about the origin of the word provides a memorable way for the audience to relate to the word.

Another means of defining is the **operational definition,** which *defines a term by revealing how it works, how it is made, or what it consists of.* The earlier description of a dasher was an operational definition revealing how a dasher is constructed. A student delivering an informative speech on rhinoplasty, or "a nose job," did so through the following operational definition:

Modern rhinoplasty is done for both cosmetic and health reasons. It consists of several minioperations. First, if the septum separating the nostrils has become deviated as the result of an injury or some other means, it is straightened with

DEFINING YOUR TERMS

Together with a group of classmates see if you can produce some topics that are problems of definition. For example, if the law allows for roving wiretaps to capure terrorists, how do law enforcers determine the differences among common criminals, terrorists, and everyday citizens? What are some other issues that are based on definitions? Share the best ideas from your group with the class.

surgical pliers. Then, if the nose is to be remodeled, small incisions are made within each nostril, and working entirely within the nose, the surgeon is able to remove, reshape, or redistribute the bone and cartilage lying underneath the skin. Finally, if the nose is crooked, a chisel is taken to the bones of the upper nose, and they are broken so that they may be straightened and centered.

An operational definition, then, defines by revealing the formula for the thing named: rhinoplasty is the surgery described in the previous sentences; a cake is its recipe; concrete is lime, cement, and water; a secretary is what a secretary does: word processing, filing, and answering phones.

Describing

A second skill of the informative presenter is distinguishing between abstract and concrete words and between general and specific words. One of the best ways to make an informative speech interesting is by using language forcefully and effectively. You can do that best if you recognize certain differences among words.

For instance, some words *refer generally to ideas, qualities, acts, or relationships:* these are called **abstract words.** Examples of abstract words are *freedom* (an idea), *mysterious* (a quality), *altruism* (an act), and *parent–child* (a relationship). Other words are more specific, or **concrete,** because they *refer to definite persons, places, objects, and acts,* such as Dr. Bettsey L. Barhorst, the Eiffel Tower, and your economics textbook. Abstract words are useful in theorizing, summarizing, and discussing and are commonly used by educated persons discussing ideas. Concrete words are most useful in relating your personal experiences, direct observations, and feelings or attitudes. The important point about abstract and concrete language is to use each where it is most appropriate.

The most frequent error in informative presentations is the use of abstract terms where concrete words would be more forceful and clear. "I have really liked some courses of study here at Northern Virginia Community College," says a student to her classmates and adds, "but others I

abstract words

Words or phrases that refer generally to ideas, qualities, acts, or relationships.

concrete words

Words that refer to definite persons, places, objects, and acts.

529

have disliked." This abstract, general statement has minimal impact. If speaking in concrete terms, the same student might say, "I have most enjoyed English, communication, and political science courses, and I have disliked courses in chemistry, mathematics, and physics." Descriptions in informative speeches should be specific, accurate, and detailed, rather than general and ambiguous.

imagery

Use of words that appeal to the senses, that create pictures in the mind.

Informative speakers should also attempt to use colorful **imagery,** *words that appeal to the senses.* A speaker describing a place might say that "the sun sets in an orange sky against the purple mountain," a victim of shock "appears lifeless, pallid, and clammy," or a manufactured meat "tastes like top-grade sirloin."

A valuable exercise for the informative speaker is to carefully review the rough draft of the speech to discover abstract, general, ambiguous words that can be replaced by concrete details.

TRY◄►THIS

Think of something that you have explained to others many times at work or at home. Does your explanation get increasingly efficient with practice? Can you practice some of your explanations from your presentation on others before you address an audience so your explanation will be easy to understand?

Explaining

explanation

A means of idea development that simplifies or clarifies an idea while arousing audience interest.

A third skill for the informative speaker is explaining an idea in words the audience can understand. An **explanation** is *a means of idea development that simplifies or clarifies an idea while arousing audience interest.*

An important step in explaining is analyzing, deconstructing, or dissecting something to enhance audience understanding. Unless you become skilled at dissecting a concept, your explanation may leave audience members more confused than they were before your speech. You have to determine what you can do to make the concept more palatable to the audience. For example, John Kenneth Galbraith, a retired professor of economics from Harvard University, wrote many books explaining economics to people who did not know very much about the subject. A close look at one of his explanations is instructive. Galbraith is trying to make the point that politicians and the public often take the voices of a few influential persons as a shift of opinion by the majority:

> On the need for tax relief, investment incentives, or a curb on welfare costs, the views of one articulate and affluent banker, businessman, lawyer, or acolyte economist are the equal of those of several thousand welfare mothers. In any recent year, the pleas by Walter Wriston of Citibank or David Rockefeller of

Chase Manhattan for relief from oppressive taxation, regulation, or intrusive government have commanded at least as much attention as the expressions of discontent of all the deprived of the South Bronx. (Galbraith, 1981)*

Galbraith is analyzing a situation: Why do the persons of economic advantage have a bigger say in our economy than the millions who live with it? His language is concrete. He is expanding on an idea with descriptive language, and he is doing so by dissecting the concept so that you can understand its parts.

Narrating

A fourth skill for informative speakers is **narrating,** *the oral presentation and interpretation of a story, a description, or an event.* In a presentation, narration includes the dramatic reading of some lines from a play, a poem, or another piece of literature; the voice-over on a series of slides or a silent film to illustrate a point in a speech; and even the reading of such information as a letter, a quotation, or a selection from a newspaper or magazine. The person who does the play-by-play account of a ball game is narrating, and so is the presenter who explains what a weaver is doing in an informative presentation on home crafts.

The person who uses narration in a speech moves just a little closer to oral interpretation of literature, or even acting, because the narration is highlighted by being more dramatic than the surrounding words. Sections of your speech that require this kind of special reading also require special practice. If you want a few lines of poetry in your speech to have the desired impact, you will need to rehearse them.

Class Activity

Provide students with the opportunity to practice narration. Have them write a fictional example that could be used as an attention-getter in their speech introduction. Ask for volunteers to read their stories to the class and receive feedback.

narrating

The oral presentation and interpretation of a story, a description, or an event; includes dramatic reading of prose or poetry.

So far in this chapter, you have learned how to select a topic for your informative speech, how to determine behavioral purposes and goals for the informative speech, how to present information to an audience, how to organize the informative speech, and how to define, describe, explain, and narrate the concepts in your speech. Now let's look at the manuscript of an informative speech delivered by a student.

Notice how the speaker gains and maintains the audience's attention, relates the topic to himself and to the audience, and forecasts the organization and development of the topic. Notice also how the speaker attempts to clarify the topic with examples high in audience interest; translates the

An Example of an Informative Speech

From Galbraith, J. K. (January 4, 1981) "The three attacks on social and economic consensus." *The Des Moines Sunday Register.*

ideas into language the audience can understand; and defines, describes, and explains. The marginal notes will help identify how the speaker is fulfilling the important functions of the introduction, body, and conclusion of an informative presentation.

Investing from Home

Topic is announced: Speaker arouses information hunger by talking about what "used to be."

In the past, ordinary people did not invest in stocks; investing was reserved for the rich and elite. In the past, even the rich people had to invest through brokers, who took a commission for services rendered both when they bought stocks and when they sold them. In the past, only the savvy reader of the *Wall Street Journal, Business Week,* and *Money Magazine* had the foggiest notion of what stocks to buy, hold, or sell. What occurred in the past is no more: Ordinary people like you and me can invest, can avoid a large brokerage fee, and can access free information that was once reserved for the elite, the rich, and the bold. Even six months ago industry experts said, "The typical online investor was male, college educated, from 32 to 42 years old, with an annual salary of $75,000" (Segal, 1998). But as David Segal (1998) says in his article "Investors Are Trading Brokers for Computers": "These days the crowd has been joined by legions of homemakers, retirees, precocious teenagers and disgruntled employees dreaming of going pro" (p. H1). The craze has even been joined by me, a lowly finance major, who has earned little this year but learned much about investing, trading, and having fun in the market and on the Net.

Topic is related to audience: Topic relevance is highlighted by "join-the-crowd" approach.

Topic is related to speaker: Speaker credibility is enhanced by her own involvement.

Forecast: Organization and development revealed: Forecast of contents.

My informative speech will introduce you to the world of personal investing, to the idea of being your own broker, and to the possibility of having some fun with your money.

Organization: First main point.

The first, and maybe most important, point of this speech is that any investing you might do because of what you learn today should not be money you might need for your mortgage, your impending marriage, or your mother's nursing home. In fact, James Glassman (1998), an expert on investing, says you should start with a "fun and games account," or FGA, which he calls "a pot of money for *playing* the market, as opposed to investing for a long-term goal such as retirement" (p. H1). So, remember, this speech is about playing with your money, not about buffetting your way to the country club set.

New term defined: FGA.

Appeal to audience's sense of adventure: Doing what could not be done before.

Some of you may already be feeling that this informative speech cannot be about you: "I've got no investments, I'm not knowledgeable about investing, and I have no reason to even want this information." Well, just to keep you interested, I will point out that five years ago you could not even do what I am suggesting today: Internet trading did not exist. But, according to David Segal (1998) in the *Washington Post,* "Today there are more than 3 million online accounts, and by 2002 that number is expected to rise to 14 million with nearly $700 billion in assets" (p. A1). Apparently, some people have a lot of FGM, fun and games money.

Appeal to join the party: Learn by knowing information.

Transition: Internal summary and forecast.

You already know that I recommend you only do online investing with FGM. Next, you need to know what stocks cost, how much or how little you have to invest. You do have to open an account with some online brokerage firm because you have to buy your stock from somebody. But unlike what it "used to be" when traditional brokers had high minimums and trades cost over $100, now trades cost as little as $8, according to David Segal (1998). According to Segal, some firms like Fidelity Brokerage want $5,000 in cash or securities to open an account, and Brown & Co. opens at $15,000; but four firms, which I have included in my handout, have no minimum investment at all: SureTrade, Quick and Reilly, National Discount Brokers, and Jack White & Co. (Looking into, 1998). You will also find on the handout their cost per stock trade and other services rendered. The second point of my speech, then, is that you can start investing your FGM at very low cost to yourself compared to what "used to be."

Cost–benefit analysis: Investing is inexpensive.

Refers to handout.

Second main point: Costs are lower than they were before.

Now you might be wondering, "How do I determine who to invest through?" Albert B. Crenshaw (1998), another expert on money and investing, says that so many financial and online service companies are on the World Wide Web today that you have many options for finding the most useful investment sources. You can see the Web addresses listed on my PowerPoint slide, but I'd like to point out a few of the more common names: Quicken.com, Yahoo, and Microsoft are among the many companies that have created websites to guide you to investment information (Crenshaw, 1998). Julio Gomez, consultant for online financial services, has a site (www.scorecard.com) that ranks more than 80 on-line brokers. He recommends starting "with an inexpensive online broker that has seedy Web site navigation and trade execution" (Burkstrand, 1998). At one website investors conduct bulletin board discussions about the advantages and disadvantages of brokerage firms (www.onlineinvestors.com.) Occasionally a competing firm plants misinformation on this bulletin board, and often the ones who do chat have complaints rather than compliments. Nonetheless, you should pay attention if the complaints about an online company are numerous (Burkstrand, 1998).

Third main point: Who to broker your account?

Presentational aid: Refer to website addresses on the board.

Presentational aid: Provides World Wide Web addresses on PowerPoint slide.

To test an online broker before doing business, Beth Burkstrand (1998) recommends trying to contact the company's customer service representative by e-mail or telephone: See if and how quickly the firm responds. Also, see if the broker provides you with tax reports, an unlimited account history, and profit and loss for each individual stock. Does the online broker have a backup way to trade in case of server overload or Internet connection failure? And, finally, how much does the company charge per trade and any ancillary services? Some firms charge extra for providing stock quotes, for making large trades, and even for talking with a human being (Burkstrand, 1998).

Inside information on evaluating online brokers: Information on how to transact a buy or sell.

So far you know that you should only invest with FGA, that you can invest small amounts, and that online brokers are ranked and discussed on the Net. Now you need to know exactly how you do a stock transaction. For the uninitiated, a broker like Charles Schwab (www.Schwab.com) will train you in one of its many offices. Online customers use schwab.com to make 66,000 orders per day, more than half of the company's daily trading volume (Knight, 1998). To actually execute a trade is simple. You fill out a form to buy or sell a certain security at a specific price, then click "send" (Burkstrand, 1998). Schwab is a discount broker that charges $39 minimum for conventional orders, $29.95 for an online stock trade, and a 20 percent discount for online trades of mutual funds. However, Datek Securities, a deeper discount broker, charges as little as

Transition: Second repetition of main points.

Conclusion: Summary and repetition of four main points.

Upbeat ending: Signals end of speech with one last piece of advice.

Support materials: Finance professors provide credible facts and figures about investing.

$9.95 for transacting a trade (Knight, 1998). How do you find out how much your stock or mutual fund costs when you buy it? The company websites provide real-time quotes, so you will know what price to pay.

My four main points are complete: Play with a fun and games account, invest modest amounts, find an online broker who provides the services you need, and learn how to transact a trade on your computer. Now I leave you with one warning: Online investing can be so much fun that "the game" gets you in trouble. Many new investors find that seeking stocks, researching them, and buying and selling them gives them such a high that they become almost obsessive about buying and selling all the time. But there is good reason to think twice before you let the game consume you. Two University of California finance professors, Barber and Odean, looked at almost 65,000 discount brokerage accounts and found that those that did the least trading earned 75 percent higher returns than those that traded the most (Glassman, 1998). That is good enough reason for me!

I hope you will keep my handout, which tells you how to set up an online account, and I hope you learned a lot today about online trading. Whether you ever choose to do it or not, I hope you found the topic an interesting one to learn about. The online trading craze is definitely sweeping the investment business.

Endnotes

Burkstrand, B. (1998, August 23). Taking the trading floor to the home front: Choosing the right broker on the Internet isn't always easy. *The Washington Post*, p. H1.

Crenshaw, A. (1998, August 23). Cash flow: Answers about money at a website near you. *The Washington Post*, p. H1. [The websites: www.quicken.com, www.quote.yahoo.com, and www.Investor.msn.com.]

Glassman, J. (1998, August 23). Internet is ideal for a "fun" account. *The Washington Post*, pp. H1, H15.

Knight, J. (1998, August 23). Schwab, clients save money online. *The Washington Post*, p. H4.

Looking into online trading. (1998, August 23). *The Washington Post*, p. H4.

Segal, D. (1998, August 23). Investors are trading brokers for computers: By going online, Wall Street is just a keystroke away. *The Washington Post*, pp. H1, H15.

The immediate purpose of this informative presentation was to inform the audience about online investing. The long-term purpose of the speech was to enable the audience to know why people might choose to invest from home, how much or little to invest, how to select and evaluate an online broker, how to find a security in which to invest, and how to actually transact a buy or sell. The presenter introduced some new vocabulary: FGA, online accounts, Internet trading, minimum investment, and online broker. Finally, the presenter appealed to the audience to listen, and to learn about the information, by portraying home investing as a new, even amusing activity and, hopefully, a profitable one as well.

Chapter Review

SUMMARY

In this chapter you have learned the following:

- Preliminary information that you need to know in informing others includes
  - The intent and goal of informative presentations.
  - The kinds of topics that are most appropriate.
  - The kinds of immediate behavioral purposes of informative presentations and how to determine if you have fulfilled them.
- Strategies for informing others include
  - Generating information hunger, an audience need for the information.
  - Achieving information relevance by relating information to the audience.

- Using extrinsic motivation, reasons outside the speech itself for understanding the presentation's content.
- Shaping the informative content requires
  - Limiting the number of main points.
  - Limiting the number of generalizations.
  - Selecting language the audience can understand.
  - Using concrete specifics to illustrate an abstract idea.
  - Including humor or wit when appropriate.
  - Revealing how the information meets audience needs.
  - Avoiding information overload.

◗ VIDEO LINK: CAMPUS-COMMUNITY CONNECTION'S INFORMATIVE PURPOSE

Video Episode 4: "Senior Seminar"

Informative speaking requires that you generate information hunger, achieve information relevance, use extrinsic motivation, select content, and avoid information overload. In "Senior Seminar," during the planning process of the Campus-Community Connection show, you can observe the discussions of Susan, Claire, Mike, and Enrique about the topic of cohabitation. After viewing "Senior Seminar," consider how the show has the potential to raise information hunger, achieve relevance for the audience, tap into extrinsic motivation, and avoid information overload. Based on your analysis, was cohabitation a good topic?

ISSUES IN COMMUNICATION: LEARNING TO TEACH

This Issues in Communication narrative is designed to provoke individual thought or discussion about concepts raised in the chapter.

Huan Yi works for a company that sells financial software to small- and medium-size businesses; his job is to show customers how to use the new software. He spends two weeks with each client demonstrating the features and functions of the software most applicable to the client's needs. The first few months on the job were difficult—he often left a client feeling that even after two weeks he hadn't been able to show the employees everything they needed to know. It's not that they weren't interested—they obviously appreciated his instruction and showed a desire to learn. Huan couldn't figure out if the software was difficult for them to understand or if he was not doing a good job of teaching.

During the next few months, Huan started to see some patterns. He would get to a new client site and spend the first week going over the software with the employees—what it could do, how it worked, and what they needed to learn. He usually did this instruction in shifts, with different groups of employees listening to him lecture. He had developed one handout, but he mostly relied on the company's manual to determine what topics to cover. He always reached his goal of going over the manual from cover to cover with each

group of employees. Then he would spend the next week installing the program and helping individuals troubleshoot.

Huan realized that during the week of troubleshooting and answering questions, he ended up addressing the same issues over and over, especially about technical terms and functions. He was frustrated because he felt that these topics had been covered very well during the first week. He was also annoyed because most of the individuals with whom he worked seemed to have retained very little information from the first week. They asked very basic questions and often needed prompting from beginning to end. At first he wondered if these people were just a little slow, but then he began to get the distinct feeling that some of the problem might be his style of presenting the information.

Apply what you have learned about the informative speech as you ponder and discuss the following questions: What was Huan's immediate behavioral goal? Was he successful in reaching this goal? In what specific ways would an understanding of information hunger and relevance, extrinsic motivation, informative content, and information overload give Huan insight into what is going wrong? What skills could Huan use to become a more effective informative speaker?

KEY TERMS

Use the *Human Communication* CD-ROM and the *Online Learning Center* at www.mhhe.com/pearson to further your understanding of the following terminology.

Abstract words	Extrinsic motivation	Informative content
Antonym	Imagery	Interest
Comparison	Immediate behavioral	Narrating
Concrete words	purposes	Operational definition
Contrast	Information hunger	Rhetorical questions
Etymology	Information overload	Significance
Explanation	Information relevance	Synonym

SELF-QUIZ

 Go to the self-quizzes on the *Human Communication* CD-ROM and the *Online Learning Center* at www.mhhe.com/pearson to test your knowledge.

ADDITIONAL RESOURCES

Facsnet. A website dedicated to improving journalism through education. www.yearbook.com Especially good for science and technology, biotechnology, land use, energy, business and economics, law and government. Includes an annotated Associated Press digest.

Foundation for American Communication Site (FACS). A search engine for the news media. www.yearbook.com or www.Directoryof NewsSources.com. Search for experts by key words, topic, or participant. Ask a question of the experts.

REFERENCES

Ausubel, D. (1960). The use of advance organizers in the learning and retention of meaningful material. *Journal of Educational Psychology, 51,* 267–272.

Baird, J. A. (1974). The effects of speech summaries upon audience comprehension of expository speeches of varying quality and complexity. *Central States Speech Journal, 25,* 119–127.

Cofer, N. C. (1961). *Verbal learning and verbal behavior.* New York: McGraw-Hill.

Ernest, C. (1968). Listening comprehension as a function of type of material and rate of presentation. *Speech Monographs, 35,* 154–158.

Galbraith, J. K. (1981, January 4). The three attacks on social and economic consensus. *The Des Moines Sunday Register.*

Gruner, C. R. (1970). The effect of humor in dull and interesting informative speeches. *Central States Speech Journal, 21,* 160–166.

McGuire, M., Stillbourne, L., McAdams, M., & Hyatt, L. (1997). *Internet handbook for writers, researchers, and journalists.* New York: Guilford.

McGuire, S. (1998, August 24). More blood for Ireland: Will the peace survive a brutal bombing? *Newsweek,* p. 31.

Pence, O. L. (1954). Emotionally loaded argument: Its effectiveness in stimulating recall. *Quarterly Journal of Speech, 40,* 272–276.

Petrie, C. R., Jr. (1963). Informative speaking: A summary and bibliography of related research. *Speech Monographs, 30,* 79–91.

Petrie, C. R., Jr., & Carrel, S. D. (1976). The relationship of motivation, listening, capability, initial information, and verbal organizational ability to lecture comprehension and retention. *Speech Monographs, 43,* 187–194.

Tucker, C. D. (1964). An application of programmed learning to informative speech. *Speech Monographs, 31,* 142–152.

Wheeless, L. R. (1974). The effects of attitude, credibility, and homophily on selective exposure to information. *Speech Monographs, 41,* 329–338.

CHAPTER EIGHTEEN

You cannot convince a
man against his will.

SAMUEL JOHNSON

A woman convinced
against her will is of the
same opinion still.

LEONA HUGHES

We are more easily
persuaded, in general, by
the reasons that we
ourselves discover than by
those which are given to
us by others.

BLAISE PASCAL

Persuasive Presentations

What will you learn?

When you have read and thought about this chapter, you will be able to:

1. Identify four action goals of persuasive speaking.
2. Distinguish between immediate behavioral purposes and ultimate goals.
3. Describe and utilize persuasive-speaking strategies.
4. Recall four ethical guidelines for persuasive speaking.
5. State and utilize some persuasive-speaking skills.
6. Reveal some strategies for resisting persuasive appeals.

Few students think they will ever give a persuasive speech, but they admit that they are likely to be asked to introduce new products, convince others to use new methods, and talk with fellow workers about complying with policies and procedures. All of these efforts are simply variations of a persuasive presentation. In this chapter you will first learn what persuasion is. Then you will learn how to prepare a persuasive presentation, when to use some strategies of persuasion, and how persuasion can be perceived differently in cultures and co-cultures. Because persuasion is perceived with suspicion in our culture, you will explore some ethical problems related to persuasion. Finally, you will learn some ways to protect yourself from unwanted persuasive efforts; in other words, you will learn some strategies for resisting persuasive appeals.

Discussion Question

Ask students to provide examples of times that someone tried to coerce, manipulate, or persuade them. Use the examples to illustrate differences between these concepts.

Group Activity

Divide students into four groups. Assign each group one of the four action goals: continuance, deterrence, adoption, and discontinuance. Each group should generate five examples of persuasive speeches approriate for their assigned goal. Groups should discuss their examples with the class.

coercion

Forcing people to think or behave as you wish.

Edward's coworkers chose him to give the final presentation to CompuWork's board of directors. CompuWork had hired him and a team of three other consultants to perform a thorough evaluation of its business, to recommend organizational reforms, and to improve the company's bottom line. A recent MBA graduate, Edward was worried that the board of directors would not take his recommendations seriously. The directors were executives with successful career tracks. His three coworkers did not seem to think the board's status would be a problem.

Georgia grew up in a tough, inner-city neighborhood. Her family did not have the money to help her attend college, but she was determined to get a good education. In high school she studied hard, worked to save as much money as she could, and volunteered to help younger children learn to read. During Georgia's senior year in high school, her chemistry teacher helped her apply for different scholarships that ultimately allowed her to get a bachelor's degree. After graduation, Georgia became an advocate for the university's scholarship program, volunteering to speak to groups of alumni to encourage them to give generously so that others like her would be able to go to school. At first she relied solely on her personal experience when talking to people, but she soon learned that she needed more than this approach to persuade people to contribute to the scholarship fund.

Like Edward and Georgia, most of us will need to give persuasive presentations during our lifetimes. The goal of this chapter is to prepare you as both a creator and a receiver of persuasive messages.

What Is Persuasion and What Are the Goals of Persuasive Presentations?

manipulation

Tricking people or using fraudulent means to change people's behavior.

ability to choose

Making a decision based on information and ideas.

Many people have a mistaken view of how persuasion works. For instance, some people think persuasion is the skillful manipulation of images to get people to do something they would not otherwise do. To them, persuasion is seduction, getting their way with people by influencing them against their will. Actually *forcing people to think or behave as you wish* is not persuasion but **coercion.** A related phenomenon involves *tricking people or using fraudulent means to gain compliance;* this is not persuasion but **manipulation.** Neither coercion nor manipulation is close to persuasion as portrayed in this text. Why? Because both coercion and manipulation bypass a person's **ability to choose,** *to make a decision based on sound information and ideas.*

Communication scholars see persuasion not as coercion or manipulation but as a more noble pursuit of the best ideas, most workable solutions, and most effective support for an idea through effective speaking. The best speakers know how to assemble an effective persuasive message through their knowledge of critical thinking, and they use the same tools to analyze what others are saying.

Persuasion is *an ongoing process in which verbal and nonverbal messages shape, reinforce, and change people's responses* (Miller, 1980). Rarely do people change greatly as a result of a one-shot persuasive effort. Instead, people usually change as a result of a **persuasive campaign:** because of *ongoing exposure to messages from speakers, newspapers, magazines, broadcasts, chat rooms, friends, and relatives.* Immediate change may be possible for behavior that is of little importance to us (e.g., changing our brand of toothpaste), but changes in life-style (e.g., daily exercise) or belief (e.g., religious beliefs) ordinarily continue through a lifetime unless dislodged over time by contrary messages from credible sources.

These multiple messages *shape* our responses by pushing us to act or think in a certain way (Miller, 1980). In the past, you might have disliked dancing, but because your closest friend loves to dance, you changed your behavior over time until you now enjoy dancing. A single persuasive speech can *start* to push an audience in a direction desired by the speaker.

Persuasive messages can also *reinforce* past behavior or beliefs—that is, reward a person for persisting in a certain response or for avoiding a certain response. In persuasive speaking, the general goal of reinforcing consists of two action goals: continuance and deterrence. **Continuance** means that *you encourage the audience to continue its present behavior or beliefs,* such as using seat belts, going to synagogue, or eating low-fat foods. **Deterrence** means that *you encourage the audience to avoid an activity or a belief,* such as using drugs, smoking, or joining a gang.

Persuasive messages can also *change* people's actions or thoughts. Under this general goal of changing an audience's responses are the action goals of adoption and discontinuance. **Adoption** is *inducing the audience to accept a new idea, attitude, behavior, belief, or product,* such as starting each day with a nutritionally balanced breakfast. **Discontinuance** means that *the audience is encouraged to stop doing or believing something,* such as voting Republican, eating junk foods, or drinking alcoholic beverages (Fotheringham, 1966). Think of shaping, reinforcing, and changing as very broad general goals of persuasion, and the action goals—continuance, deterrence, adoption, and discontinuance—as the "acting out" of those goals.

You can improve your chances of persuading an audience if you write out the ultimate goal of your presentation and your action goals, or immediate behavioral purposes. **Ultimate goals** are *purposes that you wish to fulfill with additional messages and more time—perhaps days, months, or years.* **Immediate goals** are *purposes that you wish to accomplish during the speech or within minutes or hours.* (Figure 18.1 illustrates the

---

persuasion

An ongoing process in which verbal and nonverbal messages shape, reinforce, and change people's responses.

persuasive campaign

An ongoing series of related messages from speakers, newspapers, magazines, broadcasts, chat rooms, friends, and relatives that can change one's responses.

continuance

Persuading an audience to continue present behavior or beliefs.

deterrence

Persuading an audience to avoid an activity or a belief.

adoption

Inducing an audience to accept a new idea, attitude, behavior, belief, or product and to demonstrate that acceptance through behavioral change.

discontinuance

Inducing an audience to stop doing something or thinking in a certain way.

ultimate goals

Purposes that a speaker wishes to fulfill with additional messages and more time.

GENERAL GOALS	ACTION GOALS	EXPECTED BEHAVIOR	IMMEDIATE GOALS	ULTIMATE GOALS
To shape	To move toward action goals	To move toward expected behavior	To move toward immediate goals	To move toward ultimate goals
To reinforce	Continuance	Keep doing it	Continue now	Continue later
	Deterrence	Don't do it	Avoid now	Avoid later
To change	Adoption	Start doing it	Start now	Start later
	Discontinuance	Stop doing it	Stop now	Stop later

Figure 18.1   The relationship among persuasive goals.

immediate goals

Purposes that a speaker wishes to accomplish during the speech or shortly after it.

relationships among the various persuasive goals.) For example, a student delivering a persuasive presentation against jogging might write down the following as an ultimate goal:

> The ultimate goal of my persuasive presentation is to convince people who jog that they should quit [discontinuance] and to convince people who do not jog that they should never start [deterrence].

The same presenter might state her immediate behavioral purposes as:

> One of my immediate behavioral purposes is to have the audience write down at the conclusion of my presentation the three harmful effects of jogging on the body: shin splints, bone bruises, and knee problems. A second immediate behavioral purpose of my presentation is to have the joggers in the audience start reducing their workout times to avoid problems encouraged by fatigue.

The persuasive presenter need not reveal the ultimate goal of the message itself but, ordinarily, should reveal the immediate behavioral purposes of the presentation. Audience members are more likely to write down the harmful effects of jogging if they are told of that expectation early in the presentation. They may resist the persuasive presenter, however, if they know that the ultimate goal of the presentation is to reduce the audience's workout times.

Class Activity

Have student write down three topics that they might explore for their persuasive speech along with their ultimate goal for each topic. Ask volunteers to share their goals and as a class classify those goals as continuance, deterrence, adoption, and/or discontinuance.

Many communication teachers will want you to use the general goals of shaping and changing and the action goals of adoption and discontinuance. They may even discourage presentations with the general goal of reinforcing and the action goals of deterrence and continuance. One of the reasons for encouraging you to give persuasive presentations with adoption and discontinuance action goals is that you and the teacher will be better able to observe change in the audience. With deterrence and continuance action goals, the audience's behavior may remain the same, but to attribute that lack of change to your speech would be risky.

What Are Some Persuasive Speech Topics?

Chapter 17 on informing others mentioned that the perception of a topic as informative or persuasive depends not only on the topic but also on the presenter and the audience. A presenter's **intention**—*how the speaker wants the audience to respond*—may be to produce change in an audience, but how the audience receives the message actually determines whether the message is perceived as informative or as persuasive. A topic like "equal pay for women" could be presented as informative by including pay scales and percentages of pay differences in your presentation. "Equal pay for women" also could be persuasive by including arguments for challenging and changing the current system. Even if a presenter's intent is to inform, a female giving an informative presentation on equal pay for women might be perceived by her audience as advocating a position. The main point to remember is that in a persuasive speech you are trying to change an audience's position on some issue; changing an audience assumes that the receivers have a position on the issue and that they are not neutral or ignorant about the topic.

Chapter 13, Topic Selection and Audience Analysis, provided a detailed account of how to use brainstorming and inventories to find topics. Approaches that may serve as shortcuts to finding a topic are to consider first those issues that you care about. Then look through newspapers and magazines, listen to talk radio, watch TV news and talk shows, and search the Internet for issues that interest you. Another shortcut is to look through topics that students have already used for their persuasive speeches to see if any of them give you some ideas. Following are some possibilities:

Toughen immigration policies	War is immoral
Improve relations with refugees	Celibacy for teens
Use foreign aid as a weapon	Against cohabitation
Strengthen the military	Favor gay adoption
Use mediation, not might	Improve race relations

intention

How the speaker wants the audience to respond.

Discussion Question

Ask students to think about situations where the speaker may not want to reveal her or his ultimate goal to the audience. Is it ethical to not reveal one's goal?

Teaching Tip

Give students a copy of the evaluation form you intend to use for the persuasive speech. Review elements of the form and discuss your expectations. Compare and contrast this form to the evaluation form used for the informative speech. What new requirements are included for the persuasive speech? Sample evaluation forms are provided in the instructor's manual.

How Do You Persuade an Audience?

You can persuade an audience in a variety of ways. Researchers Marvin Karlins and Herbert I. Abelson (1970) observed, "Information by itself almost never changes attitudes." In addition to offering information in support of your persuasive message, you can attempt to persuade an audience by using motivational appeals, your source credibility, and logical or emotional appeals; by organizing your materials effectively; and by observing ethical guidelines for persuasion.

Video Activity

Ask students to view the video segment "On the Air with Campus-Community Connection." Have students analyze the strategies used by both speakers to make their persuasive claims. Was one speaker more effective than the other? Were some types of appeals more persuasive than others?

Class Activity

To help students distinguish between motivational, emotional, and logical appeals, ask them to complete the exercise "Mass Appeal" found in the instructor's manual.

Motivational Appeals

The word *motivation* is based on a Latin term that means "to move," which is how the term is used in everyday conversations: "What was his motivation in buying that expensive car?" "She had plenty of motivation for getting a job"; or "His motive was to act just like the other firefighters." If you boil down motivation to its essential ingredients, you can see that three forces move people to behave in one way or another (McConnell, 1977).

One motivating force is *what our bodies tell us to do.* This physical basis of motivation explains our need for air, water, and food. You can get along without air for less than three minutes, without water for only a couple of days, and without food for only a few weeks. Having unpolluted air to breathe, clean water to drink, and desirable food to eat takes much human energy, but our basic bodily needs motivate us to do what is necessary to preserve these resources.

The second motivating force is *what our minds tell us to do.* This psychological motivation is based on our sense of rationality, as well as on our emotions, feelings, and perceptions. You are moved to do some things because you think doing so is reasonable. You may do other things because you feel good about doing them. You may avoid still other activities because they make you feel bad about yourself. The human mind motivates us to act in ways that keep us comfortable.

The third motivating force is *what other people want us to do.* This third force is a powerful social motivator that encourages us to conform to roles and norms. You may act like a student because your fellow students reinforce you when you do and punish you when you do not. You may attend classes because that is what students are to do. You might find yourself doing any number of activities because family, friends, and coworkers expect and reward such behavior.

Human behavior is very complicated. No explanation of why human beings behave the way they do is entirely satisfactory. Simply knowing the three kinds of motivational forces will not permit you to elicit the behavior you seek. Nonetheless, the most effective persuasive speakers—advertisers, politicians, and lawyers—have learned how to analyze their audiences—consumers, voters, and juries—so that they are more often successful than unsuccessful in reaching their objectives.

TRY ◄ ▶ THIS

What motivational appeals tend to work on you? Do you tend to do what others wish for you, or do the wishes of others cause you to rebel? Think carefully about what moves you to action. Do you think the same motivations that influence you also influence your audience?

Emotional Appeals

Emotional appeals are *attempts to persuade audience members to change an attitude or a behavior through an appeal—usually in a narrative form—to their emotions.* Although logical and emotional appeals are often seen as diametrically opposed concepts, most of our behavior and beliefs are based on a mixture of emotional and rational "reasons." A speaker may persuade an audience to accept his or her immediate behavioral purposes for emotional, rather than logical, reasons. A story about one person's bad experience with the campus bookstore may inspire many persons in the audience to take their business to another store. The experience may have been a one-in-a-thousand situation, the episode may have been as much the customer's fault as the manager's, or such a bad experience may never have happened before. Such is the power of our emotions that they can persuade us to defy the law, fight another nation, or ignore evidence. As one writer stated:

> The creature man is best persuaded
> When heart, not mind, is inundated:
> Affect is what drives the will:
> Rationality keeps it still.*

The appeal that has received the most attention from researchers is the *fear appeal.* Janis and Feshbach (1953) examined three levels of fear appeals in communication on maintaining dental hygiene and found that a weak threat works better than a moderate threat, which works better than a strong threat. On the other hand, Powell (1965) used strong and weak fear appeals in a civil defense message that threatened loved ones and found more opinion change when the fear appeal was strong. These results are contradictory, but the research on reassurance with fear appeals is not. Your fear appeals are likely to work better if you reveal how the audience can avoid the fearsome consequences of a behavior or belief. For example, you could say, "Not brushing your teeth can lead to gum disease and tooth loss, so listen to my tips on dental hygiene." Omitting reassurance does not influence the audience's ability to recall facts from the speech, but a speech with reassurance results in greater shifts of opinion than one without reassurance. Also, a presenter who includes reassurance is regarded by the audience as a better speaker than one who does not (Cope & Richardson, 1972).

Fear appeals are just one kind of emotional appeal commonly found in presentations. Other examples of possible emotional appeals are

emotional appeals

Attempts to persuade audience members to change an attitude or a behavior through an appeal—usually in a narrative form—to their emotions.

---

*Reprinted from Marvin Karlins and Herbert I. Abelson, *Persuasion: How Opinions and Attitudes Are Changed* (2nd ed). Copyright © 1970 by Springer Publishing Company, Inc., New York. Used by permission.

testimonials at funerals about the virtues of the deceased, appeals to loyalty and dedication at retirement ceremonies, appeals to patriotism in times of crisis, and appeals to justice in times of legal strife.

Logical Appeals

logical appeals

Propositions and evidence used to persuade an audience.

Motivational appeals and speaker credibility are just two tools for persuading an audience; a third important method is the use of reasoning or logic to convince an audience. The main ingredients of **logical appeals** are *propositions and evidence*.

A *proposition* is a statement that asserts or proposes something: "The United States should have uniform regulations for child support"; "The city should reduce the fines for traffic offenses"; or "The college should change its definition of 'a student in good standing.'" Notice that a proposition always recommends a change in the status quo, the way things are right now. The primary method of persuading an audience that a current policy should be changed and another policy should be adopted is through the use of evidence.

evidence

Any material that supports a proposition.

Evidence, *any material that supports a proposition,* is central to the persuasive process (Reinhard, 1988). The persuasive speaker can use a wide array of evidence to demonstrate the wisdom of retaining present practices or changing current policies, such as quotations from authoritative persons, conclusions from studies and reports, or experiences of individuals injured or helped by current policies. The underlying principle in logical appeals is that the audience should accept the side that presents the most convincing or the "best" evidence to support itself. In other words, our behavior or changes in behavior should be based on the best evidence; any change should be consistent with the persuasive presenter who provides the most effective evidence.

Discussion Question

What type of evidence is most persuasive when making a decision on what college to attend?

Logical appeals can also be refuted; that is, they can be attacked. Another persuasive speaker can analyze the situation suggested in a proposition and find the argument flawed. The opposing persuasive presenter may find that the authorities who were quoted were biased, that the reports and studies were flawed, or that better evidence would invite a different conclusion.

Finally, to recognize that the world does not run by logic or evidence alone is important; sometimes beliefs and behaviors are irrational or not based on evidence. A persuasive presenter might present considerable evidence on why you should eat legumes and cheese instead of meat without changing audience behavior or beliefs on that subject. The persuasive presenter is always faced with the disconcerting fact that even the best evidence in support of a persuasive proposition might not alter audience beliefs or behavior. Human beings are complicated and their responses to messages may not be what the presenter predicts. For example, an attorney may follow all the rules of law and logic, present the best possible evidence to a jury, and still lose the case because the jurors' hearts trumped their heads.

Cultural/Co-cultural Note

PEOPLE THINK DIFFERENTLY

The use of argument, evidence, and logic can be seen as a European-derived manner of thinking unendorsed either by non-European cultures or North America's own co-cultures. Yook and Albert (1998), for example, found that Korean students as a group were significantly less likely to negotiate with a teacher over matters of grading and learning than were a group of American students. Foss and Griffin (1995) explain a feminist alternative to traditional persuasion in which the goal is not to change, attack, and vanquish the opponent but to achieve understanding through "invitational rhetoric." Sullivan and Goldswig (1995) note that even the Supreme Court unexpectedly adopted "a relational approach to moral reasoning" (p. 167) instead of the usual patriarchal, Western, European, legalistic approaches. Remember different cultures and co-cultures may adopt quite different approaches to negotiating, arguing, and persuading.

Organizational Considerations

The organizational patterns used most often in persuasive presentations are problem/solution, cause/effect, and topical-sequence, patterns that you can review from Chapter 15. Besides choosing a basic pattern of organization, you need to consider how much to say in your introduction.

In informative presentations, you usually say exactly what you want your audience to learn. In persuasive presentations, you may not want to say your ultimate goal. You might not want to state your immediate purpose or ultimate goal because audience acceptance may depend on your series of arguments and examples. You do not want them to stop listening at the outset. For example, some women upon hearing that you are presenting a feminist point of view may stop listening, but if they heard first that you were proposing more job opportunities, better pay, and less discrimination, they might have listened. Sometimes you withhold the statement of immediate purpose and ultimate goal because the audience is not likely to accept your point of view until you have presented your **arguments,** *your propositions, justifications, and evidence.* You might, therefore, omit your ultimate goal until the audience is more prepared.

Other organizational considerations in persuasive speaking concern placing your arguments, presenting one or more sides of the issue, deciding

Writing Assignment

Have students write a short paper on the organizational plan for their persuasive speech. Students should incorporate answers to the four organizational consideration questions for persuasive speeches found in the text.

arguments

Propositions, justifications, and evidence used to persuade.

whether to include counterarguments, and using familiar or novel arguments in your speech:

1. *Should my best arguments come first, in the middle, or last in my persuasive presentation?* Arguments presented first or early in the body of the message seem to have more impact in presentations on controversial issues, on topics with which the audience is uninvolved, on topics the audience perceives as interesting, and on topics highly familiar to the audience. On the other hand, arguments seem to have more impact on an audience later in a persuasive presentation when audience members are involved in the issue, when the topic is likely to be less interesting, and when the issue is moderately unfamiliar to the audience (Janis & Feshbach, 1953). No research to date indicates that the most important arguments should be presented in the middle of a presentation. The middle is the place where audience attention is likely to wane, so the effective presenter usually builds in human-interest stories and interesting supporting materials to maintain audience attention.

2. *Should I present one side of the issue, both, or many?* A persuasive presenter should present one side of an issue when the audience is friendly, when the presenter's position is the only one the audience is likely to hear, and when the presenter is seeking immediate, but temporary, change of opinion. A persuasive presenter should address both sides or many sides of an issue when the audience initially disagrees with the speaker, or when the audience will likely hear other sides from other people (Powell, 1965). Presenting both sides or multiple sides to a hostile audience may make the speaker seem more openminded or less rigid to the audience. Also, presenting the other sides of the issue reduces the impact of **counterarguments,** or *rebuttals to your arguments.*

3. *Should I refute counterarguments?* The best advice is to refute counterarguments before proceeding to your own position on the issue, especially when the audience is likely to know the counterarguments already (Karlins & Abelson, 1970). If you favor freedom of choice on the abortion issue and your audience is familiar with the opposing side, then you should refute the known counterarguments—point out their relative weaknesses or flaws—before you reveal your own position on the issue.

4. *Should I use familiar or novel arguments in my persuasive presentation?* On most topics, you will have to acknowledge familiar arguments, and possibly refute them. However, *novel* arguments, or arguments the audience has not heard before, have more impact than familiar ones (Sears & Freedman, 1965). A student who delivered a persuasive presentation in favor of gun control pointed out that a common counterargument from anticontrol forces was that gun registration would provide national enemies with a ready-

counterarguments

Rebuttals to an argument.

made list of gun owners. The student who favored gun control pointed out that the membership list of the National Rifle Association already provided an extensive list of gun owners that could be used by national enemies. The argument was novel and served to nullify the claim made by the anticontrol side on the issue. You, too, should seek novel arguments in support of your own case and against the positions of others. Old, familiar arguments may be somewhat useful in your persuasive presentation, but arguments the audience has not heard before have greater impact.

The **Monroe motivated sequence** is *a problem-solving format that encourages an audience to become concerned about an issue.* Widely acclaimed for its usefulness in organizing speeches (Ehninger, 1970), the sequence has five steps:

1. *Attention.* You must gain and maintain audience attention, and you must determine a way to focus audience attention on the content of your speech.
2. *Need.* Once you have the audience's attention, you must show audience members how the speech is relevant to them. You must arouse a need for the change you suggest in your persuasive speech.
3. *Satisfaction.* Your speech either presents the information the audience needs or is a solution to their needs. You satisfy the audience by meeting their needs with your plan.
4. *Visualization.* You reinforce your idea in the audience's minds by getting audience members to *see* how your information or ideas will help them.
5. *Action.* Once the audience has visualized your idea, you plead for action. The audience might remember your main points in an informative speech and state them to others, or the audience may go out and do what you ask in a persuasive speech.

The Monroe motivated sequence is an appropriate organizational pattern for persuasive presentations, especially when the audience is reluctant to change or to accept a proposed action. See an illustration of the sequence in Figure 18.2.

Speaker Credibility

In chapter 12 you learned that **source credibility** is *the audience's perception of your effectiveness as a speaker* and that the concept has five dimensions: expertise, trustworthiness, dynamism, common ground, and identification. Recall also that a speaker does not have to exhibit all five dimensions; sometimes one dimension, such as the speaker's trustworthiness, is the sole source of credibility. You would probably favor expertise over dynamism in a mechanic, trustworthiness over expertise in a spiritual leader, and expertise over common ground in a physician.

Video Activity

Tape several commercials. In class view the commercials and have students analyze them to determine whether they follow Monroe's motivated sequence. If not all elements are present, are other elements implicit or implied?

Monroe motivated sequence

A problem-solving format that encourages an audience to become concerned about an issue; especially appropriate for a persuasive speech.

CD-ROM Activity

Ask students to view the animation titled "Monroe's Motivated Sequence" found on the accompanying student CD-ROM. The animation illustrates the process of planning a message following Monroe's sequence.

source credibility

The audience's perception of your effectiveness as a speaker.

Active Art

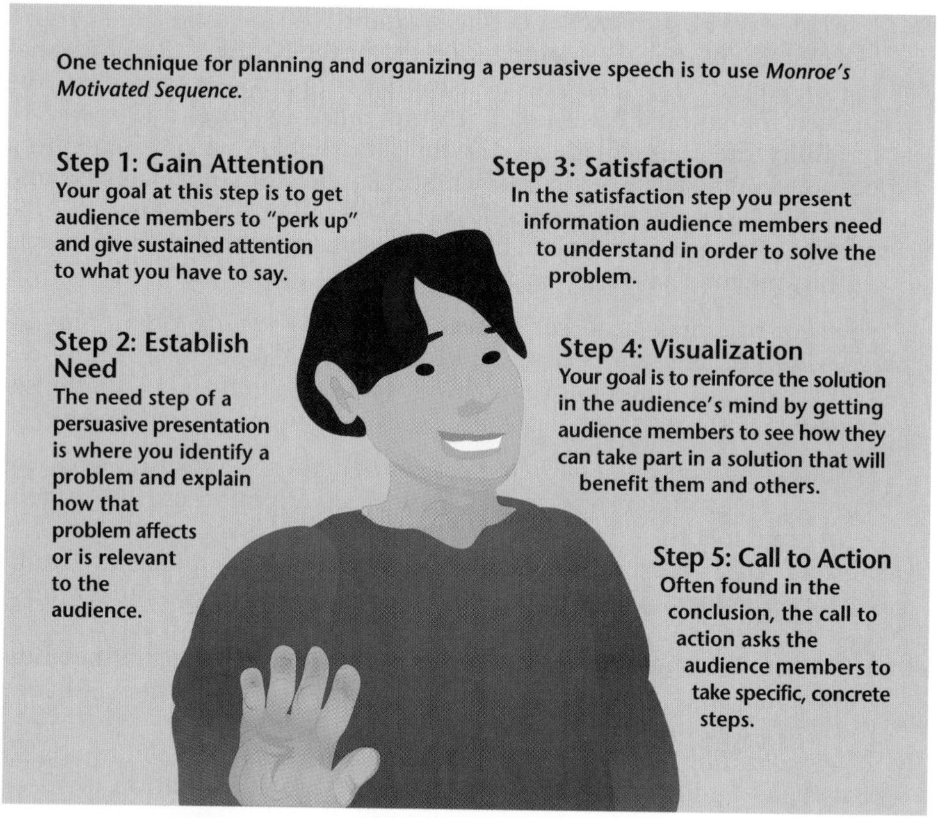

One technique for planning and organizing a persuasive speech is to use *Monroe's Motivated Sequence*.

Step 1: Gain Attention
Your goal at this step is to get audience members to "perk up" and give sustained attention to what you have to say.

Step 2: Establish Need
The need step of a persuasive presentation is where you identify a problem and explain how that problem affects or is relevant to the audience.

Step 3: Satisfaction
In the satisfaction step you present information audience members need to understand in order to solve the problem.

Step 4: Visualization
Your goal is to reinforce the solution in the audience's mind by getting audience members to see how they can take part in a solution that will benefit them and others.

Step 5: Call to Action
Often found in the conclusion, the call to action asks the audience members to take specific, concrete steps.

Figure 18.2   Monroe's motivated sequence.

Discussion Question

What steps can be taken to prevent the likelihood of the boomerang effect occurring as a result of your persuasive speech?

boomerang effect

An unintended situation in which the speaker and the message induce an audience response that is the opposite of what the speaker intended.

Who and what you are can make a powerful difference in your effectiveness as a persuasive presenter. A highly credible presenter has more impact on an audience than one with low credibility. Also, a persuasive presenter perceived as similar to the audience is more likely to be effective than one who is perceived as dissimilar. Sometimes a highly credible presenter can attain more attitude change by simply asking for more change (Hovland & Pritzker, 1957).

All presenters need to avoid asking for too much change, however, lest they invite a **boomerang effect,** *an unintended situation in which the speaker and the message induce an audience response that is the opposite of what the speaker intended.* For instance, the presenter wants the audience members to vote Republican, but they find him and his message so repugnant that they are less likely than before the presentation to vote Republican.

You can signal the origins of your credibility to your audience by describing how you earned the right to speak on the topic. Perhaps your major will help: A nuclear engineer has the authority to speak on nuclear

energy; a business major is a credible source on buying stocks and bonds; a physical education major can speak with authority on exercise programs. Maybe your experience is the key to your credibility. Your years in the military may have given you some insights into military waste. Your years as a mother and homemaker may have given you the authority to speak on managing time effectively, raising children, or relating to a spouse. Or your part-time job at a fast-food restaurant may permit you to speak with some authority on the minimum wage.

Whatever the origins of your credibility, remember to reveal them early in the presentation. Your authority may very well provide a reason for the audience to listen. If you reveal your credibility late in the presentation, the audience may have paid little attention because they did not know you spoke with authority on the topic.

Another caution is in order. Although you must demonstrate your credibility to the audience, you can go too far in self-disclosing. Psychologists Berger and Vartabedian (1985) showed that as a speaker's prestige increases, the appropriateness of self-disclosure, as determined by the audience, decreases. Thus people who are high in prestige should avoid high levels of personal revelation. Some personal information can be offered by anyone, but perhaps no speaker should "tell all" in attempting to establish credibility.

Ethical Considerations

Ethics *are a set of principles of right conduct.* Many of our standards for ethical behavior are codified into law. We do not slander or libel someone who is an ordinary citizen. We do not start a panic that can endanger the lives of others. And we do not advocate the overthrow of our government.

Many principles of ethics are not matters of law, but violations of these unwritten rules do have consequences. No law exists against pointing out acne sufferers in the audience during your speech on dermatology

---

Discussion Question

Ask students to complete the exercise "Hidden Persuasion" found in the instructor's manual. Later, have students discuss whether the use of subliminal advertising is ethical.

---

ethics

A set of principles of right conduct.

A "free" speech to an unsuspecting audience ends with a blatant appeal to buy the speaker's tapes. Was his appeal ethical in your opinion? Why or why not?

or having your audience unknowingly eat cooked hamster meat, but audience members may find your methods so distasteful that they reject you and your persuasive message.

The following are some of the generally accepted ethical standards that govern the preparation and delivery of a persuasive presenter.

Class Activity

Using ideas found in this section as well as ideas generated by the class, develop a class credo of ethics for persuasive speeches. Post the credo in your classroom.

1. *Accurately cite sources.* When you are preparing and delivering your speech, you should be very careful to gather and state your information accurately. Specifically, you should reveal from whom you received information. Making up quotations, attributing an idea to someone who never made the statement, omitting important qualifiers, quoting out of context, and distorting information from others are all examples of ethical violations.

2. *Respect sources of information.* Internet sources are sometimes the best available information and sometimes the worst. Show respect for your sources of information by revealing as completely as possible the credibility of your sources. This rule extends to respect for persons you interview. These people are willing to share information with you, so it behooves you to treat them and their information with respect in person and in your presentation.

3. *Respect your audience.* Persuasion is a process that works most effectively with mutual respect between presenter and receiver. Attempts to trick the audience into believing something, lying to the audience, distorting the views of your opposition, or exaggerating claims for your own position are all ethically questionable acts. A presenter should speak truthfully and accurately; the best persuasive presenters can accurately portray the opposing arguments and still win with their own arguments and evidence. Audiences can be very hostile to a person who has tricked them or who has lied, distorted, or exaggerated information simply to meet an immediate behavioral purpose or an ultimate goal.

4. *Respect your opponent.* Persuasive speeches invite rebuttal. Nearly always someone inside or outside your audience thinks your ideas or positions are wrong. A good rule of thumb is to respect your opponent, not only because he or she may be right but also because an effective persuasive presenter can take the best the opposition has to offer and still convince the audience he or she should be believed. The idea that you should respect your opponent means you should not indulge in name calling or in bringing up past behaviors that are irrelevant to the issue. You should attack the other person's evidence, sources, or logic—not the person. Practical reasons for observing this rule of ethics are that few of the issues about which people persuade are ever settled, that you may find in time that your opponent's position is better in many respects than your own, and that you will have to live with many issues not resolved in the manner you most desire.

You may get the impression from these four ethical guidelines that every persuasive speaker must be part angel. Not quite. The ethical rules for persuasive speaking allow for critical analysis of arguments and ideas, for profound differences of opinion, for the weighing of evidence and supporting materials, and for the swaying of the audience to your point of view. All of these strategies work best if you obey the ethical guidelines that call for the accurate citation of sources, respect for sources of information, respect for your audience, and respect for your opponent.

What Are Some Persuasive-Speaking Skills?

Just as an informative speaker must learn skills in defining, describing, explaining, and narrating, a persuasive speaker must learn skills in arguing and providing evidence.

Remember that an argument consists of propositions, justifications, and evidence. In persuasive presentations, a proposition embodies what you want the audience to believe or do—for example, to believe that all young people should spend two years in the military or in some form of public service, to give up individual rights for increased security, and to restrict immigration from hostile nations. The speaker presents evidence to get the audience to accept the proposition. To be persuasive, evidence must meet the tests of evidence and believability.

Your evidence must meet the **tests of evidence,** *questions you can use to test the validity of the evidence* in your speeches or in the speeches of others:

tests of evidence

Questions that can be used to test the validity of evidence.

1. *Is the evidence consistent with other known facts?* For instance, did the speaker look at a relatively large number of student co-ops to determine that student co-ops are successful? Have any student co-op stores failed?

2. *Would another observer draw the same conclusions?* Has anyone other than the speaker determined that other student co-ops are successful? What does the speaker mean by "success"?

3. *Does the evidence come from unbiased sources?* Does the vice-president for student affairs have anything to gain by favoring student co-op bookstores? Who made the claim that students will get better value for their used books? Who said other schools have established successful student co-ops?

4. *Is the source of the information qualified by education and/or experience to make a statement about the issue?* The vice-president may be well educated, but what does she know about co-op bookstores? What about the qualifications of the sources of the information on used books or successful co-ops?

5. *If the evidence is based on personal experience, how typical is that personal experience?* Personal experience that is typical, generalizable, realistic, and relevant can be good evidence.

6. *If statistics are used as evidence, are they from a reliable source; comparable with other known information; and current, applicable, and interpreted so that the audience can understand them?*

7. *If studies and surveys are used, are they authoritative, valid, reliable, objective, and generalizable?* A study done by persons who favor student co-op bookstores, for instance, would be questionable because the source of the study is biased.

8. *Are the speaker's inferences appropriate according to the data presented?* Does the presenter go too far beyond the evidence in concluding that students should establish their own co-op bookstore?

Writing Assignment

Ask students to write a short paper analyzing how evidence used to support their persuasive speech meets the 10 tests of evidence.

9. *Is important counterevidence overlooked?* Often, in our haste to make a positive case, we ignore or omit counterevidence. What evidence against student co-ops is left out?
10. *What is the presenter's credibility on the topic?* Has the speaker earned the right to speak on the topic through research, interviews, and a thorough examination of the issue? Has the speaker had experience related to the issue?

The answers to these 10 questions are important. Evidence that meets these tests has met the first requirement of good evidence.

The second requirement of good evidence is **believability:** *Does the audience believe, trust, and accept the evidence?* Finding evidence that meets the tests of evidence is difficult enough, but at least the presenter has some guidelines. Believability is more mysterious; however, audience analysis can help a presenter determine which kinds of evidence will be most believable to a particular group of listeners. For instance, a speaker addressing a group of fundamentalist Christians may know that evidence from scripture will fall on friendly ears and be accepted as proof; that same evidence may not be believed by groups who do not accept the authority of the Bible. The effective persuasive presenter knows all the major arguments for and against a persuasive proposition. He or she chooses the evidence to be used in the presentation both because the evidence meets the tests of evidence and because audience analysis indicates that this evidence is most likely to be believed.

believability

A criterion of good evidence—the audience must trust and accept the evidence.

An Example of a Persuasive Presentation

Having read much about persuasion and how to influence others, we turn now to an annotated persuasive presentation that illustrates many of the concepts introduced in the chapter. You should read the presentation carefully for its strengths and its weaknesses. What methods does the presenter use to influence the listeners? Do the arguments and evidence meet the tests discussed in this chapter? What could the presenter have done differently that would have made the message more appealing to you?

Race and Health

Today I want to talk with you about the link between race and health and what you can do about the issue. You can see that I am a white person and a male, so you might think this topic is not appropriate for me. What you do not see is that I have relatives who are called "people of color" because my brother-in-law is African American, my uncle is Filipino, and all of my nieces and nephews are interracial, a mixture of black and white. Also present in our community is a rich mixture of Latinos, mostly from Mexico, who came originally for field work. Add to them the many refugees and immigrants brought here by churches from Croatia, Kosovo, Vietnam, Ukraine, Serbia, Sudan, Somalia, and other nations

Topic announced

Speaker establishes credibility on the topic

*Credibility on
ethnicity established*

Reminder of topic

*Credibility based on
major career plans,
and preparation*

*Oral footnote on
authorative source*

*PowerPoint provides
visual aids*

*Statistics used as
supporting material
for argument*

*Facts and figures
from a national report*

Reminder of the topic

Oral footnote

where their lives were threatened by wars. Finally, the immediate area has a number of tribes, reservations, and Indian lands, especially Sioux and Cherokee bands of plains and woods Native Americans. So looks can be deceiving. I have black and Asian relatives, and you live in a community with dozens of ethnic groups from around the world. What does race or ethnicity have to do with health?

Well, I am also a major in food and nutrition, and I plan to make my career as a public health advocate. My personal interest in health encourages me to read widely and to listen intently to issues of health. For example, I read recently in *the Washington Post* (October 15–21, 2001) an article entitled "We're Living Longer, Healthier" with the subhead "A new report says life expectancy rates are the highest ever, and infant mortality is down." The article was a U.S. government report by Arialdi M. Minino, a demographer and statistician at the National Center for Health Statistics, which produced its report in October 2001.

Among the statistics relevant to race and health were these figures which I have included on the PowerPoint presentation:

- While women live almost 80 years on average, men live about 6 years less at 74 years of age on average.

- While white women live to an average of 80 years, black women die 5 years earlier at an average of 75 years.

- While white men live to an average of 75 years, black men die almost 6 years earlier at closer to 68 years of age.

- While the highest death rates were in Puerto Rico, Mississippi, and the District of Columbia—all with substantial minority populations—the lowest death rate was in Hawaii, the only state with a majority Asian population.

The good news in Minino's report from the National Center for Health Statistics was that life expectances went up, and national death rates went down. Also, the life expectancy of minority groups showed improvements larger than for whites and the population as a whole. Look at the PowerPoint presentation and you will see that death rates fell around 3 percent for Asian, Hispanic, and African-American men while the death rate for white men fell only half of that figure.

Another piece of good news is that death from heart disease has, according to the *Washington Post*, "fallen steadily since 1950" and cancer rates have fallen since 1990. Why should we be concerned, then, if the public health picture appears to be improving?

The reason is that in spite of this overall rosy picture of improvement in our nation's public heath, we continue to have wide disparities in who dies from what. The disparities are especially large when we look more closely at race and health.

On October 22, 2002, Katherine Lanpher's *Midmorning* program on Minnesota Public Radio featured the topic of health and race. Take a quick look at the PowerPoint presentation for some the statistics that emerged from a study by the Minnesota Department of Health.

PowerPoint provides visual aids

- Asian women are much more likely to die of cervical cancer than are other women in the population.
- Black men are more susceptible to death by prostate cancer than are other men in the population.
- Black women die of breast cancer at higher rates than other women.
- Native Americans have a diabetes rate that is 600 percent higher than that of other racial groups.
- Tuberculosis is a health threat to many immigrants and refugees from other countries.

Specific, concrete information on race and health

These statistics provide evidence that in some cases disease and death are linked to race in America.

Some of you are probably thinking that disease and death may be linked more strongly to economics than to race. For example, you might think that poor people in minority groups are more likely to die of some specific disease because they have less access to health care. Janet Malcolm, commissioner of the Minnesota Department of Health, testified on the radio program that the Minnesota statewide study corrected for income levels and found that the same diseases dominated racial groups regardless of income. So apparently we cannot erase the racial link by claiming the wealth or poverty accounts for the difference.

Analysis and reasoned discourse on the topic

However, access and equal treatment may be part of the problem in the link between race and health. As one Spanish-speaking participant observed, most equal-opportunity clinics have white physicians and nurses, many of whom do not speak the language of their patients. Are these patients treated the same as English-speaking white people in the clinics in a better part of the city? Studies have already demonstrated that women and black men are treated less aggressively for heart problems, still the leading cause of death in America. Quite possibly people of color, non-English-speaking individuals, and people without insurance receive different treatment than do others. Thus, access to first-rate medical treatment can be part of the problem as is the lack of black and Spanish-speaking receptionists, nurses, and doctors.

Specific information on race and health

Because of time constraints I just have to hope you are starting to be convinced that race and health are linked. I need to move on to some possible solutions to this issue. One answer comes from Professor Stephen Thomas, director of the University of Pittsburgh's Center for Minority Health. Another contributor to KCCD-FM's program, he said that the state with the best practices to combat the race and health issue was Ohio. Notice that Professor Thomas is from Pennsylvania, so he is singing the praises not of his own state but of a neighboring state.

Problem explained, the speaker moves to possible solutions

Fifteen years ago, Ohio decided to do something about the big disparity between black and white people's health. What that state did right, according to Dr. Thomas, was that Ohio established neighborhood-based health concerns.

Testimony from an expert

Analysis of a possible solution to race and health issues

Their concerns went beyond providing clinics and medical care centers in places that were previously ignored. What Ohio did was to environmentally scan neighborhoods for obstacles to good health. No safe place to play? That obstacle made exercise difficult, a problem that the neighborhood could target for solution with playgrounds and parental supervision. No good diet? Many poor neighborhoods had fast food but no grocery store. Such neighborhoods negotiated for fresh food and easier access to groceries. Too many kids and adults smoking? The neighborhood cracked down on bad practices and promoted better health by encouraging vendors to obey the laws on underage smoking. The

Specific examples

Indian bands in Minnesota have a program with the acronym WOLF, which stands for "Work Out, Low Fat," to encourage Indian kids to exercise and eat less fat to discourage the scourge of diabetes.

Challenge to listeners

Of course each of us can and should take personal responsibility for our health. Most people take better care of their cars than they do caring for themselves. Everybody dies from something, but often death can be delayed or denied by how you treat yourself. If you have a car, you probably take it in every three or four months for an oil change. Why not treat yourself at least as well as you treat your vehicle? One good way to handle your own health is to have a physical at least once a year around the time of your birthday.

Action plan for listeners with specific concrete examples

Also, you can scan your own personal environment. One in four American adults still smoke, and too many of our youth are starting a habit that is extremely difficult to stop. Smoking kills more people than does air pollution, and lack of exercise encourages both heart and lung diseases. Before you run out to protest pesticides, irradiated foods, and industrial pollution, you should see what you are doing to yourself to avoid health problems now and in your future. You cannot do anything about your ethnic origins, but you can do plenty to lead a healthy life.

Summary/review of contents

Today I have tried to demonstrate that race and health are related, that some ethnic groups are more susceptible to certain diseases than are other groups, and that at least one state has taken charge of the problem. I ended today by challenging you to do something about your own health. White people suffer in large numbers from obesity and die of heart disease and cancer just like other

Specific recommendations for ethnic groups

ethnic groups. Black American males die disproportionately from prostate cancer, and black American women die disproportionately from breast cancer. Asian women seem unusually susceptible to cervical cancer, Native Americans to diabetes, and many immigrants and refugees to TB. Spanish-speaking Latinos may not receive the same medical care as their English-speaking neighbors. No racial group is immune to the big killers, but all racial groups and individuals can do more to manage the problem of group and personal health. Because Americans are among the most overweight people in the world, perhaps we should all do as the Native American health group recommends: cry WOLF, for Work Out, Low Fat.

Final challenge to all listeners

TRY ◀▶ THIS

How do you avoid telemarketers? What method of avoiding telemarketers do you find most satisfying? Do you feel guilty about any of your methods of avoidance?

Listed below are some measures you can take to resist persuasion, not only in public presentations but also on the telephone, from salespeople, and in advertising:

How to Resist Persuasion

1. *Your best form of resistance is avoidance.* You do not have to watch or read advertising, go into stores where you do not intend to buy, listen to telemarketers, or watch half-hour television "infomercials."

2. *You should exercise healthy skepticism about all messages.* Persuaders who are seeking easy prey look for the uneducated, the desperate, the angry, the very young, the very old, and the unsuspecting. They avoid people who are educated, articulate, cautious, and careful. You should use your knowledge of argumentation, evidence, and proof to analyze claims.

3. *On serious matters, you should check claims with other, unbiased sources.* A good rule is to verify any persuasive claims with at least two other sources of information. A politician tells you that lower taxes will be good for you. What do the editorials, the political commentators, and the opposition say about that plan? Consumer magazines, especially those that take no advertising, are less likely to be biased, as are news sources that embrace objectivity.

4. *You should check out the credibility of the source.* Be suspicious if a salesperson will not reveal the phone numbers of satisfied customers, if a business is new or changes location often, and if a speaker has a questionable reputation for truth or reliability. Credible sources have people, institutions, and satisfied audiences who can vouch for them.

5. *You should not be in a hurry to accept a persuasive appeal.* Most states have laws that allow even a signed contract to be rejected by the customer in the first 24 to 48 hours—in case you have second thoughts. Accepting claims on impulse is a dangerous practice that you can avoid by never making an important decision in the context of a sales pitch. Have you ever heard of a businessperson who refused to take the money the next day?

6. *You should question the ethical basis of proposed actions.* Angry people are easy to turn to violence, desperate people willingly consider desperate measures, and frustrated people can be easily convinced to undermine. You need to ask if the proposed action is self-serving, if the proposal pits one group against another, and if the idea is going to be good for you when viewed in retrospect.

7. *You should use your knowledge and experience to analyze persuasive claims.* A claim that sounds too good to be true probably is. If you have a "gut feeling" that a claim seems wrong, you should find out why. You should use all you know about logic, evidence, and proof to see if the persuader is drawing a sound conclusion or making an

Discussion Question

Ask students to describe situations where they were persuaded to do something they later regretted. How could they take steps to prevent similar situations in the future?

Learn to be wary about good deals. Use your brain to protect yourself.

inferential leap that is justified by the evidence. Finally, all evidence should be open to scrutiny.

8. *You should use your own values as a check against fraudulent claims.* If someone is trying to get you to do something that runs counter to what you learned in your religion, in your home, about the law, or from your friends, you should be wary. Sales always enrich the seller but rarely the buyer. You can choose to sacrifice, but you should not sacrifice unwittingly. Your values are good protection against those who would cheat you. You should ask the question, What would my parents, my friends, my neighbors, my professor, or my religion think of this decision?

9. *Check what persuaders say against what they do.* You might add: Judge them more by what they do than by what they say. Talk may not be cheap, but words cost less than deeds, and the proof of what a person says is in his or her behavior. Many an "education governor" has cut the budget for education. You learn to trust people who do what they say; you learn to distrust those who say one thing and do another.

10. *Use your freedom of expression and freedom of choice as protection against unethical persuaders.* In the United States, you can hear competing ideas and the choice is yours. You can educate yourself about issues and ideas by reading, watching, and listening. Education and learning are powerful protection against persuaders who would take advantage of you. Use your freedoms to help defend yourself.

Now that you know 10 suggestions for resisting persuasion, you can practice the strategies for keeping others from manipulating your mind and your pocketbook.

Chapter Review

SUMMARY

In this chapter you have learned the following:

- Persuasion is a process of social influence characterized by four action goals:
  - Adoption: The audience tries a new behavior.
  - Discontinuance: The audience ceases an established behavior.
  - Continuance: The audience persists in an established behavior.
  - Deterrence: The audience avoids an unpracticed behavior.
- Receivers determine whether a presentation is informative or persuasive or both by how they perceive the message.
- Three forces motivate us to behave in one way or another.
  - What our bodies tell us to do motivates us.
  - What our mind tells us to do motivates us.
  - What others want us to do motivates us.
- Traditional strategies of social influence included source credibility, logic or reasoning, and emotional strategies.

- Organization can produce social influence.
  - Placement of arguments and evidence can produce different results.
  - Stating one side of an argument or both or many makes a difference.
  - Refuting arguments the audience might hear can make a difference.
  - Using familiar or novel arguments and evidence can make a difference.
- Ethical guidelines for social influence include
  - Citing sources accurately.
  - Collecting information accurately.
  - Respecting the audience's intelligence.
  - Respecting your opponent's point of view.
- Ten "tests of evidence" provide a means of evaluating your own and others' persuasive attempts, though audiences may or may not believe your words even when they do meet all the tests.
- Ten guidelines for resisting persuasion provide a way to protect yourself from unethical persuaders.

◑ VIDEO LINK: PERSUASIVE APPEALS BY MR. WEISS AND DR. STERN

Video Episode 5: "On the Air with Campus-Community Connection"

Persuasive speaking involves the use of motivational, emotional, and logical appeals to change audience members' attitudes, beliefs, or values. Watch "On the Air with Campus-Community Connection" and determine how the two speakers use the various forms of appeal. Do the two speakers present persuasive messages? Are there ways in which the messages could be made more effective? What goal do you think the two speakers have for their audiences? Do they want to achieve deterrence? Adoption? How do you think mediated persuasive messages might differ from more traditional public-speaking messages?

ISSUES IN COMMUNICATION: BEAUTY AND DIETING

This Issues in Communication narrative is designed to provoke individual thought or discussion about concepts raised in the chapter.

Jody Hubbard is a dietician and nutritionist who travels around the state to speak at middle, junior high, and high schools. She primarily speaks to students in health classes, but sometimes the school will arrange for her to speak to several different groups of girls. Her biggest concern is the emphasis our culture places on thinness and the negative ways this affects young women today. Jody has a Ph.D. in nutrition, but, more important, she has personal experience—her mother taught her to diet when she was only eight years old.

Jody has created several different presentations which she gives to different types of audiences, and she tries to establish an emotional connection with the students so that they will feel comfortable asking questions or talking to her privately. She shows them pictures and images from popular culture of beautiful women

and explains how computers are used to make the women look even more thin and "beautiful" than they are in real life. She describes how the definition of *beauty* has changed over the years and even from culture to culture. She then talks about health issues and the physical damage that can occur as a result of dieting. Finally, she addresses self-esteem and the notion that a person's sense of beauty must include more than how much a person weighs.

Sometimes, Jody feels that she succeeds in persuading some students to stop dieting; other times, she feels that she fails.

Apply what you have learned about influencing others as you ponder and discuss the following questions: What were Jody's action goals? What types of appeal did she make to persuade her audience? How did she seek to gain credibility in students' eyes? About what ethical considerations would Jody need to be especially careful?

KEY TERMS

Use the *Human Communication* CD-ROM and the *Online Learning Center* at www.mhhe.com/pearson to further your understanding of the following terminology.

Ability to choose
Adoption
Arguments
Believability
Boomerang effect
Coercion
Continuance
Counterarguments

Deterrence
Discontinuance
Emotional appeals
Ethics
Evidence
Immediate goals
Intention
Logical appeals

Manipulation
Monroe motivated sequence
Persuasion
Persuasive campaign
Source credibility
Tests of evidence
Ultimate goals

SELF-QUIZ

Go to the self-quizzes on the *Human Communication* CD-ROM and the *Online Learning Center* at www.mhhe.com/pearson to test your knowledge.

REFERENCES

Berger, J. M., & Vartabedian, R. A. (1985). Public self-disclosure and speaker persuasiveness. *Journal of Applied Social Psychology, 15,* 153–165.

Brody, M. (1998). *Speaking your way to the top: Making powerful business presentations.* Needham Heights, MA: Allyn and Bacon.

Cope, F., & Richardson, D. (1972). The effects of measuring recommendations in a fear-arousing speech. *Speech Monographs, 39,* 148–150.

Ehninger, D., (1970). Argument as method: Its nature, its limitations, and its uses. *Speech Monographs, 37,* 101–110.

Ehninger, D., Gronbeck, B. E., & Monroe, A. H. (1984). *Principles of speech communication* (9th brief ed.). Glenview, IL: Scott, Foresman.

Fitch, S., & Mandziuk, R. (1997). *Sojourner Truth as orator.* Westport, CT: Greenwood.

Foss, S. K., & Griffin, C. L. (1995). Beyond persuasion: A proposal for an invitational rhetoric. *Communication Monographs, 62,* 2–19.

Fotheringham, W. (1966). *Perspectives on persuasion.* Boston: Allyn and Bacon.

Gass, R. H., & Seiter, J. S. (1999). *Persuasion, social influence, and compliance gaining.* Needham Heights, MA: Allyn and Bacon.

Hamilton, G. (1998). *Public speaking for college and career* (5th ed.). New York: McGraw-Hill.

Hovland, C., & Pritzker, H. (1957). Extent of opinion change as a function of amount of change advocated. *Journal of Abnormal and Social Psychology, 54,* 257–261.

Janis, I. S., & Feshbach, S. (1953). Effects of fear-arousing communications. *Journal of Abnormal and Social Psychology, 48,* 78–92.

Karlins, M., & Abelson, H. I. (1970). *Persuasion: How opinions and attitudes are changed* (2nd ed.). New York: Springer.

Kearney, P., & Plax, T. (1999). *Public speaking in a diverse society* (2nd ed.). Mountain View, CA: Mayfield.

Lesikar, R. V., Pettit, J. D., & Flatley, M. (1993). *Basic business communication* (6th ed.). Boston: Irwin.

McConnell, J. V. (1977). *Understanding human behavior: An introduction to psychology.* New York: Holt, Rinehart and Winston.

McGuire, M., Stillbourne, L., McAdams, M., & Hyatt, L. (1997). *Internet handbook for writers, researchers, and journalists.* New York: Guilford.

Miller, G. R. (1980). On being persuaded: Some basic distinctions. In M. E. Roloff & G. R. Miller, *Persuasion: New directions in theory and research.* Beverly Hills, CA: Sage.

Powell, F. A. (1965). The effects of anxiety-arousing messages when related to personal, familial, and impersonal referents. *Speech Monographs, 32,* 102–106.

Reinhard, J. C. (1988). The empirical study of the persuasive effects of evidence: The status after 50 years of research. *Human Communication Research, 15,* 3–59.

Sears, D., & Freedman, J. (1965). Effects of expected familiarity with arguments upon opinion change and selective exposure. *Journal of Personality and Social Psychology, 2,* 420–426

Yook, E. L., & Albert, R. D. (1998). Perceptions of the appropriateness of negotiation in educational settings. A cross-cultural comparison among Koreans and Americans. *Communication Education, 47,* 18–30.

glossary

A

ability to choose 540
Making a decision based on information and ideas.

absolute criteria 291
Criteria for selecting alternatives that must be met; giving the group no leeway.

abstract words 529
Words or phrases that refer generally to ideas, qualities, acts, or relationships.

abstractions 81
Simplifications of what words stand for.

accommodation 214
The nondominant individual participates with the dominant group without losing his or her cultural identity.

accurate 146
The extent to which premises in deductive arguments are truthful and verifiable.

action model 21
A depiction of communication as one person sending a message and another person or group of persons receiving it.

active listening 140
Involved listening with a purpose.

active perception 39
Perception in which our minds select, organize, and interpret that which we sense.

adaptors 109
Nonverbal movements that you might perform fully in private but only partially in public.

adoption 541
Inducing an audience to accept a new idea, attitude, behavior, belief, or product and to demonstrate that acceptance through behavioral change.

affect displays 109
Nonverbal movements of the face and body used to show emotion.

affection 191, 267
The emotion of caring for others and/or being cared for by them.

agenda setting 344
The determination of the topics discussed by individuals and society on the basis of media attention.

aggressive mode 215
Those behaviors perceived as hurtfully expressive, self-promoting, and assuming control over the choices of others.

aggressiveness 187
Assertion of one's rights at the expense of others and care about one's own needs but no one else's.

alternative organizations 312
Employing organizations that define themselves at least somewhat in opposition to the mainstream and are established and maintained with the principle of worker control.

analog 105
Continual variable, measurable, physical quantities; nonverbal communication is analogic.

analogy 438
A comparison of things in some respects, especially in position or function, that are otherwise dissimilar.

androgynous   197
A term used in reference to persons who possess stereotypical female and male characteristics.

anticipatory socialization   242, 317
Process through which individuals develop a set of expectations and beliefs concerning how people communicate in particular occupations and in formal and informal work settings.

antonym   528
A word that means the opposite of another word.

anxiety uncertainty management   180
A theory that suggests that people who find themselves in unfamiliar cultures feel uncertainty, which leads to anxiety.

arbitrary   79
The quality of words that states that they have no inherent meanings; they have only the meanings people give them.

argumentativeness   187
The quality or state of being argumentative; synonymous with contentiousness or combativeness.

arguments   145, 547
Propositions, justifications, and evidence used to persuade.

articulation   119, 491
Coordination of the mouth, tongue, and teeth to make a word understandable by others; a component of enunciation.

artifacts   121
Ornaments or adornments we display that hold communicative potential.

assertive mode   214
Self-enhancing, expressive communication that takes into account both self and other's needs.

assigned groups   271
Groups that evolve out of a hierarchy where individuals are assigned membership to the group.

assimilation   213
Individuals from the nondominant group attempt to "fit in" the dominant group.

asynchronous communication   348
Delays occur in the communication interaction and each participant must take turns being the sender and receiver.

attitude   403
A predisposition to respond favorably or unfavorably to a person, an object, an idea, or an event.

attribution   51
The assignment of meaning to people's behavior

audience analysis   398
The collection and interpretation of data on the demographics, attitudes, values, and beliefs of the audience obtained by observation, inferences, questionnaires, or interviews.

audience interest   402
The relevance and importance of the topic to an audience; sometimes related to the uniqueness of the topic.

audience knowledge   402
The amount of information the audience already has about the topic.

audio-video conferencing   350
Use of the Internet or a network to connect two or more multimedia-capable computers for live, interactive conversations using visual and auditory channels of communication.

autocratic leaders   274
Leaders who maintain strict control over their group.

automatic attention   137
The instinctive focus we give to stimuli signaling a change in our surroundings, stimuli that we deem as important, or stimuli that we perceive to signal danger.

avoidance   214
A conscious attempt not to engage with people in the dominant group.

avoiding   177
In Knapp's relational development model, the stage characterized by partners' reluctance to interact, active avoidance, and hostility.

axiom   179
Statement accepted as true without proof.

B

bargaining   195
The process in which two or more parties attempt to reach an agreement on what each should give and receive in a relationship.

behavioral flexibility   197
The ability to alter behavior to adapt to new situations and to relate in new ways when necessary.

behaviorally based question   240
A question that focuses on an applicant's past actions and behaviors to determine how he or she will perform in the future.

belief   403
A conviction; often thought to be more enduring than an attitude and less enduring than a value.

believability   555
A criterion of good evidence—the audience must trust and accept the evidence.

bibliographic references   431
Complete citations that appear in the "references" or "works cited" section of your speech outline.

bibliography   475
A list of sources used in a presentation.

bipolar question   238
A question that limits answer options to two choices.

bit of information   138
Any organized unit of information including sounds, letters, words, sentences, or something less concrete, like ideas.

blind peer review   341
Anonymous review of articles submitted for publication in professional journals by other professionals in the discipline.

bodily movement   498
What the speaker does with his or her entire body during a speech presentation.

body   453
The largest part of the presentation, which contains the arguments, evidence, and main content.

bonding   173
In Knapp's relational development model, the stage in which partners commit to each other.

bookmarks   426
A feature of most Web browsers that stores links for immediate retrieval without entering the URL each time you want to access the site.

boomerang effect   550
An unintended situation in which the speaker and the message induce an audience response that is the opposite of what the speaker intended.

brainstorming   291, 392
A creative procedure for generating ideas and potential solutions to problems.

brakelight function   473
A forewarning to the audience that the end of the presentation is near.

bulletin board system (BBS)   349
Text-based asynchronous communication tool that allow users to disseminate information to a large number of people.

bureaucracy   309
An organizational structure characterized by a division of labor, rigid hierarchy of authority, and downward communication that enforces formalized rules and procedures for behavior.

C

captive audience   400
An audience that has not chosen to hear a particular speaker or speech.

cause/effect pattern   467
A method of organization in which the presenter first explains the causes of an event, a problem, or an issue and then discusses its consequences, results, or effects.

celebrity testimony   436
Statements made by a public figure who is known to the audience.

central tendency   55
The perceptual error of viewing everyone as average or neutral.

chain of command   309
Clear lines of authority.

channel   181, 336
The means by which a message moves from the source to the receiver of the message.

charisma   273
An extreme type of referent power that inspires strong loyalty and devotion from others.

chronemics   115
Also called temporal communication, the way people organize and use time.

chronological résumé   250
A document that organizes credentials over time.

circumscribing   177
In Knapp's relational development model, the stage marked by a decrease in partners' interaction, time spent together, and depth of sharing.

clearinghouse question   239
A question worded to assure an interviewer that all essential information is provided.

cliché   84
An expression that has lost originality and force through overuse.

closed question   238
A question worded to restrict the response, often asking for specific information or supplying answer options from which the respondent chooses.

closing   238
The stage of an interview indicating its termination.

closure   47
The tendency to fill in missing information in order to complete an otherwise incomplete figure or statement.

co-culture   42, 212
A group whose beliefs or behaviors distinguish it from the larger culture of which it is a part and with which it shares numerous similarities.

code   18
A systematic arrangement of symbols used to create meanings in the mind of another person or persons.

code sensitivity   225
The ability to use the verbal and nonverbal language appropriate to the cultural or co-cultural norms of the individual with whom you are communicating.

coercion   273, 540
(1) A form of punishment that attempts to force compliance with hostile tactics. (2) Forcing people to think or behave as you wish.

cognitive modification   372
An anxiety-reducing technique designed to bolster the novice speaker's confidence by positive thinking.

cognitive paradigms   279
Ways of looking at the world based on individuals' attitudes, beliefs, values, and perceptions.

cohesiveness   285
The attachment members feel toward each other and the group.

collectivist cultures   219
Cultures that value the group over the individual.

colloquialisms   83
Words and phrases that are used informally.

common ground   378
Also known as co-orientation, it is the degree to which the speaker's values, beliefs, attitudes, and interests are shared with the audience; an aspect of credibility.

communication   10
The process by which meaning is exchanged between individuals through a common system of symbols, signs, or behavior.

communication apprehension (CA)   366
An individual's fear or anxiety associated with either real or anticipated communication with another person or persons.

communication competence   28
The ability to effectively exchange meaning through a common system of symbols, signs, or behavior.

communication networks   315
Patterns of relationships through which information flows in an organization.

communication situation   143
The context in which communication is occurring.

communicative competencies approach   275
A leadership theory focusing on the communicative behaviors of leaders as they exercise interpersonal influence to accomplish group goals.

communibiological perspective   368
The idea that communication apprehension represents individuals' expression of inborn, biological functioning.

comparison   528
A means of defining by pointing out similarities between the known and the less known.

competence   377
The degree to which the speaker is perceived as skilled, reliable, experienced, qualified, authoritative, and informed; an aspect of credibility.

complementarity   181
The idea that we sometimes bond with people whose strengths are our weaknesses.

complementary relationships   170
Relationships in which each person supplies something the other person or persons lack.

complementation   104
Nonverbal and verbal codes add meaning to each other and expand the meaning of either message alone.

compliance-gaining   192
Those attempts made by a source of messages to influence a target to perform some desired behavior that the target otherwise might not perform.

compliance-resisting   193
Refusal of targets of influence messages to comply to requests.

computer catalog   423
An electronic database containing information about materials in a library.

computer-mediated communication (CMC)   336
Human-to-human communication using networked computer environments to facilitate interaction.

conclusion   473
The last part of the presentation; a summary of the major ideas that is designed to induce mental or behavioral change in an audience.

concrete language   91
Words and statements that are specific rather than abstract or vague.

concrete words   529
Words that refer to definite persons, places, objects, and acts.

confirmation   60
Feedback in which others treat us in a manner consistent with who we believe we are.

confrontational tactics   215
Belligerent attempts to make the dominant groups hear your position.

conjunctive task   287
A task for which no one group member has all the necessary information, but each member has some information to contribute.

connotative meaning   80
An individualized or personalized meaning of a word, which may be emotionally laden.

constructivist model   23
A theory of communication which posits that receivers create their own reality in their minds.

content message   152
The actual facts and ideas contained in the spoken statements of a communicator.

context   23
A set of circumstances or a situation.

contingency approach   275
An approach to studying leadership that assumes group situations vary, with different situations (contingencies) requiring different leadership styles.

continuance   541
Persuading an audience to continue present behavior or beliefs.

contradiction   104, 175
(1) Verbal and nonverbal messages conflict.
(2) In dialectic theory, each person in a relationship has two different ideas for maintaining the relationship.

contrast   528
The comparison of unlike things.

contrast effects   55
Comparison of people or their behavior with the characteristics or behavior of other people.

control   170, 267
(1) The ability to influence others, our environment, and ourselves. (2) The ability to influence an interview through the use of status, prestige, and custom.

cooperative   312
A business owned and democratically controlled by its users.

counterarguments   548
Rebuttals to an argument.

cover letter   251
A short letter introducing you and your résumé to an interviewer.

crisis management   320
The use of public relations to minimize harm to the organization in an emergency situation that could cause the organization irreparable damage.

criteria   290
The standards by which a group must judge potential solutions.

critical listening   141
Listening that challenges the speaker's message by evaluating its accuracy, meaningfulness, and utility.

critical thinking   143
Analyzing the speaker, the situation, and the speaker's ideas to make critical judgments about the message being presented.

cultivation effect   346
Heavy television and media use leads people to perceive reality as consistent with the portrayals they see on television.

cultural competence   94
The ability of individuals and systems to respond respectfully and effectively to people of all cultures, classes, races, ethnic backgrounds, and religions in a manner that recognizes, affirms, and values the worth of individuals, families, and communities and protects and preserves the dignity of each.

cultural relativism   216
The belief that another culture should be judged by its context rather than measured against your own culture.

culture   42, 76, 212, 343
A system of shared beliefs, values, customs, behaviors, and artifacts that the members of a society use to cope with one another and with their world.

customer service encounter   321
The moment of interaction between the customer and the firm.

D

dating   92
Specifying when you made an observation, since everything changes over time.

deceptive communication   186
The practice of deliberately making somebody believe things that are not true.

decode   74
The process of assigning meaning to others' words in order to translate them into thoughts of your own.

decoding   19
The process of assigning meaning to the idea or thought in a code.

deductive arguments   145
Arguments using general propositions to make conclusions about a specific instance.

definitions   438
Determinations of meaning through description, simplification, examples, analysis, comparison, explanation, or illustration.

delivery 484
The presentation of a speech by using your voice and body to reinforce your message.

democratic leaders 274
Leaders who encourage members to participate in group decisions.

demographic analysis 401
The collection and interpretation of data about the characteristics of people, excluding their attitudes, values, and beliefs.

denotative meaning 80
The agreed-upon meaning or dictionary meaning of a word.

dependence power 184
Control over a relationship held by a person who is committed to the relationship but perceives the partner to be less committed and who has a number of viable relationship alternatives.

descriptiveness 90
The practice of describing observed behavior or phenomena instead of offering personal reactions or judgments.

designated leader 273
Someone who has been appointed or elected to a leadership position.

deterrence 541
Persuading an audience to avoid an activity or a belief.

dialectic 175
Tension that exists between two conflicting or interacting forces, elements, or ideas.

dialectic of expression/privacy 175
Tension between wanting to self-disclose and be completely open while also wanting to be private and closed.

dialectic of integration/separation 175
Tension between wanting to be separate entities and wanting to be integrated with another person.

dialectic of stability/change 175
Tension between wanting events, conversations, and behavior to be the same while also desiring change.

dialogue 14
The act of taking part in a conversation, discussion, or negotiation.

differentiating 177
In Knapp's relational development model, the stage in which partners emphasize their individual differences rather than their similarities.

digital 105
Discrete or separate items; words are digital.

digital divide 354
A growing gap between those who have access to technology and those who do not.

discipline 11
An area of academic study.

disconfirmation 60
Feedback in which others fail to respond to our notion of self by responding neutrally.

discontinuance 541
Inducing an audience to stop doing something or thinking in a certain way.

disjunctive tasks 287
Tasks which require little coordination and which can be completed by the most skilled group member working alone.

distributed leadership 276
A leadership theory explicitly acknowledging that each member is expected to perform the communication behaviors needed to move the group toward its goal.

division of labor 309
How a given amount of work is divided among the available human resources.

downward communication 309
Superiors initiate messages to subordinates.

dyadic communication 25
Two-person communication.

dynamism 378
The extent to which the speaker is perceived as bold, active, energetic, strong, empathic, and assertive; an aspect of credibility.

E

economic production orientation   306
Organizations that manufacture products and/or other services for consumers.

ectomorph   110
Body type that is characterized by a tall, thin, and sometimes frail person.

electronic mail   349
Use of the Internet or a computer network to send addressable messages to another person connected to the Internet or network.

emblems   109
Nonverbal movements that substitute for words and phrases.

emergent groups   271
Groups resulting from environmental conditions leading to the formation of a cohesive group of individuals.

emergent leader   273
Someone who becomes an informal leader by exerting influence toward achievement of a group's goal but who does not hold the formal position or role of leader.

emergent organizational networks   316
The informal, naturally occurring patterns of communication relationships in organizations.

emoticons   158
Typographic symbols showing emotional meaning.

emotional appeals   545
Attempts to persuade audience members to change an attitude or a behavior through an appeal—usually in a narrative form—to their emotions.

emotional labor   322
Jobs in which employees are expected to display certain feelings in order to satisfy organizational role expectations.

emotional proof   145
Also called pathos, proof based on feelings and emotions.

empathic listening   140
Listening with a purpose and attempting to understand the other person.

empathy   140
The ability to perceive another person's worldview as if it were your own.

emphasis   104
Nonverbal cues strengthen verbal messages.

encoding   19, 75
The process of translating your thoughts into words.

endomorph   110
Body type that tends to be short, soft, and round.

enthymemes   146
Deductive arguments in which one or more parts are left out.

enunciation   119, 490
Pronunciation and articulation to produce a word with clarity and distinction so it can be understood.

environment   319
Organizations and individuals with whom organizational representatives have direct contact.

ethics   28, 295, 551
(1) A set of moral principles or values. (2) Rules and standards for the conduct and practices of group members.

ethnocentrism   216
The belief that your own group or culture is superior to other groups or cultures.

etymology   528
The historical origin of a word.

euphemism   84
A polite, more pleasant expression used instead of a socially unacceptable form.

evidence   439, 546
(1) Data or information from which you can draw a conclusion, make a judgment, or establish the probability of something occurring. (2) Any material that supports a proposition.

examples   434
Specific instances used to illustrate your point.

expectancy violation theory   115
The communicative impact of violations of personal space expectations.

experimenting 173
In Knapp's relational development model, the stage in which partners attempt to discover information about each other.

expert power 273
Power based on the value other members place on the leader's knowledge or expertise.

expert testimony 436
Statements made by someone who has special knowledge or expertise about an issue or idea.

explanation 438, 530
A means of idea development that simplifies or clarifies an idea while arousing audience interest.

explicit-rule culture 221
A culture in which information and cultural rules are explicit, procedures are explained, and expectations are discussed.

extemporaneous mode 485
A carefully prepared and researched speech delivered in a conversational style.

external communication 319
Verbal and nonverbal messages enabling members of an organization to coordinate its activities with those in its environment.

extrinsic motivation 523
A method of making information relevant by providing the audience with reasons outside the speech itself for listening to the content of the speech.

eye contact 497
The extent to which a speaker looks directly at the audience.

F

face 64, 220
(1) The socially approved and presented identity of an individual. (2) People's need for a sense of self-respect in a communication situation.

facework 64
Verbal and nonverbal strategies that are used to present one's own varying images to others and to help them maintain their own images.

facial expression 496
Any nonverbal cue expressed by the speaker's face.

feedback 18, 140, 336
The listener's verbal and nonverbal responses to the speaker and the speaker's message.

feminist organization 312
An organization that embraces collectivist decision making, member empowerment, and a political agenda of ending women's oppression.

figure 46
The focal point of a person's attention.

figures of speech 85
Sets of words whose meaning go beyond the meaning of the words that comprise them.

first impression 53
Our initial opinion about people upon meeting them.

first-person observation 144
Observations based on something that you personally have sensed.

fluency 492
The smoothness of delivery, the flow of words, and the absence of vocalized pauses.

formal communication 315
Messages that follow prescribed channels of communication throughout the organization.

formal role 281
Also called positional role, an assigned role based on an individual's position or title within a group.

frozen evaluation 92
An assessment of a concept that does not change over time.

functional classification system 306
A classification of organizational types based on the primary purposes for organizing and developing organization within society.

functional résumé 251
A document that organizes credentials by type of function performed.

fundamental attribution error 51
In judging other people, the tendency to attribute their successes to the situation and their failures to their personal characteristics.

G

gatekeeping   343
The process of determining what news, information, or entertainment will reach a mass audience.

gender   277
The learned characteristics associated with masculinity and femininity.

gestures   494
Movements of the head, arms, and hands to illustrate, emphasize, or signal ideas in the speech.

grammar   18
The rules of function in language.

grapevine communication   317
Informal interactions.

ground   46
The background against which a person's focused attention occurs.

group climate   284
The emotional tone or atmosphere members create within the group.

group culture   277
The socially negotiated system of rules that guide group behavior.

group decision support system (GDSS)   293
Interactive network of computers with specialized software allowing users to generate solutions for unstructured problems.

groupthink   286
An unintended outcome of cohesiveness where the desire for agreement takes precedence over critical analysis and discussion.

H

halo effect   54
A positive generalization of all attributes based on one attribute, which can be negative or positive.

hearing   133
The act of receiving sound.

heterogeneous   400
Characterized by many differences among individuals in an audience.

heterosexist language   87
Language that implies that everyone is heterosexual.

hierarchy   309
Formal organizational authority based on the office held and the expertise of individual officeholders.

high-context (HC) cultures   220
Cultures like these of the Asian Pacific Rim and Central and South America where much of the meaning is "preprogrammed information" understood by the receiver and transmitted also by the context in which the transaction occurs.

high self-monitors   64
Individuals who are highly aware of their impression management behavior.

home page   426
The first page on a website.

homogeneous   400
Characterized by similarities among individuals.

horizontal communication   316
Messages between members of an organization with equal power.

hostile work environment sexual harassment   325
Conditions in the workplace that are sexually offensive, intimidating, or hostile and that affect an individual's ability to perform his or her job.

hurtful messages   186
Messages that create emotional pain or upset.

hyperlink   424
A link in a WWW document that leads to another website or to another place within the same document.

hypothetical question   240
A question that requires the interviewee to describe how he or she would behave in specific situations.

I

identification   379
Young adults' sense of self and self-worth as a dimension of source credibility.

illustrators   109
Nonverbal movements that accompany or reinforce verbal messages.

imagery 530
Use of words that appeal to the senses, that create pictures in the mind.

immediate behavioral purposes 521
Actions a speaker seeks from an audience during and immediately after a speech.

immediate goal or purpose 455, 541
What a speaker wishes to accomplish during his or her presentation or shortly after it.

implicit-rule culture 221
A culture in which information and cultural rules are implied and already known to the participants.

important criteria 291
Criteria for evaluating alternatives that should be met, but the group has some flexibility.

impression formation 351
Making inferences about another person's personality, values, and traits.

impression management 64
The control (or lack of control) of the communication of information through behavior.

impromptu mode 485
Delivery of a speech without notes, plans, or preparation; characterized by spontaneity and informal language.

inclusion 170, 267
(1) The state of being involved with others.
(2) The degree to which each party wants to participate in an interview and wants to include others in the interview.

indexing 92
Identifying the uniqueness of objects, events, and people.

individualistic cultures 217
Cultures that value individual freedom, choice, uniqueness, and independence.

inductive arguments 145
Arguments using specific pieces of evidence to draw a generalization.

inference 93, 144, 406
A tentative conclusion drawn from observation, based on some evidence.

inflection 119
The variety or changes in pitch.

influence 192
The power to affect other people's thinking or actions.

informal communication 316
Any interaction that does not generally follow the formal structure of the organization but emerges out of natural social interaction among organization members.

informal role 282
Also called a behavioral role, a role that is developed spontaneously within a group.

information 313
A product (outcome) of communication that serves to help people understand and predict the world around them.

information hunger 522
The audience's need for the information contained in the speech.

information literacy 157
The ability to recognize when information is needed and to locate, evaluate and effectively use the information needed.

information overload 526
A situation that occurs when the quantity or difficulty of the information presented is greater than the audience can assimilate within the given time.

information relevance 523
The importance, novelty, and usefulness of the topic and the information.

informational question 239
A question worded to clarify an answer that appears to be vague or superficial.

informative content 524
The main points and subpoints, illustrations, and examples used to clarify and inform.

initiating 173
In Knapp's stages of relational development, the short beginning period of a relationship.

instant messaging (IM)   349
A text-based form of synchronous communication which allows users to connect two computers over the Internet and have a "conversation" through their computers.

integrating   173
In Knapp's relational development model, the stage in which partners start mirroring each other's behavior.

integration-goals orientation   307
Organizations that help to mediate and resolve discord among members of society.

intensifying   173
In Knapp's relational development model, the stage in which partners become more aware of each other and actively participate in the relationship.

intention   543
How the speaker wants the audience to respond.

intentionality   107
The purposefulness of nonverbal codes.

interaction model   21
A depiction of communication as one person sending a message and a second person receiving the message and then responding with a return message.

intercultural communication   210
The exchange of information between individuals who are unlike culturally.

interest   517
Curiosity about a topic.

internal organizational communication   314
The symbolic interaction that occurs within organizations and among organizational members.

internal reference   431
Brief notation indicating a bibliographic reference that contains the details you are using in your speech.

Internet   340, 424
A global network of interconnected computer networks.

Internet relay chat (IRC)   349
A text-based synchronous communication system that allows multiple users to interact in real time via the Internet.

interpersonal communication   25, 169
The personal process of coordinating meaning between at least two people in a situation that allows mutual opportunities for both speaking and listening.

interpersonal dominance   193
A relational, behavioral, and interactional state that reflects the actual achievement of influence or control over another via communicative actions.

interpersonal relationship   168
The association of two or more people who are interdependent, who use some consistent patterns of interaction, and who have interacted for an extended period of time.

interpretation   49
The process of assigning meaning to stimuli.

interpretive perception   49
Perception that involves a blend of internal states and external stimuli.

interview   235
A dyadic communication context with a purpose or goal.

interview guide   237
An outline of topics and subtopics to be covered.

interview schedule   237
A list of major questions and follow-up questions; the schedule is a useful tool in keeping the interview focused on the topic or issue of concern.

intrapersonal communication   24
The process of understanding and sharing meaning within the self.

introduction   446
The first part of the presentation; its function is to arouse the audience and to lead into the main ideas presented in the body.

involvement   394
The importance of the topic to the speaker; determined by the strength of the feelings the speaker has about the topic and the time and energy the speaker devotes to that topic.

irony   85
Words that express something different from, and often opposite to, their literal meaning.

J

jargon 86
The technical language developed by a professional group.

jealousy 185
Possessive watchfulness of the partner or suspicion about potential rivals for the partner's affections.

job description 244
A document that defines the job in terms of its content and scope.

justification 145
The evidence used to support propositions.

K

key-word outline 463
An outline consisting of important words or phrases to remind the speaker of the content of the presentation.

kinesics 108
The study of bodily movements, including posture, gestures, and facial expressions.

L

laissez-faire leaders 274
Leaders who take almost no initiative for structuring a group discussion.

language 74
A code consisting of symbols, letters, or words with arbitrary meanings that are governed by rules and used to communicate.

lay testimony 436
Statements made by an ordinary person that substantiate or support what you say.

leader 273
A person who influences the behavior and attitudes of others through communication.

leadership 272
A process of using communication to influence the behaviors and attitudes of others to meet group goals.

leading question 240
A question worded to elicit a particular response from an interviewee.

lecture cues 155
Verbal or nonverbal signals that stress points or indicate transitions between ideas during a lecture.

lecture listening 154
The ability to listen to, mentally process, and recall lecture information.

leniency 55
The consistent evaluation of people (or objects) in an overly positive manner.

linear communication 336
Communication that flows primarily from the sender to the receiver with little or no feedback from the receiver to the sender.

listening 133
The active process of receiving, constructing meaning from, and responding to spoken and/or nonverbal messages. It involves the ability to retain information, as well as to react empathically and/or appreciatively to spoken and/or nonverbal messages.

listserv 349
E-mail-based discussion groups.

logical appeals 546
Propositions and evidence used to persuade an audience.

logical proof 145
Also called logos, proof based on reasoning.

long-range goal 455
What you expect to achieve over a time period longer than the day of your presentation.

long-term memory 139
Our permanent storage place for information including but not limited to past experiences, language, values, knowledge, images of people, memories of sights, sounds, and smells, and even fantasies.

low self-monitors 64
Individuals who communicate with others with little attention to the responses to their messages.

low-context (LC) cultures   219
Cultures like United States and Scandinavia where communication tends to be centered on the source with intentions stated overtly and with a direct verbal style.

M

main points   456
The most important points in a presentation; indicated by Roman numerals in an outline.

maintenance functions   282
Behaviors that focus on the interpersonal relationships among members.

management information system (MIS)   313
System designed and implemented to help manage organizations' varied information needs.

managers   309
Persons responsible for making decisions and directing activities to accomplish primary organizational goals.

manipulation   540
Tricking people or using fraudulent means to change people's behavior.

manuscript mode   486
Delivery of a speech from a script of the entire speech.

marginalized groups   213
People who are made to feel like outsiders in other people's world.

mass communication   26, 335
A process in which professional communicators using technological devices share messages over great distances to influence large audiences.

meaning   10
The shared understanding of the message constructed in the minds of the communicators.

mediated communication   335
Any form of communication that takes place using electronic means.

memorized mode   486
Delivering a speech that has been committed to memory.

mesomorph   110
Body type that is proportioned, average in height, athletic, trim, and muscular.

message   17, 336
The verbal or nonverbal form of the idea, thought, or feeling that one person (the source) wishes to communicate to another person or group of people (the receivers).

message analysis   144
Evaluating the process by which information or knowledge was discovered as well as evaluating specific elements of the message content.

metaphors   85
Comparisons among unlike objects or concepts in which a common feature is highlighted.

metatalk   83
Talk in which meaning is not literal.

mindfulness   140
Being fully engaged in the moment.

Monroe motivated sequence   549
A problem-solving format that encourages an audience to become concerned about an issue; especially appropriate for a persuasive speech.

M-time   222
The monochrononic time schedule, which compartmentalizes time to meet personal needs, separates task and social dimensions, and points to the future.

multiuser environments   350
Web-based virtual worlds where participants can interact and engage in fantasy role-playing.

muted group theory   213
The idea that women were largely silenced by men when women's ideas were unvalued, underestimated, and sometimes unheard.

N

narrating   531
The oral presentation and interpretation of a story, a description, or an event; includes dramatic reading of prose or poetry.

negative face   64
The desire to be free from constraint and imposition.

negative feedback   140
Verbal and nonverbal responses intended to disconfirm the speaker and the speaker's message.

netiquette   77
Internet etiquette.

network   244
An intricate web of contacts and relationships designed to benefit the participants.

neutral question   240
A question that requires an answer consistent with candidates' positions on an issue, with their beliefs, with their attitudes and values, or with the facts as they know them.

neutralization   176
Managing dialectics by compromise.

noise   19
Any interference in the encoding and decoding processes that reduces message clarity.

nonverbal codes   18, 107
All symbols that are not words, including bodily movements, use of space and time, clothing and adornments, and sounds other than words.

nonverbal communication   102
The behaviors of people, other than their use of words, which have socially shared meaning, are intentionally sent or interpreted as intentional, are consciously sent or consciously received, and have the potential for feedback from the receiver.

nonword sounds   119
Sounds such as *mmh, huh,* and *ahh* and pauses or absence of sound used for effect in speaking.

norms   280, 318
Informal rules for group interaction created and sustained through communication.

nudging question   239
A question that motivates further interaction.

O

objectics   121
Also called object language, the study of the human use of clothing and other artifacts as nonverbal codes.

objective statement   249
An articulation of your goals.

observation   93, 144, 405
Description of what is sensed; seeing and sensing the behavior and characteristics of an audience.

online résumé   251
A résumé in plain text (ASCII) or in hypertext language (HTML) and posted on the Web.

open question   238
A question worded to permit freedom in the length and nature of the response.

operational definition   90, 528
Definition that identifies something by revealing how it works, how it is made, or what it consists of.

organization   46, 305
The grouping of stimuli into meaningful units or wholes.

organizational assimilation   317
Processes through which individuals become integrated into the culture of an organization.

organizational chart   315
Visual depiction of formal communication networks.

organizational communication   305
Ways in which groups of people both maintain structure and order through their symbolic interactions and allow individual actors the freedom to accomplish their goals.

organizational culture   318
A pattern of beliefs, values, and practices shared by the members of an organization.

organizational image   320
Mental picture of an organization that is descriptive and evaluative.

organizational patterns   464
Arrangements of the contents of a presentation.

organizational politics   318
The exercise or negotiation of power.

organizational stakeholder   320
Any person or group that has an interest, right, claim, or ownership in an organization.

organizational structure 308, 464
Patterns of relations and practices created through the coordinated activities of organizational members.

organizations 305
Social collectives, or groups of people, in which activities are coordinated to achieve both individual and collective goals.

outline 454
A written plan that uses symbols, margins, and content to reveal the order, importance, and substance of a presentation.

P

paralinguistic features 119
The nonword sounds and nonword characteristics of language, such as pitch, volume, rate, and quality.

parallel form 458
The consistent use of complete sentences, clauses, phrases, or words in an outline.

paraphrasing 90
Restating another person's message by rephrasing the content or intent of the message.

participatory organizations 310
Organizations that value workplace democracy.

passive mode 214
An attempt to separate by having as little to do as possible with the dominant group.

passive perception 39
Perception in which people are simply recorders of stimuli.

pattern-maintenance goal orientation 307
Organizations that promote cultural and educational regularity and development within society.

pause 489
The absence of vocal sound used for dramatic effect, transition, or emphasis of ideas.

perception 39
The process of becoming aware of objects and events from the senses.

perceptual constancy 41
The idea that our past experiences lead us to see the world in a way that is difficult to change; that is, our initial perceptions persist.

perceptual defense 54
A defense mechanism in which you ignore or minimize damaging or harmful information.

personal experience 422
Use of your own life as a source of information.

personal idioms 194
Unique forms of expression and language understood only by individual couples.

personal inventory 393
A speaker's survey of his or her reading and viewing habits and behavior to discover topics of personal interest.

personal proof 146
Also called ethos, proof based on personal expertise or authority.

persuasion 541
An ongoing process in which verbal and nonverbal messages shape, reinforce, and change people's responses.

persuasive campaign 541
An ongoing series of related messages from speakers, newspapers, magazines, broadcasts, chat rooms, friends, and relatives that can change one's responses.

phatic communication 75
Communication that is used to establish a mood of sociability rather than to communicate information or ideas.

physical communities 352
The actual communities we live in—our neighborhoods and cities.

pitch 119, 488
The highness or lowness of a speaker's voice; technically, the frequency of sound made by vocal cords.

politeness 65
Our efforts to save face for others.

political-goals orientation   307
Organizations that generate and distribute power and control within society.

positive face   64
The desire to be liked and respected.

positive feedback   140
Verbal and nonverbal responses intended to affirm the speaker and the speaker's message.

power   273
Interpersonal influence that forms the basis for group leadership.

pragmatics   75
The study of language as it is used in a social context, including its effect on the communicators.

primary question   239
A question that introduces areas of inquiry and is coherent in itself.

problem questions   290
Group questions which focus on the undesirable present state and imply that many solutions are possible.

problem/solution pattern   469
A method of organization in which the presenter describes a problem and proposes a solution to that problem.

process   10
An activity, exchange, or set of behaviors that occur over time, e.g., in relationships.

productivity   308
The ratio of input to output.

profanity   85
Language that is disrespectful of things sacred, commonly known as "swearing."

projection   54
Our belief that others are fundamentally like us.

pronunciation   119, 491
The conformity of the speaker's production of words with agreed-upon rules about the sounds of vowels and consonants, and for syllabic emphasis.

proof   439
Evidence that is sufficient to convince your audience of the truth of a claim.

propositions   145
Statements the speaker is trying to prove.

proxemics   112
The study of the human use of space and distance.

proximity   48, 180
(1) The principle that objects which are physically close to each other will be perceived as a unit or group. (2) Term referring to location, distance, range between persons and things.

P-time   222
The polychronic time schedule, where a culture views time as "contextually based and relationally oriented."

public communication   26
The process of generating meanings in a situation where a single source transmits a message to a number of receivers who give nonverbal and, sometimes, question-and-answer feedback.

public relations (PR)   320
The management of communication between an organization and its publics.

punishment power   273
A form of power where the leader withholds something followers want and need.

Q

quality   119, 308
(1) The unique resonance of one's voice, such as huskiness, nasality, raspiness, and whininess. (2) Level of performance outcome measured in ability to meet or exceed stakeholders' expectations.

quality circle   310
A small group of employees that meets regularly on company time to recommend improvements to products and work procedures.

questionnaire   408
A set of written questions developed to obtain demographic and attitudinal information.

quid pro quo sexual harassment   325
A situation in which an employee is offered a reward or is threatened with punishment based on his or her participation in a sexual activity.

R

racist language 87
Language that insults a group because of its color or ethnicity.

rate 119, 488
The speed at which speech is delivered, normally between 125 and 190 words per minute.

reasonable person rule 325
Legal concept used by courts to determine whether a "reasonable person" would find behavior in question offensive.

receiver 16
A message target.

recency 55
Assessment of a person at the current time on the basis of recollection of recent information.

reference librarian 423
A librarian specifically trained to help find sources of information.

referent power 273
Power based on others' admiration or respect.

reflective question 239
A question that verifies information when accuracy is a concern.

reframing 176
Managing dialectics by transformation of needs so they are no longer regarded as opposites.

regionalisms 86
Words and phrases that are specific to a particular region or part of the country.

regulation 105
Nonverbal cues are used to monitor and control interactions with others.

regulators 109
Nonverbal movements that control the flow or pace of communication.

rejection 60
Feedback in which others treat us in a manner that is inconsistent with our self-definition.

relational deterioration 177
In Knapp's model, the process by which relationships disintegrate.

relational development 173
In Knapp's model, the process by which relationships grow.

relational maintenance 174
In Knapp's model, the process of keeping a relationship together.

relational messages 152
Messages which address the feelings of one person in relation to another or the feelings of one person about the relationship he or she has with another.

relational uncertainty 236
A state of suspicion or doubt.

relationship-oriented groups 271
Also called primary groups; groups that are usually long-term and exist to meet our needs for inclusion and affection (love, esteem).

repetition 104
The same message is sent both verbally and nonverbally.

responsiveness 181
The idea that we tend to select our friends from people who demonstrate positive interest in us.

reward power 273
A form of power where the leader gives followers resources they want and need.

rhetorical questions 522
Questions asked for effect, with no answer expected.

rituals 194
Formalized patterns of actions or words followed regularly.

role 42, 281
The part an individual plays in a group; an individual's function or expected behavior.

rough draft 459
The preliminary organization of the outline of a presentation.

S

Sapir-Whorf hypothesis 76
A theory that our perception of reality is determined by our thought processes and our thought processes are limited by our language and, therefore, that language shapes our reality.

schema   139
Organizational "filing systems" for thoughts held in long-term memory.

search engine   425
A program on the Internet that allows users to search for information.

secondary question   239
A question that pursues the trail of information discovered in the response to a previous question.

second-person observation   144
A report of what another person observed.

selection   44, 176
(1) The process of neglecting some stimuli in the environment to focus on other stimuli. (2) Managing dialectics by choosing one need over the other.

selective attention   44, 137
The tendency, when we expose ourselves to information and ideas, to focus on certain cues and ignore others.

selective exposure   44
The tendency to expose ourselves to information that reinforces rather than contradicts our beliefs or opinions.

selective perception   45
The tendency to see, hear, and believe only what we want to see, hear, and believe.

selective retention   45
The tendency to remember better the things that reinforce our beliefs than those that oppose them.

self-actualization   58
According to Maslow, the fulfillment of one's potential as a person.

self-awareness   56
An understanding of and insight into one's self, including one's attitudes, values, beliefs, strengths, and weaknesses.

self-centered functions   282
Behaviors that serve the needs of the individual at the expense of the group.

self-concept   58
An individual's evaluation of himself or herself, that is, an individual's self-appraisal.

self-disclosure   187
The process of making intentional revelations about oneself that others would be unlikely to know and that generally constitute private, sensitive, or confidential information.

self-efficacy   63
The belief in one's capabilities to organize and execute the sources of action required to manage prospective situations.

self-esteem   60
The feeling an individual has about his or her self-concept, that is, how well the individual likes and values himself or herself.

self-fulfilling prophecy   57
The idea that we behave and see ourselves in ways that are consistent with how others see us.

self-image   59
The picture an individual has of himself or herself; the sort of person an individual believes he or she is.

self-managed approach   374
Reducing communication apprehension by self-diagnosis and application of appropriate therapies.

self-managed work teams   311
Groups of workers who are given the freedom to manage their own work.

self-presentation   63
The way we portray ourselves to others.

self-serving bias   52
In assessing ourselves, the tendency to attribute our own successes to our personal qualities and our failures to the circumstances.

semantics   75
The branch of language study that is concerned with meaning.

sentence outline   461
An outline consisting entirely of complete sentences.

separation   176, 214
(1) The nondominant individual resists interactions with the dominant group, preferring instead to relate more exclusively with his or her own group. (2) Managing dialectics by fulfilling one need in some situations and the other in different situations.

sex   277
The biological reproductive characteristics with which we are born.

sexist language   87
Language that excludes individuals on the basis of gender.

sexual harassment   324
Unwelcome, unsolicited, repeated behavior of a sexual nature.

short-term memory   138
A part of memory that acts as a temporary storage place for information.

significance   517
The importance, meaningfulness, or consequenses of a message for an audience.

signposts   472
Ways in which a presenter signals to an audience where the presentation is going.

silence   119
The lack of sound.

silent probes   239
To refrain from saying anything for a brief time, letting the respondent fill in the silence.

similarity   49, 181
(1) The principle that elements are grouped together because they share attributes such as size, color, or belief. (2) The idea that our friends are usually people who like or dislike the same things we do.

skills approach   371
Reducing communication apprehension by improving skills such as by taking a public speaking course.

slang   84
A specialized language of a group of people who share a common interest or belong to a similar co-culture.

sleeper effect   380
A change of audience opinion caused by the separation of the message content from its source over a period of time.

small-group communication   26, 269
The interaction of a small group of people to achieve an interdependent goal.

social attractiveness   181
A concept that includes physical attractiveness, how desirable a person is to work with, and how much "social value" the person has for others.

social exchange theory   182
Economic model which suggests that we develop relationships on the basis of their rewards and costs.

social penetration theory   172
A theory that explains how relationships develop and deteriorate through the exchange of intimate information.

solution questions   290
Group questions which slant the group's discussion toward one particular option.

somatotype   110
Body type which is comprised of a combination of height, weight, and muscularity.

source   16, 335
(1) A message initiator. (2) Someone who shares information, ideas, or attitudes with someone else.

source credibility   146, 375, 549
The extent to which the speaker is perceived as competent to make the claims he or she is making.

spatial/relations organization   466
A method of organization in which the presenter reveals how things relate to each other in space, position, and visual orientation.

stagnating   177
In Knapp's relational development model, the stage of deterioration marked by the partner's lack of activity, especially together.

stakeholders   292
Groups of people who have an interest in the actions of an organization.

state anxiety   368
Anxiety engendered by a specific situation.

statistics   437
Numbers that summarize numerical information or compare quantities.

stereotype   216
A generalization about some group of people that oversimplifies their culture.

stereotyping   53, 87
Oversimplifying or standardizing a person because of her or his group membership.

stimulus cues   139
Words, images, smells, and/or tastes that signal us to activate information held in schema.

strategic choices   413
What you choose to do in your speech, from the words to the arguments.

street language   87
Language that consists of highly informal words or phrases, often specific to one area, that are used to demonstrate unity.

structuration   306
The process of formating and maintaining structures through verbal and nonverbal communication, which establishes norms and rules governing members' behaviors.

style   247
The overall tone created by your linguistic and aesthetic choices.

style approaches   274
A leadership theory focusing on the pattern of behaviors leaders exhibit in groups.

subjective perception   39
Your uniquely constructed meaning attributed to sensed stimuli.

subpoints   456
The points in a presentation that support the main points; indicated by capital letters in an outline.

substitution   105
Nonverbal codes are used instead of verbal codes.

supporting materials   434
Information you can use to substantiate your arguments and to clarify your position.

supportiveness   285
An atmosphere of openness created when members care about each other and treat each other with respect.

surveys   435
Studies in which a limited number of questions are answered by a sample of the population to discover opinions on issues.

syllogism   145
Deductive arguments that have a major premise, a minor premise, and a conclusion.

symbolic interactionism   56
The process in which the self develops through the messages and feedback received from others.

symmetrical relationships   171
Relationships between people who mirror each other or who are highly similar.

synchronous communication   348
Members of the communication interaction interact in real time, and each participant is simultaneously a sender and receiver.

synonym   528
A word that means approximately the same as another word.

syntax   18, 75
A set of rules about language that determines how words are arranged to form phrases and sentences.

systematic desensitization   373
Combining deep relaxation with fear-inducing thoughts to reduce communication apprehension.

T

tactile communication   116
The use of touch in communication.

task functions   282
Behaviors that are directly relevant to the group's task and that affect the group's productivity.

task-oriented groups   271
Also called secondary groups, groups formed for the purpose of completing tasks, such as solving problems or making decisions.

terminating   177
In Knapp's relational development model, the stage of deterioration in which the partners are no longer seen as a pair by themselves or others.

testimonial evidence   435
Written or oral statements of others' experience used by a speaker to substantiate or clarify a point.

tests of evidence   554
Questions that can be used to test the validity of evidence.

time-sequence pattern   465
A method of organization in which the presenter explains a sequence of events in chronological order.

tolerating ambiguity   225
Being open-minded about differences.

topical-sequence pattern   470
A method of organization that emphasizes the major reasons an audience should accept a point of view by addressing the advantages, disadvantages, qualities, and types of persons, places, or things.

trait anxiety   368
Anxiety described as persistent behavior of a continuing nature.

transaction model   21
A depiction of communication as communicators simultaneously sending and receiving messages.

transition   471
A bridge between sections of a presentation that helps the presenter move smoothly from one idea to another.

trust   284
A group climate characteristic where members believe they can rely on each other.

trustworthiness   377
The degree to which the speaker is perceived as honest, fair, sincere, honorable, friendly, and kind; an aspect of credibility.

U

ultimate goals   541
Purposes that a speaker wishes to fulfill with additional messages and more time.

uncertainty-accepting cultures   220
Cultures that tolerate ambiguity, uncertainty, and diversity.

uncertainty reduction theory   178, 351
A theory that upon first meeting, strangers seek to reduce the uncertainty that they have about the other person.

uncertainty-rejecting cultures   221
Cultures that have difficulty with ambiguity, uncertainty, and diversity.

uniform resource locator (URL)   425
An address on the Web where particular information is located.

upward communication   316
Messages flowing from subordinates to superiors.

utilization of liaisons   214
Relating to the dominant group through others with a shared cultural identity or with a trusted individual from the dominant group.

V

valid   146
In deductive arguments, when the conclusion logically flows from the logical combination of the major and minor premises.

value   404
A deeply rooted belief that governs our attitude about something.

veracity effect   186
The assumption that messages are truthful.

verbal aggressiveness   323
An individual's communication that attacks the self-concepts of other people in order to inflict psychological pain.

verbal citations   432
Oral explanations of who the source is, how recent the information is, and the source's qualifications.

verbal codes   18
Symbols and their grammatical arrangement, such as languages.

virtual communities   352
Collections of people who populate discussion boards and/or multiuser environments on the Internet.

virtual libraries   425
Websites which provide links to sites that have been reviewed for relevance and usability.

visual aids   500
Any items that can be seen by an audience for the purpose of reinforcing a message.

visualization   373
A process of picturing one's self succeeding to reduce communication apprehension.

vocal cues   119
All the oral aspects of sound except words themselves; part of paralinguistic features.

vocal variety   492
Vocal quality, intonation patterns, inflections of pitch, and syllabic duration; a lack of repetitious patterns in vocal delivery.

vocalized pauses   489
Breaks in fluency; filling in silences with meaningless words or sounds that negatively affect an audience's perception of the speaker's competence and dynamism.

volume   119, 489
The loudness or softness of a person's voice.

voluntary audience   400
A collection of people who choose to listen to a particular speaker or speech.

W

Web browser   425
A tool for viewing pages on the WWW.

within-group diversity   277
The presence of observable and/or implicit differences among group members.

working memory   137
The part of our consciousness that interprets and assigns meaning to stimuli we pay attention to.

workplace aggression   323
All communication by which individuals attempt to harm others at work.

workplace democracy   310
A system of governance which truly values individual goals and feelings (e.g., feelings of equitable remuneration, the pursuit of enriching work, and the right to express oneself) as well as typical organizational objectives (e.g., effectiveness and efficiency) and actively fosters the connection between those two sets of concerns by encouraging individual contributions to important organizational choices.

workplace violence   323
Instances involving direct physical assaults.

World Wide Web (WWW)   424
A feature of the Internet that links together all the individual websites.

Chapter 16

PHOTOS: p. 482, Bob Daemmrich Photo, Inc.; p. 490, Robert Brenner/PhotoEdit; p. 495, Najlah Feanny/Stock Boston

Chapter 17

PHOTOS: p. 514, Bob Daemmrich/ Stock Boston; p. 519, B. Daemmrich/The Image Works; p. 525, Michael Newman/ PhotoEdit

Chapter 18

PHOTOS: p. 538, Bob Daemmrich Photo Inc.; p. 552, Jake Schoellkopf/AP/Wide World Photos; p. 560, Laura Dwight/PhotoEdit